Critical Reading in the Content Areas

First Edition

EDITOR

Glenda Moss

Indiana University–Purdue University, Fort Wayne

Glenda Moss, Assistant Professor of Secondary Education at Indiana University–Purdue University, Fort Wayne (IPFW) and Associate Director of the Appleseed Writing Project–Indiana, attended East Texas State University (now Texas A & M at Commerce, Texas) to earn a B.A. in English and History in 1972 and served as a teaching assistant for three semesters while taking graduate classes in History. In 1974, she received her Texas Teacher Certification from Abilene Christian University. She received her M.Ed. from The University of Texas at Tyler in 1983 and her Professional Administrative Certification in 1996. She taught on the middle school level from 1985 until 1998 at which time she began her doctoral studies in educational leadership. She received her Ed.D. from Stephen F. Austin State University in the summer of 2001 and began teaching at IPFW in the fall of 2001. Moss has transitioned her pre-service English and Social Studies methods courses to a field-based high school site, where students learn to implement critical reading and content instruction theory into practice.

McGraw-Hill/Dushkin

2460 Kerper Blvd, Dubuque, IA 52001

Visit us on the Internet
http://www.dushkin.com

Credits

1. **Critical Literacy Theory**
   Unit photo—Getty Images/Doug Menuez
2. **Culture of Literacy**
   Unit photo—Mel Curtis/Getty Images
3. **Adolescent Motivation for Literacy**
   Unit photo—Ryan McVay/Getty Images
4. **Textbook Reading and Comprehension**
   Unit photo—© Getty Images/Doug Menuez
5. **Content Area Reading Strategies Across the Cirriculum**
   Unit photo—© Getty Images/Royalty Free
6. **Assessing Literacy and Content**
   Unit photo—© Getty Images/Royalty Free
7. **Critical Literacy Perspectives**
   Unit photo—PhotoLink/Getty Images

Copyright

Cataloging in Publication Data
Main entry under title: Annual Editions: Critical Reading in the Content Areas, 2004/2005
1. Critical Reading in the Content Areas—Periodicals. 1. Moss, Glenda, comp. II Title: Critical Reading in the Content Areas

ISBN 0–07–297073–1   658'.05   ISSN 1550–4670

First Edition

Cover image © Andrew Ward/Life File/Getty Images

Printed in the United States of America   1234567890QPDQPD987654   Printed on Recycled Paper

Editors/Advisory Board

To the Reader

In publishing ANNUAL EDITIONS we recognize the enormous role played by the magazines, newspapers, and journals of the public press in providing current, first-rate educational information in a broad spectrum of interest areas. Many of these articles are appropriate for students, researchers, and professionals seeking accurate, current material to help bridge the gap between principles and theories and the real world. These articles, however, become more useful for study when those of lasting value are carefully collected, organized, indexed, and reproduced in a low-cost format, which provides easy and permanent access when the material is needed. That is the role played by ANNUAL EDITIONS.

The concept of critical reading in the content areas began to appear as professional education requirements in secondary teacher education programs in the mid seventies and eighties. At the university where I teach, the course requirement for secondary education majors first appeared in the 1985 edition of the Administrative Rules of the Indiana State Board of Education (ISBE). The reading requirement purpose stated, "This shall develop understanding of reading problems encountered by secondary students in subject-matter oriented materials."

Initial legislative action in Indiana, that resulted in the establishment of content area reading requirements for teachers, was prompted by low reading scores among K-12 students on national reading tests. Indiana was near the bottom of the fifty states. The teacher education requirement is consistent with the 2002 NCATE Curriculum and Content Area Standards:

INFORMATION LITERACY STANDARDS

Standard 1: The student who is information literate accesses information efficiently and effectively.

Standard 2: The student who is information literate evaluates information critically and competently.

Standard 3: The student who is information literate uses information accurately and creatively.

INDEPENDENT LEARNING

Standard 4: The student who is an independent learner is information literate and pursues information related to personal interests.

Standard 5: The student who is an independent learner is information literate and appreciates literature and other creative expressions of information.

Standard 6: The student who is an independent learner is information literate and strives for excellence in information seeking and knowledge generation.

SOCIAL RESPONSIBILITY

Standard 7: The student who contributes positively to the learning community and to society is information literate and recognizes the importance of information to a democratic society.

Standard 8: The student who contributes positively to the learning community and to society is information literate and practices ethical behavior in regard to information and information technology.

Standard 9: The student who contributes positively to the learning community and to society is information literate and participates effectively in groups to pursue and generate information.

When I interviewed for a professorship, the hiring committee members and broader faculty indicated that one of the courses I would teach was "Critical Reading in the Content Areas." I understood the concept to be that secondary teachers in the content areas must view themselves as reading teachers along side content teachers. Secondary teachers must instruct students on strategies for reading and comprehending the various content texts utilized in middle school and high school instruction.

As I began to design my edition of the course, I purposed to ensure that pre-service teachers become actively engaged, critical readers as they engaged texts addressing critical reading in the content areas. Rather than lecturing about reading, I designed assignments to engage students in reading to learn. I conducted multiple literature searches to access current research articles on a number of topics to be covered in the course. These included literacy landscapes, models of comprehension, comprehension strategies, pre-reading, expanding vocabulary, writing in the secondary classroom, literature across the curriculum and throughout life, assessing literacy and content learning, reading history texts, reading math texts, reading science texts, reading social studies texts, transmission of culture through texts, and literacy needs of diverse students. Besides reading a chapter in two textbooks each week, my students read 3-5 journal articles and then wrote reflective-reflexive responses in preparation for dialoguing about a topic each week. Students are engaged in active critical reading and professionally developing themselves as critical readers in the process of learning skills and strategies they can transfer to teaching in their secondary content areas.

I had been considering proposing a book project that would compile current literature on the above topics to meet my course textbook needs. I recently learned about *Annual Editions* when one of my own publications appeared in the *Annual Editions: Multicultural Education 03/04*, I thought this would be a perfect way to do what I had in mind. There are numerous textbooks to choose from for the content areas reading course, but these—like most textbooks—are limited to a sweeping overview of information. The readings in *Annual Editions: Critical Reading in the Content Areas 04/05*, provide students with the opportunity to look at original research projects and to critically analyze them. This *Annual Edition* provides a supplemental text to current textbooks, and use of supplemental journal texts meets with the best practices for engaging learners in content learning.

Glenda Moss

Glenda Moss
Editor

Contents

UNIT 1
Critical Literacy Theory

Three articles establish a conversation base for the practice of teaching students to critically read content area texts.

UNIT 2
Culture of Literacy

Four articles discuss the concept of school culture and provide pre-service teachers, in-service teachers, and administrators with the opportunity to critically analyze the connection between policies, practices, and school culture.

The concepts in bold italics are developed in the article. For further expansion, please refer to the Topic Guide and the Index.

UNIT 3
Adolescent Motivation for Literacy

Three articles explore affective elements of content area reading and present strategies for motivating the secondary student to read in the content area.

UNIT 4
Textbook Reading and Comprehension

Eight articles raise critical issues with regard to textbooks and measurable verbal skills and discuss models for building vocabulary within content area reading.

The concepts in bold italics are developed in the article. For further expansion, please refer to the Topic Guide and the Index.

UNIT 5
Content Area Reading Strategies Across the Curriculum

Seven articles provide content area pre-service teachers, in-service teachers, and administrators with a cross-curricular look at reading in the content areas. Articles address reading in the following subject areas: math, science, and social studies.

The concepts in bold italics are developed in the article. For further expansion, please refer to the Topic Guide and the Index.

The concepts in bold italics are developed in the article. For further expansion, please refer to the Topic Guide and the Index.

UNIT 6
Assessing Literacy and Content

Three articles present various aspects of assessing literacy in the content area and challenge teachers and policy makers to consider alternative means of assessment that move beyond standardized testing.

UNIT 7
Critical Literacy Perspectives

Six articles raise critical issues of reading, texts, and cultural politics.

The concepts in bold italics are developed in the article. For further expansion, please refer to the Topic Guide and the Index.

The concepts in bold italics are developed in the article. For further expansion, please refer to the Topic Guide and the Index.

Topic Guide

This topic guide suggests how the selections in this book relate to the subjects covered in your course. You may want to use the topics listed on these pages to search the Web more easily.

On the following pages a number of Web sites have been gathered specifically for this book. They are arranged to reflect the units of this *Annual Edition.* You can link to these sites by going to the DUSHKIN ONLINE support site at *http://www.dushkin.com/online/.*

ALL THE ARTICLES THAT RELATE TO EACH TOPIC ARE LISTED BELOW THE BOLD-FACED TERM.

Adapting textbooks
33. Assisting Students with Difficult Textbooks: Teacher Perception and Practices

Assessment
27. Giving Voice to Middle School Students Through Portfolio Assessment: A Journey of Mathematical Power
28. Dismantling the Factory Model of Assessment

Book discussions
24. Celebrating Literature in a Comprehensive Middle School Program

Collaborative learning
6. Improving Young Adolescent Literacy Through Collaborative Learning

Content area literacy
25. Literature for Children and Young Adults in a History Classroom

Content area reading
8. Affective Dimensions of Content Area Reading
9. Activating Student Interest in Content Area Reading
19. Developing Critical Understanding of the Specialized Language of School Science and History Texts: A Functional Grammatical Perspective

Critical instruction
34. Dialogue in Teaching is Critical Instruction

Critical literacy
1. Exploring the Links Between Critical Literacy and Developmental Reading
2. Saving Black Mountain: The Promise of Critical Literacy in a Multicultural Democracy
6. Improving Young Adolescent Literacy Through Collaborative Learning

Culture of literacy
4. Creating a Middle School Culture of Literacy
7. A Culture of Literacy in Science

Developmental reading
1. Exploring the Links Between Critical Literacy and Developmental Reading
5. Building Sound Literacy Learning Programs for Young Adolescents

Diverse learners
33. Assisting Students with Difficult Textbooks: Teacher Perception and Practices

Information presentation
29. Tales from Two Textbooks: A Comparison of the Civil Rights Movement in Two Secondary History Textbooks
30. The Story of Ourselves: Fostering Multiple Historical Perspectives

Learning theory
8. Affective Dimensions of Content Area Reading

Literacy learning
10. Enhancing Young Adolescents' Motivation for Literacy Learning

Motivation and learning
9. Activating Student Interest in Content Area Reading
10. Enhancing Young Adolescents' Motivation for Literacy Learning

Multicultural teaching
2. Saving Black Mountain: The Promise of Critical Literacy in a Multicultural Democracy

Questioning strategies
17. The Directed Questioning Activity for Subject Matter Text

Reading abilities
12. Assessing Students' Skills in Using Textbooks: The Textbook Awareness and Performance Profile (TAPP)

Reading and learning
26. Using Alternative Assessment to Provide Options for Student Success

Reading and understanding
11. Reading and Understanding Textbooks

Reading and writing
7. A Culture of Literacy in Science

Reading strategies
8. Affective Dimensions of Content Area Reading

Scaffolding strategy
18. Scaffolding Adolescents' Comprehension of Short Stories

Scaffold Reading Experience
13. Fostering Students' Understanding of Challenging Texts

Searches
14. Searching for Information in Textbooks

Social practice
3. What Do We Mean By Literacy Now?

Substituting
32. Guidelines for Adapting Content Area Textbooks: Keeping Teachers and Students Content

Teaching literacy
5. Building Sound Literacy Learning Programs for Young Adolescents

Textbook comprehension
16. Teacher-Directed and Student-Mediated Textbook Comprehension Strategies
17. The Directed Questioning Activity for Subject Matter Text
18. Scaffolding Adolescents' Comprehension of Short Stories
27. Giving Voice to Middle School Students Through Portfolio Assessment: A Journey of Mathematical Power
31. Using Textbooks with Students Who Cannot Read Them

Textbook reading
15. Teachers' Views of Textbooks and Text Reading Instruction: Experience Matters

World Wide Web Sites

The following World Wide Web sites have been carefully researched and selected to support the articles found in this reader. The easiest way to access these selected sites is to go to our DUSHKIN ONLINE support site at *http://www.dushkin.com/online/*.

AE: Critical Reading in the Content Areas 04/05

The following sites were available at the time of publication. Visit our Web site—we update DUSHKIN ONLINE regularly to reflect any changes.

General Sources

U.S. Department of Education
http://www.ed.gov/pubs/TeachersGuide/

Government goals, projects, grants, and other educational programs are listed here as well as many links to teacher services and resources.

UNIT 1: Critical Literacy Theory

English Learning Area
http://www.discover.tased.edu.au/english/critlit.htm

This site provides a definition of what critical literacy is as well as some ways it can be applied in the classroom.

Journal for Pedagogy, Pluralism, and Practice
http://www.lesley.edu/journals/jppp/4/shor.html

This site provides an overview of critical literacy.

ERIC Digest
http://www.cal.org/ncle/DIGESTS/critlit.htm

This site provides examples of how to apply critical reading in the classroom.

Beyond the Basics
http://ei.cs.vt.edu/~wwwbtb/book/chap6/critical.html

The World Wide Web can be a very useful tool, especially to the topic of critical reading as this site states.

Critical Literacy Links
http://io.uwinnipeg.ca/~taylor/cllinks.htm

Links to various sites associated with critical reading are provided at this site.

Alameda County Library
http://write2read.aclibrary.org/word.asp

This site gives a different perspective as to why critical reading is so important.

What is Critical Literacy
http://www.sil.org/lingualinks/literacy/ReferenceMaterials/GlossaryOfLiteracyTerms/WhatIsCriticalLiteracy.htm

This site contains information and links about critical reading.

UNIT 2: Culture of Literacy

Archived Information
http://www.ed.gov/pubs/FamLit/transfer.html

How does literacy play a part in our social life? This site helps to answer that question.

UNIT 3: Adolescent Motivation for Literacy

LinguaLinks
http://www.ethnologue.com/LL_docs/index/Motivation(Literacy).asp

This site contains glossary entries and bibliography citations from a large number of books and journals.

Research in Adolescent Literacy
http://grants1.nih.gov/grants/guide/rfa-files/RFA-HD-03-012.html

This site contains background information on The National Institute of Child Health and Human Development.

UNIT 4: Textbook Reading and Comprehension

Education World
http://www.education-world.com/a_curr/profdev034.shtml

Take a look at this site for information on a wide variety of education related topics.

Council for Learning Disabilities: Infosheet About Reading Comprehension
http://www.cldinternational.org/c/@OcSfc397ooeTg/Pages/home.html

This is the link for the Council for Learning Disabilities site.

National Council of Teachers of English (NCTE)
http://www.ncte.org/middle/teaching/111157.htm

For various strategies on educating see this site.

Teaching Strategies and Techniques
http://www.ldonline.org/ld_indepth/teaching_techniques/strategies.html

This site is a resource for various strategies and techniques.

UNIT 5: Content Area Reading Strategies Across the Curriculum

Reading in the Content Area - Baltimore County Public Schools
http://www.bcpl.net/~dcurtis/readingcontent/

This site is a resource for Reading in the Content Area.

Reading Quest Resources
http://curry.edschool.virginia.edu/go/readquest/links.html

This is a site containing a general list of links to resources about content reading and comprehension strategies.

UNIT 6: Assessing Literacy and Content

The National Research Center on English Learning and Achievement
http://cela.albany.edu/

See this site for upcoming books, articles, newsletters, and reports on English literacy.

Strategic Literacy Initiative
http://www.wested.org/stratlit/

This site contains various information on strategic literacy.

The Partnership for Reading
http://www.nifl.gov/partnershipforreading/adolescent/

This site provides a list of workshops as well as an overview for adolescent literacy.

www.dushkin.com/online/

Literacy Assessment
http://www.ncrel.org/sdrs/areas/issues/content/cntareas/reading/ li7lk29.htm
   Provided here is a list of literacy assessment techniques.

UNIT 7: Critical Literacy Perspectives

Critical Issue: Addressing Literacy Needs in Culturally and Linguistically Diverse Classrooms
http://www.ncrel.org/sdrs/areas/issues/content/cntareas/reading/ li400.htm
   This site addresses diversity in the classroom.

We highly recommend that you review our Web site for expanded information and our other product lines. We are continually updating and adding links to our Web site in order to offer you the most usable and useful information that will support and expand the value of your Annual Editions. You can reach us at: *http://www.dushkin.com/annualeditions/.*

UNIT 1
Critical Literacy Theory

Unit Selections

1. **Exploring the Links Between Critical Literacy and Developmental Reading**, Mellinee Lesley
2. **Saving Black Mountain: The Promise of Critical Literacy in a Multicultural Democracy**, Rebecca Powell, Susan Chambers Cantrell, and Sandra Adams
3. **What Do We Mean By Literacy Now?**, Jerome C. Harste

Key Points to Consider

- What is critical literacy?

- What is a "deficit model" of instruction?

- How can critical literacy contribute to reading development among diverse secondary students?

 **Links: www.dushkin.com/online/**
These sites are annotated in the World Wide Web pages.

English Learning Area
http://www.discover.tased.edu.au/english/critlit.htm

Journal for Pedagogy, Pluralism, and Practice
http://www.lesley.edu/journals/jppp/4/shor.html

ERIC Digest
http://www.cal.org/ncle/DIGESTS/critlit.htm

Beyond the Basics
http://ei.cs.vt.edu/~wwwbtb/book/chap6/critical.html

Critical Literacy Links
http://io.uwinnipeg.ca/~taylor/cllinks.htm

Alameda County Library
http://write2read.aclibrary.org/word.asp

What is Critical Literacy
http://www.sil.org/lingualinks/literacy/ReferenceMaterials/GlossaryOfLiteracyTerms/WhatIsCriticalLiteracy.htm

What do we mean by critical literacy? When I first began to design the syllabus for my edition of a secondary education course, "Critical Reading in the Content Areas," I had to consider how I would define critical literacy. From experience as a middle school teacher, I knew what many of my colleagues in East Texas meant. It was "critical" that students attain reading skills to pass the state reading test. Critical reading was discerning what was the "main idea" in a given selection on a test. Critical reading was distinguishing between fact and opinion. Critical reading was finding the answers to comprehension questions. Critical reading on the state math test included paying attention to the information that was given and the question that was being asked. It was deciding if the reading problem entailed addition, subtraction, multiplication, or division. Critical to reading math was possession of an understanding of key vocabulary such as quotient, product, estimate, less than, and greater than. In other words, critical reading referred to reading for the purpose of coming up with the correct answer on a standardized test.

I personally believe that secondary education courses in reading such as the one required at my university were instituted as a response to the low scores on standardized reading tests. Such courses were intended to focus secondary pre-service teachers' attention to the role that reading plays in learning across the curriculum. Clearly, learning to read has always been central to elementary curriculum, whereas, individual subject matter has traditionally been central to secondary course curriculums. The gap between the elementary culture of literacy and the secondary social culture, visible in extracurricular activities,

is clear. A focus on reading in the secondary content areas is an attempt to bridge this gap.

As I began to design my edition of "Critical Reading in the Content Area," my definition of critical literacy was influenced by my participation in the Scholar-Practitioner Doctoral Program at Stephen F. Austin University. Educational leadership in this doctoral program was defined by a critical perspective for the purpose of addressing educational issues of equity, gender, and race within the K-12 school setting as well as the broader field in general. Thus, critical reading in the content area had a different connotation to me. Critical suggested that secondary teachers must examine their textbooks for the ways we culturally educate students. Rather than simply focusing on reading to find answers for a test, pre-service teachers must consider literacy as reading, writing, speaking, and listening in the context of the classroom embedded in the school, embedded in the local community, embedded in the state and nation. Literacy is embedded in the political state of education and society. Critical literacy as an ideal could be defined as central to democracy.

With these two perspectives in mind, the first unit of this annual edition presents articles to stimulate critical thinking and dialogue within the critical literacy discourse. In "Exploring the Links Between Critical Literacy and Developmental Reading" (2001), Mellinee Lesley challenges instructors to address developmental reading through critical literacy pedagogy. The author presents persuasive evidence to promote critical literacy for academic success. She problematizes the "deficit model" approach to developmental reading in favor of critical literacy.

In order to create meaningful lives, students must develop critical literacy skills and use them. In "Saving Black Mountain: The Promise of Critical Literacy in a Multicultural Democracy," Rebecca Powell, Susan Chambers Cantrell, and Sandra Adams define critical literacy as central to the promotion of democracy in a multicultural society. Teachers are challenged to recognize that literacy is more a matter of making meaning out of words than developing a set of skills. Likewise, in "What Do We Mean by Literacy Now?", Jerome C. Harste challenges readers to consider literacy as social practice and raises critical questions about how educators define literacy, whose definition is advantaged, and who benefits from curriculum decisions. Each of these articles will challenge educators on all levels to think critically about what critical literacy means in a diverse, democratic society.

Exploring the links between critical literacy and developmental reading

Restructuring the curriculum of a remedial reading course to incorporate a critical literacy pedagogy led to skill improvements for the students.

> Through all my experiences with people struggling to learn, the one thing that strikes me most is the ease with which we misperceive failed performance and the degree to which this misperception both reflects and reinforces the social order. Class and culture erect boundaries that hinder our vision…and encourage the designation of otherness, difference, deficiency…[S]ome of our basic orientations toward the teaching and testing of literacy contribute to our inability to see. To truly educate in America, then, to reach the full sweep of our citizenry, we need to question received perception, shift continually from the standard lens. (Rose, 1989, p. 205)

Mellinnee Lesley

Mike Rose speaks to my experiences both as a student and as a teacher. I think first of the ways I have failed students in my hurried evaluations of their literacy, but I realize that even my little failures have taught me an immense amount as a teacher. To keep learning, I must keep assessing myself. I must have "failures" to be able to recognize and know success. I must misperceive in order to perceive. I like this passage because it reminds me to think differently about literacy, how I teach it, and how to recognize it in its most nascent forms.

The story recorded here is one of students' successful formulation of literacy as measured in test scores, reading interest inventories, and written artifacts. It's also one of success for me as a teacher, taking a huge risk to revamp an entire developmental reading program for my university. It took a great deal of risk to try to sell a pedagogy of critical literacy to instructors and graduate assistants with minimal amounts of training in literacy in general and absolutely no comprehension of constructivist approaches to literacy (Atwell, 1998; Johnston, 1992; Noguchi, 1991) let alone any understanding of the domain of critical literacy (Bee, 1993; Brady, 1995; Ellsworth, 1992; Freire, 1995; Giroux, 1993; Lankshear & McLaren, 1993; Shor, 1996).

The other risk occurred in the classroom with my own students. Attempting to evoke a pedagogy of questions (Freire, 1995), bring students out of "intel-

lectual Siberia" (Shor, 1996), and deal with resistance (Bigelow, 1990; Ellsworth, 1992; Lather, 1992) was not easy. In some ways these actions paralleled the professional development work I undertook with the other instructors and graduate assistants. Unlike some of the other instructors, my students were able to navigate the process of critical literacy and come to a measured level of "conscientization" (Freire, 1995), working through false consciousness (Lather, 1992) and resistance (Ellsworth, 1992; Lather. 1992) to obtain a new degree of control over their literacy development, histories, and futures. To say the least, learning more about the possibilities in enacting critical literacy with a "remediated" population of students was an important experience for me as a teacher.

Local and national trends in developmental studies

The current status of basic skills, "remediated" courses in English, reading, and mathematics has reached a critical juncture in the history of developmental studies programs in higher education across the U.S. Every year enrollment in such noncredit courses increases along with student attrition and academic failure rates (The Institute for Higher Education Policy, 1998). This increase in remedial student population is concomitant with an overall increase in the number of students attending college, thanks to open enrollment admission standards (The Institute for Higher Education Policy, 1998).

While attention to developmental studies programs tends to be nonexistent in institutions of higher education, remediation constitutes a core function of these programs (Brittain, 1982; The Institute for Higher Education Policy, 1998). A 1995 survey conducted by the National Center for Education Statistics (NCES) found that 78% of higher education institutions offered at least one remedial reading, writing, or mathematics course. All too often, pedagogy in developmental studies courses is "hit or miss" with little, if any, oversight of the curriculum and staff responsible for teaching these courses. In such courses, our most academically at-risk students are subjected to part-time adjunct instructors and teaching assistants with very little institutional efficacy or permanency. Another concern with developmental studies courses lies with the fact that there are no national criteria to determine placement in such courses. In other words, there are no standards for what constitutes "college-level" work and consequently what constitutes remedial college work. This phenomenon peculiar to developmental studies further alienates these courses from the intellectual rigor that is heralded in the academy proper.

At my university, we offer developmental course in mathematics, English, and reading to provide students with prerequisite skills for entry into college-level coursework. From the fall 1994 semester to the fall 1998 semester, the average percentage of first-year students enrolled in English 100 was 49.3%. In the same period, the average percentage of first-year students in Reading 100 was 27.5%. Despite the numbers of students enrolling in developmental studies courses, the status of these courses has remained low. The developmental reading course, for instance, had been moved from the Reading Education program to administration by Student Academic Services in the early 1980s. Locating Reading 100 in a service program heightened the nonacademic reputation of the course. With this shift in administrative placement, Reading 100 suffered from little administrative oversight and no curricular attention. As a result of my preliminary research on the developmental reading program a year prior to conducting this study, Reading 100 was returned to the oversight of the Reading Education Program in the Department of Curriculum and Instruction. This simple yet important shift signaled the transition of this course from marginalized to a status of more import, recognizing the relationship of this course to subsequent credit courses offered in the institution.

In an effort to ameliorate the current status of developmental studies courses, I was appointed to chair a committee to study the problems afflicting these courses. While the committee addressed issues related to the problems troubling our developmental studies courses, the greatest concern was over the pedagogy of these courses. I was appointed as the Coordinator for Reading 100 and permitted to teach one section of the class during the fall 1999 semester.

Prior to my appointment as the coordinator, Reading 100 consisted of weekly vocabulary drills, basic comprehension of brief texts (paragraphs), and eye exercises to increase students' reading rates (speed reading). The course concluded with a full-blown research paper. The course did not ask students to do any reading of the sort that would be required of them in a university-level academic setting. Furthermore, Reading 100 was predicated on a restrictive philosophy of remediation that taught basic skills with repetitive drills. Another glaring problem with the design of this course was the fact that the curriculum followed an illogical practice of teaching lower level drill activities and then expecting students to write a research paper. Little emphasis was placed on reading "real" texts or the interconnectedness of reading and writing, and certainly no attempt was made at reflexive practice or evoking a pedagogy of critical literacy. These identified weaknesses in the pedagogy of Reading 100 led to my research and restructuring of the course to reflect constructivist notions of literacy as well as a pedagogy of critical literacy.

Collecting the data

Broadly stated, the objective for this research was to design an alternative pedagogy for a developmental studies reading course offered at an open enrollment state university. In an attempt to foster the successful literacy acquisition required to survive in a university setting, I examined the effects of enacting a critical literacy pedagogy within the course. The curriculum developed in this study emphasizes the interrelatedness of processes of reading and writing as well as critical reading and writing within an academic discourse community. Consequently, the pedagogy presented in the new course incorporated research from the domains of critical literacy, adult literacy, emergent literacy, and developmental studies in order to shed light on developmental reading programs in higher education.

The following research questions guided my study:

1. What happens when students enrolled in a basic skills reading course experience critical literacy (reading and writing conscientization) as an entrance into academic modes of discourse?

2. To what extent do the students enrolled in this course construct or begin to construct themselves as readers and writers through the means of critical reflection and critical literacy pedagogy?

To answer these questions I first had to design a literacy program where critical literacy was a curricular goal. Consequently, I began by restructuring the course around the following tenets that I would require of all Reading l00 instructors:

- Writing will be used primarily as a tool for strengthening processes of reading/thinking/ learning.

4

- Texts will consist of Mike Rose's (1989) book *Lives on the Boundary*, readings chosen from the Freshman Seminar Reader, and selections chosen by the instructor.
- "Basic skills" in reading (e.g., summarizing, synthesizing, developing inference, developing vocabulary) will be embedded in the processes of reading "real" texts and explicitly taught as mini-lessons that are to be applied to immediate experiences with reading and responding to reading.
- Themes for the course will emphasize translation into academic modes of discourse (especially critical and analytical reading), "territories" for reading (Atwell, 1998) (how people read or learn to read in authentic venues), and literacy narratives.

Goals for the students included the following:

- Reconstruct their identities as readers and writers,
- Develop fluency in using writing as a tool for thinking,
- Develop skills to foster critical and analytical reading ability, and
- Develop metacognitive awareness about their reading processes.

With these tenets and goals, I grounded the course in a constructivist philosophy (Vygotsky, 1978). Through the texts chosen for the course, the reflective assignments, and the first student goal, I also set the stage for establishing a pedagogy of critical literacy in the course.

I collected data through qualitative interpretive (Erickson, 1986) methods. However, I also collected quantitative data from norm-referenced test scores and surveys. My stance was primarily that of a teacher-researcher (Cochran-Smith & Lytle, 1993, 1999). There were 22 students enrolled in my course. As recent graduates from high school, all of the students in the course could be categorized as "traditional" students. Fourteen of the students were female, and eight were male. Eight of the students were Hispanic, two were African American, and one was Native American.

Data sources for the study consisted of pre- and poststudy Nelson-Denny Test scores, interest inventories, and responses to literature; writing samples; transcripts from focus group interviews and class discussions; archives of student writing; and a reflective journal of my experiences as a teacher. I analyzed each source of qualitative data through linguistic coding according to Fairclough's (1995) work on critical discourse analysis and Vine and Faust's (1993) work on situated reading. With these tools for analysis, I looked specifically for trends in students' reflection and self-ascribed literacy labels. I also coded the data for personal connections students were making in reading, intertextual connections in their reading and writing, and instances of critical observations about developmental studies. Through all this analysis, I was looking for trends in students' abilities to read the texts

analytically as well as position themselves as readers in the broader contexts for literacy the institution entails (e.g., developmental studies). As revealing as the qualitative data was, the most compelling data were the increases made in students' reading scores on the on Nelson-Denny Test. (See Figure 1.)

FIGURE 1
Nelson-Denny Reading Test results

Year	Section number	Beginning*	Ending*
Fall 1998	104	11.5	10.5
Fall 1998	101	9.0	8.4
Fall 1998	102	8.6	9.1
Fall 1998	103	10.9	9.9
Fall 1999	101	9.1	9.8
Fall 1999	102	9.9	12.0
Fall 1999	103	10.0	10.9
Fall 1999	104	8.8	9.1
Fall 1999	105	9.1	10.2

*Average grade equivalency as scored on the Nelson-Denny Reading Test

Developmental reading

Focusing as it does on a lack of vocabulary and comprehension skills, research on developmental reading methods is almost exclusively predicated on a deficit model of learning. Developmental reading courses are similarly constructed as "college success" courses with a great deal of emphasis placed on study skills and content area reading strategies (Barksdale-Ladd & Rose, 1997). Nearly two decades ago, Brittain (1982) found that college reading instruction invariably fell into one of the following two categories: (a) courses where reading was constructed as a series of study skills, and (b) courses where reading was constructed in relation to a combined content area course. While Laine, Laine, and Bullock (1999) found that successful developmental reading instruction is contingent upon innovative teaching and learning strategies, little research to date has been conducted on evoking critical literacy pedagogy in either of Brittain's two categories within the framework of a developmental reading course (see McFarland, Dowdey, & Davis, 1999 for an exception). This study fills a gap in the research on developmental reading programs, where basic skills in reading are reconceptualized through the lens of critical literacy.

In my study, basic skills of reading (e.g., comprehension, vocabulary development, inference, synthesis)

were subsumed into a larger framework of critical literacy. Critical literacy is defined by researchers such as Lankshear and McLaren (1993), Giroux (1993), Bee (1993), Brady (1994), and others as literacy that begins with a rising consciousness of not merely the functionality of print but also the power of language to both silence and give voice to instances of oppression in issues of socially determined disparities. In this vein of consciousness, Paulo Freire (1995) wrote that students first had to read the world before they could read the word. Emergent literacy research (Avery, 1993; Calkins, 1994; Cooper, 1993; Morrow, 1997) espouses a similar philosophy, that children read their environment long before they begin to decode print. In other words, literacy at all levels always begins with the impetus of the context for reading, writing, and speaking. The impetus of the context for students in developmental reading courses exists within a system of social stratification. The construction of developmental studies courses by the larger academic community as subacademic courses teaching subacademic skills creates a relevant context for developmental studies students to delve into issues of power from a personal, experiential vantage point.

Students in basic skills courses need to read the world of the academy before they can read and write for an academic community. Critical pedagogues (e.g., Shor, 1996) would argue that we cannot successfully invite students into the world of academic reading by drilling them in a series of disconnected subskills in literacy. Rather, we must give them complete, contextualized reading and writing experiences first and then work on skills through student-driven assessment and instruction. Similarly, we must redefine the concept of "basic skills" in reading through the stance of critical literacy. While this is a seemingly compelling argument in favor of critical literacy in a developmental reading course, fully realizing critical literacy in such a context is problematic. The definition and experience of critical literacy is so utterly dependent upon the students' relationships with the texts of their lives that the story of critical literacy within the population of "remedial" students is always, necessarily, delicately contingent upon these relationships.

In the section of Reading 100 that I taught, critical literacy began with a pedagogy of questions (Freire, 1995) pertaining to discussions surrounding the nature of a developmental studies course in reading. These initial dialogues were pivotal in establishing a culture conducive to critical literacy. The dialogues were difficult for me as a teacher because some students expressed open hostility to being placed in the course based on an arbitrary score on the ACT test, receiving no credit toward graduation, and being required to pay for it.

Rose's (1989) account of remediation, tracking, and the academy in *Lives on the Boundary* served as the core text for the course. This text further fueled class discussions about the perceived unfair placement of students into the course. From this text, students read, wrote, and

talked about the larger system of developmental studies across the U.S. as well as their own experiences. The assignments I gave students to keep a dialogue journal, write in-class reflective essays, compile a reader's resource notebook, and write a literacy narrative facilitated their learning and growth from skill development to critical reflection and questioning.

Bound by university guidelines and expectations for developmental studies coursework, I wasn't able to negotiate course assignments to the extent that Shor (1996) did. I did, however, seek to provide assignments that were student-driven. The assignments for the class began with an in-class dialogue journal. This journal consisted of students first responding to class readings and discussions and then responding to their classmates' responses. I also participated in this weekly activity. I included this assignment as a mechanism to give each student a chance to voice ideas and receive feedback on these ideas. The journals also gave students less structured opportunities for writing practice. Over time, students began to generate more in-depth responses and questions with their audience in mind. The following exchange from a dialogue journal exemplifies the beginning of student reflection on their educational experiences.

Student 1: If I was designing a reading developmental class I would do pretty much the same things that we are doing in here but I would have prepared students for things like this in earlier grades so they wouldn't have to take these courses in college. I think reading should be taught by understanding what you are reading along with how to read a certain word.

Student 2: I agree they should prepare students in earlier grades and maybe they wouldn't fall behind in college. Understanding what you read might make the reading more interesting.

Mellinee: What happened in your earlier school experiences that led to your having to take a developmental studies course in reading? What were you not taught?

Student 1: I don't think that there really is anything that I haven't learned, that maybe I should've learned. Maybe I don't comprehend all the time but I don't think that it is to the point where I should have to take a basic reading class in college, but that's what the test proved. (Dialogue journal, September, 1999)

In addition to modeling writing and responding for my students, I was also participating in learning through joining this activity.

Students also kept a reader's resource notebook. The purpose of this assignment was for students to create an archive to assist them in their reading and literacy skills.

The notebook provided students with an opportunity to personalize skill aspects of their learning in a contextualized and systematic fashion. The reader's resource notebook was a compilation of vocabulary encountered in course readings, notes from class discussions on the readings, and reading strategies that worked for the student. I presented this assignment largely as an investigative tool for students to explore the mechanics of their literacy development. As such, it served the purposes of both skill exploration and metacognitive awareness development.

Every class period, we concluded with a summary of what we did on one side of an index card and what we learned on the other side. These cards not only helped students distill key ideas and recall class events, but also served as data for me. With the cards, my students were able to give me continual and instant feedback on each class. I was also able to monitor my students' literacy development (e.g., questioning, reflection, analysis, rising consciousness) through their observations of the class. The following are examples of responses to one class:

What did we do?

- Today we read pp. 111–114 and got into groups and discussed what went on and how Mike Rose is dealing with what is going on. We responded in our journals about our literacy lessons.
- We read out of *Lives on the Boundary* and David gave his presentation on a soccer player.
- Article presentation; went over Monday dialogue journals; read 111–114 in *Lives on the Boundary*; discussion in small groups about what we read; Nov. 1 class feedback.
- Discussed our journal topic, heard David's presentation. Read pgs. 111–114, got in small groups.
- We did dialogue journals and students volunteered to read from pg. 111–114 in *Lives on the Boundary*. We read 11/1/99 What did we do/What did we learn and I explained the info I got from it.

What did we learn?

- I learned how Mike Rose feels about students. I learned what other students are learning about Mike Rose.
- I learned what *tracking, resistance,* and *remediation* meant.
- Mike Rose really cares about the kids.
- What I learned was that the children Mike Rose taught live in very harsh environments.
- How others felt about *Lives on the Boundary*, the literacy words *tracking, resistance,* and *remediation*.
- Everybody will have trouble in some subject, but you can't let it take you down. Never give up.

- We learned different people's ideas in their journal and what Mike Rose's students' lives are like.
- I learned what Dr. Lesley does with these cards. I realized that remediation will help in the long run.

(Class archive, November 3, 1999)

From these statements, I could tell how many of my students were developing reading skills such as inference (e.g., how Mike Rose *really* felt about his students), empathy (e.g., how my students felt about the students in the book), and critical analysis (e.g., how concepts of tracking, remediation, and resistance figured into the book).

Another assignment in the course consisted of in-class reader response essays written about excerpts from *Lives on the Boundary*. On one occasion toward the end of the semester, I asked students to revise essays written in the previous class to include five vocabulary words from their reader's resource notebooks. I used this revision request to demonstrate for the students Noguchi's (1991) notion of the ways writing signifies class distinctions. By incorporating and applying the academic vocabulary students were encountering in their writing, they were able to begin to emulate the discourse patterns of the academy. This assignment demonstrated the students' growing control of academic discourse. By couching the assignment in terms of social class markers in discourse, I was attempting to move students toward a critical literacy insight on the ways language intertwines with societal power.

The final assignment was to write a literacy narrative (Soliday, 1994) of the story of how students acquired literacy. Through this assignment students noted social and emotional "disconnects" in their education and their lives at times when they were supposed to be developing literacy. For instance, one student wrote the following:

> Reading out loud in front of the class way always a challenge for me. My problem was that I would get nervous because I wouldn't want to mess up in front of my friends. But, of course I would get really nervous and mess up or I couldn't pronounce a word correctly. Sometimes the other students would giggle when I would read or make fun of me. So, therefore, I didn't have a strong self-confidence and I wouldn't push myself to do better because I thought I couldn't be as smart as them. (December, 1999)

Another student wrote about similar disconnects in his literacy narrative:

> From first grade to the fifth grade it got harder and easier at the same time if that makes sense. Reading was the easy part; it was the whole English part that through me off. I understood what a noun and a verb was but I didn't know how to use them. So I was screwed so to speak. Teachers at my elementary school had other

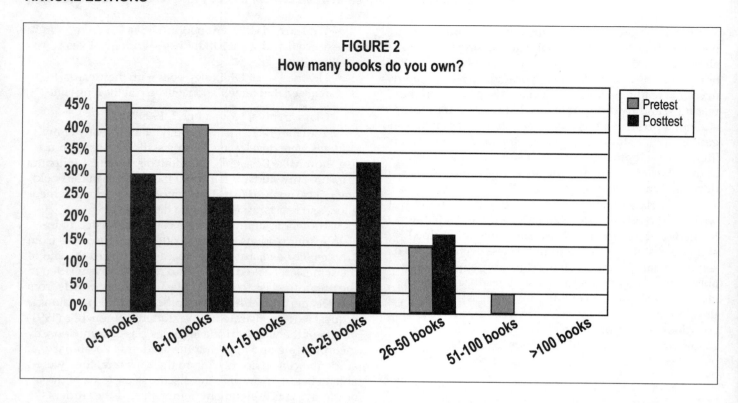

FIGURE 2
How many books do you own?

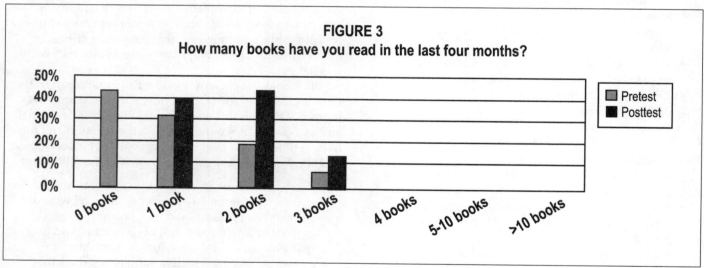

FIGURE 3
How many books have you read in the last four months?

things to worry about or they just didn't care. A teacher later on in the sixth grade stumbled across my disability and I was placed in a chapter one class where I was basically taught everything over again. To my disbelief it help. I was teased and picked on for being in the class. The teasing took a toll on my self-esteem. I felt really small and stupid and that caused me to drop the whole idea of reading except in school. My reading skill dropped once again and I didn't care. (December, 1999)

One of the most powerful literacy narratives was written by a student who through our discussions of expanding literacy beyond written texts, realized her literacy was disconnected at home long before she learned to decode print. This student wrote:

As I was growing up I learn many ways of reading. I learn how to read my father's attitude, I learn to read books from school and on my own, I learn to take care of my younger brothers and sister by reading my mother, I also read feeling and objects to write my poetry.

Since I can remember my father has had a drinking problem. I always knew what to do and how to act after reading him for a few years. Some days my dad would come home smelling weird and had blood shot eyes. I never understood what that was all about, I just knew he was going to be a different

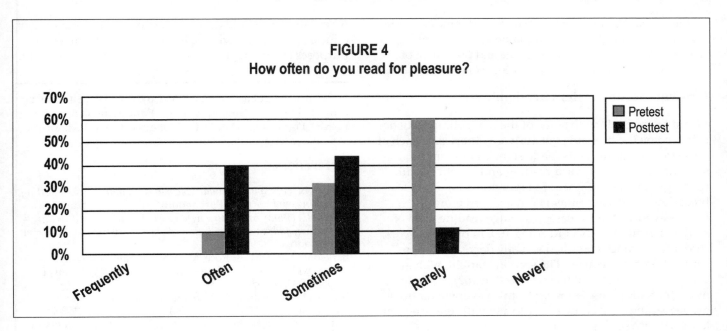

FIGURE 4
How often do you read for pleasure?

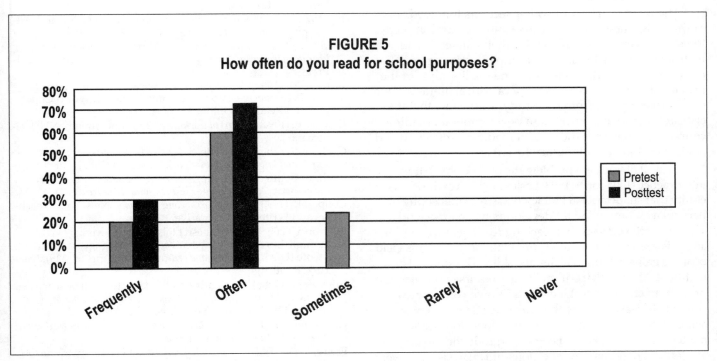

FIGURE 5
How often do you read for school purposes?

person from hours before. At first I would see that my dad's walk was weak and he wore a wicked smile. I would walk by him to see if he had that strong bitter smell on him. Once I smelled that ugly odor I had to think fast, I had to think of ways to tell my mom without him knowing. By reading his actions I learned to act fast and think quickly. As I watched him speak to my mother his words were mixed, his voice was very sharp and deep. Each time he would start talking, he would talk about all the happy and good times they had. Then he moves on to all the bad things that happen between them, after that he gets very angry and he would take his

anger out on my mother. As I was reading him I knew that I had to do something, once he started to raise his voice. (December, 1999)

These examples of students' writing and reflection about their literacy development mark the beginning of a journey of self-awareness within a larger social and academic structure facilitated by critical literacy. My approach to critical literacy was to bring critical reflection on constructions of literacy into the course content. The themes of the course initiated from this point as we explored concepts of being present, place, silence, play, teachers, community, justice, and transformation. We found that what's transformative for one student within a critical literacy context may not be for the next. Also, simply approaching literacy in relationship to critical reflection about the status of language and placement of courses within a university leads to critical literacy.

Critical literacy fosters academic success

I want to conclude with some of the compelling statistics collected on the pre-and poststudy inventories. In each of these measures, students made significant gains, and students' attitudes toward reading and practices with reading improved. (Please see Figures 2–5 for a breakdown of these results.) Perhaps even more impressive was the increase in average reading level of students in all sections of Reading 100. In previous years, students' reading scores had actually decreased upon completion of the course. The section I taught, with an explicit focus on critical literacy (section 102), made the most dramatic gains—moving from an average ninth-grade reading level equivalency to a twelfth-grade equivalency. (Please see Figure 1.)

The instructors for the other sections followed some of the assignments for the course and did not complete Rose's *Lives on the Boundary* with their classes. These instructors similarly did not attempt a pedagogy of critical literacy in their sections. The results support the previously cited research in favor of critical literacy. If we can learn anything from this study it's the fact that it's critical for students enrolled in developmental reading courses to experience the level of reading—reflection and analysis—that critical literacy fosters.

Critical literacy is a problematic philosophy to translate into practice (Ellsworth, 1992; Lesley, 1997). Yet the ideals of equity that shape critical literacy make the philosophy particularly compelling for developmental course work. This research suggests that teaching reading as a complex analysis even to "remediated" populations of students yield positive gains in students' literacy skills. The study also highlights the fact that critical literacy occurs in practice as a process. In effect, critical literacy is its own content area for students to master before they can enact a pedagogy of action. Introducing critical literacy to "developmental" readers begins students' successful introduction to academia where complex questions and analysis of answers drive inquiry in every discipline. If "remedial" students are to survive in the world of the academy, they cannot do so through lower level drill practice. They must learn to read analytically, beginning with their own circumstances of tracking, social stratification, and marginalization.

From this experience, I have come to believe that critical literacy fosters critical questioning and thinking and thus enhances students' comprehension skills in reading. Certainly, this study warrants further longitudinal investigation into the potential of academic success that critical literacy pedagogy fosters for developmental students. Finally, my attempt in this study to enact critical literacy hinged on my ability to create an environment where students could develop their own understanding of critical reading and writing in the academy. Eminent purposes for literacy compel us all to engage more deeply.

Lesley teaches at Eastern New Mexico University. She may be contacted there at Reading/Literacy Education, Station 25, ENMU, Portales, NM 88130, USA. She may be reached by e-mail at mellinee.lesley@enmu.edu.

References

Atwell, N. (1998) *In the middle: New understandings about writing, reading, and learning*. Portsmouth, NH: Heinemann.

Avery, C. (1993) *And with a light touch: Learning about reading, writing, and teaching with first graders*. Portsmouth, NH: Heinemann.

Barksdale-Ladd, M., & Rose, M. (1997). Qualitative assessments in developmental reading. *Journal of College Reading and Learning, 28*(1), 34–55.

Bee, B. (1993). Critical literacy and the politics of gender. In C. Lankshear & P. McLaren (Eds.), *Critical literacy: Politics, praxis, and the postmodern*. Albany, NY: State University of New York Press.

Bigelow, W. (1990). Inside the classroom: Social vision and critical pedagogy. *Teachers College Record, 91*, 437–448.

Brady, J. (1995). *Schooling young children: A feminist pedagogy for liberatory learning*. Albany, NY: State University of New York Press.

Brittain, M. (1982). *Development and remedial reading instruction for college students*. Paper presented at the 9th World Congress on Reading, Dublin, Ireland.

Calkins, L. (1994). *The art of teaching writing*. Portsmouth, NH: Heinemann.

Cochran-Smith, M., & Lytle, S. (1993). *Inside/outside: Teacher research and knowledge*. New York: Teachers College Press.

Cochran-Smith, M., & Lytle, S. (1999). The teacher research movement: A decade later. *Educational Researcher, 28*, 15–25.

Cooper, P. (1993). *When stories come to school*. New York: Teachers and Writers Collaborative.

Ellsworth, E. (1992). Why doesn't this feel empowering? Working through the repressive myths of critical pedagogy. In C. Luke & J. Gore (Eds.), *Feminisms and critical pedagogy* (pp. 90–119). New York: Routledge.

Erickson, F. (1986). Qualitative methods in research on teaching. In M.C. Wittrock (Ed.), *Handbook of research on teaching* (3rd ed., pp. 119–161). New York: Macmillan.

Fairclough, N. (1995). *Critical discourse analysis: The critical study of language*. New York: Longman.

Freire, P. (1995). *Pedagogy of hope: Reliving* Pedagogy of the Oppressed. New York: Continuum.

Giroux, H. (1993). Literacy and the politics of difference. In C. Lankshear & P. McLaren (Eds.), *Critical literacy: Politics, praxis, and the postmodern* (pp. 367–377). Albany, NY: State University of New York Press.

The Institute for Higher Education Policy. (1998, December). *College remediation: What it is, what it costs, what's at stake*. Washington, DC: Author.

Johnston, P. (1992). *Constructive evaluation of literate activity*. New York: Longman.

Laine, M., Laine, C., & Bullock, T. (1999). Developmental reading in the United States: One decade later. *Research and Teaching in Developmental Education, 15*(2), 5–17.

Lankshear, C., & McLaren, P. (1993). *Critical literacy: Politics, praxis, and the postmodern*. Albany, NY: State University of New York Press.

Lather, P. (1992). Critical frames in educational research: Feminist and poststructural perspectives. *Theory Into Practice, 35*(2), 70–71.

Lesley, M. (1997). The difficult dance of critical literacy. *Journal of Adolescent & Adult Literacy, 40,* 420–424.

McFarland, K.P., Dowdey, D., & Davis, K. (1999). *A search for nontraditional pedagogies in teaching developmental reading and writing*. (ERIC Document Reproduction Service No. ED 432 784)

Morrow, L.M. (1997). *Literacy development in the early years: Helping children read and write*. Boston: Allyn & Bacon.

Noguchi, R. (1991). *Grammar and the teaching of writing: Limits and possibilities*. Urbana, IL: National Council of Teachers of English.

Rose, M. (1989). *Lives on the boundary*. New York: The Free Press.

Shor, I. (1996). *When students have power: Negotiating authority in a critical pedagogy*. Chicago: University of Chicago Press.

Soliday, M. (1994). Translating self and difference through literacy narratives. *College English, 56,* 511–526.

Vine, H., & Faust, M. (1993). *Situating readers: Students making meaning of literature*. Urbana, IL: National Council of Teachers of English.

Vygotsky, L.S. (1978). *Mind in society*, Cambridge, MA: MIT Press.

Saving Black Mountain: The promise of critical literacy in a multicultural democracy

Students learned that their spoken and written words had the power to influence others.

Rebecca Powell, Susan Chambers Cantrell, Sandra Adams

We live in an era where multinational corporations wield unprecedented power; where special interest groups largely determine state and national political and economic agendas; where the gap between the rich and poor has reached dangerous proportions; and where what goes on in schools is often determined not by parents or educators, but by corporate interests. When popular power diminishes, then so does democracy.

What is the connection between democracy, literacy, and power? What can teachers do to challenge current inequities that exist between rich and poor, white and black, men and women? In this article, we explore answers to these questions by presenting a project undertaken by fourth graders in Kentucky that has aptly been called "Saving Black Mountain." The students who were involved in this project reside in a small U.S. community that is adjacent to Lexington, the second largest city in the state of Kentucky. The issues facing these students are very different from those of their Appalachian peers, yet these central Kentucky students chose to join forces with students from the mountainous region of eastern Kentucky to save the highest peak in the state from destruction by strip mining. In the process, the students learned a great deal about the hardships of their fellow citizens from Appalachia. They also learned that in a democratic society, their voices can make a difference.

To provide a theoretical framework for examining this project, we begin by exploring the concept of "democracy" and what it means in a multicultural society. Next, we outline several assumptions of critical literacy and suggest that it is important in realizing a strong democracy. We then show how the Saving Black Mountain project exemplifies critical literacy in action.

Linking democracy, equity, and literacy instruction

As educators, we are not accustomed to thinking of literacy instruction as having democratic aims. Rather, literacy is typically associated with economic aims—with producing efficient and productive workers who can help to maintain a nation's competitive edge. On a systematic and regular basis, we are bombarded with messages about the inadequacy of public education in general, and literacy instruction in particular. Recent controversies that dichotomize various instructional methodologies (e.g., whole language versus phonics, literature-based versus skills-based) and legislative decisions in several states to return to a "phonics only" instructional model are reflections of a larger political and social debate, a debate that involves who has the power to determine what gets taught in schools, how it gets taught, and even what constitutes literate behavior. Questions that focus solely on methodology (i.e., which methods will lead to the highest levels of student achievement) largely ignore issues of power and how that power works in society to enable and to oppress.

Democracy literally means power of the people. In a democratic system the populace—not special interest groups or the wealthier members of society—has the authority to govern. In an ideal democratic society, there is no aristocracy, but rather "an aristocracy of everyone" (Barber, 1992). Elsewhere, Barber (1984) contrasted a "thin" or representative form of democracy with a strong, participatory form. In strong democracies, people are directly involved in the decision-making process. (See also Arblaster, 1987; Sehr, 1997; Wood, 1988.)

Equity is consistent with a strong democratic system. In other words, the struggle for equity is a struggle to give "power to the people"—not just some people, but all people. In a multicultural society, realizing the goal of equity would mean that everyone had a voice—persons of color, the poor, and others who historically have been underrepresented. Note that equity does not mean the realization of individual personal interests; rather, it means that every person will have an integral role in determining what is best for the common good. A strong democracy that is grounded in equity involves mutual inquiry, collaboration, and compromise.

What role does literacy play in a strong, equitable, democratic system? In addressing this question, it's important to acknowledge that literacy is a social process. That is, it involves communication with others across time and space. In a strong democratic system, oral and written communication are essential. John Dewey, the famous American educational philosopher, conceived of democracy as a form of "associated living." Democracy would be at risk, he argued, when there was divisiveness in society, as when groups failed to interact with one another. In characterizing Dewey's ideas about democracy, Noddings (1995) wrote,

> Do people communicate freely across the lines of class, religion, race, and region? Whenever groups withdraw from connection, isolate themselves, and become exclusive, democracy is endangered...an isolationist society has by its very isolation risked its status as a democracy because it has lost "free points of contact" and opportunities to inquire beyond its own borders.

Dewey also argued that democracy is a process; that is, it is not a static type of governance, but rather involves the continuous formation of community. Thus, democracy is never stagnant or complete, but it is always "in the making." Thus, contrary to popular opinion, which suggests that a democratic community can be forged only through conformity of ideas (e.g., E.D. Hirsch's approach in his infamous 1988 theory of "cultural literacy"), Dewey maintained that democracy depends upon collaborative inquiry to arrive at mutual aims—aims that benefit the whole community rather than a select few.

Establishing mutual aims requires that we talk to one another, truly listen to others' perspectives, and value the opinions of those who are different from us. Thus, as Powell (1992, 1999) has argued, literacy instruction in a democracy ought to help students to communicate effectively with all persons in a multicultural society and to see the value of literacy for their own lives and for social, political, and economic transformation. We would argue that a democratic agenda requires a critical literacy—one that acknowledges the differentials of power in society and seeks to realize a more equitable, just, and compassionate community. It is to this topic that we now turn.

Conceptualizing a critical literacy

In recent years, whole language pedagogy has emerged as a means not only for literacy instruction, but also for individual empowerment (Edelsky, 1991). Critical literacy moves beyond holistic theory in that it confronts societal issues of power and dominance head on. A primary goal of critical pedagogy is to promote democracy by working toward a more just and equitable society.

We suggest that there are three basic underlying assumptions of critical literacy. First, critical literacy assumes that the teaching of literacy is never neutral but always embraces a particular ideology or perspective. Second, critical literacy supports a strong democratic system grounded in equity and shared decision making. Third, critical literacy assumes that literacy instruction can empower and lead to transformative action. We shall examine each of these assumptions.

Assumption 1: Literacy instruction can never be neutral. The teaching of literacy requires that we make certain decisions about what is taught and how it is taught. Critical theorists have argued that these decisions are not neutral but are based upon our perceptions of what constitutes literate behavior in a given social context. For instance, schools historically have reinforced the standards of those who have the power to define appropriate language use. Hence, the "hillbilly" discourse of eastern Kentucky and the black vernacular of students of color are deemed inadequate (and even deficient) within the educational institution, despite the fact that both are systematic and highly complex linguistic forms. Similarly, our choice of texts is a political decision, and despite recent trends popularizing multicultural literature, many of our textbooks remain largely monocultural and present what Banks (1995) referred to as "mainstream academic knowledge". Hence, the cultural knowledge of students of color and other underrepresented groups becomes relegated to the margins of what is considered "essential knowledge."

Beyond this, however, critical theorists would argue that how we teach literacy is also problematic. Traditional instructional approaches define literacy as a series of discrete skills that can be codified and transmitted to students. When students master these skills, they are deemed "literate." This model of literacy assumes that knowledge is "culture free" and that it can be constructed by those outside the world of the classroom. Skills-based instruction presumably removes literacy from its social and cultural contexts by presenting it as a mere tool for transmitting seemingly objective information. Thus, rather than using written language to promote creative and critical thought, literacy instruction becomes reduced to providing ritualized, mechanical responses or to producing the "right" answer in response to predetermined questions (Shannon, 1990). Thus, knowledge acquisition is controlled through both the content and structure of the curriculum materials.

Absent in such models is an acknowledgement that literacy is both a social and a cultural phenomenon. That is, it is created and used in social contexts to communicate with others—to express our ideas, to share our stories, to give us a voice. In contrast, the literacy of school often controls, marginalizes, and silences. Giroux (1992) wrote that

> Dominant approaches to reading limit the possibilities for students to mobilize their own voices in relation to particular texts. In its dominant form, literacy is constructed in monolithic rather than pluralistic terms. Literacy becomes a matter of mastering either technical skills, information, or an elite notion of the canon.

Holistic approaches to literacy instruction validate the social and cultural nature of literacy by focusing on authentic uses of written language and by insisting that children read and write for real purposes and real audiences (Edelsky, 1991). A critical view of literacy takes holistic teaching into the political domain by assuming that no knowledge is neutral but is always based upon someone's perception of reality, someone's perspective of what is important to know (Apple, 1993; Edelsky, 1999; Powell, 1999). Hence, critical teachers view texts as artifacts to be deconstructed in order to determine their underlying assumptions and hidden biases. What are the relations of power that are embedded in the text? What images are being promoted in terms of race, ethnicity, gender, and socioeconomic class? Whose interests are being served by this text, and whose are being marginalized? Taking a critical stance requires that we address issues of equity; thus, questions such as these become prominent in classrooms that promote a critical literacy.

Assumption 2: Critical literacy is consistent with a strong democratic system. As we indicated earlier, a strong democracy requires equity or shared decision-making power. Thus, a critical literacy promotes democracy by challenging inequities in society. Students learn how power works to promote particular interests over others, such as by denigrating the cultural knowledge, language, and experiences of subdominant populations while simultaneously elevating the status of dominant cultural knowledge, language, and experiences. These messages of inferiority and superiority are subtle yet powerful, and they become part of our taken-for-granted assumptions about the world.

A critical literacy helps students to unlock the hidden cultural assumptions and biases of texts. For instance, Australian educator Jennifer O'Brien had her 5- to 7-year-olds read junk mail critically by asking them to consider who benefits from Mother's Day advertisements (Luke, O'Brien, & Comber, 1994). The children compared the images of the mothers in the catalogues to "real" mothers and, contrary to the characteristics of many of their mothers, they found that most of the women in the catalogues were young, Anglo Australian, and pretty. The children also conducted a student survey on their mothers' gift preferences and found that mothers actually desired many things for Mother's Day that were not represented in the catalogues, such as leisure time, appreciation, and "peace and quiet," as well as items like tickets to the movies and photographs. Through their activities, the children were asked to take a critical stance toward the messages found in popular texts.

Critical literacy also promotes a strong democracy in that students are encouraged to consider all sides of an issue in the decision-making process, including views of persons whose perspectives traditionally have been marginalized or even silenced in schools and in society. The "transformative knowledge" of marginalized populations is given prominence in the curriculum, as students read and hear about the experiences and practices of historically underrepresented groups (Banks, 1995, 1997). Students become engaged in writing, sharing, and discussing stories and information that have relevance in their everyday lives. They explore current social issues and address problems in their community, "giving voice to the voiceless" (McElroy-Johnson, 1993) as they read and listen to the narratives of persons whose experiences differ from their own. In this way, critical literacy becomes "real-world" literacy that is truly functional—students are asked to read "the world" in addition to "reading the word" (Freire & Macedo, 1987).

Assumption 3: Literacy instruction can empower and lead to transformative action. Contrary to skills-based models that assume literacy instruction can be neutral, critical literacy is "consciously political" in that it intentionally promotes the basic tenets of democracy: freedom, justice, equality. Students are encouraged not merely to engage in a critical reading of a text, but also to take action. So, for instance, Australian educator Barbara Comber (1999) told about a primary teacher who involved her students in a study of the low number of trees in their community. Because trees are a commodity in South Australia, they are found more frequently in the affluent suburbs, and therefore can be considered a marker of one's socioeconomic status. As a result of their study, the students became involved with an urban renewal project in their area. They invited key government personnel to come to their school to respond to their questions and developed and mailed their own design to the people in charge of the project.

Similarly, students in Bob Peterson's fifth-grade class investigated Native American stereotypes in their school's books and classrooms. Subsequently, they decided to take action by teaching first graders about what they had found (Peterson, 1994). The students in Maria Sweeney's fourth-grade class chose to write and perform a play about apartheid after viewing a film on the subject. Sweeney (1999) wrote about similar projects done with students that led to social action: posters that were hung around the school and in store windows condemning racism, sexism, ageism, and classism; and picture books her students created for the school library that told the alternative view of Columbus's "discovery" of America.

Critical literacy goes beyond providing authentic purposes and audiences for reading and writing and considers the role of literacy in societal transformation. The students in these classrooms are learning a great deal more than how to read and write. They are also learning about the power of literacy—their literacy—to make a difference.

We shall now describe the project undertaken by fourth graders in Kentucky that illustrates the transformative potential of critical literacy. These children took a political stand and used their power as citizens to save a mountain from the destruction of strip mining.

Saving Black Mountain: A critical literacy project

> They scrape off the mountain, fill the valleys below. I can't drink my water, my well has sunk low. The scars stretch across her, her face looks so sad. The children are crying, the people are mad.
>
> Song written by Jessamine County, Kentucky, students

The southern Appalachian region of the United States has been marked by both economic and cultural exploitation. In the late 1800s and early 1900s, southern Appalachia was discovered by outside capitalistic investors, who descended upon the region in the years after the Civil War and bought up mountain land for its rich coal and timber reserves (Eller, 1982). Often land was purchased through "broad form deeds," which gave the mineral rights to speculators, leaving the surface land to be used for agricultural purposes.

Eventually many of the smaller land holdings became consolidated, and a few mining companies managed to gain a monopoly over the coal industry in the region. The coal barons also gained control of the local economic and political systems, establishing company towns and company stores where goods could be purchased only on credit or through company scrip. Between 1900 and 1930, over 600 such towns were established in the southern Appalachian region.

During World War I, with expanded production and increased profits, most operators left the company towns for a more comfortable life in the city. Many independent coal producers sold out to larger companies, leaving the coal fields in the hands of absentee owners who often had even less concern for the local residents. Dependence upon a single industry left the region subject to the fluctuations of the national economy, and with rising land prices, increasing taxes, and a more competitive market, local residents found that they could no longer sustain a self-sufficient agricultural economy.

Even today, mountain people in areas such as eastern Kentucky depend largely on the coal industry for their livelihoods. A survey conducted two decades ago of 80 counties in six Appalachian states revealed that 40% of the land and 70% of the mineral rights were owned by corporations (Beaver, 1983). The coal companies continue to wield tremendous power, and local residents have often had little input on how the land is to be used. Thus, while Appalachia has unlimited wealth in terms of natural resources, these resources have generally added to the coffers of a few individuals and corporations—many of whom do not even reside in the region—leaving Appalachia barren and its residents impoverished.

The struggle of the local population to gain control of their land and resources has been continuous and characterized by a number of grassroots movements and labor strikes. This struggle for local autonomy continues through the work of committed individuals and community action groups. For instance, residents gained a major victory in 1988 when a state constitutional amendment was passed that eliminated the coal industry's right to strip mine under the authority of broad form deeds without the landowner's permission. At the same time that eastern Kentuckians have been fighting for their rights, however, the rest of the nation continues to see Appalachia as a region of ignorance and inferiority. That image reinforces the tendency to "blame the victims" for their own plight and therefore undermines a broader democratic response.

Even within the state of Kentucky, there is divisiveness between the mountainous region of eastern Kentucky, the urban areas of central and northern Kentucky, and the rural western part of the state. While there have been a few initiatives to break down the images and stereotypes associated with eastern Kentucky, school children typically know very little about persons from other parts of the state. Thus, students in Kentucky often have erroneous images of other populations within their own state and are largely ignorant of the issues and problems that those others face. This divisiveness hinders the development of mutual goals that are so critical to a democracy.

In 1998 that situation changed for the fourth-grade students at Rosenwald-Dunbar Elementary in Jessamine County, which is located in the bluegrass region of central Kentucky just south of Lexington. One of their teachers, Sandy Adams (third author), who is a firm believer in inquiry-based learning, asked her students to choose a project that interested them. The children had been learning about Black Mountain, the highest peak in Kentucky, in their social studies textbook. After Adams told them that the mountain was slated to be strip mined, the children decided that they wanted to learn more. Soon the entire fourth grade became involved, and the students were arranging field trips, interviewing miners, and working with eastern Kentucky activists to halt the destruction of Black Mountain.

Initially it was not the students' intention to save the mountain. Rather, consistent with responsible democratic inquiry, their purpose merely was to learn about the issue so that they might address it from a position of knowledge rather than ignorance. They took a critical stance, talking with those in the region who benefitted from strip mining as well as those who opposed it. In those interviews, they discovered that many miners and their families depended upon coal mining for their livelihoods and thus supported the strip mining of "Big Black." Two students' comments illustrate their dilemma:

I guess we did go against strip mining, but we knew what the other people's perspective was. It's kind of a hard thing. You don't want to take those jobs away from the people....

You have to look at how the coal miners feel. When we were doing this project, we were always thinking of them and how they have to support their families.

At the same time, however, the students conducted research on the impact of strip mining on the natural environment, and their findings eventually led to their decision to fight to preserve the mountain.

At the time of the project, Jericol Mining Company had applied for a permit to expand its surface mining operations on Black Mountain. As part of the application process in Kentucky, companies are required to provide information on the environmental impact of their mining operations. Other groups are also permitted to submit petitions for consideration, at which point a public hearing is required prior to acting on the company's application. Further, while the application is being considered, mining is prohibited. Because of the unique habitat at higher elevations on the mountain, a petition had been filed by Kentuckians for the Commonwealth to declare elevations above 3,000 feet on Black Mountain unsuitable for mining. Hence, when the students visited the mountain, they were surprised to find that strip mining was occurring. They were also disturbed when they examined water samples from wells and streams and learned from local residents that their water sources had been contaminated.

The fourth graders then began what can only be considered an all-out fight to save Black Mountain. They decided to make a second trip there to gather more information for their project. They wrote to individuals to solicit funds to continue their campaign and subsequently collected thousands of dollars for the project. They alerted local newspapers and television stations and arranged for press conferences to talk about the mountain's future, and they even organized a "Hands Across the Mountain" rally with students from eastern Kentucky to raise public awareness. The Rosenwald-Dunbar students also wrote to the governor and to various state representatives to make their opposition known.

As part of their research, the students met with mining company officials in order to hear their perspective on the surface mining of Black Mountain. During the meeting, the children presented their findings and asked the officials to respond to their report. Company representatives tried to dissuade the students by stating that the facts they were presenting were false. Their teacher tells what transpired as follows:

The Coal Council came here from Frankfort and the Office of Surface Mining came from Bell County. An official from the Coal Association more or less told a student that she had made up facts in front of all these kids. She was standing there after handing him her writing and he made it a point to say "these facts are not true." So she looked around the room for help, but when she had gathered her thoughts she said, "Well, I used your [Web] site for a source." He didn't say anything else. But they came in and presented their side. We thought that was only fair.

In October of 1998, the students submitted a proposal to the Director of Permits of the Department for Surface Reclamation and Enforcement, urging the Department to consider alternatives to strip mining. This 10-page proposal included an analysis of the problem, data on the unique plant and animal life on the mountain, a rationale for the students' suggestions, and five recommendations. The proposed recommendations reflect the students' awareness of the complexity of the issue and the need to consider economic as well as environmental concerns:

1. Choose another mountain or area that is not so special to the people. And, that is not such a big part of our history. There is coal everywhere in Kentucky, not just Black Mountain.

2. Do underground mining. It's not the easiest or cheapest way, but it will save most of the stuff on top, and you can still get the coal out.

3. If the coal companies...are still going to strip mine Black Mountain, just don't mine near the highest peak. That way, the animals and plants that need high elevation, some of them will still live, and at least that part of the mountain will still be elegant.

4. Ashland Incorporated should buy the land, and not let the coal companies mine it.

5. Kentucky could maybe buy the mountain and turn it into a state park. Then it would still be lovely, people could still enjoy it, and the plants and animals could still live. (Submitted by a fourth-grade student at Rosenwald-Dunbar Elementary School)

In early December of the same year, a group of fourth-grade students from Rosenwald-Dunbar joined eighth

Students' purposeful literacy activities

Reading activities	Writing activities	Oral language activities	Instructional lessons
literary pieces related to the project	notetaking and documentation	storytelling sessions (e.g., Jack Tales)	brainstorming
feedback from readers (letters)	letters to the governor, state representatives, newspapers	presentations to various legislative committees	inquiry lessons (e.g., skimming, main ideas, supporting details)
research using books, articles, and Internet sources	response journals	presentations to Harlan County residents	in-class discussions based on information learned
various government documents	on-demand writing (writing prompts) tied to the project, to prepare for state test	presentations at colleges and universities	lessons on Kentucky government, citizenship, democracy, citizens' rights
newspaper articles/press releases on the project	writing in a variety of genres (e.g., personal narratives, articles, proposals, persuasive essays, reports)	presentations to/interviews with coal company representatives	lessons involving planning field trips, ceremonies, presentations
writing of other students	petitions and surveys	presentations to other students	formal reading lessons
legislature and mining company agreements	songs and poetry related to the project	interviews with Appalachian residents	lessons on effective writing in various genres
social studies textbook	statewide e-mails to students in other districts	interviews conducted by the news media (newspapers and television stations)	lessons on Appalachian culture (e.g., mountain music, quiltmaking)

graders from Harlan County in eastern Kentucky to present their findings to the legislature's joint committee on Agriculture and Natural Resources. With microphones in hand and with the aid of videotapes, transparencies, and posters that their classmates had created, the students spoke about the need to save Black Mountain. They urged the legislators to consider developing the mountain for tourism rather than for strip mining. One Harlan County student who argued for the economic benefits of tourism had a father who had been forced to quit his job as a miner because of illness. Another student, however, advocated for strip mining because he reasoned that preventing mining on Black Mountain could cause people to be out of work. One representative wrote a letter in response to the students' presentation:

I was impressed by the presentation concerning mountaintop removal mining on Black Mountain. I am opposed to mountaintop removal on that particular mountain, and that is why I invited your group to appear before the Interim Agricultural and Natural Resources Environmental Committee.

I urge you to continue your efforts and to appear at the public hearing to be held sometime in late January 1999....

Largely as a result of the students' efforts, a compromise agreement was reached in May 1999 between coal operators and Kentuckians for the Commonwealth whereby 1,850 acres on Black Mountain would be saved from logging and strip mining. The agreement also called for a 18,915-acre conservation area, with the state purchasing some of the timber and coal rights from the owners. Jericol Coal also agreed to make changes in existing strip mining permits and to develop a sediment control plan. In a subsequent newspaper article, teacher Sandy Adams was quoted as saying, "Who would have thought that kids could save a mountain?" (Rutledge, 1999).

Critical literacy in action

Consistent with a whole language perspective, it is clear that these fourth graders were involved in a number of authentic, purposeful literacy activities through their involvement in the Saving Black Mountain project. The Table summarizes the various activities in which the children were engaged.

All of the language arts strands included in the Kentucky Program of Studies were targeted: reading, writing, speaking, listening, observing, inquiring, and using technology. In addition, the project incorporated all of the fourth-grade social studies strands, including historical perspective of Kentucky, geography, economics, government and civics, and culture and society.

We would argue, however, that this project also exemplifies critical literacy in that the children learned about the transformative potential of literacy in a democratic society. As we outlined earlier, critical literacy involves confronting the non-neutrality of knowledge and texts (both spoken and written) and is consistent with a strong democratic system. The perspectives of historically marginalized groups are welcomed and alternative viewpoints are sought, as they are seen as necessary ingredients for informing the decision-making process. As with the Saving Black Mountain project, critical literacy often leads to social action as students begin to discover and internalize the problems of society, thereby leading to more transformative uses of written and oral language. Thus, critical literacy is real-world literacy in that it is integral to the discovery of societal inequities and subsequent action. For the students involved in this project, uncovering hidden agendas and learning about both sides of the issue were essential as they sought to understand the problems associated with Black Mountain. Consistent with a critical agenda, literacy also became an important avenue for realizing a strong democracy, one where the voices of those with historically limited power are truly heard.

Earlier in this article, we presented the ideas of John Dewey, who suggested that democracy is a form of "associated living" that can be sustained only through the interaction of diverse populations. Through the Black Mountain project, students in central Kentucky collaborated with students and community activists from the eastern part of the state to realize a common goal: the saving of a mountain. In the process, they learned about the problems faced by the Appalachian population, whose history and experiences have resulted in lives that vary significantly from populations elsewhere in the state. For instance, the students learned about economic and environmental conditions that mountain people must endure daily as a result of corporate power: land erosion, contaminated water, black lung disease. By talking with families and environmental activists in the region, they also learned how the local people have fought back. Thus, rather than merely learning about Appalachia through seemingly neutral facts found in a textbook, these children personalized the experiences of their mountain neighbors, thereby reading the *world* as they learned to read the *word*.

Beyond this, however, these students learned that literacy can make a difference. For them, literacy has power. When asked in interviews what this project meant to them, the students had various responses:

I think it made us feel special. We were a part of what was happening, and we helped save a part of Kentucky.

We made a difference. We changed people's lives.

Writing, getting something published, or sending something to the government, you don't think you're going to do that. Once you start, you push yourself as far as you can go until you achieve what you are trying to achieve. And we really did.

The interviews quoted were held nearly a year later, while the students were in fifth grade, yet it was evident that the children still had a great deal of enthusiasm for the project. Shortly after the interviews took place, a group of these students traveled to Washington, D.C., to accept the youth environmental education award presented by the U.S. Environmental Protection Agency.

Perhaps the students who benefitted the most from the project were special-needs students who had struggled with reading and writing in the past. One such young man reported that before the project he was considered a "behavior problem," and he hated reading and writing. He told us that during the project, however, he never got in trouble; if his teacher gave him the choice of playing outside or writing for the project, he'd probably write. Another special-needs student was proud that, as the result of a letter he had written to a local professor, he was able to raise US$500 for the project.

The Saving Black Mountain project shows what can be accomplished when we take seriously the importance of literacy for promoting democracy in a multicultural society. In reflecting about the project, an eastern Kentucky community activist (who wished to remain anonymous), told us that

The kids in Harlan County started the project to try to save Black Mountain from the devastating effects of mountaintop removal, but their efforts only gained mostly local attention. When the kids from central Kentucky joined in with their interest, their voices, their visits to inspect the potential destruction, the news media found it quite interesting that small "outsiders" cared enough to join the fight.... Those children came in here, and even they realized what these coal companies were about to do to our state's highest peak, so they went home and told their parents and everyone who would listen. Only then did the legislators from central Kentucky and the rest of the state take on the cause and join in the effort to rescue Black Mountain from total destruction. Thankfully, the state is in the process of buying Black Mountain to enshrine the peak for all of us to continue to enjoy. We owe so much to all of the children who took on the crusade to make a difference in the world, starting with southeastern Kentucky. I only wish that they will continue to believe in themselves, to know that they are a very important part of what we call democracy, because their voices were heard; they were sincere in their beliefs, and they didn't give up.

As teachers of literacy in a multicultural society, we have a choice. We can either teach literacy as a series of skills, or we can teach it as if words matter. Through the Saving Black Mountain project, the students who were involved discovered that words—their words—could have the power to effect change. While some of the adults who were involved sometimes doubted the children's ability to have an impact, teacher Sandy Adams said the students never gave up: "Somehow, in the back of my mind, I knew these kids could make a difference." We would suggest that this is what literacy in a democracy ought to be about.

Powell and Cantrell teach at Georgetown College in Kentucky (400 E. College Street, Box 275, Georgetown, KY 40324, USA). Adams is a student-based inquiry consultant with the Jessamine County Schools.

References

Apple, M.W. (1993). *Official knowledge: Democratic education in a conservative age.* New York: Routledge.

Arblaster, A. (1987). *Democracy.* Minneapolis, MN: University of Minnesota Press.

Banks, J.A. (1995). Multicultural education and curriculum transformation. *Journal of Negro Education, 64,* 390–400.

Banks, J.A. (1997). *Educating citizens in a multicultural society.* New York: Teachers College.

Barber, B.R. (1984). *Strong democracy: Participatory politics for a new age.* Berkeley, CA: University of California Press.

Barber, B.R. (1992). *An aristocracy of everyone: The politics of education and the future of America.* New York: Ballantine.

Beaver, P.D. (1983). Participatory research on land ownership in rural Appalachia. In A. Batteau (Ed.), *Appalachia and America: Autonomy and regional dependence* (pp. 252–266). Lexington, KY: University Press of Kentucky.

Comber, B. (1999, November). *Critical literacies: Negotiating powerful and pleasurable curricula—How do we foster critical literacy through English language arts?* Paper presented at the 89th annual conference of the National Council of Teachers of English, Denver, CO.

Edelsky, C. (1991). *With literacy and justice for all: Rethinking the social in language and education.* Bristol, PA: Falmer Press, Taylor & Francis.

Edelsky, C. (1999). *Making justice our project: Teachers working toward critical whole language practice.* Urbana, IL: National Council of Teachers of English.

Eller, R.D. (1982). *Miners, millhands, and mountaineers: Industrialization of the Appalachian South, 1880–1930.* Knoxville, TN: University of Tennessee Press.

Freire, P., & Macedo, D. (1987). *Literacy: Reading the word and the world.* South Hadley, MA: Bergin & Garvey.

Giroux, H. (1992). Textual authority and the role of teachers as public intellectuals. In C.M. Hurlbert & S. Totten (Eds.), *Social issues in the English classroom* (pp. 304–321). Urbana, IL: National Council of Teachers of English.

Hirsch, E.D., Jr. (1988). *Cultural literacy: What every American needs to know.* New York: Vintage.

Luke, A., O'Brien, J., & Comber, B. (1994). Making community texts objects of study. *Australian Journal of Language and Literacy, 17,* 139–149.

McElroy-Johnson, B. (1993). Giving voice to the voiceless. *Harvard Educational Review, 63,* 85–104.

Noddings, N. (1995). *Philosophy of education.* Boulder, CO: Westview.

Peterson, B. (1994). Teaching for social justice: One teacher's journey. In B. Bigelow, L. Christensen, S. Karp, B. Miner, & B. Peterson (Eds.), *Rethinking our classrooms: Teaching for equity and justice* (pp. 30–33). Milwaukee, WI: Rethinking Schools.

Powell, R. (1999). *Literacy as a moral imperative: Facing the challenges of a pluralistic society.* Lanham, MD: Rowman & Littlefield.

Powell, R.E. (1992). Goals for the language arts program: Toward a democratic vision. *Language Arts, 69,* 342–349.

Rutledge, K. (1999, May 6). Big victory for Big Black: Young activists celebrate agreement to limit mining. *The Jessamine Journal,* pp. 1, 7A.

Sehr, D.T. (1997). *Education for public democracy.* Albany, NY: SUNY Press.

Shannon, P. (1990). *The struggle to continue: Progressive reading instruction in the United States.* Portsmouth, NH: Heinemann.

Sweeney, M. (1999). Critical literacy in a fourth-grade classroom. In C. Edelsky (Ed.), *Making justice our project: Teachers working toward critical whole language practice* (pp. 96–114). Urbana, IL: National Council of Teachers of English.

Wood, G.H. (1988). Democracy and the curriculum. In L.E. Beyer & M.W. Apple (Eds.), *The curriculum: Problems, politics, and possibilities* (pp. 166–187). Albany, NY: SUNY Press.

From *The Reading Teacher* Vol. 54, No. 8, May 2001, pages 772-781. Copyright © 2001 by The International Reading Association. Reprinted with permission.

What Do We Mean by Literacy Now?

Jerome C. Harste

Every now and then we really do have breakthroughs in our understanding of literacy. Two of the most recent insights are "multiple literacies" and "literacy as social practice." Instead of one literacy, there are multiple literacies (Street, 1995). In addition to language, humans have developed a variety of ways to mean (art, music, movement, etc.). This is what the humanities are all about as well as why malls have background music. It is also why visual-text literacies (e.g., electronic computer games) are so appealing and compelling to our young.

The notion of multiple literacies has several implications for how we think about literacy. Different cultural groups have different ways of making meaning. This is what we find fascinating about travel. How many of us have not been fascinated with totem poles in Alaska or the hula in Hawaii? Even further, different cultural groups induct their children into literacy in different ways. Literacy means different things to different groups. Closer to home, school literacy may be very different from "everyday literacy" or even literacy as the parents of your students may be thinking about it.

Instead of thinking about literacy as an entity (something you either have or don't have), thinking about literacy as social practice can be revolutionary. When coupled with the notion of multiple literacies, literacy can be thought of as a particular set of social practices that a particular set of people value. In order to change anyone's definition of literacy, the social practices that keep a particular (and often older) definition of literacy in place have to change.

In terms of your classroom, it is important to ask, What kinds of social practices are in place and, as a result, how is literacy being defined? Who benefits from this definition of literacy? Who is put at jeopardy? What social practices would I have to put in place to make the everyday literacies that students bring with them to school legitimate? What kinds of things would I have to do to show that I honor the home literacies that students bring with them to school? What would I have to do to expand what it means to be literate in the 21st century?

This is not a matter of walking away from what we already know. A good language arts program for the 21st century continues to be comprised of three components—meaning making, language study, and inquiry-based learning, *but* (and this is a big *but*) the emphasis is different.

Meaning-Making

M. A. K. Halliday (1975) taught us that language did not develop because of one language user but rather because of two, and they wanted to communicate. Language is first and foremost a social meaning-making process. Most of what we know about language we have learned from being in the presence of others (Wells, 1986).

What this means for the 21st-century classroom is that students are going to continue to have lots and lots of opportunities to mean, not only in the form of reading and writing, but also in the form of visual-text literacies. I maintain that writing begins in voice. If you can get students to write "what is on their minds," the rest may not take care of itself, but you will have come a long way toward creating a potentially great literacy program. Barbara Kamler and Michelle Fine (2001) argue that we have to help students "relocate the personal," by which they mean that once students have expressed what is on their minds, we need to help them see how "the social"—meaning social, historical, and cultural forces—have been at play to position them in particular ways. These are the new social practices that need to be added to our process writing program. I like this position as it acknowledges what we teachers of writing already know: No one can write from nowhere.

In reading, we must continue to have "grand conversations" over literature (Peterson and Eeds, 1990). Literature study and literature discussion are cultural practices that an important segment of our society values and that, more likely than not, we as English language arts educators are mandated to pass on to future generations. Nonetheless, it is now obvious that we need to expand the canon so that all participants can see themselves in the literature, not as "other" but as the main character. This is why the use of multicultural literature is so important as well as why the use of literature that raises important social issues is key to making reading relevant (Harste, et al., 2000; Leland, et al., 2002).

While what materials we read is an issue, even more of an issue is what social practices we institute around our discussion of books. I like to think of it as opening up spaces in the curriculum for starting some much needed new conversations. We need to teach in such a way that students enjoy literature and at the same time come to see that language is never innocent. "Whose story is this?" "What would the story look like if it had been told by someone very different (in terms of race, gender, age, etc.) from the current author?" "What is being taken for granted and what other ways are there to think about this thing being discussed?"

Hilary Janks (2002), in her keynote address at the Annual Convention of the National Council of Teachers of English, pulled a text off the Web and showed how easy it can be to create those spaces that encourage conversation about social practices. It was a poster developed by the United Nations High Commissioner for Refugees (2002) entitled, "Spot the Refugee." It was meant to change people's attitudes towards refugees. The poster showed 40 Lego dolls all in different dress, with the following text:

> SPOT THE REFUGEE
>
> There he is. Fourth row, second from the left. The one with the moustache. Obvious really. Maybe not. The unsavory-looking character you're looking at is more likely to be your average neighborhood slob with a grubby vest and a weekend's stubble on his chin. And the real refugee could just as easily be the clean-cut fellow on his left. You see, refugees are just like you and me. Except for one thing. Everything they once had has been left behind. Home, family, possessions, all gone. They have nothing. And nothing is all they'll ever have unless we all extend a helping hand…"

On a first reading with students, a teacher might want to explore what connections the students are making with the text and what meanings they are getting out of the text. I would do this with the strategy, "One Observation, One Connection, One Surprise, One Question" (Short, Harste w/Burke, 1996). Figure 1 explains this strategy. On a second reading, let students begin to interrogate the text by building from what students have said. For instance, students might discuss how the authors of the poster have, probably unwittingly, paired refugees with "unsavory-looking characters" or described them as "slobs" who "wear grubby vests" and have "a weekend's stubble on their chin." Students might count the number of male and female dolls in the poster to find that three-fourths of them are male, leaving the impression that refugees are mainly unsavory men who are poor and need a helping hand. Certainly the impression given is that they are not skilled.

One Observation, One Connection, One Surprise, One Question

1. Give 4 sticky notes to each student.
2. On separate sticky notes, students are asked to jot down one observation, one connection, one surprise, and one question they have as a result of reading the text being studied.
3. Once students have their sticky notes, have them get in groups of 4 or 5 to share.

Note: As a variation, the sticky notes containing questions can be collected and run off on a single sheet of paper. In new groups, students can come together to discuss and answer the questions that have been generated by classmates. A whole class discussion should follow.

**Credit for this strategy is given to Jennifer Story (seventh-grade teacher, Dole Middle School, Honolulu, Hawaii) and Lee Heffernan (second-grade teacher, Childs Elementary School, Bloomington, Indiana).

Figure 1.

Discussions of this sort represent a new set of practices around what it means to be a reader. What I would argue is that students in the 21st century are going to have to be able to interrogate text for purposes of understanding how authors position readers. To be literate is to be able to elect what identity one wants to take on as well as what position one wants to take relative to the issues raised in texts.

> **Instead of thinking about literacy as an entity (something you either have or don't have), thinking about literacy as a social practice can be revolutionary.**

Language Study

Too often in the past we have reduced the study of language to phonics in reading, and spelling and grammar in the area of writing. I would argue that has never been good enough, but even more so when it comes to preparing 21st-century literate beings.

Rather than think in terms of phonics, spelling, and grammar, I believe it is helpful to think about what kinds of literacy one needs in order to read things critically. Bill Green (in Comber & Green, 1998) calls this "instrumental literacy."

Instrumental literacy is made up of all of those proficiencies one needs in order to be able to access a text and understand what it is doing to readers. In the case of our "Spot the Refugee" text, a reader not only has to be able to decode the text but understand how the authors use language to get certain work done. To make this concrete, notice their use of "he." The use of "he" reinforces the notion that refugees are men. Notice also how refugees become "they." All of a sudden, refugees are "othered." They may look like us, but they are a very different group of people; if not grubby, then certainly helpless. In this instance, the author uses pronouns to do the work. In other texts, other devices may be used, such as "Iraq Bombed," as if there were no agent involved in the bombing and hence no one has to take responsibility.

I think most of what is exciting about language falls well above the phoneme and grapheme level of text, and yet we do very little to help students understand how language works. Students need to be invited to become linguistic detectives as well as encouraged to practice writing texts that do different kinds of work. It is especially important that "everyday texts" be an integral part of our language arts program as this is where literacy is occurring in the lives of students. Many people, in fact, argue that today's youth learn more about literacy and what it means to be literate *outside* of school than they do in school (Nixon, 1998; Manning, 1999; Vasquez, 2000). In school, students can learn to examine the literacies that operate on them outside of school and how they might position and reposition themselves differently in the outside world. Critical literacy, Hilary Janks says (2001), is about language and power, language and access, diversity, and redesign. No matter how it is said, literacy in the 21st century is not a spectator sport.

Inquiry-Based Learning

Probably the one thing we can be sure of is that we are handing tomorrow's adults problems of some magnitude—poverty, homelessness, pollution, over-utilization of our natural resources ... the list goes on. There are no magic answers to these problems, nor is it likely that such problems, will be solved simply or single-handedly. Given this "reading" of our times, it should surprise no one that I am an advocate of inquiry-based collaborative learning (Harste, 1990, 1993).

What I want to see in curriculum is lots and lots of opportunities for students to explore their own inquiry questions using reading, writing, and other sign systems as tools and toys for learning. For the 21st century, I want to produce learners who know how to use art, music, drama, etc., to reposition themselves, gather information, change perspectives, re-theorize issues, and take thoughtful new social action.

Curriculum has historically been organized around the disciplines. Students move through the school day by going from English to social studies to science to any number of other disciplinary studies. Donald Graves (1994) called this "the cha-cha-cha curriculum." Students tick off subjects like it is a checklist: "Taken earth science; done with that." Even in college, they say: "Taken women's studies; done with that." Rather than invite students to use earth science or gender as a lens to examine their world, we've inadvertently reinforced the notion that they are "done with that." This is why, in part, the redesign of curriculum begins with reflexivity; the self-reflective interrogation and critique of what it is we have been doing. Rest assured, we have all had our hand in the cookie jar.

Don't get me wrong. I think the disciplines are important. But they are only important in relationship to the inquiry questions of learners. It is for this reason that I want curriculum to begin with what is on students' minds; with what makes them itch; with what questions they have. Disciplines can and should be introduced as perspectives that students can take in un-

packing and understanding issues. The same is true of the arts. Curricular invitations to explore what something looks like in art or in music can be absolutely illuminating.

If we return to "Stop the Refugee," all kinds of questions might be pursued. How many refugees are really men as opposed to women? If one does one's homework, what one finds is that 80 percent of all refugees are women rather than men. So who, we might ask, is being served by the visual text in this poster? Clearly not men. They are already seen as wolves after little gullible girls from our fairy tales. This poster only reinforces such stereotypical thinking.

Conclusion

If asked to critique education, I would argue that too often in the past our English language arts curricula have focused on meaning making with a half hour of phonics thrown in. For the most part, studying language in terms of what work it does and how it does it has been left out, as has providing daily opportunities to inquire into problems of personal and social relevance to learners. No wonder, then, that students learn more about literacy on the streets than they do at the chalkface. This has to change. The real question that each of us has to ask is, "What kind of literate being should inhabit the 21st century?" Asked differently, "What kind of lives do we want to live and what kind of people do we want to be?" For my part, I want critically literate beings who know how language works and can use it to make meaning and reposition themselves in the world in a more democratically thoughtful and equitable manner.

> **Students in the 21st century are going to have to be able to interrogate text for purposes of understanding how authors position readers.**

Jerome C. Harste is Distinguished Professor of Language Education at Indiana University. He can be reached at harste@indiana.edu.

Bibliography

Comber, B., & Green, B. (1998). *Information technology, literacy, and educational disadvantage*. Adelaide: South Australia Department of Education, Training, & Employment.

Graves, D. (1994, July). *Inviting diversity through writing*. Keynote address given at the 4th Annual Meeting of the Whole Language Umbrella (audiotaped), San Diego, CA.

Halliday, M. A. K. (1975). *Learning to mean: Explorations in the development of language*. London: Edward Arnold.

Harste, J. C. (1990). Inquiry-based instruction. *Primary Voices, K–6, 1* (1), 3–8.

Harste, J. C. (1993). Literacy as curricular conversations about knowledge, inquiry, and morality. In M. Ruddell & R. Ruddell (Eds.), *Theoretical models and processes of reading* (4th ed., pp. 1220–1242). Newark, DE: International Reading Association.

Harste, J. C., with Breau, A., Leland, C., Lewison, M., Ociepka, A., & Vasquez, V. (2000). Supporting critical conversations in classrooms. In K. M. Pierce (Ed.), *Adventuring with books (12th ed., pp. 507–554). Urbana, IL: NCTE.*

Janks, H. (2001, May). *Critical literacy: Models, methods, and motivations.* Keynote address given at the co-sponsored IRA/NCTE Critical Perspectives on Literacy Task Force Preconvention Institute, Annual Meeting, International Reading Association, New Orleans, LA.

Janks, H. (2002, November). *Critical literacy: Deconstruction and reconstruction* (mimeographed). Keynote address given at the Annual Convention of the National Council of Teachers of English, Atlanta, Georgia.

Kambler, B., & Fine, M. (2001). *Relocating the personal: A critical writing pedagogy.* Albany: NY: State University of New York Press.

Leland, C. H., & Harste, J. C., with Berghoff, B., Bomer, R., Flint, A. S., Lewision, M., & Moller, K. (2002). Critical literacy. In A. A. McClure & J. V. Kristo (Eds.), *Adventuring with books* (13th ed., pp. 465–487). Urbana, IL: NCTE.

Manning, A. (1999). *Frameworks for locating practice* (mimeographed). Presentation given at a Mount Saint Vincent University Open Learning Course, Mississagua, Ontario, Canada.

Nixon, H. (1998). Fun and games are serious business. In J. Sefton-Green (Ed.), *Digital diversions: Youth culture in the age of multimedia.* London: UCL Press.

Peterson, R., & Eeds, M. (1990). *Grand conversations.* New York: Scholastic.

Short, K. G., Harste, J. C., with Burke, C. L. (1996). *Creating classrooms for authors and inquirers.* Portsmouth, NH: Heinemann.

Street, B. (1995). *Social literacies: Critical approaches to literacy in development, ethnography, and education.* London: Longman.

United Nations High Commissioner for Refugees (2002). *UNHCR Lego posters.* Web site: www.unhcr.org.ch.

Vasquez, V. (2000). Our way: Using the everyday to create a critical literacy curriculum. *Primary Voices K–6,* 9 (2),8–13.

Wells, G. (1986). *The meaning makers: Children learning language and using language to learn.* Portsmouth, NH: Heinemann.

UNIT 2
Culture of Literacy

Unit Selections

Key Points to Consider

- What is a culture of literacy?

- What culture dominates secondary schools?

- What are the signs and symbols of a culture of literacy?

- How can teachers contribute to developing a culture of literacy in secondary schools?

 **Links: www.dushkin.com/online/**
These sites are annotated in the World Wide Web pages.

Archived Information
http://www.ed.gov/pubs/FamLit/transfer.html

I have already alluded to the role that culture plays in the educational process. Whether we define critical literacy as skills for mastery learning or as a critical thinking process in which students construct meaning out of texts—books and environment—we must consider how to build a culture of literacy. Having included reading, writing, speaking, and listening in the definition of critical literacy, it is easier to grasp the concept that a culture of literacy would include each of these functions. In a history classroom, a culture of literacy would move beyond the students reading one assigned textbook; defining persons, places, and things; answering section questions; taking notes; memorizing information; and taking multiple choice, matching, fill-in-the-blank, and short answer type tests.

I believe that in a culture of literacy, students would read multiple texts to bring out diverse views on events and issues. Students would critically think about the reasons why events happened and how the consequences are being played out in society today. Ethical and moral decision making is a topic that cannot be avoided in a culture of literacy. Building on Goodman's reference to John Dewey's perspective, Democratic or civic education parallels cultures of literacy. Dewey believed that education was the foundation to a Democratic society, but his definition of education was a critical one in which students participated in the construction of meaning. It is the participation that is the foundation of a democratic society. Each must exercise his or her voice in the construction of community.

In my course, "Critical Reading in the Content Area," my students engage in a critical reading activity in which they work in teams of five to eight people to design a change process. While students are reading two to four journal articles and two textbook chapters each week in preparation for class dialogues, they also spend 45 minutes to an hour each class period with a small group of peers, grappling with how to activate an entire school towards building a culture of literacy. It is only after about the fourth meeting that my students begin to realize that they are in the very process they are trying to design. It is only through the dialogical process, where all voices begin to be heard, that the students experience the development of a democratic community. They eventually realize, they cannot construct another school's culture of literacy; they can only design a dialogical process through which the members of any school can engage in literacy practices to express their views and grow to understand other members' views. A culture that fosters the open and free exchange of ideas is the beginning of a culture of literacy.

The articles in this section discuss the concept of school culture and provide pre-service teachers, in-service teachers, and administrators with the opportunity to critically analyze the connection between policies, practices, and school culture. Learners will be challenged to consider the concept of building a culture of literacy through policies and practices. Secondary educators are challenged to consider the dichotomy between the culture of literacy in elementary schools and the culture of sports that is clearly visible in secondary schools. I feel the movement towards prescriptive reading-centered curriculums of elementary schools who are bound to federally funded reading programs is anti-democratic and thus counter the development of a culture of literacy as defined by critical thinking. The focus on reading in elementary grades does, however, create a culture of literacy, even if it is limited to a mastery level.

In "Creating a Middle School Culture of Literacy" (1997), Robert Feirsen contrasts the void of a culture of literacy experienced by students as they transition from elementary school to middle school. Feirsen appeals to middle school educators to transform the culture for the sake of literacy. In "Building Sound Literacy Learning Programs for Young Adolescents through Collaborative Learning" (1997), Judith L. Irvin presents six different methods found in secondary schools for teaching literacy: no reading instruction, remedial reading courses, developmental reading courses, reading in the content area, integrated language arts programs, and thematic learning. In "Improving Young Adolescent Literacy Through Collaborative Learning" (1997), Karen D. Wood, Rachel L. McCormack, Diane Lapp, and James Flood present collaborative learning as an ideal instructional strategy for meeting the social and developmental needs of secondary students as a way of promoting critical literacy. Finally, in "A Culture of Literacy in Science" (2002), Donna Hooker Topping and Robert Ann McManus describe a middle school science room in which the science teacher cares about reading and writing and uses the two in science as part of the school-wide accountability for literacy. It takes the commitment of all stakeholders to create a culture of literature in the secondary school context.

Educators interested in shifting their classroom, school, or community towards a culture of critical literacy are encouraged to begin by using these articles and the remaining articles in this *Annual Edition* as texts for engaging in dialogue with colleagues, students, administrators, and community members. While the articles do not contain the answers as in a how-to manual, they provide texts to stimulate critical dialogues. It is in the dialogue as a democratic process—critical literacy of speaking and listening—that the change has a chance to take place.

Creating a Middle School Culture of Literacy

Robert Feirsen

Walk into an elementary school and take a look around. In all likelihood, the sights and sounds of literacy will barrage your senses. At one entrance, a bulletin board may display student writing under a catchy, alliterative tide. In a classroom, students may be publishing their latest poems, while others are conferencing with peers and teachers as they work toward their final drafts. A stroll down a hallway may find a cluster of students sprawled outside a classroom, reading a book by a noted children's author. Over the main office door, a sign enlivened by a smiling face may greet visitors with the announcement. "Welcome to our school—a community of readers!"

Elementary schools often preach consistent messages about the importance of reading, writing, listening, and speaking. Daily routines are supplemented by special assemblies, contests, author visits, guest readers, reward systems, and parent workshops. Together, they focus attention on the central importance of becoming literate members of the community.

Follow elementary students into middle school, however, and observe a startling change: the zeal and enthusiasm noted during earlier days get tempered, and the drive for literacy appears to wither. Several factors account for this dramatic turn of events. Middle school students manifest a significant change in levels of motivation. Students once focused on pleasing the adults in their lives develop an emerging sense of independence and a greater need for acceptance by peers (Wolf, 1991). Emotional peaks and valleys consume much time and energy (Irvin, 1990). Social pressures and the media place an emphasis on being part of the crowd; no one wants to be labeled "geek." Self-concept and confidence in one's abilities to master new challenges often take a nosedive (Eccles, Midgley, Wigfield. Buchanan, Reuman, Flanagan, & Mac Iver, 1993). Through all this turmoil runs an emphasis on action. Many middle schoolers therefore agree with Atwell's (1987) student Melissa, who commented, "I don't like to read because I think reading is boring. I like to do things. I'll read the sports pages and comic books but that's it because it's JUST SO BORING [emphasis in original]".

Reading, writing, and more formal forms of speaking also find themselves competing with a host of other endeavors during the day. Athletics, cocurricular programs, responsibilities at home, flirting, visiting with friends, and other early adolescent activities occupy much of the available free time. As a result, "When reading doesn't happen in school, it's unlikely to happen away from school, which means it's unlikely to happen at all" (Atwell. 1987, p. 156).

The picture, however, does not have to remain bleak. In fact, middle school educators have enormous potential to forge literate environments that encourage lifelong learning. As noted by the Carnegie Council on Adolescent Development, "Cognitive development during early adolescence is not on hold" (1989). Research and experience confirm that middle level students are greatly interested in the world around them; they are eager to investigate such concerns as personal and group identity, morals and values, change, and participation in the complexities of the adult world (George, Stevenson, Thomason, & Beane, 1992). Learning activities that encourage exploration of these intriguing areas and that allow students to flex their newly discovered cognitive abilities for critical thinking and abstraction will create a student body that is "ripe to be hooked" (Atwell, 1987) by academic matters.

The remainder of this article provides information that middle level educators can use to develop dynamic school cultures that feature a strong emphasis on literacy and actively engage students in the quest for growth. After defining "school culture," the article discusses how cultures are created and sustained. Middle school practices are then examined for the cultural messages they may communicate to students. In its final sections, the article describes how literacy may be enshrined as a core value of school life. Specific, age-appropriate practices that create excitement about literacy are presented as models for change.

The Elements of School Culture

Discussions of school culture assume that educational institutions behave in much the same manner as other organizations. In this view, schools are miniature societies and powered by a set of core understandings that guide and structure interactions among stakeholders. Accordingly, "organizational culture is a composite of the values and beliefs of the people within the organization" (Karpicke & Murphy, 1996). Sergiovanni (1984) defined school culture as "the collective programming of the mind that distinguishes the members of one school from another" (p. 9).

Culture is composed of several elements, some relatively easy to discern. Others are well-hidden beneath the surface of day-to-day operations. Symbols of culture, for example, include organizational slang, memos, office arrangements, and objects and locations around the school building upon which special meanings have been conferred (e.g., a faculty lounge chair reserved for a veteran teacher.) Heroes, another cultural level, serve as role models for the school; their accomplishments become part of an oral history handed down from one generation to another. Rituals and ceremonies establish mechanisms for conducting interactions; they acknowledge and celebrate notions of both what is central and what is only tangential to the school's mission. Social networks pass along and interpret information about members of the school community and events deemed significant. Beliefs, consciously held understandings about right and wrong, provide measuring sticks against which actions can be evaluated. At the deepest level, shared values represent broad feelings, usually held out-of-awareness, about what is good and what is bad, normal or abnormal, or appropriate or inappropriate. These values are not open to discussion; instead, they are taken for granted as natural parts of the environment. In short, culture defines what is and what should be (Corbett, Firestone, & Rossman, 1988).

Once established, organizational cultures tend to sustain themselves through the processes of socialization, affirmation, and recruitment. Stakeholders "learn the ropes" through such mechanisms as orientation programs; rule-setting; role modeling; formal and informal interactions with peers, supervisors, and subordinates; and a consistent set of sanctions and censures that defines what is acceptable. Group activities confirm core understandings through celebrations, rituals, verbal and non-verbal communication that interprets the meaning of events, and the anointment of heroes who personify attributes held in high regard. Those identified as villains, of course, receive condemnation with similar intensity for faults that violate beliefs and values held in common.

At the same time, an informal social network provides credit and support to those who conform to approved standards and criticizes those who push the boundaries beyond acceptable limits. This "cultural broadcasting system" transmits news and editorials about school activities through highly efficient channels. In many schools, de facto historians on the staff recount previous innovations tried and found wanting, while power-broker "priests" offer or deny benedictions to the actions of various members of the school community (Deal, 1985). Over time, stakeholders develop a sixth sense that tells them whether or not a given action or idea will receive a warm collective greeting or a series of icy stares.

When students enter middle school, they receive cultural messages about literacy that appear markedly different from the ones they encountered only a few months before. Gone are the highly visible symbols that enliven elementary school corridors and classrooms.

Once established, school cultures tend to perpetuate themselves. By defining what is reasonable and possible, cultures provide on-the-job satisfaction for staff members whose views are most aligned with shared practices, beliefs, and values. Those who find it difficult to blend their own needs and views with prevailing ideas may look for other jobs or be counseled to leave; others learn to squelch actions and statements that are incompatible with the mind-sets of supervisors and peers. When turnover occurs, potential replacements may be screened for their abilities to blend with others. Over time, this search for good matches tends to eliminate from hiring consideration those who might upset the cultural boat. The outcome is a set of common understandings that accepts current ways of doing things and constrains the search for alternatives.

When added to the volatile young adolescent mix of developmental challenges and social pressures, the culture of middle schools may therefore complicate an already difficult quest for enhanced levels of student literacy.

Middle School Culture and Literacy

Without question, middle level programs have been heavily influenced by their secondary school heritage. In contrast to elementary schools, programs and practices have often reflected a traditional high school emphasis on the separation of content areas, tracking, teaching for coverage rather than deep understanding, formalized systems of midterms and finals, and lecturing as the dominant mode of instruction (George et al., 1992). These circumstances have made it difficult to sustain school-wide efforts to heighten literacy. Understanding the cultural significance of these influences is a necessary first step on the road to creating developmentally appropriate environments for learning.

When students enter middle school, they receive cultural messages about literacy that appear markedly different from the ones they encountered only a few months before. Gone are the highly visible symbols that enlivened elementary school corridors and classrooms. In place of the energetic mixture of reading and writing displays to which elementary teachers and students devote so much time are hallways dominated by lockers, perhaps interrupted by the occasional showcase holding neat, finished products from art or technology. Classroom bulletin boards may offer samples of student work, but they may just as easily appear lifeless with nothing except announcements, calendars, and commercially designed posters to occupy the space. Large areas such as the cafeteria, gymnasium, and auditorium may be similarly adorned with little of academic consequence; students accustomed to seeing invitations to join the school community in reading and writing may instead view school logos, pictures of team mascots, and statements of rules and regulations.

Activity patterns differ inside classrooms as well. The reading corner, a prominent feature of primary and intermediate grades, becomes an artifact of the past; and floor mats, classroom libraries, and reading charts are nowhere to be found. Imaginative reports on books, perhaps represented by dioramas, mobiles, and character dress-up days, are replaced by the more traditional book reports, literary essays, and multiple choice tests. Spelling and vocabulary lists substitute for inventories developed from personal interactions with print; individual choice in reading and writing topics is often eliminated for the sake of covering the assigned curriculum and preparing for the demands of high school. Visits to the library become less frequent; and when they do occur, they are often dominated by an emphasis on teacher-directed research rather than the exploration, oral reading, and book sharings of earlier years. Even the writing process, a validated cornerstone of many approaches to literacy instruction, may be jettisoned in order to accommodate the needs of 40-minute periods.

Middle school rituals and celebrations also may offer few connections to the theme of literacy. Sustained, silent reading periods may prove difficult to implement on a consistent basis without wreaking havoc with the master schedule or past practices. Similarly, guest authors and special assemblies devoted to literature and drama may become rare occurrences. Sadly, awards for reading, writing, and speaking, proffered with such frequency in the earlier grades, may lose their standing among students who no longer view these honors as "cool" and among faculty members hesitant to expose to potential embarrassment the strongest students in their classes.

Tracking, a common feature of many middle schools, adds further complications by separating students into the more challenging higher tracks and the bottom groups composed of reluctant readers and writers. Lower expectations follow these students; and they are frequently provided with skills-based exercises, rarely confronting an assignment that requires extended writing, independent reading, or formal speech (Wheelock, 1992). By the end of their middle school years, students from the lower tracks regard books as obstacles rather than facilitators to school success.

Report cards and parent-teacher communications send cultural messages as well. Regardless of the specific format utilized, elementary schools place considerable emphasis on reporting progress in reading. Grades and teacher comments specifically targeted toward reading, however, often disappear at the middle level, subsumed under the more general headings of "English" or "language arts." In addition, content area instructors frequently lack a good background in the teaching of reading, writing, and study skills (Thomas, 1993). Uncertain of the validity of their own suggestions for the improvement of performance, they send concerned parents to see specialists or English teachers (who often have similar gaps in their academic preparation) when literacy deficits are noted. As a result, the statement, "I'm not a reading teacher," often resonates through the halls by the end of parent-teacher conference day.

Middle schools do affirm some values with considerable emphasis and consistency, particularly the importance of teacher control and student discipline (Eccles, Wigfield, Midgley, Reuman, Mac Iver, & Feldlaufer, 1993). Unfortunately, the expression of these values in daily school life may limit rather than encourage academic growth and the risk-taking essential for learning new habits of mind. When added to the volatile young adolescent mix of developmental challenges and social pressures, the culture of middle schools may therefore complicate an already difficult quest for enhanced levels of student literacy.

Creating a Culture of Literacy

Middle school cultures that promote literacy cannot be simply willed into existence as Fullan (1993) noted, "You can't mandate what matters". Similarly, one-shot inservice seminars will not remove deep-seated skepticism about the feasibility of changing adolescent attitudes and behaviors. Above all, superficial change efforts will not reach down into murky layers of organizational culture, the "symbolic webbing" that holds together the many and varied aspects of schooling (Deal, 1990).

Educators concerned with the process of cultural change should instead utilize a wide-angle lens to determine how the elements of the school day interact with each other to create subtle messages about the place of literacy in middle school affairs. This examination of the social and institutional landscape should include assessments of the overt and covert effects of school activities, formal and informal communications, official and unofficial traditions, reward and penalty systems, status hierarchies, funding patterns, classroom design, leadership styles, decision-making structures, and stakeholder interactions. In this way, the "hidden" outcomes of actions may be identified and the implicit values and beliefs that drive collective behavior and structure the school environment may be discerned.

Armed with an understanding of the complexities of school culture, members of the school community can then draft plans that establish or reinforce the importance of literacy as a cornerstone of middle school life. Strategies should align all aspects of organizational behavior, including administrative activities (Sashkin & Sashkin, 1993), to create a powerful blend that surrounds students with continuous support for improvement. When successful, these efforts will create an ambience and vitality appropriate for middle schools yet reminiscent of the elementary school devotion to making every student a skilled reader, writer, speaker, and listener.

A blueprint for action might include or extend the following approaches:

- Encouraging adults to serve as role models by allowing themselves to be seen reading books and writing for a variety of purposes. For example, one middle school established a book club that enabled faculty members to read and discuss works of literature drawn from many genres. Students who caught teachers and administrators in the act of being literate recognized that a love for language can be a significant component of adult life.
- Establishing the library as a symbolic center of the school universe. Through motivating contests, dynamic programming that addressed student interests, faculty collaboration, the utilization of information technology, and the judicious

use of available funds, a school created a "user-friendly" library that served as many students' second home.

- Encouraging research on subjects of interest to young adolescents. Allowing students in one middle school to select their own topics for a graduation exhibition communicated an awareness of pupil needs and aroused the motivation spawned by emerging interests (George et al., 1992).
- Using many formats to elicit reactions to books will encourage sharing, heighten interest in the world of print, and transmit the enthusiasm for reading and writing felt by adult role models. Parents in particular can provide invaluable assistance in this endeavor; good books can anchor a Parents and Children Read Together evening (Vossler, 1996) that reaffirms the strength of shared values and beliefs.
- Telling stories about students, teachers, and other members of the school community who have demonstrated a commitment to literacy or achieved success in areas related to reading, writing, and speaking. Stories are told around schools all the time, and they have extraordinary power to highlight cultural values (Deal, 1985) Harnessing this potential would create an oral tradition and a set of heroes that may inspire others.
- Developing celebrations that recognize achievements in literacy for individuals, families, interdisciplinary teams, and the school in general. Far from being trite, special assemblies, awards, and contests heighten engagement and remind members of the school community about what is considered important; a pep rally for reading can become as prized as one for athletics. Celebrations that applaud effort and involvement will encourage the participation of students from all points along the achievement continuum, not just those who are most skillful and practiced.
- Identifying literacy as an area of focus for site-based decision making teams. Group deliberations may produce practical, creative suggestions for achieving literacy goals; and dialogue with parent representatives may inspire efforts to create meaningful literacy experiences outside, as well as inside, the schoolhouse. A reading committee (Irvin, 1990), for instance, could plan special events related to reading, writing, and public speaking while affirming the importance of working cooperatively to raise student performance levels.
- Empowering teacher teams and facilitating dialogue across grade levels and subject areas (Clark & Clark, 1996). As faculty members share perspectives, they may recognize the need for collaborative effort to solve problems. In addition, they may learn that strategies to teach reading and writing are not as mysterious as they once seemed. Team efforts to raise reading levels, for example, will almost certainly demonstrate that literacy is intimately connected with heightened mastery of subject content. Productive by-products of such conversations may also include the redefinition of literacy efforts to include technical reading, writing, and speaking, as well as a consensus-based commitment to reducing the stranglehold of "coverage."
- Focusing staff development initiatives on promoting literacy. Instruction in this area may reduce teacher hesitation to address student deficits. At the same time, it can provide teach-

ers with an arsenal of tools, including flowcharts, webs, and sorting trees that have valuable, task-specific applications in the various content areas (Hyerle, 1996).

- Including reading and writing specialists in all aspects of instructional design. If greater literacy is our quest, we should encourage participation by those with the richest academic background in this area. Elevating the status of these staff members will inform decisions and simultaneously proclaim the importance of new goals.
- Conducting a "culture audit" on a regular basis. Examining organizational action and stakeholder behavior will provide the data needed to determine the extent to which values and beliefs are shared. Plans then can be drafted to enhance or support the drive for literacy (Champy, 1995).

Conclusion

Middle schools face serious challenges in their efforts to increase literacy levels among their students. As always, each building must respond to the developmental, academic, and social demands that confront young adolescents. In addition, educators must recognize that achieving basic competency in areas related to literacy is no longer sufficient; energies should be focused on attaining the high standards of pupil performance required for success in an increasingly competitive environment.

Our actions must also reflect the awareness that middle schools are not simply passive vehicles for students as they move from elementary to high school. The collective effects of school policies, practices, and implicit values transmit strong messages to teachers and students about the significance of literacy and the importance of increasing levels of achievement. To create environments that engage students in the consistent pursuit of ever-higher goals, middle schools must go beyond traditional staff and curriculum development approaches; they need to develop cultures that broadcast a clear commitment to literacy and support the attainment of this outcome in word and deed. In this way, they will define skillful reading, writing, listening, and speaking as "the way we do things around here" (Deal & Kennedy, 1982).

Robert Feirsen is the principal of W. T Clarke Middle School, East Meadow, New York.

References

Atwell, N. (1987). *In the middle: Writing, reading, and learning with adolescents.* Portsmouth, NH: Heinemann.

Carnegie Council on Adolescent Development. (1989). *Turning points: Preparing American youth for the 21st century.* New York: Carnegie Corporation.

Champy, J. (1995). *Reengineering management: The mandate for new leadership.* New York: Harper Collins.

Clark. D. C., & Clark, S. N. (1996). Building collaborative environments for successful middle level school restructuring. *Bulletin of the National Association of secondary School Principals. 80*(578), 1–16.

Corbett. H. D., Firestone. W. A., & Rossman, G. B. (1987). Resistance to planned change and the sacred in school culture. *Educational Administration Quarterly. 23*(4), 36–59.

Deal, T. E. (1985). The symbolism of effective schools. *Elementary School Journal, 85*, 601–620.

Deal, T. E. (1990). Reframing reform. *Educational Leadership. 47*(8), 6–12.

Deal, T. E., & Kennedy, A. A. (1982). *Corporate cultures: Rites and rituals of corporate life*. Reading, PA: Addison-Wesley.

Eccles, J. S., Midgley, C., Wigfield, A., Buchanan, C. M., Reuman, D., Flanagan, C., & Mac lver, D. (1993). Development during adolescence. *American Psychologist, 48*(2), 90–101.

Eccles, J. S., Wigfield, A., Midgley, C., Reuman, D., Mac lver, D., & Feldlaufer, H. (1993). Negative effects of traditional middle schools on students' motivation. *Elementary School Journal, 93*(5), 553–574.

Fullan, M. G. (1993). lnnovation, reform, and restructuring strategies. In G. Cawelti (Ed.), *Challenges and achievements of American education.* (pp. 116–133). Alexandria, VA: Association for Supervision and Curriculum Development.

George, P. S., Stevenson, C., Thomason, J., & Beane, J. (1992). *The middle school—and beyond*. Alexandria, VA: Association for Supervision and Curriculum Development.

Hyerle, D. (1996). *Visual tools for constructing knowledge*. Alexandria: VA: Association for Supervision and Curriculum Development.

Irvin, J. L. (1990). *Reading and the middle school student: Strategies to enhance literacy*. Boston: Allyn and Bacon.

Karpicke, H., & Murphy, M. E. (1996). Productive school culture: Principals working from the inside. *Bulletin of the National Association of Secondary School Principals,. 80*(576), 26–34.

Sashkin, M., & Sashkin, M. G. (1993). Leadership and culture building in schools. In W. E. Rosenbach & R. L Taylor (Eds.), *Contemporary issues in leadership* (pp. 201–211). Boulder. CO: Westview Press.

Sergiovanni, T. J. (1984). Leadership and excellence in schooling. *Educational Leadership 41*(5), 4–13.

Thomas, J. W. (1993). Promoting independent learning in the middle grades: The role of instructional support practices. *Elementary School Journal. 93*(5), 575–591.

Vossler, J. M. (1996). When danger threatens. *Middle School Journal. 27*(3),47–51.

Wheelock, A. (1992). *Crossing the tracks: How untracking can save America's schools*. New York: New Press.

Wolf, A. E. (1991). *Get out of my life, but first could you drive me and Cheryl to the Mall?: A parent's guide to the new teenager*. New York: Noonday Press.

From *Middle School Journal* Vol. 28, No. 3, January 1997, pages 10-15. Copyright © 1997 by National Middle School Association. Reprinted with permission from National Middle School Association.

Building Sound Literacy Learning Programs for Young Adolescents

Judith L. Irvin

Becoming literate, like other developmental tasks, is not fully accomplished during early adolescence. Like developing a self-identity, becoming an abstract thinker, or becoming adept at social interactions, literacy is generally nor fully achieved until high school or beyond.

"During the middle grades, young adolescents face increasing demands on their literacy skills. They are asked to read and write much more than in the earlier grades, and they are assigned reading and writing tasks that increase in complexity" (Davidson, 1990). Students must make a significant shift from "learning to read" to "reading to learn" (Herber, 1970, 1978, 1984). For some students, this shift becomes a fairly large leap because teachers and materials do not provide for a deliberate transition. Yet, for many of our nation's students, no systematic instruction in reading is given past grade five (Irvin & Connors, 1989).

Chall (1983) described the failure to make a smooth transition to reading to learn as the fourth grade slump. The reading and writing instruction students received during the elementary years was primarily comprised of stories and other narrative material. Many middle grades students are at a complete loss when faced with the demands of science and social studies texts. More silent reading, less reading aloud, more independent learning, more study and remembering material, and more expository material all increasingly challenge middle grades readers.

In this article, I present the predominate approaches for addressing middle school literacy learning. In the past two decades, literacy learning has been considered more broadly. Previously, more traditional approaches isolated the teaching and learning of reading and writing from other language areas. Literacy includes all of the language areas of reading, writing, speaking, and listening. Most of the literature and research, however, focuses on reading. Where applicable, I will include a discussion of

writing, speaking, and listening. I will conclude this article by describing five components for implementing and sustaining a successful literacy learning program for middle grades students.

Status of Reading Programs

Little research on middle level literacy learning practices and programs exists, and the few surveys we have generalize to secondary programs (Early, 1973; Freed, 1972; Greenlaw & Moore, 1982; Hill, 1975; Witte & Otto, 1981). One national survey (Irvin & Connors, 1989) was designed to describe the nature and extent to which reading is taught in middle level schools. Using that survey data, and extending it with my experience with middle level schools across the nation, I perceive six patterns of reading instruction: (a) no systematic instruction, (b) remedial reading course, (c) developmental reading course, (d) content area reading with a reading specialist usually available as a resource to a team or grade level, (e) integrated language arts, and (f) integrated curriculum using a thematic approach. Each approach has strengths and difficulties, and all can be found in middle level schools today.

No systematic reading instruction

Although it is unreasonable to expect that any student could acquire enough reading competence by the fifth grade to carry him or her through middle school, high school, and adult life. almost half of the middle schools offer no systematic reading instruction or make it available only for remedial readers or as an elective (Irvin & Connors, 1989).

A departmentalized organization coupled with secondary trained teachers who, generally, do not feel comfortable teaching reading partially account for many middle grades students being deprived of systematic instruction in reading beyond grade five. Surprisingly, many students acquire the reading competence they need to progress academically; but, then, many do not.

Remedial reading Course

The Remedial Reading Course and Reading Lab are usually pull-out courses for students reading below grade level and typically include instruction in reading skills, vocabulary development, and comprehension. Approximately one-third of middle schools offer a semester-long remedial reading course at all grade levels (Irvin & Connors, 1989). The primary source of reading material is narrative, and often little transfer occurs between what is learned in a remedial reading course and reading required in content area courses. Students who receive isolated skill instruction and more experience with stories still must face the daily challenge of reading their science and social studies textbooks. Recognizing the problem of applying reading skills in social studies and science, some remedial reading teachers use content area books to help students become more successful readers of expository text by teaching them chapter mapping, text structures, and vocabularly development strategies.

Developmental reading course

These courses are designed to be a normal part of a student's progression through the curriculum, not a remedial course. This type of reading instruction seems to be the most preferred in middle level schools today, occurring in about 60% of them (Irvin & Connors, 1989).

Developmental reading courses are most heavily emphasized at the sixth grade level, and the time and the requirement is reduced at the seventh and eighth grade levels. Most schools require reading for a semester or a year in the sixth grade. For seventh and eighth graders. reading instruction is commonly offered through "the wheel" which generally refers to a slot in the school schedule when students may take exploratory courses such as art or keyboarding. Students who are below grade level are sometimes advised to take reading courses repeatedly on "the wheel."

This type reading course usually includes the development of comprehension, vocabulary, flexible reading rates, and study strategies. Materials used in these courses range from skill materials and worksheets, to basal textbooks, to student-chosen literature, to materials dealing with study strategies.

When school budgets are slashed, often the developmental reading class is the first to go. Similar to remedial reading courses, these developmental courses are sometimes isolated from the reading realities of the rest of the student's day. When reading teachers, though, coordi-nate and integrate the use of learning strategies and vocabulary development with the objectives of content area teachers, students have more authentic reading experiences and have the opportunity to grow into the more complex reading and writing tasks that the middle grades demand.

Content area reading

The recommended approach to content area reading is one in which teachers collaborate to present content and learning strategies concurrently. Students are given direct instruction in reading strategies as they learn content and, ideally, a reading resource teacher is available to work with content teachers. This approach enhances reading, thinking, and study skill ability while increasing students' knowledge of content. Thus, one main reason that this method of content area reading instruction is desirable and effective is that it allows direct application of reading strategies to content.

This orientation to reading instruction has been attempted since the early 1900s (Moore, Readence, & Rickleman, 1983) and was more or less emphasized throughout the first half of the century. Content area reading instruction re-emerged with the publication of Herber's (1970, 1978) *Teaching Reading in the Content Areas*. Integrating reading and content instruction, however, does not seem to be widely applied across the country (Gee & Forester, 1988; Irvin & Connors, 1989; Witte & Otto, 1981) and most content area teachers do not see reading instruction as their responsibility. Some lack administrative support or leadership, and some simply do not know how to enhance the reading and writing abilities of their students.

> **Teachers often expect students to complete such tasks as writing summaries or answering essay questions in tests, but most teachers do not teach students how to write in an expository mode.**

If reading in the content areas has been neglected over the years, then writing in the content areas has been all but forgotten. Teachers often expect students to complete such tasks as writing summaries or answering essay questions on tests, but most teachers do not teach students how to write in an expository mode (Gahn, 1989). When students do write, they generally do not have an authentic audience. They write for a teacher for purposes of evaluation. Gebhard (1983) suggested finding real audiences such as peers or younger children to help students learn to write clear and meaningful expository pieces. Strategies such as webs, semantic feature analysis, and structured overviews can assist students in structuring their writing in the content areas. Reading and writing, certainly, can be learned together to help students understand the Structure of expository text.

Integrated language arts

An integrated language arts approach is based on the premise that reading, writing, speaking, listening, and thinking are interrelated processes and is being implemented by a growing number of teachers through a reading/writing workshop (Anders & Pritchard, 1993; Roe, 1992). Atwell (1987) introduced the workshop in her book *In the Middle: Writing, Reading, and Learning with Adolescents* as a way of motivating young adolescents to write about self-selected books, to talk to others about their writing and their reading, and to participate in the evaluation of their work and the work of others. Atwell (1990) elaborated on writing to learn in her book *Coming to Know: Writing to Learn in the Intermediate Grades*. In *Seeking Diversity: Language Arts with Adolescents*, Reif (1992) refined the workshop by sharing stories of student reading and writing. These three books and the stories of numerous language arts teachers sharing their experiences through articles and presentations at conferences have encouraged teachers in many schools to request two-hour blocks of time for students to read and write. Atwell and Reif advocated "mini-lessons," as the need arose, for students in the reading and writing process. Authentic literacy experiences and assessment (reading real books and writing for real audiences), and allocating plenty of time for reading, writing, and reflection also are important components of this approach.

Workshop and workshop-like approaches to teaching literacy in the middle school are a giant leap from the spelling on Monday, reading on Tuesday, grammar on Wednesday approach that unfortunately continues to dominate in schools. Some teachers find the workshop difficult to manage and it seems to be most effective when offered in a longer-than-one-hour time period with fewer students. While a more integrated language arts program is a vast improvement over the fragmented approach, one problem that sometimes develops is the neglect of content-based learning strategies. A middle school literacy program is most effective when students are involved in wide reading of novels and other books and are also taught the learning strategies of content area reading. Helping young adolescents develop literacy abilities consistent with increased demands is a complex task which includes instruction in both narrative and expository materials.

Thematic learning

A few schools have implemented a curriculum that integrates content around themes. For example, in one middle school, 30 students remain with one teacher for a three-hour block of time to learn social studies, language arts, and reading. Themes derived from social studies content naturally lend themselves to the use of literature which enhances understanding of content. Ideally, learning strategies for both narrative and expository text are taught in relation to learning new content. "By themselves, strategies have no useful function. They exist only as a means of understanding, creating, and communicating information, ideas, and feelings from the knowledge base…purposeful integration cannot occur unless teachers understand the relationships between content and strategies" (Roehler, Foley, Lud & Power, 1990). Thematic or whole learning holds much promise for middle grades teaching and learning. The pioneers that create meaningful learning environments and experiences for developing literacy abilities and acquiring new content will provide the models for others to emulate and reformulate for their students.

During the past few decades, literacy learning programs have changed with philosophical changes about language acquisition. Although still in practice in some middle level schools, teaching reading and writing skills isolated from other language areas and from content instruction seems to be giving way to literacy instruction that is more integrated with the entire curriculum. Reading/writing workshop, learning strategies taught in content areas, and literacy instruction integrated with thematic study are all promising directions for literacy development during the middle grades.

Components of a Successful Middle Level Literacy Program

Literacy programs for young adolescents tend to come and go depending on administrative leadership and support, expertise and enthusiasm of teachers, and budget restraints. Educators generally agree that continued literacy instruction for middle grades students is beneficial, but few middle schools have been able to implement and sustain a quality program. In my experience, practices to create literate environments for young adolescents vary widely. Middle level educators need documentation of effective programs that include teachers' reflections of what seems to work for their students. In my opinion, a successful middle grades literacy learning program accomplishes the following:

1. Facilitates the language development of students. Any program, curriculum, or instructional methodology must incorporate the developmental tasks of early adolescence. Language development parallels growth in the ability to engage in abstract thinking and parallels the maturation of social skills. It seems natural, then, to use the social proclivity of young adolescents to enhance their literacy and thinking abilities. Such methods as cooperative learning, peer editing, and paired reading can strengthen and support literacy learning while accommodating developmental tasks.

Integrating all of the language areas for authentic audiences helps students see the relevance in becoming competent readers and writers. Chat modes, posting writing on the Internet, or producing a radio play for younger students all provide students with meaningful tasks for literacy development and, at the same time, natural ways of interacting with peers and adults.

2. Focuses on the process of learning. Reading instruction of two decades ago focused on skill development. That is, if students could find the main idea, detect a sequence, locate information, and make an inference, it was reasoned that they could read. To provide an analogy, soccer players spend many hours developing their skill in ball dribbling. All of that work pays off when a player dribbles past the opposing defenders then strategically makes a nice cross to a teammate who is open at the far goalpost. Skills only take a player so far unless he or she has a strategy for making a goal. Literacy instruction today emphasizes learning strategies—those approaches that coordinate the various reading and writing skills to make sense to the learner. Just as the soccer player must monitor the field for player position, time remaining, and a possible tackle, readers and writers must monitor their progress, understanding, and purpose for reading and writing. This process is called metacognition, and since it involves abstract thinking, it is not generally fully developed until about age 15.

Research on prior knowledge and metacognition has helped educators understand the complexity of literacy learning. Activating and using prior knowledge while learning new content and reflecting on understandings should be the focus of instruction rather than any particular skill. Content-based strategy instruction, reading/writing workshop, and thematic learning tend to support this emphasis on the process of learning.

3. Integrates the language arts. Reading, writing, speaking, and listening are interconnected and recursive processes. Reading and writing, in the majority of schools, have been taught separately. Good writers are often good readers; similarly, good readers are often good writers. Knowledge of one process appears to reinforce knowledge of the other, and students "derive learning benefits across reading and writing when they understand that connections exist" (Shanahan, 1990). Most language arts teachers recognize these logical connections, but literacy learning is much more powerful if connections are made in the content areas as well.

Literacy should also be taught and reinforced across the curriculum, using social studies, music, art, science, and mathematics content. Literacy learning is a process; it has no content. For students to become literate, they have to read, write about, speak, and listen to something. That something is found in the content areas and in literature.

> **Such methods as cooperative learning, peer editing, and paired reading can strengthen and support literacy learning while accommodating developmental tasks.**

4. Provides strategy-based instruction across the curriculum. Learning how to read and write expository text is different from learning how to read and write narrative text, but it is equally important. Teaching students to set purposes and use strategies for reading a variety of texts will help them become fluent, strategic, and versatile learners. Strategy-based instruction across the curriculum takes work, staff development, coordination, and leadership. Reading resource teachers or curriculum specialists are often instrumental in helping teachers provide balanced literacy instruction.

5. Sustains a recreational reading and read aloud program. Usually, a school reading committee provides leadership for book fairs, reading break time, book exchanges, and any special school-wide activities. These activities indicate a school-wide commitment to reading improvement, provide opportunities to involve parents, and carry a strong message to the community. A read aloud program can occur within language arts classes or it can be a school-wide effort. Young adolescents should be "read aloud to every day from a variety of texts, including nonfiction" (Anders & Pritchard, 1993). This practice creates a common experience and a forum for responding orally and in writing and can be a major ingredient in vocabulary development.

Conclusion

It is clear that young adolescents need instruction to become literate and handle the demands of continued schooling and adulthood. They need this instruction as much as continued learning in mathematics or science. Yet, many schools do not offer reading instruction for middle grades students, or, if they do, it is provided for remedial students only. Emerging models such as reading/writing workshop, thematic approaches, and content-based strategies across the curriculum are promising approaches for creating literate environments. Implementation is the easy part, however; sustaining and improving a literacy learning program is more difficult.

I have presented what I consider to be the essential components of a successful middle grades literacy program. My ideas have evolved over the years based on what I know about the developmental tasks of early adolescence, philosophical shifts in language acquisition, and practices in middle level schools. As middle level literacy educators, we need consistent and repeated documentation of effective programs that create literate environments for young adolescents and motivate them to continue their journey to become proficient readers and writers. I welcome conversations that add to or adjust my thinking about the components of effective middle level literacy programs. It is my hope that renewed interest in creating more literate environments for our students will lead to programs that become an integral, systematic, and sustained part of the middle school program.

References

Anders, P. L., & Pritchard, T. G. (1993). Integrated language curriculum and instruction for the middle grades. *The Elementary School Journal*, 93(5),611–624.

Atwell, N. (Ed). (1990). *Coming to know: Writing to learn in the intermediate grades*. PORTSMOUTH, NH: Heinemann.

Atwell, N. (1987). *In the middle: Writing, reading, and learning with adolescents*. Portsmouth, NH: Heinemann.

Chall, J. (1983). *Stages of reading development*. New York: McGraw Hill.

Davidson, J. (1990). Literacy in the middle grades. *Educational Horizons*, 68(2), 74–77.

Early, M. J. (1973). Taking stock: Secondary school reading in the 70s. *Journal of Reading*. 16(5),364–373

Freed, B. F. (1972). *Teaching reading in secondary schools: Survey of state departments of education and selected school districts*. Philadelphia, PA: Research for Better Schools.

Gahn, S. (1989). A practical guide for teaching writing in the content areas. *Journal of Reading*, 32(6), 525–531.

Gebhard, A. O. (1983). Teaching writing in reading and the content areas. *Journal of Reading*. 27(3), 207–211.

Gee, T. C., & Forester, N. (1988). Moving reading instruction beyond the reading classroom. *Journal of Reading*, 31 (6), 505–511.

Greenlaw, J. M., & Moore, D. M. (1982). What kinds of reading courses are taught in junior and senior high school? *Journal of Reading*, 25(6),534–536.

Herber, H. L. (1970). *Teaching reading in content areas*. Englewood Cliffs, NY: Prentice-Hall.

Herber, H. L. (1978). *Teaching reading in content areas*. Englewood Cliffs, NY: Prentice-Hall.

Herber, H. L. (1984). Subject matter texts: Reading to learn: Response to a paper by Thomas H. Anderson and Bonnie B. Armbruster. In R. C. Anderson, J. Osborn, & R. J. Tierney (Eds.), *Learning to read in American schools: Basal readers and context texts* (pp. 227–234). Hillsdale, NJ: Lawrence Erlbaum .

Hill, W. R. (1975). Secondary reading activity in western New York: A survey. *Journal of Reading*, 19(1), 13–19.

Irvin, J. L., & Connors, N. A. (1989). Reading instruction in middle level schools: Results of a U.S. survey. *Journal of Reading*, 32(4), 306–311.

Moore, D. W., Readence, J. E., & Rickelman, R. J. (1983). An historical exploration of content area reading instruction. *Reading Research Quarterly*, 18(4), 421–438.

Reif, L. (1992). *Seeking diversity: Language arts with adolescents*. Portsmouth, NH: Heinemann.

Roe, M. F. (1992). Reading strategy instruction: Complexities and possibilities in middle school. *Journal of Reading*, 36(3), 190–197.

Roehler, L. R., Foley, K. U., Lud, M. T., & Power, C. A. (1990). Developing integrated programs. In G. G. Duffy (Ed.), *Reading in middle school* (pp. 184–199). Newark, DE: International Reading Association.

Shanahan, T. (1990). Reading and writing together: What does it really mean? In T. Shanahan (Ed.), *Reading and writing together: New perspectives for the classroom* (pp. 1–19). Norwood, MA: Christopher-Gordon.

Witte, P. L., & Otto, W. (1981). Reading instruction at the postelementary level: Review and comments. *Journal of Educational Research*, 74(3), 148–158.

Author's Note: This article is drawn from the author's forthcoming book, *Reading and the Middle School Student: Strategies to Enhance Literacy* (Second Edition) Boston: Allyn and Bacon.

Judith L. Irvin teaches at Florida State University, Tallahassee.

Improving Young Adolescent Literacy Through Collaborative Learning

Karen D. Wood, Rachel L. McCormack, Diane Lapp & James Flood

Given the social nature of adolescents, the growing emphasis on grouping and pairing students for instructional purposes is a welcome match. Schools across the nation are discouraging the lecture approach wherein the teacher is the sole purveyor of information in favor of collaborative learning where students get in groups to share their thinking, engage in discussions, and solve various problems.

Increasing interest in collaborative learning has led to numerous questions regarding its origin, research-based benefits, and strategies and procedures for classroom implementation. In this article, we address some of the most frequently asked questions and offer practical suggestions to help ensure successful use.

What Is the Difference Between Cooperative Learning, Collaborative Learning, and Flexible Grouping?

In many instances, the terms cooperative learning and collaborative learning are used interchangeably. However, certain researchers such as David and Roger Johnson, Spencer Kagan, and Robert Slavin are associated with the term "cooperative" learning and have labeled their publications and approaches accordingly (Johnson & Johnson, 1991; Kagan, 1994; Slavin, 1995).

According to Davidson (1994), "collaborative" models of learning focus on the creation of personal meaning and understanding through dialogue and discussion. Proponents of collaborative learning, he maintains, tend not to micromanage, that is to break tasks into specific rewardable, component parts. Advocates of cooperative learning approaches, for the most part, tend to be more structured with an emphasis on specific behaviors and rewards.

We believe that students must be able to cooperate (get along with others) to collaborate (work together toward a common goal); therefore, we use the term "collaborative" learning in this article because we feel it is more inclusive. We also advocate flexible grouping as a means of implementing collaborative learning. Flexible grouping is not a static, rigid approach to learning. On the contrary, it involves the formation of many group arrangements to coordinate with class and teacher goals. In flexible grouping, students might be grouped by interest or need; they might be asked to read with a partner, join a heterogeneous group to retell math processes, or share their group projects with the entire class (Radencich, McKay & Paratore, 1995).

Is Collaborative Learning a New Concept?

The earliest study on collaborative learning reported in the professional literature dates back to 1897 (Johnson & Johnson in Brandt, 1987). Since that time, hundreds of studies have been conducted attesting to the validity of employing grouping techniques in the classroom. Prominent educators such as John Dewey and Colonel Frances Parker long advocated classrooms in which learning is a collaborative effort. More recently, Pearson and Raphael (1990) suggested that information can be conveyed via the notion of a "cognitive apprenticeship," which is based on the model of "mentor helping novice" that has characterized entry into certain crafts and professions. Interest in group learning has become an international crusade with research conducted in Israel, West Germany, Canada, and Nigeria, to name a few. In fact, according to Johnson and Johnson (Brandt, 1987), there is more evidence for collaborative learning than any other aspect of education. It can be said that collaborative learning is the individualized instruction of the present and the future (Wood & Algozzine, 1994).

What are the Research-based Benefits of Collaborative Learning?

Through analyses of the extensive research on grouping, it has been consistently shown that students in collaborative learning situations score higher on achievement tests than students learning by other methods (Johnson and Johnson, 1991; Slavin, 1995). Further, according to reviews by Kagan (1994), Lehr (1984), Johnson & Johnson (1985), and Stevens and

Slavin (1995), many other benefits of collaborative learning have emerged including: (a) higher motivation to learn and greater intrinsic motivation; (b) improvement of both tutor and tutee: (c) increased self-esteem: (d) more positive perceptions about the intentions of others: (e) decrease of negative competition: (f) greater acceptance of differences (academically handicapped students were more accepted socially by their peers): (g) a decrease of dependence on the teacher: (h) improvement in mathematics, reading vocabulary, comprehension; and language expression; and (i) improvement in the achievement of students labeled as gifted. In fact, research has shown that students at all ability levels can benefit from collaborative learning experiences (Graves & Graves, 1983; Slavin, 1989).

What Can I Do to Ensure Successful Implementation in My Classroom?

To implement collaborative learning experiences successfully in the classroom, the teacher must begin by establishing an atmosphere of responsible learning and caring in which negative comments are not tolerated. It may be necessary to extend or re-emphasize existing classroom rules such as "stay in your groups," "speak softly," and "respect others." To further ensure success and avoid chaos, the teacher may want to make decisions about placement in groups before starting the lesson. Another important point is to use a variety of grouping strategies to avoid boredom and to allow students the opportunity to interact with all class members.

Lapp and Flood (1992) suggested seven steps for successful collaborative learning as follows:

- Identify Objectives: Before formalizing groups, it is important to specify the academic objective of the topic being presented.
- Orient Students: Before using collaborative learning, students should be oriented to the rationale, procedures, and expected outcomes of the instructional activity. Students need to be told that cooperation is the key to successful learning in this teaching mode.
- Design Teams: Four things related to team design should be considered: team size, team composition, materials, and room arrangements.
- Explain Team Rules: Explain to students what the rules are for working in teams and what the team tasks are that students will be expected to complete.
- Monitor and Facilitate Group Interactions: While students are working, it is important for teachers to circulate and observe each group to determine the problems the members may encounter when they are working with one another.
- Prepare Students for Learning from their Textbooks: Students need to know how and when to use the textbooks during the collaborative learning experience. It is important to remember that not all collaborative experiences need to be drawn directly from the students textbook.
- Evaluate Group and Individual Success: Collaborative learning is successful only if every member of the team is involved. To be sure this occurs teams will need to be evaluated and observed regularly.

How Can Collaborative Learning Experiences Be Used with Subject Matter Teaching?

Because literacy instruction goes hand in hand with social studies instruction in many instances, students' abilities often complement each other. For example, in one classroom when students read *War Comes to Willy Freeman* (Collier & Collier, 1990), a story about a freed African American slave girl during the Revolutionary War, students were able to share with each other what they already knew about slavery and the Revolutionary War, regardless of their reading ability. In addition to providing new information about African Americans who fought for the colonists during the Revolution, the story enhanced what they were learning about the Revolutionary War in the more traditional social studies classes. It also provided students with opportunities to be creative, learn and refine writing skills, and work in collaboration with their peers.

The teacher used a reading model that implemented a variety of grouping configurations and provided learning opportunities to connect social studies with the language arts. An example of a lesson organizer used in planning lessons according to this model is provided in Figure 1 (See also Paratore, 1991). Named "Take Five" by the students, the model includes the following components: (a) Get Ready, (b) Read, (c) Reread, (d) Respond, and (e) React.

Get Ready. While reading the book *War Comes to Willy Freeman* (Collier & Collier, 1990), all students were kept at the same pace, reading approximately one chapter or 15 pages per day. Before reading the selection, the whole class met with the teacher to prepare for the reading and to activate students' background knowledge and experiences. The students described events that had occurred in the previous chapters, providing a transition into what was going to be read. They also made predictions and related personal events to rationalize their predictions. The students then presented a focus for reading by posing questions to their peers to ponder while reading. Finally, technical words, historical terms, and other difficult vocabulary were developed with the help of the teacher. These prereading activities, accomplished in a whole class format, provided an opportunity for all students to share their ideas and expertise.

Read. Students read the chapter, or pages assigned for the day, silently. While reading, they were asked to jot down ideas in their response journals to use in their discussions.

Reread. Students formed peer dyads, or combined two dyads, to reread all or part of the selection. Because middle grade students are often reluctant to reread a selection, a new focus was given. Students were also given the opportunity to find a 2-3 page excerpt with dialogue and engage in a theatrical reading, with each student taking the part of a character. In either case, students were encouraged to "think aloud" (Barr, Sadow, & Blachowicz, 1995; Davey, 1983) to make their thinking public and enhance their comprehension and recall of the topic.

Respond. Working in the same groups, in new pairs, or independently, the students wrote responses to the selection in their response journals. Sometimes the responses were prompted, sometimes they were personal reactions to what stu-

Figure 1

Take Five Reading Lesson Plan

Title: _____

Chapter/Pages: _____

Date: _____

Get Ready

___ Build and access background knowledge: _____

_____

_____

_____

___ Vocabulary: _____

_____

_____

___ Set Purpose: _____

_____

___ Questions: _____

_____

___ Strategy/Concept Mini-lesson: _____

_____

_____

Read

___ Read Aloud ___ Silent ___ Pairs ___ Other

Reread

Set Purpose: _____

_____

___ Read Aloud ___ Silent ___ Pairs ___ Other

Respond:

Oral Response: _____

_____

_____

Written Response: _____

_____

_____

React

___ Whole Class ___ Silent ___ Pairs ___ Other

*Extra Help: _____

**Enrichment: _____

(Developed by R. L. McCormack)

dents had read, and sometimes the responses were specific tasks which related to the mandated language and curriculum.

React. The students and teacher reacted to each other's comments, questions, and journal responses in small group and whole class discussions. Sometimes the discussions were teacher-facilitated; other times they were student-led. The students' reactions were an integral part of the model. In these discussions, students practiced being competent language users by elaborating, confirming, seeking clarification, extending each other's meanings, and practicing turn taking strategies.

Using the *Take Five* model, students worked in a number of grouping situations. The make-up of these groups rarely remained static; they varied from day to day and book to book. In addition to working independently, the students were given opportunities to collaborate with friends, more able peers, and teachers.

Are There Some Effective, Not Too Difficult to Manage Collaborative Learning Strategies to Use in the Classroom?

Some collaborative learning strategies are quite complex in terms of their group arrangement, student tasks, and student movement from group to group. These techniques can cause some educators to feel overwhelmed by the complexity of collaborative learning. However, there are some less complex and effective collaborative learning strategies that can be implemented in any classroom. One of these is the Cooperative Reading Activity (Opitz, 1992).

Students were encouraged to "think ahead" to make their thinking public and enhance their comprehension and recall of the topic.

With the Cooperative Reading Activity, a teacher divides students into heterogeneous groups and gives them the responsibility for the initial learning and presentation of a particular topic. Reading selections are determined by the teacher. Individual accountability is required since students read the selection on their own, prior to meeting with team members.

Designing a cooperative reading activity

1. Choose a piece of expository text. Textbook selections with headings and subheadings are a great source for this activity.
2. Determine the number of groups you would like to have. Generally groups of four students work best.
3. Divide the reading selection into sections so that each group of students has about the same amount of text. Make one 5 x 7 index card for each student. Write the title of the reading section at the top of card. This card will be used to record important information about the reading.
4. Make copies of the text. Make enough so that each student has a copy of the section that he or she is responsible for reading. Use a colored highlighter to clearly mark the sections. You may also want to highlight the title of the reading section on the 5 x 7 cards that you created so that students can easily determine their groups.

Procedure for a cooperative reading activity

1. Introduce the reading selection by accessing students prior knowledge. Introduce any key vocabulary and set a purpose for reading.
2. Tell students that they will be reading a certain section of the text depending on the card they select and writing three facts that they think everyone in the class should know about their section of reading. Distribute the cards and sections of text.
3. Give students a specific amount of time to complete their individual reading and fact finding. When the time is over, have students meet with the other members of their group and share their important facts.
4. Next have each group make a list of details they all agree upon as important and write these on a sheet of chart paper. Tell students to begin by recording the facts that all members of the group may have selected individually and then add other facts that they all agree are also important.
5. Finally, have each group take a turn presenting their list to the class. Post the charts and have students write the facts that each group presented.

What About Students Who Cannot Read the Material Presented in the Whole Class Session?

The *Take Five* model described previously provides a variety of options for students who are unable to read materials independently presented in whole class sessions. For example, the vocabulary and concepts introduced in the book. *War Comes to Willy Freeman* (Collier & Collier, 1990) caused some difficulties for less able students. Often they had difficulty placing the story historically in time, understanding the detailed descriptions of some of the settings, and deciphering the sequence of events. However, the whole-class prereading discussion, in which everyone participated, provided enough support for less able students.

When the students were asked to read the selection silently, additional support was available for these less able readers. The teacher led a group of these students, and others who asked for more intervention, to guide the reading of the selection. The teacher and students shared in the active reading of the text by taking turns "thinking aloud," adjusting their predictions, and asking new questions. Passages were often reread, verbal summaries were elicited, and spontaneous talk about the events in the text were encouraged. When it was time for the students to respond in their response journals, they discussed their ideas first. then wrote their responses in cooperation with a peer or the teacher. To reread the selection, they often paired up to choose a small excerpt of the chapter to read orally. Although it would have been prohibitive for some of the less able readers to read the selections independently at first, the added support and strategic interventions aided their ability to read the same text that was being read by their peers.

How Are Grades Assigned?

In classrooms where thematic instruction is integrated with varied grouping practices, students can share in the responsibility for assessing their performance. Their flexibility in working with others and autonomy when making choices prepares them to find ways in which they can improve their performance, measure their own growth, and set goals.

The authentic experiences in which the students participate are often reflected by the artifacts they choose to represent their growth. This is sometimes difficult in districts where a mandated curriculum supersedes student choice. A compromise can be attained through a series of tasks, which, while complying with mandated curriculum guidelines, allows students to creatively demonstrate new skills and concepts.

During the reading of *War Comes to Willy Freeman* (Collier & Collier, 1990), the students and teacher were faced with this dilemma. Seeking to satisfy the grade level English requirements, the teacher combined the reading of the story with guidelines suggested by the language arts curriculum. She devised a series of tasks that, while measuring comprehension of the book, provided evidence that the students were learning other skills. The students' response journals already contained an eclectic array of writing samples. She merely added another requirement to the contents of the journals. The students, using a task sheet for guidance, were asked to show evidence at some time during the reading of the book, that they could demonstrate particular skills. They used a scoring rubric to grade these strategic responses in collaboration with their peers, and then conferenced with the teacher (Figure 2).

Figure 2

Scoring Rubric for Strategic Responses to Literature

4
- Clear, well-defined topic sentence.
- Main ideas and major points are elaborated upon.
- Transitional devices are used.
- Controlled organizations.
- Effective variety of sentence structure and length.
- No major mechanical errors.

3
- Topic sentence states the main idea satisfactorily.
- Some major points and main ideas are elaborated upon.
- Some transitional devices are used.
- Predictable pattern in sentence structure and length.
- Adequate organization.
- Few major mechanical errors.

2
- Topic sentence does not clearly state the main idea.
- Unelaborated details.
- Irrelevant details may be included.
- Few, if any transitional devices are used.
- Attempts at organization.
- Simplistic sentence structure.
- Some major mechanical errors which interfere with communication.

1
- No topic sentence.
- Very limited detail.
- Unsuccessful attempt at organization.
- Inappropriate sentence structure.
- Numerous major mechanical errors which interfere with communication.

(Developed by R. L. McCormack)

For example, the students had been instructed in the steps for writing persuasive compositions and had been given many opportunities for guided practice. The steps for writing a persuasive composition were conspicuously posted in the classroom. After reading half of *War Comes to Willy Freeman* (Collier & Collier, 1990), a group of students cooperatively wrote a persuasive composition about Sam Fraunces' Tavern, the setting for most of the book (Figure 3). On their task sheets they gave themselves a score of 4 and stated in their comment, "We followed the steps and made it interesting". The teacher concurred (Figure 4).

Using this procedure for all the tasks, the students combined skills they learned in class to produce some strategic responses to the literature they read. Friendly letters and business letters—which were woven into the reading block to enable all students to produce meaningful artifacts, often in collaboration with their peers—were also part of the curriculum. Then, after sufficient practice commensurate with each students strengths and weaknesses, the same scoring rubric was used to assess individual performance on the same tasks.

Figure 3

Cooperative Composition about Sam Fraunces' Tavern

Why You Should go to San Fraunces' Tavern

Sam Fraunces' tavern is one of the best in New York. This place is a place where you can go and relax, talk to friends and just plain have a good time. Ask any British soldiers and he'll tell you... "It's a great place to talk to someone in private, without a waitress snooping around."

In addition to being relaxed, if you need a waitress, you've got a waitress. If you want to talk alone, she will go away as quickly as she came. But if you get hungry, she will come and bring you some of the best food around.

Moreover, you could order an appetizer to get you started, a meal to fill you up and a sweet dessert to top off the night. Or you could just come for tea or a mug of the best beer you ever tasted. The beer is always cold and foamy for you. If you're looking for a good time and a good meal, come to Sam Fraunces' tavern.

Figure 4

Task Sheet for Collaborative Learning Groups

Lit Club/Assessment

Name: _____

Book: War Comes to Willy Freeman

Dates: Jan / Feb 1996

✓ Student   __ Teacher

TASK	DATE	GRADE	COMMENT
Friendly Letter			
Business Letter			
Persuasive Composition	1/96	4	We Followed the steps and it was interesting
Time order Paragraph			
Summary			

OBSERVATIONS:

How Much Time Should Be Allotted To Grouping in Any Given Day? Lesson?

No set parameters exist concerning the amount of time students should spend on collaborative learning activities. However, three important considerations should be kept in mind when determining the amount of time to spend on grouping.

First, some units of instruction and their accompanying activities lend themselves to a substantial amount of group work, others do not. Therefore, it is necessary to keep a big picture of the curriculum in mind when planning for collaborative learning experiences. Use collaborative learning experiences where they fit into overall curriculum plans. Figure 5 illustrates just one example of a weekly schedule in which collaborative learning activities are used across all subject areas.

Second, students need time to explore topics on their own and develop their own understandings. For collaborative learning to be effective, students need to have unique experiences to bring to the group for sharing and discussion. Third, practice makes perfect for both students and teachers. As teachers begin to use collaborative learning in their classroom, they will find that their ability to plan instruction, monitor groups, and manage behavior improves. Additionally, as students are given opportunities to work with their peers, their own skills in group work will improve.

How Will Students Know and Carry Out Their Responsibilities in a Group?

Effective collaborative learning requires three conditions (Rapp-Ruddell, 1996): (a) Activities must have students working in pairs or small-group teams with clearly articulated goals. These goals may be determined through teacher decision, student decision, or a combination of the two. (b) Students need to sit at tables or group desk arrangements with free access to resource materials so they can work together with the least amount of noise, movement, and confusion. (c) Working arrangements and procedures must be structured to increase student efficiency and decrease problems. For example, rules establishing the number of students who can be out of their seats or at a given resource area at a time set limits on the amount of classroom movement and instills a sense of responsibility in students.

Figure 5

A Sample Weekly Schedule For Collaborating Learning Experiences

	MONDAY	TUESDAY	WEDNESDAY	THURSDAY	FRIDAY
Language Arts and Social Studies	*Take Five Model:* groups predict/ pose questions. re: *War Comes to Willy Freeman*	Students write in response journals while reading	In *peer dyads*, students engage in theatrical reading	Students *respond* in groups to teacher prompt about being a slave	*Pair* and *small group* discussion of events/characters in book.
Science	Demonstration on "Sources of Pollution" Whole Class	Students engage in *Cooperative Reading Activity*	Students work in groups to read and record facts	Groups discuss their charts with the class	Research Groups continue; Students write facts from each chart presented.
Math	Teacher models use of percentages on overhead —Whole Class	Students practice in pairs—*Tutorial Grouping*	Students practice individually	Progress test is given	Students grouped according to *Need*

(Adapted from Practical Strategies for Improving Instruction, by K.D. Wood, 1994, Columbus, OH: National Middle School Association. Copyright 1994. Reprinted with permission.)

Another method that ensures that students are responsible for the task they are assigned is to designate a role for each student in the group. Some common group member roles include:

- Initiator—a student who explains the objective (what is to be accomplished)
- Summarizer—a student who makes sure that everyone understands what is being learned
- Researcher—a student who finds the materials needed by the group
- Recorder—a student who keeps track of what is being learned
- Monitor—a student who makes sure that everyone stays involved
- Communicator—a student who shares information with the whole class or the teacher

How Can Grouping/Collaborative Learning Strategies Be Used with Gifted Students?

An important feature of collaborative grouping is that groups should be flexible. This means that students can be grouped differently for different activities depending on the purposes set forth. In some situations teachers may find it most suitable to have gifted students in their own group. In other situations, they may be dispersed among several groups. Their distribution in the group structure should be determined by the instructional objectives. Possible bases for grouping learners include: skills development, interest, work habits, prior knowledge (content), prior knowledge (strategies), task/activity, social, random, and students' choice (Flood, Lapp, Flood, & Nagel, 1992).

Summary

In this article we have outlined the research and theory that supports the use of collaborative learning as a means of improving literacy for young adolescents. We have also posed a number of frequently asked questions and shared suggestions and practical strategies for classroom implementation. In addition to its soundness as a means of conveying information, collaborative learning provides a viable and motivating way to capitalize on the social needs of young adolescents. Collaborative learning holds great potential for improving both the intellectual and the social abilities of middle grades students.

References

Barr, R. Sadow, M. Blachowicz, C. (1995). *Reading diagnosis for teachers: An instructional approach*. White Plains, NY: Addison Wesley.

Brandt, R. (1987). On cooperation in schools: A conversation with David and Roger Johnson. *Educational Leadership, 45*(3), 1+19.

Collier, C. & Collier, W. (1990). *War Comes to Willy Freeman*. New York: Scholastic.

Davidson, N. (1994). Cooperative and collaborative learning: An integrated perspective. In J. Thousand, R. Villa, & A. Nevin (Eds.),

Creativity and collaborative learning: A practical guide to empowering students and teachers (pp. 13–30). Baltimore: Paul H. Brooks Publishing.

Davey, B. (1983). Think aloud: Modeling the cognitive processes of reading comprehension. *Journal of Reading, 27*(1), 44–47.

Flood, J., Lapp, D., Flood, S., & Nagel, G. (1992). Am I allowed to group? Using flexible patterns for effective instruction. *The Reading Teacher, 45*(8), 608–616.

Graves, N., & Graves, T. (1983). The cultural context of prosocial development: An ecological model. In D. Bridgeman (Ed.), *The nature of prosocial development: Interdisciplinary theories and strategies* (pp. 39–46). New York: Academic Press.

Johnson, D. W., & Johnson, R. T. (1991). *Learning together and alone* (3rd ed.). Boston: Allyn and Bacon.

Johnson, R. T., & Johnson, D. W. (1985). Student-student interactions: Ignored but powerful. *Journal of Teacher Education* 36, 22–26.

Kagan, S. (1994). *Cooperative learning*. San Juan, CA: Kagan Cooperative Learning.

Lapp, D., & Flood, J. (1992). *Teaching reading to every child* (3rd ed.). New York: Macmillan.

Lehr, F. (1984). Cooperative learning. *Journal of Reading, 27*, 458–460.

Opitz, M. (1992). The cooperative reading activity: An alternative to ability grouping. *The Reading Teacher, 45*, 736–738.

Paratore, J. R., (1991). Flexible grouping: Why and how. *The leadership letters: Issues and trends in reading and language arts*. Columbus, OH: Silver Burdett Ginn.

Pearson, P. D., & Raphael, T. E. (1990). Reading comprehension as a dimension of thinking. In B.F. Jones & L.I. Idol (Eds.), *Dimension of thinking and cognitive instruction: Implications for reform*. Vol. 1 (pp. 209–240). Hillsdale, NJ: Lawrence Erlbaum.

Radencich, M. C., McKay, L. J., & Paratore, J R (1995). Keeping flexible groups flexible: Grouping options. In M. C. Radencich & L. J. McKay (Eds.), *Flexible grouping for literacy in the elementary grades. (pp. 25–41) Boston: Allyn and Bacon.

Rapp-Ruddell, M. (1996). Engaging students interest and willing participation in subject area learning. In D. Lapp, J. Flood, & N. Farnan (Eds.), *Content area reading and learning* (pp. 95–110). Boston: Allyn and Bacon.

Slavin, R. E. (1989). A cooperative learning approach to content areas: Jigsaw teaching. In D. Lapp, J. Flood, & N. Farnan (Eds.), *Content area reading and learning* (pp. 330–346). Englewood Cliffs. NJ: Prentice-Hall.

Slavin, R. (1995). *Cooperative learning* (2nd ed.). Needham Heights, MA: Allyn and Bacon.

Stevens, R. J. & Slavin, R. E. (1995). The cooperative elementary school: Effects on students' achievement, attitudes, and social relations. *American Educational Research Journal, 32*(2), 321–35l.

Wood, K. D. (1994). *Practical strategies for improving instruction*. Columbus, OH: National Middle School Association.

Wood, K. D., & Algozzine, B. (Eds.). (1994). *Teaching reading to high risk learners: A unified perspective*. Boston: Allyn and Bacon.

Karen D. Wood teaches at the University of North Carolina, Charlotte.

Rachel L. McCormack is a reading consultant for the Plymouth, Massachusetts, Public Schools.

Diana Lapp teaches at San Diego State University.

James Flood teaches at San Diego State University.

From *Middle School Journal* Vol. 28, No. 3, January 1997, pages 26-34. Copyright © 1997 by National Middle School Association. Reprinted with permission from National Middle School Association.

A Culture of Literacy in Science

*A community of readers and writers in a middle school science class
learn science and develop a passion for learning.*

Donna Hooker Topping and Roberta Ann McManus

The science teacher's classroom is a typical middle school science room, but those who enter it become immersed immediately in a culture of literacy. Harry Potter peers from a poster that says, "Reading Can Take You Anywhere." A prominent glow-in-the-dark bulletin board reminds students to use the SQ3R (survey, question, read, recite, and review) plan when they read their science texts. Magazines and brochures on tables and windowsills invite the eye to linger. A stop sign above an over-flowing bookcase says, "STOP—Take the time to read and enjoy." The daily *Philadelphia Inquirer* sits in a place of honor, rarely left folded for long, as students gravitate to it to find out more about science-related events, or just to check the latest sports scores, comics, or horoscopes.

Today Mike and Pablo are putting the finishing touches on a poster that displays magazine pictures and newspaper headlines that students have been clipping about science in the news. It will join several other posters, similarly assembled, that hang on the wall to remind students that science is present in the real world, not just in school. Knowing that his teacher leaves home before the early morning news shows air, Jake says to her,

I heard on *Good Morning America* this morning that the Centers for Disease Control say we don't have enough smallpox vaccine for all of us.

Without prompting, Jake picks up the newspaper and finds the related article. Steve goes to the computer and clicks on a search engine to read more about it. Jen returns *Horrible Science: Disgusting Digestion* (Arnold, 1998) to the circulating science library at the left of the teacher's lab desk. As she crosses off her name on the sign-out sheet, she tells Stacy it was "totally gross." Stacy picks it up and signs it out. Keisha shows her teacher the draft of the letter she has written requesting information for the class on recycling, and the teacher approves it for printing out on school letterhead stationery. Students gather around Timmy, who has brought *Mad Magazine* from home, and laugh at take-offs on Rube Goldberg's machines. All of this happens before the bell rings.

The Science Teacher Cares About Reading and Writing

High engagement in literacy is typical in this classroom because the teacher is a reader and writer who regularly talks about reading and writing with her students. By this time of the year, she has taught them strategies for tackling science texts. She has "thought aloud" the strategies for reading and writing in science that have worked for her. She has joined them in writing in journals, jotting ideas that help them reflect on the science concepts they have just read or heard about. They have talked about how the typical television news show account of a scientific event would fill only a paragraph of a newspaper and how newspaper and Internet sites tell much more. She has shared with them the books that she reads for pleasure and encouraged them to do the same. She has assembled a collection of science-related books that she encourages them to check out and read on their own.

This teacher is not a language arts teacher, a reading specialist, or a librarian. She teaches middle school science. After earning a bachelor's degree in secondary education biology 28 years ago, she entered her classroom thinking that her job was to teach *science*, never thinking that part of her job would be to help students transfer their reading and writing skills into science. This was middle school, after all! That sort of instruction took place in the elementary schools. When her students stumbled and fell while attempting to read and write about science, she couldn't understand it. No one had warned her about this problem.

Not willing to let a single student fall by the wayside, however, she joined forces with the district reading supervisor, who was interested in finding ways to help middle and high school students develop their learning strategies in content-area subjects. Now, she still claims that teaching science is her primary responsibility, but her broader goals extend beyond science content. She wants to impart the processes of learning and the passion for literacy.

The bell to start the period rings. Holding up a book from her circulating science library, she says,

> Listen to this. "The stomach-brooding frog swallows her eggs or tadpoles into her stomach. When they turn into froglets, they leave via Mom's mouth." You should see the picture! It has the baby peeking out of the mother's mouth. It looks as though she is going to burp up her baby! This book is called *Amazing Frogs and Toads* (Clarke, 1990), and it's here if you'd like to check it out.

Damien stretches forward in his seat and says, "I get it first!" The teacher often begins class with a brief sales pitch for one of the books she has purchased at yard sales, at used book sales, or through book clubs—traditionally the province of language arts teachers only. The titles all relate to science, but they are not textbooks. Through this circulating library, she invites students to *read*, period, at a time when pleasure reading is often trumped by the competing lures of adolescence. Students take her up on her invitation and discover that reading science can be fun. At the end of the period, Damien rushes to get to *Amazing Frogs and Toads* before Liz and Charmaine, leaving them to search for books that the teacher "sold" last week.

During this crucial period of their lives, students should have an opportunity to forge bonds with significant adults.

Her students work at different rates. Bothered by the idea that the reward for completing work efficiently should be busywork, the teacher writes DIRT—Daily Independent Reading Time—on her chalkboard each day to direct students to what they may do when they complete assignments. During this time, students can read *anything* whether it is science-related or not. Most often, however, they gravitate to the interesting science books in her classroom library. Her school district, like most today, is preoccupied with standards and state testing. Supported by studies by Baumann and Duffy (1997), Krashen (1988), and Pilgreen (2000) that indicate that students' pleasure reading enhances their reading performance and academic work, she knows that DIRT is not a waste of time.

Ultimately, however, her job is to help students learn science. Her science curriculum is in the forefront of her teaching, but the processes of literacy help her deliver that curriculum. She often introduces units and lessons by reading aloud from articles and books that directly relate to her current lessons and units, concurring with Jim Trelease, who says, "Far from suggesting the curriculum be abandoned, I say it should be enriched and brought to life by story" (1989). For a unit about diseases, she reads aloud about Alexander Fleming's accidental discovery of penicillin from *Serendipity: Accidental Discoveries in Science* (Roberts, 1989). While the teacher is reading, she sees Melissa get up and go to the bookshelf. She pauses. Melissa says, "Oh, keep going. There's another book over here that tells about this same thing." After searching through the shelves, she finds the book—one that she had read during DIRT.

Guiding Reading and Writing in Science

Students in this class not only become interested in reading science, but they also learn how. After reading aloud an account of the discovery of Lyme disease, for example, the teacher gives students an article about it from a science journal. Some argue that difficult readability should preclude the use of such sources, but this teacher regularly provides primary source material—from magazine and newspaper articles, pamphlets, brochures, and the Internet—for the latest updates in science. She accommodates the difficulty in readability by previewing the Lyme disease article and giving students a printed guide that calls their attention to key facts, ideas, and organizational patterns in the text. The guide invites their responses and provides a chart on which they can organize the information that they find.

She helps students develop a repertoire of strategies for dealing with science and other content-area texts. Reading guides (Wood, Lapp, & Flood, 1992) alert students to the text's organization and key ideas. K-W-L (Ogle, 1986) helps students think about what they *know, want* to know, and what they *learned* from texts and lectures. RAFT (Santa, 1988) helps them strengthen the clarity of their writing by assuming different roles, writing to different *audiences* in different *formats* about the topics that they study in her class.

She and the reading supervisor have devised a strategy that they call Text Boxes to help students slow down their reading and monitor their comprehension when reading difficult texts about unfamiliar topics. The boxes of a reading guide correspond with the paragraphs, diagrams, and photos on a particular page of the text. Each box has two columns; students take notes about important facts and ideas in the first, and reflect and question the text in the second. They have developed the Listen-Stop-and-Write technique, breaking the teacher's lecture into three-minute segments interspersed with two-minute writing periods, which helps students focus on their listening and note-taking (Topping & McManus, 2002). The teacher also designs assessments to re-inforce learning. For example, just be-fore students take a test on DNA, she plays a short clip from the movie *Jurassic Park* and asks students to watch, lis-ten for, and list the DNA vocabulary mentioned in this film. Brains acti-vated and geared toward science, stu-dents perform well on the test.

> **She has assembled a collection of science-related books that she encourages students to check out and read on their own.**

Schoolwide Accountability for Literacy

The school is committed to creating lifetime readers. During a once-a-week, school wide sustained silent reading period, everyone—stu-dents, teachers, administrators, and support personnel—reads silently from self-selected books. After-ward, everyone writes a response to what they have read. These writings are not book reports; rather, they are opportunities to respond to books by reflecting on what in the books has amazed them, surprised them, or made them laugh. The sharing of these reflections among adults and adolescents are the "grand conversations" about which Atwell (1987) writes.

> **She often introduces unit and lessons by reading aloud from articles and books that directly relate to her current lessons and units.**

The school's adults savor the rela-tionships that they develop with stu-

dents by sharing their respective reading experiences. Maria's favor-ite subject to read about was drag-ons. She knew how they ate, their favorite names for their babies, and how they escaped from tight spots. The teacher was impressed and said so. With the conversation link now open, Maria became comfortable enough to ask the teacher for help in science. Kristina was reading Tom Clancy's *Rainbow Six*, and the teacher noticed that this book kept reappearing week after week during sustained silent reading time. Not wanting to be without a book, Kris-tina kept this book in her locker from week to week. The teacher, also a Tom Clancy fan, feigned shock:

> How can you possibly leave my fa-vorite author in a stuffy old locker and only read him once a week? Doesn't the suspense kill you?

The teacher and Kristina devel-oped a friendly, teasing relationship. Debby began to read romance novels during sustained silent reading time and shared complaints with the teacher every time the bell rang to end the reading period. One day, the teacher heard a fight outside the classroom door. She went into the hall and saw Debby and another girl clawing and screaming at each other. Summoning her best teacher stare, the teacher said, "Get to your home-rooms." Debby looked at the teacher, stopped fighting, and walked into homeroom, while the other girl con-tinued to protest. In homeroom, the other students challenged Debby. "Why did you stop fighting her?" Debby said, "'Cuz she [the teacher] is my friend; we talk about books" (Topping & McManus, 2002).

Adolescence is a turbulent time, at best. During this crucial period of their lives, students should have an opportunity to forge bonds with sig-nificant adults through literacy. The science teacher hopes that her stu-dents will not only learn science, but

will also learn the skills and rewards of literacy that will continue throughout their lives. Establishing a community of readers and writers is the place to start.

References

Arnold, N. (1998). *Horrible science: Disgusting digestion.* New York: Scholastic.

Atwell, N. (1987). *In the middle: Writing, reading, and learning with adolescents.* Portsmouth, NH: Heinemann Boynton/Cook.

Baumann, J. F., & Duffy, A. M. (1997). *Engaged reading for pleasure and learning: A report for the National Reading Research Center.* Athens, GA: National Reading Research Center.

Clarke, B. (1990). *Eyewitness juniors: Amazing frogs and toads.* New York: Alfred A. Knopf.

Krashen, S. (1988). Do we learn to read by reading? The relationship between free reading and reading ability. In D. Tannen (Ed.), *Linguistics in context: Connecting observation and understanding* (pp. 269–298). Norwood, NJ: Ablex.

Ogle, D. M. (1986). K-W-L: A teaching model that develops active reading of expository text. *The Reading Teacher.* Newark, DE: International Reading Association.

Pilgreen, J. (2000). *The SSR handbook: How to organize and manage a sustained silent reading program.* Portsmouth, NH: Heinemann.

Roberts, R. M. (1989). *Serendipity: Accidental discoveries in science.* New York: John Wiley.

Santa, C. M. (1988). *Content reading, including study systems: Reading, writing, and studying across the curriculum.* Dubuque, IA: Kendall/Hunt.

Topping, D. H., & McManus, R. A. (2002). *Real reading, real writing: Content area strategies.* Portsmouth, NH: Heinemann.

Trelease, J. (1995). *The new read-aloud handbook.* New York: Penguin.

Wood, K. D., Lapp, D., & Flood, J. (1992). *Guiding readers through texts: A review of study guides.* Newark, DE: International Reading Association.

Donna Hooker Topping (Donna.Topping @millersville.edu) is an assistant profes-sor of education at Millersville Univer-sity, 220 Stayer Education Center, Millersville, PA 17551;

Roberta Ann McManus (robertam @zoominternet.net) is a science teacher at Penns Grove Middle School, Oxford Area School District, Oxford, PA 19363.

From *Educational Leadership*, November 2002, pages 30-33. Reprinted with permission of the Association for Supervision and Curriculum Development. © 2002 by ASCD. All rights reserved.

UNIT 3
Adolescent Motivation for Literacy

Unit Selections

8. **Affective Dimensions of Content Area Reading**, Alan M. Frager
9. **Activating Student Interest in Content Area Reading**, Carla Mathison
10. **Enhancing Young Adolescents' Motivation for Literacy Learning**, Nancy B. Mizelle

Key Points to Consider

- How can teachers motivate secondary students to read textbooks?

- Which reading strategies would best meet the needs of students in the content area?

- How do instructional strategies contribute to creating a positive learning environment?

 **Links: www.dushkin.com/online/**
These sites are annotated in the World Wide Web pages.

LinguaLinks
http://www.ethnologue.com/LL_docs/index/Motivation(Literacy).asp
Research in Adolescent Literacy
http://grants1.nih.gov/grants/guide/rfa-files/RFA-HD-03-012.html

While today I have a doctorate and teach pre-service teachers methods of secondary English and social studies instruction, I was a reluctant reader in junior high and ninth-grade following a slow start in elementary school. I can still remember the trauma of daily reading class in first grade, when I would stand with the rest of the black birds against the back wall and wait for my turn to read. Since the teacher explained how she was the mother bird and we were the baby birds, I did not look forward to eating worms, as she had explained the analogy of her having to tell us words we did not know. Neither the basal readers nor the instructional strategy was very motivational.

Junior high was not much improvement. I wrote book reports from the book jackets and thought that the only homework was that which required me to write something to turn in the next day. I remember taking notes during world history, but more than that, I remember students tapping one for true and two for false on the chapter tests. The teacher, who was also the school basketball coach, read 25 statements and we wrote "T" or "F." We exchanged papers and then called out our grades to him. Science was not much different in junior high. The football coach was nice to us and would let us color pictures in our science workbook.

I was halfway through ninth-grade when we got a new English teacher. She assigned us to read *A House of Seven Gables*. There are two things I remember about the experience that changed my academic life. First, my teacher believed I could read even though I did not believe that I could. She motivated me to read chapters in the book at home by telling me to read all the words I knew on the assigned pages. Even when I could not answer any of the four or five comprehension questions each day, she gave me full credit if I had read all the words on the pages that I knew. She trusted that if I turned in a three by five card with my name on it, that meant I had read all the words I knew. She had told me not to turn in a card if I did not complete the reading. The other thing I remember is how interesting the discussions were in class. Everyone got to say what he or she thought about what we had read. I never talked, but I enjoyed listening without fear of embàrrassment or failure. Even though I never was able to answer any of the daily quiz questions until the last couple of chapters in the book, I felt proud that I read a complete novel for the first time in my life.

We read several novels that semester, and with each one I grew to comprehend what I was reading. I can still remember our discussions about what we would have done if we had found the pearl in John Steinbeck's novel. I remember the teacher asked us questions that resulted in us thinking about how we would make value decisions. I grew to love reading literature as a way to think about myself in relationship to self and others in the world where I lived. I started reading my history and biology texts because it seemed like our texts were integrated. Novels were a different text through which to understand society. Studying history made more sense as we talked about the lives of the people in novels and our own lives in the present. Our teachers did not talk about constructivism back then, but those of us who were surviving the schooling ritual were doing so by making meaning out of our learning experiences.

In keeping with the definition of critical literacy as participatory construction of meaning, it is easy to understand that teaching is more than dispensing information to students. Critical to developing a culture of literacy discussed in unit two is engaging students in the process of meaning making. How can secondary content area teachers interest and motivate adolescents to engage texts beyond the traditional purpose of finding answers to section reviews in order to pass chapter tests at the end of a unit of study?

Most pre-service teachers learn about motivation theory in their educational psychology classes. Building a positive classroom environment is just as important on the secondary level as it is in elementary schools. INTASC (1992) standard # 5, Motivation and Learning Environment, states, "The pre-service teacher uses an understanding of individual and group motivation and behavior to create a learning environment that encourages positive social interaction, active engagement in learning, and self-motivation." Motivation theory plays an integral role in literacy development, as teachers must find ways to capture students' interest in content area texts.

The articles in this unit explore affective elements of content area reading and present strategies for motivating the secondary student to read in the content area. In "Affective Dimensions of Content Area Reading" (1993), Alan M. Frager connects affective learning theory with practical reading strategies and addresses the affective dimensions of content areas reading. The author focuses on the affective stage of the reading process to identify causes and solutions to reading problems. Pre-reading, during reading, and post-reading strategies are suggested. In "Activating Student Interest in Content Area Reading" (1989), Carla Mathison addresses the problem of students not completing reading homework assignments and the role that motivation plays in reading. The author gives five strategies for generating student interest in content area reading: analogies, personal anecdotes, disrupting readers' expectations, challenging students to resolve a paradox, and novel and conflicting information or situation. In "Enhancing Young Adolescents' Motivation for Literacy Learning" (1997), Nancy B. Mizelle discusses the concerns of middle school teachers about young adolescents' motivation for literacy learning in the content area. Specifically, she focuses on classroom strategies educators in the fields of motivation and literacy have identified as beneficial.

Creating interest in all subjects is important. Math and science teachers must look for ways to allow students to personalize their learning. When students are encouraged to investigate the ways that math and science are present in the world around them, reading their textbooks can be integrated with reading their social environment.

Affective Dimensions of Content Area Reading

There is an affective dimension to even factual, nonfictional accounts. Effective strategies combining affective and cognitive elements of instruction can motivate students to read content area textbooks with awareness.

Alan M. Frager

Affect and motivation play a significant if not paramount role in content area reading. Reading to learn requires that a reader begins by engaging the text—opening the book and starting to read it—and continues by interacting with the text—comprehending, interpreting, and assimilating the author's ideas within the framework of the reader's prior knowledge and experience.

The act of reading calls upon a learner's inner resources which at first appear to be mostly cognitive. For example, educational psychologists like Bloom and Piaget have explained "comprehension," "interpretation," and "assimilation" as dimensions of cognitive hierarchies. Yet, these same dimensions depend upon inner resources that are affective, such as interest, self-confidence, control of negative feelings and procrastination, and willingness to take risks.

Understanding and appreciating the affective dimensions of content area reading may help teachers address some of the most frustrating and debilitating problems in schools today. One major problem occurs when students who are quite able readers choose not to read selections of content area texts assigned by the teacher. Of equal concern is when students do read the assigned texts but fail to employ reading strategies that are conducive to learning.

The purpose of this article is to help teachers address the problems of students who are not reading content area materials strategically or even not reading at all. By looking at affective aspects in different stages of the reading process, we can find some of the causes as well as solutions to these problems. This will shed new light on some familiar instructional methods that have been developed and used primarily for reasons of cogni-

tive development and will show how these methods may contribute to motivation to reading content area materials.

Prereading

The prereading phase has received much attention as reading educators have come to appreciate that "the single most important factor influencing new learning is what the learner already knows" (Ausubel 1968). Under the name schema theory (Anderson & Pearson, 1984; Rumelhart, 1980), this idea has been a force of transformation in reading instruction. Reading, which was once defined as the reader's application of word recognition and comprehension skills, has been redefined by many as the connection of the reader's prior knowledge to the author's ideas presented in the text. Within this framework teachers can understand the importance of instruction that is provided before the reading of a text and builds or activates a reader's prior knowledge.

Examples of methods that activate readers' prior knowledge are abundant: prereading questions, anticipation guides, ReQuest, PreP, and others. Prereading questions and anticipation guides, for example, accomplish this task by eliciting readers' responses to some of the same ideas and concepts they will encounter after reading the text, sometimes in the form of postreading questions. With the PreP activity (Langer, 1981), teachers ask students to "Tell anything that comes to your mind when you hear the word *bacteria*" (or any word that is the topic discussed in the text to be read). Given the simplicity and educational logic of prereading activities, we must wonder why content teachers rarely use these reading methods (Ratekin et al., 1985; Smith & Feathers, 1983).

Without diminishing this cognitive perspective, we can gain new understandings of prereading activities by looking at their affective dimensions. One of these with great value in the prereading stage is confidence. For prereading activities to have the intended cognitive benefit, readers need to feel confident that they have prior knowledge about a subject, a feeling too frequently lacking.

My experience in teaching questioning strategies to pre- and inservice teachers has taught me that a common first response of secondary school students to a general question like "What do you know about_____?" is "I don't know anything." Sadker and Sadker's (1985) study of 100 classrooms in four U.S. states also found that many students don't respond at all to teacher questions: "We were concerned that so many students—approximately one-fourth of our study—treated classroom discussion as a spectator sport and did not get involved in any interaction with teachers."

But this is certainly no surprise: When teachers ask students to disclose their prior knowledge about bacteria or any other topic discussed in a text, students must have confidence to risk revealing what is at best a partial knowledge and at worst a complete misconception. Common sense tells us that students aren't going to take risks with possible wrong answers when classroom rewards are given only for right answers.

An indication that confidence is at the center of a student's decision to participate in a prereading discussion is the way students' participation in discussion is responsive to teacher praise, which boosts confidence. Both the Sadkers' study and one by Morine-Dershimer (1982) suggest a strong link between teacher praise and student participation in discussion.

Though it is not broached in these studies, I believe that a key element in a teacher's ability to use praise to activate students' prior knowledge of content area topics is a teacher's appreciation of how students can be intelligently wrong. This element is keenly captured in Ault's (1984) article describing the imaginative and perceptive thinking in children's misconceptions about topics in science and math.

For example, Ault describes a first grader having trouble solving addition problems with Cuisenaire rods who exclaims, "I can't find the zero rod!" While the utterance was technically wrong because a zero rod cannot exist, the remark also showed a high level of intelligence. It expressed an issue raised by many mathematicians before Cantor, whose work on sets in the late 19th century departed from the use of length as the fundamental object in mathematics.

Teachers should understand that students' prior knowledge of content area topics is supposed to be incomplete, naive, and in some cases completely misconceived; if they knew everything the text would relate about the topic, there would be no need to read it. Likewise, teachers need to appreciate and praise students for the risk taken in revealing their prior knowledge—naiveté and all—because it leads to more involvement in learning with the text and within the classroom.

A second affective dimension of the prereading stage is interest. The effect of interest on comprehension can be inferred by considering how interest increases attention, which improves comprehension. More direct evidence of the effect of interest on comprehension comes from the experience of teachers and parents who have observed young readers understand texts considered too difficult for them when those texts are related to their interests (Maria, 1990). Generating and developing students' interest about a subject in a content area text should be an integral part of every prereading instructional sequence.

Current scholars in the field of content area reading have described a variety of ways to address a reader's interest through prereading activities. Richardson and Morgan (1990) propose that readers assess their interest through an exploration of their prior knowledge, including what they know about the text, like about the topic, and understand about the purpose for reading.

Pace et al. (1989) give a similar recommendation, to "help students become more reflective about and evaluate their own ideas, their observations, others' observations, and contradictions." In their view, this approach is crucial in understanding text presenting scientific concepts because prior knowledge, especially in science, is more than the reader's concepts and beliefs; it also includes the reader's commitment to those concepts and beliefs. They remind us that people have personal attachments to their commitments, which makes some beliefs and concepts more resistant to revision.

Manzo and Manzo (1990) advocate the ReQuest procedure as a prereading activity precisely because "it encourages students to develop their own purposes for reading by reducing many of the 'risks' or inhibitions involved in class participation." ReQuest helps students to develop confidence in themselves as well as interest in reading through its rhythm of teacher and students taking turns asking questions about the text. By modeling the teacher's methods of questioning, especially prediction-type questions—"what might happen next?"—students can gain confidence as their questioning skill increases. These same skills promote engagement with the text and more interest, as the reading reveals answers to questions and confirmations of predictions.

During reading

Louise Rosenblatt (1983) has explained how readers decide as they begin reading a text whether to direct more attention to the information they can carry away from the reading or to the range of feelings elicited from the associations with the text. To illustrate that these two different purposes are frequently unknown or ignored by teachers, she often referred to a poem in a third-grade workbook that was printed under the heading "What facts does this poem teach you?"

For Rosenblatt, the juxtaposition of poetry, which is "an event in which the reader draws on images and feelings stirred up by the words of the text," with an efferent purpose statement (after the Latin *effere*, to carry away) produced an oxymoron on the order of a low calorie banana split. Her concept of an efferent/aesthetic continuum (Rosenblatt, 1988) helps teachers understand that readers' purposes always have both cognitive and affective aspects in proportions that vary with texts and contexts.

I have taught many students for whom the only perceived experience with a nonfiction text has been of an efferent nature:

read to memorize for a test. Students have often told me their nonfiction content area texts, even those used in my classes, were "cold" and "just plain factual" as if for cognitive response only. While strictly speaking their feeling of coldness was an affective response to the texts, my discussions with students have shown me that the vast majority of them have at best a very narrow range of affective responses to nonfiction.

To develop a wider range of affective responses to content area texts, teachers might begin by looking at the reverse of Rosenblatt's poem in a workbook example and ask: What feelings does this science text teach you? While there are as many answers to this question as there are texts, I think three are of particular importance: the feelings of wonder, beauty, and adventure.

In his book *Superstrings and the Theory of Everything*, F. David Peat (1988), a science writer who explains developments in quantum physics for the general public, not only captured the wonder of science in current attempts to answer questions about the beginning of the universe and the origin of time, but also reflected on why science makes us wonder. To Peat, ideas in science are "like patterns in a kaleidoscope which move and transform until some new pattern swings into perception."

This phenomenon of kaleidoscopic wonder is perfectly expressed in the scientific question "Why are all snowflakes different?" that is driving a new branch of science called chaos. James Gleick (1987) included in his best-selling book called *Chaos* a set of color photographs of Koch curves, the Mandelbrot Set, and fractal clusters, which illustrate the beauty of this new science. They are images that have a familiar parallel in the beauty of natural science seen at every scale, from the amoeba to the galaxy.

To Lewis Thomas (1980), a physician and science writer, another feeling science evokes is "high adventure":

It is the very strangeness of nature that makes science engrossing. That ought to be at the center of science teaching. There are more than seven-times-seven types of ambiguity in science. The poetry of Wallace Stevens is crystal-clear alongside the genetic code. . . .[Science is] the wildest of all explorations ever undertaken by human beings, the chance to catch close views of things never seen before, the shrewdest maneuver for discovering how the world works.

History texts teach feelings, also. It is easy to understand this by keeping in mind that history is a story of human experience. As Meltzer (1987) explained in his foreword to *The American Revolutionaries: A History in Their Own Words:* "It was people who made the Revolution, not abstract social and economic and political forces. Who were the new Americans? What did they hope for? What did they worry about? What did it *feel* like to make the modern world's first democratic republic and write its new Constitution?"

By attending and responding to the affective dimension of content area texts, students can learn more while reading. One way content area teachers can promote this awareness and response is to balance textbook reading with trade books that discuss the same content. Since textbooks are third-hand

sources—predigested, chopped-up versions of knowledge constructed from original (primary) sources and commentaries on original sources (secondary)—they frequently fail to capture the sense of adventure and wonder that accompany discoveries in all fields.

The science books *Superstrings, Chaos,* and *Late Night Thoughts* cited above are trade books written by authors much closer to the primary sources of the content than textbook authors. Readers of these trade books not only learn the science content but also feel the excitement and awe of the authors as they experience the story of the discoveries unfolding.

Another way of helping students respond in affective ways to content area reading material is to teach them to monitor and express their affective responses to the reading along with their cognitive responses. An example of this method is reported by Smith and Dauer (1984), who propose that students use a code to record their responses on strips of paper they affix to the margins of the pages they are reading. The authors explain: "For example. The code for a social studies textbook might be 'A' = Agree, 'B' = Bored, 'C' = Confused, 'D' = Disagree, 'M' = Main Idea. For an assignment in a science textbook, the code might be 'C' = Clear, 'D' = Difficult, 'I' = Important, 'S' = Surprising." When students identify feelings of boredom and confusion as well as surprise, they are learning about the elements of as well as the obstacles to comprehension. This is important because awareness of the elements and obstacles of comprehension is a first step in developing control over them.

Ability to overcome the affective obstacles that occur during reading may be the critical characteristic that better readers have and poorer readers lack. Estes's pilot study (1987), in which elementary through high school students of varying abilities were given a passage to read on a topic about which they all knew enough to make comprehension possible, showed that better readers seemed to persist in their attempts to overcome obstacles and make sense of the reading, while less able readers were seen giving up, "resigning themselves to another failure to understand."

Sharon Smith (1982) reported similar findings in her study of college students encountering a difficult text; to successfully overcome obstacles to comprehension and complete the reading, the students in her study required awareness and control of affective responses, like confronting negative feelings, summoning up positive feelings, and creating positive self images.

While students in Smith's study and the better readers in Estes's study seemed to have learned to identify and overcome affective obstacles to comprehension without direct instruction, the large number of readers who do not have these abilities suggests that direct instruction in this area, like the Smith-Dauer coding strategy, is warranted.

After reading

The after-reading part of the reading process consists of activities that help readers share and extend their comprehension of the text, including discussion, writing, and rereading. The most common after-reading activity in content area classes is known as recitation, a form of classroom verbal interaction in which teachers review and quiz students about the reading they were assigned (Sizer, 1984). Studies like Sadker & Sadker's (1985), however, show that in recitation activities students tend to give literal-level, short, unelaborated responses.

A recent study by Alvermann & Hayes (1989) indicated that teachers' patterns of verbal interaction with students during after-reading activities are resistant to intervention efforts; even providing teachers with instruction and close reflection on strategies for improving class discussions was not effective in generating "a more meaningful give-and-take between teacher and students."

Many methods for helping teachers improve classroom discussions focus on cognitive levels of teacher questions and student responses, such as using Bloom's Taxonomy of Educational Objectives: The Cognitive Domain. While cognitive analyses of after-reading activities have significant value, much also can be gained by looking at the affective dimensions of the social relationships among teachers and students in these activities.

These social relationships are illustrated well in Frank Smith's (1986) conception of a classroom "literacy club," where teachers and students help each other with reading and talk about what they have read recently, "the way readers normally behave in the world outside school." Smith highlights the affective dimensions of the social relationships in these clubs as their most critical elements. One rule is *no coercion,* because "it is the essence of clubs that their activities are entered into freely," A second rule is *no status*, meaning that teachers should not be obviously in control of the club.

Instead of coercion and control, which Smith says lead to intimidation, insecurity, and dependency, teachers should concentrate on providing help when help is needed by assuming the role of most experienced club member. This role is empowering to students, and the results are "growth, assurance, and independence".

Dillon's (1989) ethnographic study of a rural secondary, low-track, English-reading classroom illuminates Smith's premise that status, or social relationships among the teacher and student, have affective consequences for students. Dillon found that "Appleby," an effective teacher who was a primary focus of the study, had much success in leading discussions after reading assignments because he "allowed his students to interact with each other and with him, in the way they spoke with their peers and adults in their family/community."

Dillon observed that while students often talked sarcastically and would interrupt Appleby and other students, there was no evidence of disrespect displayed or felt; "rather the interruptions were filled with excitement and persistence related to presenting one's thoughts. Students' use of Black dialect was also typical during reading lessons. Appleby allowed students to use their dialect in his classroom because they were comfortable with it and more effective communicators".

Dillon's study is instructive also in showing that for secondary, low-track students, teachers need to incorporate techniques that help students develop positive feelings towards involvement in afterreading activities. In an interview, Appleby explained some of these techniques:

> I let them run their mouths more; I challenge them more, maybe I talk to them more, ask them for feedback, get personal and use nicknames…I let them work together more than most of their other teachers would do, I imagine…I pretty much give them responsibility for their own behavior…with some of these kids they're not going to remember who wrote *The Pearl* or *Of Mice and Men* —but they did something in my class—they got involved in a book, and they got involved in something—they use their imagination—they had a good experience.

While Smith and Dillon suggest that it is the social relations among students and the teacher that are critical in the after-reading phase of instruction. Bernhardt (1987) explains how the students' and teacher's "social" relations toward the text are important also. She contrasts the view of the text as an "authority figure containing facts which students must extract and reproduce" with the view of the text as a participant with which students interact in a knowledge construction process based on the reader's prior knowledge and the author's ideas.

A vivid example cited is an aside offered by a student who had read a passage on Martin Luther and answered the teacher's recitation questions about it:

> Amy: You know, I never knew Martin Luther King knew German.
>
> Teacher: [disdainfully] Amy, there is Martin Luther and there is Martin Luther King.

Amy's reading and recitation had enabled her to answer questions correctly while constructing a concept quite different from what the author intended.

Bernhardt suggests that instead of deferring to the authority of the fact that the two men had similar names but were quite different, the teacher could have reframed Amy's statement more positively—noting her comprehension monitoring and interest in the topic—and helped Amy discover the differences between the two men on her own. Using the text as a participant, not "the authority," in a classroom requires helping students gain both confidence and ability in making independent and mature interpretations of text.

Webb (1982) proposes making texts participants by using a technique based on Rogers' nondirective therapy and the uses of subjective criticism in discussing literary texts. She invites a student to join her sitting on chairs in front of the class and begins a dialogue focusing on the student's personal responses and associations to the text he or she has read. The dialogue usually begins with a question like "What do you think is important about this story?" and ends with "What is the most important word in the story? The most important scene? The most important action?" With this technique, Webb signals clearly to students that their feelings and interpretations are important; the student, the text, and the teacher are equal partners in a conversation.

Conclusion

Though reading to learn is a process that has both cognitive and affective components, the cognitive components in content area reading receive exclusive attention in many schools, where knowledge is measured in cognitive terms: right or wrong answers given or the number of facts memorized. Improving aspects of students' reading that are primarily cognitive is important but not sufficient to address reading problems students have in today's schools.

Alternative instructional approaches based on reader response theory like the reading workshop (Atwell, 1987; Willinsky, 1990), can also be very useful, especially in expanding students' range of affective responses to text, because they provide students with choice in their reading and a sense of ownership. However, these are unlikely to fully address student needs in content areas for two reasons.

First, the "dining room table" conversations about books that Atwell describes and promotes are predominately about works of fiction, not the nonfiction texts so widely used in content area courses. Second, due to unique traditions and conceptions of learning and teaching in the different content areas, teachers of the natural and social sciences are much more likely to maintain teacher-centered classrooms than are language teachers (Barnes, 1975).

The concepts and strategies described in this article are as applicable in a content area class where the teacher directs the majority of students' assigned text reading as they are in classes where the teacher's role does not go beyond modeling the behaviors of mature readers. In either case, teachers need to help students develop confidence that they have prior knowledge about the subject in the text to be read. Students' interests in subjects and texts should be developed as well as incorporated in choosing reading materials for classroom use.

While students are reading a content area text, they should know that responding to the author means experiencing the feelings generated by the words as well as thinking about the concepts. Teachers should help students monitor their feelings during reading and learn to identify and overcome feelings that present obstacles to comprehension.

When students have completed the reading, teachers need to be aware that activities that help students share and extend their comprehension employ social relations in which students' feelings are critical. Where the teacher or the text are viewed as the authority, students learn to be insecure and dependent. Where the teacher and text are viewed as participants in a conversation, students can learn to become confident and independent interpreters of text.

Teachers who can understand and appreciate how the affective dimensions of reading complement the cognitive dimensions should experience more success in teaching content area reading.

Frager teaches in the Department of Teacher Education at Miami University (Oxford OH 45056, USA).

References

Alvermann, D.E., & Hayes, D.A. (1989). Classroom discussion of content area assignments: An intervention study. *Reading Research Quarterly,* 21, 305–335.

Anderson, R.C., & Pearson, P.D. (1984). A schema-theoretic view of the basic processes in reading comprehension. In P. D. Pearson (Ed.), *Handbook of reading research.* New York: Longman.

Atwell, N. (1987). *In the middle: Writing, reading, and learning with adolescents.* Montclair, NJ: Boynton/Cook.

Ault, C.R. (1984) May). Intelligently wrong: Some comments on children's misconceptions. *Science and Children,* 21, 22–24.

Ausubel, D.P. (1968). *Educational psychology: A cognitive view.* New York: Holt, Rinehart & Winston.

Barnes, D. (1975). *From communication to curriculum.* Harmondsworth, UK: Penguin.

Bernhardt, E.B. (1987). The text as a participant in instruction. *Theory into Practice,* 26(1), 32–37.

Dillon, D.R. (1989). Showing them that I want them to learn and that I care about who they are: A microethnography of the social organization of a secondary low-track English-Reading classroom. *American Education Research Journal,* 26(2) 227–259.

Estes, T. (1987). Illusions (and realities) of schema theory. *Seventh Yearbook of the American Reading Forum,* 1–6.

Gleick, J. (1987). *Chaos.* New York: Viking Penguin.

Langer, Judith A. (1981). From theory to practice: A prereading plan. *Journal of Reading,* 25, 152–156.

Manzo, A. & Manzo, U. (1990). *Content area reading: A heuristic approach.* Columbus, OH: Merrill.

Maria, K. (1990). *Reading comprehension instruction: Issues and strategies.* Parkton, MD: York Press.

Meltzer, M. (1987). *The American revolutionaries: A history in their own words.* New York: Thomas Crowell.

Morine-Dershimer, G. (1982). Pupil perceptions of teacher praise. *Elementary School Journal,* 82(5) 421–434.

Pace, A.J., Marshall, N., Horowitz, R., Lipson, M.Y., & Lucido, P. (1989). When prior knowledge doesn't facilitate text comprehension: An examination of some of the issues. *Cognitive and social perspectives for literacy research and instruction (38th Yearbook).* Chicago, IL: National Reading Conference.

Peat, F.D. (1988). *Superstrings and the theory of everything.* Chicago, IL: Contemporary Books.

Ratekin, N., Simpson, M.L., Alvermann, D.E., & Dishner, E.K. (1985). Why teachers resist content area reading instruction. *Journal of Reading,* 28, 432–437.

Richardson, J., & Morgan, R. F. (1990). *Reading to learn in the content areas.* Belmont, CA: Wadsworth.

Rosenblatt, L. (1983). The reading transaction: What for? In R. Parker & F. Davis (Eds.), *Developing literacy: Young children's use of language.* Newark, DE: International Reading Association.

Rosenblatt, L. (1988). *Writing and reading: The transactional theory* (Technical Report No. 416). Urbana. IL: Center for the Study of Reading. (ERIC Document Reproduction Service No. ED 292 062)

Rumelhart, D.E. (1980). Schemata: The building blocks of cognition. In R.J. Spiro, B.C. Bruce, & W.F. Brewer (Eds.) *Theoretical issues in reading comprehension.* Hillsdale, NJ: Erlbaum.

Sadker, D., & Sadker, M. (1985). Is the O.K. classroom O.K.? *Phi Delta Kappan.* 66, 358–361.

Sizer, T.R. (1984). *Horace's compromise: The dilemma of the American high school.* Boston, MA: Houghton Mifflin.

Smith, F. (1986). *Insult to intelligence.* New York: Arbor House.

Smith, F.R., & Feathers, K.M. (1983). The role of reading in content area classrooms: Assumption vs. reality. *Journal of Reading.* 27, 262–269.

Smith, R.J., & Dauer, V.L. (1984). A comprehension monitoring strategy for content area teachers. *Journal of Reading,* 28, 144–147.

Smith, S. (1982). Learning strategies of mature college students. *Journal of Reading,* 26, 5–12.

Thomas, L. (1980). *Late night thought on listening to Mahler's Ninth Symphony.* New York: Viking.

Webb, A.J., (1982). Transactions with literary texts: Conversations in classrooms. *English Journal,* 71(3), 56–60.

Willinsky, J. (1990). *The new literacy.* New York: Routledge.

From *Journal of Reading* Vol. 36, No. 8, May 1993, pages 616-622. Copyright © 1993 by The International Reading Association. Reprinted with permission.

Activating Student Interest in Content Area Reading

Carla Mathison

Mr. Sloane's initial enthusiasm for his third period class was quickly thwarted when he realized that his social studies students couldn't answer questions about text material. They simply hadn't done the homework reading that had been assigned after the introductory lesson to the chapter had been presented. His frustration was exacerbated by the realization that his entire lesson, which was based on an understanding of concepts presented in the initial lesson and reinforced in the text assignment, would have to be placed on hold or completely eliminated so that in-class time could be used to read the textbook.

Mr. Sloane's lament reflects the frustration of many teachers who find their instructional plans impeded by their students' failure to read the textbook. In a survey of English, math, science, social studies, physical education, art, and home economics teachers, Rieck (1977) discovered that, although 97% of these teachers assigned reading material in their courses, a disappointingly high percentage of these same teachers (38%) reported that most students didn't do the reading. Although conducted over a decade ago, Rieck's survey supports what is still obvious in today's classrooms.

Why is it that students do not read their textbooks? Factors such as inability and low interest may account for some aspects of the problem. Many teachers, believing that the problem is inability, have tried diligently to use instructional strategies that help students improve their ability to read expository text. Such learning-from-text strategies include mapping techniques (Alvermann, 1986; Flood & Lapp, 1988), summarizing techniques (Brown, Campione, & Day, 1981; Taylor, 1982), constructing graphic organizers (Dansereau, Holley, & Collins, 1980; Jones, 1985), questioning strategies (Ciardiello, 1986; Gilmore & McKinney, 1986; Raphael & Pearson, 1982), and applying one's prior knowledge (Bransford & Johnson, 1972; Pearson, Hansen, & Gordon, 1979).

If the problem was only inability, it would seem that once students were armed with these strategies and were able to read their textbooks, they would do so. But many of us who spend countless hours working with high school teachers and students realize that ability alone may not be enough to induce students to open their books. What students can do and what they choose to do remain two intertwined but subtly different instructional concerns. The focus of instruction needs to include an emphasis on the factors that motivate students to read their textbooks as well as factors that enhance reading ability.

Motivation has been defined as the magnitude and direction of behavior—the choices we make about what experiences or goals we will pursue or avoid and the degree of effort we will exert toward the accomplishment of these goals (Keller, 1983). A great deal of one's motivation, regardless of age, may occur because of self-predicted success. But even when success is a given, educators are often perplexed by students who lack the interest needed to motivate themselves to read their book.

There is increasing evidence that interest plays a critical role in determining what students learn and remember from their expository reading (Anderson, 1982; Hidi, Baird, & Hildyard, 1982). A recent study by Anderson, Shirey, Wilson, and Fielding (1987) revealed that interest accounted for approximately the same amount of variance in recall as did standard reading scores on reading performance.

Realizing the significant role that interest plays in motivating learning from text, educators must ask: *How can we generate student interest in content area reading?*

How is interest stimulated?

While research on interest-promoting techniques is somewhat scant, five general strategies have been identified that seem to have potential for linking readers and text. These include: (1) using analogies, (2) relating personal anecdotes, (3) disrupting readers' expectations, (4) challenging readers to resolve a paradox, (5) introducing novel and conflicting information or situations.

Using analogies. The careful use of analogies, making the "strange familiar and the familiar strange," promotes interest by connecting readers' prior knowledge with new information (Hayes & Tierney, 1982; Singer & Simonsen, 1989; Weil, Joyce, & Kluwin, 1978). Analogies provide students with "cognitive hooks" (Ausubel, 1968) upon which to hang new information. Analogical thinking helps students make critical schematic connections that might otherwise be difficult to establish. Possibly, one of the major reasons analogies are often effective in stimulating interest is that they allow students to initially work with knowledge and ideas with which they are more secure. At the same time, analogies create intrigue because they cause students to look at their past experiences and knowledge in different and new ways (see Example 1).

Relating personal anecdotes. In his article entitled *Confessions of a Textbook Writer*, McConnell (1978) suggests that an author's use of personal anecdotes captures interest because these anecdotes help readers personalize the information they read. This sharing from author to reader can be paralleled in the classroom with teachers and their students. Students are normally curious about the personal lives of their teachers. Teachers can capitalize on this curiosity by sharing experiences they have had or situations they have encountered, which can help students appreciate the importance and relevancy of the text passages they will be reading (see Example 4 below). The use of analogies and personal anecdotes often promotes interest in the textbook because they give students a personal context in which to place the new information they read.

Disrupting readers' expectations. Like all of us, our students have a natural tendency to confine themselves to those domains in which they already feel safe. But again like us, students can become bored and uninterested in learning if left unchallenged to reach beyond these comfortable arenas of knowledge and thought. This boredom and lack of interest is often seen in students' textbook reading behaviors (Mandler, 1982; Schank, 1979, 1982). By disrupting students' learning expectations, teachers can induce a temporary state of surprise and confusion that heightens students' interest in textbook information (see Example 4).

Challenging students to resolve a paradox. Presenting students with factual information that contradicts their present knowledge and beliefs creates what educational psychologists Bruce Joyce and Marsha Weil (1986) refer to as "dynamic disequilibrium." Numerous developmental learning theorists have described the strong human drive to regain cognitive equilibrium (Erikson, 1950; Harvey, Hunt, & Schroder, 1963; Piaget, 1952). This phenomenon makes the introduction of paradoxical situations a robust interest-promoting technique, because students can be directed to their textbook to find information they will need to resolve the paradox and return to a state of equilibrium (see Example 2).

Introducing novel and conflicting information or situations. Zuckerman (1971, 1978) found that interest can be triggered by the introduction of novel and conflicting information. In a book entitled *Instructional Message Design* (1978), Fleming and Levie support Zuckerman's findings: "Specifically, attention is drawn to what is novel, to whatever stands in contrast to immediate past experience or to life-long experience".

Teachers have long realized the attention-getting value of novelty in instruction. But initial attention does not necessarily lead to sustained interest. Fleming and Levie further explain that "attention is drawn and held by complexity". Teachers can ensure students' continued interest in new information by focusing students' attention more keenly on conflicting ideas within the new information. Students can then be directed to use the text to help them examine and resolve these conflicts (see Example 3).

More textbook authors are using these interest promoting strategies to sustain student interest during reading. Yet, an author's efforts are fruitless if that book remains unopened. The challenge to teachers is to use these same techniques to develop prereading instruction to stimulate students' interest. Let's step inside several classrooms to see how this might be done.

Interest-promoting strategies for content area reading

• **Classroom example 1**
Interest-promoting strategy: Use of an analogy
Grade: 6
Subject: Health science
Reading assignment: Keeping the heart healthy

Ms. Johnson's sixth-grade students had been studying the organs of the body and their functions. The following lesson segment was designed to aid students in learning about the location and function of the main arteries and veins leading to and leaving from the heart. Subsequent reading was to be a section of the chapter entitled "Keeping Your Heart Healthy."

Before assigning the reading, Ms. Johnson showed students an overhead transparency of a city map.

She asked them to identify the "heart" of the city while drawing a heart shape over the center of the city. Next, she asked them to locate the major roads leading into and out of the city. As students identified these roads, she traced over them for emphasis.

Ms. J: "Take a good look at this map. Does it remind you of the heart? In what ways?"

Katie: "Well, the city is like our heart and big roads are like the big veins and arteries that go into and out of our heart."

Peter: "If the heart didn't have its veins and arteries, it wouldn't get any blood so we would die. If the city didn't have any roads, it wouldn't get any people so it would be like a ghost town."

Ms. J: "Very good. Now, I want you to think about something. What happens to these big roads during rush hour traffic?"

Sam: "They get crowded and it takes longer to get where you want to go."

Ti: "One time, we were going downtown and there was a big wreck. All the cars were stopped for almost an hour."

Ms. J: "So, we would probably all agree that when the roads are clear, it's much easier to get in and out of the heart of the city. But, when they're crowded or 'clogged' it gets much harder. The same thing can happen to the roads or veins and arteries leading to and from your heart. Now, we all know we don't have little cars driving around in our veins and arteries, but sometimes those veins and arteries do get clogged. Tonight, for your homework, you're going to be reading about some things that make it hard for your veins and arteries to get all the blood to the heart that it needs. Why is that important information for you to know?

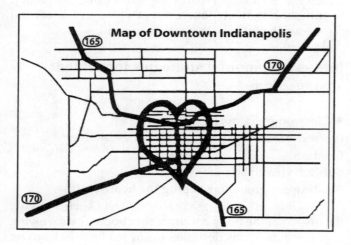

Map of Downtown Indianapolis

Using information from the lesson, students talked briefly about the importance of their hearts. Ms. Johnson passed out the following study guide.

Home study guide
for "Keeping Your Heart Healthy"

(1) Before you begin reading pages 87–94, look up the following words in the glossary and write a brief definition for each one.

diet _____

_____

exercise _____

_____

cholesterol_____

_____

blood pressure _____

_____

blood clot _____

_____

(2) Think about the questions below as you read. We will talk about your answers to these questions tomorrow.

  (a) What is the difference between healthy and unhealthy arteries and veins?

  (b) How can the arteries and veins leading to and from your heart become unhealthy?

  (c) How can you keep your heart healthy?

  (d) How are your veins and arteries similar to the roads we discussed today?

Then she said: "Look at your study guide. Before you begin reading tonight, look up these terms in your glossary and write down their meanings. You probably recognize some of these terms already, don't you? Your job is to figure out what each of these terms has to do with keeping your heart strong and healthy. Your reading will help you do this. Look over the questions I've asked you. After you read, try to answer those questions. We will talk about your answers tomorrow."

Ms. Johnson stimulated students to read the text by providing an analogy to which they could relate. When using analogies, it is important to focus students' attention on the salient relationships between situations. Ms. Johnson carefully directed students to see key analogous relationships between the city's major roads and the heart's major arteries and veins. Any other similarities (or differences) between the two situations are not relevant and could be distracting or misleading.

● Classroom example 2
Interest-promoting strategy: Challenging students to resolve a paradox
Grade: 11
Subject: U.S. history
Topic: The U.S. homefront during W.W. II

Mrs. Gonzalas's class of 11th graders had been learning about the political, social, and economic climate surrounding the Second World War. The intended reading assignment which was to climax the following discussion described the impact of the war on the U.S. homefront (see Mathison, 1989).

As Mrs. Gonzalas put the reading assignment on the board, she initiated discussion by saying, "So far, we have learned that one of the major reasons World War II was fought was because Germany, under Adolf Hitler's rule, was persecuting a group of people (the Jews) because of their race. In Germany, Jews were forced to leave their homes. They were sent to concentration camps. Families were separated and often never saw one another again.

"Think about how you would feel if this ever happened to you and your family. As you think about your feelings, try to complete the sentences I've started for you on the board: 'I would be frightened because....' 'I would be sad because....' 'I would be angry because....' "

After they completed their sentences, several students shared their thoughts with the class. Then Mrs. Gonzalas introduced the following paradoxical situation:

"In a country like the United States, do you think this could ever happen to you?" [The students are given several minutes to verbalize their feelings.] "Can you believe that, during World War II, while we were fighting against Hitler, our government decided to do a similar thing to a group of people in our own country? In tonight's reading assignment, you'll find out who these people were."

"I'm putting five questions on the board for you to think about as you read tonight's assignment. We will talk about each of these questions tomorrow.

(1) What was the ethnic origin of the people who were persecuted in the U.S. during World War II?
(2) How did we persecute these people?
(3) How was this persecution similar to what Hitler did to the Jews in Germany?
(4) Why did we treat these people the way we did?
(5) Even though we may not do it in the same way, do you think certain groups of people in the U.S. are persecuted today because of their ethnic origins? Who are they? Why do we do this?"

Mrs. Gonzalas's plan for promoting student interest in the reading assignment was well sequenced. She initially engaged students in a brief writing activity designed to personalize the emotions surrounding the devastating persecution of self and family experienced by European Jews. As her students evoked and expressed the fears, sadness, and anger this situation would cause them, Mrs. Gonzalas fueled both their affective and cognitive arousal by introducing an unsettling paradox. It is important to note that Mrs. Gonzalas did not help students resolve the paradox immediately. Instead, she directed them to the reading assignment as a means to begin this resolution process.

•**Classroom example 3**
Interest-promoting strategy: Introducing new and conflicting information or situations.
Grade: 9
Subject: American citizenship
Topic: Equal rights and opportunities

The ninth-grade students in Mr. Chang's class were about ready to embark on the investigations of a new topic in their American Citizenship course: the laws and regulations concerning equal opportunities for all U.S. citizens. Mr. Chang began by engaging students in a cooperative learning activity that was followed by reading information about laws and regulations developed to promote equal opportunity in the U.S.

Students were divided into two groups and Mr. Chang explained his performance expectation for both groups.

He then distributed a written description of a situation involving discrimination to Group 1 and a different version of the same situation to Group 2.

Group #1—Situation description: You are the lawyers representing the Rodriques family in a court case. Mr. and Mrs. Rodriques wanted to rent a large apartment for themselves and their three young children. They found an apartment that was affordable and just the right size. Excited to move in, Mr. and Mrs. Rodriques filled out the necessary paperwork and gave it to Mrs. Simmons, the landlady.

The next day, Mrs. Simmons called the Rodriqueses to tell them she had decided not to rent the apartment to them because they have children. She explains that she does not allow children in her apartment complex because they make too much noise and leave their toys on the sidewalks where other tenants might trip over them. She also says that she is afraid they will drown in the swimming pool located in the center of the apartment complex.

Mr. and Mrs. Rodriques are very upset. They feel that they are being unfairly discriminated against because they have children.

As the lawyers for the Rodriques family, your job is to convince the judge that the Rodriqueses have a right to live anywhere they want to as long as they can pay the rent. In your group:

(1) Write as many reasons as you can why the Rodriques family should be allowed to move into the apartment. Make sure your arguments make sense and seem fair.
(2) Choose a spokesperson who will present your case to the judge.

Group #2—Situation description: You are the lawyers representing Mrs. Simmons in a court case. Mrs. Simmons is a kind, elderly lady who has owned an apartment complex for a long time. As the landlady, Mrs. Simmons takes a great deal of pride in keeping the apartment complex attractive and safe for her tenants, most of whom are senior citizens.

Recently, Mr. and Mrs. Rodriques inquired about a vacant apartment Mrs. Simmons had advertised. When Mrs. Simmons found out that Mr. and Mrs. Rodriques had three young children, she decided that she would not rent the apartment to them. Mrs. Simmons told the Rodriqueses that children often leave toys on the sidewalk making it unsafe for her elderly tenants. She was also concerned that the children might drown in the swimming pool located in the center of the apartment. complex. In general, she believes that her apartment complex is not a good place for children.

Mrs. Simmons is now being sued by Mr. and Mrs. Rodriques because they feel she unfairly discriminated against them because they have children.

As the lawyers for Mrs. Simmons, your job is to convince the judge that Mrs. Simmons, as the owner of the property, has the right to decide who should live there and who should not. In your group:

(1) Write as many reasons as you can why Mrs. Simmons has the right to make the decision she made. Make sure your arguments make sense and seem fair.

(2) Choose a spokesperson who will present your case to the judge.

Mr. Chang gave students 15 minutes to generate their reasons and to formulate their arguments. Then he asked them to return their desks to the normal position in preparation for the 'trial', and said, "I am the judge hearing this case today. The spokespersons for Mrs. Simmons and Mr. and Mrs. Rodriques will each be granted three minutes to present their cases." After the spokespersons presented their cases, Mr. Chang told them what the next steps would be.

"You both have represented your clients well. I must say this is a difficult case. Like real judges, I'm going to have to do some research on how cases similar to this one have been resolved in the past. As a matter of fact, you will be reading about several court cases very similar to this one in your text tonight. How were those cases resolved? Why did the judges in each case make the decisions they made?

"Instead of me making the final decision in this case, we'll try to figure out what is fair tomorrow. In order to do this well, you'll want to read pages 236-248 very carefully. As you read, get ready for tomorrow's discussion by asking yourself the questions you see on the board. Copy them onto a piece of paper to take home:

(1) In the Youngstown, Arizona case, what did the judge decide?

(2) Do you agree with the judge's decision? Why? Why not?

(3) What seem to you to be the strongest arguments for and against discrimination in housing?"

Mr. Chang presented students with a situation involving conflicting beliefs and perspectives. By asking students to generate arguments on their "clients'" behalf, Mr. Chang sparked the intellectual and emotional energy of his students.

Who is right? Who will win? Why? Mr. Chang leaves the answers to these questions suspended temporarily, advising students that many arguments and answers can be drawn from information found in the text. He further challenged students to be prepared for tomorrow's discussion by drawing from text information to substantiate the final judgment they will make about the Rodriques vs. Simmons case.

•**Classroom example #4**
Interest-promoting strategies: Use of personal anecdote/ disrupting readers' expectations
Grade: 4
Subject: Geography
Topic: Climate and temperature of deserts

Mr. Bolger's fourth-grade students were studying landforms on the planet Earth. The subsequent reading was about the climatic characteristics of the desert. Before assigning the reading, Mr. Bolger told the following story about himself:

"When I was 18 years old, some friends and I decided that we would like to go camping in the desert. We knew the desert got very hot, so what kinds of clothing do you think we took with us?"

Mr. Bolger wrote the students' responses on the board, and then continued: "Very good! You're naming all the things we packed: shorts, tee shirts, a hat to shield us from the burning sun, and a sweatshirt or sweater for the evenings. All of these items would be useful in the desert. But, guess what happened? We had to come home the same day we left because we didn't bring some other types of clothing we needed. Our whole camping trip was spoiled. I was so disapointed!"

Tonight, you're going to read about the climate of the desert. If you read these pages carefully, you'll never make the same mistake I did. In fact, after you've done your reading, try to make a list of the types of clothing you would take with you if you were going camping in the desert. I am passing out a piece of paper to each of you so you can make your list. We'll share our clothing lists tomorrow so be ready to explain why you listed the clothing you did."

Study guide

Read pages 55-61 in your science book. When you have finished, make a list of clothing you would take with you on a camping trip to the desert. Be ready to explain why you would take the clothing you put on your list. (Note: *Only list clothing.* We will talk about other important items to take with you tomorrow.)

The Happy Desert Camper's Clothing List

_____

_____

_____

_____

_____

_____

Mr. Bolger captured his students' interest in reading the text by sharing a personal experience about a potentially fun experience that turned into a disaster. He also used his awareness of common misperceptions about desert temperatures to disrupt students' expectations. In combination with one another, these two strategies provided compelling reasons for students to interact with their textbook. By providing students with the Happy Desert Camper's Clothing List sheet, Mr. Bolger also gave students a postreading activity that promoted application and relevancy.

Meaningful learning

As we learn more about instructional strategies that increase students' technical abilities to understand what they read, we must recognize that ability alone does not ensure successful student/text interaction. Activating student *interest* in content area reading is a critical instructional concern. The choices our students make about when to read and what to read depend heavily upon the level of personal investment they have in the subject matter. In their book entitled *Thinking in Context*, Hyde and Bizar (1989) offer this reflection on the reading learning process: "It is a major task in our teaching for thinking to provide experiences for students that not only engage them intellectually but also sustain their emotional involvement... They must feel that they will find *meaningfulness* in what we ask them to do".

Helping students create a more compelling and purposeful relationship with their textbooks will certainly facilitate their ability to learn in our classrooms. But perhaps more importantly, the identification of reading as a means by which one can pursue and expand his or her personal interests has tremendous implications for adult literacy and lifelong learning. As teachers, we must provide our students with experiences that help them develop an orientation to reading, not as a compulsory task, but as an enriching and fulfilling endeavor.

References

Alvermann, D. (1986). *Adaptive webbing*. Paper presented at the Baltimore City School Staff Development Day, Baltimore, MD.

Anderson, R. (1982). Allocation of attention during reading. In A. Flammer & W. Kintsch (Eds.), *Discourse processing*. Amsterdam: North-Holland.

Anderson. R., Shirey, L., Wilson, P., & Fielding, L. (1987). Interestingness of children's reading material. In R.E. Snow & M. Farr (Eds.), *Aptitude, learning, and instruction, Volume 3: Cognitive and affective process analyses* (pp. 287–299). Hillsdale, NJ: Erlbaum.

Ausubel, D. (1968). *Educational psychology: A cognitive view*, New York: Holt, Rinehart & Winston.

Bransford, J., & Johnson, M. (1972). Contextual prerequisites for understanding: Some investigations of comprehension and recall. *Journal of Verbal Learning and Verbal Behavior, 11*, 717–726.

Brown, A., Campione, J., & Day, J. (1981). Learning to learn: On training students to learn from text. *Educational Researcher, 10*, 14–21 .

Ciardiello, A. (1986). Teacher questioning and student interaction: An observation of three social studies classes. *The Social Studies, 77*, 119–122.

Dansereau, D., Holley, C., & Collins, K. (1980). *Effects of learning strategy training on text processing*. Paper presented at the annual meeting of the American Educational Research Association, Boston.

Erikson, E. (1950). *Childhood and society*. New York: Norton.

Fleming, M., & Levie, H. (1978). *Instructional message design: Principles from the behavioral sciences*. Englewood Cliffs, NJ: Educational Technology Publications.

Flood, J., & Lapp, D. (1988). Conceptual mapping: Strategies for understanding information texts. *The Reading Teacher, 41*, 780–783.

Gilmore, A., & McKinney, C. (1986). The effects of student questions and teacher questions on concept acquisition. *Theory and Research in Social Education, 14*, 225–296.

Harvey, 0., Hunt, D., & Schroder, H. (1963). *Conceptual systems and personality organization*. New York: John Wiley & Sons.

Hayes, D., & Tierney, R. (1982). Developing readers' knowledge through analogy. *Reading Research Quarterly, 17*, 256–280.

Hidi, S., Baird, W., & Hildyard, A. (1982). That's important, but is it interesting? Two factors in text processing. In A. Flammer & W. Kintsch (Eds.), *Discourse processing* (pp. 63–75). Amsterdam: North-Holland.

Hyde, A., & Bizar, M. (1989). *Thinking in context*. New York: Longman.

Jones, B. (1985). *Research-based guidelines for constructing graphic representations of text*. Paper presented at the annual meeting of the American Educational Research Association, Chicago.

Joyce, B., & Weil, M. (1986). *Models of teaching* (3rd ed.). Englewood Cliffs, NJ: Prentice-Hall.

Keller, J. (1983). Motivational design of instruction. In C. Reigeluth (Ed.), *Instructional design theories and models: An overview of their current status* (pp. 383–436). Hillsdale, NJ: Erlbaum.

Mandler, G. (1982). The structure of value: Accounting for taste. In M. Clark & S. Fiske (Eds.), *Affect and cognition* (pp. 3–36). Hillsdale, NJ: Erlbaum.

Mathison, C. (1989). Stimulating and sustaining student interest in content area reading. *Reading Research and Instruction, 28*, 76–83.

McConnell, J. (1978). Confessions of a textbook writer. *American Psychologist, 33*, 159–169.

Pearson, P.D., Hansen, J., & Gordon, C. (1979). The effect of background knowledge on young children's comprehension of explicit and implicit information. *Journal of Reading Behavior, 11*, 201–209.

Piaget, J. (1952). *The origins of intelligence in children*. New York: International University Press.

Raphael, T., & Pearson, P.D. (1982). *The effect of meta-cognitive strategy awareness training on students' question answering behavior* (Tech. Rep. #238). Urbana, IL: University of Illinois, Center for the Study of Reading.

Rieck, B. (1977). How content teachers telegraph messages against reading. *Journal of Reading, 20*, 646–648.

Schank, R. (1982). *Dynamic memory: A theory of reminding and learning in computers and people*. London: Cambridge University Press.

Schank, R. (1979). Interestingness: Controlling inferences. *Artificial Intelligence, 12*, 273–297.

Singer, H., & Simonsen, S. (1989). Comprehension and instruction in learning from text. In D. Lapp, J. Flood, & N. Farnan (Eds.) *Content area reading and learning* (pp. 43–57). Englewood Cliffs, NJ: Prentice-Hall.

Taylor, B. (1982). Text structure and children's comprehension and memory for expository material. *Journal of Educational Psychology, 74*, 323–340.

Weil, M., Joyce, B., & Kluwin, B. (1978). *Personal models of teaching*. Englewood Cliffs, NJ: Prentice-Hall.

Zuckerman, M. (1978). The search for high sensation. *Psychology Today* (February), 38–46, 96–97.

Zuckerman, M. (1971). Dimensions of sensation seeking. *Journal of Consulting and Clinical Psychology, 36*, 45–52.

Mathison teaches educational psychology at San Diego State University (San Diego CA 92182, USA).

From *Journal of Reading* Vol. 33, No. 3, December 1989, pages 170-176. Copyright © 1989 by The International Reading Association. Reprinted with permission.

Enhancing Young Adolescents' Motivation for Literacy Learning

Nancy B. Mizelle

"It is hard. It takes so much time. Many nights I sit down at the kitchen table after supper to read and correct papers, and I do not get up until it is time to go to bed. But I stick with it because I see how motivating it is for the kids."

—Mrs. Pritchett, an 8th grade teacher using a writing workshop approach for the first time

Young adolescents' motivation is, indeed, a critical factor in their literacy learning. When middle school students are motivated, when they are enthusiastic about literacy learning, they are more likely to engage in literacy activities than when they are not motivated: they write avidly (Oldfather, 1993) and read more on their own (Ley, Schaer, Dismukes, 1994). When students express interest in what they are reading, they also are more likely to use a variety of learning strategies to help them understand their reading and monitor their understanding (Garner, 1987; Mizelle, Hart, & Carr, 1993; Paris, Lipson, & Wilson, 1994). Their use of learning strategies, in turn, leads to an increased sense of self-confidence and to further interest and use of learning strategies (Borkowski, 1992). In the words of one group of eighth graders, students have to be interested before they "get it;" if they are bored "it [doesn't] register." When they are interested though, they "learn much quicker" and "want to learn it more," even to the point of "going to the encyclopedia to look it up" (Mizelle, 1992).

As young adolescents make the transition into and move through middle school, they seem to become less interested in literacy learning (Bintz, 1993; Ley et al., 1992; Mullis, Dossey, Campbell, Gentile, O'Sullivan, & Latham, 1994; Oldfather & McLaughlin, 1993). Mullis and associates (1994) for example, reported that, of the 9-year-olds surveyed in 1992, 56% read for fun on a daily basis, while only 37% of the 13-year-olds read daily for fun. At the same time, 16% of the 9-year-olds, compared to 31% of the 13-year-olds, read for fun only once a month or even less frequently.

Students who are not motivated or interested in literacy learning have become a critical concern for teachers. In a recent national poll, teachers were asked to identify and rank problems related to literacy that warranted research; they indicated that their first priority was to find ways to motivate students and to create their interest in reading (O'Flahaven,

Gambrell, Guthrie, Stahl, Baumann, & Alvermann, 1992). With middle school teachers, I also find that, whether the course I am teaching is about middle school curriculum, assessment, or teaching and whether the teachers are preservice or inservice, they want to know "how to motivate their students" to work on reading and writing activities. Teachers raise questions about student motivation in class and they often, in projects of their choosing, focus on strategies to foster student motivation in literacy activities.

The purpose of this article is to begin to address the concerns of middle school teachers about young adolescents' motivation for literacy learning. Specifically, it focuses on classroom strategies educators in the fields of motivation and literacy have identified as beneficial. I write with the hope that this article will challenge and guide you in your thinking about your own students; I do not write to give you a prescription for your classroom.

Classrooms Environments That Enhance Young Adolescents' Motivation for Literacy Learning

Theoretically, this article is based on the idea that motivation is a natural desire to learn in positive ways (McCombs & Pope, 1994). Motivation is not viewed as something that needs to be fixed or done to a student, rather it is something that needs to be fostered. Motivation to learn varies from student to student and is based on students' conscious beliefs and values (Stipek, 1993).

Furthermore, the classroom context is a critical factor in young adolescents' motivation for literacy learning (Moore, 1995; Oldfather & McLaughlin, 1993). In classrooms where students feel that being successful is linked to their making progress and improvement rather than getting high grades and where they feel their teacher values students' effort and learning more than their high ability, students are more likely to be interested and engaged in learning (Ames, 1992; Oldfather & McLaughlin, 1993).

Within the middle school classroom, six broad dimensions of organization seem to influence a student's motivation for literacy learning (Ames, 1992; Epstein, 1988). They include the type of tasks students are assigned, the way authority is distributed in the classroom, the way students are rewarded and recognized, the way students are grouped, the type of evaluation that is emphasized, and the way time is allocated. It is these classroom dimensions—Task, Authority, Reward, Grouping, Evaluation, Time: TARGET (Epstein, 1988, 1989)—that provide the framework for this article as it addresses the question: What can I, a middle school teacher, do in my classroom to foster students' motivation for literacy learning?

Tasks

Tasks, in general, involve what students are asked to learn as well as the type of learning activities and assignments they are given to do (Ames, 1992; Epstein, 1988). They are related to "the content and sequence of the curriculum, the design of classwork and homework, the level of difficulty of the work, and the materials required to complete assignments" (Epstein, 1988, p. 93). Students are more interested and actively engaged in literacy learning when teachers provide a variety of classroom activities that make learning interesting, that are personally challenging to students, and that students view as meaningful and important (Ames, 1992; Miller, Adkins, & Hooper, 1993; Pope & Beal, 1994; Stewart, Paradis, Ross, & Lewis, 1996). They are also more engaged when teachers help them establish realistic short-term goals for completing assignments (Ames, 1992; Davey, 1993) and help them develop and use strategies to plan and monitor their work (Ames, 1992; Caverly, Mandeville, & Nicholson, 1995; Kos, 1991).

Students' engagement in literacy activities further depends on their understanding of why they should be engaged (Benware & Deci, 1984; Brophy, 1986). When students are given a reason for doing an activity, they are more likely to become involved in it (Brophy, 1986). Even more importantly, when they are told to learn material "so that they can teach someone else," students are more likely to work to understand the material than when they are told to learn the material because it is on the test (Benware & Deci, 1984).

Ideas for classroom practice
Assignments/Activities. Providing a variety of interesting literacy activities for young adolescents may involve having students read from different genres, respond to readings in a variety of ways, or write to various audiences. Students may, for example, respond to reading assignments through journals (Berger, 1996; Hancock, 1993); through dramatic presentations, informal discussions, or literature circles (Noll, 1994); or through visual or pictorial representations (Naughton, 1993/1994; Wilhelm, 1995).

Providing a variety of tasks also may involve having middle school students collect interesting sentences from their reading to share with the class (Speaker & Speaker, 1991); incorporating trade books, newspapers, and magazines into your science or social studies curriculum (Lapp, Flood, & Ranck-Buhr, 1995); or reading aloud daily to students (Anders & Pritchard, 1993; Lee & Neal, 1993). While reading aloud is generally thought of as more appropriate for younger children, I learned from personal experience that it is also motivating for middle school students. The one time I remember my daughter requesting that I read a particular book was when she was in the sixth grade and she asked me to read a book her teacher had read aloud in class.

When students are given a reason for doing an activity, they are more likely to become involved in it.

Tasks that middle school students find personally challenging and motivating are authentic reading and writing activities rather than assignments that focus on drill and skill (Pope & Beal, 1994; Miller et al., 1993; Stewart et al., 1996). They are more motivated by complex tasks that involve reading and writing longer segments and lengthy discussions than they are by simple tasks that "require underlining, copying, or the writing of single words or sentence fragments" (Miller et al., 1993). Middle school students also indicate that they prefer teachers who help them with difficult textbooks by teaching them strategies to use on their own, instead of helping them by using outlines and overheads to point out important information or by discussing key ideas before giving the reading assignment (Schumm, Vaughn, & Saumell, 1992). In other words, students seem to prefer the challenge of "figuring it out" on their own, to having the teacher tell them what to learn.

Relevant literacy activities for middle school students are those that relate to their needs and interests and bridge the students' "world outside school to the world in the classroom" (Cousin, Aragon, & Rojas, 1993). Two ways to provide students with relevant literacy activities are to plan curriculum that meets the needs of middle school learners and to plan activities that make connections to the community. Curriculum that is responsive to young adolescents' needs includes literature with characters, settings, or conflicts with which students can identify (Gentile, & McMillan, 1994; Pope & Beal, 1994). Relevant curriculum is designed to "encourage students actively and purposefully to use the tools of speaking, listening, reading, and writing to pursue meaningful ideas" (Anders & Pritchard, 1993). It is also designed so that the different forms of language—speaking, listening, reading, and writing—work and develop together. Two structures that support this integrated literacy curriculum are the reading and writing workshop (Pollak, 1994) and integrating language across the curriculum (Anders & Pritchard, 1993).

Connecting literacy learning to the community may be accomplished by bringing the community in (Moniuszko, 1992) or by sending students out into the community (Cousin et al., 1993; Shah, 1986). Moniuszko (1992) found, for example, that her students were eager to read and research topics like the Federal Bureau of Investigation and tornadoes when she invited local experts in to speak.

Goals/Strategies. As young adolescents make the transition into middle school, they are faced with the challenge of more and more complex literacy assignments—content texts to read, nightly homework assignments, research papers, and projects. Many have not, however, developed the skills they need to be successful (Irvin, 1990). Therefore they lack the motivation to learn from such literacy activities (Borkowski, 1992). According to Davey (1993), one way to help students is to focus on strategies they can use to manage their study time. The process she outlines includes an explanation of the value of daily and long-term planning and instruction in task-analysis strategies. Students are taught to ask: What are my goals? How can I break long-term goals into short-term goals? What do I need to accomplish my goals? How long will it take to accomplish them? To help students with goal setting, Davey also included instruction in the use of daily planning charts and weekly and monthly calendars.

Authority

Authority relates to the roles the teacher and students play in making decisions about literacy learning in the classroom and the sense of control that students have over their literacy learning (Ames, 1992; Epstein, 1988; Unrau & Ruddell, 1995). To foster young adolescents' motivation, it is important to provide them opportunities to be actively involved in making decisions and to develop a sense of ownership in the literacy learning process (Ames, 1992; Bintz, 1993). In the classroom this means that all, not just a few, students have choices about activities. It means that all students make decisions about how to proceed with their learning and are given the opportunity to develop the strategies they need to learn on their own to investigate and explore the world of literacy (Caverly et al., 1995; Epstein, 1988; Pope & Beal, 1994; Stewart et al., 1996).

Ideas for classroom practice

Active involvement. Students responding to teacher-initiated questions about a story are "actively" engaged in learning, but in a very limited way (Epstein, 1988). Active involvement that fosters students' motivation for literacy learning involves more. "A broader definition of students as active learners includes participation with teachers in selecting topics for study and discussion, [as well as] deciding how long to work to master skills before being evaluated, when to continue with deeper study of a topic, when to ask for help to understand difficult concepts, and many other decisions" (Epstein, 1988). To ensure that all middle school students are given the opportunity to engage actively in literacy learning, it is important for teachers to be effective discussion facilitators (Barton, 1995; McAuliffe, 1993). According to Barton (1995), teachers need to listen carefully to students and teach students to listen to each other; teachers need

to know when to speak, when not to speak, and how to encourage reluctant students to speak. Teachers also need to be able to activate and to use students' prior knowledge and to develop questions to help stimulate discussion if all students are to be actively engaged in classroom activities.

Choice. Middle school students' interest in literacy learning is dependent on the opportunities they have to make choices (Stewart et al., 1996). Students may choose the topic for their social studies research paper, which book they will read next, what they will read during "free reading," and with whom they will work on their next literature response project. On some occasions students may exercise free choice like when they design their own response project; on other occasions they may choose from among a variety of activities like when they choose whether to use a concept map or a written outline to organize the key ideas for a science topic (Stevenson & Carr, 1993). Both ways of providing students choice are appropriate as long as they are given "real" choices—as long as students perceive, for example, that they are choosing from a group of equally attractive assignments or from a group of equally difficult books (Ames, 1992). Otherwise, students choosing "any book they want to read" may select a book that is not really challenging and thereby undermine their interest in the task.

Strategies. For students to feel that they can take responsibility for their own literacy learning, they need to develop a variety of cognitive and metacognitive strategies for understanding and remembering narrative and expository or information text (Baker & Brown, 1984; Malone & Mastropieri, 1992; Mizelle, 1995; Paris, Wasik, & Turner, 1991). Middle school students need to be able, for example, to make predictions, to question their understanding of text, and to summarize text (Palincsar & Brown, 1984). They need to recognize when they do not understand what they are reading, to identify why they are not understanding (e.g., became distracted), and to know what to do to "fix" the problem (e.g., reread the section) (Garner, 1987).

Middle school students' strategy development may involve instruction of special strategies such as prediction and summarization with the strategy being taught individually or as one of a group of strategies (Caverly et al., 1995; Maxworthy & Barry, 1992; Palincsar & Brown, 1984). Palincsar and Brown (1984), for example, used teacher scaffolding and reciprocal interaction between the teacher and a small group of students to teach students to predict, clarify, self-question, and summarize with science text. In another example, in a whole class setting, Caverly et al. (1995) used a combination of direct instruction, teacher modeling, and small group work to teach students to make predictions, to recognize text structure, and to summarize text information.

Middle school students' strategy use may also be developed through the use of a variety of more teacher-directed strategies like anticipation guides, compare-contrast charts, concept maps, graphic organizers, and dialogue journals (Bean, 1995; Duffelmeyer, 1994; Naughton, 1993/1994; Randall, 1996; Wood, 1995). Using anticipation guides, for example, helps students develop their ability to make predictions and set goals for reading text (Duffelmeyer, 1994); using information charts helps them summarize text and organize their ideas (Randall,

1996); and using visual imagery helps students identify the main ideas in text (Naughton, 1993/1994).

Tasks that middle school students find personally challenging and motivating are authentic reading and writing activities rather than assignments that focus on drill and skill.

While it is beyond the scope of this article to outline the details of providing middle school students strategy instruction, it is important to note that students need to learn strategies in context (Craig & Yore, 1995; Maxworthy & Barry, 1992). Students need to be able to use a variety of strategies including some that are specific to different types of content text (Craig & Yore, 1995). It also seems that students learn strategies best when they are taught in a context that is meaningful to them (Maxworthy & Barry, 1992).

Reward and Recognition

The reward structure in the middle school classroom involves the ways students are recognized and rewarded for their progress and achievement (Ames, 1992; Epstein, 1988). The types of rewards, the reasons for rewards, and the distribution of rewards are all important components of the reward structure. Drawing on the work of Covington and Beery (1976), Ames recommends the following guidelines to promote a positive attitude toward learning:

1. Recognizing individual student effort, accomplishments, and improvement.
2. Giving all students opportunities to receive rewards and recognition.
3. Giving recognition and rewards privately so that their value is not derived at the expense of others. (Ames, 1992)

While these recommendations run counter to the reading contests and perfect-paper bulletin boards frequently seen in schools, it is important to remember that the rewards and recognition we use indicate those things we value (Epstein, 1988). Recognizing individual student improvement in private emphasizes that we value learning by all students: recognizing a few students publicly indicates that we are more concerned about the achievement of perfection by a few.

Ideas for classroom practice

The validity of these recommendations is seen in students' enthusiastic responses to teachers' personal comments in student journals (Fuhler, 1994; Hancock, 1993). Hancock (1993), for example, described her experience as follows:

> Although the need for encouragement declined, the enthusiasm from the students toward the teacher/researcher comments did not. As journals were returned each day, the students savored the comments before

moving on to the next chapter of reading and responding. As with all journals, the enthusiasm and effort for the character journal can be sustained when the readers/writers know that someone cares about and appreciates their level of involvement.

The validity of these recommendations is also seen in students' lack of enthusiasm for grades (Oldfather & McLaughlin, 1993). When young adolescents were faced with an increased emphasis on grades in their transition into middle school, some felt grades helped because "you can kind of tell how you are doing", but most disagreed that grades helped with learning or reflected how hard a student worked.

Middle school students want to know "Is it going to be graded?" If so, the next question usually is "How long does it need to be?" Grades may help you get students to turn in assignments, but they do little to encourage students to be truly interested and engaged in reading or writing activities (Stipek, 1993). Grades and public recognition also discourage students from taking on challenging tasks; the risk is just too great. When the reward is a grade, students are more concerned with getting the assignment done and done well enough to get a good grade than they are with learning.

While the research is clear that grades undermine students' intrinsic motivation for learning, they, nevertheless, are a reality of the world in which most teachers live. What can middle school teachers do to minimize the negative effects of grades and support students' motivation for literacy learning? It is important to begin by decreasing references to grades (Stipek, 1993). Students do not need to be constantly reminded that they are being graded on a project or that they will get a bad grade if they do not "pay attention"; and when students do ask about grades, encourage them to focus on what they are learning rather than the grade. It is also important to set your classroom up so that all students feel that they can be successful. For some, this may involve helping them learn to establish short-term goals so that they can focus on what they are learning rather than being overwhelmed by the enormity of the assignment; for others this may involve allowing students to choose, at least part of the time, projects that highlight their strengths (e.g., artistic or musical talent), rather than their weaknesses (e.g., their writing ability).

Grouping

The grouping structure relates to the ability of students to work together effectively in school activities (Ames, 1992). Student motivation is enhanced in a classroom environment where individual students feel accepted as a member of the group and as if they belong to the group as a whole. When students feel that the classroom environment focuses more on students cooperating with each other rather than on competing with each other, they are more motivated to learn. When they feel their ideas are respected and valued, when their thoughts and ideas are "honored," young adolescents are more motivated to engage in literacy activities (Oldfather, 1995).

Student motivation also is related to the teacher's willingness to provide a variety of opportunities for cooperative group learning in heterogeneous groups (Ames, 1992; Irvin, 1990; Livdahl, 1993; Pope & Beal, 1994). As students work together in groups, they learn to recognize and focus on their strengths; they also gain peer support and help in their areas of weakness. As teachers structure a classroom to include cooperative learning groups, they contribute to students' increased sense of confidence and, thereby, their increased intrinsic motivation in literacy learning (Borkowski, 1992).

Ideas for classroom practice

Cooperative literacy learning in a middle school classroom may be as simple as one student turning to a neighbor to discuss the answer to a question or as complex as Reciprocal Teaching where the teacher scaffolds the development of reading strategies with a small group of students (Palincsar & Brown, 1984). Cooperative learning experiences may take place in dyads, in small groups, or in large groups; they may involve students working together for one day or across several days; and they may be based on student self-selection or teacher assignment. No particular organizational scheme is "best"; each is important for supporting different aspects of students' literacy development (Hiebert, 1991).

> Although whole class contexts may be ideal for fostering a sense of community among students, few students get the opportunities in whole class settings to share their unique interpretations of books. Peer dyads and groups allow students to read with one another and to share ideas, but peers rarely scaffold learning for one another in ways that encourage students to develop new strategies like predicting. Teacher-led instruction in small or large groups provides the scaffolding that students need, but application of these strategies will depend on the chance to read or write independently.

Even though middle school students seem to want to spend all, or at least much, of their time talking to each other, just putting them together in groups does not mean that they will automatically work together effectively. For group activities to work and support students' motivation, young adolescents need to be taught how to work in groups. They need to learn, for example, how to offer constructive criticism, how to solve problems that involve personal relationships, how to share the responsibility of completing an assignment, how to establish goals for a particular assignment, and how to evaluate their progress related to their goals. Perhaps most importantly, for young adolescents to work together effectively, they need to experience a classroom where respect for the ideas and feelings of all students is modeled and encouraged (Oldfather, 1993).

Evaluation

The evaluation dimension of the classroom involves the different methods used to observe and assess student learning (Ames, 1992: Epstein, 1988). An evaluation plan that supports students' motivation involves a variety of assessment strategies that focus on progress, improvement, and mastery; it provides students with opportunities to make improvements in their work; and it makes student evaluation private. A supportive classroom environment also encourages students to view making mistakes as a part of learning rather than as a sign of failure. The specific evaluation strategies that support students' interest in learning concur with the authentic assessment practices described in the literacy literature (Ediger, 1986; Katz, 1994; McAuliffe, 1993; Ruddell, 1995).

Ideas for classroom practice

According to Ruddell (1995), a literacy assessment plan for middle school students should be "broad-based, flexible, and capable of capturing students' multiple abilities and propensities". It should focus on learning and improvement and should involve students in their own assessment—allowing them to set goals for their own literacy activities, to engage in self-evaluation of their literacy work, and to select pieces of their own work for teacher assessment. Assessment in middle schools should also support the integration of the different areas of literacy development (reading, writing, speaking, and listening) and the integration of literacy learning and content area learning. Results should be reported consistently and in ways that are useful for students.

Portfolio assessment is particularly appropriate for encouraging middle school students' interest in literacy learning (Katz, 1994; Ruddell, 1995). A portfolio system of assessment allows students to demonstrate what they are learning and how they are improving; it involves students in meaningful ways in the assessment process; and it provides for a variety of projects—letters, poems, plays, essays (see Rief, 1990, 1992 and Tierney, Carter, & Desai, 1991 for more details). Furthermore, portfolios do not need to be limited to traditional written pieces. They may include art work, project papers, photographs, sketches, and mapping exercises; reading response log, learning log, or double-entry journal, or writing from assigned readings; a reading log or dated list of books read; letters to peers, pen pals, teachers, or community leaders; group work, papers, and products; vocabulary journal; out-of-school reading, writing, and art work; and lesson and unit assessments (Ruddell, 1995).

While portfolio assessment supports middle school students motivation for literacy learning, it is a mistake to think that just introducing portfolios into a classroom assessment system will increase students' interest. If, for example, students are not involved in choosing pieces to include in their portfolio or if students are assessed on the rough draft as well as the final draft of a paper, then the motivating potential of the portfolio method of assessment is undermined. It is also a mistake to think that introducing portfolios into the classroom is the only way to increase students' interest in literacy learning. The keys to motivating evaluation practices are providing students a variety of experiences that allow them to be involved and allow them to focus on improvement and mastery. Students helping the teacher design the rubric for their social studies paper, students working together on an assessment, students giving oral presentations of research done on a topic of their choice, students redoing work, some students working on a dramatic presentation while others are at work on a collage or mural—all of these are scenes from classrooms where young adolescents are interested and engaged in literacy learning.

Time

Time as a factor in students' motivation to learn concerns the pace of instruction, as well as the amount of time students are given to complete activities and assignments (Ames, 1992; Epstein, 1988). It is also closely related to the way time in the classroom is structured in response to the individual needs of a diverse student population.

Ideas for classroom practice

Organizing a classroom that is responsive to the literacy needs of young adolescents seems to involve both "taking time" (McAuliffe, 1993) and "giving time" (Ames, 1992; Stewart et al., 1996). Middle school teachers need to take time to listen to students, respond to students' questions, and to discuss reading assignments with students (McAulliffe, 1993). When teachers do take time, middle school students understand and are more interested and involved in literacy learning.

Middle school teachers also need to give students time (Ames, 1992; Oldfather, 1995; Stewart et al., 1996). They need to give students flexibility in the way they use their time and the opportunity to plan how they will use their time (Ames, 1992). Consider, for example, the student who has access to a computer at home. Might not that student be more interested in spending class time in the library looking for additional resources, than in going to the computer lab with every one else to type in a rough draft?

In addition, middle school teachers need to give students extended periods of time to read and write—time to think about their writing and time to spend actually involved in reading—to foster students' interest in literacy activities (Oldfather, 1995; Stewart et al., 1996). Stewart and associates (1996) summarized the powerful influence "time to read" has on young adolescents' development as literacy learners:

> Providing time for reading sends a message to students that reading is valued and is an important venue for learning.
>
> Once time is provided, the other bubbles can form and coalesce. Specifically, choice leads to interest and ownership, interest and ownership to practice, and practice to speed and fluency. Speed and fluency result in increased comprehension and retention (i.e., reading proficiency). With increased reading proficiency comes additional benefits both within and outside reading class, leading to students' enhanced sense of accomplishment. With accomplishment comes a growing sense of empowerment. Students complete assignments more readily, begin to gain control over their reading lives, feel less victimized by reading, and for the first time enjoy reading.

Conclusion

The question is this: How should all these ideas work together? Providing young adolescents with interesting, relevant, and challenging tasks; incorporating more authentic measures of assessment; providing students opportunities to work in heterogeneous groups; allowing students to choose; incorporating instruction on learning strategies; rewarding students for improvement and providing students longer periods of time to read and write—all are crucial for fostering young adolescents' interest in literacy learning. Each of the TARGET structures—Tasks, Authority, Rewards, Grouping, Evaluation, Time—is important and no one structure is more important than the others. Instead they are related to each other and to some extent overlap (Ames, 1992). If all six dimensions are not coordinated, the positive impact of work in one area (e.g., providing students longer periods of time to read and write) may be undermined by failure to attend to another area (e.g., limiting students' choice of reading material). In other words, as a middle school teacher, whether you consider yourself a literacy or content area teacher, it is important for you to consider each of these different dimensions in your classroom as you work to support young adolescents' motivation about literacy learning.

An evaluation plan that supports students' motivation involves a variety of assessment strategies that focus on progress, improvement, and mastery.

I began this article with a quotation from Mrs. Pritchett, my son's eighth-grade language teacher; now, I want to explain why. Mrs. Pritchett is an experienced teacher who decided to try something very different the year Will was in her class. In place of a more traditional emphasis on grammar, she implemented a writing workshop. Throughout the year, students wrote from their own experiences; they wrote and rewrote; and they maintained a year-long portfolio. Mrs. Pritchett read and reread; she was constantly in the process of writing comments and providing feedback; and when the fire drill bell sounded, she went in search of her notebook of anecdotal comments on each student rather than a grade book. Within the structure of a writing workshop, this teacher offered students tasks that were challenging and relevant; the opportunity to choose; various group activities; evaluation that related specifically to their improvement in writing; and time to work at their own pace. She offered them the rewards of personal satisfaction and feelings of competence.

Mrs. Pritchett's students responded to her efforts with enthusiasm and demonstrated a genuine interest in writing that, for many, has continued into high school. Furthermore, her students' increased motivation in writing, inspired Mrs. Pritchett, subsequently, to use the same strategies to foster students' motivation in reading and other aspects of literacy learning. As you take the ideas and suggestions presented in this article, my hope is that, rather than being overwhelmed by the challenge of restructuring your classroom to support young adolescents' interest in literacy learning, you will be encouraged by Mrs. Pritchett's success.

Nancy B. Mizelle teaches at the University of Georgia, Athens.

References

Ames, C. (1992). Achievement goals and the classroom motivational climate. In D. Schunk, & J. Meece (Eds.), *Student perceptions in the classroom.* Hillsdale, NJ: Lawrence Erlbaum Associates.

Anders, P. A. & Pritchard, T. G. (1993). Integrated language curriculum and instruction for the middle grades. *The Elementary School Journal.* 93(5), 611–624.

Baker, L. & Brown, A. L. (1984). Metacognitive skills and reading. In P. D. Pearson (Ed.), *Handbook of reading research* (pp. 353–394). New York: Longman.

Barton, J. (1995). Conducting effective classroom discussions. *Journal of Reading.* 38(5), 346–350.

Bean, T. W. (1995). Strategies for enhancing text comprehension in middle school. Special Section: Literacy instruction and assessment in the middle school. *Reading and Writing Quarterly: Overcoming Learning Difficulties.* 11(2), 163–171.

Berger, L. R (1996). Reader response journals: You make the meaning and how. *Journal of Adolescents & Adult Literacy,* 39(5), 380–385.

Benware, C. & Deci, E. L. (1984). Quality of learning with an active versus passive motivational set. *American Educational Research Journal.* 21, 755–766.

Bintz, W. P. (1993). Resistant readers in secondary education: Some insights and implications. *Journal of Reading,* 36(8), 604–615.

Borkowski, J. C. (1992). Metacognitive theory: A framework for teaching literacy, writing, and math skills. *Journal of Learning Disabilities.* 25(4), 253–257.

Brophy, J. (1986). On motivating students. (Occasional paper No. 101). East Lansing, MI: Institute for Research on Teaching.

Caverly, D. C., Mandeville, T. F., & Nicholson, S. A. (1995). PLAN: A study reading strategy for informational text. *Journal of Adolescents Adult Literacy.* 39(3), 190–199.

Cousin, P. T., Aragon, E., & Rojas, R. (1993). Creating new conversations about literacy: Working with special needs students in a middle school classroom. *Learning Disability Quarterly.* 16(4), 282–298.

Covington, M. C., & Beery, R. G. (1976). *Self worth and school learning.* New York: Holt, Rinehart & Winston.

Craig, M. T., & Yore. L. D. (1995). Middle school students' metacognitive knowledge about science reading and science text: An interview study. *Reading Psychology,* 16(2), 160–213.

Davey, B. (1993). Helping middle school learners succeed with reading assignments: A focus on time planning. *Journal of Reading,* 37(3), 170–173.

Duffelmeyer, F. A. (1994). Effective anticipation guide statements for learning from expository prose. *Journal of Reading,* 37(6), 452–457.

Ediger, M. (1992). The middle school student and interest in reading. *Reading Improvement.* 29(3), 171–173.

Epstein, J. L. (1988). Effective schools or effective students: Dealing with diversity. In R. Haskins & D. MacRae (Eds.), *Policies for America's public schools: Teacher equity indicators* (pp. 89–126). Norwood, N: Ablex.

Epstein, J. L. (1989). Family structures and student motivation: A developmental perspective. In C. Ames & R. Ames (Eds.), *Research on motivation in education* (Vol. 3, pp. 259–295). New York: Academic.

Fuhler, C. J. (1994). Response journals: Just one more time with feeling. *Journal of Reading,* 37(5), 400–405.

Garner, R. (1987). *Metacognition and reading comprehension.* Norwood, NJ: Ablex.

Gentile, L. M., & McMillan, M. M. (1994). Critical dialogue: The road to literacy for students at risk in middle schools. *Middle School Journal.* 25(4), 50–54.

Hancock. M. R. (1993). Character journals: Initiating involvement and identification through literature. *Journal of Reading,* 37(1), 42–50.

Hiebert, E. H. (1991). Literacy contexts and literacy processes. *Language Arts.* 68(2), 134–139.

Irvin, J. L., (1990). *Reading and the middle school student: Strategies to enhance literacy.* Needham Heights, MA: Allyn and Bacon.

Katz, C. A., (1994). Putting an end to lonely street. *Journal of Reading.* 38(2), 94–96.

Kos, R. (1991). Persistence of reading disabilities: The voices of four middle school students. *American Educational Research Journal.* 28(4), 875–895.

Lapp, D., Flood, J., & Ranck-Buhr, W. (1995). Using multiple text formats to explore scientific phenomena in middle school classrooms. Special Section: Literacy instruction and assessment in the middle school. *Reading and writing Quarterly: Overcoming Learning Difficulties.* 11(2), 173–186.

Lee, N. G., & Neal, J. C. (1992). Reading rescue: Intervention for a student "at promise." *Journal of Reading,* 36(4), 276–282.

Ley, T. C., Schaer, B. B., & Dismukes, B. W. (1994). Longitudinal study of the reading attitudes and behaviors of middle school students. *Reading Psychology.* 15(1), 11–38.

Livdahl, B. S. (1993). "To read it is to live it, different from just knowing it. "Journal of Reading. 37(3), 192–200.

Malone, L. D., & Mastropieri, M. A. (1992). Reading comprehension instruction: Summarization and self-monitoring training for students with learning disabilities. *Exceptional Children.* 58(3), 270–279

Maxworthy, A. G., & Barry, A. (1992). Can middle school students summarize? *Reading Horizons.* 32(3), 191–198.

McAuliffe, S. (1993). A study of the differences between instructional practice and test preparation. *Journal of Reading,* 36(7), 524–530.

McCombs, B. L., & Pope, J. E. (1994). *Motivating hard to reach students.* Washington, DC: American Psychological Association.

Miller, S. D., Adkins, T., & Hooper, M. L. (1993). Why teachers select specific literacy assignments and students reactions to them. *Journal of Reading Behavior.* 25(1), 69–95.

Mizelle, N. B. (1992). Middle grade students' motivational processes and use of strategies with expository text. Unpublished doctoral dissertation. University of Georgia, Athens.

Mizelle, N. B. (1995, April). *Transition from middle school into high school: The student perspective.* Paper presented at the annual meeting of the American Educational Research Association. San Francisco, CA.

Mizelle, N. B., Hart, L. E., & Carr, M. (1993, April). *Middle grade students' motivational processes and use of strategies with expository text.* Paper presented at the annual meeting of the American Educational Research Association, Atlanta, GA.

Moniuszko, L. K. (1992). Motivation: Reaching reluctant readers age 14–17. *Journal of Reading,* 36(1), 32–34.

Moore, D. W. (1995, December). *Contexts for literacy in secondary schools.* Paper presented at the annual meeting of the National Reading Conference, New Orleans.

Mullis, I. V. S., Dossey, J. A., Campbell, J. R., Gentile, C. A., O'Sullivan, C., & Latham, A. S. (1994). *Report in brief: NAEP 1992 trends in academic progress.* Washington, DC: National Center for Education Statistics. U. S. Government Printing Office.

Naughton, V. M. (1993/1994). Creative mapping for content reading. *Journal of Reading.* 37(4), 324–326

Noll, E. (1994). Social issues and literature circles with adolescents. *Journal of Reading.* 38(2), 88–93.

O'Flahavan, J., Gambrell, L. B., Guthrie. J., Stahl. S., Baumann. J. F., & Alvermann, D. E. (1992, August/September). Poll results guide activities of research center. *Reading Today.* p. 12.

Oldfather, P. (1993). Students' perspectives on motivating experiences in literacy learning. *(Perspectives in Reading Research Series)* Athens, GA: National Reading Research Center), Universities of Georgia and Maryland.

Oldfather, P. (1995). Commentary: What's needed to maintain and extend motivation for literacy in the middle grades. *Journal of Reading*, 38(6), 420–422.

Oldfather, P., & McLaughlin, H. J. (1993). Gaining and losing voice: A longitudinal study of students continuing impulse to learn across elementary and middle level contexts. *Research in Middle Level Education*. 17(1), 1–26.

Palincsar, A. S., & Brown, A. L. (1984). Reciprocal teaching of comprehension-fostering and comprehension-monitoring activities. *Cognition and Instruction*. 1(2), 117–175.

Paris, S. G., Lipson, M. Y., & Wixson, K. K. (1994). Becoming a strategic reader. In R. Ruddell, M. R. Ruddell, & H. Singer (Eds.), *Theoretical models and processes of reading* (4th ed., pp. 788–837). Newark, DE: International Reading Association.

Paris, S. G., Wasik, B. A., & Turner, J. C. (1991). The development of strategic readers. In R. Barr, M. L. Kamil, P. Mosenthal, & P. D. Pearson (Eds.), *Handbook of reading research: Volume II* (pp. 609–640). New York: Longman.

Pollak, J. P. (1994). A workshop approach to reading and writing: Why does it work for middle level learners? *Reading Improvement*. 31(3), 145–148

Pope, C., & Beal, C. (1994). Building pathways for at-risk students and their teachers. *Voices from the Middle*. 1(2),3–10.

Randall, S. N. (1996). Information charts: A strategy for organizing student research. *Journal of Adolescent & Adult Literacy*. 39(7), 536–543.

Rief, L. (1990). Finding the value in evaluation: Self-assessment in the middle school classroom. *Educational Leadership*.47(6), 24–29.

Rief, L. (1992). *Seeking diversity: Language arts with adolescents*. Portsmouth, NH: Heinemann.

Ruddell, M. R. (1995). Literacy assessment in middle level grades: Alternatives to traditional practices. Special Section: Literacy instruction and assessment in the middle school. *Reading and Writing Quarterly: Overcoming Learning Difficulties*. 11(2), 187–200.

Schumm, J. S., Vaughn, S., Saumell, L. (1992). What teachers do when the textbook is tough: Students speak out. *Journal of Reading Behavior,* 24(4), 481–503.

Shah, D. C. (1986). Composing processes and writing instruction at the middle/junior high school level. *Theory into Practice*. 25(2), 109–116.

Speaker, Jr., R. B., & Speaker, P. R. (1991). Sentence collecting: Authentic literacy events in the classroom. *Journal of Reading*. 35(2), 92–95.

Stewart, R. A., Paradis, E. E., Ross, B. D., Lewis, M. J. (1996). Student voices: What works in literature-based developmental reading. *Journal of Adolescent & Adult Literacy*. 39(6), 468–478.

Stevenson, C., & Carr, J. F. (1993). *Integrated studies in the middle grades: "Dancing through walls"*. New York: Teachers College Press.

Stipek, D. J. (1993). *Motivation to learn: From theory to practice* (2nd ed.). Needham Heights, MA: Allyn and Bacon.

Tierney, R J., Carter, M. A., & Desai, L. E. (1991). *Portfolio assessment in the reading-writing classroom*. Norwood, MA: Christopher-Gordon.

Unrau, N. J., & Ruddell, R. B. (1995). Interpreting texts in classroom contexts. *Journal of Adolescent & Adult Literacy*. 39(1), 16–27.

Wilheim, J. D. (1995). Reading is seeing: Using visual response to improve the literary reading of reluctant readers. *Journal of Reading Behavior*. 27(4), 467–503.

Wood, K. D. (1995). Guiding middle school students through expository text. Special Section: Literacy instruction and assessment in the middle school. *Reading and Writing Quarterly: Overcoming Learning Difficulties*. 11(2), 137–147.

UNIT 4
Textbook Reading and Comprehension

Unit Selections

Key Points to Consider

- Do content area classroom teachers have the time necessary to assess secondary students' reading needs?

- Who is responsible for teaching secondary students how to read and comprehend textbooks?

- What strategies will empower secondary students to read and comprehend their textbooks?

 **Links: www.dushkin.com/online/**
These sites are annotated in the World Wide Web pages.

Education World
  http://www.education-world.com/a_curr/profdev034.shtml
Council for Learning Disabilities: Infosheet About Reading Comprehension
  http://www.cldinternational.org/c/@OcSfc397ooeTg/Pages/home.html
National Council of Teachers of English (NCTE)
  http://www.ncte.org/middle/teaching/111157.htm
Teaching Strategies and Techniques
  http://www.ldonline.org/ld_indepth/teaching_techniques/strategies.html

Have content area textbooks been simplified? Is oversimplification of textbooks the cause of poor literacy skills and low performance scores on standardized tests? If textbooks have been simplified, then why do so many secondary students continue to have difficulty reading them to learn? Do content area classroom teachers have the time necessary to assess secondary students' reading needs? Who is responsible for teaching secondary students how to read and comprehend textbooks? While this unit does not answer these questions, selected articles give teachers, counselors, and administrators research to help them talk about these critical questions as they explore solutions to secondary reading development for life-long learning.

Secondary teachers across the curriculum have been challenged to join the ranks with middle school language arts and secondary literature teachers to address reading and writing in the content areas. While language arts and literature teachers have not escaped the dilemma of working with secondary students with only elementary literacy skills, content area teachers find it problematic that they, too, are now expected to address literacy skills in the content area. One of the dominant problems facing subject area teachers with regard to literacy development is attaining strategies to assist their students who are struggling with reading the textbook. Even when we do motivate a reluctant or discouraged learner to want to read, without adequate reading skills the student will fail to comprehend what is read.

Students in any class have a wide-range of reading abilities and interests. Using multiple texts to accommodate the diverse reading levels and interests of students is one place to begin. Developing a new way of viewing textbooks as resources to teach the curriculum standards rather than the curriculum itself is another foundation to building students' comprehension levels. As a middle school language arts teacher, I made this shift over a several year period. I collected copies of literature and grammar textbooks, purchased a variety of dictionaries, thesauruses, and electronic spellers, and filled my bookshelves with novels. I quit issuing textbooks and created writing centers—a table with four chairs. In the center of each table was a set of seven different resources for the students to use as they practiced their writing skills. In this setting, reading comprehension was more a case of manual reading. My students did not read their grammar book to learn about a topic of interest but rather as a skill manual to perfect their writing within the state standard.

My social studies classroom was different. Multiple texts included biographies, maps, encyclopedias, and resource books. Each six-week grading period, my students completed social studies research projects based on topics within the curriculum. While we read the adopted textbook to gain an overview, the textbook was little more than a resource from which to choose a topic of interest to explore. I was responsible, as a social studies teacher, to teach my students how to read to locate multiple texts on their topics and how to read the multiple texts to find the parts that pertained to their topics.

Similarly, the science teacher and I worked together to teach our students how to access information and use it to explore a topic for the science fair each year. The science teacher worked with the students to decide on appropriate topics and access multiple texts in the library and on the Internet. I shared class time in my language arts class to allow students to read their science texts for background information. Students grew in their understanding that language arts, social studies, and science were all interconnected.

I have defined critical literacy from differing views within the dualism of mastery for standardized testing on the one hand and critical thinking for Democratic, social, and political engagement in a multicultural society on the other hand. I have considered the role that culture plays in learning and challenged educators to work towards the development of a culture of literacy in schools. I addressed the role of motivation and classroom environment in developing this culture of literacy. In this unit, I address the pragmatics of comprehension in literacy. Educators are presented with researched strategies for secondary reading instruction. Regardless of where a teacher is on the literacy continuum, strategies for developing secondary students' reading comprehension skills are important.

Whether a new teacher or an experienced teacher, deciding how and when to use the textbook is an ongoing concern in secondary content areas. The articles in this unit present theory and strategies for engaging secondary students in the use of their textbooks during content area instruction. They discuss reading from the perspective of finding information. The articles present suggestions for instructing secondary students on how to conduct meaningful searches to gather, use, and produce information. Teacher-based strategies and student-based strategies for improving textbook comprehension are explored. Reading/study guides to help students access information in textbooks are presented, including K - W - L, Selective Reading Guides, and Levels of Comprehension Guide. Finally, questioning strategies to aid in comprehending textbook information and move them from the concrete to abstract, higher-level thinking are presented for discussion.

Whether working with secondary students to read the adopted textbook or multiple texts to supplement understanding, all teachers must help their students acquire the reading skills necessary to access information, understand it, and use it in creative endeavors. Reading and writing across the curriculum cannot be reduced to technical skills for state test mastery, but must become meaningful resources for authentic learning.

READING AND UNDERSTANDING TEXTBOOKS

Textbooks are often used for content instruction. Students who have difficulty obtaining information and ideas from textbooks require and benefit from guidance through their reading and learning. This article will describe one type of instructional option for helping students read their textbooks with understanding.

KATHERINE E. MISULIS
Associate Professor
School of Education
East Carolina University
Greenville, North Carolina 27858

Learning content material may be a difficult and often frustrating task for students who experience reading difficulties. These students require a greater degree of structure of instructional tasks, more teacher-led guidance through the completion of these tasks, and more reinforcement of what they have learned to insure that understanding and retention occur.

Students often have difficulty grasping content from textbooks, particularly as the complexity of information and ideas increases. A number of instructional strategies can be used to help students overcome this difficulty. One of these strategies involves the use of reading/study guides.

A reading/study guide is a piece of instructional material usually in the form of a worksheet on which are placed sets of questions and activities. This material helps to guide students' reading of text material so that they acquire the important information in the text. In addition, depending on the nature and purpose of the guide, it can also help students to read and understand at various levels of comprehension. Used consistently, reading/ study guides can provide the structured guidance necessary to ultimately help students' learning of content and reading processes with greater degrees of independence.

This article will describe the suggested use of three types of reading/study guides. They are K - W - L (Ogle, 1986), the Selective Reading Guide-O-Rama (Cunningham & Shablak,

1975), and the Levels of Comprehension Guide (Herber, 1978; 1985). These reading/study guides can be used for students of all levels of academic and learning proficiency.

While any of these guides will be helpful for the reader, the teacher may want to consider using each guide for varying purposes. The K - W - L strategy can, for example, be used in the prereading and postreading parts of a lesson. It begins with a discussion and documentation incorporating the students' prior knowledge and expectations for learning. The remaining portion of the guide would be used as a postreading strategy for identifying what was learned and how that information relates to initial purposes for learning.

The Selective Reading Guide may be helpful for students needing the greatest degree of guidance and structure. It essentially "walks" students through a process of identifying information and ideas.

The Levels of Comprehension Guide is beneficial when the specific objective is to help students read and learn at several levels of comprehension: literal, interpretive, and applied. This guide helps students identify important information and ideas in the text and helps to develop higher levels of understanding and thinking beyond the information found within the text.

These reading/study guides are best applied to content instruction from the upper-elementary grade levels and above involving any subject area. This recommendation is due to the fact that it is at these grade levels that the frequency and complexity of information associated with content instruction increases and continues to increase at each higher grade level.

In order to provide sufficient assistance to students with reading problems, it is recommended that the teacher initially provide direction and guidance of students through their completion of the guides. This involves insuring that the level of difficulty of the guides is appropriate for the students' reading levels. The teacher may provide verbal direction and guidance, perhaps reading the items from the guide to the students. As students are better able to identify information and acquire ideas related to the content independently, then the teacher would provide less immediate direction, perhaps allowing students to complete the guides with greater independence.

Each guide is appropriate for approximately one instructional lesson. The teacher may wish to use reading/study guides often with those students who experience difficulty in reading and for those who need extra assistance. On the other hand, the guides can be used selectively, with parts of the textbook that present greater difficulty for students.

The guides may be used flexibly with the entire class, or with small cooperative groups, or by individual students. Regardless of their use, it will be beneficial if students have the opportunity at some point in the lesson to discuss their responses with each other. Discussion helps the learners clarify their own understanding, while at the same time it promotes learning of new, perhaps different perspectives related to the topic. Students can "add" their information and ideas together for the benefit of even more learning.

An overview of each of the study guides along with discussion related to their use, follows.

K - W - L STUDY GUIDE DESCRIPTION

The K - W - L strategy helps to guide students through their learning of content. It helps them think about what they already know about a topic. It then provides a framework or reading/study guide for students to use as they develop purposes for learning, and then think about what they have learned.

In this strategy, "K" stands for "What I KNOW," "W" stands for "What I WANT to Learn," and "L" represents "What I LEARNED." The column type framework for K - W - L is placed on an overhead transparency or on the chalkboard. In addition, each student is given a copy which constitutes the reading/study guide for the lesson.

To use this strategy, before reading, the teacher involves students in an activity in which they brainstorm everything they know about the topic to be studied. The teacher and students write this information under the "K" (What I Know) column. In addition, the teacher and students categorize this information to promote greater understanding of concepts and of the anticipated organization of the information. The categories are placed under the "K" column.

Next, before reading the text, the teacher leads a discussion with the students to identify what information they want to

learn. This anticipated information is written as a set of questions and is placed under the "W" column (What I Want to Learn).

The students then read the text. After reading, they identify what was actually learned through the text. This information is recorded under the "L" column (What I Learned).

The K - W - L strategy incorporates the use of a reading/study guide which helps students bring into the learning experience what they know about a topic and then what they have learned. With teacher-direction and guidance through the lesson, it provides a framework within which students identify and note important information related to the topic.

SELECTIVE READING GUIDE-O-RAMA DESCRIPTION

The Selective Reading Guide-O-Rama consists of a set of directives related to the material being read. The directives are usually in the form of questions or activities to which the student is to respond while reading the content segment.

In preparing a Guide-O-Rama, the teacher first identifies the specific goals and purposes for reading a segment of text. The teacher then identifies the relevant and specific portions of the text which correspond with the goals and purposes. Having identified what the student is to learn in the related reading material, the teacher next identifies specific tasks which would be required by the student to acquire the essential pieces of information and concepts. The specific tasks become the Guide-O-Rama.

The Selective Reading Guide-O-Rama provides structured guidance in helping students identify important information in text. It also helps them to think about ideas related to the information presented.

LEVELS OF COMPREHENSION GUIDE DESCRIPTION

The Levels of Comprehension Guide provides structured guidance in helping students read and think at three levels of comprehension: literal, interpretive, and applied.

In describing levels of comprehension, the literal level focuses on the students' identification of information and facts in the text segment. The interpretive level focuses on having students interpret the information, make inferences, and draw conclusions. At the applied level, students extend their thinking by considering information and ideas in the text plus their own prior knowledge and experiences similar to the critical/evaluative and creative levels of comprehension.

In attempting to construct a levels of comprehension guide, the teacher initially identifies the overall instructional goals and associated important ideas and information related to the content. The guide is in three parts corresponding to Level I (Literal), Level II (Interpretive), and Level III (Applied). In Level I, the teacher identifies important pieces of information that the author states in the text. These are written as a set of statements which reflect the literal level of comprehension. Level II consists of a series of statements which reflect the interpretation of information or inferences to be made from the text. Level III consists of a set of phrases or statements which are very broad or general in nature, reflecting information and ideas in the text and which are conducive to having students express their own opinions based upon experience. For each level, the students must place a check mark beside each statement which can be supported. Importantly, the students must also cite evidence and provide reasons to justify their responses.

The levels of comprehension guide helps students identify important information, interpret the meaning of that information, and then think about the information and ideas in the text with respect to their own opinions and ideas. Used within cooperative group settings, the guide provides the stimulus to generate more ideas and to cause reflection of what is being learned, through discussion.

Summary

Content instruction often involves the use of textbooks as an important resource. For many students, reading textbooks is a challenging and difficult task. Reading/study guides can help students to acquire the important information and ideas associated with textbooks and with content instruction.

References

Cunningham, D., and S. L. Shablak. 1975. Selective reading guide-o-rama: the content teacher's best friend. *Journal of Reading,* 18(5): 380-382.

Herber, H. L. 1978. *Teaching Reading in Content Areas.* 2nd ed. Englewood Cliffs, New Jersey: Prentice-Hall.

Herber, H. L. 1985. Levels of comprehension: an instructional strategy for guiding students' reading. *In Reading, Thinking, and Concept Development,* edited by T. L. Harris and E. Cooper 195-211. New York: The College Board.

Ogle, D. M. 1986. K - W - L: A teaching model that develops active reading of expository text. *The Reading Teacher,* 39(6): 564-570.

Assessing students' skills in using textbooks

The Textbook Awareness and Performance Profile (TAPP)

The TAPP is a way for teachers to identify student strengths and weaknesses in reading and understanding textbooks. It can help teachers plan their instruction for individual students.

Rebecca Bell Sammons;
Beth Davey

Much recent attention has focused on identifying alternative, more authentic reading assessment strategies. These strategies should provide information considered more relevant than standardized tests for classroom teachers and reading specialists in that they provide a better match for the range of skills students are called upon to use regularly in school (Calfee, 1992). Furthermore, these classroom-based assessments may reveal individual strengths and needs that help or hinder students' successful completion of related activities. Increasingly, checklists, surveys, teacher made tests, informal reading inventories, and portfolios that reflect the curriculum provide an alternative to standardized test scores (Hiebert, 1990)

One area that has not been considered in developing alternative techniques for assessment is students' proficiency in using textbooks. When approaching a textbook reading assignment, students can differ in their prior knowledge of the topic, their awareness of textbook parts, their understanding of the task, and their use of learning and reading strategies (Archambeault, 1992; Valencia & Pearson, 1987). Thus, individual readers may follow widely divergent pathways in their attempts to learn from textbooks.

This article describes an interview procedure that teachers or reading specialists can use to gain information about how students in fourth grade and above learn from textbooks. This procedure can help identify individual students' areas of strength and areas of need when they undertake tasks requiring them to read textbooks.

The Textbook Awareness and Performance Profile (TAPP) was originally developed in a clinical setting to give students tasks that would parallel school demands and to provide evaluative information about their differ-

ing abilities to use textbooks. In addition, the TAPP was designed for diagnostic and instructional use by teachers and reading specialists in the classroom.

Description of the TAPP

The TAPP has three sections: (1) a metacognitive interview to investigate the student's perceptions of how the textbook is used both in and out of the classroom; (2) a series of tasks to assess the reader's ability to interact with the textbook; and (3) a summary sheet to record observed strengths and needs. In addition, directions for the examiner within each section provide guidance on what to say to the student and what to look for as the student completes each task.

Metacognitive interview. Students are asked to respond to open-ended questions that explore their understandings about what the teacher or reading specialist does with the textbook in terms of assignments, activities, and tests. They are also asked to describe what strategies they use to learn from the text. This interview provides information about students' perceptions of textbook use both in and out of class, and it may reveal possible misconceptions.

Textbook tasks. Students complete activities designed to identify strengths they bring to interacting with textbooks as well as areas of need. For example, they are instructed to provide an oral summary after listening to a paragraph or two read out loud by the teacher, reading specialist, or other examiner. This summary reveals the reader's ability to comprehend the passage and to identify main ideas and relevant details.

Textbook Awareness and Performance Profile (TAPP)

Student name:_____ Date: _____

Case no.: _____ Grade:_____ Age:_____

Examiner: _____

Textbook reference:_____

Class book is used in: _____

A. Metacognitive interview

A1. Asking the student what the teacher does with the text

What do you use this book for? When? Where?

Do you enjoy using it? Why?

How often do you use this book? (daily? weekly? not often?)

What does your teacher do with this book? (read out loud? show you information? give assignments?)

What kind of assignments and activities does your teacher give?

What does your teacher have you do with this book? (read out loud? answer questions at the end? read for a test?)

Is the book used in class or for homework? Is it used as a supplement to other books?

Have you had any guidance in how to use this text? If so, what?

How are you tested on this text? (essay? multiple choice? short answer?) Are you allowed to look back to the text during a test?

A2. Asking what the student does with the text

Do you prefer to read this textbook silently or out loud? Why?

What do you do when you come to something that you don't know or don't understand?

Do you ever go back and reread? When do you go back and reread?

How often do you use the pictures? Do they help you?

What things do you do to help you remember information?

What things do you do to help you study for a test?

How well do you think you read this text? (not very well? okay? very well?)

B. Textbook tasks

B1. Listening evaluation

Directions: Ask the student to identify where he or she currently is in the text. Find a place *beyond* that point that will be new to the student. Select a paragraph or two that is well organized and that can stand alone.

a. Summary: [Page: ___, Paragraph(s): ___]

Directions: "I'm going to read out loud to you, and your job is to listen. When I'm finished, I'll ask you to give me a summary of what you heard." After reading to the student say, "Please tell me what this passage was mostly about. Anything else?" Continue asking until the student says no. Look for ability to provide main ideas, recall supporting details, and organizational patterns such as sequence or cause-effect relationships.

How well did the student summarize?

	Not very well		Moderately well		Very well
	1	2	3	4	5
Provided main ideas		—	—	—	—	
Provided relevant details		—	—	—	—	
Provided well-organized summary		—	—	—	—	

Included unnecessary detail   Yes _____   No _____

Needed prompting   Yes _____   No _____

Comments:

b. Notetaking [Page: ___, Paragraph(s): ___]

Directions: "I'm going to read some more to you now, and your job is to take notes on what you hear so that you can tell me a lot more about it. When I'm finished, I'll ask you to share your notes with me." After reading to the student say, "Please tell me what this passage was mostly about. You can use your notes." Look for ability to organize and to produce clear, complete notes. Evaluate the efficiency of notetaking. Attach student notes.

(continued)

Textbook Awareness and Performance Profile (TAPP) (cont'd.)

How well did the student use a notetaking strategy?

	Not very well		Moderately well		Very well
	1	2	3	4	5
Provided main ideas		—	—	—	—
Provided relevant details		—	—	—	—
Provided well-organized notes		—	—	—	—
Provided complete notes		—	—	—	—
Was efficient with notetaking		—	—	—	—
Included unnecessary detail	Yes _____		No _____		

Follow-up questions:

Have you been shown how to take notes?	Yes _____		No _____
Who showed you?			
Did you find that helpful?	Yes _____		No _____
Do you ever take notes in class?	Yes _____		No _____
When?			
Do you know *why* you should take notes?	Yes _____		No _____
Why?			

Comments:

B2. Silent reading evaluation:

Directions: Continue forward from this point in the textbook. Select a paragraph or two that is well organized and that can stand alone.

a. Summary: [Page: _____, Paragraph(s): _____]

Directions: "Now it's time for you to read silently. When you're finished, I'd like you to look up so that I know you're done. Then I'll ask you to give me a summary of what you read." Show the student where to begin reading and where to end. After the student finishes reading say, "Please close the book and tell me what this passage was mostly about. Anything else?" Continue asking until the student says no. Evaluate in terms of organizational patterns and ability to identify main points and recall supporting details. Note problems of reading rate.

How well did the student summarize after silent reading?

	Not very well		Moderately well		Very well
	1	2	3	4	5
Provided main ideas		—	—	—	—
Provided relevant details		—	—	—	—
Provided well-organized summary		—	—	—	—
Silent reading rate		—	—	—	—
Included unnecessary detail	Yes _____		No _____		
Needed prompting	Yes _____		No _____		

Directions: Open the book to the place where the student was reading. Say, "I'm going to give you the book to use however you wish." Ask the student detail questions based on the material just read. Evaluate in terms of locating strategies.

How well does the student locate information in a text?

	Not very well		Moderately well		Very well
	1	2	3	4	5
Used textbook efficiently to answer questions		—	—	—	—
Provided correct responses		—	—	—	—

Comments:

b. Underlining: [Page: _____, Paragraph(s): _____]

Directions: "I'd like you to continue to read silently. As you read I'd like you to lightly underline the important information. I will erase it for you when you are done." Evaluate in terms of the organizational strategy used to identify main points.

(continued)

Textbook Awareness and Performance Profile (TAPP) (cont'd.)

How well does the student underline key points in a text?

	Not very well		Moderately well		Very well
	1	2	3	4	5

	Not very well		Moderately well		Very well
Underlined key information (key words, topic sentences)					
Underlined relevant detail					
Underlined unnecessary detail	Yes _____		No _____		
Underlined too much	Yes _____		No _____		
Underlined too little	Yes _____		No _____		

Comments:

c. Vocabulary: [Page(s): _____]

Directions: Look ahead in the text and pick out 3 or more key vocabulary words. Write words on index cards or on a sheet of paper. Show the student each word and say, "What does ___ mean? How do you know?" Ask the student to read the word as it appears in context in the textbook and say, "Now tell me what you can about this word based on what you read." Evaluate in terms of knowledge of word meanings in isolation and from context.

Words selected:

How well does the student identify words in isolation and from context?

	Not very well		Moderately well		Very well
	1	2	3	4	5

Provided complete meaning of words in isolation

Word 1: _____

Word 2: _____

Word 3: _____

Word 4: _____

Provided complete meaning of words from context

Word 1: _____

Word 2: _____

Word 3: _____

Word 4: _____

Comments (including definitions provided by the student):

d. Scanning: [Page: _____]

Directions: Read ahead and find a detail or date on the page. Say, "I'd like you to locate _____ on this page." Evaluate in terms of ability to scan for specific details. Note problems with timing and accuracy.

How well does the student scan for specific details?

	Not very well		Moderately well		Very well
	1	2	3	4	5
Used a scanning strategy					
Scanned accurately					
Scanned efficiently					

Comments:

e. Headings and other graphics: [Page: _____]

Directions: Find a page with several headings or graphics. Then say, "Where on the page may I find information related to_____?" Evaluate in terms of ability to locate information efficiently.

(continued)

Textbook Awareness and Performance Profile (TAPP) (cont'd.)

How well does the student use headings and other graphics?

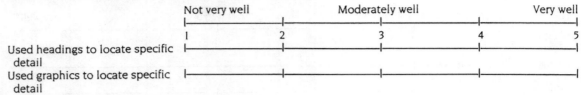

	Not very well		Moderately well		Very well
	1	2	3	4	5
Used headings to locate specific detail					
Used graphics to locate specific detail					

Comments:

B3. Awareness of textbook parts
Table of contents and index:

Directions: Select specific information that the student can locate in the table of contents or in the index. Close the textbook and say: "Tell me quickly where you can find [*specific detail*]? Where would I find information related to [*broad category*]? What can I expect to learn about [*broad category*]? I am going to give you the book to use however you wish." Evaluate in terms of ability to use table of contents and index.

How well does the student use the table of contents? How well does the student use the index?

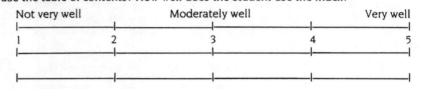

	Not very well		Moderately well		Very well
	1	2	3	4	5
Used table of contents efficiently					
Used index efficiently					

Comments:

C. Summary sheet
C1. Observed strengths
C2. Observed needs

In addition, students' use of a notetaking strategy is assessed after they hear a section of text read. This provides information about the organization, completeness, and efficiency of an individual student's approach to notetaking as well as the reader's ability to identify main ideas and relevant details.

A number of textbook tasks are included to evaluate students' strategy use after they have read a short passage silently. They are again asked to provide an oral summary and are also instructed to locate details in the text. In addition, they may be told to underline key points, to identify the meanings of words in the passage, to scan a paragraph for specific facts, or to use headings and other graphics to locate additional information. An understanding of how proficiently a reader uses each of these strategies adds to the overall picture of observed strengths and needs in textbook use.

Students are also asked to use the textbook to show where they would expect to find information about a broad category like the Industrial Revolution or a more specific detail such as the introduction of weaving machinery. This activity evaluates how efficiently each reader uses the table of contents and the index. Assessing students' awareness of textbook parts is important because of the increased emphasis in schools on project work that requires an ability to locate information prior to reading.

Summary sheet. A final section has been included in the TAPP for synthesizing the findings from the individual textbook tasks. Writing a statement of observed strengths and needs clarifies a teacher's or reading specialist's understanding of the student's ability to use expository text. The TAPP helps the professional see which strategies should then be encouraged in the classroom and which areas require further instruction.

Guidelines for use

The TAPP is designed for use with students in Grades 4 and above (age 9 through adult). It has been pilot tested with middle school and high school students in a clinical setting as part of a diagnostic battery used to assess reading performance.

The individual evaluation takes approximately 45-60 minutes. If time is limited, sample components may be selected and evaluated in depth. Alternatively, the complete TAPP can be given in two sections: On the first day, do the metacognitive interview and the listening evaluation; later do the silent reading evaluation.

Students should be encouraged to choose the textbook used for the TAPP. Science, math, social studies, history, or health textbooks are all suitable choices. We recommend that the examiner preview the textbook if possible, preparing an index card to provide quick reference to the page numbers and sections of text that will be used. While notes can be recorded during the interview, we also recommend tape recording the session. This will help in checking for accuracy later. Photocopies of the relevant pages from the textbook as well as any written products generated by the students during the evaluation can also be attached to the TAPP for future reference.

Throughout administration of the TAPP, the examiner should focus on assessing the student's strengths and needs. To provide the most complete assessment, the TAPP should be used with more than one textbook. For example, students could select one textbook they really like to use and one they do not like. In addition, samples of textbook evaluations might be compiled over time and used as an ongoing record of a student's ability to use textbooks.

Application to instruction

Teachers or reading specialists can use the TAPP to design an instructional program that builds on students' strengths to address observed needs. For example, during pilot testing of the TAPP, one sixth grader said that he took notes to help him remember information in class and to study for a test at home. He did indeed use an adequate notetaking strategy to complete the textbook task, but he was unable to remember much information when asked to provide an oral summary of a passage. A teacher or reading specialist might want to encourage him to use his notetaking strength to improve his ability to summarize text—e.g., during activities such as class discussions instead of relying on notetaking purely as a memory aid.

In another case, Michael, an 11th grader, chose his history textbook for the TAPP. During the metacognitive interview, he said that his history teacher had the students use the book almost daily. Typically, they outlined the chapters and completed worksheets of questions related to the main points. Michael stated that his preferred strategies for remembering the textbook's information were to reread what he did not understand and to outline.

On the TAPP textbook tasks, Michael showed strengths locating literal information in a passage, recalling specific details after reading silently, taking notes quickly and accurately, and using the table of contents and the index. However, he appeared to lack both knowledge of expository text structure and organizational skills for summarizing main ideas and details. In addition, he demonstrated a need to acquire a more efficient scanning strategy to locate information, and he failed to integrate information across sentences for meaning.

Although he had been taught how to outline chapters and said he used the strategy to help him remember information, Michael would probably benefit from instruction that would both improve his outlines and provide alternative strategies for interacting with expository text.

Conclusions

The TAPP provides a technique for assessing students' awareness and skills in using textbooks. The information gained from the metacognitive interview and from the textbook activities may be used to identify strategy preferences and areas of strength as well as to pinpoint areas of need on specific tasks. In addition, a description of general textbook use can be generated by completing the summary sheet of observed strengths and needs. This information may be useful for diagnostic purposes in planning instruction for a particular student, or it may guide teachers and specialists in designing an integrated approach to textbook use in the classroom.

Sammons is a doctoral candidate in reading education at the University of Maryland (1117 Benjamin Building, College of Education, College Park MD 20742-1175, USA). Davey teaches reading education at the same university.

References

Archambeault, B. (1992). Personalizing study skills in secondary students. *Journal of Reading*, 35, 468–472.

Calfee, R.C. (1992). Authentic assessment of reading and writing in the elementary classroom. In M.J. Dreher & W.H. Slater (Eds.), *Elementary school literacy: Critical issues* (pp. 211–226). Norwood, MA: Christopher-Gordon.

Hiebert, E.H. (1990). The role of teacher-based information in statewide assessment of literacy learning. In P. Afflerbach (Ed.), *Issues in statewide reading assessment* (pp. 57–72). Washington, DC: ERIC Clearinghouse on Tests, Measurements, and Evaluation.

Valencia, S., & Pearson, P.D. (1987). Reading assessment: Time for a change. *The Reading Teacher*, 40, 726–732.

From *Journal of Reading* Vol. 37, No. 4, December 1993/January 1994, pages 280-286. Copyright © 1993/1994 by The International Reading Association. Reprinted with permission.

Fostering Students' Understanding of Challenging Texts

Susan Watts & Michael F. Graves

In an attempt to expose students to a variery of sources of information and increase their interest and involvement with social studies issues, many middle school teachers are deliberately incorporating a variety of types of texts into their social studies curricula. A text one seventh grade teacher, whom we will call Linda, found particularly intriguing was David Macaulay's *Castle* (1977). This book presents an in-depth study of 13th century English castles through both text and illustrations, and Linda saw it as a very informative sidebar highlighting one facet of the medieval period her class was studying. Macaulay's text and award-winning illustrations have the potential to enhance students' understandings of the structure and purposes of medieval castles, emphasizing medieval peoples' need for security. It presents an abundance of opportunities for students to investigate the physical, social, geographic, and political factors influencing the construction of castles.

Linda's Approach

Excited about the book, and realizing that the topic and illustrations should generate a good deal of interest, Linda approached her lesson on *Castle* with optimism. Her plan was fairly typical of those she routinely used in working with relatively-short reading selections, and not unlike the Directed Reading Activity (Betts, 1946; Tierney, Readence, & Dishner, 1995) she had been introduced to in her reading methods class some years earlier.

Linda established background for the selection by asking students to share what they already knew about castles and listing their ideas on the chalkboard. Students discussed the fact thar castles are very large, are strong, may have drawbridges and motes, are used by kings and queens, are old, and are found mainly in Europe. She then read aloud the preface of *Castle*, which explains that, although the castle described in the book is fictional, the circumstances of its creation are based on the real attempt of the English to conquer Wales, and the book describes the actual building processes and physical appearance of castles existing at that time.

To motivate her students for the selection, Linda asked them what they thought it would be like to live in a castle and let them discuss their ideas for a few minutes in small groups. After setting the stage for reading, she introduced five words that she thought her students might have difficulty with: *fortress, landward, apprentice, flanked,* and *bailiff.* Although she had identified several other words that she thought would be new to her students, she did not include them in her vocabulary instruction because they were either defined in the glossary or could be gleaned from context. Linda concluded her introductory activities by asking students to read to discover some of the factors Kevin, the nobleman who built the castle, takes into account as he builds the castle and how the castle itself reflects these concerns.

After students had read, Linda opened a discussion of the text with, "So, what did you learn about Lord Kevin's main concerns as he built the castle and the ways in which the finished castle reflected these concerns?" Her plan was to list her students' ideas on the chalkboard and work with them to discover the main themes driving the creation of the castle. And, for the next 20 minutes or so, she did list ideas on the board. But she increasingly realized that all too many of the ideas were her own. To be sure, students had gleaned some information from the text and illustrations, but not a lot; and the knowledge they did have seemed fragile, a bit disjointed, and incomplete. Also, students were definitely confused on some points. "They said the castle was built on an outcrop. What's an outcrop?" Michael asked. "Why did Lord Kevin need to build such a big home?" Wanda wanted to know. "Wouldn't something more like an ordinary house be big enough for his family?" And, Reggie complained, "They keep talking about an inner curtain and an outer curtain, but I don't think I know what they mean."

What we want to achieve is generative knowledge–knowledge that does not just sit there but functions richly in people's lives to help them understand and deal with the world.

It was clear from the students' questions and comments that they had not really understood the text, had not made much use of the pictures and diagrams or the glossary, and really were not very interested in the topic. By the time Linda listened to and tried to answer all of her students' questions and fill in the knowledge gaps they displayed, the period was over and she felt disappointed and somewhat frustrated. Although she had initially planned to continue the exploration of *Castle* on the following day, she was not sure what to do now. While the session had not been a disaster, neither had it been a real success. As she drove home, Linda was still pondering the question of how she might have created a more effective lesson.

Of course, virtually any lesson leaves some room for improvement, and there are a variety of perspectives from which we might look at strengthening Linda's lesson. Here, we focus on two instructional constructs—the notion of Teaching for Understanding (Perkins, 1992; Perkins & Blythe, 1994) and the concept of Scaffolding Reading Experiences (Graves & Graves, 1994)—that offer some answers to her question.

Teaching for Understanding

The notion of Teaching for Understanding, particularly as it is described by Perkins (Perkins, 1992; Perkins & Blythe, 1994), provides a valuable perspective for viewing Linda's teaching and considering how fuller understanding might be fostered in Linda's classroom and in a myriad of other classrooms. As Perkins and others (e.g., Bruer, 1994; Gardner, 1994; Resnick, 1987; Sizer, 1984) have repeatedly noted, many of today's students are not developing the sort of deep and thorough knowledge that will enable them to use that knowledge in the increasingly complex and demanding world outside of school. As British philosopher Alfred North Whitehead explained over 50 years ago (Whitehead, 1929), much of the knowledge that children and even college students gain in school is inert—fragile, tip-of-the-iceberg information that might enable them to choose a correct answer on a multiple-choice test but is not lasting and does not serve much purpose in the real world. Or, as Perkins (1992) has recently put it, in all too many cases our instruction does not produce the retention, understanding, and active use of knowledge that we expect education to foster. What we want to achieve, Perkins explains, is "generative' knowledge—knowledge that does not just sit there but functions richly in people's lives to help them understand and deal with the world".

We thoroughly agree, and Perkins offers a number of suggestions about how we can help students construct such generative knowledge. Two of these—the notion that we need to very specifically identify and very clearly articulate the understanding goals we hope students to achieve and the notion that we need to continually strive to connect topics to students' lives and to other topics in the curriculum (Perkins & Blythe, 1994)—are particularly relevant in the present case.

We will begin by considering Linda's goals, making certain that they are clearly identified and articulated as what we want students to accomplish. Linda's first goal was to increase stu-

dents' understanding of the structure and purpose of medieval castles, emphasizing the matter of security. Her second goal was to have students investigate the physical, social, geographic, and political factors influencing the construction of castles. In Perkins' terms, to have students make connections between castles and other facets of medieval life. Both of these are worthy goals and provide students with many opportunities for understanding, but in keeping with Perkins' concerns we would add a third goal—for students to make connections between castles and things they are more familiar with, things closer to their own lives.

To what topics closer to students' lives can we connect the topic of medieval castles? One answer is fortified structures. Many students know something about forts in the United States—the Alamo, for example—and comparing medieval castles to U.S. forts gives students an opportunity to explore the similarities and differences in these diverse ages and to realize how people's desire to protect themselves has persisted over time. Additionally, almost all students know something about contemporary "forts"—the walled and hidden houses of Beverly Hills that protect movie and television stars from the prying eyes of the rest of us, the "gate-guard" communities that are becoming increasingly common throughout the country, and the White House with its recently fortified perimeter.

Thus, students can make connections between the remote topic of castles and matters closer to their lives by, for example, considering why the castle described in Macaulay's book is made of stone, why many American forts in the expanding western frontier were wooden structures, and why wood would be a poor choice for the fortifications that surround the White House. As another example of making connections, students might consider the social forces that influence the construction of fortified structures. Why was the castle in Macaulay's book built? Why did Americans of frontier days build the forts they did? What has prompted the recent development of gate-guard communities? What about the recent fortifications added to the White House? Examining each of these questions helps make the information in Macaulay's book tangible, interesting, meaningful, and informative for students.

A Framework for Supporting Students' Understanding of Text

As we move toward suggesting a revised set of activities to assist students in reaching the three goals we have just listed, we should first say that Linda was definitely on the right track. Her pre- and postreading activities certainly helped students to achieve the limited comprehension they did. We suggest that what derailment occurred took place because Linda did not systematically examine and take into account the relationship among three critical factors—the students, the text they are reading, and their purposes for reading it—which operate in any learning situation (Jenkins, 1979). Clearly, her students needed more instructional support in order to achieve the two goals she had set, and they would need still more support to achieve both those goals and the additional goal of connecting their learning about castles to their lives.

A Scaffolded Reading Experience (SRE), the second instructional concept we focus on here, can be useful in planning and providing that support. The key concept underlying the SRE is that of a scaffold or temporary support that the teacher uses to assist students completing challenging tasks. "A scaffold," as Anderson (1989) explains, "is a temporary and adjustable structure that enables the accomplishment of a task that would be impossible without the scaffold's support".

As shown in Figure 1, an SRE has two phases, a planning phase and an implementation phase. During the planning phase, the three learning factors identified by Jenkins—the students, their purposes for reading, and the text to be read—are considered. Then, during the implementation phase, a carefully selected set of pre-, during-, and postreading activities are created to support this particular group of students in reading this text to achieve these purposes.

Prereading activities prepare students to read the upcoming selection. They serve a number of functions, including getting students interested in reading the selection, reminding students of things they already know that will help them understand and enjoy the selection, and preteaching aspects of the selection that students may find difficult. Prereading activities are particularly important because only with adequate preparation will students achieve full understanding of what they read. Prereading options include motivating students, relating the reading to students' lives, activating background knowledge, building text-specific knowledge, preteaching vocabulary, preteaching concepts, questioning, predicting, direction setting, and suggesting reading strategies.

During-reading activities include both things that students themselves do as they are reading and things that teachers do to assist them as they are reading. During-reading options include silent reading, reading to students, guided reading, oral reading by students, and modifying the text.

Postreading activities serve a variety of purposes. They provide opportunities for students to synthesize and organize information gleaned from the text so that they can retain what they have learned, relate the newly-learned information to their existing knowledge, and actually use this synthesis of information in dealing with their world. They provide opportunities for students to evaluate an author's message, his or her stance in presenting the message, and the quality of the text itself. They provide opportunities for both teachers and students to evaluate students' understanding of the text. And they provide opportunities for students to respond to a text in a variety of ways, to reflect on the meaning of the text, to compare differing texts and ideas, to imagine themselves as one of the characters in the text, to synthesize information from different sources, to engage in a variety of creative activities, and to apply what they have learned within the classroom walls to the world beyond the classroom. Postreading options include questioning, discussion, writing, drama, artistic and nonverbal activities, application and outreach activities, and reteaching.

In all, the SRE framework presents 18 possible activities, far too many to be used with a single selection. Again, however, this is a list of options. From this set of possibilities, a teacher chooses only those that are appropriate for his or her particular students who are reading a particular text for a particular purpose.

Figure 1

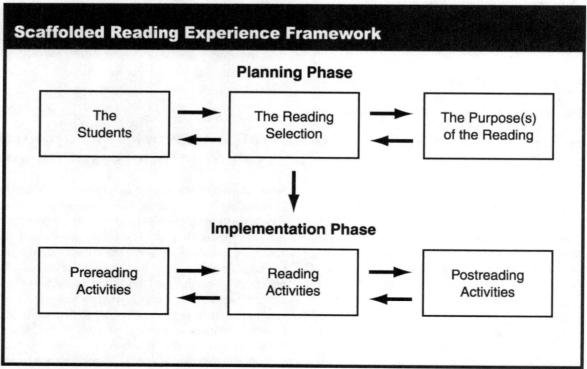

Taking a Closer Look at the Castle Text

As we just noted, one feature of the learning situation that requires consideration is the text itself. Linda certainly considered the appropriateness of *Castle* for her students, but she was so impressed with the quality of writing and illustrations that she did not think about the unique challenges the book might pose for them.

A thorough perusal of the text with an eye out for both challenges and teaching opportunities for this particular group of students and their purposes for reading the text is the first requisite for constructing a powerful reading experience. In reviewing *Castle*, we discovered several facets of the book that would challenge even the most competent seventh grade reader. First, the book is expository in nature, but it is not a textbook. Some of the features it shares with textbooks are its glossary and the inclusion of diagrams and content specific illustrations. Other than that, however, it is formatted much the way a storybook is formatted, with no headings or bold print and no paragraphs introducing and summarizing main sections. Understanding the book requires much more careful reading the students often give narratives.

Second, the book presents a heavy concept load in two ways. For one thing, many of the concepts presented are challenging. For example, the author goes into great detail about European castles built for the purpose of protecting territory and power—a concept only vaguely familiar to 20th century, American seventh graders. For another, a large number of concepts are presented. Students need to slow down as they read, to ask themselves whether they understand the ideas they encounter, and to reread, ask questions, and make use of textual aids when understanding is thwarted; they also need to determine just what is important among the myriad of ideas the book presents.

Third, the book includes a lot of difficult vocabulary. Although there is a glossary and several of the words are defined in context, if these aids are to be of value students must actually use the glossary and context to glean the meanings of words that are unfamiliar.

What Might an SRE for Castle Look Like?

In creating a sample SRE for *Castle*, we will use Linda's class as our target readers. They are a fairly typical group of 12 and 13-year-olds in a large city, 32 in number—14 boys and 18 girls: African Americans, Asian Americans, Caucasians, and Native Americans with independent reading levels ranging from about fifth grade to 11th or 12th grade.

The purposes for reading *Castle*, as we have already noted, are threefold: (a) to increase students' understanding of the structure and purpose of medieval castles, paying particular attention to the matter of security; (b) to give students an opportunity to make connections between various facets of medieval life; and (c) to give students an opportunity to make connections

among various features of medieval life, castles and the need for security, and matters closer to their own lives.

Given these goals, what Linda had done to prepare her students for reading *Castle* was on the right track but insufficient. She had, in fact, used several of the prereading activity options that comprise an SRE. She had activated background knowledge, built some text specific knowledge, pretaught vocabulary, given students a purpose for reading, provided motivation for reading, and then had the students read and discuss the text—in one period! We believe this text and these students require more in order to achieve the reading goals.

Prereading activities

Because getting off to a good start is always important, and because it's doubly important with a challenging text that might otherwise frustrate students, we would preface students' reading with a healthy set of prereading activities—four of them in all.

Relating the reading to students' lives. Since the book depicts events that occurred nearly 700 years ago and in another part of the world and because one of our goals is to have students make connections between that world and their own, we would begin with an activity relating the reading to students' lives. We might begin by asking if they could think of any modern houses that are like castles and show pictures of the houses of wealthy people including celebrities, politicians, and CEO's of large corporations. Students could then discuss similarities and differences between castles and these present day houses with partners and then contribute to a large group discussion on the topic. In that discussion, we would prompt consideration of the fact that security is a major concern of the occupants of these "modern-day castles" and was probably a concern for castle owners hundreds of years ago.

Building text-specific knowledge. Macaulay's illustrations provide a wealth of information, but many students would profit from instruction as to how to interpret them. To get students off to a good start in this direction, we might put the words "illustration" and "diagram" on the chalkboard, ask students to explain how the two are similar and how they are different, and explain that Macaulay uses both illustrations and diagrams to supplement his written presentation. We would also point out that the graphic and written materials complement each other in such a way that comprehension is increased when the reader goes back and forth between the two. To make the suggestions concrete and be sure that students understood what we were suggesting, we would use several transparencies of graphics and sentences excerpted from the book. With the first transparency or two, we would think aloud as we considered the illustration and the text, exemplifying the thinking processes that we used as we considered how the illustrations amplified the textual information. With the remaining transparencies, we would call on students to think aloud and model their thinking as they considered how the illustrations amplified the text. If students needed help in doing this, we would of course scaffold their efforts and coach them as necessary.

Suggesting strategies. Just because a glossary is available does not mean students automatically use it. Consequently, early in the school year, we would present a short unit on using a glossary generally following the approach to strategy instruction suggested by Collins, Brown, and Holum (1991)—describing the procedure, modeling it for students, scaffolding their efforts as they work with glossaries, evaluating their efforts and giving them feedback, and gradually fading our assistance and allowing students to become independent in using glossaries. Since students have already had instruction in using glossaries, at this time we would simply tell them that *Castle* includes a glossary, and ask them to recall what a glossary is, where it is located in a book, and why authors include it in books. We would suggest that they use the glossary when they come to words that are new to them, and we would remind them that some unknown words will not be in the glossary and they will have to use context or the dictionary to glean the meanings of these terms.

In all, the Scaffolded Reading Experience framework presents 18 possible activities. From this set of possibilities, a teacher chooses only those that are appropriate for his or her particular students who are reading a particular text for a particular purpose.

Predicting and direction setting. As a final prereading activity, we would ask students what is likely to be included in a book about building a single castle, have them brainstorm some possibilities, and put these on the board. Then, we would encourage them to read both to find out how Lord Kevin deals with security for his castle and to discover what other considerations influence the way Lord Kevin builds the castle.

During reading activities

Guided reading. In addition to having students read the text silently, as Linda did, we would give them a particular suggestion to guide their reading and make it an active process. Specifically, we would suggest that students consciously create mental pictures as they read and compare their mental pictures to the pictures drawn by the author as they encounter them. To get them started here, we would think aloud about a mental picture that we might conjure up and then compare it to a picture from the text.

Postreading activities

Three postreading activities seem particularly appropriate here—questioning, a discussion, and an artistic activity.

Questioning. We would begin postreading activities by soliciting students' responses to the two directions we gave them just before they began reading—to find out how Lord Kevin deals with security for his castle and to discover what other considerations influence the way Lord Kevin builds the castle. We would do this orally, putting responses on the board and, with the aid of the class, filling in gaps and correcting misconceptions.

Discussion. Here we suggest a particular sort of discussion, one based on another idea we have borrowed from Perkins (1994), that of a "design conversation." Although design conversations are applicable to a number of topics, they are particularly applicable to our consideration of *Castle* because they focus specifically on how the form of an object fits its function, a central concern throughout our work with the book. As described by Perkins (1994), design conversations focus on five questions that help learners think deeply about a topic. Here are the five design questions applied to *Castle*: (a) What are the purposes of castles such as the one described in *Castle?* (b) What is the structure of such castles? (c) What are some specific examples or model cases of such castles—and of present day "castles"? (d) What are the explanatory arguments for castles? and (e) What are the evaluative arguments for castles? (Questions d and e require students to explain how the structure of castles fits their purpose and then *evaluate* how well castles fit their purposes by listing pros and cons.)

We would provide these questions a few days before the conversation is to take place and assign students the task of finding specific answers to the third question through their own research. Then, on the day of the conversation, we would have students form eight groups of four and ask each group to hold its own design conversation, after which each group would contribute its line of reasoning in a whole-class design conversation. Next, we would provide closure and additional attention to our goal of connecting the past with the present by asking the class as a whole to apply the design questions to modern day castles. Finally, we would leave students with something concrete to take away with them by having them create two semantic maps based on their design conversation. At the center of one map would be the term "Castles of the Past," and at the center of the other the term "Modern Day Castles." The design questions—purposes, structure, examples, explanatory arguments, and evaluative arguments—would radiate from the center of each map, and students' responses to each question would fall under those headings.

An artistic activity. This activity provides an opportunity for students to create their own castles. First we would encourage students to determine what the primary purpose of their castles is and to design them accordingly, stressing however the point that all castles had to be secure. It would be helpful to enlist the aid of an art teacher to help students come up with structural designs and materials that would achieve certain effects while we worked with them on aligning their designs to their purposes and using the information presented in *Castle* and class discussions to help them in their own castle creations. Finally, once students had completed their castles, we would ask them to present their work to the class, once more considering connections between the Middle Ages and the present by discussing medieval and present-day influences on their castles.

Concluding Remarks

In all, our SRE for *Castle* has included eight activities and probably occupied the class for four or five days. This is a lot of time, and yet time is necessary for fostering deep understanding. As we move toward the 21st century, school reform movements are focused on promoting deep knowledge and critical thinking across the curriculum (Goodlad, 1990; Lewis, 1995). Meeting these calls for reform will frequently require extended treatment of topics. These calls for reform will also require increased decision-making on the part of the teacher in creating instructional situations conducive to higher-level learning.

In this article, we have examined the challenge of facilitating deep understanding of content presented through text with an in-depth look inside one classroom at one particular point in time. By considering Linda's classroom, we have shown one way to foster deep understanding by tailoring instructional activities to a specific group of students, a specific reading selection, and specific instructional goals. Of course, our plan is just one of several that would foster such understanding; different teachers would choose different combinations of activities. Just as our choices were guided by the students in Linda's class, the book *Castle*, and our goals for instruction, individual teachers will make their own choices—some very different from ours—in their work with other reading selections, other students, and other instructional goals; and in doing so they will facilitate real understanding in their students.

References

Anderson, L. M. (1989). Classroom instruction. In M. C. Reynolds (Ed.), *Knowledge bases for the beginning teacher* (pp. 101–111). Oxford, England: Pergamon.

Betts, E. A. (1946). *Foundations of reading instruction.* New York: American Book.

Bruer, J. (1994). *Schools for thought. A science of learning in the classroom.* Cambridge, MA: The MIT Press.

Collins, A., Brown, J. S., & Holum, A. (1991). Cognitive apprenticeship: Making thinking visible. *American Educator, 14*(4), 6–11, 38–46.

Gardner, H. (1994). On teaching for understanding in the disciplines—and beyond. *Teachers College Record,* 96, 198–218

Goodlad, J. I. (1990). Better teachers for our nation's schools. *Phi Delta Kappan, 72,* 185–194.

Graves, M. F., & Graves, B. B. (1994). *Scaffolding reading experiences: Designs for students success.* Norwood, MA: Christopher-Gordon.

Jenkins, J. J. (1979). Four points to remember: A tetrahedral model of memory experiments. In L. S. Cermak & F. I. M. Craik (Eds.), *Levels of processing in human memory.* (pp. 429–446) Hillsdale, NJ: Erlbaum.

Lewis, A. C. (1995). An overview of the standards movement. *Pbi Delta Kappan,* 76,744–750.

Macaulay, D. (1977). *Castle.* Boston: Houghton Mifflin.

Perkins, D. (1992). *Smart scbools: From training memories to educating minds.* New York: The Free Press.

Perkins, D. (1994). *Knowledge as design: A handbook for critical and creative discussion across the curriculum.* Pacific Grove, CA: Critical Thinking Press.

Perkins, D., & Blythe, T. (1994). Putting understanding up front. *Educational Leadership,* 51(5), 4–7.

Resnick, L B. (1987). *Education and leaming to think.* Washington, D. C.: National Academy Press.

Sizer, T. B. (1984). *Horace's compromise: The dilemma of the American high school today.* Boston: Houghton Mifflin.

Tierney, R. J., Readence, J. E., & Dishner, E. K. (1995). *Reading strategies and practices: A compendium* (4th ed.). Boston: Allyn & Bacon.

Whitehead, A. N. (1929). *The aims of education and other essays.* New York: Macmillan.

Susan Watts & Michael F. Graves teach in the Department of Curriculum and Instruction at the University of Minnesota, Minneapolis.

From *Middle School Journal* Vol. 29, No. 1, September 1997, pages 45-51. Copyright © 1997 by National Middle School Association. Reprinted with permission from National Middle School Association.

Searching for information in textbooks

Mariam Jean Dreher

Reading comprehension research has almost always focused on reading to understand or recall the contents of a passage (Calfee & Drum, 1986). Yet another type of literacy task—the search task—is increasingly important and involves different processes than reading to learn an entire passage.

In a search task, the goal is to locate specific information. Indeed, students engaged in a search task would want to avoid examining the entire contents of the material. Instead, they would use features such as headings and indexes to eliminate irrelevant information while targeting critical portions.

This article will define search, explain why we should be concerned with it, describe research on high school and college students' searching, and offer suggestions for search instruction.

What is search?

In a search task, a reader attempts to locate information for specific purposes. For example, if a reader is asked to define a new term, it is not necessary for him or her to read an entire chapter; instead he or she might go directly to a glossary or to an index. Whether the reader uses textbooks, reference materials, or documents, the purpose is not to recall or understand all the material but to locate only the information that is needed.

Is search the same as skimming and scanning? These two processes are certainly part of the search process. In fact, when a search task is a simple find-one-fact type of task they may be identical. But typically skimming or scanning is part of a larger search strategy.

Is it the same as other reading skills? There is increasing recognition of the need to distinguish search tasks from other literacy tasks. For example, in examining adult literacy levels, the U.S. National Assessment of Educational Progress (NAEP) differentiated "three qualitatively different aspects of reading comprehension" (Kirsch & Jungeblut, 1986): (a) locating information in text, (b) producing and interpreting text information, and (c) generating a theme or organizing principle from text information. Similarly, Guthrie and Mosenthal (1987) have argued that search tasks do not involve the same processes as traditional reading comprehension tasks and, therefore, need to be studied in their own right.

There is also research evidence to support the contention that text search is distinct from traditional reading comprehension

tasks. Guthrie found that college students' performance on passage recall did not help predict their success on a search task (Guthrie & Dreher, 1990). Yussen and Stright (1991) confirmed these results. Similarly, in a factor analysis of engineers' and technicians' reading performance, Guthrie and Kirsch (1987) showed that text comprehension and locating were clearly differentiated.

How prevalent are search tasks?

The demand for locating information is quite common. In the workplace, adults have been found to spend more time on reading to locate information than for any other purpose (Guthrie, Seifert, & Kirsch, 1986; Kirsch & Guthrie, 1984; Mikulecky, 1982). As Mosenthal and Kirsch (1989) explained, in school students *learn to read* and *read to learn*; but beyond school, we *read to do*. However, even in school, teachers ask students to read and locate answers, to locate supporting conclusions, and to locate information on particular topics for reports.

Indeed, analyses of curricular materials suggest that locating skills are part of the goals. For example, a study of several social studies programs for elementary schools concluded that locating information was among the skills that all the programs claimed to address (Armbruster & Gudbrandsen, 1986). Similarly, studies of secondary classrooms suggest that locating information is a typical requirement in worksheets and end-of-chapter questions (e.g., Smith & Feathers, 1983).

How skilled are we?

In 1985, the U.S. National Assessment of Educational Progress (NAEP) surveyed the literacy skills of young adults, ages 21-25 (Kirsch & Jungeblut, 1986). One major concern in this assessment was prose literacy, defined as "skills and strategies needed to understand and use information from texts that are frequently found in the home or community" The NAEP prose literacy scale includes locating information in text.

The NAEP results indicated that about 95% of young adults were estimated to be proficient at the lower end of the prose literacy scale. At this level, readers are asked to complete tasks such as matching a single feature in a question with appropriate information in a text. For example, readers might be asked to locate a statement in a six-paragraph newspaper article telling what a swimmer ate to keep up her strength during a marathon.

But as the tasks increase in complexity, the percentage of young adults who can successfully perform them decreases. Only about 37% of the young adults were estimated to be proficient at a three-feature locating task in a newspaper article. Such a task would entail considering three information categories at once. For example, a question might require attention to people, action, and situation categories in order to locate information on what a town did to help it decide what to do with the toxic waste dump left behind by a defunct factory.

What do errors tell us?

Several research studies have been conducted on the text search performance of high school and college students. These studies indicate striking inefficiency on the part of many students. For this article, a secondary analysis of the original data from three of these studies (Dreher & Brown, 1990; Dreher & Guthrie, 1990; Guthrie & Dreher, 1990) was conducted. The aim of this analysis was to identify instructional interventions by examining the responses of unsuccessful or inefficient searchers.

• Research on high school students

Dreher and Guthrie (1990) studied 34 Grade 11 students who were enrolled in average or better classes. They were asked to locate information in a life sciences textbook that they had not previously used. They were instructed to use the book in any way they wished in order to locate the answers to the questions. The two questions were presented individually in counterbalanced order. When the students believed they had found the answers, their responses were accepted whether or not they were correct.

One of the questions, "What are cocci?" (answer: spherical bacteria), required only locating the meaning of a single term. *Cocci* was an entry in the glossary and the index. All but one student successfully answered this question; the single incorrect response was from a student who mistook it for *coccyx* and answered "tailbones" without examining the textbook.

The other search question was more complex: "What are the three characteristics of living things?" (answer: movement, growth, reproduction). It required locating three pieces of information—all three could be found in the same section of the chapter. Either the table of contents or the index could be used to locate the appropriate area of the text. The table of contents contained a section labeled "characteristics of living things" and the index contained entries for *living things, characteristics of* and *characteristics, living things.*

Only 18 of the 34 students (53%) answered the three-characteristics question correctly. These results parallel the NAEP young adult data in that the number of accurate responses dropped off dramatically when the complexity of the search task increased.

Do students' incorrect responses suggest the nature of the problem? Table 1 categorizes the responses of the 16 students who offered incorrect answers to the three-characteristics ques-

Table 1

Incorrect search responses by high school students

Incorrect response pattern	Number of students
Located appropriate text pages but did not extract the correct information	9
Settled for selecting answers from close to right spot (e.g., the first page of the right chapter)	3
Did not use textbook (offered an answer based on prior knowledge)	2
Used index but never found an entry leading to an appropriate text page	1
Made a lucky stab but failed to take full advantage (selected a somewhat related section heading from table of contents, which happened to open with a paragraph summarizing the points from the correct chapter)	1

Text used: life sciences textbook for secondary school.
Question asked: "What are the three characteristics of living things?"

tion. Nine of these students located one or more of the correct pages but failed to extract the correct information. Another 3 students located the beginning of the relevant chapter but did not search beyond its first page; instead they simply selected three terms from that first page.

Thus, 12 students either located appropriate pages or were very close to them. When the responses of these 12 were analyzed, it was interesting that 7 of these students had settled on terms that appeared in boldface on the pages they had examined, or that appeared in a box highlighting vocabulary words. Their responses indicate that they had learned that high-lighted terms are important. However, truly aberrant responses, such as *time-lapse photography* as a characteristic of living things, suggest that some students simply found a highlighted term and did not evaluate or monitor the appropriateness of the response.

In short, most of the students who were unsuccessful started the search in an appropriate way. However, they frequently failed to complete the task successfully and appeared to take the first answers available, often a boldface term. This suggests that they did not fully understand the use of boldface or that they did not monitor or evaluate their own responses. It should be recalled that these students were not poor readers; all were in at least average classes.

• Research on college students

Dreher and Brown (1990) studied 28 college students engaged in search tasks in individual sessions using a psychology textbook. This article discusses their performance on two search tasks, each requiring them to locate one piece of information. One of these questions contained a searchable term—"Explain the moral reasoning of children who think that accidentally

Table 2

Incorrect search responses by college students on a task with no stated search term

Search response	Number of students	Type of error
Located appropriate text page but did not extract the correct information	11	9 wrong answers (5 were boldface headings from correct page) 2 ran out of time
Located right chapter but not correct text page	3	1 wrong answer 2 ran out of time
Located related chapter	6	1 wrong answer 5 ran out of time

Text used: a college psychology textbook.
Question: "Why does the moon seem to be moving through the clouds on a windy night?"
Answer: induced motion.
Correct chapter in textbook: "Perception."
Related chapter: "Sensory Processes," prior to target chapter.

breaking 15 cups is worse than intentionally breaking 1 cup" (answer: they attribute blame according to the amount of damage regardless of intention). Both *moral reasoning* and *children, moral reasoning of* were in the index.

The other question required the subjects to generate a searchable term because no terms in the question were in the index or glossary. It was "Why does the moon seem to be moving through the clouds on a windy night?" (answer: induced motion).

For the moral reasoning question, the success rate was 57%. But for the moon-motion question, with no searchable term, only 29% were successful. As with the three-characteristics question, students' responses were examined to see what they revealed about text search difficulties.

(1) *A task with no stated search term.* The few college students who were successful on the moon question located the answer by going to the table of contents and selecting the chapter on perception, or by going to the index and looking up either motion or perception.

But 20 out of these 28 students were unsuccessful. Fourteen—the top two categories in Table 2—were able to get to the right chapter by using the index or table of contents or both. Of these 14, 11 actually viewed the right page but failed to extract the correct information; 5 of them selected an incorrect boldface heading that appeared on the page (the correct answer did appear in boldface type, but these 5 students selected another boldface heading on the page).

The last category in Table 2 indicates that several students never located the right chapter. Most of these students never offered an answer since they were not close to the target area.

The majority of students who were unsuccessful on this question seemed to be able to select an appropriate category to search. They got to the right chapter and even the right page, but they either were unable to extract an answer or extracted an inappropriate answer, which they appeared not to evaluate. As in the three-characteristics question, some misused the boldface cues. In addition, several students were not able to locate the right chapter because they were not able to generate an appropriate search term.

It should be noted that in this study, subjects were stopped after 5 minutes, so some would probably have obtained a correct answer with more time. But those who offered incorrect answers almost always had plenty of time left to evaluate their answers, yet did not do so. Indeed, the high school students in the previous study had no time limit, yet their performance was similar.

(2) *A task with a stated search term.* These college subjects also received the moral reasoning question (in counterbalanced order). Table 3 summarizes the findings. The bottom category in this table shows that 2 students never made it to the appropriate chapter. While the top two categories show that almost all were able to get to the right chapter, only half of those who made it to the chapter actually viewed the target page. The only boldface heading on this page was "Moral Reasoning," a term that was in the question; hence, no one selected it as an answer.

As with the harder moon-motion question, the majority of people who were unsuccessful on this question seemed to be able to select an appropriate category to search. They were able to locate the right chapter and some even the right page, but they either were unable to extract an answer or extracted an inappropriate one. And a few seemed not to be able to formulate an appropriate search term.

• **A second example with college students**

In another study with a different kind of question and task, Dreher and Guthrie (1987; see also Guthrie & Dreher, 1990) had 23 college students answer questions using a textbook chapter accessible on a microcomputer. Of interest here is tracking the routes these students took in relation to the scores they earned on their answers.

These students used a menu to select from several information-access systems—glossary, index, table of contents, scan chapter, browse. The scan-chapter feature simulated a reader flipping through a text by displaying each page at a rate of 2 seconds per page. In the browse feature, starting at the beginning, subjects could browse through the chapter forward or backward at their own speed.

The question required subjects to locate and integrate information about five earth science terms and to use this information to infer the relationship among the terms in a written response. The question was "Explain how the following terms

Table 3
Incorrect search responses by college students on a task with a stated search term

Search response	Number of students	Type of error
Located appropriate text page but did not extract the correct information	5	4 wrong answers 1 ran out of time
Located right chapter but not correct text page	5	2 wrong answers 3 ran out of time
Located related chapter	2	1 wrong answer 1 ran out of time

Text used: a college psychology textbook.
Question: "Explain the moral reasoning of children who think that accidentally breaking 15 cups is worse than intentionally breaking 1 cup."
Answer: They attribute blame according to the amount of damage, regardless of intention.
Correct chapter: "Psychological Development."
Related chapters: "Social Information Processing" and "Thought and Language."

are related to each other: *bacteria, humus, lichens, mechanical agents, solute.*" Answers were rated from 0 to 15 points depending on how well subjects did on defining and identifying the relationship among the terms.

What do the approach routes of college students reveal? There was a good deal of variety in the routes they took (recorded by the computer) in searching the text.

The Figure here maps out the college students' initial search patterns—the first four choices made by each of the subjects. For example, Student A chose the glossary (gl), then the index (in), and finally, the index (in) again; this student's essay was rated 13 points. Student T chose the browse option (br), then the glossary (gl), then browse again, then the table of contents (tc). The + means this student made more than four choices. Student T's essay received a 3 rating.

Few students had exactly the same route. Yet some general statements can be made. The last column shows the average essay score for students with the same initial choice. On the average, students who chose to begin with a more specific access system (glossary, index, table of contents) did better than those who chose a broader initial route (scan or browse) or who arbitrarily selected a particular page to start with. Selecting a nonspecific first choice—when key search terms are stated—suggests a failure to formulate a specific goal before searching.

Why might students be having trouble?

Research evidence on the type and amount of content area reading that students actually do may help explain why many students have trouble with search tasks. Despite the prevalence of textbooks at all levels of schooling (Goodlad, 1976, 1984), students may have used texts for narrow purposes or they may have used their texts minimally, relying instead on teacher lectures.

Tierney (1982), for example, found that high school students reported a restricted range of study strategies. Their most common pattern was to simply read through a chapter while trying to memorize portions of it.

Others have found that students may not actually read textbooks to the extent that has been assumed (Anderson, 1979; Anderson & Armbruster, 1984). Since less than 5% of class time at the high school level is devoted to reading (Goodlad, 1984), one would assume that most textbook reading occurs outside school. But Smith and Feathers (1983) concluded that little reading is actually assigned and that many students view their teachers' lectures as equally or more important than their content area textbooks for obtaining information.

Similarly, Ratekin, Simpson, Alvermann, and Dishner (1985) found that in junior and senior high school classes the teacher, not the textbook, was the primary information source. Because students could rely on the teacher to develop new concepts, it was possible to perform adequately without reading the book.

Ratekin et al. also noted that instruction did not include teaching students to read and learn from their content area textbooks. Although there is variation in classroom practice, many students may have had little experience using such features as an index, glossary, or table of contents, which search tasks require. (See Alvermann & Moore, 1991, for a review of research on secondary school reading practices.)

What can we do?

Research on the use of content area textbooks suggests that more use of textbooks for varied purposes would help improve search skills. But beyond that it seems likely that search performance could be improved by instruction that takes into account the responses of unsuccessful or inefficient searchers.

Characteristics of unsuccessful searchers can be identified from an analysis of high school and college students' responses in the differing search tasks discussed above. In Table 4, these characteristics appear in the middle column, where they can be seen to map onto the search processes in the first column, based on the model of locating information that has been proposed by Guthrie and Mosenthal (1987; see also Guthrie, 1988; Guthrie & Dreher, 1990). The model proposes five components involved in locating information: (a) goal formation, (b) category selection, (c) information extraction, (d) integration, and (e) recycling.

In other words, a student engaged in a text-search task would need to (a) formulate a goal or plan of action, (b) select appropriate text sections or categories for inspection (e.g., table of contents, text pages), (c) extract relevant information from the

Initial search patterns shown by college students on a computerized earth sciences search task

First four choices in the search				Student	Essay score	Mean essay score of students making same first choice
1	2	3	4			

Tree diagram of search patterns:

- gl
  - in
    - in — : A, 13
    - ra — : B, 5
    - — — : C, D, 5, 8
  - tc
    - in — ra : E, 11
    - — : F, 4
    - sc — pp + : G, 3
    - — — : H, 12
  - sc — tc — in + : I, 3

Mean essay score of students making same first choice: 7.11

- tc
  - in
    - in — tc + : J, 7
    - ra — gl : K, 10
    - — — : L, 9
  - ra — in — gl + : M, 2
  - — — — : N, 9

Mean essay score: 7.00

- in
  - ra — in — : O, 5
  - br — ra + : P, 10
  - gl — tc — pp + : Q, 5

Mean essay score: 6.67

- sc — gl — in — : R, 4

Mean essay score: 4.00

- br
  - ra — — : S, 4
  - sc — pp — ra : T, 3
  - gl — br — tc + : U, 3

Mean essay score: 3.33

- pp — in — ra — : V, 5
  - — — : W, 1

Mean essay score: 3.00

br = browse	ra = review assignment	
gl = glossary	sc = scan chapter	
in = index	tc = table of contents	
pp = particular pages	+ = student made more than 4 choices	

inspected categories, (d) integrate the extracted information with prior knowledge, and (e) recycle through the preceding processes until the search task is completed.

Thus, if learners are unclear about the goal, if they select inappropriate categories, if they fail to extract or integrate the appropriate information, or if they fail to recognize the need for more information, then their locating performance will be inefficient or unsuccessful.

Table 4 thus shows the relationship of processes in Guthrie and Mosenthal's search model to characteristics of unsuccessful searchers. The match between students' text search difficulties and these components suggests the value of converting a cognitive model of locating information into an instructional device. Accordingly, Table 4 also presents examples of questions that students can be taught to use to guide their monitoring of text search tasks. The aim of such instruction would be for students to internalize a self-monitoring routine.

The need for teaching such a self-monitoring procedure is evident in the conclusions of Simpson (1984), who noted that high school and college students often fail to engage in self-reg-

ulating activities such as planning, checking, and evaluating outcomes. Similarly, in a review of metacognition and comprehension in adult readers, Baker (1989) concluded that "adults do evaluate and regulate their ongoing efforts to understand, although there is considerable room for improvement".

Both Baker and Simpson were referring to traditional reading and studying, but their observations also appear to characterize the text-search performance of many high school and college students. Indeed, the results from text-search research are consistent with classic research in problem solving in which performance is linked to a systematic approach to a problem. For example, Bloom and Broder (1950) observed that unsuccessful problem solvers began "with no apparent plan for solution, more or less plunging in, not knowing what was to come next".

In short, search is distinct from the usual concept of "reading comprehension," and it is also a common workplace and school requirement. But many students are not very effective at it. Consequently, students need practice and instruction to aid them. The self-monitoring questions in Table 4 can be used in providing such instruction.

Table 4

How unsuccessful searchers' characteristics relate to a model of the search process

Search response	Searchers' problems	Questions for student self-monitoring
Goal formation	Failure to formulate a specific goal before searching (e.g., not using specific search terms when they are present)	Exactly what information do I need?
Category selection	Inability to locate an appropriate text section	How should I approach this material? How is the material organized? What are the available features?
Information extraction	Misuse of potentially helpful text features (e.g., about half of the incorrect responses by high school students were boldface terms that appeared near the correct answers)	Is the information I need located here? Does the information I have located make sense?
Integration	Failure to monitor the appropriateness of the response	Do I need to combine this information with other material that I have located or already know?
Recycling	Failure to evaluate the response and look further. (occurs in tasks both with and without time limits)	Do I have all the information that I need? If not, I should continue searching.

*Model proposed by Guthrie and Mosethal.

References

Alvermann, D.E., & Moore, D.W. (1991). Secondary school reading. In R. Barr, M.L. Kamil, P. Mosenthal, & P.D. Pearson (Eds.), *Handbook of reading research,* vol. 2 (pp. 951–983). New York: Longman.

Anderson, T.H. (1979). Study skills and learning strategies. In H.F. O'Neil, Jr. & C.D. Spielberger (Eds.), *Cognitive and affective learning strategies* (pp. 77-98). New York: Academic Press.

Anderson, T.H., & Armbruster, B.B. (1984). Studying. In P.D. Pearson (Ed.), *Handbook of reading research* (pp. 657–680). New York: Longman.

Armbruster, B.B., & Gudbrandsen, B. (1986). Reading comprehension instruction in social studies programs. *Reading Research Quarterly, 21,* 36–48.

Baker, L. (1989). Metacognition, comprehension monitoring, and the adult reader. *Educational Psychology Review, 1*(1),3–38.

Bloom, B.S., & Broder, L.J. (1950). *Problem-solving processes of college students: An explanatory investigation* (Supplementary Educational Monographs, No. 73). Chicago: University of Chicago Press.

Calfee, R., & Drum, P. (1986). Research on teaching reading. In M.C. Wittrock (Ed.), *Handbook of research on teaching* (3rd ed.) (pp. 804–849). New York: Macmillan.

Dreher, M.J., & Brown, R. (1990). *Planning prompts and searchable terms in textbook search tasks.* Paper presented at the National Reading Conference, Miami, FL.

Dreher, M.J., & Guthrie, J.T. (1987). *Tracking inspection and extraction during textbook chapter processing via computer.* Paper presented at the National Reading Conference, St. Petersburg Beach, FL.

Dreher, M.J., & Guthrie, J.T. (1990). Cognitive processes in textbook chapter search tasks. *Reading Research Quarterly, 25,* 323–339.

Goodlad, J.I. (1976). *Facing the future: Issues in education and schooling.* New York: McGraw-Hill.

Goodlad, J.I. (1984). *A place called school: Prospects for the future.* New York: McGraw-Hill.

Guthrie, J.T. (1988). Locating information in documents: Examination of a cognitive model. *Reading Research Quarterly, 23*(2), 178–199.

Guthrie, J.T., & Dreher, M.J. (1990). Literacy as search: Explorations via computer. In D. Nix & R. Spiro (Eds.), *Cognition, education, and multimedia: Exploring ideas in high technology* (pp. 65–114). Hillsdale, NJ: Erlbaum.

Guthrie, J.T., & Kirsch, I.S. (1987). Distinctions between reading comprehension and locating information in text. *Journal of Educational Psychology, 79,* 220–228.

Guthrie, J.T., & Mosenthal, P. (1987). Literacy as multidimensional: Locating information and reading comprehension. *Educational Psychologist, 22,* 279–297.

Guthrie, J.T., Seifert, M., & Kirsch, I.S. (1986). Effects of education, occupation and setting on reading practice. *American Educational Research Journal, 23,* 151–160.

Kirsch, I., & Guthrie, J.T. (1984). Adult reading practices for work and leisure. *Adult Education Quarterly, 34,* 213–232.

Kirsch, I., & Jungeblut, A. (1986). *Literacy: Profiles of America's young adults.* Princeton, NJ: Educational Testing Service.

Mikulecky, L. (1982). Job literacy: The relationship between school preparation and workplace actuality. *Reading Research Quarterly, 17*(3), 400–419.

Mosenthal, P., & Kirsch, I. (1989). Lists: The building blocks of documents. *Journal of Reading, 33,* 58–60.

Ratekin, N., Simpson, M., Alvermann, D.E., & Dishner, E.K. (1985). Why content teachers resist reading instruction. *Journal of Reading, 28,* 432–437.

Simpson, M.L. (1984). The status of study strategy instruction: Implications for classroom teachers. *Journal of Reading, 28,* 136–142.

Smith, F.R., & Feathers, K.M. (1983). Teacher and student perceptions of content area reading. *Journal of Reading, 26,* 348–354.

Tierney, R.J. (1982). Learning from text. In A. Berger & H.A. Robinson (Eds.), *Secondary school reading: What research reveals for classroom practice* (pp. 97–110). Urbana, IL: National Conference on Research in English/ERIC Clearinghouse on Reading and Communication Skills.

Yussen, S., & Stright, A. (1991). *Simple searching to find information in a textbook.* Paper presented at the American Educational Research Association meeting, Chicago, IL.

Dreher directs the Reading Center at the University of Maryland (College Park MD 20742, USA).

From *Journal of Reading* Vol. 35, No. 5, February 1992, pages 364-371. Copyright © 1992 by The International Reading Association. Reprinted with permission.

Teachers' views of textbooks and text reading instruction: Experience matters

Experienced high school teachers become freer in the ways they use their content area textbooks. They're also more likely to teach students how to use the text, according to responses to this survey. And guess which teachers make most use of the textbook—those in schools where teachers choose the books.

Deborah Menke
Beth Davey

It is a widely held assumption in the United States that textbooks play a dominant role in the education of secondary students. Indeed, descriptive research has documented the prevalence of textbooks in content classrooms (Moore & Murphy, 1987). Moreover, the belief that cultural reproduction is one of the goals of schooling has led many teachers to rely on textbooks as an approved source of this information (Moore & Murphy, 1987). Apple (1992) describes textbooks as artifacts that play a "major role in defining whose culture is taught." If textbooks bear such a powerful role in schooling, their use in the classroom needs examination.

Although there is a scarcity of research on actual reading practices in secondary classrooms (Dillon, 1989), one source of information on text use comes from surveys conducted with various groups of content area teachers. The purpose of these surveys has been to describe how teachers view reading and how they use textbooks in their classrooms.

Using a paper and pencil survey, Rieck (1977) investigated teacher and student perceptions about reading in their classrooms. Thirty-three of the 34 content area teachers surveyed said that they required reading in their subject areas, and 20 teachers said that they thought most students read the assignments.

Researchers then surveyed 300 students of the teachers who had indicated that they believed that their students did *not* read the assignments. Eighty-one percent of these students said they didn't read the assignments, 73% reported that they were not required to discuss assigned reading in class, and 95% indicated that teachers merely assigned pages to be read without providing any purpose for reading.

In contrast to these somewhat discouraging findings, Lipton and Liss (1978) reported that English teachers in their study devoted 66% of their time "specifically to teaching reading." Moreover, foreign language teachers reported teaching reading, on the average, 64% of the class time, social studies teachers reported doing so 28% of their class time, and science teachers reported that 11% of their time was spent on teaching reading.

On the other hand, Spiegel and Wright (1984) found little interest by biology teachers in promoting student reading skills. In rating the importance of textbook characteristics, the teachers judged learning from text features to be significantly less important than having features that would add to the text's attractiveness. Although the teachers indicated that they prepared students for reading by preteaching important vocabulary and concepts, they did not rate as important those aspects of text that would promote independent student comprehension. This group of teachers also indicated that they did not depend on the text for determining the order and content of their teaching topics.

The apparent lack of interest by teachers in text features to assist comprehension found by Spiegel and

Wright (1984) is reflected in a more recent survey by Gee and Forester (1988). Forty-four percent of 466 teachers surveyed nationwide indicated that they believed reading instruction was not the responsibility of content area teachers. Although 30% reported that they believed content area teachers lacked the confidence needed to participate in reading instruction, 29% indicated that they believed that many teachers do not feel that secondary reading programs are necessary. Further, the majority of teachers in this study felt that teachers did not have time to plan a program incorporating content area reading instruction into their classrooms.

Finally, Davey (1988) found that secondary teachers in her survey reported incorporating some specific comprehension promoting activities in their classrooms. Forty-five secondary teachers indicated that they frequently had students answer questions at the end of the chapters, that they overviewed the text selections before giving assignments, and that they expected the students to read most of the text. However, this same group only rarely or occasionally gave students time to read in class, taught students how to use the textbook, used different texts with different readers, or changed texts when it was evident that students could not read them.

Although these secondary teachers said they frequently expected their students to read the whole text, only 20% of the teachers in Davey's sample actually assigned the text for reading. In fact, only about a third of them reported reliance on their textbooks either for lectures or assigned reading. Rather, most indicated that they used the textbook to supplement instruction, for group work, or for activities.

One might conclude from the surveys reported above that content area teachers are ambivalent about the place of textbooks in their classrooms and the appropriateness of reading instruction at the secondary level. Although it appears that many teachers feel reading instruction is not the province of secondary teachers (Gee & Forester, 1988), teachers also report that they do use comprehension-enhancing teaching methods (Davey, 1988; Spiegel & Wright, 1984). While teachers do make text reading assignments (Davey, 1988; Lipton & Liss, 1978; Rieck, 1977), it appears that students use their texts primarily without teacher assistance (Conley, 1987; Holdzkom, 1987) and with teachers often failing to review reading assignments.

The present study

Why are some secondary teachers unclear or ambivalent about the place of textbooks in student learning of content? One possibility, not considered in the prior survey research, is that degree of classroom teaching experience may shape attitudes and approaches concerning the role of textbooks in learning. Much recent research has described how teachers' thought processes, which drive classroom teaching behaviors, are influenced by classroom experience (Clark & Peterson, 1986).

For example, Calderhead's research using student teachers, beginning teachers, and experienced teachers (Calderhead, 1981, 1983) has indicated that more experienced teachers have more complex knowledge structures concerning the nature of their students, allowing them to anticipate needed instructional adjustments for optimal learning. Likewise, there is evidence that degree of experience plays a role in teachers' elaborated knowledge of what actually happens in classrooms (Clark & Peterson, 1986). Such knowledge would presumably assist secondary teachers in designing optimal content learning lessons.

Against this backdrop, our study questioned the effect of teaching experience on content teachers' use of textbooks in the classroom. Specifically our research question was: How do teachers at three levels of teaching experience (preservice, beginning, and experienced) differ in their reported use of textbook materials?

Sixty-one secondary teachers, grouped according to teaching experience, participated in this study. The experienced teacher group (N = 21) had 6 or more years of service. The beginning teacher group (N = 15) had 1 to 5 years of teaching experience. The preservice teacher group (N = 25) were all senior undergraduate students. All subjects volunteered to participate in the study.

A survey instrument validated by Davey (1988) was employed in this new study. Items were designed to tap use of textbooks and instructional practices.

Thirteen items asked teachers to rate the frequency of their use of particular strategies and practices, using a scale of 1 to 4 (rarely or never, occasionally, frequently, or most of the time). The survey also included five open-ended questions requesting information on textbook selection, typical classroom use of text, and attitudes towards content area texts. Subjects were asked to respond thoughtfully and honestly to the survey items without conferring with other teachers. The task was completed anonymously and was untimed.

The five open-ended questions were scored independently by two raters blind to subjects' teaching experience. First, verbatim responses were place on individual index cards. Response categories were set when two or more teachers provided acceptable examplars.

For example, several teachers provided the following responses to Question 2, How do you typically use your textbooks?: "Have students read aloud," "assign reading and assignments based on reading," "I would have reading from the text at home and in class," "I ask students to read a selection." All such response examples were coded as representing the assigned reading category.

Two raters verified the categories and examples with a .89 proportion of agreement. Discrepancies were resolved through discussion.

Table 1
How secondary school content area teachers rate their uses of their class textbook

Survey items	Teachers' mean ratings of textbook uses, with (standard deviations)		
	Preservice teachers	Beginning teachers (1-5 years)	Experienced teachers (6 or more years)
1. I give students time to read the text silently in class.	1.96 (.84)	2.53 (1.06)	2.90** (1.26)
2. I use one textbook primarily.	2.52 (1.04)	2.93 (1.27)	2.23 (1.22)
3. I teach students how to use the textbook.	2.52 (.96)	2.60 (1.18)	3.14* (1.15)
4. I assign students only portions of the text to read.	3.00 (1.00)	3.26 (1.16)	3.19 (1.03)
5. I give independent homework assignments from the text.	3.00 (.76)	2.73 (.88)	2.66 (1.15)
6. I have students answer questions at the end of the chapter.	2.76 (.92)	3.26 (.70)	2.23** (1.09)
7. I use different texts with different students.	2.00 (1.00)	2.33 (1.29)	2.28 (1.18)
8. I rely on text information for my lectures or discussions.	2.84 (.98)	2.80 (1.14)	2.04** (.97)
9. I overview the text selection before giving an assignment.	3.68 (.47)	3.13 (.99)	3.61 (.86)
10. I ask students to read from the text orally.	2.52 (.91)	2.33 (.81)	1.92 (1.02)
11. I change texts when I see students can't read them well.	2.28 (1.06)	2.00 (1.19)	2.33 (1.23)
12. I give text assignments for students to work in small groups or teams.	2.00 (.86)	2.46 (.63)	2.52 (1.07)
13. I expect students to read most of the text.	2.48 (1.12)	2.40 (.98)	2.57 (1.28)

Note: Ratings were on a 1-4 scale, where 1 = rarely or never. 2 = occasionally, 3 = frequently, and 4 = most of the time.
*$p<.10$
**$p<.05$

Each item was scored for frequency of category information for each subject. When subjects provided information germane to more than one category for an item, it was scored as a proportion (i.e., .33 would be the score for one category from three responses to a single item).

Experience tells

Table 1 presents mean frequencies and standard deviations for the 13 survey items by the three groups of subjects.

A one-way multivariate analysis of variance procedure was conducted using each scale item as a sepa-

Table 2
Teacher responses to open-ended questions about textbook selection and use

Survey questions and categories of free responses	Mean proportion of responses in each category		
	Preservice teachers	Beginning teachers (1-5 years)	Experienced teachers (6 or more years)
1. How are your text materials selected?			
By country, state, district decision	.33	.18	.33
Principal, department chairperson	.11	.09	.06
School or department committee	.11	.27	.25
Primarily the teacher	.30	.41	.37
2. How do you typically use your textbook?			
Supplement instruction	.32	.50	.21
Discussion/group work	.04	.02	.08
As a source of activities	.11	.17	.23
Assigned reading outside class	.23	.17	.15
As a guide, outline, or basis for lectures and instruction	.23	.09	.32
3. What things keep you from the most effective use of your textbook?			
Time constraints	.07	.21	.23
Student characteristics	.27	.15	.31
System requirements	.18	.06	.04
Text limitations	.20	.35	.17
My limitations	.00	.00	.04
4. What do you like about your textbooks?			
Content	.37	.36	.33
Organization of ideas	.07	.13	.11
Visuals, graphics, print	.11	.07	.14
Questions and activities	.06	.12	.08
Readability	.20	.15	.20
5. What do you dislike about your textbooks?			
Content	.45	.35	.22
Organization of ideas	.00	.09	.06
Visuals, graphics, print	.02	.00	.02
Questions and activities	.10	.09	.17
Readability	.00	.06	.00

Note: Response to a question was valued at 1. If a teacher gave more than one category of response to a single question, the value was divided among those response categories.

rate dependent variable. When multivariate effects were statistically significant using a Wilks' lambda statistic, univariate analyses were performed for each survey item. All statistical tests were conducted at $p<.05$.

Overall, a significant multivariate effect was found for teacher experience, $F(26,92)=1.99$, $p<.009$. Univariate analyses and post hoc Scheffe tests revealed significant effects for the following survey items:

Item 1. I give students time to read the text silently in class, $F(2,58)=4.6$, $p<.013$. Preservice teachers rated this lower than did experienced teachers.

Item 6. I have students answer questions at the end of the chapter, $F(2,58)=5.3$, $p<.008$. Beginning teachers rated this higher than most experienced teachers.

Item 8. I rely on text information for my lectures or discussions, $F(2,58)=3.9$, $p<.0244$. Experienced teachers rated this lower than beginning or preservice teachers.

Table 2 depicts mean proportions of teacher responses to open-ended items according to categories of information provided. Across the five open-ended items, 79% of all responses could be coded according to our framework of information categories.

The major difference between experienced and less experienced teachers on open-ended questions appeared to be the degree to which less experienced teachers depend on the textbook to structure their classrooms. Although on the scaled questions experienced teachers did not appear to assign much reading, in the open-ended questions experienced teachers reported providing more time for in-class reading and using the text less often as a supplement to instruction. Experienced teachers tended to use the texts as a source of lecture topics and activities.

Overall, degree of teaching experience appeared to play an important role in several aspects of textbook use in secondary content classrooms.

There was evidence from the scale items that more experienced teachers may teach students how to use the textbooks more frequently than do either preservice or beginning teachers and that they may be more likely to employ group or team learning strategies than do less experienced teachers. These descriptive findings await further empirical verification with perhaps larger groups of teachers.

The open-ended responses indicated that most teachers, regardless of experience, rarely used their textbooks as a source of discussion or for group work. Teachers were most likely to use the text to supplement instruction or as a basis for lectures. Only 18% of the total sample indicated that they used the text for assigned reading outside the classroom.

The overall results from this survey are thus quite congruent with the findings and observations reported elsewhere (Alvermann & Hayes, 1989; Davey, 1988; Hinchman, 1987; Lipton & Liss, 1978; Rieck, 1977). Indeed, the description provided by Smith and Feathers (1983a, 1983b) and Ratekin, Simpson, Alvermann, and Dishner (1985) of a teacher-as-information-giver in the classroom has been supported to some degree by what teachers reported here.

Why is it that these teachers overall reported that they used the text so little for assigned reading or discussion? Table 2 suggests that student characteristics and text limitations prevent many teachers (48% of this sample) from the most effective use of their textbooks. But there is another unexplored influence, also related to text use, that has not been mentioned in the literature.

When responding to the open-ended questions concerning what they liked or disliked about their texts, 49% of the teachers in this survey indicated that content and readability were important text characteristics. However, it has been pointed out previously (Barrett, 1989) that teachers are often not instrumental in text selection. Realizing that teacher use of text might be related to the text selection process, we reanalyzed the ratings provided by the two groups of teachers currently teaching (beginning and experienced).

In the reanalysis we categorized the ratings of these two groups according to the proximity of the selection process to the teachers actually using the text. We developed two categories: (1) text selected at the state, county, district, or principal level, and (2) text selected by school or department committee, department chairperson, or individual teacher. We also examined the teachers' responses to the open-ended questions (questions 4 and 5) soliciting information about what the teachers liked or disliked about their textbooks. From this information we categorized the teachers as providing neutral, positive, or negative evaluations of their texts.

For teachers who had their text chosen at the state, county, district, or principal level, we found that 77% indicated either a negative (42%) or a neutral (35%) evaluation of their texts. Of this same group, only 8% said they used their text for assigned reading.

On the other hand, for teachers reporting that the text is chosen by the school or department committee, department chairperson, or the individual teacher, we found that only 12% indicated a negative evaluation of their text and 36% a neutral evaluation. Also of this group, 21% reported using the text for assigned reading. This figure is nearly three times that reported by teachers who have their text externally selected.

These findings suggest that teachers might have been more involved in the effective use of textbooks in their classrooms if they were more closely involved in the text selection/adoption process.

This survey did not find much evidence of reading strategy instruction occurring in the secondary classroom, and overall it appeared that text reading is not heavily promoted in U.S. content area classrooms regardless of teacher experience level. Our survey results suggest that one reason is that teachers need to be more involved in the text adoption process. Further research may illuminate other factors and help determine what explicit or implicit strategy instruction is occurring. Thorough interviews and observations of classroom teachers could provide important information concerning their attitudes toward and practices with text materials.

References

Apple, M.W. (1992). The text and cultural politics. *Educational Researcher, 21,* 4-11.

Alvermann, D.E., & Hayes, D.A. (1989). Classroom discussion of content area reading assignments: An intervention study. *Reading Research Quarterly, 25,* 296-322.

Barrett, M. (1989). Textbooks and teachers: A new relationship in reform. *Momentum, 38,* 45-47.

Calderhead, J. (1981). A psychological approach to research on teachers' classroom decision-making. *British Educational Research Journal, 7,* 51-57.

Calderhead, J. (1983, April). *Research into teachers' and student teachers' cognitions: Exploring the nature of classroom practice.*

Paper presented at the annual meeting of the American Educational Research Association, Montreal, Quebec, Canada.

Clark, C.M., & Peterson, P.L. (1986). Teachers' thought processes. In M.C. Wittrock (Ed.), *Handbook of research on teaching.* New York: Macmillan.

Conley, M.W. (1987). Teacher decision-making. In D.E. Alvermann, D.W. Moore, & M.W. Conley (Eds.), *Research within reach: Secondary school reading* (pp. 142-152). Newark, DE: International Reading Association.

Davey, B. (1988). How do classroom teachers use their text books? *Journal of Reading, 31,* 340-345.

Dillon, D.R. (1989). Showing them that I want them to learn and that I care about who they are: A microethnography of the social organization of a secondary, low-track English reading classroom. *American Education Research Journal, 26,* 227-259.

Gee, T.C., & Forester, N. (1988). Moving reading instruction beyond the reading classroom. *Journal of Reading, 31,* 505-511.

Hinchman, K. (1987). The textbook and three content-area teachers. *Reading Research Quarterly, 26,* 247-263.

Holdzkom, D. (1987). Readability. In D.E. Alvermann, D.W. Moore, & M.W. Conley (Eds.), *Research within reach: Secondary school reading* (pp. 80-92). Newark, DE: International Reading Association.

Lipton, J.P., & Liss, J.A. (1978). Attitudes of content area teachers towards reading. *Reading Improvement, 15,* 294-299.

Moore, D., & Murphy, A. (1987). Selection of materials. In D.E. Alvermann, D.W. Moore, & M.W. Conley (Eds.), *Research within reach: Secondary school reading* (pp. 94-108). Newark, DE: International Reading Association.

Ratekin, N., Simpson, M.L., Alvermann, D.E., & Dishner, E.K. (1985). Why teachers resist content reading instruction. *Journal of Reading, 28,* 432-437.

Rieck, B.J. (1977). How content area teachers telegraph messages against reading. *Journal of Reading, 28,* 646-648.

Smith, F.R., & Feathers, K.M. (1983a). The role of reading in content classrooms: Assumption vs. reality. *Journal of Reading, 27,* 262-267.

Smith, F.R., & Feathers, K.M. (1983b). Teacher and student perceptions of content area reading. *Journal of Reading, 26,* 348-354.

Spiegel, D.L., & Wright, J.D. (1984). Biology teachers' preferences in textbook characteristics. *Journal of Reading, 27,* 624-628.

Menke is a graduate student at the University of Maryland, College Park, and an instructional aide for Montgomery County Public Schools, Maryland. She can be contacted at 6322 Walhonding Road, Bethesda MD 20816, USA. Davey teaches at the University of Maryland, College Park, USA.

From *Journal of Reading* Vol. 37, No. 6, March 1994, pages 464-470. Copyright © 1994 by The International Reading Association. Reprinted with permission.

Teacher-Directed and Student-Mediated Textbook Comprehension Strategies

Describes a variety of teacher-directed and student-mediated strategies that can improve the text comprehension skills of mainstreamed students.

Catharine J. Reynolds
Spencer J. Salend

Students spend a considerable amount of time using textbooks both during regular class time and homework time. Studies indicate that 70% to 90% of classroom teachers' decisions are based on the textbook (Muther, 1985). Therefore, it is critical that teachers employ instructional strategies to help mainstreamed students comprehend information presented in print.

A variety of strategies are available to assist mainstreamed students in gaining information from textbooks. Some of these strategies are teacher directed, requiring the teacher to modify the text or create additional instructional materials to accompany the text. Others are mediated by students and provide students with a systematic approach to reading and understanding without teacher intervention. Both types of strategies are designed to enable students to process information and focus on critical ideas. Both must be used in the context of effective instruction.

The purpose of this article is to present and describe teacher directed and student-mediated text comprehension strategies. Additionally, guidelines for assessing the treatment acceptability or reasonableness of these strategies from the teachers' perspective will be discussed.

Teacher-Directed Strategies

When mainstreamed students have reading scores below grade level, teachers have a variety of options available to ensure student success. Teachers may decide to have these students use the same textbook as the rest of the class and use supplementary materials that provide an organizational structure for gaining important information.

One such technique is constructing a preliminary overview such as an advance organizer or preview for the material to be read (Lenz, 1983). These overviews direct student attention to main ideas, critical concepts, new vocabulary, and important facts or relationships necessary to an overall understanding of the subject presented. By placing basic words, phrases, or sentences on an overhead transparency or blackboard, or by providing each student with a handout of the overview, teachers can briefly describe those ideas that may be new to students and relate the information to prior experiences. For example, a timeline of geologic eras or a partially completed plot outline of a short story might assist students in learning essential concepts and relationships as they read. Constructing such a framework also helps teachers to clarify for themselves which information they want to emphasize for lecture, discussion, and testing purposes.

A study guide is another accommodation that may assist students in text comprehension by emphasizing major headings and cueing students to respond to specific parts of the text. A study guide usually requires students to respond to questions in the order in which the concepts appear in the text. Sometimes text page numbers are placed next to each question to help students locate information. Teachers may decide to prepare a study guide for all students and mark those questions that relate to critical content. Mainstreamed students could contract for a grade of C on the condition that they successfully complete those questions on the study guide and similar test questions.

A similar organizational tool is an outline of the chapter containing major headings, subheadings, and details. Initially, a teacher can construct a slot outline that omits only key words from the outline. Eventually, the number of words provided can be faded to a skeletal outline so that students decide which concepts are critical to their comprehension. The outline structure also can be taught to students in the context of taking lecture notes.

Teachers can also use a semantic feature analysis (SFA) to facilitate text comprehension (Bos, Anders, Filip, & Jaffe, 1989). Initially, teachers delineate the content into superordinate, coordinate and subordinate concepts and vocabulary. A relationship chart is then developed by listing the superordinate concept as the title, the coordinate concepts as important ideas across the top of the chart, and the subordinate concepts down the left margin of the chart. Before reading the selection, students define key terminology and important ideas in their own minds. Then, using the relationship chart, students predict the relationship between the key terms and the main ideas as positive (+), negative (–), none (0), or unknown (?).

Color coding is another teacher-directed strategy that may assist students in focusing on critical information. In color coding words or sentences, Wood and Wooley (1986) suggest that teachers ask themselves if the material is something the student should retain one, or five, years from now. Highlighter pens of at least three different colors can be used, one color for important terms, another for definitions, and a third for significant facts. The teacher can highlight one text and then allow students to highlight their own texts or just refer to the highlighted text when reading or answering questions. This procedure must be cleared with a school administrator since books are permanently altered.

For those students whose poor decoding skills detract considerably from their ability to comprehend, it may be necessary to tape the text or read it orally. Rose and Beattie (1986) found that listening to a prerecorded tape of material or the teachers' oral reading prior to reading aloud improved students' accuracy rate in oral reading. Although a straight reading can be helpful to students who learn best by listening, comprehension can be fostered by inserting summaries, emphasizing vocabulary words, explaining graphic information, or instructing students to listen for answers to specific questions (Wood & Wooley, 1986).

Another approach is to have a peer read the text whose reading skills are at or above grade level. This might be done in the context of a cooperative learning task so that the listener would be given the task of recording answers

to questions found in a study guide or at the end of the chapter. Community volunteers or older students who are considering teaching as a future profession also might be enlisted as readers.

"Preliminary overviews direct student attention to main ideas, critical concepts, new vocabulary, and important facts or relationships necessary to an overall understanding of the subject presented."

Because of the need for content area textbooks with low readability, more publishers have been producing texts or workbooks that can serve as acceptable alternatives for students who, even with the previously mentioned modifications, are not able to succeed in the regular classroom. If the alternative text closely parallels the standard text, teachers may find this to be a workable strategy.

However, if salient information is not covered in the alternative text, teachers may want to reconstruct the standard text. This may be done in several ways. Teachers can indicate to students that they need to read only specific parts of chapters, or they can reproduce the pages, deleting extraneous information. Another strategy found to be effective in improving comprehension is to insert a question prior to or after each paragraph or section (Wong, 1979, 1980).

A final alternative is to rewrite part or all of the text. This is a labor-intensive task and should be done with teachers who are given training for how to lower readability and additional paid time beyond the regular school day. It is important that cohesive ties such as coordinate and subordinate conjunctions not be eliminated from the text under the assumption that fewer words and simpler sentences translate into easier reading. Clear pronoun reference and word substitution contribute to the understanding of relationships that promote comprehension (Armbruster & Anderson, 1988). Signal words within the text (e.g., first, second, next) or numbered lists in a vertical format also can clarify the order inherent in concepts. Furthermore, text comprehension is improved when a topic sentence for each paragraph is easily identifiable and the final sentence makes a logical transition to the next paragraph. Frequent boldfaced headings that accurately describe the subsequent text are helpful during initial reading and later review. Wood and Wooley (1986) provide additional excellent guidelines for simplifying the readability of text.

> "For example, a timeline of geologic eras or a partially completed plot outline of a short story might assist students in learning essential concepts and relationships as they read."

Graphic information can be a valuable addition to print. However, some figures or charts are excerpted from other sources, with little attempt to explain the content and format or relate to the text. The meaning of graphics should be self-evident (e.g., via captions, symbols, or labels) and should be referred to at the appropriate place within the text. Questions regarding maps, graphs, or tables should be embedded in the text so that all types of visual presentations become valuable learning tools.

Text modification also may involve the use of technology to supplement or substitute parts of the text. Printed materials have been adapted into computer software programs that assist students in mastering content (Burnette, 1987). Computer-assisted instruction (CAI), which presents textbook material in a concise and interesting format, is increasingly more available. Well designed CAI presents text in organized, logical sections followed by a strategy prompt to remind students to answer a related question or practice a skill (Keene & Davey, 1987). Also, programs that integrate videos with computer programs such as *The Voyage of the Mimi* (Burns, Hawkins, & Midian-Kurland, 1985) can be worthwhile supplements to textbook materials. Programs that are interactive allow for frequent feedback, remediation, and multiple correct answers. Similarly, video disc technology that follows the principles of good curriculum design can enhance the efficiency of the learning process (Carnine, 1989).

Student-Mediated Strategies

Student-initiated strategies do not require teachers to spend as much preparatory time modifying materials as do teacher-directed strategies. However, it is essential that these strategies be taught to students in a systematic fashion so that they eventually will be able to apply them to multiple situations. Once students are identified as needing to learn a reading comprehension strategy, they must be convinced that the learning strategy will benefit them.

Some students may have already acquired or developed inefficient strategies. Assessment should involve an identification of the components of the strategy that students are currently implementing. Then it is possible to determine which aspects of an efficient strategy are missing or which unnecessary steps students are employing. This can be done by asking students to work through a comprehension task out loud. By identifying those steps of an efficient strategy that students are already using, the teacher can save time in instruction and help students develop their strengths.

Acquisition of efficient strategies depends on use of sound learning principles such as the teaching sequence suggested by the staff of the University of Kansas Institute (Schumaker et al., 1983). After assessment and task analysis of the strategy, the teacher should model each step aloud for the students. For example, the teacher might skim through a chapter pointing out boldfaced headings, new vocabulary, or graphic material, and making predictions about the general content being covered or formulating questions to be answered while reading. Then the students should verbally rehearse the steps until they are able to explain them easily in the proper order. Next, students are ready to apply the steps to controlled materials, those that are written on their independent reading level. Once an established criterion level is obtained, students can practice the strategy on the regular classroom test. It is particularly helpful if the strategy is taught or reinforced by the regular classroom teacher at the beginning of the year or semester. Then the teacher can provide feedback as to which steps students need to relearn or practice further to mastery.

Perhaps the best known and most longstanding strategy for teaching students to approach content systematically is SQ3R (Robinson, 1961). The acronym represents five steps:

1. **S**urvey. Scan the entire reading assignment, noting headings, topic sentences, summaries, maps, tables, or pictures to get an overview of the material.
2. **Q**uestion. Formulate questions by rephrasing headings or captions to establish reader expectancies that can then be confirmed or altered.
3. **R**ead. Read to answer the questions, taking notes if necessary.
4. **R**ecite. Answer the questions without reference to text or notes in order to test comprehension and store in memory.
5. **R**eview. Reread text and notes in areas that were not clearly explained and enumerate major headings and ideas.

A similar strategy developed at the University of Kansas Institute for Learning Disabled Students is Multipass (Schumaker, Deshler, Alley, Warner, & Denton, 1982). The strategy includes three steps or "passes":

1. *Survey Pass.* As in SQ3R, students read only titles, headings, illustrations, chapter summaries, and so forth. They then paraphrase the information gained in skimming.
2. *Size-Up Pass.* Students read the chapter questions and determine which ones they can't answer. Rather than read the entire text, students skim the chapter, using headings as cues, and locate the an-

swer. They then orally paraphrase the answer, without reference to the text.

3. *Sort-Out Pass.* Students test themselves on the chapter questions, checking off those they can answer immediately and returning to the text to locate forgotten information.

Idol (1987) has found that a critical thinking map is successful with high school students who have reading comprehension difficulty but adequate word recognition skills. Students use a critical thinking map that allows them to make interpretations of the text as opposed to predictions about what will happen next. The map includes *five* components the students must complete:

1. *Important Events.* The salient events, points, or steps that are explicitly stated in the text are recorded in one of several formats: compare/contrast, pro/con, or chronologically.

2. *Main Idea/Lesson.* The implicit or explicit message of the text is stated.

3. *Other Viewpoints/Opinions.* Readers use their background knowledge to supply additional information the author may not have stated.

4. *Reader's Conclusions.* Readers decide whether the author's conclusions are valid.

5. *Relevance to Today.* The readers draw conclusions between past and present events.

As described previously, this strategy must be taught using teacher modeling, practice, and feedback. Students should be able to use the strategy independently and respond to questions regarding each part of the critical thinking map.

Students also can increase their text comprehension skills by using self-questioning techniques (Clark, Deshler, Schumaker, Alley, & Warner, 1984). Clark et al. (1984) devised a self-questioning procedure in which students (a) formulate *who, what, where, when,* and *why* questions; (b) delineate question types with symbols; and (c) mark the correct answers within the selections with a corresponding symbol. Additional self-questioning procedures have been developed by Wong and Jones (1982) and Wong, Wong, Perry, and Sawatsky (1986).

Some students may benefit from use of paraphrasing (Schumaker, Denton, & Deshler, 1984). While reading a selection, students respond in their own words to questions they have identified as relating to the text's main points. It is important that paraphrased statements be complete and logical sentences.

Treatment Acceptability

In selecting an appropriate strategy to modify text comprehension, educators need to consider several factors. One critical factor is treatment acceptability (Martens,

Peterson, Witt, & Cirone, 1986). Treatment acceptability relates to the degree to which educators feel a teaching strategy is easy to implement.

Brown (1988) identified reasonableness as another variable in assessing treatment acceptability. She defined reasonableness with respect to (a) the amount of time it requires for teachers to develop and implement the strategy, (b) the compatibility of the strategy with the teacher's teaching style, and (c) the cost of the strategy. Examining the impact of the instructional modification on the targeted student and other classroom peers also is an important dimension of treatment acceptability (Salend, in press).

The student-mediated and teacher-directed text comprehension strategies previously discussed vary in their treatment acceptability. In general, student-mediated strategies tend to be less time-consuming to develop, less intrusive, and less costly for teachers. However, they may not be as effective as teacher-directed strategies because students may fail to implement them properly or to apply them to a variety of appropriate situations. Similarly, teacher-directed strategies may be time-consuming to develop but easy to implement. Therefore, in determining the treatment acceptability of an instructional strategy, educators should address the following:

1. What are the student's strengths, weaknesses, and unique needs?

2. Given the student's strengths, weaknesses, and unique needs, is the proposed instructional modification likely to be effective?

3. How much time does it take to develop and implement the instructional modification?

4. How does the presentation mode of the instructional modification affect the student's performance and the teacher's style?

5. How does the response mode of the instructional modification affect the student's performance and the teacher's style?

6. Is the proposed instructional modification consistent with the integrity of the course and the grading system?

7. What is the impact of the instructional modification on the targeted student? Other students?

Summary

In order to benefit from instruction, mainstreamed students need to be able to gain information from textbooks and other print materials. This article reviewed a range of teacher-directed and student-mediated strategies that can be employed to improve the text comprehension skills of mainstreamed students. Teachers should consider several factors in selecting appropriate text comprehension strategies for their mainstreamed students.

References

Armbruster, B.B., & Anderson, T.M. (1988). On selecting considerate content area textbooks. *Remedial and Special Education, 9*(1), 47–52.

Bos, C.S., Anders, P.L., Filip, D., & Jaffe, L.E. (1989). The effects of an interactive instructional strategy for enhancing reading comprehension and content area learning for students with learning disabilities. *Journal of Learning Disabilities, 22*, 384–390.

Brown, J. (1988, March). *Preventing classroom failure: Small modifications make a big difference.* Paper presented at a meeting of the Council for Exceptional Children, Washington, DC.

Burnette, J.M. (1987). *Adapting instructional materials for mainstreamed students.* Reston VA: Council for Exceptional Children.

Burns, G., Hawkins, J., & Midian-Kurland, D. (1985). *The voyage of the Mimi.* New York: Holt, Rinehart & Winston.

Carnine, D. (1989). Teaching complex content to learning disabled students: The role of technology. *Exceptional Children, 55*, 524–532.

Clark, F., Deshler, D.D., Schumaker, J.B., Alley, G., & Warner, M. (1984). Visual imagery and self-questioning: Strategies to improve comprehension of written material. *Journal of Learning Disabilities, 17*, 145–149.

Idol, L. (1987). A critical thinking map to improve content area comprehension of poor readers. *Remedial and Special Education, 8*(4), 28–40.

Keene, S., & Davey, B. (1987). Effects of computer-presented text on LD adolescents' reading behaviors. *Learning Disability Quarterly, 70*, 283–290.

Lenz, B.K. (1983). Using advance organizers. *The Pointer, 27*(2), 11–13.

Martens, B.K., Peterson, R.L., Witt, J.C., & Cirone, S., (1986). Teacher perceptions of school-based interventions. *Exceptional Children, 53*, 213–223.

Muther, C. (1985). What every textbook evaluator should know. *Educational Leadership, 42*, 4–8.

Robinson, F.P. (1961). *Effective study.* New York: Harper & Row.

Rose, T.L., & Beattie, J.R. (1986). Relative effects of teacher-directed and taped previewing on oral reading. *Learning Disability Quarterly, 9*, 193–199.

Salend, S.J. (in press). *Effective mainstreaming.* New York: Macmillan.

Schumaker, J.B., Denton, P.H., & Deshler, D.D. (1984). *The paraphrasing strategy.* Lawrence: University of Kansas.

Schumaker, J.B., Deshler, D.D., Alley, G.R., & Warner, M.M. (1983). Toward the development of an intervention model for learning disabled adolescents: The University of Kansas Institute. *Exceptional Education Quarterly, 4*(1), 45–74.

Schumaker, J.B., Deshler, D.D., Alley, G.R., Warner, M.M., & Denton, P.H. (1982). Multipass: A learning strategy for improving reading comprehension. *Learning Disability Quarterly, 5*, 295–304.

Wong, B.Y.L. (1979). Increasing retention of main ideas through questioning strategies. *Learning Disability Quarterly, 2*, 42–47.

Wong, B.Y.L. (1980). Activating the inactive learner: Use of questions/prompts to enhance comprehension and retention of implied information in learning disabled children. *Learning Disability Quarterly, 3*, 29–37.

Wong, B.Y.L., & Jones, W. (1982). Increasing metacomprehension in learning disabled and normally achieving students through self-questioning training. *Learning Disability Quarterly, 5*, 228–240.

Wong, B.Y.L., Wong, R., Perry, N., & Sawatsky, D. (1986). The efficacy of a self-questioning summarization strategy for use by underachievers and learning disabled adolescents in social studies. *Learning Disabilities Focus, 2*, 20–35.

Wood, J.W., & Wooley, J.A. (1986). Adapting textbooks. *The Clearing House, 59*, 332–335.

Catharine J. Reynolds, PhD, is currently an assistant professor in the Special Education Program at SUNY/The College at New Paltz. **Spencer J. Salend,** EdD, is currently a professor in the Special Education Program at SUNY/The College at New Paltz. Address: Catharine J. Reynolds, SUNY/The College at New Paltz, 307 Old Main Bldg., New Paltz, NY 12561.

From *Academic Therapy* Vol. 25, No. 4, March 1990, pages 417-427. Copyright © 1990 by PRO-ED, Inc. Reprinted with permission.

The Directed Questioning Activity for subject matter text

Randall James Ryder

Subject matter curricula often require teachers to use texts containing concepts and vocabulary unfamiliar to students. In this situation, students' comprehension can be improved by means of various instructional techniques. Prior to reading, teaching vocabulary (Omanson, 1985; Stahl, Jacobson, Davis, & Davis, 1989) or presenting main concepts (Barron, 1969; Hayes & Tierney, 1982; Slater, 1985) can improve students' overall understanding. During reading, strategies employing study guides and teacher-directed questioning may be useful for promoting background knowledge, establishing a purpose for reading, and facilitating various levels of comprehension.

The Directed Questioning Activity (DQA) introduced here is a teacher-directed questioning strategy to be used in class with subject matter textbooks containing unfamiliar or difficult concepts. The activity acknowledges the difficulty many students experience with higher level comprehension questions, the need for teachers to guide students in responding to these questions, and students' need to develop their own comprehension strategies. The DQA's purpose is to help students improve their understanding of text through the use of advance cognitive organizers and question placement strategies and through the teacher's posing of higher level comprehension questions. Initially the DQA is highly directed by the teacher,

but as students acquire an understanding of its inherent strategies, the teacher gradually transfers instructional responsibility to them. The DQA should help students achieve goals the teacher sets for them and lead to successful reading experiences that increase students' knowledge in a given subject—knowledge that will eventually assist them to apply comprehension strategies independently.

The components of the DQA are based on a number of observations. First, the DQA is designed to be used with expository text, which is more common than other sorts of text (Just & Carpenter, 1987) and is also usually organized according to a hierarchical structure of main ideas and supporting details that can provide obstacles to comprehension (Taylor, 1982). Teacher-directed questions can lead students to better understand concepts in exposition and provide them with strategies for dealing with text's structure.

A second observation underlying the DQA recognizes that when students read to answer the teacher's questions, their attention to the reading and their understanding of information targeted by the questions improves (Reynolds & Anderson, 1982). Furthermore, questions provided by the teacher facilitate the recall of details and main ideas more than do questions generated by students (Andre & Anderson, 1978-1979).

Rationale

While the DQA may appear similar to Stauffer's (1969) Directed Reading-Thinking Activity (DRTA), it is distinct in a number of ways. First, the DRTA directs students to make predictions or define their own purpose for reading narrative text by generating open-ended questions. With the DQA, on the other hand, the teacher defines students' purpose for reading and asks questions throughout the reading. By directing students' attention to certain text elements in this way, the teacher attempts to relate specific text details to the students' own prior knowledge. Through these structured questions and the teacher's modeling of responses for higher level questions, students will develop their own strategy for comprehending expository text.

Second, the DQA, unlike the DRTA, actively promotes student comprehension monitoring by allowing the teacher to direct learning through instruction that focuses on restructuring information in text. Because students tend to pay attention when the teacher asks the questions, strategies to promote higher level thinking can be prepared well in advance of the lesson. The DRTA, on the other hand, encourages students to make their own predictions and set individual purposes for reading. Providing all students with immediate feedback on their individual predictions can be difficult to manage, and the teacher's attention to strategies may be limited to those that students might develop spontaneously.

Finally, the DQA directs students to monitor comprehension of information and then directs them to engage in what Aulls (1982) refers to as "backward inferencing." During this backward inferencing students seek to clarify, confirm, or infer meaning from the linking of new and old information, thereby expanding their understanding of text.

Components

The DQA consists of two instructional components: text explicit and text implicit instruction. In text explicit instruction, various activities are presented prior to reading to promote students' comprehension; text implicit instruction presents activities during reading to focus students' attention on key concepts and to promote higher level thinking skills. The teacher, therefore, initially assumes the role of facilitating students' text understanding, then gradually begins to coach students in their collaborative and individual efforts to apply selected strategies.

Text explicit instruction. In this component of the DQA, the teacher provides students with an overview of concepts or vocabulary contained in a portion of the reading assignment. First, the teacher identifies the reading objectives. The teacher then surveys the text to identify concepts that may best be grouped for instruction. Finally, the teacher determines if supplemental information is needed.

While a number of instructional activities are useful for previewing concepts or vocabulary prior to reading, the DQA is best suited to use of the structured overview (Barron, 1969), a graphic representation of concepts or vocabulary that displays content deemed important by the teacher. In this presentation, information is organized from general to specific. The overview can contain information that is absent from the text or can supplement text information that may be unclear to students.

Figure 1 gives an example of the steps a teacher may take in establishing goals for reading and designing a structured overview with a selection on photosynthesis.

Adhering to certain guidelines when designing the structured overview will increase the likelihood that it will assist students to comprehend the text and achieve the teacher's objectives. Teachers should consider the following when constructing the overview:

1. The overview should proceed from the general to the specific.
2. Categories should be displayed in a manner that places parallel content on the same visual plane. In Figure 1, step 3, the categories "Products for other living organisms" and "Products for the plant" are side by side to emphasize their equal importance.
3. The overview should present only content relevant to the teacher's objectives—it should not necessarily map the entire content of a given reading. If the text omits something relevant to the teacher's objective, that material should be included in the structured overview.
4. The overview should allow for student input and involvement. The overview is often more effective when students are allowed to contribute their knowledge to it. The teacher can leave certain portions of the overview blank and elicit students' background knowledge to fill in missing pieces. Students may also be asked to skim a reading once the overview has been presented, with the objective of finding additional information. The teacher can provide page and paragraph references to help students find appropriate portions of the reading.
5. The overview should display a minimal number of words. If an overview contains too many words, students are likely to become confused and overwhelmed

by visual information. It is better to present several simple, concise overviews than to use a single overview to display every piece of information.

When deciding on the content for a structured overview, teachers should not assume that the section or chapter divisions in a text translate into appropriate conceptual chunks. Teachers should instead rely on the objectives they have set for their students with a particular reading assignment and their awareness of their students' abilities and prior knowledge to design appropriate prereading activities.

Text implicit instruction. This stage of the DQA directs students to respond to questions as they read and to reread to gather information necessary to answer higher level comprehension questions. Questioning students during reading promotes active involvement with the text as well as increased comprehension, particularly for readers who may not otherwise reflect upon what they are reading (Anderson & Biddle, 1975; Graves & Clark, 1981). Such questions draw the reader's attention to objectives and help the reader to evaluate and categorize text information (Levin & Pressley, 1981).

The DQA suggests two types of questions to direct at students while they read. The first is the prequestion. Prequestions should not be confused with prereading questions that frequently require students to make a prediction or assess their background knowledge. Prequestions are presented to students immediately before they read portions of a text, for the purpose of providing the objective for reading. The questions are discussed only after the student has read the assigned passage.

The amount of reading required to answer a prequestion may vary from a paragraph to a number of pages, depending on the conceptual load of the text, the students' prior knowledge of the concepts it contains, and the objectives for reading. Students should be asked only one

Figure 1
Steps in text-explicit instruction

Step 1: Teacher identifies the following learning objectives:
  1. Students will understand the role of sunlight in the process of photosynthesis.
  2. Students will understand what products are produced by plants as a result of photosynthesis.
  3. Students will understand how plants store starch and sugar during the process of photosynthesis.
  4. Students will understand that the process of photosynthesis is vital to the survival of all plants and animals.
Step 2: Teacher examines concepts presented in text and chunks them for class presentation.
  Chunk 1: The products of photosynthesis.
  Chunk 2: The process of photosynthesis.
  Chunk 3: The role of photosynthesis in the food chain.
Step 3: Teacher creates a prereading activity to address each chunk. (The following overview addresses the first chunk.)

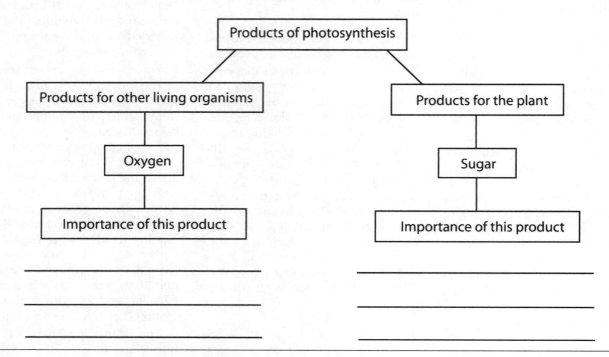

or two prequestions for each portion of a text assignment; too many questions can be distracting. Once the prequestions have been answered, students can focus on additional questions or reflect on the reading in order to respond to higher level questions.

The second type of question is the adjunct question, which is presented to students immediately after they have read a portion of the text. These questions cue the reader to reflect on a limited amount of text to emphasize particular details or concepts. This signaling of important points alerts the reader to information related to the teacher's objectives and draws the reader's attention to information that

may be necessary for understanding subsequent related concepts.

While both pre- and adjunct questions have been shown to enhance comprehension beyond the level that is achieved with traditional postreading questions (Anderson & Biddle, 1975), certain characteristics of both text and reader will dictate the type of question most likely to increase students' understanding. Prequestions appear to be more effective when (1) the text contains a high concept load, (2) the text is poorly written, or (3) it is desirable that students acquire a limited number of the concepts presented in the material. Prequestioning is generally also effective when teachers want to di-

rect students' attention to a specific objective during reading.

Adjunct questions appear to be more appropriate when (1) the text does not contain a high concept load, (2) it is desirable that students reflect on multiple concepts in the reading, (3) it is desirable to have students reread in response to higher level questions, and (4) it is desirable to have students link a series of questions that lead to a higher level of understanding.

To continue with the lesson dealing with photosynthesis, an example of the use of a prequestion and an adjunct question is shown in Figure 2. In this example, the prequestion directs students' attention to specific

Figure 2
Pre- and adjunct questions for a text passage

Teacher objectives
1. Students will understand the function of chloroplasts in the process of photosynthesis.
2. Students will understand how the process of photosynthesis aids plants in their survival.

Prequestion
What is the function of the chloroplasts in the process of photosynthesis?

Text excerpt

The process of photosynthesis

Photosynthesis is the food-making process that takes place in the leaves of plants. The process, which takes place only during the day, begins with the plant making use of the energy in sunlight. Light makes contact with the cells in the plant that contain chloroplasts. It is the green pigment in the plant's chloroplasts that absorbs the energy in light and converts it into chemical energy that is stored in the plant cells. In each plant cell, small bodies called chloroplasts draw water which the plant has removed from the soil. The water is split into atoms of hydrogen and oxygen inside the chloroplast. Through a chemical process, the hydrogen combines with carbon dioxide from the air and sugar is produced. Oxygen produced in this chemical process is given off by the plant. Sugar can be used by the plant immediately, or it can be converted into starch and stored in the plant for later use. Without photosynthesis, plants would be unable to produce the nutrients and oxygen which are essential to human survival.

Adjunct question
How does the process of photosynthesis allow the plant to survive during various types of climatic conditions? For example, how can plants survive a mild drought?

---

text concepts. This limits attention to specific ideas relative to the teacher's objectives.

The use of prequestions has several advantages. First, when text has a high conceptual load, the reader has opportunity to discard information not pertinent to the stated question. Second, prequestions improve students' recall of text information (Denner & Rickards, 1987).

Conversely, the use of prequestions also has limitations. Since their attention is directed to a limited number of concepts, students are less likely to acquire other text information.

Adjunct questions like those shown in Figure 2 can promote higher level thinking skills through a teacher-directed strategy of question "staging." Staging questions means directing students to reread in order to restructure information obtained from lower level questions and link that information to arrive at an inference.

Lower level questions can first be presented on an overhead projector, thereby limiting the number of questions under consideration and in-

creasing the likelihood that students will focus on the teacher's objectives. This is of particular importance with adjunct questions, since students tend to read the question and then read to locate an answer, much as with prequestions.

In the text excerpt shown in Figure 2, readers could first be asked a series of literal questions and then called on to use their answers to formulate a response to an inferential question. Figure 3 gives an example of this staging activity for our lesson on photosynthesis.

To introduce students to staged questions, the teacher should model the process with familiar text. This will increase the likelihood that students' attention will be directed to a strategy for constructing an inference rather than to the content addressed in the questions. This modeling should continue over a period of time with a variety of texts to allow students to observe staging over diverse content. Finally, the teacher can model the staging of an inference with content that may not be familiar. At this point, it is important for the teacher to elaborate his or her own

Figure 3
Staged questions

Adjunct question 1: What does the chloroplast do with the light energy provided by the sun?

Adjunct question 2: When does photosynthesis take place?

Adjunct question 3: Once the light energy is absorbed by the chloroplast, what does the plant do with it?

Inference question: Using the information obtained from the preceding questions, can you suggest why photosynthesis occurs only during the sunlight hours?

---

metacognitive processes for the students. The greater the detail provided by the teacher, the more likely students will acquire insight into the restructuring of literal information.

In noting the importance of metacognition, Roehler and Duffy (1984) have suggested the teacher provide students with tasks that guide comprehension by making them aware of what they know and don't know while they read. Staged questions provide this by first guiding students through the meaning-gathering process with literal level questions, then extending their comprehension through selective presentation of higher level questions. As students attempt to respond to staged questions, the teacher can provide additional guidance in arriving at inferential understanding.

The DQA in independent reading

The DQA as presented thus far is highly dependent on the teacher's ability to direct students' attention while reading expository text. Ultimately the goal of the DQA, however, is to increase students' ability to regulate their own reading. With guidance, students can learn to create and apply structured overviews and questioning strategies and to stage inferential understanding. In circumstances where a text contains numerous concepts, students have little background information, or if too many objectives are given, students' success during independent reading will be severely reduced. However, without an instructional framework that can be transferred from a classroom setting to a personal one (as can the DQA), the student will never succeed in becoming an independent thinker.

The DQA's transition from a teacher-directed to a self-regulated strategy can be achieved through teacher modeling and student collaborative modeling. The first step in the process, teacher modeling, requires a concise description of the purpose of the strategy and a recognition of students' level of back~ ground knowledge. Vocabulary, examples, and analogies used in modeling should be familiar to students. Suggestions for modeling the DQA strategies include the following:

• *Structured overviews.*
  1. Provide an oral summary of a portion of a reading assignment. From this summary, display terms and topics on the board or an overhead. Describe for students main and subordinate topics, placing these topics in ascending order visually. Using your background knowledge, present terms from the reading that describe attributes or characteristics of the topics and your rationale for selecting those terms. Place these terms under the appropriate topics.
  2. Have the students skim a passage to identify topics or concepts and note terms that are descriptive of those topics. Ask them to provide a rationale for the inclusion of those terms.

• *Pre- and adjunct questions.*
  1. Using the structured overview, generate questions that address its content. These questions can seek to clarify or extend information or can address causal relations.
  2. Demonstrate a process for generating adjunct questions that extend or elaborate on the information addressed in the prequestions.

• *Staged questions.*
  1. Summarize the information addressed in the pre- and adjunct questions. Note common concepts and attributes they address. Attempt to draw relationships between this information that could generate inferential questions.
  2. Formulate questions that go beyond information addressed in the pre- and adjunct questions by asking "What isn't directly stated in the reading that I would like to know about that topic or concept?" Demonstrate to students that they will not always arrive at an answer to this question with information stated in the text.

Once the teacher has repeatedly modeled the process of restructuring literal information to derive inferential understanding, students can engage in the DQA in groups. Thorough descriptions of the mechanics of structuring collaborative learning environments are provided by Slavin (1983) and Johnson and Johnson (1975). Applying a strategy in a collaborative group situation reduces the cognitive effort necessary from each individual and it allows each group member to observe others engaging in portions of thinking strategies that each must eventually apply independently (Brown & Palincsar, 1987).

Collaborative modeling mirrors the process described for teacher modeling. Following the steps modeled by the teacher, students assume the responsibility of assisting one another in the construction of structured overviews, pre- and adjunct questions, and staged questions. The teacher should monitor group progress closely and supplement the group modeling when difficulty is experienced. As each component of the DQA is addressed by the collaborative groups, they may describe their efforts to the entire class. This description provides additional insight into the strategies of the DQA and reviews lesson content that may not have been comprehended by a particular group.

Understanding and learning

The DQA provides students with a purpose for reading and initiates a process whereby readers begin to monitor their comprehension as they interact with text concepts. Unlike the Three Level Guide (Vacca & Vacca, 1989), the DQA stresses (1) asking questions of various levels rather than using statements and (2) posing pre- and adjunct questions during reading rather than presenting statements at the conclusion. The DQA is an instructional activity that acknowledges students' difficulty in dealing with subject matter text containing a high conceptual load or text that requires students to link concepts as they read. By advancing strategies that allow the teacher to direct the reader's attention to important concepts in a structured and sequential manner and by displaying a process for linking concepts to lead to higher level thinking, the DQA aids students' understanding of teacher-defined objectives and provides them with a strategy for learning from subject matter text.

References

Anderson, R.C., & Biddle, W.B. (1975). On asking the people what they are reading. In G.H. Bower (Ed.), *The psychology of learning and motivation* (vol. 9). New York: Academic.

Andre, M.E.D.A., & Anderson, T.H. (1978-1979). The development and evaluation of a self-questioning study technique. *Reading Research Quarterly, 14,* 605-623.

Aulls, M. (1982). *Developing readers in today's elementary school.* Boston, MA: Allyn & Bacon.

Barron, R. (1969). The use of vocabulary as an advance organizer. In H.L. Herber & P.L. Anderson (Eds.), *Research on reading in the content areas: First Report.* Syracuse, NY: Syracuse University Reading and Language Arts Center.

Brown, A.L., & Palincsar, A.S. (1987). Reciprocal teaching of comprehension strategies: A natural history of one program for enhancing learning. In

J.D. Day & J. Borkowski (Eds.), *Intelligence and exceptionality: New directions for theory, assessment and instructional practice* (pp. 81-132). Norwood, NJ: Ablex.

Denner, P.R., & Rickards, J.P. (1987). A developmental comparison of the effects of provided and generated questions on text recall. *Contemporary Educational Psychology, 12,* 135-146.

Graves, M.F., & Clark, D.L. (1981). Effects of adjunct questions on high school low achievers. *Reading Improvement, 18,* 8-13.

Hayes, D.A., & Tierney, R.J. (1982). Developing readers' knowledge through analogy. *Reading Research Quarterly, 17,* 256-280.

Johnson, D.W., & Johnson, R.T. (1975). *Learning together and alone.* Englewood Cliffs, NJ: Prentice Hall.

Just, M.A., & Carpenter, P.A. (1987). *The psychology of reading and language comprehension.* Boston, MA: Allyn & Bacon.

Levin, J.R., & Pressley, M. (1981). Improving children's prose comprehension: Selected strategies that seem to succeed. In C.M. Santa & B.L. Hayes (Eds.), *Children's prose comprehension: Research and practice.* Newark, DE: International Reading Association.

Omanson, R.C. (1985). Knowing words and understanding texts. In T.H. Carr (Ed.), *The development of reading skills* (New Directions for Child Development, No. 27, pp. 35-54). San Francisco, CA: Jossey-Bass.

Reynolds, R.E., & Anderson, R.C. (1982). Influence of questions on the allocation of attention during reading. *Journal of Educational Psychology, 7,* 623-632.

Roehler, L.R., & Duffy, G.G. (1984). Direct explanation of comprehension processes. In G. Duffy, L. Roehler, & J. Mason (Eds.), *Comprehension instruction.* White Plains, NY: Longman.

Slater, W.H. (1985). Teaching expository text structure with structural organizers. *Journal of Reading, 28,* 712-718.

Slavin, R.E. (1983). *Cooperative learning.* White Plains, NY: Longman.

Stahl, S., Jacobson, M.G., Davis, C.E., & Davis, R.L. (1989). Prior knowledge and difficult vocabulary in the comprehension of unfamiliar text. *Reading Research Quarterly, 24,* 27-43.

Stauffer, R. (1969). *Directing reading maturity as a cognitive process.* New York: Harper & Row.

Taylor, B. (1982). Text structure and children's comprehension and memory for expository material. *Journal of Educational Psychology, 74,* 323-340.

Vacca, R.T., & Vacca, J.R. (1989). *Content area reading* (3rd ed.). Glenview, IL: Scott, Foresman.

Ryder teaches in the Department of Curriculum and Instruction at the University of Wisconsin-Milwaukee and can be reached at PO Box 413, Erderis 357, Milwaukee WI 53201, USA.

From *Journal of Reading* Vol. 34, No. 8, May 1991, pages 606-612. Copyright © 1991 by The International Reading Association. Reprinted with permission.

Scaffolding adolescents' comprehension of short stories

This article describes an approach to assisting
seventh-grade students' comprehension of individual
texts with a Scaffolded Reading Experience or SRE.

by David N.E. Fournier, Michael F. Graves

After falling out of favor for some years, comprehension strategies instruction has recently regained considerable interest. Such widely read and influential publications as Snow, Burns, and Griffin's *Preventing Reading Difficulties in Young Children* (1998); the National Reading Panel's Report *Teaching Children to Read* (2000); Pressley's "What Should Reading Comprehension Instruction Be the Instruction Of?" (2000); and Armbruster, Lehr, and Osborn's *Put Reading First* (2001) have all emphasized the importance of comprehension strategies instruction.

This is a fortunate turn of events because comprehension strategies instruction is important. These influential publications, however, fail to consider another type of comprehension instruction—instruction that focuses on assisting students in reading, comprehending, and learning from individual texts. Tierney and Cunningham (1984) described comprehension instruction that focused on individual texts as "learning from text" and distinguished it from strategy instruction or "learning to learn from text". This distinction is further clarified by Pearson and Fielding (1991), who noted that the purpose of instruction in learning from text is "to increase students' comprehension of prose" while the purpose of instruction in learning to learn from text is "to increase students' *ability* to learn from prose" (emphasis in orginal).

By arguing that learning from text is receiving little attention at the present time, we are not suggesting that it has been forgotten. For example, the International Reading Association's position statement on adolescent literacy (Moore, Bean, Birdyshaw, & Rycik, 1999) devoted a paragraph to learning from text, noting that "many teaching practices are available for supporting adolescent learners". The RAND Reading Study Group report

Reading for Understanding (Snow, 2001), recommended research on comprehension and on content area reading that would appear to include some research on learning from text.

The fact remains, however, that very little attention is being given to learning from text. This is very unfortunate. As the authors of the RAND report explicitly and forcefully pointed out, "The demand for literacy skills is high and increasing. The U.S. economy demands a universally higher level of literacy achievement than at any prior point in history, and it is reasonable to believe that literacy demands will increase in the future" (Snow, 2001). Yet, while the demand for high-level reading skills is great and increasing, the most recent National Assessment of Educational Progress data available, the *NAEP 1999 Trends in Academic Progress* (Campbell, Hombo, & Mazzeo, 2000), indicated that the reading skills of U.S. high school students have remained unchanged over the past 30 years—the entire period that NAEP data have been available.

Obviously, we need to use all the tools at our disposal to improve the reading skills of our students, and instruction that promotes learning from text is certainly one possible tool. If more students fully understand what they read, learn from their reading, realize that they have successfully understood and learned from what they read, and enjoy reading, the better their chances will be to become the sort of competent lifelong readers and learners the times require (Graves, Juel, & Graves, 2001). Moreover, such positive experiences with the texts they read are particularly crucial for less able readers (McGill-Franzen & Allington, 2001). Thus, methods that assist students in comprehending individual texts are well worth investigation.

This article describes one such method—an approach termed a Scaffolded Reading Experience or SRE (Graves & Graves, 1994, in press) that I (Fournier) used with significant success in my seventh-grade class. Included is an outline of the scaffolded reading experiences that I created. The article also describes a classroom study of the effect of using SREs and discusses what was learned from that study.

The Scaffolded Reading Experience framework

The key concept underlying the Scaffolded Reading Experience is that of *scaffolding*, providing support to help learners bridge the gap between what they know and can do and the intended goal. This is frequently singled out as one of the most effective instructional procedures available (Bransford, Brown, & Cocking, 2000; Cazden, 1992; Rosenshine & Meister, 1992). Scaffolding, as Pearson (1996) pointed out, "allows us, as teachers, to intervene in an environment and provide the cueing, questioning, coaching, corroboration, and plain old information needed to allow students to complete a task before they are able to complete it independently". But what exactly is

scaffolding? As defined by Wood and his colleagues (Wood, Bruner, & Ross, 1976)—the first to use the term *scaffolding* in its educational sense—it is "a process that enables a child or novice to solve a problem, carry out a task, or achieve a goal which would be beyond his [or her] unassisted efforts".

Training wheels on a bicycle are an excellent example of scaffolding. They are adjustable and temporary, providing the young rider with the support she or he needs while learning to ride a two-wheeler. Without an aid of this sort, the complex task of learning to pedal, balance, and steer all at one time would be extremely difficult, if not impossible. The scaffold—training wheels—allows the learner to accomplish a goal, to be successful at riding a bicycle, and happily pedal her or his way into a wider world.

The SRE takes the concept of scaffolding and incorporates it in a framework for guiding students' reading. As shown in Figure 1, an SRE has two phases—a planning phase and an implementation phase. During the planning phase you consider your students, the text they are reading, and the purposes for reading. During the implementation phase you select pre-, during-, and postreading activities that will lead students to a successful reading experience. The SRE framework is

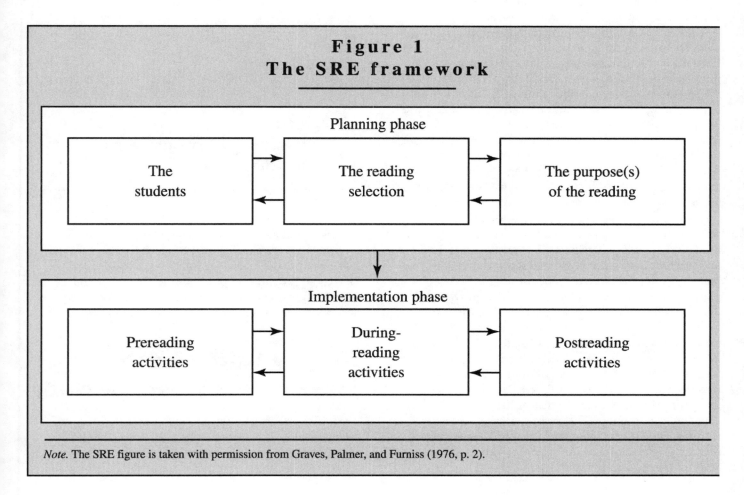

Figure 1
The SRE framework

Planning phase

| The students | → ← | The reading selection | → ← | The purpose(s) of the reading |

Implementation phase

| Prereading activities | → ← | During-reading activities | → ← | Postreading activities |

Note. The SRE figure is taken with permission from Graves, Palmer, and Furniss (1976, p. 2).

appropriate for virtually any combination of students, texts, and purposes; but the specific pre-, during-, and postreading activities you employ in any particular situation will differ greatly. In general, with less proficient students, more difficult selections, and more challenging purposes, more scaffolding is needed. Conversely, with more proficient students, less difficult selections, and less challenging purposes, less scaffolding is needed. The scaffolded framework is flexible and adaptable in that it presents a variety of options—sets of pre-, during-, and postreading options—from which you choose those best suited to lead a particular group of students to success. The options we suggest are shown in Figure 2.

Prereading activities prepare students to read the upcoming selection. They serve a number of functions, helping students to engage with and comprehend text. These functions generate student interest in the text, remind them of relevant knowledge, and preteach aspects of the selection they may find difficult, such as complex concepts and troublesome words. Of course, students can read many texts without prereading assistance; but when texts are challenging or when you want students to understand them deeply, prereading activities can set the stage for a truly productive and rewarding reading experience.

During-reading activities include things that students do as they are reading and things that you do during that time to assist them—students' reading silently, your reading to them, their taking notes as they read, and the like.

Postreading activities provide opportunities for students to synthesize and organize information gleaned from the text so that they can understand and recall important points. They also provide opportunities for students to evaluate an author's message, his or her stance in presenting the message, and the quality of the text itself. Students may also respond to a text in a variety of ways—reflecting on the meaning of the text, comparing differing texts and ideas, engaging in a variety of activities that will refine and extend their understanding of what they learn from the text, and applying what they have learned to the world beyond the classroom.

As Figure 2 indicates, the SRE framework we used presents 20 possible types of activities—far too many to be used with a single selection. Again, however, this is a list of options. From this set of possibilities, you choose only those that are appropriate for your students as they read a particular text for a particular purpose. (For those familiar with guided reading, we point out that SREs differ from guided reading in several ways. For example, SREs do not include any essential elements, SREs are applicable at any grade level, and SREs are intended for challenging texts as well as for less challenging ones. For further information on these two approaches, see Fountas & Pinnell, 1996; Graves & Graves, 1994, in press; and Tierney & Readence, 2000.)

The individual activities suggested by the SRE framework (e.g., building background knowledge, preteaching vocabulary) are supported by a substantial body of theory and research (see Graves & Graves, 1994,

Figure 2
Optional activities in an SRE

Prereading activities
   Relating the reading to students' lives
   Motivating
   Activating background knowledge,
   Building text-specific knowledge
   Preteaching vocabulary
   Preteaching concepts
   Prequestioning, predicting, and direction
      setting
   Suggesting strategies

During-reading activities
   Silent reading
   Reading to students
   Guided reading
   Oral reading by students
   Modifying the text

Postreading activities
   Questioning
   Discussion
   Writing
   Drama
   Artistic and nonverbal activities
   Application and outreach activities
   Reteaching

in press), and the approach has generally received favorable reviews (Berskin, 1995; Readence, Moore, & Rickelman, 2000; Tierney & Readence, 2000). However, as Tierney and Readence pointed out, there is no research specifically investigating complete SREs. The study described here is a response to this lack of research.

The two Scaffolded Reading Experiences used in the study

Scaffolded reading experiences were created for two short stories—"Last Cover" by Paul Annixter (1994) and "The Medicine Bag" by Virginia Driving Hawk Sneve (1994). "Last Cover" is approximately 3,800 words long and depicts the protagonist's strong bond with a pet fox and explores his conflict with his father who doesn't understand his artistic talents. "The Medicine Bag" is approximately 3,200 words in length and illustrates how a young boy comes to understand the significance of his Native American culture by connecting with his great-grandfather prior to the old man's death. Both stories were taken from a section called "Doors to Under-standing" in a seventh-grade literature anthology titled *Literature and Language* (McDougal Littell, 1994). Each SRE spanned four days. I provided all relevant instruction.

Day 1 with "Last Cover." I introduced the story's general topic and had students write brief personal responses to the following prompts regarding the close ties people sometimes form with animals: "Why do you think some people develop such close ties with animals?" and "What can pets offer in friendship that people cannot?" These prompts were designed to motivate students, activate their background knowledge on pets, and allow them to establish a relationship to the story through their personal experiences with pets. Students' responses then became springboards for small-group discussions followed by large-group sharing.

After the large-group sharing, I read the first paragraph of the story, directed small groups to brain-storm what the story might be about, and had the groups share their responses in a class discussion.

I next presented a brief preview to the class. The preview sought to involve students by asking them to think of a time when they didn't understand a family member's decision. I noted that in "Last Cover" the main character is misunderstood by his father, gave a brief overview of a part of the story, and prompted students to see how the conflict between the main character and his father is resolved.

Finally, I continued reading the story aloud, completing about three pages of it and interspersing factual and inferential guiding questions such as "What is the father's opinion of the fox early on in the story?" and "Although he may express himself differently, how is Colin similar to his father?"

Day 2 with "Last Cover." The day began with students answering a personal response question about the antagonist's reasons for instigating the main conflict, "Why doesn't Colin's father appreciate his artistic talents?" Then students wrote journal responses for the protagonist (projecting his thoughts regarding his father and pet fox) and for the father (considering his thoughts and feelings about his son and his perspective on the fox). Students shared their journal responses in small groups during a class discussion and then made individual predictions about whether the main character's conflict with his father would be resolved by the story's end. After the discussion, I read the rest of the

story aloud, again posing factual and inferential questions along the way.

Day 3 with "Last Cover." As their first postreading activity, students in small groups answered factual and inferential questions on selected quotations from the story such as the following.

- "From the first, the tame fox had made tension in the family". How do different views of Bandit cause tension in the family?
- "There was something rare and secret, like the spirit of the woods, about him; and back of his calm, straw-gold eyes was the sense of a brain equal of a man's. The fox became Colin's whole life". How does Bandit come to be Colin's "whole life"?

The groups then shared their answers with the class.

Day 4 with "Last Cover." For a culminating postreading activity, students worked in pairs writing logical contin-uations of the story. They used the last two sentences of the story as a writing prompt. Pairs then presented their continuations to the class.

This concluded the SRE for "Last Cover." The SRE for "The Medicine Bag" began the following week.

Day 1 with "The Medicine Bag." The class began by writing personal responses to prompts such as "What is your cultural heritage?" and "How is this cultural heritage important to you?" These prompts were designed to help students think about the importance of their cultural heritages and the value of ethnicity in general.

Next, I read the first four paragraphs aloud and facil-itated a class discussion of predictions for what the story would be about. Students then wrote who, what, when, why, and how questions about the story.

After this, students read the story silently to themselves while completing a slightly modified version of a Character Analysis Grid (Buehl, 1995). This graphic organizer, shown in Figure 3, was designed to facilitate students' exploration of the main character's actions, dialogue, and thoughts; treatment by other characters; and evidence of change.

Day 2 with "The Medicine Bag." Students continued their reading and completed the Character Analysis Grid. Next, I facilitated a postreading class discussion, calling on students to share details from their Character Analysis Grids.

I asked students to respond in their journals to the following two prompts:

- Write a journal entry for Martin exploring his thoughts and feelings when his great-grandfather first arrives at his home.

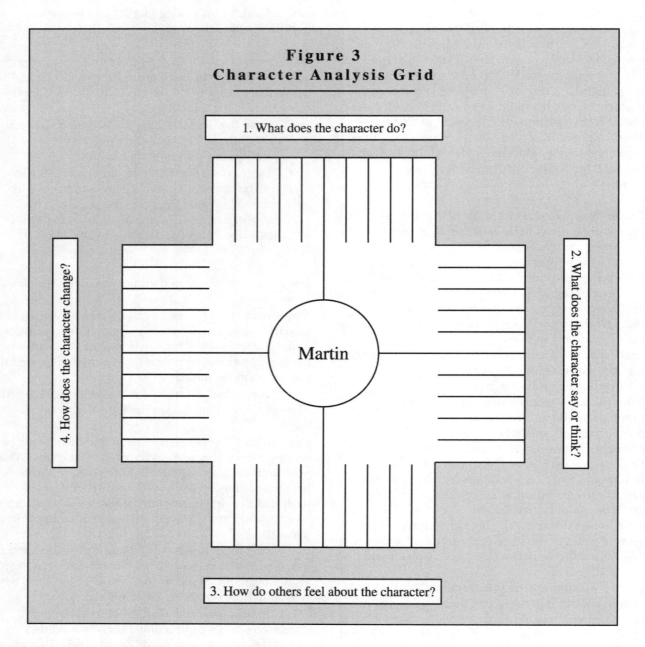

Figure 3
Character Analysis Grid

1. What does the character do?

4. How does the character change?

Martin

2. What does the character say or think?

3. How do others feel about the character?

- Write another entry for Martin exploring his thoughts and feelings about his great-grandfather at the end of the story.

Day 3 with "The Medicine Bag." Students individually presented their journal entries to the class, which took the entire period.

Day 4 with "The Medicine Bag." Working in pairs, students considered two key quotations that suggest a logical continuation of action: "After the bag is yours, you must put a piece of prairie sage within and never open it again until you pass it on to your son" and "Two weeks later I stood alone on the lonely prairie of the reservation and put the sacred sage in my medicine

bag". They then wrote a continuation to the story using the following prompt.

- At the end of the story, we learn Martin does put a piece of prairie grass in the medicine bag. Imagine he is older now with his own son, and outline a brief sequel to the story describing the circumstances of how he passes the medicine bag on to his son.

This concluded the SRE for "The Medicine Bag."

The classroom study

We investigated the effects of these SREs in a classroom study. I conducted the study as my Master of Education project at the University of Minnesota under the supervision of Michael Graves. At Minnesota, M.Ed. students design their projects in a course titled "Practical Research." This course stresses the importance of both internal and external validity, presents quantitative and qualitative approaches as valuable and often complementary methods, and extols the value of generalizability. At the same time, the course emphasizes that generalizability is an elusive and often only partially realized goal. In keeping with this position, we view the results of this study as validation for the SRE approach, an indication of what SREs can achieve, and a suggestion of what they may accomplish in other contexts.

Participants in this study were 50 students from two seventh-grade English classes in a suburban, midwestern U.S. middle school of approximately 1,300 students. One class consisted of 25 students (10 male, 15 female) of high scholastic achievement, the other of 25 students (11 males, 14 females) of low to moderate scholastic achievement.

The study extended over two weeks. Students in the two classes read "Last Cover" during the first week of the study and "The Medicine Bag" during the second week. The SRE treatments were counterbalanced across the stories; that is, one class received the SRE for "Last Cover," and the other received the SRE for "The Medicine Bag." The dependent measures were a multiple-choice comprehension test for each story and a Likert scale probing students' attitudes toward the stories and the SREs. As noted, each SRE lasted four days. The fifth day of each week was used for the test and attitude survey.

When reading the story without an SRE, each class read silently on the first day and completed the comprehension questions and attitude survey on the second day. During the remainder of the week, they received a lesson on poetic concepts, worked in pairs responding in writing to a poem that illustrated these concepts, and shared their responses with the class.

The results of the comprehension test are shown in Table 1. As can be seen, students scored higher on comprehension for both stories when receiving the SRE and also, therefore, when the scores are averaged across both stories. A two-way analysis of variance with treatment and story as independent variables show that the overall effect of treatment was significant, $F(1, 96) = 21.48, p < .01$, while both the effect of story and the story x treatment interaction were not ($p > .05$). The SREs had a significant positive effect on students' comprehension of both stories.

Because "Last Cover" and "The Medicine Bag" ranged in difficulty, and because one class received the SRE with "Last Cover" and the other with "The Medicine Bag," in order to compare the effect of the SRE for the two classes we needed to standardize the students' comprehension scores. We did this by converting the students' raw scores to what are called z-scores. We could then compare the z-scores of students in the two classes to get an accurate picture of the effects of the SREs. This comparison showed that 21 of the 25 students in the high scholastic achievement class scored better when they

Table 1 Percent correct on the comprehension test		
	Without the SRE	With the SRE
"The Medicine Bag"	69	86
"Last Cover"	68	77
Average across the two stories	68	81

received the SRE and 19 of the 25 students in the low to average scholastic achievement class scored better when they received the SRE. Thus, while the SRE helped a few more students in the high scholastic achievement class, it obviously helped the majority of students in both classes.

In reporting the results of the attitude survey, we combined the "strongly disagree" and "disagree" results and termed them "disagree" and the "strongly agree" and "agree" results and termed them "agree." These results—except those for Question 5, which differed when students did and did not receive an SRE—are shown in Table 2. Students responded more positively to every question when receiving SREs. With SREs, students' responses indicated that they liked the story more, were more likely to recommend the story to friends, found the language of the story easier to understand, understood the main event and conflict better, considered the story itself easier to comprehend, and strongly endorsed the use of SRE activities.

As noted, Question 5 differed when students did and did not receive an SRE. When students received an SRE, Question 5 read "The reading activities helped me understand the story better." Responses to this question showed that 6% disagreed, 30% had no opinion, and 64% agreed. When students did not receive an SRE, Question 5 read "Some sort of explanation or learning activities would have helped me better understand this story." Responses to this question showed that 20% disagreed, 36% were undecided, and 44% agreed. Thus, when they received an SRE, nearly two thirds of the students believed that it helped them understand the story.

What we learned from the study

Clearly, SREs can increase students' comprehension of short stories. Averaged across the two stories, students' comprehension with an SRE was 19% higher than without an SRE.

Table 2
Students' responses to the attitude questionnaire (in percents) with and without an SRE

		Disagree	Undecided	Agree
1. I liked the story.	SRE	0	20	80
	No SRE	12	30	58
2. I would recommend this story to a friend.	SRE	4	18	58
	No SRE	36	28	36
3. The story's language was easy to read.	SRE	0	8	92
	No SRE	4	6	90
4. I understood the main events and conflicts in the story.	SRE	0	12	88
	No SRE	4	14	82
6. Having students do activities relating to a story before, during, and after reading the story is a good idea.	SRE	6	26	68
	No SRE	6	36	58
7. I felt the story was at or below my reading level.	SRE	6	16	78
	No SRE	12	14	74

This is a substantial gain. Similarly, students' attitudes toward all aspects of the story and to the instruction they received were more positive when they received an SRE. This is no small matter, for helping seventh graders develop positive attitudes toward reading and toward school is at least as much of a challenge and at least as important as improving their comprehension of what they read. With respect to our opening remarks, in which we lamented the current lack of attention to instruction that facilitates students' learning from text, we provide some evidence for the effectiveness of instruction aimed at learning from text. The addition of learning from text instruction, such as that provided in SREs, helped students comprehend nearly 20% more of their texts than they would have without such instruction. Twenty percent is a considerable gain in knowledge. And while knowledge is by no means the sole end of schooling, it is arguably one of the most important sorts of capital we can provide for students (Bransford et al., 2000; National Research Council, 1999; Snow, 2001).

Still, as the two of us have found to be almost always the case over our combined 40 years of teaching, using SREs has costs as well as benefits. In this case, the most serious cost is the amount of time required by robust SREs such as those used here. The SRE treatments required significantly more time than the control treatments. That is a real cost that we cannot always afford.

Two arguments, however, suggest that the increased time required for SREs is sometimes justified. First, as

Perkins (1992), Newmann (1996), Wiggins and McTighe (1998), and Pressley (2001)—as well as many others—have argued, all too frequently we fail to take the time to teach for true understanding, that is, to teach in such a way that learners understand what they read, remember important information, and use what they learn in the world outside of school. Teaching for understanding takes time, and we must be willing to spend that time to foster deep understanding. The second argument to justify the time spent on SRE activities comes from considering the nature of the activities. Many of them—for example, taking the perspective of the son and then of the father and interpreting figurative language in "Last Cover," and reflecting on the significance of one's cultural heritage and interpreting the Character Analysis Grid in "The Medicine Bag"—engage students in the sorts of higher level, constructivist, open-ended experiences that lead them to become the creative problem solvers required in the 21st century.

Thus, while we admit that robust SREs like those described here take time, we also argue that it is both necessary and desirable to sometimes take the time. We leave it to individual teachers to consider just when learning from text activities are appropriate for their classes. Teachers who are considering using SREs in their classes may find the samples available on the Web at http://www.onlinereadin+gresources.com of some interest.

Fournier teaches middle school English. He may be contacted at 355 Cimarron Road, Apple Valley, MN 55124, USA, or by e-mail at dave.fournier@district196.org. Graves teaches at the University of Minnesota in Minneapolis.

REFERENCES

Annixter, P. (1994). Last cover. In *Literature and language* (pp. 523–530). Evanston, IL: McDougal Littell.

Armbruster, B.B., Lehr, F., & Osborn, J. (2001). *Put reading first: The research building blocks for teaching children to read.* Jessup, MD: National Institute for Literacy.

Berskin, A. (1995, March). Professional book brag. *Instructor*, p. 82.

Bransford, J.D., Brown, A.L., & Cocking, R.R. (2000). *How people learn: Brain, mind, experience, and school* (expanded edition). Washington, DC: National Academy Press.

Buehl, D. (1995). *Classroom strategies for interactive learning.* Schofield, WI: Wisconsin State Reading Association.

Campbell, J.R., Hombo, C.M., & Mazzeo, J. (2000). *NAEP 1999 trends in academic progress: Three decades of student performance.* Washington, DC: Department of Education.

Cazden, C.B. (1992). *Whole language plus: Essays on literacy in the United States and New Zealand.* New York: Teachers College Press.

Driving Hawk Sneve, V. (1994). The medicine bag. In *Literature and language* (pp. 558–565). Evanston, IL: McDougal Littell.

Fountas, I.C., & Pinnell, G.S. (1996). *Guided reading: Good teaching for all children.* Portsmouth, NH: Heinemann.

Graves, M.F., & Graves, B.B. (1994). *Scaffolding reading experiences: Designs for student success.* Norwood, MA: Christopher-Gordon.

Graves, M.F., & Graves, B.B. (in press). *Scaffolding reading experiences: Designs for student success* (2nd ed.). Norwood, MA: Christopher-Gordon.

Graves, M.F., Juel, C., & Graves, B.B. (2001). *Teaching reading in the 21st century.* Boston: Allyn & Bacon.

Graves, M.F., Palmer, R.J., & Furniss, D.W. (1976). *Structuring reading activities.* Washington, DC: Educational Resources Information Center/National Council of Teachers of English.

McDougal Littell. (1994). *Literature and language.* Evanston, IL: Author.

McGill-Franzen, A., & Allington, D. (2001, June/July). Summer reading: Improving access to books and opportunities to read. *Reading Today, 18*, p. 10.

Moore, D.W., Bean, T.W., Birdyshaw, D., & Rycik, J.A. (1999). *Adolescent literacy: A position statement.* Newark, DE: International Reading Association.

National Reading Panel. (2000). *Report of the National Reading Panel: Teaching children to read.* Bethesda, MD: National Institute of Child Health and Human Development.

National Research Council. (1999). *Improving student learning: A strategic plan for education research and its utilization.* Washington, DC: National Academy Press.

Newmann, F.W. (1996). *Authentic achievement: Restructuring schools for intellectual quality.* San Francisco: Jossey-Bass.

Pearson, P.D. (1996). Reclaiming the center. In M.F. Graves, P. van den Broek, & B.M. Taylor (Eds.), *The first R: A right of all children* (pp. 259–274). New York: Teachers College Press.

Pearson, P.D., & Fielding, L. (1991). Comprehension instruction. In R. Barr, M.L. Kamil, P.B. Mosenthal, & P.D. Pearson (Eds.), *Handbook of reading research* (Vol. 2, pp. 815–860). White Plains, NY: Longman.

Perkins, D. (1992). *Smart schools: From training memories to educating minds.* New York: Basic Books.

Pressley, M. (2000). What should reading comprehension instruction be the instruction of? In M. Kamil, P.B. Mosenthal, P.D. Pearson, & R. Barr (Eds.), *Handbook of reading research* (Vol. 3, pp. 545–561). Mahwah, NJ: Erlbaum.

Pressley, M. (2001). Comments on reading for understanding: Towards an R&D program in reading comprehension. Available online at http://www.rand.org/multi/achievementforall/reading/

Readence, J.E., Moore, D.W., & Rickelman, R.J. (2000). *Prereading activities for content area reading and learning* (3rd ed.). Newark, DE: International Reading Association.

Rosenshine, B., & Meister, C. (1992). The use of scaffolds for teaching higher-level cognitive strategies. *Educational Leadership, 49*(7), 26–33.

Snow, C.E. (2001). *Reading for understanding: Toward an R&D program in reading comprehension.* Santa Monica, CA: RAND Education. Available online at http://www.rand.org/multi/achievement-forall/reading/

Snow, C.E., Burns, S.M., & Griffin, P. (1998). *Preventing reading difficulties in young children.* Washington, DC: National Academy Press.

Tierney, R.J., & Cunningham, J.W. (1984). Research on teaching reading comprehension. In P.D. Pearson (Ed.), *Handbook of reading research* (pp. 609–654). White Plains, NY: Longman.

Tierney, R.J., & Readence, J.E. (2000). *Reading strategies and practices: A compendium* (3rd ed.). Boston: Allyn & Bacon.

Wiggins, G., & McTighe, J. (1998). *Understanding by design.* Alexandria, VA: Association for Supervision and Curriculum Development.

Wood, D.W., Bruner, J.S., & Ross, G. (1976). The role of tutoring in problem-solving. *Journal of Child Psychology and Psychiatry, 17*(2), 89–100.

From *Journal of Adolescent & Adult Literacy* Vol. 46, No. 1, September 2002, pages 30-39. Copyright © 2002 by The International Reading Association. Reprinted with permission.

UNIT 5

Content Area Reading Strategies Across the Curriculum

Unit Selections

Key Points to Consider

• Whose responsibility is it to teach secondary students to read?

• Is reading a math, science, and social studies textbook different from reading a novel?

• Do reading strategies cross curriculums?

 **Links: www.dushkin.com/online/**
These sites are annotated in the World Wide Web pages.

Reading in the Content Area - Baltimore County Public Schools
http://www.bcpl.net/~dcurtis/readingcontent/

Reading Quest Resources
http://curry.edschool.virginia.edu/go/readquest/links.html

Reading in the content area, reading and writing across the curriculum, and reading to learn are all phrases frequently heard by secondary in-service and pre-service teachers. All teachers must become reading and writing teachers no matter what subject they teach. Students must read and write to learn in the content areas.

I remember the exciting discovery that History and Science textbooks had some of the same information. I was in the ninth grade. It was the first time I experienced integration of the various subjects I was studying. I noticed that the study of history sometimes relied on the sciences, especially anthropology, archeology, and geology. Before my discovery, textbooks were something I only used for defining terms and answering section questions for a grade. The weeks and months of school had a rhythm to them. Define terms, answer section questions, take notes, and take a test. It was only when the teachers assigned projects that I read to find information. That reading was in the library and not in my textbook.

While I began to read my World History and Biology texts towards the end of my freshman year in high school as well as all of my Physics assignments my sophomore year, it was during my high school American History class that I first realized the importance of reading my textbooks as a way to learn. I was a junior in high school in 1967. At that time, we studied about the discovery and colonization of North America by Europeans up to World War II. Our teachers used to joke about how students studied the same material in fifth-grade, eighth-grade, eleventh-grade, and freshman year in college. The teachers also used to joke about how we never studied the present because no teacher ever got past WWII. It was not too many years later that the study of American History was divided by the Colonial Period through the Civil War for eighth-grade and Reconstruction through the present in high school.

The school I went to offered the academic core subjects. We did not have a band, shop, or art classes. We had choir two times a week to prepare us for singing at church. We had football and basketball at our school, but we did not have a football field and indoor gym until my senior year. Our school was considered a college-prep school—80% of us went to college and over 50% received at least a bachelor's degree. My junior college English instructor told me that he and his colleagues loved to have graduates from my high school in their classes because they could count on us having read the classics. I only say that to indicate that our school's textbooks must have been acceptable. I still have my history books from sixth, seventh, and eighth-grades. The copyright date of this Catholic School History Series was 1950, yet it was my text in 1964.

I also have the eighth-grade and ninth-grade HBJ American History Series that were used in many public schools in the late eighties and early nineties. The copyright was 1986. My 1950 eighth-grade American History book ended with the explosion of the atomic bomb. The last chapter is titled WORLD CONFLICT, which covers the election of Woodrow Wilson, Revolution in Mexico, World War I, League of Nations, the Depression of 1929, The New Deal, Communism, Naziism, the dictator nations, and World War II. These are all covered within 24 pages of text, 419-442, that are half the size of my 1986 textbook pages and typed in a 14-font type. Based on my personal, reflexive analysis, I would have to disagree with Hayes, Wolfer, and Wolfe (1996) that schoolbook simplification has resulted in the decline in SAT-verbal scores. My 442-page history book, published in 1950, had pages half the sizes of current textbooks and type that is in 14 font. It was much simpler than the two-volume HBJ American

History text published in 1986. Volume I, colonization through the Civil War, contains 675 pages in 12-font type. A student would have to also cover another 390 pages in 12-font type to complete a study through WWII as covered in my 1950 text. By rough calculations, I think a student has nine times more text to read about the same time period, colonization through WWII, than I did in 1967. I do not believe that textbooks have been simplified. I believe they are becoming more and more complex with each year's edition, and teachers in the content areas must step up to the challenge of teaching their students how to access the information and use it in meaningful ways. We must not foster a form of "aliteracy" as defined by Brozo and Simpson (2003) as the "decision of literate individuals not to use their literacy." We must find ways to engage secondary students in reading to learn in the subject areas.

In this unit, articles provide content area pre-service teachers, in-service teachers, and administrators with a cross-curricular look at reading in the content areas. Articles address reading in the following subject areas: math, science, and social studies. "Developing Citical Understanding of the Specialized Language of School Science and History Texts: A Functional Grammatical Perspective" (1999), by Len Unsworth, focuses on the specialized language of Science and History textbooks used in school and points out the importance of developing a broad range of literacy skills needed for students to function in the academic content area setting. "The Effect of Learning Mathematical Reading Strategies on Secondary Students' Homework Grades" (1997), by Elliott Ostler, lists and discusses how terminology, eye patterns, graph/text interaction, and reading direction are four key factors that distinguish reading math texts from other informational texts.

This section also addresses how teachers can supplement their textbook with literature. Articles address the concept of reading as a social life skill that can be used to supplement and enhance learning in the core academic areas, arts, and technology-centered careers. "Celebrating Literature in a Comprehensive Middle School Program" (1997), by Marguerite Cogomo Radencich and Anita Meyer Meinbach, features the successful use of book discussions at Southwood Middle School in their effort to develop a comprehensive literature program. The book discussions are conducted under the program title of "Grand Conversations." "Literature for Children and Young Adults in a History Cassroom" (1994), by Judy E. Van Middendorp and Sharon Lee, describes the powerful impact children's literature can have in the content areas.

Reading in the content area does not have to be limited to textbooks. Students can be encouraged to celebrate literature through content area topics. With this approach, students may begin to picture reading as a life-long process for attaining information and celebrating literature.

Developing critical understanding of the specialised language of school science and history texts

A functional grammatical perspective

This article demonstrates the practicality of functional grammatical descriptions of language in understanding the difficulties students encounter with the specialised language of school science and history texts.

Len Unsworth

Developing the range of literacies needed by students from diverse backgrounds to effectively negotiate school learning is a complex task. One aspect of current endeavours to prepare teachers for this task in Australia is addressing the interconnections of learning in content areas and learning to control the grammatical forms that construct and communicate knowledge in those content areas. This has involved teachers learning to use descriptions of language based on systemic functional linguistics (Halliday, 1994; Martin, 1992; Matthiessen, 1995) to understand the distinctive language and literacy demands of particular content areas. Although these functional descriptions of language are not a sufficient resource for improving content area literacy and learning, they have provided a very productive, practical impetus toward improved teaching and learning practices.

The work of junior secondary school science teacher Margaret Watt was reported by Macken-Horarik (1996), showing how functional descriptions of language

informed explicit teaching of the language of science texts as an integral part of teaching the science content. Watt's 10-week classroom program dealt with explanations of animal and human reproduction. She thought that students should progress from their everyday understanding of the topic to systematic, technical understanding. But she also wanted them to problematize their knowledge in scientific, technological, and social terms. This progression from the domain of the everyday to that of the reflexive and critical and the progression in the types of texts the students needed to negotiate is summarised by Macken-Horarik as follows:

In learning about in-vitro fertilisation, for instance, students typically deal first with texts which are close to immediate experience, as in *Information for IVF patients*. Later, they move into texts which generalise across a set of experiences, for instance *The IVF program at Royal Prince Alfred Hospital*, and then into texts which explore issues raised by contradictory experiences of the IVF program, e.g., *Do the costs of IVF outweigh the benefits?* (1996, p. 247)

A great deal of explicit teaching at the level of grammar and overall text organization and a lot of scaffolding of students' learning were involved in making such shifts in reading and responding to different types of texts. The science teacher worked with her students on functional descriptions of the language of the texts they were reading and writing, describing her practice thus:

[I] explicitly model the language demands of the genre. I show them and tell them how to do it; step one, two, three et cetera. I show the connectors, the processes. I am really down at the language level. And then they have the means for dealing with language on their own. They can deconstruct texts even in exams. The language functions are there even in short-answer questions. (Macken-Horarik, 1996, p. 273)

It is important to understand that being "really down at the language level" involves this teacher in drawing on functional grammatical knowledge that is quite different from that of traditional or formal grammar. Whereas the latter are associated with instructing students about "correct" or "standard" syntactic structures, systemic functional grammar is primarily concerned with the roles of various elements of a clause in simultaneously constructing three different types of meaning: Ideational meanings are concerned with material, mental, and verbal events—who or what is involved in them and the circumstances surrounding them; interpersonal meanings are concerned with the roles and nature of the relationships (in terms of status, power, affect, etc.) among speakers and listeners and readers and writers; textual meanings are concerned with the organization of information in terms of orienting the reader/listener to what is familiar and what is new in the text. So a functional description of language can show the ways in which grammatical choices influence both how and what meanings are conveyed. It is some of these functional grammatical concepts that I will explain and illustrate in this article. More comprehensive accounts relevant to teachers are also readily available (Butt, Fahey, Spinks, & Yallop, 1995; Collerson, 1994; Gerot & Wignell, 1995).

Margaret Watt's science students' achievements in developing a high level of technical understanding of reproduction technologies and in demonstrating informed critical appraisal of contemporary textual material on the topic are evident in the samples of student writing discussed by Macken-Horarik (1996). Elementary school teachers and children are also effectively integrating functional grammatical knowledge into their classroom literacy work (Derewianka, 1995; Williams, 1994, 1995; Williams & French, 1995; Williams, Rothery & French, 1994, 1995) and specifically addressing the language of content area texts (Collerson, 1997; Derewianka & Schmich, 1991).

This article provides a brief introduction to the ways in which functional grammatical concepts can be used in developing an understanding of the distinctive literacy demands of school science and history texts. We will consider the following key issues:

- distinguishing the grammar of specialised knowledge from the grammar of everyday language;
- understanding the complete interconnections of content area learning and learning to control the grammatical forms characteristic of texts in different content areas;
- using functional grammatical concepts to differentiate the literacies of different content areas; and
- developing functional grammatical knowledge as a tool for critical literacy.

From the grammar of talk to the grammar of writing

The following text is an example of talk in an everyday casual conversation:

First she told me about the wedding and then she just kept going on about their families and she even told me about the cars and all that but she never even asked me one question and so I got fed up and I interrupted her and I said, "Mavis, look, I've just got to hang up now" and I just sort of put the phone down.

Notice here that we have one sentence that consists of 10 clauses:

First she told me about the wedding | | and then she just kept going on about their families | | and she even told me about the cars and all that | | but she never even asked me one question | | and so I got fed up | | and I interrupted her | | and I said, | | "Mavis, look, I've just got to hang up now" | | and I just sort of put the phone down.

This is very typical of spoken language. This kind of grammatical structuring is also typical of students' talk in learning experiences at school. In the following example (Hammond, 1990), a student is talking about the novel *Z for Zachariah* (O'Brien, 1975):

Like I reckon he would have been really nice but now that he's been to all the towns and seen like there's no life or anything and he comes into the valley and sees Ann and sees life and he just wanted power over her because he's never had power or anything before. (Hammond, 1990, p. 36)

In English, written medium tends to pack information more densely than spoken medium. This is achieved through greater use of lexical items (content words) in comparison with grammatical items (structure words). The piece of student talk we have just looked at is repeated below with the lexical items underlined:

Like I <u>reckon</u> he would have been really <u>nice</u> but now that he's been to all the <u>towns</u> and <u>seen</u> like there's no <u>life</u> or anything and he <u>comes</u> into the <u>valley</u> and <u>sees</u> <u>Ann</u> and <u>sees</u> <u>life</u> and he just <u>wanted</u> <u>power</u> over her because he's never had <u>power</u> or anything before.

There are 14 lexical items distributed over 10 clauses. Following Halliday's (1994) method of dividing the number of lexical items by the number of clauses, we can calculate that this text has a lexical density of 1.4. This is fairly typical of the spoken medium, which generally has a lexical density of about 2 (Halliday, 1993). In written texts, when language is more planned and more formal, the lexical density is higher—usually about 4 to 6 lexical items per clause and sometimes higher in texts dealing with technical or abstract concepts (Halliday, 1993). The following sentence from a senior high school history text has 15 lexical items in 2 clauses—a lexical density of 7.5.

Although the <u>league</u> <u>sought</u> <u>cooperation</u> between <u>classes</u>, its <u>determination</u> to <u>re-establish</u> the <u>integrity</u> and prosperity of <u>Australia</u> <u>marked</u> it as <u>largely</u> <u>representing</u> <u>business</u> and <u>professional</u> groups. (Tudball, 1991, p. 404)

For students who are confident users of spoken English but lack familiarity with the grammar of the written form, the greater lexical density of school texts can contribute to comprehension difficulties.

Even the written medium of information books intended primarily for elementary school students is much more lexically dense than spoken language. Consider the following excerpt from a book called *Spiders*:

<u>Spiders</u> are not <u>insects</u>. || They always <u>have</u> <u>eight</u> <u>jointed</u> <u>legs</u>, || not <u>six</u> as <u>insects</u> <u>have</u>, || and they never <u>have</u> <u>wings</u>. || The <u>feeling</u> <u>organs</u> on their <u>head</u> are not <u>antennae</u> but <u>leg-like</u> <u>structures</u> <u>called</u> <u>palps</u>. || <u>Spiders</u> all <u>have</u> a <u>pair</u> of <u>poison</u> <u>fangs</u> and several <u>pairs</u> of <u>spinnerets</u> || which <u>produce</u> <u>silk</u>. (Bender, 1988, p. 6)

Here there are 28 lexical items and 7 clauses—a lexical density of 4. So there is quite a lot of content or information packed into this text. How is this achieved? In contrast to the Zachariah excerpt, many of the lexical items in the Spiders text occur within groups of words that construct single entities—"feeling organs," "leg-like structures called palps," "poison fangs." These groups of words that constitute single entities are known as noun groups. By expanding the noun groups to include more lexical items (content words), a greater amount of information can be included within each clause.

As children progress through the education system they need to learn to deal with the distinctive grammar of written texts with their proportionately lower number of clauses and greater complexity within the clause. Consider for example this *single-sentence, single-clause* extract from an information book called *Killing for Luxury*.

Many of the wild animals traded in the luxury market have been so reduced in numbers that they are in danger of extinction (Bright, 1988, p. 5)

If you were telling someone this information, how many clauses would you need? The following is one attempt at "talking out" this text:

Hunters kill some wild animals || so that they can sell them to traders || who then sell them to manufacturers || who make luxury products out of parts of the animals' bodies. || The hunters have killed so many of these wild animals that there are hardly any of them left || and there is a danger that they will die out completely. (two sentences and 6 clauses)

You will notice that it is not just a matter of using more clauses. A significant aspect of this "talking out" is turning single noun groups (nominalisations) into noun + verb structures. We can see how these noun groups (nominalisations) are built into texts by looking at the first 2 clauses in the introduction to *Killing for Luxury*.

Man has always killed animals. The killing was traditionally for food and clothing. (Bright, 1988, p. 4)

In the first clause the noun groups (man; animals) are indeed things. But in the second clause, the first noun group is a nominalisation: "The killing." It is a simple noun group structure:

The	killing
Article	Thing

The Thing is actually realising an event, which implies an action. Turning verbs into nouns is a very common occurrence in English.

Consider the following excerpt from *Vanishing Habitats*:

All over <u>the</u> <u>world</u> <u>wetlands</u> are threatened by <u>drainage</u> and <u>conversion</u> to <u>arable</u> <u>land</u>. (Simon, 1987, p. 21)

The noun groups are underlined. The first two (<u>the</u> <u>world</u>; <u>wetlands</u>) are clearly "things" in the everyday sense. But <u>drainage</u> and <u>conversion</u> are Things only in language—they are abstract or pseudo things. In a more spoken explanation of this phenomenon the events would be realised as action verbs:

All over the world people <u>are</u> <u>draining</u> more and more of the wetlands and <u>converting</u> them to arable (farming) lands so there is a danger that the wetlands will disappear.

The highly nominalised and lexically dense language of specialised knowledge is highly functional. It is necessary to the construction and communication of higher order, specialised knowledge. For example, Martin (1993d), in discussing the linguistic construction of the scientific classification of electrical conductors and insulators, drew attention to the nominalisation of potentiality in the noun group "the ability to carry electricity." He pointed out that usually in spoken language potentiality is expressed by the modal verb *can*, which is not gradable—substances either can or can't conduct electricity. But once potentiality is nominalised, it becomes gradable—a low/medium/high ability to conduct electricity. The nominalisation is necessary to establish a category of substances whose ability to conduct electricity is intermediate between conductors and insulators. In other words the construction of this specialised knowledge "depends on the grammar of writing—on a process of nominalisation which makes available meanings that are not readily available in the spoken form" (Martin, 1993d, p. 95).

Students whose experience of language use has made them more familiar with such distinctive grammatical features of written language have an advantage in accessing specialised knowledge that is characteristically constructed in these typically written grammatical forms. The next section will further outline some ways in which the grammar of the written mode is an integral part of content area learning in school science and history.

Controlling the characteristic grammatical and discourse forms of content area learning

Compare the beginnings from the pieces of writing by two Year 6 students (Figure 1) after they had visited a Museum of Applied Arts and Sciences. The students had talked about their excursion in class, and the teacher asked them to write about the three exhibits they liked the best. Notice that the first student writes as she or he speaks, and the way she or he deploys clauses reflects this. The example in Figure 2 shows the persistence of the grammar of talk in the writing of an older student.

Christie (1984) demonstrates that the difficulty this student experiences is not so much at the level of genre or text type (much less spelling), but has more to do with the writer's lack of technical knowledge of the field being written about. The student also writes as she or he speaks. Building up knowledge of the field will entail using the grammatical forms more typical of written text.

There is much more to understanding the language of particular subject areas than learning the specialised vocabulary and learning to read and write the genres or text types that are valued in the discipline—important as these aspects certainly are. The significance of the role of the grammar of written language in content area learning was recently addressed by Wells (1994):

> Through engaging with written texts in relation to the topics that they study in school, therefore, children gradually reconstitute their lexicogrammar in the more abstract written mode… Thus, in learning to reconstrue experience in terms of the semantic structures of written language, children construct what Vygotsky refers to as "scientific concepts." That is to say, it is written texts—and the talk about them—that provide the discursive means for the development of the "higher mental functions." (pp. 81–82)

Figure 1
Spoken and written media in students' writing

I like the Strasburg clock because it was a real clock and it was a good clock because it had the apostles were moving around.	At the museum a lot of things interested me but three things interested me the most they were the Planetarium, the Railway engines, and the Mineral Wealth of Australia.
1 sentence - 4 clauses	1 sentence - 3 clauses

Adapted from Christie (1984, p. 96) *Children writing: Study Guide.* Geelong, Australia: Deakin University Press.

There are, of course, a range of grammatical differences between spoken and written language, which have been extensively documented (Halliday, 1985; Hammond, 1990; Perera, 1984). For the moment we will focus on just one major difference to which Wells (1994) has drawn attention. This is the extensive use of "grammatical metaphor" in written texts (Halliday, 1985; Halliday & Martin 1993a, 1993b; Martin, 1992, 1993b, 1993c), in particular the concept of nominalisation previously discussed.

Nominalisation is one form of grammatical metaphor and it refers to

> a substitution of one grammatical class, or one grammatical structure by another; for example, his departure instead of he departed. Here the words (lexical items) are the same; what has changed is their place in the grammar. Instead of the pronoun he + verb departed, functioning as Actor + Process in a clause, we have determiner his + noun departure, functioning as Deictic + Thing in a nominal group. (Halliday & Martin, 1993a, p. 79)

Grammatical metaphor is essential to the construction of specialised knowledge in language and this has been well established by Halliday and Martin (1993b) and by Martin (1993a, 1993c). For example, Martin (1993a) shows how nominalisation is a key resource in defining technical terms:

The production of rock waste by mechanical processes and chemical changes

is called

weathering

In this example the compaction and distillation of the meaning of the technical term *weathering* must be in a nominalised form ("The production of…"). The events that occur during weathering then can be grammatically equated with the nominal form of the single technical term.

Students who write effectively in curriculum areas are clearly able to use grammatical metaphor for this purpose. The following example is from a student's written explanation of why rainwater isn't salty (nominalisation underlined):

The vapour condenses into droplets of liquid water, forming clouds. If the vapour is chilled enough, it condenses into ice crystals and falls as snow. <u>This great unending circulation of the</u> earth's <u>waters</u> is called the water cycle.

Nominalisation is also functional in facilitating the development of a chain of reasoning. In order to lead on to the next step you have to be able to summarise what has gone before as the point of departure. Halliday and Martin (1993b, p. 131) illustrate the simplest form of this as follows:

...both ethyne and nitrogen oxide are kinetically stable...

The kinetic stability of nitrogen oxide shows...

By expressing a series of events as a Thing, those summarised events can then assume a participant role in the next part of the explanation. So nominalisation is one of the means by which the explanation is able to progress through the cause and effect sequence.

Figure 2
Spoken medium in writing of an older student

Christie, F. (1984). *Children writing: Study guide.* Geelong, Australia: Deakin University Press. Reprinted with permission.

You can see this is in the explanation of "bending light" (Taylor, 1989), which has been reformatted in Figure 3 to show the use of nominalisation. Events that are initially expressed as verbs are subsequently summarised and expressed as Things in the noun group:

So "travels more slowly" becomes "this slowing down" and then the Thing ("this slowing down") is what makes the light change direction. Similarly, the verbal structure "change direction" becomes a Thing in the noun group, "The bending of light." This is equated with another Thing, "refraction" and this "makes your legs look shorter than they really are." Examples of the deployment of these grammatical resources from secondary school history texts are shown in Figure 4.

In the first example in Figure 4, the verb form "help pay" becomes the classifying adjective "assisted" and the verb "migrate" is nominalised as "migration." In the second example "given their discharges" is nominalised as "The demobilization." Martin (1993b, p. 243) points out that nominalisation is the means by which the "New" information in the Rheme (at the conclusion) of one clause is summarised and located as "Given" information in the Theme (at the beginning) of the next clause and so on. As Wells (1994) reminds us, for many students this kind of structuring will not be familiar from their everyday language experience and they will need to "gradually reconstitute their lexicogrammar in the more abstract written mode". Furthermore, for many students this does not occur spontaneously. It will need carefully scaffolded experience with written texts and explicit teaching of knowledge about language. We could, of course, provide many other kinds of examples of the functionality of the grammar of written language in constructing specialised knowledge (see for example, Martin, 1993e). What is clear even from this abbreviated account is that effective access to knowledge and understanding in curriculum areas entails access to the grammatical resources characteristic of the written mode.

Using a functional model of language to differentiate content area literacies

Functional descriptions of language provide a metalanguage capable of describing the characteristic features of the language common to all content areas, but different content areas deploy the linguistic resources of English in distinctive ways. One of the most useful practical accounts of content area literacies is the recently published material from the Write It Right project conducted by the Disadvantaged Schools Program (DSP) in the Metropolitan East Region of the New South Wales Department of School Education at the Erskineville DSP Centre (Coffin, 1996; Humphrey, 1996; Iedema, Feez, & White, 1994; Rothery, 1995). Some aspects of this work have also been discussed and developed by Rothery (1996), van Leeuwen and Humphrey (1996), and Veel (1997).

Figure 3
The use of nominalisation in an explanatory text in school science

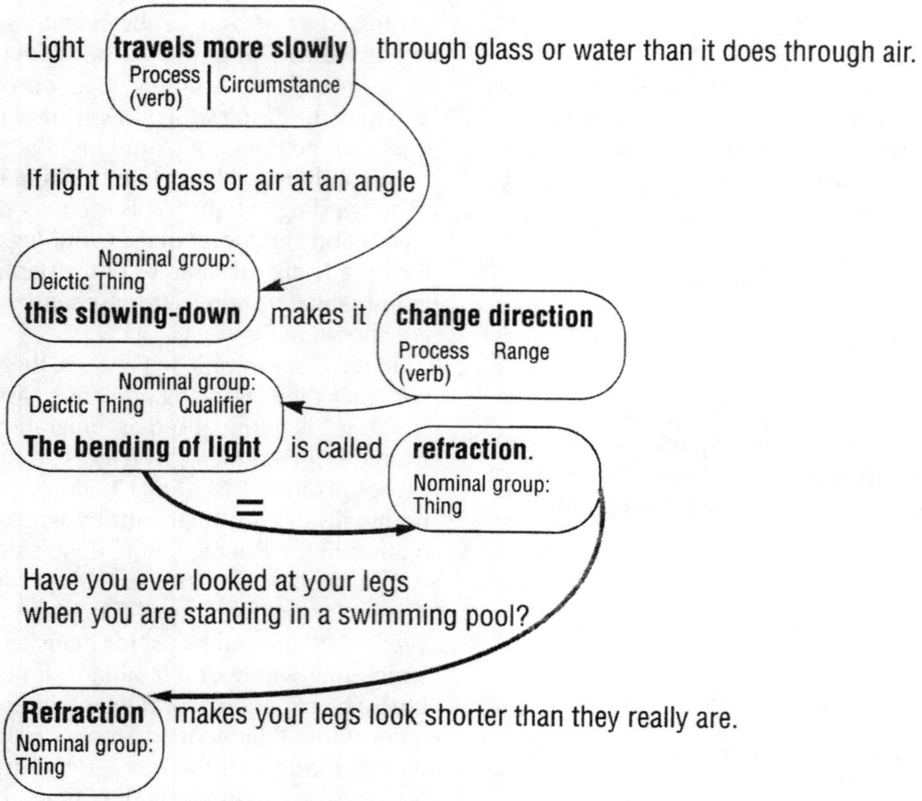

Light [**travels more slowly**] through glass or water than it does through air.
      Process (verb) | Circumstance

If light hits glass or air at an angle

Nominal group:
Deictic Thing
this slowing-down) makes it (**change direction**
                                  Process   Range
                                  (verb)

Nominal group:
Deictic Thing   Qualifier
The bending of light) is called (**refraction**.
                                       Nominal group:
                =   Thing

Have you ever looked at your legs
when you are standing in a swimming pool?

Refraction \ makes your legs look shorter than they really are.
Nominal group:
Thing

Figure 4
Use of nominalisation in secondary school history texts

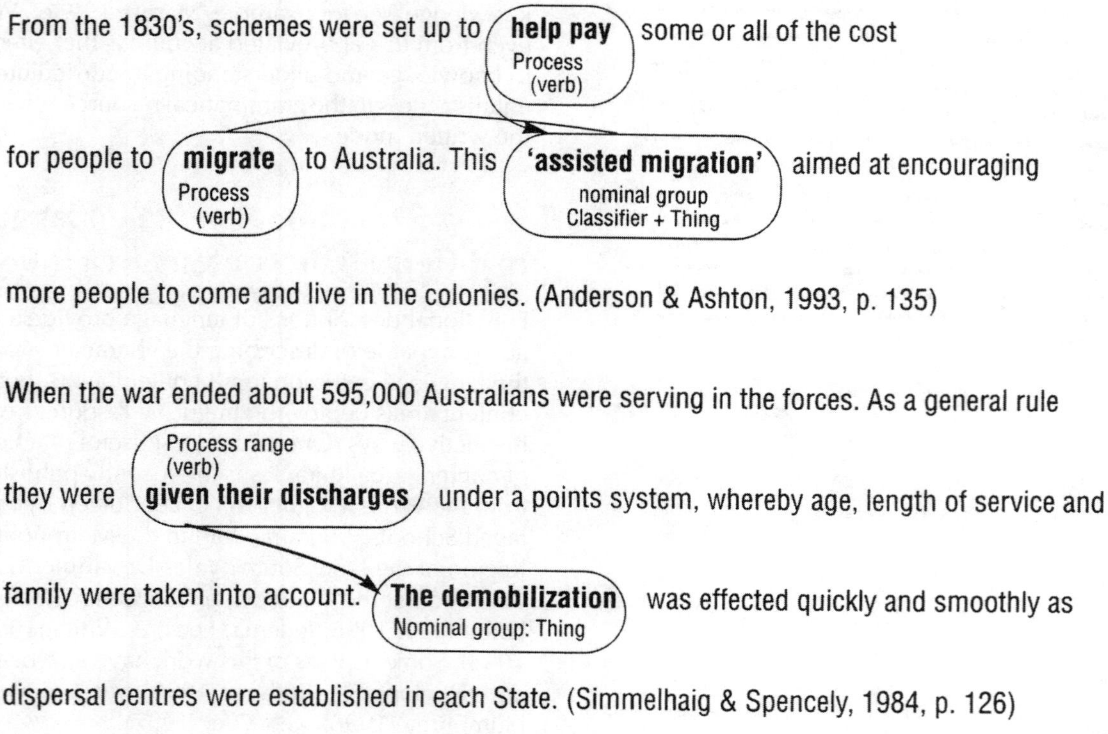

From the 1830's, schemes were set up to (**help pay**) some or all of the cost
                                            Process
                                            (verb)

for people to (**migrate**) to Australia. This (**'assisted migration'**) aimed at encouraging
                 Process   nominal group
                 (verb)   Classifier + Thing

more people to come and live in the colonies. (Anderson & Ashton, 1993, p. 135)

When the war ended about 595,000 Australians were serving in the forces. As a general rule

                 Process range
                 (verb)
they were \ **given their discharges**) under a points system, whereby age, length of service and

family were taken into account. (**The demobilization**) was effected quickly and smoothly as
                                    Nominal group: Thing

dispersal centres were established in each State. (Simmelhaig & Spencely, 1984, p. 126)

Article 19. Developing critical understanding of the specialised language of school science and history texts

Here I will focus briefly on some of the different ways language is used in science and history confining exploration to the different role played by nominalisation in the discourses of these school subject areas. The disciplines of history and science are viewed quite differently by most people and the language forms that construct these distinctive types of knowledge are also quite different, demanding different kinds of literate practices for their interpretation.

Science is a technical discourse (Martin, 1993b) since it builds up an alternative perspective on phenomena to that of common sense—a technical, scientific perspective. In school science this means taking common sense as a starting point and translating or constructing specialised knowledge from there. A good deal of this work involves building up meanings, accumulating them, and then equating them with, or distilling them into, a technical term. We can see this in the following text about the water cycle:

> Where does our rain come from? It all begins with the sun shining on the seas, rivers and puddles or your wet clothes on the washing line. The water becomes warm and tiny bits of water, too small to see, rise into the air as water vapour. This drying is called evaporation.

> As the water vapour rises higher into the air it cools. It changes back into minute drops of water forming clouds. This cooling back into water is called condensation. (McClymont, 1987, p. 8)

"This drying" is a nominalisation that compacts the meanings built up in the previous clauses. This compacted meaning is then translated into a technical term. "This drying" is identified with the (technical) nominalisation "evaporation" by the linking verb group "is called." The same manoeuvre occurs again in the second paragraph with "This cooling back into water is called condensation."

In the following example explaining winds several clauses are reduced into a single term, "convection current," in this way.

> Air begins to move when the sun heats the land and warms the air above. Molecules in the air move faster when they are heated and the air starts to expand. It becomes less dense than the surrounding air. At the same time, cooler, heavier air is drawn in below to replace the rising air. This circulation of air is called convection current. (Morgan, 1996, p. 10)

This text makes the whole process of "convection currents" available for use in further explanation as a single technical term without the need for cumbersome reiteration of what has already been dealt with.

While the language of subjects like science and geography are characterised by the development of this kind of technicality, Martin (1993b) pointed out that the discourse of history, by contrast, is not essentially a technical one:

> Aside from a small set of terms referring to periods of time (the Middle Ages, the Dark Ages, the Renaissance, etc.) and possibly some distinctive -isms (e.g., colonialism, imperialism, jingoism, etc.), relatively few technical terms are used; and where they are used they tend to be borrowed from other disciplines rather than established by the historical discourse itself (e.g., socialism, capitalism, market forces, etc.). (Martin, 1993b, p. 226)

As Martin went on to explain, the fact that the discourse of history is not technical does not make it any easier to read. This is because the language of history can be very abstract. And it is the use of grammatical metaphor that constructs this abstraction. Veel and Coffin (1996) showed that as students move from the genres or text types that chronicle history (biographical recount, historical recount) to genres or text types that explain and interpret history (e.g., historical account, factorial explanation, consequential explanation, analytical exposition) the presence of people as participants is effaced. Instead of people involved in processes, these event sequences are nominalised and, as abstract noun groups, they are related to other abstract noun groups.

Martin (1993b, p. 224) provided the following example:

> The enlargement of Australia's steel-making capacity, and of chemicals, rubber, metal goods and motor vehicles all owed something to the demands of war. (p. 224)

Notice that the nominalisations here ("The enlargement of Australia's steel-making capacity..." and "the demands of war") are not technical terms, but there is no mention of human agency. This can be easily seen if you try to "talk out" this text into the grammar of spoken language.

> The Australian Government and factory owners built more factories because Australians needed to make more steel and other goods than they had before so that they could supply more and more products because many more of these products than before were needed to replace the ones that were being quickly consumed as soldiers used them to fight the enemy.

The bundling together of events and their construal as abstract "Things" or noun groups through the grammatical resource of nominalisation is a functional aspect of the language of history. Nominalisation becomes a means of facilitating the writers' purpose. This occurs in a variety of ways (see Coffin, 1996). Once phenomena are "grammaticalised" as noun groups they have the potential for greatly extended description, classification, and qualification. For instance "opposition to the government's initiatives" can become:

Figure 5
Using nominalisation to texture information build up in a school history text

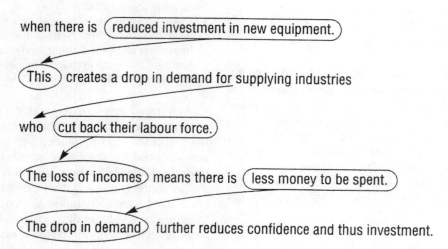

Adapted from Tudball, 1991, p. 358

extensive opposition to the government's initiatives

extensive violent opposition to the government's initiatives

extensive violent civil (or military) opposition to the government's initiatives

and so on. In addition, as indicated previously, the representation of events as nominalisations and hence as abstract nouns in the clause, enables them to be located in Theme position at the beginning of the clause. This facilitates the texturing of information build-up in explanatory texts, so that what is introduced as new events at the end of one clause, is summarised and restated as familiar information or Given in Theme position as the point of departure in the next clause.

Figure 5 illustrates this texturing with a section from a history text dealing with the Depression of the 1930s in Australia.

Although nominalisation is used functionally in both science and history, it creates different kinds of discourses in these content areas—a highly technical discourse of school science and a relatively nontechnical but highly abstract discourse of school history. There has been further exploration of this grammatical resource in the construction of distinctive discourses in other content areas (see for example, Veel, in press, on the role of nominalisation in mathematics education). A wide range of grammatical resources are integral to the construction of texts that are specific to content areas. Learning in content areas means learning to read, write, and talk about texts in the various content areas. Teachers' efforts to facilitate this learning will be enhanced through their own gradually increasing understanding of the role of grammatical concepts in the textual construction of content area knowledge and understanding.

Developing functional grammatical knowledge as a tool for critical literacy

> It is estimated, in fact, that if rainforest destruction occurs at the present rate, by the end of the century nearly half of the world's plant and animal species will be wiped out. (Humphrey, 1996, p. 154)

This text, like all texts, is not an innocent statement of fact. Like all texts, it deploys a variety of grammatical means of "colouring" its argument to position the reader to see it from the writer's viewpoint. By showing students these colouring techniques, teachers help them to see the "constructedness" of the texts, so that they are less likely to simply take the text at face value but may be more aware of its deliberate positioning of them as readers.

One familiar aspect of colouring in the above text is the use of emotive words like *destruction* instead of, say, *logging* and *wiped out* instead of *become extinct*. But notice also how whoever is doing the estimating is not mentioned, so grammatically speaking the agentless passive voice is used to present the information as if it were unassailable. While many grammatical techniques for colouring arguments are used across content areas, some grammatical forms characteristic of particular content areas can be identified as key colouring strategies in that curriculum area. Frequently used strategies in school history (Coffin, 1996) are summarised in Figure 6 and then further illustrated and discussed below.

History deals with the accumulation of events over long periods of time, so it tends to bundle such sequences of events together and package them as if they were a Thing. Hence we have periods of time like "the Depression," "the Gold Rushes," or "the Chinese Revolution." The grammatical resource being used is again nominalisation. As Coffin (1996) pointed out,

Figure 6
Frequently used "colouring" strategies in school history texts

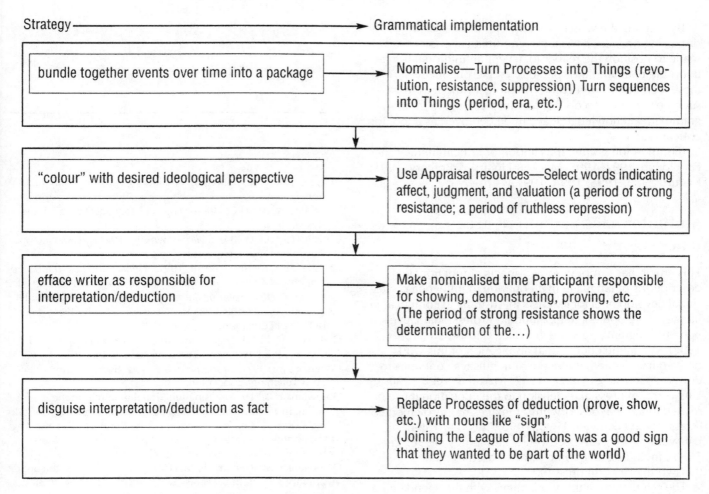

This makes it possible for a whole series of separate events, for example, attacking, burning, destroying, fighting, and resisting, to be condensed into a single nominal group such as "this period of Black resistance." (p. 91)

The particular nominalisation selected to do this condensing of events is strongly linked to the ideological and cultural perspective of the writer of the history. Compare the following possible nominalisations all condensing events over the same time span:

this period of black resistance

this period of early conflict

this period of black lawlessness

this period of black violence

this period of violent suppression of blacks

As nominalisations these periods of time can participate in a process as in the following example:

The period of violent suppression provided a catalyst for organised resistance.

Periods of time as noun groups can become the Appraiser—time and events themselves are responsible for proving, demonstrating, and showing. In this way the role of the historian/writer as interpreter is obscured and what is really an interpretation becomes naturalised as fact and hence unquestionable. For example:

The period of black resistance *showed* how strongly Aboriginal people resisted the invasion.

Deductions of this kind can be further abstracted from the writer responsible for them by choosing a grammatical structure that avoids verbs like *showed*, *demonstrated*, or *proved*. Instead a less straightforward way of "grammatical-ising" deduction is to use a noun like *sign*, which can then be qualified by *good*. The deductive process has been nominalised in the following example:

Joining the League of Nations was a clear *sign* that the country wanted to be part of the rest of the world. (Coffin, 1996, p. 155)

By effacing the writer as interpreter of events and disguising deductions as facts, grammatical choices are made to position the reader to accept an interpretation as unproblematic and indisputable. By alerting readers to these techniques, it becomes possible for them to resist such positioning. To do this readers need the kind of grammatical knowledge that can be deployed as a tool for critical reading.

(For more on grammar as a tool for critical literacy see Fairclough, 1992, 1995; Macken-Horarik & Rothery, 1991; Martin, 1989, 1995, 1996, 1997.)

Multiliteracies in content area teaching and learning

This article has sampled some aspects of functional descriptions of language that continue to influence professional development for teachers in Australia in content area literacy development (e.g., National Professional Development Program: New South Wales Consortium, 1996, 1997). While the educational application of this work derived from systemic functional linguistics continues to develop (Christie & Martin, 1997; Martin & Veel, 1998; Unsworth, in press a), extension to the educational use of related functional descriptions of images has also emerged (Kress & van Leeuwen, 1990, 1996; O'Toole, 1994, Unsworth, 1997; van Leeuwen & Humphrey, 1996; Veel, 1998), including electronic screen-based formats (Unsworth, 1997, in press b).

The orientation of this work aligns with the agenda for a pedagogy of multiliteracies as proposed in the *Harvard Educational Review* by the New London Group (1996). This group [Courtney Cazden (Harvard, USA); Bill Cope (University of Technology Sydney, Australia); Norman Fairclough (Lancaster University, UK); Jim Gee (Clark University, USA); Mary Kalantzis (James Cook University of North Queensland); Gunther Kress (University of London, UK); Allan Luke (University of Queensland, Australia); Carmen Luke (University of Queensland, Australia); Sarah Michaels (Clark University, USA); Martin Nakata (James Cook University of North Queensland, Australia)] advises that the multiliteracies for the future will need to be built on

an educationally accessible functional grammar; that is, a metalanguage that describes meaning in various realms. These include the textual and the visual, as well as the multi-modal relations between the different meaning-making processes that are now so critical in media texts and texts of electronic media. (p. 77)

Unsworth is head of the Division of Graduate Studies at the University of Sydney. He may be contacted at the Faculty of Education, University of Sydney, New South Wales 2008, Australia.

REFERENCES

Butt, D., Fahey, R., Spinks, S., & Yallop, C. (1995). *Using functional grammar: An explorer's guide.* Sydney: Macquarie University, National Centre for English Language Teaching and Research.

Christie, F. (Ed.). (1984). *Children writing: Study guide.* Geelong, Australia: Deakin University Press.

Christie, F., & Martin, J. (Eds). (1997). *Genres and institutions: Social processes in the workplace and school.* London: Cassell.

Coffin, C. (1996). *Exploring literacy in school history.* Sydney: Disadvantaged Schools Program, New South Wales Department of School Education.

Collerson, J. (1994). *English grammar: A functional approach.* Sydney: Primary English Teaching Association.

Collerson, J. (1997). *Grammar in teaching.* Sydney: Primary English Teaching Association.

Derewianka, B. (1995). Using functional grammar in the classroom. In J. Murray (Ed.), *Celebrating the differences, confronting literacies: Conference papers from the Australian Reading Association National Conference Sydney July 1995.* Melbourne: Australian Reading Association.

Derewianka, B., & Schmich, M. (1991). Factual texts in the upper primary school. In E. Furniss & P. Green (Eds.), *The literacy connection* (pp. 58–78). Melbourne: Eleanor Curtain.

Fairclough, N. (Ed.). (1992). *Critical language awareness.* London: Longman.

Fairclough, N. (1995). *Critical discourse analysis: The critical study of language.* London: Longman.

Gerot, L., & Wignell, P. (1995). *Making sense of functional grammar.* Sydney: Gerd Stabler, Antipodean Educational Enterprises.

Halliday, M.A.K. (1985). *Spoken and written language.* Geelong, Australia: Deakin University Press.

Halliday, M.A.K. (1993). Some grammatical problems in scientific English. In M.A.K. Halliday & J.R. Martin (Eds.), *Writing science: Literacy and discursive power* (pp. 69–85). London: Falmer.

Halliday, M.A.K. (1994). *An introduction to functional grammar* (2nd ed.). London: Edward Arnold.

Halliday, M.A.K., & Martin, J.R. (1993a). General orientation. In M.A.K. Halliday & J.R. Martin (Eds.), *Writing science: Literacy and discursive power* (pp. 2–21). London: Falmer.

Halliday, M.A.K., & Martin, J.R. (1993b). *The model.* In M.A.K. Halliday & J.R. Martin (Eds.), *Writing science: Literacy and discursive power* (pp. 22–50). London: Falmer.

Hammond, J. (1990). Is learning to read and write the same as learning to speak? In F. Christie (Ed.), *Literacy for a changing world* (pp. 26–53). Hawthorn, Australia: Australian Council for Educational Research.

Humphrey, S. (1996). *Exploring literacy in school geography*. Sydney: Disadvantaged Schools Program, New South Wales Department of School Education.

Iedema, R., Feez, S., & White, P. (1994). *Media literacy*. Sydney: Disadvantaged Schools Program, New South Wales Department of School Education.

Kress, G., & van Leeuwen, T. (1990). *Reading images*. Geelong, Australia: Deakin University Press.

Kress, G., & van Leeuwen, T. (1996). *Reading images: The grammar of visual design*. London: Routledge.

Macken-Horarik, M. (1996). Literacy and learning across the curriculum: Towards a model of register for secondary school teachers. In R. Hasan & G. Williams (Eds.), *Literacy and society* (pp. 232–278). London: Longman.

Macken-Horarik, M., & Rothery, J. (1991). *Developing critical literacy: A model for literacy in subject learning*. Sydney: Metropolitan East Disadvantaged Schools Program.

Martin, J.R. (1989). *Factual writing: Exploring and challenging social reality*. Oxford, England: Oxford University Press.

Martin, J.R. (1992). *English text: System and structure*. London: Benjamins.

Martin, J.R. (1993a). Genre and literacy—modelling context in educational linguistics. *Annual Review of Applied Linguistics, 13,* 141–172.

Martin, J.R. (1993b). Life as a noun: Arresting the universe in science and humanities. In M.A.K. Halliday & J.R. Martin (Eds.), *Writing science: Literacy and discursive power* (pp. 221–267). London: Falmer.

Martin, J.R. (1993c). Literacy in science: Learning to handle text as technology. In M.A.K. Halliday & J.R. Martin (Eds.), *Writing science: Literacy and discursive power* (pp. 166–202). London: Falmer

Martin, J.R. (1993d). Technicality and abstraction: Language for the creation of specialized texts. In M.A.K. Halliday & J.R. Martin (Eds.), *Writing science: Literacy and discursive power*(pp. 203–220). London: Falmer

Martin, J.R. (1993e). Technology, bureaucracy and schooling: Discourse resources and control. *Cultural Dynamics, 6*(1), 84–130.

Martin, J.R. (1995). Reading positions/positioning readers: JUDGMENT in English. *Prospect: A Journal of Australian TESOL, 10*(2), 27–37.

Martin, J.R. (1996). Evaluating disruption; symbolising theme in junior secondary narrative. In R. Hason & G. Williams (Eds.), *Literacy in society* (pp. 124–171). London: Longman.

Martin, J.R. (1997). Analysing genre: Functional parameters. In F. Christie & J.R. Martin (Eds.), *Genres and institutions: Social processes in the workplace and school* (pp. 3–39). London: Cassell Academic.

Martin, J.R. & Veel, R (Eds.). (1998). *Reading science: Critical and functional perspectives on discourses of science*. London: Routledge.

Matthiessen, C.M.I.M. (1995). *Lexicogrammatical cartography: English systems*. Tokyo: International Language Sciences Publishers.

National Professional Development Program. (1996). *Literacy across the key learning areas: Years 7&8*. Sydney: New South Wales Department of School Education.

National Professional Development Program. (1997). *Literacy in the middle years of schooling* [CD-ROM].

The New London Group. (1996). A pedagogy of multiliteracies: Designing social futures. *Harvard Educational Review, 66*(1), 60–91.

O'Brien, R (1975). *Z for Zachariah*. New York: Atheneum.

O'Toole, M. (1994). *The language of displayed art*. Leicester, England: Leicester University Press.

Perera, K. (1984). *Children's reading and writing*. Oxford, England: Blackwell.

Rothery, J. (1995). *Exploring literacy in school English*. Sydney: Disadvantaged Schools Program, New South Wales Department of School Education.

Rothery, J. (1996). Making changes: Developing and educational linguistics. In R. Hasan & G. Williams (Eds.), *Literacy in society* (pp. 86–123). London: Longman.

Unsworth, L. (1997). Scaffolding reading of science explanations: Accessing the grammatical and visual forms of specialized knowledge. *Reading, 31*(3), 30–42.

Unsworth, L. (Ed.). (in press a). *Researching language in schools and communities: Functional linguistic perspectives*. London: Cassell Academic.

Unsworth, L. (in press b). Explaining school science in book and CD ROM formats: Using semiotic analyses to compare the textual construction of knowledge. *International Journal of Instructional Media, 26*(2).

van Leeuwen,T., & Humphrey, S. (1996). On learning to look through a geographer's eyes. In R. Hasan & G. Williams (Eds.), *Literacy in society* (pp. 29–49). London: Longman.

Veel, R. (1997). Learning how to mean scientifically speaking: Apprenticeship in scientific discourse in the secondary school. In F. Christie & J.R. Martin (Eds.), *Genres and institutions* (pp. 161–195). London: Cassell.

Veel, R. (1998). The greening of school science: Ecogenesis in secondary classrooms. In J.R. Martin & R. Veel (Eds.), *Reading science: Critical and functional perspectives on discourses of science* (pp. 14–151). London: Routledge.

Veel, R. (in press). Language, knowledge and authority in school mathematics. In F. Christie (Ed.), *Pedagogy and the shaping of consciousness: Linguistic and social processes*. London: Cassell Academic.

Veel, R., & Coffin, C. (1996). Learning to think like an historian: The language of secondary school history. In R. Hasan & G. Williams (Eds.), *Literacy and society* (pp. 191–231). London: Longman.

Wells, G. (1994). The complementary contributions of Halliday and Vygotsky to a "Language-based Theory of Learning." *Linguistics and Education, 6*(1), 41–90.

Williams, G. (1994, December). *Semiotic mediation and childrens development of knowledge about language*. Paper presented at the International Language Education Conference, University of Hong Kong.

Williams, G. (1995). *Learning systemic functional grammar in primary schools*. Style Council Macquarie Conference Proceedings. Sydney: Dictionary Research Centre, Macquarie University.

Williams, G., & French, R. (1995). *The Haberfield Grammar Club*. Paper presented to the Australian Systemic Functional Linguistics Conference, University of Melbourne.

Williams, G., Rothery J., & French, R. (1994). *Children learning systemic functional grammar in Year Six*. Plenary address to the Australian Systemic Linguistics Conference, University of Queensland.

Williams, G., Rothery J., & French, R. (1995, July). *Children learning functional grammar in practice*. Conference Institute, Australian Reading Association Annual Conference, Sydney.

SCHOOL TEXTS

Anderson, M., & Ashton, P. (1993) *Focus on Australian history*. Melbourne: Macmillan Education.

Bender, L. (1988). *Spiders*. London: Franklin Watts.

Bright, M. (1988). *Killing for luxury*. London: Franklin Watts.

McClymont, D. (1987). *Water*. London: Macdonald.

Morgan, S. (1996). *Weather*. Sydney: Allen & Unwin.

Simmelhaig, H., & Spenceley, G. (1984). *For Australia's sake: A history of Australia's involvement in nine wars*. Melbourne: Nelson.

Simon, N. (1987). *Vanishing habitats*. London: Franklin Watts.

Taylor, B. (1989). *Science starters: Bouncing and bending light*. London: Franklin Watts.

Tudball, L. (1991). *Australian perspectives: Australian history for senior students*. Brisbane: Jacaranda Press.

From *Journal of Adolescent & Adult Literacy* Vol. 42, No. 7, April 1999, pages 508–521. Copyright © 1999 by The International Reading Association. Reprinted with permission.

Learning from social studies textbooks:
Why some students succeed and others fail

Some texts demand more reading energy—a repertoire of reading abilities to cope with both the text's surface and its deep structure. Happily, there are ways to help students compensate for inadequate reading energy.

Elton G. Stetson
Richard P. Williams

There can be little doubt that a large number of American students cannot understand their social studies textbooks, and the empirical evidence over-whelmingly supports this perception (Hill & Erwin, 1984: Lunstrum, 1987). Regardless of how one perceives the difficulty level of these textbooks, research reveals that the failure rate from reading them ranges from a low of 50% (Wait, 1987) to a high of 92% (Sellars, 1987/1988).

Why some students learn from their social studies textbooks and others do not can be explained rather easily. The answer lies in four basic assumptions about reading textbooks, which apply particularly to social studies materials.

Assumption 1—Readers possess a repertoire of abilities, defined as reading energy, that are brought to any reading task.

Assumption 2—Textbooks contain two kinds of energy requirements which must be met in order to be understood: surface structure (decoding) requirements and deep structure (comprehension) requirements.

Assumption 3—Learning from textbooks depends largely upon readers' ability to exert energy in sufficient amounts to meet both surface structure and deep structure requirements of the text.

Assumption 4—When reading energy is not sufficient, students tend to consume so much of their energy deciphering the surface structure that energy needed to comprehend and remember factual information, terms, concepts, and the deeper meaning of the text is simply not available.

To understand these assumptions in depth, it is necessary to explore more closely the reader, social studies textbooks, and the interaction of the two. The purpose of this article, then, is to examine the skills readers bring to the reading act, print requirements of social studies textbooks, why breakdowns in learning sometimes occur during reader interaction with text, and possible solutions.

Readers and reading energy

When students read a social studies textbook, they bring to the task their own personal repertoire of reading energy which consists of at least three interrelated abilities: (a) skill in decoding surface structure of the text, (b) previously acquired knowledge and perceptions about the topic, and (c) the language skills they possess for combining information obtained from decoding the text with their previously acquired knowledge and perceptions in order to create meaning from the text.

Skill in decoding print is the ability to decipher the surface structure of the text and to translate print to speech. To decode well, one must not only translate letters to sounds, divide sounds into appropriate parts, and recognize words on sight, one must also be able to use these skills rapidly and automatically. There is ample support for the importance of surface structure skills in the reading process (Bradley & Bryant, 1978; Butler & Hains, 1979; Ehri & Wilce, 1979; Perfetti, Finger, & Hogaboam, 1978; Perfetti & Lesgold, 1979; Vellutino, 1977; West & Stanovich, 1979), and the connection between efficient word processing, automaticity, and good comprehension has also been clearly established (Calfee & Drum, 1985: Gough, 1985; Manis, 1985; Stanovich, 1986; Stanovich, Cunningham, & West, 1981; Torgesen, 1986).

As skill with surface structure improves, and as that skill is used more rapidly and becomes more automatic, the amount of reading energy consumed for decoding print is greatly reduced, leaving more energy available for comprehension. However, while skill in decoding is necessary, it is never sufficient in itself because it is possible to decode rather fluently and still not comprehend. For example, some have had the experience of studying Spanish and being able to read it aloud after only a few lessons while never learning to understand what was read.

A second component of reading energy is topical knowledge, the information one possesses beforehand about a specific topic (Harris & Sipay, 1990). This includes competence with the vocabulary, facts stored in memory, concepts attained, and possession of a schema system about the topic which has been created in the mind by the readers. Extracting meaning from social studies textbooks depends on what a reader already knows about the topic.

The amount of prior knowledge one possesses is one of the more accurate predictors of comprehension ability (Marr & Gormley, 1982; Pearson, 1985), and the influence of one's schema system on comprehension of text has been clearly established (Anderson & Pearson, 1984; Bartlett, 1932; Minsky, 1975; Rosenblatt, 1978).

According to Gillet and Temple (1990), schemata are like frameworks in a person's brain around which previously acquired topical information is organized. This framework contains holes that can be filled in by new information from the text being read. When new information is taken in during reading, an attempt is made to place it in one of the holes of the schema system where it makes sense. Sometimes this works, while at other times the new information makes no sense at all.

Some readers with a lot of topical knowledge have well-formed schema systems which make deriving meaning from new information easier and learning from textbooks highly probable. Conversely, the less topical knowledge

readers possess, the more nebulous their schema systems tend to be, and the likelihood that learning will occur is greatly diminished.

Competence with language is a third component of reading energy and is considered by many as the single most important ingredient for success in reading social studies materials (Butler, Marsh, Sheppard, & Sheppard, 1985; Horn & Packard, 1985; Ruddell, 1974).

Gardner and Hatch (1989) refer to language facility as the ability to use linguistic and logical-mathematical symbolization. This involves a reader's knowledge of general vocabulary, the amount of general information stored in memory, the ability to solve problems without regard to subject matter and, according to Gardner and Hatch, the capacity to discern logical or numerical patterns, to reason in complex situations, and to be sensitive to the different functions of language.

One's language system acts both as the mixing bowl in which the newly decoded print and the previously acquired knowledge about the topic are blended together and as the filter or schema system through which this newly blended information passes in an attempt to create meaning.

Before leaving this part of the discussion, we want to be sure that no one is left with the notion that there are only three components to reading energy or that components not discussed here are any less important. For example, knowing the purpose for reading social studies material, possessing or acquiring an interest in the topic, and having confidence in the ability to learn information from reading are also vital components of reading energy. When present, this kind of reading energy can be so powerful that weakness in the other three components can actually be overcome. In its absence, learning from social studies textbooks can be brought to a complete halt in spite of the strength of the reader's other skills and knowledge.

Social studies textbooks

Independent of the reader, social studies textbooks have reading energy requirements that must be met in order for them to be understood.

There are a number of factors in a text that influence the ease or difficulty with which it is understood. One major factor—and the one with which students must deal first—is the surface structure of the textbook itself, that is, length of sentences, number of polysyllabic words, and the numerous graphophonic (letter-sound) combinations.

Determining readability levels of textbooks is typically based on these factors, and readability studies have shown rather consistently that social studies textbooks: (a) are more difficult to read than textbooks in many other subject areas; (b) often require more reading energy than their targeted students possess; and (c) vary as much as 4 or more years in reading difficulty from one passage to another, even within the same text (DuVall, 1971; Hill & Erwin,

1984; Johnson, 1970/1971, 1975, 1977; Sellars, 1987/1988; Turner, 1968; Wait, 1987).

A second factor is the deep structure of the text, including the amount and difficulty of important vocabulary, the complexity of the concepts to be learned, and the sheer volume of facts typically found in social studies textbooks.

Finally, the way in which authors organize a text, communicate its goals, present information within an understandable context, and ask appropriate questions of students can have a significant effect on how user friendly a text can be. Unfortunately, there is mounting evidence that many social studies textbooks do a poor job of communicating such information clearly to the reader (Armbruster & Gudbrandsen, 1986; Crismore, 1983).

Students in upper grades tend to have more reading energy than those in lower grades. Correspondingly, social studies textbooks used in higher grades tend to have higher energy requirements than those used in lower grades.

While students' reading energy and the energy requirements of textbooks both increase from one grade level to the next, it must be kept in mind that, even among students of the same age or grade, significant variations exist in individual reading energy. Similarly, a social studies textbook will vary significantly in its energy requirements from one paragraph to the next and from one sentence to the next even within the same paragraph.

Interacting reader and text

It is important now to examine what happens when the reader and social studies textbook interact. Understanding a passage requires an effective and efficient interaction between the reader and text which is realized through two separate but interactive steps.

In the first step, the student uses whatever reading energy is necessary to mediate the surface structure requirements of the text—reading the words. The result of this initial interaction is a decoding of the symbols to inner or oral language. Adequate surface structure skills provide the reader with the tools to decode print. As important as decoding may be, however, comprehension cannot be presumed until this first interaction is supported by the second.

The second step takes place simultaneously and interactively with the first. In it, the reader employs reading energy left over from decoding to match the deeper structure of the text—vocabulary, facts, and concepts—with the schema system the reader has developed in which all previously acquired language skills and knowledge of the topic have been placed.

To get meaning from social studies texts, then, the reader needs sufficient reading energy to accommodate both the surface structure of text and its deep structure of meaning. Figure 1 illustrates this.

Naturally, reading is far more complex than for us to suggest that first one decodes and second the decoded language leads to comprehension. Most experts believe

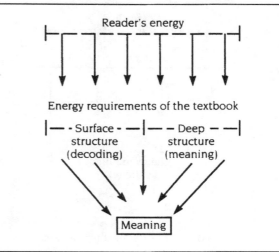

Figure 1
Distributions of reading energy

reading is a skill of interaction in which the reader decodes and comprehends back and forth interactively and simultaneously (Rumelhart, 1985; Stetson, 1983). The two terms are separated here merely to define them and identify their attributes.

Regardless of how the two interact, there is general agreement that both decoding and comprehension are necessary if students are to succeed in reading the social studies text (Duffy & Roehler, 1986: Finn, 1985; Heilman, Blair, & Rupley, 1986).

Comprehension:
Success or failure

Illustrating successful and unsuccessful reading is relatively easy. Using shorter lines to represent less energy and longer lines to represent more energy, one can readily see in Figure 2 that while the energy requirements of the textbook are the same in both scenarios, the reading energy of the student in Scenario A exceeds the textbook's requirements, and the reading energy of the student in Scenario B is less than required.

Here are two students in the same room reading the same social studies text. Yet, the probability of learning from textbook reading is very high for the student in Scenario A and equally low for the student in Scenario B.

When the reading energy available to the reader exceeds that required by the text, as illustrated for Reader A, both decoding and comprehension typically occur with relative ease. An example of this is when the teacher reads aloud to the class from the social studies text. The teacher's energy is so clearly superior to that required by the text that oral reading is easy, fluent, and automatic and comprehension is obvious.

Figure 2
Easy and difficult reader–textbook interactions

Scenario A
An easy reader–text interaction

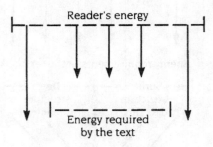

Scenario B
A difficult reader–text interaction

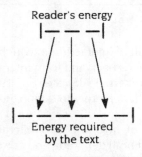

Figure 3
Result of insufficient reading energy on comprehension

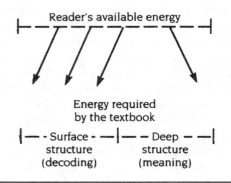

For a student, on the other hand, whose reading energy fails to measure up to that required by the social studies textbook, as illustrated for Reader B, a variety of problems are likely to occur, including failure to learn.

When reading energy becomes inadequate, students are forced subconsciously to make decisions about how their reading energy will be used. Unless taught otherwise, most readers will unknowingly give priority to decoding the surface structure. When this occurs, as illustrated in Figure 3, failure to learn is almost assured.

This tendency might be attributed in part to the emphasis given in the early grades to mastering decoding skills, phonic skills, reading accuracy, and fluency and to "sounding good." Regardless of the cause, when reading energy is shifted disproportionately to surface structure, the remaining reading energy is often insufficient for social studies comprehension.

The student may sound fluent during oral reading, a feat which often leads teachers and students to believe that comprehension is also occurring, but this is not necessarily the case. Gillet and Temple (1990) explain this phenomenon: "they get so involved in puzzling out the words, by their sounds, that they pay less attention to the meaning of the passage… Their brain is so absorbed there is little left for comprehending higher-order information".

To compound matters, these students typically lack prior knowledge about the topic. That weakens their schema systems, which consequently diminishes their ability to understand and assimilate new information about that topic (Myer, 1977). What new information they might read in the text fails to make sensible connections in their schema systems and is often not understood or is misunderstood.

This is especially true with nonfiction materials such as social studies (Marshall & Gluck, 1978-79). Even those who function adequately reading fiction often begin to experience great difficulty in the intermediate grades when the reading of nonfiction increases dramatically (Richards, 1978).

The result of inadequate reading energy may be that it is sufficient for fluency but not for comprehension. And, while sounding good might be appreciated by the teacher who judges good reading on the basis of fluency and accuracy, sounding good is hardly the primary objective of social studies teachers, who want students to acquire new terms, learn concepts, remember facts, and understand relationships.

In the end, unfortunately, the amount of new information learned may not be enough to affect the knowledge base to any extent and is almost always insufficient for these students to pass tests over the social studies material.

Solutions

The ability to comprehend requires that students not only possess sufficient reading energy to meet the requirements of the social studies textbook but also distribute that energy to meet both surface and deep structure requirements of the text. When energy is not sufficient or not distributed appropriately, comprehension is likely to suffer without some form of intervention.

Ultimately, it is the teacher, sometimes motivated by students or parents, who must seek ways to increase the probability that learning will occur. There are four basic ways this can be accomplished: (a) increase the reading energy of students to match that required of social studies textbooks; (b) teach students to use less energy for decoding in order to have more available for comprehension; (c) decrease the energy requirements of social studies textbooks until they more closely match that of readers; and (d) when the gap between reader energy and text requirements is too great, eliminate the need to read altogether.

Increase reader's energy. There are a number of dependable strategies for increasing students' reading energy rather quickly. One is to preview new materials with students prior to formal instruction. Students are directed to survey the chapter, doing four things: (1) silently read the initial paragraphs that serve as the introduction; (2) silently read the boldface headings and the first sentence of every paragraph within each major section of the chapter; (3) read summary paragraphs in their entirety; and (4) conclude with a spontaneous recitation in which students discuss what they read, what they learned, and what the chapter is basically all about.

This 20-30 minute activity, usually conducted on the first day of a new chapter or unit, meets two very important prerequisites for effective learning. First, it exposes readers to new information that, once added to their knowledge base, increases their reading energy and strengthens their schema systems for social studies. Second, surveys provide readers with advanced organizers or maps of where the author will take them in the chapter. Because social studies textbooks tend to be poorly organized (Thorpe, 1986/1987), it is important that surveys allow students to create their own organization.

A second strategy is to preteach key vocabulary. The more key words that are foreign to students, the more time they waste using the context to decipher word meanings, which disrupts comprehension (Harris & Sipay, 1990; Perfetti, 1985). Preteaching key vocabulary (a) increases a student's specific word knowledge about the topic, (b) increases overall reading energy, and (c) allows the reader to devote additional energy to comprehension.

Concerning effective methods for teaching key vocabulary. Nelson-Herber (1986) recommends direct instruction. In deciding which words to preteach, Harris & Sipay (1990) suggest that teachers ask the following questions:

1. How important is the word to understanding the text?
2. How likely is the word's particular meaning to be understood?
3. Does the context reveal the meaning and do the students have the skill to use that contextual information?
4. Does the text define the word and how adequate is the definition?
5. How important to future learning is the word's meaning?

In addition to preteaching key words, key concepts and important statements should also be taught in advance. There is ample evidence that when teachers take time to teach specific information prior to students reading the text, comprehension of the text improves (Beck, Omanson, & McKeown, 1982; Calfee & Drum, 1985: Ruddell & Speaker, 1985; Stahl & Jacobson, 1986).

Use available energy more effectively. Equally as important as expanding students' energy is guiding redistribution of the limited energy they possess so that less is used on surface structure, leaving more available for comprehension.

One way to effect this change is to give as little attention as possible to reading errors—especially those that have low impact on meaning—when students read aloud in class. Too much correcting is often interpreted by students to mean that good reading means "sounding good." In social studies, where the objectives are almost always content specific, focusing too much energy on the surface structure can become counterproductive. Those who believe that better accuracy produces better comprehension should keep in mind what Johnson & Baumann (1984) concluded from their summary of the research: "empirically, we have been unable to document strong support for such belief".

One of the more effective ways to get better comprehension mileage out of limited energy resources is to use repeated readings, the fast-growing practice of directing students to read materials more than once. A growing body of research supports the use of repeated reading to improve both fluency and comprehension (Dowhower, 1987, 1989; Samuels & Eisenberg, 1981; Torgesen, 1986).

In essence, the more often students reread, the more fluent reading becomes. As fluency improves, greater amounts of energy are released for use on the more important deep structure of the text.

There are many variations of repeated reading. One is paired repeated reading in which two students read passages several times, sometimes in unison and sometimes to each other (Koskinen & Blum, 1986). Another is when the teacher assigns short passages to be read silently followed by oral or choral reading and then discussion.

Reduce textbook energy requirements. One way to reduce the difficulty of social studies textbooks is to use those materials that have less difficult surface structure requirements—use easier materials to teach the same concepts. While this does not provide students with more reading energy, it does allow them to use more of the reading energy they have for comprehension.

In reading research., there is ample evidence to support the use of easy materials for teaching difficult concepts (Barr, 1982; Berliner, 1981; Tierney & Cunningham, 1984). These same concepts used in reading instruction can be applied to social studies instruction as well.

Another way to reduce textbook requirements is to narrow the concepts to be learned. Even the most capable students find it difficult to learn everything they read. Pauk

(1974) shows that even average learners forget 56% of new information within 24 hours and 92% within 14 days unless measures are taken to retain that information. As the amount of information to be processsed multiplies, the likelihood of learning and remembering decreases.

Since most students have not developed the ability to make good judgments about what should be learned and what can safely be ignored, teachers should assist students in making these decisions.

To accomplish this, prepare the chapter test first, then mark all the places in the social studies text where answers to the test questions can be found. In addition, mark other important information even though it may not be on the test.

Then teach students to watch for certain signal statements such as "this is an important paragraph" or "know this because..." or "are you prepared to identify the six New England states?" Help them understand that when you use these signal words you are alerting them to information you feel they should know because it is important or because it might be on the test.

Reduce the need to read. When all else fails, teachers should consider reading aloud to students, one of the tried and true methods for helping students learn difficult material. This learning through listening technique is more effective than student oral or silent reading for most elementary students (Harris & Sipay, 1990) and for students at all levels who have problems reading and learning (Stetson, 1983).

When teachers read aloud, all of the difficulties that energy-deficient readers have with print disappear. Teachers not only read fluently, they add important embellishments that enhance comprehension opportunities such as gestures, facial expressions, and proper use of pitch, stress, and juncture.

During listening, students no longer have to divide what little energy they have between decoding and comprehension. The need for decoding energy is completely removed from the task, allowing students to focus all their energy on meaning and remembering.

There are variations on the theme of learning through listening that can be as effective as having the teacher read aloud. One variation is that of assigning particularly important passages to a student who, after first reading the passage silently, reads it orally to the class. Another is that of making available tape recordings of the materials that may have been prepared by parent helpers, parent organizations, or student volunteers who are good readers. Most students with limited reading energy also benefit greatly when teachers follow up any silent reading assignment with group discussion about its terms, concepts, and important information.

What is crucial in all of these listening strategies is that someone is reading aloud or talking about social studies information in the text and that helps compensate for inadequate reading energy.

Summary and conclusions

Reading energy is the composite of skills readers possess to interact with decoding and comprehension requirements of the text. Some readers use more reading energy than other readers, and some textbooks require more reading energy to comprehend than others. As long as reading energy equals that required by the text, meaning is gained with relative ease. However, when the energy requirements of the text exceed that available to readers, students tend to pay more attention to the surface structure of the social studies text at the expense of meaning.

When the primary purpose for reading is to learn social studies concepts, teachers should be aware of strategies that allow students to concentrate their reading energy on meaning. Some possibilities we have mentioned include: (a) increasing students' reading energy by using surveys, preteaching vocabulary, and preteaching important concepts; (b) teaching students to shift more energy to comprehension by paying as little attention to reading errors as possible and by using the principle of repeated readings; (c) decreasing energy requirements of social studies textbooks by using easier-to-read materials, narrowing the bits of information to be learned to a more manageable number, and teaching students to watch for words that signal important information; and (d) reducing the need to learn entirely through reading by having better readers read orally and by having group discussion after silent reading.

It is reasonable to believe that we get from students what we teach them to give us. If this is true, taking reading energy into consideration when planning social studies instruction might increase the probability that our students will learn what we intend for them to learn.

Stetson teaches at East Texas State University (Department of Elementary Education, Commerce TX 75429, USA). Williams teaches in the Department of Instructional Leadership and Academic Curriculum, College of Education, at the university of Oklahoma, Norman, Oklahoma.

References

Anderson, R.C., & Pearson, P.D. (1984, January). *A schema-theoretic view of basic processes in reading comprehension.* (Tech. Rep. No. 306). Champaign, IL: Center for the Study of Reading. University of Illinois.

Armbruster, B.B., & Gudbrandsen, B.H. (1986). Reading comprehension instruction in social studies programs. *Reading Research Quarterly, 21,* 36-48.

Barr, R. (1982). Classroom reading instruction from a sociological perspective. *Journal of Reading Behavior, 14,* 375-389.

Bartlett, F.C. (1932). *Remembering: A study in experimental and social psychology.* Cambridge, England: Cambridge University Press.

Beck, I.L., Omanson, R.C., & McKeown, M.G. (1982). An instructional redesign of reading lessons: Effects on comprehension. *Reading Research Quarterly, 17,* 462-481.

Berliner, D.C. (1981). Academic learning time and reading achievement. In J.T. Guthrie (Ed.), *Comprehension and teaching: Research reviews*. Newark, DE: International Reading Association.

Bradley, L., & Bryant, P.E. (1978). Difficulties in auditory organization as a possible cause of reading backwardness. *Nature, 271*, 746-747.

Butler, B., & Hains, S. (1979). Individual differences in word recognition latency. *Memory and Cognition, 7*, 68-76.

Butler, S.R., Marsh, H.W., Sheppard, M.J., & Sheppard, J.L. (1985). Seven-year longitudinal study of early prediction of reading achievement. *Journal of Educational Psychology, 72*, 349-361.

Calfee, R.C., & Drum, P.A. (1985). Research in teaching reading. In M.C. Wittrock (Ed.), *Handbook on teaching* (3rd ed., pp. 804-849). New York: Macmillan.

Crismore, A. (1983). *The rhetoric of social studies textbooks: Metadiscourse*. (ERIC Document Reproduction Service No. ED 239 226)

Dowhower, S.L. (Fall, 1987). Effects of repeated reading on second-grade transitional readers' fluency and comprehension. *Reading Research Quarterly, 22*, 389-406.

Dowhower, S.L. (1989). Repeated reading: Research into practice. *The Reading Teacher, 42*, 502-507.

Duffy, G.G., & Roehler, L.R. (1986). *Improving classroom reading instruction: A decision-making approach*. New York: Random House.

DuVall, C.R. (1971). *A study of the measured readability level of selected intermediate grade social studies textbooks*. (ERIC Reproduction Document Service No. ED 051 049)

Ehri, L.C., & Wilce, L.S. (1979). Does word training increase or decrease interference in a Stroop task? *Journal of Experimental Child Psychology, 27*, 352-364.

Finn, P.J. (1985). *Helping children to read*. New York: Random House.

Gardner, H. & Hatch, T. (1989). Multiple intelligences go to school: Educational implications of the theory of multiple intelligences. *Educational Researcher, 18*, 4-10.

Gillet, J.W. & Temple, C. (1990). *Understanding reading problems: Assessment and instruction* (3rd ed.). Glenview, IL: Scott. Foresman/Little, Brown Higher Education Division.

Gough, P.B. (1985). One second of reading. In H. Singer & R.B. Ruddell (Eds.), *Theoretical models and processes of reading* (3rd ed., pp. 661-686). Newark, DE: International Reading Association.

Harris, A.I., & Sipay, E.R. (1990). *How to increase reading ability: A guide to developmental and remedial methods* (9th ed.). New York: Longman.

Heilman, A., Blair, T.R., & Rupley, W.H. (1986). *Principles and practices of teaching reading* (6th ed.). Columbus, OH: Charles E. Merrill.

Hill, W.R., & Erwin, R.W. (1984). The readability of content textbooks used in middle and junior high school. *Reading Psychology, 5*, 105-117.

Horn, W.F. & Packard, T. (1985). Early identification of learning problems: A meta-analysis. *Journal of Educational Psychology, 77*, 597-607.

Johnson, D.D., & Baumann, J.F. (1984). Word identification. In P.D. Pearson (Ed.), *Handbook of reading research* (pp. 583-608). New York: Longman.

Johnson, R.E. (1971). *How readable are our elementary social studies textbooks?* Paper presented at the International Reading Association Convention. Anaheim, CA. May 6-9, 1970. (ERIC Document Reproduction Service No. ED 043459)

Johnson, R.E. (1975, November). *Teachers beware: Elementary social studies textbooks are getting harder to read*. Paper presented at the Annual Meeting of the National Council for the Social Studies. Atlanta, GA. (ERIC Document Reproduction Service No. ED 115 572)

Johnson, R.E. (1977). The readability of elementary social studies textbooks is decreasing. *Social Science Record, 14*, 25-28.

Koskinen, P.S., & Blum, I.H. (1986). Paired repeated reading: A classroom strategy for developing fluent reading. *The Reading Teacher, 40*, 70-75.

Lunstrum, J.P. (1987, June). *Whatever happened to the crisis in reading in the social studies?* Paper presented at the annual meeting of the Social Science Education Consortium. Salt Lake City, UT.

Manis, F.R. (1985). Acquisition of word identification skills in normal and disabled readers. *Journal of Educational Psychology, 77*, 78-90.

Marr, M.B., & Gormley, K. (1982). Children's recall of familiar and unfamiliar text. *Reading Research Quarterly, 18*, 80-104.

Marshall, N., & Gluck, M. (1978-79). Comprehension of connected discourse. *Reading Research Quarterly, 14*, 10-56.

Minsky, M. (1975). A framework for representing knowledge. In P.H. Winston (Ed.), *A theory of computer vision*. New York: McGraw-Hill.

Myer, B. (1977). The structure of prose: Effects on learning and memory and implications for educational practice. In R.P. Anderson & S. Rand (Eds.), *Schooling and the acquisition of knowledge*. Hillsdale, NJ: Erlbaum.

Nelson-Herber, J. (1986). Expanding and refining vocabulary in content areas. *Journal of Reading, 29*, 626-633.

Pauk, W. (1974). *How to study in college* (2nd ed.). Boston, MA: Houghton Mifflin.

Pearson, P.D. (1985). *The comprehension revolution: A twenty-five year history of process and practice related to reading comprehension*. (Reading Education Report No. 57). Champaign, IL: Center for the Study of Reading. University of Illinois.

Perfetti, CA. (1985). *Reading ability*. New York: Oxford University Press.

Perfetti, CA., Finger, E., & Hogaboam, T. (1978). Sources of vocalization latency differences between skilled and less-skilled young readers. *Journal of Educational Psychology, 70*, 730-739.

Perfetti, CA., & Lesgold, A.M. (1979). Coding and comprehension in skilled reading and implications for reading instruction. In L. Resnick & Weaver (Eds.), *Theory and practice of early reading: Vol. 1* (pp. 57-84). Hillsdale, NJ: Erlbaum.

Richards, J. (1978). *Classroom language: What sorts?* London: Allen and Unwin.

Rosenblatt, L. (1978). *The reader, the text, the poem*. Carbondale, IL: Southern Illinois University Press.

Ruddell, R.B. (1974). *Reading-language instruction: Innovative practice*. Englewood Cliffs, NJ: Prentice-Hall.

Ruddell, R.B., & Speaker, R.B., Jr. (1985). The interactive reading process: A model. In H. Singer & R. Ruddell (Eds.), *Theoretical models and processes of reading* (3rd ed., pp. 751-793). Newark, DE: International Reading Association.

Rumelhart, D.E. (1985). Toward an interactive model of reading. In H. Singer & R. Ruddell (Eds.), *Theoretical models and processes of reading* (3rd ed., pp. 722-750). Newark, DE: International Reading Association.

Samuels, S.J., & Eisenberg, P. (1981). A framework for understanding the reading process. In E Pirozzolo & M. Wittrock (Eds.), *Neuropsychological and cognitive processes in reading* (pp. 31-67). New York: Academic Press.

Sellars, G.B. (1988). A comparison of the readability of selected high school social studies, science, and literature textbooks (Doctoral dissertation. Florida State University, 1987). *Dissertation Abstracts International, 48*, 3085A.

Stahl, S.A. & Jacobson, M.G. (1986). Vocabulary difficulty, prior knowledge, and text comprehension. *Journal of Reading Behavior, 18*, 309-323.

Stanovich, K.E. (1986). Cognitive processes and the reading problems of learning-disabled children: Evaluating their assumption of specificity. In J.K. Torgesen & B.Y.L. Wong (Eds.), *Psychological and educational perspectives on learning disabilities* (pp. 87-131). New York: Academic Press.

Stanovich, K.E., Cunningham, A.E., & West, R.F. (1981). A longitudinal study of the development of automatic recognition skills in first graders. *Journal of Reading Behavior, 13,* 57-74.

Stetson, E.G. (1983). Definitions, theories, and models of reading. In D. Phelps-Terasaki, T. Phelps-Gunn, & E. Stetson (Eds.), *Remediation and instruction in language: Oral language, reading, and writing* (pp. 131-157). Rockville, MD: Aspen Systems Corporation.

Thorpe, L.D. (1987). Prior knowledge and reading: An investigation of fourth grade social studies textbooks and basal readers. (Doctoral dissertation, Clarement Graduate School, 1986). *Dissertation Abstracts International, 47,* 2527A.

Tierney, R.J., & Cunningham, J.W. (1984). Research on teaching reading comprehension. In P.D. Pearson (Ed.), *Handbook of reading research* (pp. 609-655). New York: Longman.

Torgesen, J.K. (1986). Learning disabilities theory: Its current state and future prospects. *Journal of Learning Disabilities, 19,* 399-407.

Turner, D.G. (1968). *The readability of selected second grade social studies textbooks.* (ERIC Document Reproduction Service No. ED 027 968)

Vellutino, F.R. (1977). Alternative conceptualizations of dyslexia: Evidence in support of a verbal deficit hypothesis. *Harvard Educational Review, 47,* 334-354.

Wait, S.S. (1987). Textbook readability and the predictive value of the Dale-Chall, comprehensive assessment program, and cloze. (Doctoral dissertation, Florida State University). *Dissertation Abstracts International, 48,* 357A.

West, R.E. & Stanovich, K.E. (1979). The development of automatic word skills. *Journal of Reading Behavior, 11,* 211-219.

From *Journal of Reading* Vol. 36, No. 1, September 1992, pages 22–30. Copyright © 1992 by The International Reading Association. Reprinted with permission.

Reading across the great divide

English and math teachers apprentice one another as readers and disciplinary insiders

A teacher educator uses an apprentice reading project to teach new teachers about the ways they read in the content areas.

David Donahue

In an era when scholars from the sciences, social sciences, and humanities are coming together to examine multidisciplinary topics ranging from human aging and the development of cities to African American culture and cognitive science, one institution still does a remarkable job of isolating subject area learning: the U.S. secondary school, where subject area departments stand as "realms of knowledge" (Siskin, 1994). The four dominant realms—science, math, English, and social studies—are marked geographically, socially, academically, and administratively in the vast majority of schools. Often comprising a wing of the school, an academic department serves as the center for its teachers' informal conversation, professional identity, and decisions about spending, curriculum, and course assignments. In this context, teachers from different disciplines rarely meet or talk across departmental boundaries, and the opportunities for intellectual exchange are few and far between. Such schools fail to nurture learning among the teachers working there (Darling-Hammond & Sykes, 1999; Little, 1990).

As a consequence, teachers become experts at their own subject matter, but they often become less expert at the content taught in other departments. At best, science and math teachers confer about which math program meshes best with the science curriculum or English and history teachers try to synchronize teaching a novel in one class with its historical context in the other. Even these conversations, however, keep the humanities and sciences isolated from one another. In such a fragmented, specialized environment, teachers in various departments are unlikely to talk about their common role as teachers of reading. In a middle school, teachers begin to see themselves as subject area specialists, with reading relegated to English teachers or reading specialists. In a secondary school, even English teachers think of themselves as specialists in the teaching of literature and writing but rarely reading (Ericson, 2001). At the higher grade levels,

teachers assume that because students can say the words on a page they understand them as well. Too often this is not the case (Greenleaf, Schoenbach, Cziko, & Mueller, 2001).

As a teacher educator responsible for a course on reading in the subject areas, I want all new middle and secondary school teachers, regardless of discipline, to view reading as their responsibility. I also want to break down the department walls between subject areas in middle and secondary schools that prevent teachers across the profession from talking about their common duty to ensure that all students read well. As a means toward those ends, I asked the preservice teachers in the course I teach to read regularly in their discipline, to reflect in writing on their reading, and to read and respond to the writing of a colleague in another discipline. My intention was for new teachers to understand that reading is a process of making meaning from texts, to become more cognizant of their own strategies for reading, and to appreciate the different skills needed to read various genres in diverse disciplines. I also wanted new teachers to cross disciplinary divides to discover common intellectual concerns and to realize how they are both expert and novice readers depending on the type and subject matter of a text. I wanted these teachers to experience "reading apprenticeship"—a method in which the classroom teacher facilitates metacognitive conversations about reading including its personal, social, cognitive, and knowledge-building dimensions (Schoenbach, Greenleaf, Cziko, & Hurwitz, 1999).

"Reading apprenticeship" (Greenleaf et al., 2001) integrates reading with learning in the content areas of secondary schools. Based on the expertise that teachers and students in a community of readers bring to reading in their subject areas, it requires that teachers and students make explicit to themselves and one another the strategies and knowledge that they bring to reading texts in their discipline. Using the reading apprenticeship framework, teachers demystify and make visible the hidden mental activities that are part of comprehending a text. Many teachers, once aware of such strategies, would certainly be tempted to teach them in isolated lessons where students learn the strategies, practice them, and then are expected to incorporate them in their own reading. Because such expectations are no foregone conclusion, apprenticeship teachers develop their students' reading competence by building a classroom environment that brings together the multiple dimensions of reading—including the social, personal, cognitive, and knowledge-building dimensions—through metacognitive conversation (Schoenbach et al., 1999). Such conversations, making why and how one reads as much a part of subject area learning as what one reads, are described and analyzed in this article.

When teachers across the divide of English and math encounter one another over a text from one discipline or the other, what do they discuss? What are the notions of reading they hold, that they take for granted, or that they are surprised to learn are not universal when seen in the light of the other discipline? How can these conversations across the biggest disciplinary divide in secondary schools help both sides rethink what reading means? What are the implications for teachers in different disciplines as they come to see themselves as reading teachers? And what are the implications for teacher educators who want preservice teachers to implement a reading apprenticeship approach in their middle and secondary classrooms?

As the new math and English teachers described in this article read with one another across the disciplinary divide, they challenged notions that their academic disciplines are necessarily divided from each other, that they have little to say to one another, or that they address concerns exclusive only to one discipline. As a result, they came to see connections across disciplines and how English and math provide different perspectives on common themes. At the same time, they challenged simplistic notions that reading is a technical process with little differentiation across subject areas or types of text. As a consequence of these discussions, they developed a more complex view of reading, particularly its discipline- and genre-specific nature.

Reading in secondary schools

Middle and secondary school teachers find themselves charged with teaching subject matter but challenged by their students' difficulties with reading the texts that are central to so much content area instruction. As a result, many teachers call on their own "simple view of reading" as a basic, technical skill that is mastered forever and always by the end of elementary school (Gough, 1983). This assumption reinforces the notion that middle and secondary school teachers are not responsible for teaching reading, only for making sure students understand subject area content. Many teachers avoid engaging students in texts and teach content by other means (Greenleaf et al., 2001).

Many middle and secondary school teachers resist teaching reading because they think it is "someone else's job" or they face contextual constraints that make reading instruction difficult (Alvermann & Moore, 1991; Konopak, Wilson, & Readance, 1994; Moje & Wade, 1997). As a consequence,

schools are implementing reading programs, many of which rely on phonics and discrete, skills-based instruction to boost students' achievement, despite evidence that phonics instruction makes little difference beyond the first few grades (Braunger & Lewis, 1998; National Reading Panel, 2000). Most middle and secondary students who struggle to read can decode; what they need is explicit instruction in reading comprehension to understand the reasoning processes and strategies as well as the knowledge of the world, texts, and disciplinary discourses that good readers employ to understand texts (Allington, 2001; Delpit, 1995; Freedman, Flower, Hull, & Hayes, 1995; Hillocks, 1995; Pearson, 1996).

Against this background of content area teachers "working around" reading, researchers and theorists in English and math education have been pointing out connections between learning to read in these disciplines and learning these disciplines. In English, teachers and researchers have described practices such as literature circles (Daniels, 1994), question-answer-response (Raphael, 1986), storyboards (Wilhelm, Baker, & Dube, 2001), and independent reading along with conversation and interactive journal writing (Atwell, 1998) that are based on a transactional view of reading literature (Rosenblatt, 1978/ 1994). This view, which posits meaning arising through transactions between readers and texts in particular contexts, overlaps with approaches to teaching reading that develop students' metacognitive awareness and that encourage young people to connect text to themselves, other texts, and knowledge of the world. Paralleling this shift in reading and learning literature, knowledge in math as a certain and absolute entity has been challenged by conceptions of math knowledge as "a process of inquiry, ever open to doubt" (Borasi & Siegel, 2000). In much the same way that the interpretation of literature is considered a transactional and social process, the construction of meaning in math is also the product of "discourse communities" where truth is established using language in a "rhetorical contest" to convince the "community of practice" that a claim to knowledge is warranted (Borasi & Siegel, 2000). In a math classroom where learning math is conceived not as the transmission of knowledge but as a type of inquiry or as participating in a community of practice, instruction focuses on the social process of "apprenticeship" into the discipline. Such classrooms engage students in thinking similar to the kind needed to become more thoughtful readers who generate questions and construct evolving knowledge from texts.

Description of the project and study

The preservice teachers whose work is analyzed in this study were in the fifth and final year of a teacher education program in the United States at Mills College in Oakland, California. Half were completing the requirements for a credential to teach secondary school English, the other half a credential in math. All were enrolled in Reading and Writing in the Content Areas, a course required for the California secondary school teaching credential, which I teach. One of the course assignments, from

Partner teachers and their reading

Teacher	Subject area	Book	Partner	Partner's subject	Partner's book
Denise	Math	Various mathematics journal articles	Marisa	English	*Of Mice and Men*
Jackie	English	*The Amazing Adventures of Kavalier and Clay*	Louise	Math	*Elementary Linear Algebra*
Joyce	English	*The Souls of Black Folks*	Robin	Math	*Flatland*
Meg	English	*Oedipus Rex*	Ruth	Math	*Fermat's Enigma*

which all of the data for this study come, was a reading apprenticeship portfolio. The assignment was designed so new teachers could

- reflect on their own development and learning as readers,
- understand reading as an activity of making meaning and apply that understanding to teaching subject matter,
- practice strategies for making explicit the ability to read in different subject areas, and
- appreciate the disciplinary-specific nature of reading while crossing into new "reading territories."

Each preservice teacher in the class was partnered with a preservice teacher from another discipline. Whenever possible, I matched humanities teachers (English and social studies) with math and science teachers. I based this decision on past experience with preservice teachers writing to one another about their reading. When teachers in the same discipline wrote to one another, their comments tended to focus on *what* they read. When teachers wrote across the disciplinary divide separating the humanities from math and science, they were much more likely to reflect on *why* and *how* they were reading in addition to *what*. Often this additional attention to motivation and process was sparked by humanities teachers asking science or math teachers, "Why are you reading that?" or just as often, "How do you read that?" These questions frequently revealed the limited reading territories of humanities teachers. Teachers in all disciplines read novels, biographies, and even poetry. Among this small sample, only teachers in math and science routinely read nonfiction. Science and math teachers never questioned humanities teachers about why they read novels, which perhaps implies that new teachers define literacy as the ability to read literature, while humanities teachers felt no such reticence asking science and math teachers why or how they read texts rooted in those disciplines. Whether because they feared looking like philistines or because they had their own motivation and strategies for reading in the humanities, few science and math teachers asked their English colleagues to bring the same level of scrutiny to why and how they read.

Each teacher was asked to choose a text in his or her subject area that he or she had not read before but felt comfortable reading. In general, texts written for adults, rather than the adolescents they teach, worked best for this project. While math teachers chose textbooks in their discipline as well as trade books about math, English teachers read only trade books, from bestsellers to classics. The Table lists the teachers described in this article, the books they read, the teachers with whom they were partnered, and the partners' books (all names are pseudonyms).

I asked teachers in each pair to read different books because I wanted each teacher to have the experience of apprenticing and being apprenticed in subject area reading. The teachers read their books over the course of a month and wrote a reflective log once a week, focusing not only on what they read but how and why as well. These logs were exchanged weekly with the partner who responded in writing with comments and questions. For the first three weeks, students read the text of their own choice. During the fourth and final week, they each read their partner's text, crossing the disciplinary divide with the help of the partner's log to make meaning from the new text outside their area of disciplinary expertise and comfort. I provided prompts for the logs to help the teachers record their mental activities and strategies for understanding texts. These included prompts to spark predicting, picturing, making connections, identifying problems, and employing "fix-up" strategies. After they completed their reading and writing, I asked them to have a metacognitive conversation with their partner to explore the following questions:

- What have you learned about reading in your own subject area?
- What have you learned about reading outside your subject area?
- How will you use this learning to help your students make meaning from the texts you assign in your class?

For this article, I examined the reading logs of four pairs of English and math teachers. (Because there are so few math teachers in the credential program, the number of pairs writing across this particular disciplinary divide is consequently small.) I coded the writing in the logs according to themes developed inductively based on a close reading of the texts. I asked students to check the accuracy of these categorizations. The themes fell into two categories: content and processes. The content category included themes, such as truth and equality, that the math and English teachers found common to their texts specifically and their disciplines more generally. The process category included the various strategies they used to make meaning from their texts. Even when the teachers felt a degree of comfort crossing the disciplinary divide, they were fascinated by how a reading strategy was employed differently in the two disciplines, for example "chunking" comprehension of a novel at the chapter level versus "chunking" comprehension of a math text at the sentence, phrase, or word level.

The nature of this study is exploratory. Its purpose is to help teacher educators think about how to engage all new teachers in discussions about one of their most important responsibilities: ensuring that all students read well. It is also designed to spur teacher educators' reflection about how best to spark the metacognitive conversations that allow teachers to explore reading's varied dimensions and to nudge teachers over disciplinary divides that isolate them and fragment students' learning. The following sections describe how new teachers apprenticing one another to reading in their subject areas made connections across the divide and developed more sophisticated understandings of reading as a discipline-specific process. The first two sections describe new teachers across the disciplinary divide making content connections through their reading. The third section illustrates new teachers' process connections focused on reading strategies and their differentiation by discipline and genre.

Searching for truth in math and literature

Meg, an English teacher reading Sophocles' *Oedipus Rex* (trans. 1949), and Ruth, a math teacher reading *Fermat's Enigma* (Singh, 1997), found themselves engaged in conversation about the nature of truth—a discussion that was informed by their personal interests, disciplinary perspectives, and the texts they were reading together. Ruth began this conversation when she explained her thoughts about Singh's description of the Pythagorean Brotherhood, a secret society whose members were dedicated to unlocking the mystery of numbers and thereby bringing themselves closer to the gods. Ruth wrote, "This reminds me of some discussions I had as an undergraduate, where we likened mathematics to a religion of logic. In math, you can know that something is absolutely *true* and *right*." Meg responded,

I am interested in our quest for certainty—and for those things that are "true and right." Can we be sure that math is "true and right"? Could it possibly still be simply our perspective or present understanding? This idea of course spills over into my own personal questions about religion, Christianity and spirituality—which is why it is interesting to me that you made the same link.

In reply, Ruth explained mathematical proof by quoting Singh.

The idea of a classic mathematical proof is to begin with a series of axioms, statements that can be assumed to be true or that are self-evidently true. Then by arguing logically, step by step, it is possible to arrive at a conclusion. If the axioms are correct and the logic is flawless, then the conclusion will be undeniable.

Meg found Ruth's thoughts illuminating and connected to her interest in "universal truths," something she was thinking of in terms of religion and faith as well as teaching literature. She wrote,

I've been struggling with questions about if there are truly any universal truths. But this conversation, and your insight has reminded me that there are—mathematical—natural, universal truths. It has made me think a bit about how those ideas affect my understanding about different religions and my own spirituality.

At the same time, Meg acknowledged that

something inside me rebels against the idea of absolute "truths." But mathematical absolute truths seem to take me into a totally different perspective. Math seems to be a field where theory and practice (or reality) have no separation. They are the same thing.

Meg brought this focus on truth to her reading of *Oedipus Rex*. In particular, she was interested in how the audience was privy to knowledge about truth that was invisible to characters in the play and in the intersection between sight and knowledge of truth. Reflecting on the role of truth in the play, she wrote, "It is interesting to note how many people knew the 'truth' [of Oedipus's incest] but looked the other way. Now only the thought of revealing the truth and its consequences makes them shudder—not the truth itself:" When Oedipus's self-mutilation, the tearing out of his eyes, is revealed by a messenger in the play, Meg reflected,

We hear [Oedipus's] words about blindness, but only through the messenger. How interesting and ironic that the audience is not allowed to see this act, extending the metaphor of sight and blindness. Do we truly know what happened if we do not see it? I'm interested in the idea that as Oedipus "sees" the truth, he loses his sight. But the assumption is that he "sees" all, and I wonder how clear his sight is even now that he is blind. Charagos says, "Your fate is clear, you are not blind to that." We don't know what his future fate is. We know he'll be cast out, but we don't know anything else…. We as an audience could "see" the truth for most of the drama but now that we've "heard" it, we do not "see" the future.

As Meg contemplated the connections between sight and knowledge, vision and truth, Ruth shared in Meg's intellectual excitement. She responded to Meg by saying, "I love your observation about the connection to sight. It's especially relevant since Oedipus's ultimate act of self-mutilation will be to gouge out his eyes. It's fascinating to me that Sophocles pulls this metaphor out in the beginning!"

This conversation challenged notions that only some realms of knowledge are responsible for conversations, like those about truth, that in fact cut across disciplinary boundaries. These teachers came to see themselves as connected by their intellectual interests. Reading and writing across the disciplinary divide illustrated for these teachers the power of reading beyond one's own discipline and the potential for support in doing so with a colleague from another discipline. These new teachers learned to expand their "reading territory" into less familiar subjects and genres, and in the process they gained inspiration and insight, described later in this article, for helping students expand their own reading territories.

Exploring social justice in math and the humanities

Joyce, an English and social studies teacher reading W.E.B. DuBois's *The Souls of Black Folk* (1903/1993), and Robin, a math teacher reading *Flatland* (Abbott, 1884/1984), discovered common interests in connecting disciplinary reading to contemporary issues of social justice. They described their books as "not only about their subject matter, but [also having] relevant social and political implications."

Joyce connected DuBois's writing from the early 20th century to the racial climate at the beginning of the 21st. Thinking about DuBois's metaphor of waves to describe major strands of thought about racial equality after the U.S. Civil War, Joyce described social justice imagery in her mind:

> So as I read, I could see each thought as a wave, a human wave, rather than an ocean wave. He describes the first wave as being one of global cooperation, so I pictured black, brown, red, yellow, and white brothers working together. He describes the second wave as one made up of clowns, who see themselves as a third inferior race. So I pictured Bo Jangles who always accompanied Shirley Temple in all her dances, but never took center stage himself. And the last wave DuBois describes as composed of men who know not their own rights and ask for them timidly. So I pictured a man holding his hat in hand, with his head bowed, asking for what is rightfully his. DuBois's use of waves also makes me imagine the power of these waves to sweep people away, to stir up emotions, to churn up the environment.

In addition to calling upon her own knowledge to describe a scene as powerful as DuBois's, Joyce imagined her students when she read. In her journal, she cited DuBois's writing on responsibility. "So long as the best elements of a community do not feel duty bound to protect and train and care for the weaker members of the group, they leave them to be preyed upon by these swindlers and rascals" (1903/1993). She described thinking about contemporary situations that might help her students interpret such writing.

Robin's reading of *Flatland* (Abbott, 1884/1984) paralleled Joyce's in its attention to imagery and connections to contem-

porary social issues. Abbott's 19th-century British novel, narrated by A. Square, describes Flatland, a two-dimensional world of geometry where the social classes of its inhabitants are represented by different shapes, with higher status signified by more sides to the shape. Women, who are lines, represent the lowest class. Robin was struck by the similarities in class structure between the characters and contemporary U.S. society. Focusing on the inequality of women, she wrote,

> There is a separate legislature for women that centers entirely around controlling them. Because they are lines, they are only visible from certain angles. If looking at one end or the other, they can be mistaken for points and can therefore sneak up on their male counterparts and pierce them (either injuring or killing them). Women are mandated in all states of Flatland to keep up a "Peace-Cry" so they can be heard at all times. In some states, they are required to sway from side to side (shake their backsides) so they can always be seen. They are considered stupid and forgetful and because of this are treated horribly by their husbands and other men in Flatland who assume they'll forget that anyone was rude or mistreated them.

Like Joyce, Robin connected her reading to the present day, reflecting on those people "thought of as secondary citizens and why." Connecting the Flatlanders' limited knowledge of worlds beyond two dimensions to current intolerance, she continued,

> I really think that those who are racist are frightened by the unknown and therefore try to confine or downgrade groups of people who they deem lesser. It made me think of the recent proposition which banned gay marriages that passed overwhelmingly in California. That to me was as offensive and ridiculous as the restrictions on women in this book. We really haven't come that far as a society and that is disturbing.

Joyce and Robin used reading in their disciplines as a springboard to conversations like those initiated by Moses (2001) and Oakes and Lipton (1998) connecting math and the humanities curriculum to issues of equality and social justice. Summarizing their experience of reading together, Joyce and Robin concluded, "it's critical to make connections to today's world in order to gain a deeper understanding and appreciation of the texts." When working with students, they said they would also "encourage students to make those links."

Drawing on the personal and social dimensions of reading, Joyce and Robin found areas of common interest—areas that grew out of their very different disciplinary passions. Without such conversations that roam across subject area boundaries, teachers have few opportunities to see where disciplines converge and how they can inform one another. Confounding their notions that "reading is reading" regardless of subject area, these teachers also challenged the stereotype that experts in their disciplines cannot talk to one another about content.

Metacognitive conversations

In addition to writing about content themes that these new teachers found common to their texts, they engaged in metacognitive conversations about how they were reading—their strategies for making meaning, their tools for identifying and fixing problems, and their motivation for sticking with texts that proved difficult or initially uninteresting. Writing to one another, they described strategies that included relying on one another for understanding, connecting to prior knowledge or other texts, predicting, skimming, rereading, annotating, picturing, looking ahead, skipping, questioning, and "talking back to the text" (i.e., carrying on a conversation with the author of the text). In this section, I describe these teachers' awareness of how the usefulness of various reading strategies depended on the discipline or genre of text. Such awareness contributed to their understanding of reading as a complex, discipline-specific activity rather than an uncomplicated skill that looks the same in all subject areas.

Jackie, a teacher whose background is in literature, and Louise, a high school math teacher, read *The Amazing Adventures of Kavalier and Clay* (Chabon, 2000), at the time a bestseller and Pulitzer Prize-winning novel, and *Elementary Linear Algebra* (Grossman, 1987), a college textbook. To read *Elementary Linear Algebra*, Jackie relied heavily on Louise for motivation and strategies. She wrote to her partner,

> I persevered even though I was lost. I had no language for what I was looking at, but I kept trying to make meaning out of the reading by referring to your log. Your log provided me with a template for learning math…. It was only because of the relationship with you and your log that I had a structure for beginning to read the textbook.

Jackie found inspiration to stick with a difficult text, following Louise who described the key to learning math as practicing problems again and again. Jackie found, "This comment gave me hope that I could learn math—that math isn't something learned magically; it takes practice and repetition whether you are skilled at math or a novice."

In the same way that Jackie challenged her assumptions about learning math, Marisa, a secondary English teacher, noted that she challenged her preconceived notions about learning math as a mechanical, rote process after reading with Denise, a secondary math teacher. Marisa wrote,

> A bias has existed between math and English people: Math is numbers only read one way (the right way) while English is open-ended. The implication is that math is something to memorize and English is something to ponder over. While reading Denise's journals, I was pleased to see that math people (as I suspected) do indeed ponder over, get lost over, and feel excitement over numbers on a page.

Jackie and Marisa gained more sophisticated ideas about reading in math by doing so with a disciplinary insider. Their insight, gained through conversations, underscores the importance of the social dimension of reading.

While disabusing one another of stereotypical notions of reading in their disciplines, the teachers did find real differences. Math teachers frequently reminded their English colleagues that reading a math text would not be like reading a novel. Ruth wrote to Meg,

> When I'm reading a math text, I like to have a pencil and paper in hand to work on problems as I go along, constructing meaning for myself out of the math on the page, even if an "answer" is presented along with the problem. Math builds on itself, so if you haven't understood previous material, you'll be lost.

Denise wrote to Marisa about how she slowed down her reading to comprehend articles from an academic math journal.

> I wrote in the margins several times that I had to reread sentences. I believe that in math there is a lot of rereading taking place because you have to understand what is being said so that you can understand the main point. You need one thing to understand the other. Also, I could see myself breaking up sentences so that I explained one word at a time. I would decode parts of the sentence and then put it all together so that I could make sense of the whole concept. At times there was so much information that I needed to understand that I could only look at a sentence in parts.

Louise and Jackie frequently compared strategies as Jackie learned that what served her well reading a novel did not help her with a math text. *About Elementary Linear Algebra*, Jackie wrote, "There was very little that had meaning for me, so when I came to the historical biographies, I read them carefully," because these were sections where she could draw on familiar comprehension strategies. Louise, the math teacher, noted, however, "I skipped them because they didn't have anything to do with math." Louise was defining her discipline as only about understanding mathematical concepts and their applications to problems. Jackie also tried a successful strategy from reading literature to gain clarity when she was confused. "I thought I could use the fix-it strategy of reading ahead but it really was not working." Louise responded, "There is no point in going on in a math text if you haven't learned the concepts being introduced." Given perseverance, Jackie did learn a strategy, however, for making sense of terms such as vector, scalar, and matrix that stumped her when reading the text for the first time. She wrote,

> If I look ahead I might find some story problems and that might help me better understand the concepts. I find several story problems. I look at the problem, and then I refer to the answer in the back of the book. The answer clarifies the concepts for me. Now I know what a row vector is, a column vector, and a scalar. The answer provides me with the concrete example I needed to understand the concepts. I try two more story problems and check my answers. I have now begun to understand the concepts.

In a similar manner, Meg and Ruth found disciplinary differences in how they read, particularly in whether they could read ahead with only partial understanding of what they already read. Referring to the Odes in *Oedipus Rex*, Meg, the English teacher, wrote, "The chorus parts seem long, disconnected, and tedious to read. I think I will read for the story first time through and then go back to read out loud through some of these philosophical poetic sections." Comparing this reading of literature to reading math, Ruth, the math teacher, replied,

> Unlike your ability to skip over the Odes and go back later…I think coming from my background I would be more likely to think that I would have to read through that intimidating Ode word by word until I understood it, which might turn me off from continuing with the play.

Ruth, like the other math teachers such as Louise and Denise, understood the importance of persevering and not skipping ahead when reading in math, but she also came to understand how that strategy is discipline and genre specific.

Many of the teachers commented on the importance of a "story" as a hook for reading difficult texts. Initially feeling lost in *Elementary Linear Algebra*, Jackie wrote, "I am interested in the story of math." She latched on to the biographies of mathematicians, drawing vivid pictures in her mind. On first picking up *Fermat's Enigma* Meg wrote,

> The back of the book describes it as a "mesmerizing tale," and I'm excited to open it and start reading. But glancing through the book, I immediately find equations and math everywhere, and my next impulse is to shut it. This reminds me how wonderful it has been to hear the story through your [Ruth's] journal…. I'm realizing how necessary it is for me to be drawn into a discipline by a story or a narrative.

Even Ruth, the math teacher, commented, "I am more interested in the story behind the mathematics than just the math itself." When reading Meg's text, *Oedipus Rex*, she noted the importance of an engaging story and commented on her surprise that the text resembled a novel. Meg also appreciated reading *Oedipus Rex* as a narrative with a captivating plot, writing toward the end of the play, "I'm caught up in the story, even though I know what is coming…. So now I've read to the end, reading for plot even though there is no mystery of plot. How interesting."

By reading and writing with one another, the teachers gained increased awareness of the role that prior knowledge played in their understanding. Ruth drew on her deep knowledge of the history of math as she read. Mention of the famous mathematician Evariste Galois, for example, led to her following thoughts:

> What I was thinking when I read this was what I already know about Galois. He was a hotheaded young 19th-century rebel who flunked out of school and could not pass the entrance examinations for university. At the age of 21 he was challenged to a duel and died of a pistol wound in a field. The night before, knowing he was to die, he stayed up all night and com-

mitted everything he had in his head about mathematics to paper, feverishly writing all night. Most of the major theorems in Group Theory were written down by Galois in those last few hours before his death.

Meg, too, drew on prior knowledge. Of *Oedipus Rex*, she wrote, "I realize that I have never read this play although I know as 'we all do' what the story will be about." Later in her reading, she observed,

> Creon has been sent to Apollo's oracle at Delphi. I also "know" about this but not in any detail that I can remember. I wonder if we'll have to introduce Apollo and Delphi to our students for this information to register.

In response, Ruth connected Meg's questions to Hirsch's (1987) notion of "cultural literacy."

> You're right about the cultural literacy connection. I think so many "educated" people know about what *Oedipus* means, just from references to it (e.g., Freud and his complexes). I think I read the full play at some point, but mainly what I remember is the big concept of the man marrying his mother and her bearing his children. Oh, and that he plucks his eyes out at the end. I wonder, too, what a much younger person might know about the story.

Denise, writing to Marisa, found "that in math you constantly pull from prior knowledge. This prior knowledge is derived from definitions and concepts. If you do not know what one thing is, most of the time, you will be lost." In reading *Of Mice and Men* (Steinbeck, 1937/1993), Marisa did not draw on definitions but on a storehouse of disciplinary knowledge about how to read a novel, as demonstrated in her prediction after reading the first chapter of the book.

> I sense that whatever trouble that they [George and Lennie, the novel's main characters] had run from might be revealed later in the book, and the whole plot might even center on that. I think this relationship is a unique and caring one, but I think something "huge" is going to happen. I can picture them calm and free by the water, which I feel is a contrast to what surely waits at the end of the book.

As they reflected on their experience reading with others across the disciplinary divide, math and English teachers admitted that it had increased their knowledge, but they also recognized that knowledge, a key dimension of reading apprenticeship, contributed to their process of making meaning from texts. This realization raised for them a question about reading and knowledge development: How much "prior knowledge" should teachers provide students so they would read for meaning? Jackie, reflecting about her process of learning math, wrote, "I cannot be taught simply by reading the text. Math requires that a teacher demonstrate how the problem is done. The text is useful for reviewing the vocabulary and the formulas but not for learning the procedures."

While text should not be solely relied on to convey new information or develop students' understanding, these new teachers might have been concluding that text was always inappropriate or less efficient for building knowledge. This misunderstanding might have resulted from another misunderstanding—the persistent separation of learning from reading, the hard-to-dislodge view that reading is somehow passive or "less" than other forms of learning. These teachers' statements about needing background knowledge before reading cause me to reflect on the work teacher educators must do to prevent new teachers from creating a false dichotomy between reading and learning in a subject area. Such dichotomies contribute to the complaint many secondary content area teachers make: "I have too much content to cover so I don't have time to teach reading."

Preparing subject area teachers as teachers of reading

Conversations across disciplinary boundaries do not come "naturally" to preservice teachers. That is, such conversations need time and encouragement to develop. They also require teachers to challenge perceptions of themselves as "illiterate" outside their subject area specialties. Much of the value of these conversations, however, lies in their "unnatural" quality. In writing to a colleague who did not share the same knowledge about subject area or texts in the subject area, these teachers made explicit how their knowledge shaped their reading. They also discussed personal motivation for reading as well as the processes they used to make sense of texts that, to a person outside the discipline, might have seemed boring or impenetrable. In short, they apprenticed one another to reading in a foreign subject area. Louise demonstrated apprenticeship in reading by explaining how to read math with clarity and detail. She also displayed thoughtfulness and generosity to a novice math reader, Jackie, who she was apprenticing. Through Jackie's writing, Louise saw the power of stories to engage others in reading and learning math, and she learned new ways to think about supporting struggling readers in her math class. Jackie also explicitly shared background knowledge and her processes in reading, respecting Louise's less-than-novice status as a reader of fiction. In the process, Jackie, who saw herself as a reader of literature, analyzed how she read in order to teach others to read.

In another case, Meg read *Oedipus Rex* to prepare for teaching the play to her 10th graders. Meg's log illustrates the value of teachers reflecting on the reading they assign to students. Not only did Meg raise pedagogical issues about teaching *Oedipus Rex*, she also became aware of issues her students might face in reading the play and discovered strategies for helping them read a sophisticated text. For example, keeping a reflective log allowed Meg to ponder the importance of plot and suspense in reading the play. By paying attention to how she read the play's Odes (first skipping them and then returning to read them several times), she became aware of a strategy that might aid her students' comprehension. As a result of her log, not only did she realize the value of rereading the Odes, but she could also explain to her students why such a strategy is helpful.

Having seen the value of making explicit her own thinking, she is more likely to encourage such metacognitive awareness in her students.

Reading with colleagues from other disciplines has the potential to give teachers insight on the difficulty that novice readers, including their students, face when encountering texts that build on disciplinary ways of knowing and presume a certain level of knowledge in a subject area or about certain kinds of texts. While some teachers might bemoan their students' lack of subject area knowledge when they enter their classes, they are not likely to make the same complaint about other teachers. Reading across subject areas in the teacher education program leveled the reading playing field. Here were colleagues who respected one another's education and intelligence. Yet even these persons brought diverse personal experiences, values, and beliefs that challenged notions of what they assumed all literate readers shared. Their colleagues brought gaps in knowledge, incorrect information, and insecurities as readers that could not be chalked up to laziness, indifference, or resistance. As a result, these teachers had the opportunity to reconsider why some students do not read or why they do not understand what they attempt to read. They also had opportunities to reflect on how one teaches students under such circumstances to read in the disciplines.

Breaking down subject area divisions

Conversations across disciplinary boundaries about reading have the potential to mitigate the isolation and fragmentation of academic departments in most secondary schools. Through their logs, these teachers invited one another to become "initiated" in their disciplinary communities. They did so by explaining key ideas and knowledge in their fields and by providing one another with ideas for curriculum.

Most important perhaps to math and English teachers' initiation into another discipline were the connections they made and questions they asked their partners—connections and questions that went to the heart of their disciplines. Ruth and Meg asked each other about the nature of truth and proof. Robin and Joyce engaged in dialogue about equality and social justice. All these teachers wondered what role background knowledge plays in students' understanding of texts in their disciplines and how much background is needed. Reading with an experienced reader prompted the novice reader to gain a sense of wonder and provided an opportunity for what Duckworth (1987) called "the having of wonderful ideas."

Beyond the "essential questions" (Wiggins & McTighe, 1998) of their disciplines, they also shared with one another sophisticated, complex perspectives on their disciplines. As math teachers presented it, their discipline is not an exercise in "plugging and chugging" through equations where answers are right or wrong. Instead, it is a field of uncertainty and contention, vitality and relevance. English teachers portrayed a discipline where readers juxtapose their reading of classics with contemporary concerns, where readers—not only critics—give meaning to texts. Through their reading and writing, these preservice teachers shared their disciplinary loves. In the process, rather than looking only for common denominators of reading across genres and subject areas, they reveled in the particularities of reading in their fields. They helped one another gain an appreciation of reading's variability across disciplines—an understanding that serves as a first step toward building appropriate reading instruction into their subject area curriculum.

Implications of reading apprenticeship

Ball and Cohen characterized teacher professional development as "intellectually superficial, disconnected from deep issues of curriculum and learning, fragmented, and non-cumulative." Such "training" assumes teachers "need updating rather than opportunities for serious and sustained learning" (Ball & Cohen, 1999). It is unfortunate that preservice education and professional development in secondary reading often takes the "updating" approach, providing teachers with new standards, materials, and tests, but not opportunities to learn. These programs are generally designed to be "teacher proof," with the teacher serving as a technician who delivers instruction developed, or even scripted in the case of some reading programs, by others.

Describing a different course of professional education, Ball and Cohen called for changing teachers' "discourse of practice" from the "rhetoric of conclusions" to a "narrative of inquiry" (1999). While Ball and Cohen focused on teachers' inquiry into their students' learning, teachers' inquiry into their own learning (in this case learning about one's own reading processes) promotes a similar change in discourse. Many secondary content area teachers are unconscious of their own strategies as expert discipline-based readers and feel ill-prepared to help their students who struggle to make meaning from texts. These same teachers are the ones most likely to believe they can do nothing or to look for a quick fix to their students' difficulties with reading. They are the most likely to think that reading instruction means time away from exploring content or implementing decontextualized reading strategies to promote comprehension.

This project of apprentice reading across the disciplinary divide was designed to promote learning about one's own reading. It was also designed so teachers would learn about reading apprenticeship by engaging in it. As Meg noted in her final journal entry, "This assignment is exciting to me because it is one of the first ones…where I feel like we were actively making new meaning and connections ourselves." As the teachers in my class reflected jointly on their own processes as readers, not only did they gain self-knowledge, but they also gained practice in promoting colleagues' metacognition. Such practice is consistent with teacher education that honors teaching as a learning profession. It is also consistent with the conditions necessary for "the having of wonderful ideas."

As a teacher educator who values collegiality across disciplinary boundaries and who sees reading as one of the most important skills for a teacher in any discipline to develop among students, I hope that asking preservice teachers to read across the curriculum will allow them to pay more attention not only

to *what* but also to *how* and *why* they read in their discipline. By reading and writing to others outside their discipline, they can learn how to translate and then share their process of understanding as expert readers in a discipline with colleagues who are novice readers in that discipline and who, in many respects, resemble their students. By working with colleagues, they will also practice apprenticing their expertise in ways that respect not only the experience and knowledge but also the dignity of novice readers.

Donahue teaches at Mills College (Education Dept., 5000 MacArthur Blvd., Oakland, CA 94613, USA).

References

Abbott, E. (1984). *Flatland: A romance of many dimensions*. New York: Signet Classics. (Original work published 1884)

Allington, R. (2001). *What really matters for struggling readers: Designing research-based programs*. New York: Longman.

Alvermann D., & Moore, D. (1991). Secondary school reading. In M.L. Kamil, P.B. Mosenthal, P.D. Pearson, & R. Barr (Eds.), *Handbook of reading research* (Vol. 2, pp. 951–983). New York: Longman.

Atwell, N. (1998). *In the middle: Writing, reading and learning with adolescents*. Portsmouth, NH: Boynton/Cook Heinemann.

Ball, D., & Cohen, D. (1999). Developing practice developing practitioners: Toward a practice-based theory of professional education. In L. Darling-Hammond & G. Sykes (Eds.), *Teaching as the learning profession: Handbook of policy and practice*. San Francisco: Jossey-Bass.

Borasi, R., & Siegel, M. (2000). *Reading counts: Expanding the role of reading in mathematics classrooms*. New York: Teachers College Press.

Braunger, J., & Lewis, J. (1998). *Building a knowledge base in reading*. Portland, OR: Northwest Regional Educational Laboratory.

Chabon, M. (2000). *The amazing adventures of Kavalier and Clay*. New York: Picador USA.

Daniels, H. (1994). *Literature circles: Voice and choice in the student-centered classroom*. York, ME: Stenhouse.

Darling-Hammond, L., & Sykes, G. (Eds.). (1999). *Teaching as the learning profession: Handbook of policy and practice*. San Francisco: Jossey-Bass.

Delpit, L. (1995). *Other people's children: Cultural conflict in the classroom*. New York: New Press.

DuBois, W.E.B. (1993). *The souls of black folks*. New York: Alfred A. Knopf. (Original work published 1903)

Duckworth, E. (1987). *"The having of wonderful ideas" and other essays on teaching and learning*. New York: Teachers College Press.

Ericson, B. (Ed.). (2001). *Teaching reading in high school English classes*. Urbana, IL: National Council of Teachers of English.

Freedman, S., Flower, L., Hull, G., & Hayes, J. (1995). *Ten years of research: Achievements of the National Center for the Study of Writing and Literacy* (Technical Report No. 1-C). Berkeley, CA: National Center for the Study of Writing.

Gough, P. (1983). *The beginning of decoding. Reading and Writing: An Interdisciplinary Journal, 5*, 181–192.

Greenleaf, C., Schoenbach, R., Cziko, C., & Mueller, F. (2001). Apprenticing adolescent readers to academic literacy. *Harvard Educational Review, 71* (1), 79–127.

Grossman, S. (1987). *Elementary linear algebra* (3rd ed.). Belmont, CA: Wadsworth.

Hillocks, G. (1995). *Teaching writing as reflective practice*. New York: Teachers College Press.

Hirsch, E.D. (1987). *Cultural literacy*. New York: Vintage Books.

Konopak, B., Wilson, E., & Readance, J. (1994). Examining teachers' beliefs, decisions, and practices about content-area reading in secondary social studies. In C. Kinzer & D. Leu (Eds.), *Multidimensional aspects of literacy research, theory, and practice* (pp. 127–136). Chicago: National Reading Conference.

Little, J. (1990). The persistence of privacy: Autonomy and initiative in teachers' professional relations. *Teachers College Record, 91,* 509–536.

Moje, E., & Wade, S. (1997). What case discussions reveal about teacher thinking. *Teaching and Teacher Education, 12,* 691–712.

Moses, R. (2001). *Radical equations: Civil rights from Mississippi to the Algebra Project.* Boston: Beacon Press.

National Reading Panel. (2000). *Teaching children to read: An evidence-based assessment of the scientific research literature on reading and its implications for reading instruction.* Washington, DC: National Institute on Child Health and Human Development.

Oakes, J., & Lipton, M. (1998). *Teaching to change the world.* New York: McGraw Hill College Division.

Pearson, P. (1996). Reclaiming the center. In M. Graves, P. van den Broek, & B. Taylor (Eds.), *The first R: Every child's right to read* (pp. 259–274). New York: Teachers College Press.

Raphael, T. (1986). Teaching question-answer relationships, revisited. *The Reading Teacher, 39,* 516–522.

Rosenblatt, L. (1994). *The reader the text the poem: The transactional theory of the literary work.* Carbondale, IL: Southern Illinois University Press. (Original work published 1978)

Schoenbach, R., Greenleaf, C., Cziko, C., & Hurwitz, L. (1999). *Reading for understanding: A guide to improving reading in middle and high school classrooms.* San Francisco: Jossey-Bass.

Singh, S. (1997). *Fermat's enigma.* New York: Walker.

Siskin, L. (1994). *Realms of knowledge: Academic departments in secondary schools.* Bristol, PA: Falmer Press.

Sophocles. (1949). *The Oedipus cycle.* (D. Fitts & R. Fitzgerald, Trans.). New York: Harvest Books.

Steinbeck, J. (1993). *Of mice and men.* New York: Penguin Books. (Original work published 1937)

Wiggins, G., & McTighe. J. (1998). *Understanding by design.* Alexandria, VA: Association for Curriculum Development.

Wilhelm, J., Baker, T., & Dube, J. (2001). *Strategic reading: Guiding students to lifelong literacy.* Portsmouth, NH: Heinemann.

From *Journal of Adolescent & Adult Literacy* Vol. 47, No. 1, September 2003, pages 24–37. Copyright © 2003 by The International Reading Association. Reprinted with permission.s

The Effect of Learning Mathematical Reading Strategies on Secondary Students' Homework Grades

Elliot Ostler

If it ain't broke, don't fix it!" is the philosophy that I use to avoid doing certain things, such as changing the slightly leaky faucet in my bathroom. (After all, it still works pretty well!) I can't help thinking that that same philosophy affects how we regard instruction in the secondary mathematics classroom. As a teacher of mathematics, I have many times observed, and too often used, the traditional paradigm for mathematics instruction: teacher-directed demonstrations, including explanations of processes and procedures, followed by student questions and practice on written exercises. That routine seems to be a fairly comfortable and effective one for most math teachers. The problem is that, like my leaky bathroom faucet, the lecture/demonstration model doesn't work as well as it could; it tends to underuse one of the primary resources in the mathematics classroom—the textbook.

Although textbooks are not currently considered the most fashionable instructional tool, they still have the potential for a great deal of influence in today's mathematics classroom. That notion is supported by Merseth's (1993) findings that more than 95 percent of twelfth-grade mathematics teachers surveyed indicated that the textbook was their most commonly used instructional resource.

For several years, my colleagues and I used the textbook as a source of homework problems and little else. That was because a substantial portion of our textbooks was dedicated to the presentation of formal proofs and sample problem solutions, and our students had a great deal of difficulty understanding the presentations. In fact, many students find it hard to internalize new concepts and processes when they are required to read and synthesize information from the text (Bray and Armstrong 1986). The common textbook format of teaching through formal proof is what initially caused me to question the overall value of mathematics textbooks as an instructional tool.

Concern by teachers over the utility of textbooks as a teaching tool appears to be two dimensional. Some teachers claim that mathematics textbooks are devoting more space to practice problems than ever before and that process explanations have become fewer and shorter in recent years. Others argue that the problem is not inadequate description or detail but rather students' lack of specific skills and strategies to decode written mathematical solutions. Traditionally, high school classes have not required students to learn mathematics through any formal written protocol. Instead, they rely largely on process modeling by teachers and peers. That becomes an especially critical issue in those cases where teachers report relying heavily on textbook-based instruction but rarely teach students how to decipher common textbook formats and patterns in sample problem solutions or formally presented proofs (Bush 1987).

Armed with a research base that convinced me to try to incorporate textbook-based learning into my classes, I decided to make some observations related to how students used textbooks. I then devised a way to teach the reading skills that students need when reading mathematics textbooks. The purpose of this quasi-experimental study was to determine if direct instruction relating to general skills and strategies for reading mathematics textbooks significantly aided students in their ability to complete homework assignments (consisting of textbook practice problems). The general procedure of the investigation follows.

Subjects

Two classes of eleventh-grade intermediate algebra students from a rural Midwestern high school participated in the study. All students had completed the equivalent of at least two years of high school mathematics, not including the current course in intermediate algebra; none was identified as having special academic needs. A total of thirty-seven students participated in the study (twenty-three boys and fourteen girls). Twenty-one students (thirteen boys and eight girls) were enrolled in the course section that was randomly selected as the experimental group, and sixteen students (ten boys and six girls) were enrolled in the section used as the control group.

Method

Timeline

The study was conducted over a four-week period—twelve days of formal instruction, four days of review with problem solving applications, and four days of testing. The first three days of each week were devoted to formal instruction that consisted of lecture and process demonstrations by the teacher, questions from students, and time for students to work on assigned problems. The fourth day was typically spent reviewing assigned homework and learning the concepts in the context of practical applications. Tests were given on the last day of each week on the concepts covered in the textbook and were generally process oriented. I chose that format in order to follow the routine to which the teacher and students had become accustomed during the school year. Homework problems from the textbook were assigned at the end of each of the three instructional days and turned in on the Thursday prior to the test. The instructor who taught both the experimental and control groups used that weekly format.

Content

During the four-week period in which the investigation took place, the instructor used a chapter from the students' intermediate algebra textbook on conic sections. One type of conic section was presented in each of the four weeks in the following order: week 1—parabolas; week 2—circles; week 3—ellipses; and week 4—hyperbolas. The instructor assigned ten homework problems of progressive difficulty at the end of each instructional day and collected them on the Thursday of that particular week. Assignments were determined to be successfully completed if at least seven of the ten homework problems illustrated correct solutions.

Treatment

The treatment of the experimental group consisted of a general strategy for reading various mathematical text formats. The development of this strategy stemmed from earlier observations that high school students read mathematics textbooks in much the same way that they might read a story.

Those observations suggested that there are four key factors in reading mathematical text that are not factors in reading other informational text. The mathematical reading strategy presented to the students was intended not only to provide explicit skills for students to read mathematics textbooks, but also to give them insight as to why additional reading strategies are needed for successful decoding in mathematics. The four factors, which were used to develop the reading strategy that was then taught to the experimental class as the treatment, are as follows:

Terminology. The terminology component emerged from the observation that students tend either to completely skip the technical terms or try to memorize all of the terms listed at the end of a chapter before doing any reading—either of which is a potentially confusing approach. The strategy developed and taught for this component focused on the need to first identify and learn only the terminology needed for the sample problem on which a student is working. Doing so forces the student to frequently revisit the terms at the end of the chapter as he or she moves on to new problems.

Eye patterns. The eye pattern component was identified from the students' tendency to read mathematical expressions from left to right, as is done in informational text. Many mathematical expressions involving parentheses need to be read starting from the inside and moving outward in order to follow the proper sequence of steps. The strategy developed and taught from this component encouraged students to pay close attention to the appropriate order of mathematical operations.

Graph/text interaction. The graph/text interaction component was identified from observations that showed students' tendency to read an entire sample problem solution before trying to find the problem's relation to its graph. This component of the reading strategy encouraged students to stop at intermediate stages of the sample problem to identify patterns emerging simultaneously on the graph.

Reading direction. The reading direction component was identified from students' tendency to read problems from the top to the bottom, the approach they use in most other reading situations. In reading mathematics text, it is sometimes helpful for students to start with the final step of the solution and reason as to how each step was derived from the earlier stages in the problem.

Procedure

In addition to learning the four reading components during class, students in the experimental group were each given a short written description of the components to use as a reminder when they were doing their homework. The instructor taught the general reading strategy that incorporated the four components in conjunction with, and in the context of, the process demonstrations each day.

That allowed students the option of using the reading strategy to rework sample problems at home in order to clarify any misconceptions. In addition, the experimental group received daily, in-class practice time on homework problems, during which time the teacher coached students on self-instruction through the reading strategy. Students in the control group received a more traditional guided practice for homework problems during the in-class practice time.

Data Collection and Analysis

Data on homework completion were collected for two four-week periods. Baseline data were gathered for both the control and experimental groups during the four weeks prior to the initiation of the reading strategy instruction, and again during the four weeks of the investigation itself. The baselines for each group were then compared with data

collected during the four weeks of the investigation. All the data gathered and compared were in terms of "successfully completed assignments" (an assignment was considered to be successfully completed if seven of the ten assigned problems illustrated correct solutions). The number of successfully completed assignments was then divided by the total number of assignments due in order to calculate the class percentage of successfully completed assignments during each four-week period. A total of 192 student assignments was due for the control group during each four-week period, and a total of 252 student assignments was due for the experimental group during each four-week period. The total number of assignments was determined by multiplying the number of students in each group by the number of days that assignments were given. Table I shows the number of successfully completed assignments by week for each group.

TABLE 1
Assignments Completed during Baseline Period versus Treatment Period

	Total assignments	Number completed (baseline period)	Number completed (treatment period)
Week 1			
Experimental group	63	48 (76.19%)	47 (74.60%)
Control group	48	41 (85.41%)	39 (81.25%)
Week 2			
Experimental group	63	47 (74.60%)	56 (88.89%)
Control group	48	40 (83.33%)	42 (87.50%)
Week 3			
Experimental group	63	50 (79.37%)	54 (85.71%)
Control group	48	38 (79.17%)	40 (83.33%)
Week 4			
Experimental group	63	48 (76.19%)	55 (87.30%)
Control group	48	38 (79.17%)	35 (72.92%)

TABLE 2
Total Assignments Completed during Baseline Period versus Treatment Period

	Total assignments	Number completed (baseline period)	Number completed (treatment period)	Computed t-value
Experimental group	252	193 (76.59%)	212 (84.13%)	2.02*
Control group	192	157 (81.77%)	154 (80.12%)	−0.15

*$P < .05$.

Overall means were compared by group to determine if each group improved homework completion scores. A *t*-test was run to determine if either group successfully completed a significantly higher number of homework assignments during the investigation period than during the baseline period. Table 2 illustrates the means and standard deviations of homework completion scores for the baseline and investigation periods for both the control group and the experimental group. The *t*-values are also given for each group. No significant increase in the successful completion of homework assignments was evident from the baseline period to the investigation period for the control group. However, the experimental group significantly improved the successful completion of homework assignments ($p < .05$) from the baseline period to the treatment period.

Discussion

It appears that once students were given a general reading strategy designed for mathematical texts, they were more able to read and comprehend sample problem solutions from the textbook. Although students in the experimental group started out completing no more assignments than usual, a steady increase was apparent during the last three weeks of the treatment phase of the investigation. That could be partially attributed to the idea that students needed time to acclimate to the new reading strategy. Though no qualitative data were formally collected, students in the treatment group verbally reported an increased awareness and understanding of how and why textbooks were written in such a formal, proof-based format. Additionally, more than half of the students said they valued the textbook reading strategy as being generally helpful in reading the sample problems.

A detailed examination of the data from an individual standpoint did show that not all of the students in the treatment group benefited from the reading instruction. Three of the students in the treatment group experienced difficulty in using the reading strategy outside of class when the instructor was not available to answer questions. Those students actually turned in fewer assignments during the treatment phase of the investigation than during the four weeks before that phase began.

Although this study suggests that teaching reading strategies for mathematics may improve students' ability to successfully complete process-oriented textbook problems, it in no way indicates that students in the study engaged in any sort of self-analysis related to their reading patterns. Specifically, students seemed to use the reading strategy as a blueprint for decoding the types of problems seen in the one chapter of their textbook. A similar study of greater magnitude may give insight into how effective a general reading strategy would be if used for a different textbook and over a longer period of time. Also, more detailed observations into student reading patterns related to mathematics may produce a more effective and specific set of strategies.

Although the scope of this study was fairly limited, it seemed to be a successful first attempt at providing better instruction to mathematics students by giving them a new tool to fix a functional but leaky faucet. Perhaps a new philosophy will emerge: "If it ain't broke, don't fix it—just tinker to make it better."

REFERENCES

Bray, J., and J. Armstrong. 1986. *What's wrong with mathematics textbooks? Views from the field.* Denver, Colo.: Education Commission of the States. ERIC Document Reproduction Service No. ED 306 091.

Bush. W. S. 1987. Mathematics textbooks in teacher education. *School Science and Mathematics* 87 (3): 558–56.

Merseth. K. K. 1993. How old is the shepherd? An essay about mathematics education. *Phi Delta Kappan* 74 (7): 548–54.

Elliott Ostler is an assistant professor of education at the University of Nebraska at Omaha.

From *The Clearing House*, September/October 1997, pages 37-40. © 1997 by Heldref Publications, 1319, Eighteenth St., NW, Washington, DC 20036-1802. Reprinted with permission of the Helen Dwight Reid Educational Foundation.

Comprehending Multiple Texts: A Theme Approach Incorporating the Best of Children's Literature

Raymond P. Kettel and Nancy L. Douglas

Traditionally, students' experiences with literature consist of reading a single text and answering teacher directed questions. And, traditionally, that practice often disengages as many students (if not more) than it engages. So, why does this tradition linger? Perhaps it is because, like the Thanksgiving tradition of always cooking the turkey in a particular pan, we fail to consider better ways of accomplishing our goal, like buying a turkey already cooked!

We were ready to replace a tradition that was in effective for too many students, so we asked ourselves what would happen if young adolescents preceded their reading of several theme-based texts by relating their own knowledge and experience to that theme. We hoped that giving students the opportunity to read a variety of texts that all addressed a similar theme would encourage more engagement and, consequently, better comprehension. We found a sixth-grade teacher at Stout Middle School in Dearborn, Michigan, who was willing to try on a new tradition, so we began our study in Maysam Beydoun's classroom, where the majority of students mirrored the school population of mostly Arab Americans. While her students had read a variety of novels, they had had little opportunity to consider how one theme can be addressed in different genres. To introduce this concept, we introduced them to literary works of fiction and nonfiction with a common theme.

Why Use Multiple Texts?

Schema theory tells us that readers construct meaning from the information suggested by the printed page in combination with their own knowledge (Anderson, 1999). The reader's existing knowledge (schema) consists not only of knowledge gained through experiences, but that gained from other texts. Proficient readers understand texts not as isolated entities, but in relation to, among other things, other texts. Moreover, when readers apply their knowledge of past texts to current texts, they often revise and refine their comprehension of past texts (Beach, Appleman, & Dorsey, 1994).

Regrettably, literature instruction is usually focused on single texts (Beach, Appleman, & Dorsey, 1994). In analyzing students' think-aloud responses to texts, Rogers (1988) discovered that a mere 1% of students made references to other texts. Only if students saw other texts as almost identical were they able to make intertextual links. The one-text-at-a-time tradition, therefore, translates beyond an isolated reading experience to an experience that reinforces a student's belief that each text is an island, that each text does indeed stand alone.

We contend, however, that this view can be altered when teachers move from book-at-a-time teaching to multiple text–single theme teaching. Moreover, when teachers use theme as a guiding force for instruction rather than the single text, students of diverse reading abilities can benefit. Robb (2002) reminds us that getting students involved in themes makes it possible to reach students of various abilities. As teachers select books with a similar theme but of various levels of difficulty, all students can be involved in the discussion. And from that involvement comes a rise in comprehension.

Role of Theme

In searching for themes, we considered three sources: those discussed by Sutherland (1997), "strength of family life, overcoming jealously or fear, adjusting to a physical handicap"; examples shared by Huck and her colleagues (2001), "acceptance of self and others, growing, and the overcoming of fear and prejudice"; and the more detailed themes provided by Lukens (1999), "the love of family members is real and enduring; freedom is so important that it is worth even the threat of annihilation, and appearances are less important than what one is inside".

From the above examples, we have identified theme as something that is characteristic of the human condition. Like a pattern that is repeated throughout a tapestry, theme usually can be found throughout a literary piece. It can be stated explicitly or implicitly, and the same theme can be interpreted in a variety of ways. A single book can have any number of major or minor themes, with the relative value of each assigned by the individual reader (Rosenblatt, 1999).

For our project, we chose books that we thought would encourage discussion around the following themes:

1. When discrimination is practiced, people are cruel to one another.
2. People must find peaceful ways to resolve differences as war brings death and destruction.

3. Every person has a right to belong and to have a home where he or she can put down roots and grow.

4. We are all responsible for protecting and maintaining the balance of nature.

5. Our survival depends on ourselves and our reactions to problems.

Often, the most difficult consideration for preparing students to work with themes is knowing where to start. We suggest that instruction begin with a favorite book recommended by the teacher or student, one that has the potential for lively discussion and offers a wide range of possibilities for writing activities. Once the choice is made, a theme or themes from the book are decided upon, and other literary pieces of both fiction and nonfiction are chosen to accompany the first selection. In Figure 1, you'll see how we grouped books by theme, labeling each as fiction (F) or nonfiction (N), and, when important, noting the gender of the central character and the topic of the book. (Note that "topic" differs from "theme" in that "topic" merely signifies the subject of the book, such as baseball or sibling rivalry, whereas "theme" denotes deeper threads of moral or philosophical debate, such as the concepts of fair play or family bonds.) For rich discussions of theme, we found that students should read at least three of the selections and should be encouraged to read both fiction and nonfiction.

Implementing Theme-based Literature Units

When we began working with Ms. Beydoun, we found that one of her favorite books is *Petey* by Ben Mikaelsen. This book is about the difficult life of an individual with cerebral palsy, and it follows him from childhood to adulthood. We suggested that she add *The Breadwinner* by Deborah Ellis, which is about an Afghan girl, Parvana, who must dress up like a boy in order to feed her family during the repressive Taliban rule, and the nonfiction selection *Through My Eyes* by Ruby Bridges, which describes the author's experience of being the first black child to attend an all-white school in New Orleans in 1960. One theme common to these three selections is, "When discrimination is practiced, people are cruel to one another." In addition to having a shared theme, we have chosen these titles because they address current topics of concern—gender equity, Civil Rights, and the physically challenged.

One strong advantage of a multi-book, single-theme approach is that readers of all levels can participate because books of all levels can be used. So, to make sure that Mrs. Beydoun's struggling readers could participate, we also included the detailed picture book, *The Story of Ruby Bridges* by Robert Coles. For struggling readers who want to tackle more difficult works, the teacher may need to read sections of the book aloud, make the book available on tape, or pair students to read together.

Preparing for Reading

We got the students involved with the theme before they began reading any books by giving them the opportunity to think about, then discuss, and then write about discrimination. First, the students were directed to think about how people are dis-

criminated against because of their appearance, their religious beliefs, their gender, or other differences. They were asked to think about the meaning of the theme, "When discrimination is practiced, people are cruel to one another," and then consider the following quote from Dr. Martin Luther King, Jr. (1963) from his Washington D.C. speech:

There is no easy way to create a world where men and women can live together, where each has his own job and house and where all children receive as much education as their minds can absorb. But if such a world is created in our lifetime, it will be done in the United States by Negroes and white people of good will. It will be accomplished by persons who have the courage to put an end to suffering by willingly suffering themselves rather than inflict suffering upon others. It will be done by rejecting the racism, materialism, and violence that has characterized Western civilization and especially by working toward a world of brotherhood, cooperation, and peace. (quoted in Bridges, p. 54)

Next, the students were paired and asked to discuss the questions and topics below, beginning with the one most meaningful to them.

- Is discrimination ever justified? Why or why not?
- Talk about how discrimination might seem at first the popular thing to do but later turns out to be harmful and hurtful to others.

Students were then asked to independently write a first draft about the theme. They were told that their audience would be their classmates and that their ideas may come from the discussions they just had or information they had gleaned from television, reading, or observation. They were given the following prompts:

- Tell what form of discrimination you feel is most harmful and why.
- Describe a time when you felt you were experiencing some form of discrimination.
- Explain how you or someone else could help another person who is experiencing discrimination.
- Persuade the reader that discrimination is harmful.
- Write about discrimination in your own way.

Then, the students were invited to share their writing with their peers. This allowed them to hear other points of view, establish the relevance of the theme to their own lives, and begin to understand the pain and anguish caused by discrimination. Figure 2 is an example of one student's response.

Reacting to Reading

Next, students were told about book selections. All students read *Petey* by Ben Mikaelsen and then each read two or more additional books. Once the students had finished their reading, we wanted them talking and writing about how the theme was seen across texts.[1] We shifted from questions about a single text to more complicated questions that required comparisons between two or more texts. For example, all students read *Petey*,

Theme: When discrimination is practiced, people are cruel to one another.

Title	Author	Fiction/ Nonfiction	Protagonist's Gender	Topic
Petey	Ben Mikaelsen	F	Boy	Physical Disability
*Going Places	Thomas Bergman	N		Physical Disability
The Breadwinner	Deborah Ellis	F	Girl	Taliban Regime
Adem's Cross	Alice Mean	F	Boy	Kosovo Conflict
Charlie Pippin	Candy Dawson Boyd	F	Girl	Vietnam War
The Watsons Go to Birmingham—1963	Christopher Paul Curtis	F	Boy	Civil Rights
*The Story of Ruby Bridges	Robert Coles	F	Girl	Civil Rights
*Through My Eyes	Ruby Bridges	N	Girl	Civil Rights
The Devil's Arithmetic	Jane Yolen	F	Girl	WW II/Holocaust
*The Bracelet	Yoshiko Uchida	F	Girl	WW II
*My Secret Camera	Frank Dabba Smith	N	Boy	WW II/Holocaust
The Captive	Joyce Hansen	F	Boy	Slavery
Nightjohn	Gary Paulsen	F	Girl	Slavery
*Christmas in the Big House	Pat McKissack et at.	N		Slavery
Fat Chance	Leslea Newman	F	Girl	Eating Disorders

Theme: People must find peaceful ways to resolve differences as war brings death and destruction.

Title	Author	Fiction/ Nonfiction	Protagonist's Gender	Topic
Zlata's Diary	Zlata Filipovic	N	Girl	Sarajevo Conflict
*The Wall	Eve Bunting	F	Boy	Vietnam War
Sadako and the Thousand Paper Cranes	Eleanor Coerr	N	Girl	World War II/Japan
*Rose Blanche	Roberto Innocenti	F	Girl	World War II/Holocaust
*Faithful Elephants	Yukio Tsuchiya	N		World War II/Japan
*Hiroshima No Pika	Toshi Maruki	N		World War II/Japan
*Pink and Say	Patricia Polacco	F	Boy	Civil War
Charley Skedaddle	Patricia Beatty	F	Boy	Civil War
Habibi	Naomi Shihab Nye	F	Girl	Middle Eastern Conflict
*Sitti's Secrets	Naomi Shihab Nye	F	Girl	Middle Eastern Conflict

Theme: Every person has a right to belong and to have a home where he or she can put down roots and grow.

Title	Author	Fiction/ Nonfiction	Protagonist's Gender	Topic
*Erik Is Homeless	Keith Greenberg	N	Boy	Homeless
A Family Apart	Joan Lowery Nixon	F	Girl	Homeless
Monkey Island	Paula Fox	F	Boy	Homeless
Maniac Magee	Jerry Spinelli	F	Boy	Homeless
*I Was Dreaming to Come to America	Veronica Lawler	N		Immigration
*Immigrants	Martin Sandler	N		Immigration
*Journey to Ellis	Carol Bierman	F	Boy	Immigration
Bud, Not Buddy	Christopher Paul Curtis	F	Boy	Great Depression
My Louisiana Sky	Kimberly Willis Holt	F	Girl	Fitting In
*One Boy from Kosovo	Trish Marx	N	Boy	War Refugee
Pictures of Hollis Woods	Patricia Giff	F	Girl	Foster Child/Orphan

Theme: We are all responsible for protecting and maintaining the balance of nature.

Title	Author	Fiction/ Nonfiction	Protagonist's Gender	Topic
*Our Endangered Planet: Tropical Rain Forests	Cornelia Mutel & Mary Rodgers	N		Rain Forest
*Where the River Begins	Thomas Locker	F	Boy	Camping
*A River Ran Wild	Lynne Cherry	N		River Pollution
*Someday a Tree	Eve Bunting	F	Girl	Pollution/Trees
Who Really Killed Cock Robin	Jean Craighead George	F	Boy	Ecological Mystery
*Just a Dream	Chris Van Allsburg	F	Boy	Pollution
*Letting Swift River Go	Jane Yolen	F	Girl	River/Reservoir
On the Far Side of the Mountain	Jean Craighead	F	Girl	Pollution

Theme: Our survival depends on ourselves and our reactions to problems.

Title	Author	Fiction/ Nonfiction	Protagonist's Gender	Topic
Julie of the Wolves	Jean Craighead George	F	Girl	Tundra
Trial by Ice	K. M. Kostyalk	N	Boy	Tundra
Hatchet	Gary Paulsen	F	Boy	Canadian Wilderness
True Confession of Charlotte Doyle	Avi	F	Girl	Ship
The Cay	Theodore Taylor	F	Boy	Island
Out of the Dust	Karen Hesse	F	Girl	Dust Bowl
Night of the Twisters	Ivy Ruckman	F	Boy	Tornado
*Wilma Unlimited	Kathleen Krull	N	Girl	Polio
*Encounter	Jane Yolen	F	Boy	Invasion
Homeless Bird	Gloria Whelan	F	Girl	Widow/India
*Fly Away Home	Eve Bunting	F	Boy	Homelessness
Crispin: The Cross of Lead	Avi	F	Boy	Feudalism

*Picture book format

Figure 1. Literature thematic chart

Discrimination greatly harms society. Discrimination is when people are treated worse than others are because of where they come from, how they look, or what their beliefs are. It comes in many different forms and happens for many different reasons. It creates tension and it makes people dislike each other.

The mistrust that comes with discrimination is what ruins society the most. An example of mistrust is when something gets stolen and the person that was stolen from might say that it was someone whose group of people were publicly discriminated against and said to steal. As the discrimination gets worse the mistrust gets worse, and the mistrust will most likely lead to unfairness or hatred.

Worse harm comes when you have police or government officials discriminating against people, because people could be arrested for "looking suspicious" when they were just driving to a grocery store. People who are discriminated against go through hassles that a lot of people don't have to go through, like not being able to join some social groups or being pulled over for no good reason. This is an example of the unfairness in society that can break up a community.

Nowadays Arabs are discriminated against because of what happened with the World Trade Centers. What people don't realize is that a handful of Arabs did that not all of them. I heard about an incident in Detroit where police came to a crime scene and asked every witness what happened there except for the Arabs who witnessed the whole thing. That is what I meant by mistrust.

Figure 2. Omar's written response

so, Ms. Beydoun began the discussion by asking them to write about the following two questions:

1. Do you think it was right or wrong for Petey's mother to place her son in a mental institution?
2. Think about the scene of Trevor saving Petey from a snowball attack by a group of other teens. Do you think that teens today would injure or harm someone who is physically disabled? Would other teens come to that person's rescue?

One student, Jennifer, used information from the text to support her opinion, but she also relied on her own beliefs about doctors as she answered the first prompt:

I think it was right for Petey's mom to put him in a mental institution. I think his mom was right because their family couldn't afford to pay any more doctor bills. Petey was too hard to take care of, and putting Petey in a mental institution was doctor recommended, and doctors are usually right.

Adham supported his opinion about the tendency of teens to be cruel by relating to his own experiences as he discussed the second prompt:

I think that the teens today would throw snowballs at an elderly man who was disabled because in these days

people aren't comfortable with themselves and feel better when they can hit someone and that person does nothing about it. In these days I don't believe that another teen would come to the rescue of person with Petey's disability because in these days everyone is to conceited and self-involved to even think about anyone else. They would let someone wither away in the cold as long as their happy with themselves.

Once students had considered their responses to discrimination using *Petey* as a support, they moved to questions that pulled them across texts. These questions are listed below, along with representative student responses to the first three.

1. The following is the dedication in *The Story of Ruby Bridges* that Ruby's mother wrote as a tribute to her daughter:

Our Ruby taught us all a lot. She became someone who helped change our country. She was part of history, just like generals and presidents are part of history. They're leaders, and so was Ruby. She led us away from hate, and she led us nearer to knowing each other, the white folks and the black folks.

If you were the parent of a child who overcame a severe hardship as did Petey and Parvana, what would you say in your tribute to your child?

Virginia was able to discern the special characteristics that made the protagonists heroes: If I were to be Petey or Parvanas parent I would tell them don't let anyone or anything stand in your life. To Parvana, people like the Taliban would expect you to do as you are told. To Petey, no matter what the doctors or people think of you, I know you are an amazingly spectacular person. It doesn't matter to me how you look but it does matter how you act.

2. Think about how the characters from the three books that you read experienced cruelty because of discrimination. Choose two of the books and describe what lessons you have learned about what happens when people discriminate because of how people look. Include details from at least two of the selections.

Aamina is able to demonstrate what she has learned and provides information from both texts to support her opinion: In *Petey* I learned that beneath the exterior there is someone you might like. Looks can be deceiving. In the book almost everybody Petey met was scared of him and the people who didn't take the time to get to know Petey missed their chance to meet a very special person. In the story *Through My Eyes* I learned that discrimination of race can have a very lasting impression on a child. Ruby Bridges said that she always felt a sense of loss when she looked back on that hectic year. Ruby had never before met people who hated her for such mindless reasons. All of this ill will directed at Ruby gave her nightmares and lost her innocence.

3. Think about the picture book *The Story of Ruby Bridges*. Four years after this book was published, Ruby Bridges wrote her own story about herself and named it *Through My Eyes*. Explain

why you think that Ruby Bridges felt the need to write her own story. Give details from both selections to explain your answer.

Although Ron neglected to support his opinion with information from the texts, he gives a reader support for his opinion using his own prior knowledge and beliefs: Ruby Bridges may or may not have seen it absolutely vital that she retell her story as she felt it happened, but, at any rate, I shall follow with a couple of reasons why she might have done it. Firstly, if given the opportunity, I'm sure that anyone would want to let people know how you felt/feel about anything that big that you accomplished, witnessed as a child or at any point in your past years. Anyway, she might have thought that she was being made out as so much more of a "hero" or a "do-gooder" than she felt herself to be. She may have thought that she just needed to tell her side of the story. In any case, it is she alone that knows why she wrote the book, really.

Other questions that elicited thoughtful responses were:

4. Both Ruby Bridges and Parvana had to leave home each day without the company of their parents. Consider what the mothers must have been thinking while their daughters were not with them. In your opinion, which mother had the most to worry about? Give details from the story to support your answer.
5. Think about the different kinds of discrimination that were experienced by Ruby Bridges, Parvana, and Petey. Who do you feel suffered the most? Give details from at least two of the selections to support your answer.
6. Imagine that you had the opportunity to award gold medals to two of the three characters that you read about: Ruby Bridges, Parvana, and Petey. The medal represents what they did to help others. Name the two characters that you would award the medals to and tell why they are the most deserving of this award. Use information from all three selections to support your response.

As you can see, this combination of discussion, open-ended questions, and writing prompts related to multiple literary works with the same theme, regardless of reading level, gave all students an opportunity to extend their thoughts and make meaningful connections to their own lives and the world at large.

Final Thoughts

Single-theme multiple text instruction helps students understand the theme from a variety of perspectives. We realize that some students might have difficulty responding to multiple texts. Thus, we suggest that teachers consider using picture books rather than chapter books when first introducing multiple texts that explore the same theme. Also, we encourage teachers to bring in expository texts from various sources including textbooks, newspapers, the Web, and magazines to build background knowledge on either the topic or the theme. These informational selections build background knowledge that fosters comprehension (Anderson, 1999). Finally, we encourage teachers to remember that simply reading multiple texts is not enough. Students must have the opportunity for

- peer- and teacher-directed discussions,
- responding to open-ended questions,
- reflective writing, and
- making comparisons between various sources that address similar issues.

These opportunities encourage higher order thinking, deep knowledge, substantive conversation, and connections to the world beyond the classroom (Newmann, Secada, & Wehlage, 1995). More important, these opportunities improve students' understanding not only of a single text, not only of multiple texts, but of the issues that confront them in their lives.

Raymond P. Kettel is associate professor of education and **Nancy L. Douglas** is assistant professor of reading and language arts at the University of Michigan in Dearborn. They can be reached at rpkettel@umd.umich.edu and ndouglas@umich.edu, respectively.

Notes

1. Students can read these novels either during in-class readers workshop time or as at-home assignments. If students read at home, make sure to provide some time during class for literature circle meetings so students can discuss books as they read.

References

Anderson, R. C. (1999). The role of the reader's schema in comprehension, learning, and memory. In R. B. Ruddell, M. R. Ruddell, & H. Singer (Eds.), *Theoretical models and processes of reading* (pp. 469–482). Newark, DE: International Reading Association.

Beach, R., Appleman, D., & Dorsey, S. (1994). Adolescents' uses of intertextual links to understand literature. In R. B. Ruddell, M. R. Ruddell, & H. Singer (Eds.), *Theoretical models and processes of reading* (pp. 695–713). Newark, DE: International Reading Association.

Huck, S., Helper, S., Hickman, J., & Kiefer, B. (2001). *Children's literature in the elementary school.* New York: McGraw-Hill.

Lukens, R. J. (1999). *A critical handbook of children's literature.* New York: Addison-Wesley Educational Publishers.

Newmann, F. M., Secada, W. G., & Wehlage, G. G. (1995). *A guide to authentic instruction and assessment: Vision, standards, and scoring.* Madison, WI: Wisconsin Center for Education Research.

Robb, L. (2002). Multiple texts: Multiple opportunities for teaching and learning. *Voices from the Middle, 9*(4), 28–32.

Rogers, T. (1988). *Students as literary critics: The interpretive theories, processes, and experiences of ninth-grade students.* Unpublished doctoral dissertation, University of Illinois at Urbana–Champaign.

Rosenblatt, L. M. (1999). The transactional theory of reading and writing. In R. B. Ruddell, M. R. Ruddell, & H. Singer (Eds.), *Theoretical models and processes of reading* (pp. 1057–1092). Newark, DE: International Reading Association.

Sutherland, Z. (1997). *Children and books.* New York: Addison-Wesley Educational Publishers.

Celebrating Literature in a Comprehensive Middle School Program

Marguerite Cogorno Radencich & Anita Meyer Meinbach

At the beginning of the school year, the school's reading teacher read Spinelli's (1990) *Maniac Magee* to students on the Alpha Team, the school's at-risk program, as part of a thematic unit an "Heroes and Heroines." Inspired by the title character, the students initiated the "Maniac Magee Award for a Legacy of Kindness." This award is now presented annually to the student or staff member who has done the most to promote understanding, kindness, and harmony. In October, to introduce the award, the Alpha Team unanimously honored the school's principal with the award, citing him for his tremendous efforts to help all students realize their potentials. In June, the entire school voted on the recipient of the 1995 Maniac Magee Award, a cafeteria worker, "Grandma," who not only feeds over 1200 students a day but nurtures them with her warm smile and caring heart. In the final analysis, we all gain from characters like Maniac as we recognize that each kindness, each display of caring, each measure of compassion grows geometrically. Through the pages of his book, Jerry Spinelli certainly gave Southwood's staff and students a hero worthy of emulating.

Reading programs in middle schools take many forms (Duffy, 1990). Model schoolwide programs referenced in the literature often address specific aspects of reading such as reading with interdisciplinary teams (Condon & Hoffman, 1990), reading with the support of resource specialists (Radencich, Beers, & Schumm, 1993), or instructional approaches (Anders & Levine, 1990; Cowart & Fabre, 1986). The program at Southwood Middle School in Dade County (Miami) Florida went beyond these efforts in a more comprehensive planned approach where teaching and celebrating literature occur systematically through specified goals and defined components.

Initiating Events

Southwood is a visual and performing arts magnet of approximately 1400 students, primarily non-Hispanic white and black, with 25% receiving free and reduced lunch. Three years ago, Southwood's principal created a special team of faculty members and charged us with the responsibility of building a comprehensive literature program to celebrate reading and bring quality literature to the forefront of middle school education. Interestingly, both the principal and reading teacher had a strong background in elementary education and shared the perspective that quality literature should provide the framework and the pillars to support education.

Before a plan of action could be developed, literature program goals were established:

1. To instill in students the love of reading and the sense that reading is joyful.
2. To involve all members of the school's faculty in using literature to make learning come alive.
3. To provide students with an ongoing forum for sharing, discussing, and interpreting literature.
4. To provide an outreach program to extend into the community—bringing the "gift of reading" to young and old.

With these goals at the forefront, the team then brainstormed the major components intrinsic to a literature-rich program and organized them under umbrella headings. While each component in and of itself was important to achieve our goal, we realized that each also needed to work in concert with the others to bring literature alive for all students. Consequently, we realized that our literature program needed a hub, an area that brought together the many components identified.

Our hub became "the Happening," a small room decorated with poems, book jackets, a parent-drawn picture of a child reading, and related artifacts, furnished with stuffed bean bag chairs, and filled with literature, both classic and contemporary. The Happening soon became a place where reading was encouraged, a place filled with the sounds of students involved in dialogue and with the magic of reading. In short, the Happening was reminiscent of the 60s coffee houses where ideas flowed and creativity soared.

A part-time teacher was hired to create the setting that we envisioned and to coordinate the events in the Happening. This special person, with the guidance of the reading teacher, not only created an atmosphere that welcomed readers, but one that made students want to return again and again. The Happening became host to a myriad of activities—"Grand Conversations"

(Peterson & Eeds, 1990), book talks, read-alouds, guest speakers and authors, storytelling, and tutorials. In short, the Happening became a place where stories and poems took on a life of their own.

With the Happening in place, our literature team focused on the need to fill classrooms with quality literature. One team member wrote a parent involvement grant that helped fund the libraries. Of the school's 55 teachers, 42 requested and obtained classroom libraries in the first year of our project. In the second year of our celebration of literature program, our principal made funds available so that every classroom in the school could have a library.

Catalogues from the Perfection Learning (16-1000 North 2nd Ave., Logan, IA 51546) were distributed to teachers and they were asked to select two sets of books for their classrooms, each set including approximately 18-25 varied trade books with suggested grade levels. Books arrived stored in their own crates which were then easily stacked, negating the need for shelf space.

Southwood's focus on literature gave one of our team's language arts teachers the impetus to initiate and sponsor a new club, one based on a common love for reading. The club would spread the love for literature to others in the community, from preschoolers to the elderly. Word of mouth circulated the goals of this club, and in just months, the Bookworms became one of the most popular clubs on campus.

Components

Following is a more detailed description of the eight components of Southwood's literature program that have emerged since its beginnings.

Literature team

To lead the school's literature program, a literature team was created comprised of three language arts teachers, a reading teacher, the media specialist, and the assistant principal for curriculum. The reading teacher had one released period a day to support the team's goals.

The Happening and Grand Conversations

Our unique reading room, the Happening, premiered with a special ribbon cutting ceremony. Video and newspaper staff captured the moment as the principal made a brief speech and cut the ribbon. As guests entered and visited the Happening, the music of Peter, Paul, and Mary floated through the air, performed by a student guitarist. The goals of the Happening, as stated in the student newspaper, were threefold: (a) to turn kids onto reading, (b) to increase by 50% the number of books read by students, and (c) to foster family reading. The Happening would become synonymous with literature as a myriad of reading related activities were scheduled in the room throughout the year.

When the Happening's coordinator and the reading teacher participated in a session on Grand Conversations held at the conference of the National Council of Teachers of English, they realized that Grand Conversations needed to headline the roster of "happenings."

Grand Conversations are actually book discussions. The participants in Grand Conversations all read the same material and come together to discuss questions, ideas, concepts, and so forth suggested by their own interpretations of the reading.

In planning Grand Conversations, we tried to schedule books as they tied into a special monthly event or theme. The first Grand Conversation, held during Black History Month, was based on *Roll of Thunder, Hear My Cry* by Mildred Taylor (1984). The event was led by the reading teacher with ten invited students representing the gifted class, the Alpha Team, and regular classes. The quality of the discussion was most gratifying. It would be difficult for an observer to determine which students represented the gifted program, the Alpha Team, or the general school population. Students listened, reacted to the comments of others, and gained new insights and deeper understanding.

To involve teachers across disciplines in Grand Conversations, the reading teacher held a training session. Four teachers attended; two led subsequent Grand Conversations, and the others made a commitment to do the same next year. Once a teacher volunteers to lead a Grand Conversation, the date and book he or she would like to use are discussed with the Happening coordinator. Eleven copies are then ordered (one for the discussion leader and ten for the student participants). Various teachers are asked by the teacher-leader to advertise the Grand Conversation in their classrooms and to identify a specific number of students. In this way, the discussion group becomes quite heterogeneous in terms of student ability. The ten students are then given a copy of the book and a Grand Conversation Form (Figure 1).

The school's French teacher led a Grand Conversation based on Lois Lowry's (1993) Newbery Award winning *The Giver*. Students debated issues and made connections to their own lives and our world. They compared the idea of "release" with euthanasia, for example, and delved into concepts such as the importance of choice. The discussion also generated many ideas concerning the role of government, giving new meaning to the term "individual responsibility."

As the reputation of Grand Conversations grew, one of the school's special education teachers arranged to have her sister, a local elementary school media specialist, lead a Grand Conversation during Poetry Month based on Robert Frost's poem, "The Road Not Taken." To coincide with Holocaust Remembrance Day, the Happening coordinator led a Grand Conversation on Jane Yolen's (1990) *The Devil's Arithmetic*.

The Grand Conversations at Southwood have been extremely successful. In the words of one student:

> After reading a meaningful and sometimes confusing book, I feel it is necessary to discuss the book with others. Our very own Happening is the perfect environment to hold a Grand Conversation. With bean bags, a throw rug, and an understanding teacher, one can discuss a book openly.

Figure 1

The Grand Conversation Form

Student Name: _____   Date of Grand Conversation: _____

Literature to Be Discussed: Time: _____

 Title: _____   Place: _____

 Author: _____   Sponsor: _____

To prepare for your "Grand Conversation," please follow the directions below:

1. Clear the time and date with your classroom teacher as soon as possible. If he/she can't excuse you at this time, please let Ms. Friedman (Room #50) know immediately, and you will be scheduled for a different time.

2. Complete your reading of the literature before the Grand Conversation. Please do not make any marks in the book, you may use "stick-ums" if you wish to mark certain pages.

3. List any questions that occur to you as you read. (Questions might include, but are not limited to questions concerning author's meaning, questions about some aspect of the story, questions about the character(s), etc.).

 a. _____
 b. _____
 c. _____
 d. _____
 e. _____

4. Did any event or scene especially interest you, surprise you, or cause any other strong emotion? If so, please make a note of it.

 page(s) _____
 paragraph(s) _____

5. Bring the book and this sheet with you to the Grand Conversation.
 This sheet will serve as your hall pass.

In addition to the impact the Grand Conversations have made in arousing interest in literature, they have three additional benefits: (a) teachers, especially those outside the area of language arts, have learned a technique that can easily be adapted to their own classes; (b) students are able to interact with some incredible teachers outside their regular classrooms; (c) the books ordered and used for the Grand Conversations are available to be enjoyed by other students.

Along with 200 eighth graders, one language arts teacher has brought the Gift of Reading to community members—youngsters who cannot yet read, the blind, the infirm, and elderly nonreaders.

At the end of the first year of our Celebrating Literature program, students began requesting more Grand Conversations. In fact, several asked to form a special Grand Conversation Club with student mentors to provide a group of students the opportunity for regular book discussions. In year two of the program, this club was established, with the reading teacher as group sponsor. Members suggested literature for the Grand Conversations, discussed and developed skills for facilitating a Grand Conversation, and learned techniques for listening and responding.

In an effort to bridge school and community, the Happening coordinator and the reading teacher spoke with the manager of a local nationally known book shop to create a partnership. Beginning in year two of our program, Borders Book Shop became the host of our monthly Grand Conversations. Letters were sent by the Happening coordinator and the reading teacher to the head of the language arts department of area middle schools, inviting their students to join ours in a discussion of quality literature. The response was instantaneous and overwhelming. Now in year three, the Grand Conversation has literally become the talk of the town. Students from both public and private schools have made this a monthly event. A variety of genres and literary forms are being highlighted. The next Grand Conversation, for example, will focus on the short stories of O'Henry, including "The Gift of the Magi." Teachers throughout the country have called to see if they can establish Grand Conversations at book stores in their areas of the country and a high school teacher in our feeder pattern is making plans to begin a Grand Conversation for older students so the tradition can continue. The special events coordinator at Borders Book Shop, in addition to advertising the Grand Conversations in Border's monthly newsletter, is preparing a booktalk to precede each Grand Conversation to make students aware of the newest publications.

In year one of the program, the Happening played host to a variety of other literature related events. Students in the gifted program performed story tellings of legends connected with Native Americans. Students in the National Honor Society held tutorials in the Happening—they liked the quiet of the room. To celebrate the Great American Read Aloud, community members read excerpts from their favorite literature. During Poetry Month, Poetry Alive!, a professional group, performed special works of poetry. Afterwards, students in the Bookworms Literature Club attended a special poetry training session given by the stars of Poetry Alive! As phrased by a student reporter in the "What's Happening?" column of the school newspaper, "Never has poetry been spoken so clearly to students and never before have students learned how to perform poetry." The Bookworms later had the opportunity to use their training as they performed favorite poetry along with winners of the school's poetry writing contest sponsored by the Happening. When Professor Anthony Fredericks, a noted author, storyteller, and teacher at York College, visited Southwood, he trained the Bookworms on specific storytelling techniques. In this way, the Bookworms will have the skills to bring literature alive for others.

While many students and teachers had the opportunity to visit the Happening, we hoped to make the room even more accessible and hold additional events there. Unfortunately, in year two of the program, space restrictions forced the closing of the Happening. However, a section of the media center became the focal point, along with the extension at Borders Book Shop. Regardless of space constraints, the vision we had for the Happening is still evident in one form or another. A commitment to the original goals of the school's literature program has continued to guide our actions. In year three, we have also implemented the Book Buck$ program in which students earn points for reading short stories, magazine articles, and books. Extracurricular clubs are asked to conduct at least one reading-focused project, and students will participate in the "The Miami Heat Library Card Challenge." In future years, attention will be given to these activities:

- Continuation of monthly themes to add zest and give focus to the literature and activities. The themes for the third year are: The Play's the Thing (plays and playwrights); Take Me Out to the Ball Game (sports); Keepers of the Earth (environmental issues-based on the collection of Native American stories of the same name by Caduto and Bruchac, 1991); Sing a Song of Popcorn (poetry-based on the popular poetry book edited by deRegniers, 1988); and a Time for Healing (multicultural understanding).

- Additional training sessions on Grand Conversations to teachers in other regions.

- A Young Authors Day.

- Recruit members of the Grand Conversations Club from Southwood's magnet art program.

- Workshops on book binding, artistic styles, and writing to promote an involvement in the arts.

- Opportunities to showcase original student art and writing.

- An increase in the number of staff and students who visit the library Happening section not only for special events but whenever they have a free moment and wish to get lost between the pages of a book.

The Bookworms Literature Club

In their custom designed T-shirts, members of the Bookworms have worked to spread their love of books in the school and the community. The Bookworms meet once a month after school to plan and organize projects. During the district reading council's annual "Reading Day in the Mall," the Bookworms wore storybook character costumes and read to youngsters. Of all their projects to date, the Bookworms are perhaps most proud of their efforts to share literature with residents of a local nursing home. These residents were so delighted they have invited the Bookworms back again—and again. The Bookworms hope that all students will join with them on the mission of bringing the world to others—through books.

In year two our of Celebrating Literature program, the Bookworms sponsored a schoolwide book drive in which each homeroom received 20–30 contemporary and classic books of literature to supplement their classroom libraries. In addition, many books for younger children were collected and donated to a local elementary school. As a result of the tremendous success of this book drive, we would like to make this an annual event.

The Bookworms have a number of projects lined up for subsequent years:

- Establish a "Listening Library." With help from students in the school's magnet drama department, Bookworms will create audio cassettes of books selected from a list compiled by the school's reading teacher that correlate with subject area topics and themes.

- Create a "Trading Post" to which students and teachers bring used books to trade. Books not traded will go to a used book store and exchanged for other titles.

School newspaper staff

Student newspaper staff covers various Happening events and write separate "The Happening" articles for students and parents, as well as pieces on other school literacy events. In addition, newspaper staff surveyed teachers and students on their favorite books and published the results. There were eight high ranked titles in Grade 6, but clear favorites emerged in the higher grades: *Jurassic Park* (Crichton, 1990) in Grades 7 and 8 and *It* (King, 1986), closely followed by *Jurassic Park*, in Grade 9.

Media center

In addition to traditional activities associated with a media center, Southwood is adding to the literature program with a focus on technology. Students can now access a computer card catalog that "knows" exactly which titles are currently available. The system allows for multiple listings of each book as customized to the needs of the school. Plans are being made to link library computers to each other and to the rest of the school, giving teachers and students easy access to CD-ROM reference materials. Online sources will include the DIALOG databases and America Online. Students with a home computer and modem will be able to phone Southwood's library and access the school's new computer Bulletin Board System.

Computer lab

Classes have been scheduled into the computer lab to provide students with reading assessment and practice exercises. Teachers are encouraged to increase computer usage for desktop publishing. The many teachers in the school with a background in computer technology are available to help students use the various reading and writing programs. Students are encouraged to publish and share original works.

Classroom teachers

Initially, support from teachers throughout the building was solicited on a number of fronts and strongly supported by the school's administration: a door decorating contest sponsored by the Happening coordinator, use of classroom libraries, and participation in the Happening's events.

As the literature program progressed, a greater number of teachers began to buy into the concept of reading across the curriculum and the importance of having books, both to extend the subject matter and for leisure time reading. Teachers who had not requested a classroom library began asking how they could get one. Teachers with libraries were asking how they could supplement them with more books. In response to this, as mentioned earlier, several approaches provided more books for the classroom libraries. In the future, we hope to write additional grants to fund new books.

One language arts teacher and member of the literature team has supported the efforts of Celebrate Literature in a most innovative way. She originated the concept of the "Gift of Reading" and with her 200 eighth graders has brought the Gift of Reading to community members—youngsters who cannot yet read, the blind, the infirm, and elderly nonreaders. Each student volunteered five hours of talking, listening, caring, and reading. Sensitive to the needs of others, students translated readings from English to foreign languages and chose stimulating, age-appropriate material. Some found themselves reading *The Cat in the Hat* (Seuss, 1947) and playing with two-year-olds. Others read *The Wall Street Journal* and discussed the stock market with retirees.

The highlight of the Gift of Reading was the exhibit created jointly by the readers and nonreaders. There were videotaped interviews, original coloring books featuring characters and dialogue from the stories, critical reading skills posters, collages, costumes, photographs, charts, singalongs, dioramas, mobiles, and sculptures all illustrating this project. Each student wrote an expository essay describing his or her participation. It was uncertain who got the most out of the "Gift of Reading"—but judged on their essays, the students gained the most.

In preparing for the second year to celebrate literature, plans were developed to further involve the classroom teachers in reading literature. The Blueprint 2000 committee has recommended (a) a minimum of 20 minutes daily of reading in the content area (a different content area each day) and (b) Wednesday Drop Everything and Read (DEAR) time during advisement (20 minutes). Teachers were also encouraged to involve students in journal writing. During an inservice session to explain the various forms of journal writing, staff will be provided with examples of journal entries and sample reading contracts for use in lieu of traditional homework.

To provide another inservice, we invited the district reading supervisor to work with teachers by departments to model think alouds (Davey, 1983) with subject appropriate text. Based on the success of this inservice method, departmental inservice sessions were extended in years two and three to train content area teachers on the use of specific active reading strategies: K-W-L (Ogle, 1986), SQ3R (Robinson, 1941, 1970), graphic organizers, and Read and Retell (Brown & Cambourne, 1990). In addition to these departmental inservice sessions, school faculty meetings continue to feature specific skills and strategies such as inferential reading, think alouds, the Langer (1990) model of the reading process, Cornell notetaking (Pauk, 1983), and general test-taking strategies. Each subsequent year we hope to add to this list of strategies. Simmers-Wolpow, Farrell, & Tonjes (1991) report increased standardized test scores following multi-year plans of school-wide implementation of select strategies.

Tutorials

The grant-funded Student Literacy Corps from the University of Miami provided five university students to work with the Alpha at-risk students in the media center and in the Happening who were pulled from their language arts classes. Among their activities were journal writing and reading with the students. Students become quite disappointed if their tutor missed a day. The head of the University of Miami Literacy Corps, also teamed up with members from the National Junior Honor Society and residents of a local retirement village to help them tutor students with difficulty in reading and writing. During two days of training, retiree and student tutors were introduced to strategies to assist with motivation and instruction such as making big books, buddy reading with tutees, and using sight word flash cards. Packets of support information were also distributed. Included was information on rights and responsibilities for tutors and tutor/tutee dialogue journals.

Students who took part in peer tutoring already recruited additional tutors. The head of the University of Miami Literacy Corps trained these new Southwood student tutors as well.

Conclusion

Southwood Middle School is committed to bringing children and books together. We realize that we must promote books, advertise books, and totally surround students with the magic of books if we are to be successful. Originally, our four-goal program was heavily slanted toward literature. Over the course of the past three years, other areas of reading have become paramount. The planned schoolwide use of specific reading strategies has been a step in this direction. Our program is truly a collaborative effort. With the support of a dynamic, proactive administration, and an energetic, creative, and cooperative faculty, we have already begun to see our vision become reality. We hope that our program can be a catalyst for other schools attempting comprehensive literature programs. We hope some day more middle school students will remember the legacy of riches and magic they derived from the pages of the books they read.

Note

The voice in this article is that of Dr. Anita Meinbach, the school reading teacher, speaking also on behalf of Robert Kalinsky, Southwood's principal at the inception of the program, and Allen Hindman, Southwood's current principal; Carole Dien-Grant, assistant principal at the inception of the program, and Dr. Shirley Hill, current assistant principal; Harriet Friedman, coordinator of the Happening; Bea Llano, author of the parent involvement grant; Barbara Benton, sponsor of the Bookworms Literature Club; Sue Barth, a Grand Conversations facilitator; Michelle Bluestone, sponsor of The Gift of Reading; Steven Silberman, media specialist; and the entire Southwood faculty.

Marguerite Cogorno Radencich teaches in the Reading Education Department at the University of South Florida, Tampa. Anita Meyer Meinbach teaches at Southwood Middle School, Miami, Florida.

Trade Books Cited

Caduto, M., & Bruchac, J. (1991). Native American stories (from Keepers of the Earth). Golden, CO; Fulcrum.

Crichton, M. (1990). Jurassic park. New York: Knopf.

deRegniers, B.S., (Ed.). (1988). Sing a song of popcorn. New York: Scholastic.

King, S. (1986). It. New York: Viking.

Lowry, L. (1993). The giver. New York: Bantam, Doubleday, Dell.

Seuss, Dr. (Geisel, T. S.). (1947). The cat in the hat. New York: Random House.

Spinelli, J. (1990). Maniac magee. Boston: Little Brown.

Taylor, M. (1984). Roll of thunder, hear my cry. New York: Bantam.

Yolen, J. (1990). The devil's arithmetic. New York: Viking.

References

Anders, P.L., & Levine, N.S. (1990). Accomplishing change in reading programs. In G. G. Duffy (Ed.), Reading in the middle school, (2nd ed.) (pp. 157–170). Newark, DE: International Reading Association.

Brown, H., & Cambourne, B. (1990). Read and retell. Portsmouth, NH: Heinemann.

Condon, M.W.F., & Hoffman, J.V. (1990). The influence of classroom management. In G. G. Duffy (Ed.), Reading in the middle school (2nd ed.) (pp. 41–59). Newark, DE: International Reading Association.

Cowart, D., & Fabre, A. (1986, March). LEAP for success. Paper presented at the meeting of the National Association of Laboratory Schools, New Orleans.

Davey, B. (1983). Think-alouds: Modeling the cognitive processes of reading comprehension. Journal of Reading, 27, 44–47.

Duffy, G.G. (Ed.), (1990). Reading in the middle school (2nd ed.). Newark: DE: International Reading Association.

Langer, J.A. (1990). Understanding literature. Language Arts 67, 812–816.

Ogle, D.J. (1986). K-W-L: A teaching model that develops active reading of expository text. The Reading Teacher, 39, 564–570.

Pauk, W. (1983). How to study in college. Boston: Houghton Mifflin.

Peterson, R. & Eeds, M. (1990). Grand conversations. New York: Scholastic.

Radencich, M.C., Beers, P.G., & Schumm, J.S. (1993). A handbook for the K-12 reading resource specialist. Boston: Allyn & Bacon.

Robinson, F.R. (1941/1970). Effective study. New York: Harper & Row.

Simmers-Wolpm, R., Farrell, D.P., & Tonjes, M.J. (1991). Implementing a secondary reading/study skills program across disciplines. Journal of Reading, 34, 590–594.

From *Middle School Journal* Vol. 29, No. 1, September 1997, pages 15–21. Copyright © 1997 by National Middle School Association. Reprinted with permission from National Middle School Association.

Literature for Children and Young Adults in a History Classroom

JUDY E. VAN MIDDENDORP
SHARON LEE

He put his head down in his hands. "War is hard, boy. Sometimes we do a lot of things we don't want to do. A lot of very good men have been killed in this war, and all we can do is hope that it's been worth it. Maybe it hasn't. Maybe in the end we'll conclude that. But I don't think so, I think it will be worth it, despite the death and destruction." (Collier and Collier, *My Brother Sam Is Dead.* 1974, 193)

Powerful historical fiction such as this popular young adult book is generating lively discussions among students about relevant social science concepts and issues of the past, present, and future. Literature creates a positive reading environment in any classroom. Content area teachers, as well as reading teachers, can share in the benefits of literature. All teachers should model reading for different purposes, display new books, and set aside time during the day when every child has a chance to read a book of his or her choice (Atwell 1987).

Books can be used in a variety of ways, not the least of which is for enjoyment. Fiction, nonfiction, historical fiction, and poetry can be provided for the students to read on their own or can be read aloud by the teacher. Laughter and tears are equally present as students experience the lives of well-rounded characters (Common

1986) while they are learning the concepts and facts of history.

Literature can provide meaningful experiences in a history classroom in a way that a textbook cannot. This article outlines the rationale for using literature in the social sciences and describes a literature-based American history unit that was successfully implemented with eighth graders.

Why Use Children's Literature in the Content Areas?

The use of literature in the social sciences is in part a response to the many documented problems associated with history textbooks. According to Woodward (1986), many researchers find social studies and history textbooks to be poorly organized and poorly written. Their instructional design does not permit students to obtain maximum value from them. In many cases, it appears that the books are written in a vacuum with no concern for instructional considerations or the levels of interest of the students who will be reading them.

Some researchers refer to history, civics, and government textbooks as "encyclopedic" (Brandt 1989; Carroll et al. 1987; Sewall 1988a; Tyson and Woodard 1989) as there isn't enough space to give ample detail about all the topics that are covered. The size of textbooks for the social sciences are de-

scribed as overwhelming, overbearing, and intimidating (Sewall 1988b).

Two other problems associated with social studies/history textbooks are errors of commission and errors of omission. Schuster (1984), a textbook writer for twenty-three years, explains that textbook writers are compelled to tell a certain amount of truths and untruths. Many important topics and concepts are likewise omitted from history textbooks. Controversial subjects and those relating to values have been largely ignored (Carroll et al. 1987). Davis et al. (1986) describe these texts without controversy and values as boring, mindless, and bloodless narratives. The result, Elliott, Woodward, and Nagel (1986) fear, is that students subjected to this type of history "will propagate a view of country and world that is devoid of controversy, point of view or values"

Literature, on the other hand, promotes interest and involvement, and provides students with positive experiences (McMillan and Gentile 1988). Sewall (1988a) states that students "feed on the adventure and excitement that narrative history can provide". Literature enriches the content curriculum and makes it more comprehensible and memorable (Brozo and Tomlinson, 1986). "Students are a lot more likely to learn from and remember a great biography than they are to remember the blank paragraph or two in the textbook" (Ravitch 1989). The trivial facts presented in the textbook may be forgotten, but the story belongs to the student forever.

Before the advent of print, stories were the "primary means for the oral transmission of a people's history and for communicating the nature of their institutional structures, cultural practices, and spirituality. History and story were one" (Common 1986). There are four reasons, according to Common, why stories need to be a part of the social studies curriculum: (1) stories give us clues as to how we should react emotionally about historical events and the people who were involved in them; (2) reality is more easily faced through stories; (3) stories have an end and therefore are innately satisfying; and (4) teachers and students will have a shared experience, a place to start when they begin with a story. "It is the stories of individuals (heroes and villains alike) that bring history to life" (Finn and Ravitch 1988).

Common (1986) names several activities students become involved in when they meet people through literature: they vicariously reenact the events, they attempt to interpret the events, they try to interpret why the people and events are as they are, and they compare their culture with the story culture. Students especially like to read accounts of children who lived long ago. Students can compare and contrast their lives with the lives of other children. In this way they develop a strong self-identity. "Students learn that they are not alone, that they're connected through time with others who felt, hoped and feared as they do" (Downey 1986).

"History and social studies can be explained more clearly, in more depth, and in more detail through literature. The students gain more knowledge as a result. Besides the facts, they learn about the struggles, the excitement, and the challenges of life as it was in the past" (Van Middendorp 1990).

Literature provides students with important cognitive information:

facts, figures, dates. They are also learning that life isn't always fair, that life does not always exist without pain, and that not every situation results with everyone living happily ever after (Cline and Taylor 1978). In short, literature deals with human experiences, feelings, and emotions (Shumaker and Shumaker 1988). These are all important aspects of the social studies curriculum—aspects that may be overlooked by strict adherence to a text-based curriculum.

A Literature-Based Unit for Eighth-Grade U.S. History

The literature-based unit that will be discussed here focuses on pioneering. The unit, developed by the first author of this article as part of a research study on literature-based instruction, was successfully implemented by Curt Cameron, an eighth-grade U.S. history teacher in Vermillion, South Dakota. The five-week study began with the students' reading informational literature books on the concept of pioneering. Through reading, writing, and thinking, students came to the realization that they, too, could be pioneers in such fields as space travel, undersea exploration, or in medicine.

As an introduction, students read general information books about pioneering. The following books and magazines were available for students to read:

Books

Beatty, B. E. 1964. *Living in pioneer days.* New York: Holt, Rinehart & Winston.

Burns, P. C., and R. Hines. 1962. *To be a pioneer.* New York: Abingdon Press.

Havinghurst, W. 1959. *The first book of pioneers.* New York: Franklin Watts.

Kalman, B. 1981. *Early village life.* Toronto: Crabtree.

Moss, M. 1986. *The American West.* Vero Beach, Florida: Rourke Enterprises.

Parish, P. 1967. *Let's be early settlers with Daniel Boone.* New York: Harper & Row.

Magazines

Gores, M. 1983. Frontier physicians. *Cobblestone* (March): 16–19.

Laycock, G. 1986. The pioneer way. *Boy's Life* (April): 30–32.

After reading, students participated in some of the pioneer activities they had learned about, such as making butter, hasty pudding, candles, sheaths, and salt clay. The students were then involved in a critical thinking discussion about the activities. The teacher asked the students to decide which product would have been most important for the pioneers. Ryan summarized the majority vote of the class by stating that "candles were needed for both light and heat" and were therefore most important. This concept could easily have been taught by lecture, but its discovery through literature-based activities required more active involvement from the students and thus more thinking.

Students then worked in groups, each of which was assigned a different folk hero or famous pioneer to study. A text set (Harste and Short 1988) of five books or more about the

---

Titles for Text Set on Johnny Appleseed

Aliki. 1963. *The story of Johnny Appleseed.* Englewood Cliffs, N.J.: Prentice Hall.

Anderson, J. I. 1977. *I can read about Johnny Appleseed.* Mahwah, N.J.: Troll.

Gleiter, J., and K. Thomson 1987. *Johnny Appleseed.* Milwaukee: Raintree.

Hogstrom, D. C. 1983. The man with the sack on his back. *Children's Digest* April/May: 4–7.

Johnson, A. D. 1979. *The value of love: The story of Johnny Appleseed.* La Jolla, Calif.: Value Communication.

Kellog, S. 1960. *Johnny Appleseed.* New York: Morrow Junior Books.

Norman, G. 1960. *Johnny Appleseed.* New York: G. P. Putnam's Sons.

Walt Disney presents the story of Johnny Appleseed. 1969. Racine, Wisc.: Golden Press.

historical figure was provided for each group, which then had the responsibility of teaching the rest of the class about that person. The titles of the text set on Johnny Appleseed, for example, appear in the sidebar. This activity generated much discussion among the students about the factual information presented in the books. High-level thinking was evident as students grappled with the problems of inconsistent information across the texts, simplified story lines, and neglected or omitted information.

The classroom teacher also read aloud *Skitterbrain*, by Irene Brown (1978). The students compared and contrasted their daily life with that of Larnie, the young pioneer girl in *Skitterbrain*. They had a hard time relating to the everyday trials of the young girl, finding her worries trivial, mundane, and hardly worth mentioning. As Jolie put it, "This book puts me in a coma. This girl loses her cow and goes into an emotional trauma over it." They couldn't imagine how important the cow really was for the pioneer family. Jolie was forced to come to terms with someone whose values and lifestyle were very different from her own—a very important lesson to learn in social studies.

A natural extension activity that stems from reading literature is writing. Students quickly observe that reading and writing cannot be separated. After reading about folk heroes, the students began to write their own stories based on legendary characters. Other writing activities took the form of diaries and newspaper articles. Critical thinking and synthesis are evident in virtually all examples.

Extension Activities

The main emphasis of any literature-based history unit will naturally be to teach concepts related to social science. These concepts should be broader than those covered in a textbook. A teacher who is designing a unit such as this could certainly extend the classroom activities into dis-

cussions of such vital issues as racism, classism, sexism, and other moral dilemmas that may be absent in the assigned textbook. For example, in this unit, the teacher could have asked students to consider why there are few stories about minorities or legendary women characters and/or pioneers. The students could have been asked to think and write about the pioneers in the civil rights and women's movements as symbols of the pioneer spirit today.

One student activity that involved thinking and sizing was the writing of a cinquain about pioneers. A few examples follow.

Jolie:	Pioneer
Richard:	tough, strong
Jenny:	working, farming, living
Fris:	they settled the land
	People.
Dan:	Pioneers
Becky:	rough, tough
	working, cooking, farming
	Pioneers have rough lives
	Explorers.
Olivia:	Pioneer
David:	Tired, Poor
Matt:	Working, Hunting, Traveling
	A long journey ahead
	Traveler.

In the cinquain, the students compressed a large amount of information about pioneering into one succinct statement. The literacy activities and literary learning may seem secondary, but they are indeed central to the discovery of historical facts and generalizations. Each cinquain became a sort of graphic organizer for the entire unit of study.

Another writing activity asked students to synthesize what they knew about the concept of pioneering and to apply it to life as we know it today. Ryan's story about contemporary pioneers effectively demonstrates this process. His story is about a family landing on the planet Big Mic. As a passport, however, they need a Big Mac box from America. They fly back to Earth to get the box, but then the family wants to remain on Earth. "No," says the main character as the story ends, "we are

pioneers and that means explore, keep together and not be afraid of anything." Through reading and writing about pioneers, Ryan was able to think through the concept of pioneering and reproduce his knowledge in story form. His final comment in the story is truly a definition of the pioneer spirit.

As a culminating activity, students wrote an account of an imaginary trip in a covered wagon. They were instructed to include the good parts and the bad, the comforts and discomforts. The literature that they had read provided many excellent models for their own writing. During the writing process, they were able to synthesize, analyze, and evaluate life as a pioneer. They became involved in higher-order thinking skills, as well. The final paragraphs of Ryan's story sum up the hardships effectively:

> As I was going down the trails I noticed my son was all sweaty and started to get real pale. Later that day he died and we were only about three days away.
>
> We stopped and built a house where my son died and never got to Oregon.

Literature proved to be a powerful tool for these students. Through the fictional and factual accounts of life as a pioneer, they were able to discuss the topics in their own words, learn what was interesting and relevant to them, and add this knowledge to their personal concept understandings. From their written and oral reports, students proved that they knew vicariously about all aspects of pioneering: pleasure and pain, life and death. Learning from the past through literature, they learned to face today and to prepare for tomorrow.

JUDY VAN MIDDENDORP is an assistant professor in the Education Department at Briar Cliff College in Sioux City, Iowa. SHARON LEE is the director of field experiences and professor of reading at the University of South Dakota.

REFERENCES

Atwell, N. 1987. *In the middle.* Portsmouth, N.H.: Heinemann.

Brandt, R. 1989. On curriculum in California: A conversation with Bill Honig. *Educational Leadership* 47(3): 10–13.

Brown, I. B. (1978). *Skitterbrain.* Nashville, Tenn.: Thomas Nelson Inc.

Brozo, W. G., and C. M. Tomlinson. 1986. Literature: The key to lively content courses. *The Reading Teacher* 40(3): 288–93.

Carroll, J. D., W. D. Broadnax, G. Contreras, T. E. Mann, N. J. Ornstein, and J. Stiehm. 1987. What do US government and civics textbooks teach? In *We the people: A review of US government and civics textbooks.* Washington, D.C.; People for the American Way.

Cline, R. K. J., and B. L. Taylor. 1978. Integrating literature and "free reading" into the social studies program. *Social Education* 40:27–31.

Collier, J. L., and C. Collier. 1974. *My brother Sam is dead.* New York: Scholastic.

Common, K. L. 1986. Students, stories, and the social studies. *The Social Studies,* 77(3):246–48.

Davis, O. L., G. Ponder, L. M. Burlbaw, M. Garza-Lubeck, and A. Moss. 1986. *Looking at history: A review of U.S. history textbooks.* Washington, D.C.; People for the American Way.

Downey, M.T. 1986. Teaching the history of childhood. *Social Education,* 50(4): 262–67.

Elliott, D. L., A. Woodward, and K. C. Nage. 1986. Does the tail wag the dog in the social studies curriculum? *Momentum* 17(3): 46–49.

Farr, R., M. A. Tulley, and D. Powell. 1987. The evaluation and selection of basal readers. *Elementary School Journal* 87(3): 267–81.

Finn, C. E., and D. Ravitch. 1988. No trivial pursuit. *Phi Delta Kappan* 69(8): 559–64.

Harste, J. C., and K. G. Short. 1988. *Creating classrooms for authors.* Portsmouth, N.H.: Heinemann.

Holbrook, H. T. 1985. The quality of textbooks. *The Reading Teacher* 38(7): 680–83.

Huck, C. S. 1987. Literature as the content of reading. *Theory into Practice* 16(5): 363–71.

McMillan, M. M., and L. M. Gentile. 1988. Children's literature: Teaching critical thinking and ethics. *The Reading Teacher* 41(7): 876–78.

Ravitch, D. 1989. The revival of history: A response. *The Social Studies* 80(3): 89–91.

Sewall, G. T. 1988a. American History textbooks: Where do we go from here? *Phi Delta Kappan* 69(8): 553–58.

———. 1988b. American history textbooks: Their literary merit. *American Educator* 12:32–37.

Schuster, E. H. 1984. Students against the text. *C/C/T* 34:30–33.

Shumaker, M. P., and R. C. Shumaker. 1988. 3000 paper cranes: Children's literature for remedial readers. *The Reading Teacher* 41(5): 544–49.

Strickland, D. 1988. Literature: The key element in the language and reading program. In *Children's literature in the reading program,* edited by B. Cullinan. Newark, Del.: IRA.

Tyson, H., and A. Woodward. 1989. Why students aren't learning very much from textbooks. *Educational Leadership* 47(3): 14–17.

Van Middendorp, J. E. 1990. *An eighth-grade literature-based U.S. history classroom: Reactions, responses, attitudes, perceptions, and participation.* Unpublished doctoral dissertation, University of South Dakota, Vermillion.

Woodward, A. 1986. The treatment of recent U.S. history in elementary school social studies textbooks: A case study of the breadth and depth of content coverage. Paper presented at the annual meeting of the American Educational Research Association, San Francisco. (ERIC Document Reproduction Service, No. 273 541.)

From *The Social Studies,* May/June 1994, pages 117–120. © 1994 by Heldref Publications, 1319, Eighteenth St., NW, Washington, DC 20036-1802. Reprinted with permission of the Helen Dwight Reid Educational Foundation.

UNIT 6

Assessing Literacy and Content

Unit Selections

Key Points to Consider

- What is assessment?

- What is meant by alternative assessment?

- What is portfolio assessment?

- How can content area teachers assess literacy?

 **Links: www.dushkin.com/online/**
These sites are annotated in the World Wide Web pages.

The National Research Center on English Learning and Achievement
http://cela.albany.edu/
Strategic Literacy Initiative
http://www.wested.org/stratlit/
The Partnership for Reading
http://www.nifl.gov/partnershipforreading/adolescent/
Literacy Assessment
http://www.ncrel.org/sdrs/areas/issues/content/cntareas/reading/li7lk29.htm

Assessment is not a new concept. Teachers have always assessed their students in terms of content knowledge and ability to attain knowledge. Assessment has generally been more than simply grades and standardized tests. At the end of my first year in second-grade, my grades were sufficient for promotion; but after a parent-teacher conference the assessment of my parents and my teacher was that I should repeat second grade since my reading skills were low. When my daughter neared the end of fifth-grade, she declared that she was not going to middle school the next year. Her lowest report card grade was an 85 but she was the youngest and smallest student in her class. Her best friend, a fourth-grade student who had a September birthday, was not going to go to middle school for another year. My daughter and her best friend were less than 30-days difference in age. After careful consideration (assessment), the school counselor and principal agreed to let her repeat the fifth-grade since she had failed to pass the state reading test by one point.

We had failed to assess the negative atmosphere of the school due to standardized accountability testing. During my daughter's second year in fifth-grade, we began to think we had made a mistake in allowing her to repeat the grade. Where we thought she would enjoy a high level of success, she experienced the teacher and other children treating her like she was an academic failure. She was pressured to master the reading test. During two months preceding the state test, she was detained during P.E. to practice taking simulated state reading tests. The boundary between assessment of students' skills as a means for planning instruction and evaluation and drill were totally blurred. The test had become the literacy curriculum and reinforced failure to achieve levels of literacy necessary to pass the accountability test.

While educators agree with the importance of literacy in learning in K-16, assessing literacy skills in the secondary content areas has lagged behind elementary education, where literacy has been seen as central to all instruction. Content area teachers continue to debate whether literacy is part of their job as some claim that students should learn to read in elementary school as a prerequisite to reading to learn in middle and secondary schools. In this unit I begin with the presupposition that literacy instruction must continue in secondary grades and that assessment is essential to preparing instruction.

In this unit, I have included "Using Alternative Assessment to Provide Options for Student Success" (1997). Dorie Combs argues that the more teachers focus on the basics, the less children actually learn. This supported my daughter's experience with the heavy focus on drilling for the Texas Assessment of Academic Skills (TAAS) test. While Combs encourages teachers to give students options for demonstrating their knowledge and learning as an alternative to students failing within a standardized system, most teachers who work under state accountability systems continue to struggle with how to do this in practice. In "Giving Voice to Middle School Students Through Portfolio Assessment: A Journey to Mathematical Power" (1997), Karen M. Higgins and Mary Ann Heglie-King present portfolio assessment for the math classroom as a means for students to communicate their thinking, processes, and degree of understanding of concepts. In "Dismantling the Factory Model of Assessment" (2002), Frank W. Serafini presents a critical study of assessment and challenges teachers to consider replacing the Factory Model with "reflective inquiry" processes of assessment.

This unit presents several effective strategies for secondary literacy and content assessment. Secondly, several articles challenge teachers to engage in a critical examination of assessment as it is used within classroom settings and in the broader arena of standardized testing. Teachers must take up the role of literacy assessment in the secondary setting but must also take up the role of challenging standardized testing in terms of equity issues in public education. Preparing students as critical readers and critical citizens for a democratic society add to the complexity of literacy assessment. How do we assess literacy in terms of social justice issues?

Using Alternative Assessment to Provide Options for Student Success

Dorie Combs

Before heading out of the door to drive to school, I took one last look in the mirror to make sure my toga was properly wrapped. I left for school a little early that day, knowing there would be more to do than usual. When I entered the hallway I could see that already there were several students waiting at my door. One was balancing a scale model of the Acropolis, another held a shoe box containing a bright green model of Medusa, others stood around with carefully rolled posters of Plato, Archimedes, and Venus. The day of our Greek Alive festival had arrived. It was a day that made me proud to be a teacher.

The need for alternative forms of assessment has been well documented (e.g., Marzano, Pickering, & McTighe, 1993). However, methods for incorporating more authentic assessment into a middle school classroom tend to require wholesale reform, not only in the specific classrooms, but throughout the school building as well. Sometimes this systemic change, even though it might be needed, is slow to come about. Can one classroom teacher adopt new assessment strategies without revising the entire grading system?

My motivation to try something new came from frustration with too many student failures. I also felt that the standard paper and pencil tests were not getting to the heart of what I was trying to teach in my seventh grade language arts classes. The inspiration came from an inservice I attended prior to the opening of school. The presenter, Nell Westbrook, was giving ideas for working with students possessing at-risk factors. As a teacher, she had developed a system in which her students made choices about their own learning activities. A contractual point system was used to determine percentages and report card grades. Although I was not willing to be as democratic as Ms. Westbrook, I was ready to adapt her ideas to the needs of my own students. The result was a plan I called "Options."

With each theme-related unit, I prepared a menu of projects, papers, and reports. The students had to complete one of these for each grading period. Additional options could be completed for extra credit. In establishing each unit's menu, I was bound by a set of philosophical convictions: (a) the activities must be adaptable by students with a broad range of prior knowledge and achievement levels, including those with a variety of special needs; (b) the activities must allow for demonstration of understanding through a va-

riety of learning styles and modalities; and, (c) the activities must require students to demonstrate understanding of the theme, genre, culture, or historical period under study.

The term *alternative assessment* has no precise definition or standard and is often used interchangeably with *authentic assessment* and *performance assessment* (Marzano, Pickering & McTigue, 1993). Here, the purpose of alternative assessment is assumed to be to require students to use higher order thinking skills as means to demonstrate newly learned information and ideas, and apply these in new and unique ways. Specifically, in my seventh grade language arts classes, this form of alternative assessment had to serve several purposes.

What should be the purpose of Alternative Assessment in Language Arts?

Require students to use basic skills in meaningful ways

In language arts it is easy to get bogged down in the basics. Of course our students need to master basic skills, but it seems that the more we focus on the basics, the less our children actually learn. Most of us learn "the basics" as we need them. After years of moderate to poor success in math, I finally came to truly understand percentages when I became a teacher. Fractions are a snap when you are responsible for preparing most of the meals in your home. The reverse is also true. How many individuals are there who were once masters of diagramming sentences, but who cannot write a clear, concise paragraph?

The research on the teaching of grammar and mechanics is clear: these skills must be taught in the context of reading and writing (Rief, 1992). Research on human information processing indicates that we learn by integrating parts and wholes (Caine & Caine, 1991). Students have difficulty learning skills if these skills are taught in isolation. This is true of grammar and vocabulary as well as math facts, scientific principles, and important events in history. We need to be teaching both the parts as well as the whole.

> Of course our students need to master basic skills, but
> it seems that the more we focus on the basics, the less
> our children actually learn.

In order to help students grasp the importance of descriptive verbs as well as adjectives and adverbs, the class might read a novel together, stopping to analyze a particularly lyrical passage or chapter. Later, this novel can serve as a model for student writing. As a part of a unit on Families, students can write essays on a variety of timely and age appropriate topics, such as: How to be a Dependable Baby-sitter, Conflict Mediation Can Work at Home as Well as at School, It's Tough Being a Single Parent, and Divorce Can Be Difficult for Teens. Middle schoolers often enjoy writing children's picture books on topics such as *King Arthur & the Middle Ages* or *Ancient Greek Mythology*. When a real purpose and a real audience are identified, these young writers become more focused, and the spelling, grammar, and punctuation take on more importance.

Require students to use higher order thinking skills

Our middle schoolers must be required to use creative thinking to solve problems, to analyze, evaluate, and synthesize. The workplace requires these skills; many of our district and state goals require these skills; and national standards developed by various professional organizations require these skills (Marzano, Pickering, & McTighe, 1993; Carnegie Council on Adolescent Development, 1989). But more importantly, when instructional tasks are designed so that students have to think and manipulate information, our youngsters become more actively involved in their learning and, therefore, are more likely to assimilate the new information and remember it longer (Caine & Caine, 1991). I often ask both preservice and experienced teachers what they remember learning in middle school (or junior high). Unfortunately, their lists are rather short (regardless of age!). However, what they *do* remember usually involves a project, play, in-depth research paper, field trip, or other experience in which they became immersed in a topic or issue.

In a language arts class students can be asked to extend their understanding of the setting of a novel through the creation of detailed maps or travel guides. Themes can be developed into essays, letters to the school or local newspaper, or parent/teen communication guides. Allow students to express their interpretation of a major character through sculpture, painting, or collage. All of these activities require the use of analysis, evaluation, and synthesis, but each results in a unique product.

Provide alternative formats that will meet the educational needs of diverse learners in a heterogeneously grouped setting

The debate over "de-tracking" has, for most of us, moved from the question of "why?" to one of "how?" My seventh grade language arts classes included not only students gifted in language arts, but students with learning disabilities and be-

havior disorders as well. I needed a plan that provided alternatives for a variety of learning styles. How could I provide enrichment opportunities for language arts-gifted students while meeting the IEP's of students with special needs? The answer was in giving students a choice. With each new menu of options, each student could choose a medium to explore. These choices could include everything from book reports to art work, videos to models. For example, for the Mystery unit, students might choose to write a report on an author of mystery stories, write an original mystery, make a children's mystery book, or conduct an interview with an archeologist, research scientist, or private investigator. Each of these options comes with a detailed set of instructions and a scoring guide for quality control (see figure 1). However, I am careful not to establish a ceiling, but to encourage all individuals to reach their personal best.

Each of us has certain things that we do well, and other things we do poorly. While it is our job to guide children to develop areas of weakness, we should also encourage and allow our youngsters to express themselves through their preferred modalities. When working with students who have identified learning disabilities, this is critical. These children may be able to demonstrate reading comprehension orally but have great difficulty writing a complete sentence. Others may have amazing auditory memory skills but poor reading comprehension. I have known several youngsters who found handwriting to be laborious and difficult but who had a real knack for word processing. If we are too rigid in our requirements, we doom such children to failure and poor self-esteem, when, in fact, they have much to offer our world. Some students might find reading a collection of short stories to be more manageable than tackling an entire novel. Book reports presented in the form of comic strips, shadow boxes, or posters may be less tedious than a written report. I suspect there are several future comedians and actresses who got their first stand-up experience in our team "comedy club"—students with a special talent that would never be nurtured in traditional classroom dramas.

Integrate language arts processes with the content of other subjects

Schema theory tells us why it is important to integrate our teaching across content areas (Rumelhart, 1980). It is much easier to learn information about which you have prior knowledge or experience. By linking subjects together through interdisciplinary units, teachers get "more bang for their bucks." Why teach the scientific method in science during September, in social studies during October, and math problem solving in May? Teach it to everyone at the same time in September. Meanwhile, the language arts teacher can study mysteries. It is much easier to talk about inductive and deductive reasoning in relation to Sherlock Holmes if these same terms were introduced in the science class the week before. Tie in literature related to the environment and nature while the science class is studying ecology. Read historical novels that parallel the social studies curriculum. The history provides the background knowledge for the novel, while the novel gives a deeper understanding of the effects of historical events upon individuals and families.

Figure 1

Directions and Scoring Guides for Examples of Alternative Assessment

Middle Ages Option Model

Directions:

Make a model of a creature or character from the middle ages. Write a one-half to one page description of your character (tell who or what it is and its importance in the middle ages). Your model must portray the creature or character through the use of appropriate costume, props, or other attributes.

Scoring Guide

<u>25</u>	Model Portrays the character or creature and time period through the use of attire, props, and other attributes
<u>10</u>	Artistic quality
<u>15</u>	The model shows evidence of effort
<u>50</u>	A ½ to 1 page written description of the character is included

Family Unit Option
Family Tree Poster

Directions:

Make a poster of your family tree, you must go back at least 3 generations. Provide as much information about family member as possible, including but not limited to birthdate, death date (if not living), occupation, place of birth, accomplishments, etc. In addition, provide at least two anecdotes about your family's history (how they came to live in our town, special notoriety, honors, awards, medals, etc.). You must *write out* your family tree! (You may not make a copy of a commercially prepared family tree and paste it on the poster.) Make your poster attractive and neat!

Scoring Guide

<u>25</u>	Family tree includes at least three generations prior to you
<u>25</u>	In addition to names, most entries include information such as birth, death, and place of birth
<u>25</u>	Poster includes at least two anecdotes about interesting or well-known family members
<u>15</u>	Poster is neatly and attractively typed or written *by you*
<u>10</u>	Mechanics, spelling, usage

Even in the best situations, we cannot, and do not always want to, integrate *all* of our content areas. The coordination can be too time consuming, and the topics do not always mesh. The language arts teacher is blessed, however, with the opportunity to integrate with any topic. Language arts is a process class. By being aware of what your colleagues are doing in their classrooms, you can easily provide "options" that relate to their content. For example, as a part of a unit on Families students can prepare "I-Search" style reports (Zorfass & Copel, 1995) on animal families, tying in to work in science. Another assignment might require students to conduct a survey on family traditions and present the results, using percentages, in a graph. These sorts of tie-ins can become contagious, and before you know it, your students will be doing art or music that relates to your content, or the home economics teacher may spend a day or two teaching students about Appalachian culture and crafts to relate to your unit on *Where the Lilies Bloom* (Cleaver, 1970), a lovely novel that is set in the Great Smoky Mountains.

Encourage students to experiment with various media and technologies

As much as we would like to, most of us do not have access to the equipment necessary to teach all of our students how to use the same medium at the same time. Schools may have one video camera, which must be shared by a student population of 500 to 1,000 students. How then, can you possibly encourage experience with these media? By including video production as one of the options for each unit, small groups of students can work together to plan and produce a short video. Some students may have their own video equipment and can work at home (parents are often commandeered into serving as videographer on these projects), while others utilize equipment available in the media center. Individuals who otherwise might never have the opportunity or desire to attempt such a venture, may take the risk, knowing their work is not being compared to similar projects by everyone else in the class.

Such exploration and experimentation are the nature of adolescence and can plant the seeds for future proficiency.

Provide an alternative to failure

Options make up only 20% of my class grade. Being a middle school teacher, I base a great deal of the student's grade on daily participation and activities completed at home. I even use traditional paper and pencil tests and quizzes. But I was stymied by the number of children who simply seem to choose to fail. Student failure is a vicious cycle. Failure results in more failure. Yet, by the time they reach middle school, it seems that some of these youngsters have their minds made up, and they quickly get stuck in a hopeless quagmire of zeroes and low percentages.

I needed to give these students a way out—a path that might lead to success. The path was extra credit. By allowing students to complete additional options for extra credit, students who had fallen behind could get a second chance. I love to see the spark in their eyes when they ask, "How many options can I do?" and I respond, "as many as you want to do." My only requirement was that the students complete activities from a variety of categories. For example, a student could do two book reports, but only one model or poster per unit. This would ensure the student was demonstrating the use of a variety of language arts skills (research, creative writing, information writing, speaking, etc.).

The extra credit plan has had an unexpected effect. Over several years I have found that most of the students who complete extra options are, in fact, gifted in language arts or above average students. In fact, these students seem to enjoy the concept of having overall averages of more than 100%. (The fact that I cannot record more than 100% on their report card does not seem to matter.) These individuals also carefully selected a variety of options, becoming quite strategic in the gathering of educational experiences.

I have had several students become aware of the potential for failure (some students simply do not seem to grasp the concept that they are going to spend another year in the same grade, no matter how many times this is explained to them) and sincerely want to do something about it. If we were to rely solely on their obtained averages, there would be no hope; but with the extra credit and a great deal of work, some have been able to turn a failing grade around. By carefully planning the options students are allowed to do, the teacher can ensure that the individual has mastered the content and is ready to move up. There is a fine line that middle school teachers must walk. We must do all that we can to avoid failure while maintaining a certain level of academic rigor. Middle schoolers need second chances. We must provide them with multiple opportunities to succeed.

Alternative Assessment Can Help You Meet Portfolio Requirements

In Kentucky, as in several other states, students are required to complete writing and math portfolios at certain grades. These accumulations of a student's best work are compiled and re-

vised over several years. Initially, teachers taught the portfolio in isolation from the curriculum. Everything stopped while the class wrote a "portfolio piece." These contrived works tended to lack voice and purpose, therefore, receiving lower scores. Now we are learning that the best student writing (and math, for that matter) is produced when it is a natural extension of the curriculum: when the purpose is real, the audience genuine, and the voice is truly that of the writer. By adding carefully chosen writing prompts to the options list, students were able to demonstrate understanding of a theme, concept, or issue in a format which, coincidentally, met a portfolio requirement. For example, in the Kentucky Writing Portfolio, seventh graders must include one or more pieces which are written for a specific purpose, such as to explain a process or defend a position. One option which followed our reading of *Where the Lilies Bloom* was to make an Appalachian craft (e.g., a corn husk doll, soap, a wood carving) and then explain, in writing, how it was made. Another unit on famous people allowed students to write letters (using business letter style) to famous people. Many students enjoyed this activity and some even received replies. The letters were carefully written and edited. They had real purpose, a clear audience, and wonderful voice! The students had fun, without realizing they had ticked off another portfolio requirement.

I suspect there are several future comedians and actresses who got their first standup experience in our team "comedy club"— students with a special talent that would never be nurtured in traditional classroom dramas.

Alternative Assessments Are More Interesting to Share and Grade

Language arts teachers are "born to grade," but we are not born to be bored. If all 125 students write on the same topic, the students and the teacher are going to be bored. Alternative assessment strategies can provide the flexibility that students need to be motivated and enjoy their work. The result will be products that are more interesting to the teacher as well as fellow students and parents. Instead of posting row after row of copycat papers, you will have a room or display case full of all sorts of creative works.

What Suggestions Are There for Teachers Wanting to Implement Alternative Assessment Measures?

The idea of alternative assessment has been around long enough for there to be a plethora of books as well as articles on the subject. The *Dimensions of Learning* (Marzano, 1992) model, developed by the McREL Institute and published by the Association for Supervision and Curriculum Development (ASCD) provides clear, easy to follow guidelines for the development of performance based assessment, including examples of scoring rubrics. The Kentucky Department of Education has developed an extensive document *Transformations: Kentucky's Curriculum Frameworks* Volumes I & II, which gives suggestions and examples for performance assessment activities across the state's identified Learning Goals and Achievement Outcomes. Before embarking on a comprehensive alternative assessment strategy, a teacher should develop a plan that includes:

1. Rubrics or scoring guides for each assessment activity.
2. Clear, thorough directions and standards for quality.
3. Reasonable time lines for students to complete the task.
4. Reference or research materials that may be needed.
5. Hidden costs for materials and how disadvantaged students can obtain the supplies they need.
6. Forms and organizational tools for tracking student progress.
7. Logistics for evaluation of student products.
8. Storage and display of completed products.

What Do Students Think About Alternative Assessment?

Student comments about "options" ranged from, "They're fun," to, "I personally think they are kind of hard." Though many of the students complained vigorously, as middle schoolers tend to do, it was apparent that most seemed to become immersed in their work, had fun, and learned something in the process. From time to time some would even admit to being just a little excited about their project. The ultimate evaluation came when the due date arrived. The pride in their accomplishments was obvious when the completed product was brought to school. Middle schoolers want and need to have some control in their lives, particularly regarding their learning. I have discovered that these middle schoolers are full of surprises, and will often create amazing works when we give them opportunity and then get out of their way.

References

Caine, R.N., & Caine, G. (1991). *Making connections: Teaching and the human brain.* Alexandria, VA: Association for Supervision & Curriculum Development.

Carnegie Council on Adolescent Development. (1989). *Turning points: Preparing American youth for the 21st century.* New York: Carnegie Corporation.

Cleaver, V. (1970). *Where the lilies bloom.* Philadelphia: J.B. Lippincott.

Marzano, R.J. (1992). *A different kind of classroom. Teaching with dimensions of learning.* Alexandria, VA: Association for Supervision & Curriculum Development.

Marzano, R.J., Pickering, D., & McTighe, J. (1993). *Assessing Student Outcomes: Performance assessment using the dimensions of learning model.* Alexandria, VA: Association for Supervision & Curriculum Development.

Rief, L. (1992). *Seeking diversity.* Portsmouth, NJ: Heinemann Educational Books.

Rumelhart, D. (1980). Schemata: The building blocks of cognition. In R.J. Spiro, B.C. Bruce, & W.F. Brewer (Eds.), *Theoretical Issues in Reading Comprehension* (pp. 33–58). Hillsdale, NJ: Lawrence Erlbaum & Associates, Inc.

Transformations: Kentucky's Curriculum frameworks. Volumes I & II. Kentucky Department of Education, Capital Plaza Tower, 500 Mero Street, Frankfort, KY.

Zorfass, J., & Copel, H. (1995). The I-Search: Guiding students toward relevant research. *Educational Research, 27*(l), 48–51.

From *Middle School Journal* Vol. 29, No. 1, September 1997, pages 3–8. Copyright © 1997 by National Middle School Association. Reprinted with permission from National Middle School Association.

Giving Voice to Middle School Students Through Portfolio Assessment

A Journey to Mathematical Power

Karen M. Higgins & Mary Ann Heglie-King

Mary Ann, a middle school mathematics teacher, became increasingly frustrated with her students' apathy and resentment towards their learning of mathematics. This attitude is exemplified through the following journal entries from her eighth grade middle school students:

- *Mathematics, as I see it, means: algebra, hard, boring, a way to figure out a number by using other numbers, and to find the answer when someone already has the answer in their book! I don't understand it. If someone has the answer, why are you suppose to figure it out? The mysteries of school.*
- *Mathematics is a subject in school that everybody has to put up with to get a good grade. Most of them hate it and think they will never use it in later life.*
- *Mathematics is sometimes really annoying to me because I don't know why we need to know a lot of the stuff we are taught. As I see it, when are we going to use the square root of Y x 2 in a grocery store…! I don't want to do it when I don't see how I benefit in the long run.*

Knowing how prevalent this attitude was, she chose to confront her students at the beginning of the school year about their attitudes in an attempt to understand "why." They claimed there were many obstacles preventing them from succeeding in mathematics. Students complained they were afraid to open up in class and ask questions because they felt they were the only ones who did not understand what was happening. Another obstacle expressed by a majority of students was that their teachers in the past did not really explain the purpose of what they were doing in mathematics. They were learning a step-by-step approach to solving problems, but this knowledge was not perceived as having deeper meaning or purpose. As Catherine stated, "Math was just put in the curriculum to fill up space and to torture us kids."

The students also made it clear to Mary Ann that the way they were assessed and on what they were assessed played a large role in their lack of success in mathematics. Most students felt what they did from day to day in the math class was drastically different from what was on the test, even down to the at-mosphere of the room during testing time. They felt that since a large part of their grade was invested in tests, they must perform well on them. That pressure turned out to be too much for many students—they just gave up.

Mary Ann desperately wanted to change her students' attitudes and empower them to believe they could be successful in mathematics—even enjoy it! She realized she needed to do more than alter her teaching. She also needed to make some major changes in her assessment practices. The National Council of Teachers of Mathematics (1995) asserted there should be opportunities for students to enhance their learning throughout the assessment process as it is embedded in instruction. The Council encourages artifacts of mathematics learning that are routinely produced in the classroom to be an integral part of the student's assessment. They claim that the continuous assessment such artifacts provide not only facilitates the learning of mathematics, but also enhances students' self-confidence in their development of mathematical power and in their ability to communicate their mathematical understanding.

It occurred to Mary Ann that one way she could facilitate her students' development of mathematical power was by integrating portfolios into her classroom assessment system. She would give her students voice in the contents of the portfolio as well as their grades. Through this, she hoped to alter her students' attitudes and remove many of the obstacles that were preventing them from being successful.

She wondered how her students would react to becoming such active participants in their own assessment. Could the portfolios really make a difference? How would the students view the portfolios and react to the control she would give them over their grades? To answer these questions, she chose to engage in teacher research and investigate the effects of portfolio assessment on her middle school students' dispositions towards mathematics and their self-perceptions. She believed their experiences would shed a great deal of light on students' reactions to increased power in relation to the progress of assessment reform in the classroom. This study took place over the course of two trimesters. Aspects of the research were done in collaboration with a university professor who worked part-time at the school.

Portfolios and Their Impact

According to Perrone (1991), performance-based assessment or exhibits of learning were common in many nineteenth century and early progressive schools, but became less important with the rise of standardized testing (Viechnicki, Barbour, Shaklee, Rohrer, & Ambrose, 1993). According to Chittenden (1991), a recent move toward a return to more authentic forms of assessing student work are occurring because authentic assessment (a) capitalizes on the actual work of the classroom (b) enhances teacher and student involvement in evaluation, and (c) meets some of the accountability concerns of the district. Furthermore, authentic assessment, and portfolios specifically, reveals not only what students know and understand, but also how those new understandings metamorphosed.

Arter & Spandel (1992) define a portfolio as a purposeful collection of student work that tells the story of the students' efforts, progress, or achievement in given areas. This collection must include student participation in selection of portfolio content, the guidelines for selection, the criteria for judging merit, and evidence of student self-reflection. This definition supports the notion that assessment should be ongoing, capture a wide variety of what students know and can do, contain realistic contexts, communicate to students and others what is valued, show the process by which work is accomplished, and be integrated with instruction.

Paulson, Paulson, & Meyers (1991) have found that portfolios allow students to take ownership in their own assessment and offer students the opportunity to learn about learning through self-reflection. They also argue that portfolio assessment is assessment done by the student rather than to the student. Through portfolios, students are able to learn to value their own work and themselves as learners. According to Wolf (1989), portfolios also allow students to demonstrate how demanding and thoughtful they can be about shaping something about which they care.

Rogers & Stevenson (1988) claim that the guiding idea of portfolio assessment is that they can provide an opportunity for richer, more authentic, and more valid assessment of student achievement: Through portfolio assessment, educators learn what students can do when given adequate time and resources. Calfee & Perfumo (1993) found that students begin to take ownership of their portfolios very quickly, and strive to perform and do their best. They also found that the portfolio process fosters positive feelings. According to Paulson, Paulson, & Meyers (1991), everything in the portfolio does not have to be perfect the first time. Ideas come first and are valued more with portfolio assessment.

Wolf (1989) claims that portfolios reverse the message that students receive from traditional assessment approaches—such as standardized tests—that assessment comes from without and is not a personal responsibility, that what matters is not the full range of your intuitions and knowledge but your performance on the slice of skills that appear on the test, that first-draft work is good enough, and that achievement matters to the exclusion of development.

> The teacher chose to increase students' ownership in their learning and assessment in three ways: by letting them choose the contents, by having them develop the assessment criteria, and by allowing them to assess their own and each others' portfolios.

This study investigates the effect of mathematics portfolios on middle school students to see if some of these assertions hold true. It is an attempt to understand how portfolios can be used as a vehicle for increasing students' feelings of adequacy in mathematics, empowerment and ownership in their learning and assessment, and growth in self-reflection.

Overview of the Project

This study took place in a Chapter 1 middle school of approximately 560 students located in a lower to middle-class suburb of a city in Oregon with a population of about 120,000. The 40 students involved in this study came from two eighth grade block classes, a total of 21 girls and 19 boys. Each block class, approximately 120 minutes in length, was given consistent instruction in mathematics and portfolio use.

Using a stratified sampling technique so there would be an equal number of males and females, six students from each block class were randomly chosen for in-depth interviews regarding their beliefs and attitudes towards issues related to the portfolios. These interviews were conducted by the university professor with who the teacher was collaborating on this project.

To investigate the research question, the teacher instigated a series of activities in her teaching and assessment practices. The following is a brief chronology of those activities organized under the trimesters in which they occurred. More detailed explanations of the activities are provided where appropriate.

First trimester

- Students engaged in class discussions regarding what obstacles they felt were preventing them from succeeding in mathematics.
- "Working portfolios" were introduced to the students. These portfolios involved the idea of collecting math work over the course of a trimester to be retained in the room after evaluation by the teacher so that revisions could be made by the students as their understanding of the concepts occurred.

- The teacher held a class discussion around the idea of an "assessment portfolio." Students were given a list of items that they would keep to be assessed at the end of the first trimester.
- The teacher informed the class that students would have more influence over their final trimester grade by giving the portfolio a value of 25%.
- At the end of the trimester, students selected portfolio items and attached reflection sheets that stated both the requirement the piece fulfilled and why they selected it.
- Students turned in their portfolios, which were graded by the teacher.

Second trimester

- Students were informed that 50% of their final grade would be based on their portfolios.
- Students generated a list of eight items to be included in their assessment portfolio.
- Students developed the scoring guide which would be used to score their portfolios.
- Students were assisted in keeping their working and assessment portfolios. Students had been introduced to and had used a 6-point scoring guide for scoring open-ended mathematics problems throughout the year and so were familiar with scoring guides and their use in evaluating mathematics work. In small groups, students were asked to develop a 6-point scoring guide for their final assessment portfolio. The teacher compiled all of the small group ideas and returned them to the students for final revisions. Using these ideas, the class created a final scoring guide to be used by the students to assess their final portfolio at the end of the trimester. The contents of the final portfolio and the scoring guide were posted in the room next to the students' working portfolios.
- Two items for the assessment portfolio were collected at mid-trimester. Students again attached reflection sheets to the items as discussed first trimester.
- Students received more detailed instruction from the teacher on writing the reflection sheets. After the teacher received the reflection sheets she realized the students did not really have an understanding of how to capture their self-assessments in writing. She decided to make suggestions on the reflections as to how students could state more thoughtfully why they chose a particular piece. These pieces were then returned to the students for revision. After revisions were made, the piece was put into the final assessment portfolio. Two weeks later, two more pieces were turned in with reflection sheets to make sure that students had internalized the purpose of the reflection sheet.
- Portfolios were assessed by the teacher, the students, and two peers using the class generated scoring guide. The week before the final portfolio was due, students were asked to name three people in the classroom, other than the teacher, they respected or trusted enough to evaluate their portfolio. These names were collected by the teacher and two of the three names were written on a card and stapled to the student's portfolio. The portfolios were evaluated by the teacher, the student, and two other students in the classroom using the class scoring guide. Each evaluator would not know how the

other evaluators had scored the portfolio. After all four evaluations were done, the student and the other three evaluators sat down and compared scores. Every score had to be backed up with an explanation. During this discussion, a final score was given and agreed upon by all four evaluators.

- Six students from each block class were interviewed by the university professor with whom the teacher was collaborating on this project.
- Students were asked to write a short essay on the question, "What is mathematics?"

Collecting data for analysis

The teacher kept a journal during the course of the year where she recorded her questions and assessment events, reflected on her teaching, and made observation and class discussion notes. On a regular basis, she discussed her research with the teacher research support group at the school and the university professor with whom she was collaborating on this project.

Based on individual criterion statements from the student interviews, criteria categories were determined using a comparative technique. This task involved comparing one individual criterion statement with the next, then forming new categories if the information in the criterion statement did not "fit" with those that had been previously determined. This process was continued until all criterion statements were categorized into discrete sets.

The Journey to Mathematical Power

During the interviews, students talked about how the portfolios represented them mathematically, how they felt about increased ownership in their grades, and how they had grown in their abilities to be self-reflective. As they embarked upon their complex journeys to mathematical power, their eyes were opened to a different world—an assessment system that enabled them to show their mathematical understandings in new ways.

How did the students consider the portfolios a reflection of themselves and their mathematical abilities?

It appeared as if the students did believe that the portfolios reflected who they were as students of mathematics. Eight of the 12 students said that the portfolios would tell they were good mathematics students and discussed characteristics to back their claims. The three students who claimed that the portfolio showed they were not good mathematics students based their perception on lack of understanding rather than effort. There was one student who stated the portfolio showed what they had learned from their teacher. It was interesting that when the students talked about the portfolio contents with the university professor, they discussed traits about themselves which were not physically evident within the portfolio—such as effort, listening, and the absence or lack of understanding of a mathematical concept.

When students were asked to identify the most important piece in their portfolio and state why it was important, six of the students chose a particular piece because it exemplified their abilities in mathematics. One student said, "My algebraic expressions because I believe that it shows I can do higher math and I will need it in high school." Four students chose pieces that illustrated improvement in their math abilities. As one student said, "A book assignment. I look at it and the first time I got a really bad grade and I didn't understand hardly any of it. Then, after I learned better, I figured out what I didn't understand and then I could redo it and it made more sense." Three of the 12 students chose their most important piece because they liked the work involved. One of these students said, "I put in my problem solving piece because I like problem solving and brain busters the most." Two other students chose their most important piece to reflect the type of math they will be using in their careers as adults. Only one of the 12 students based her reasoning on the fact that the piece had a good grade on it.

What were students' reactions to their active involvement in their own assessment through increased ownership in the contents and assessments of their portfolios?

The teacher chose to increase students' ownership in their learning and assessment in three ways: (a) by letting them choose the contents of the portfolio second trimester, (b) by having them develop the assessment criteria for the portfolios, and (c) by allowing them to assess their own and each other's portfolios, knowing that the portfolios would be 50% of their second trimester's grade.

Students' second trimester choices for their portfolios indicated that they were beginning to broaden their perspectives of the discipline of mathematics and to view the presence of mathematics in other subject areas and in potential career choices. (See Figure 1 for a listing of first and second trimesters' portfolio contents.) They also chose to include a piece that showed improvement, which could indicate some control over and knowledge of their own abilities in mathematics.

The students developed the scoring guide for their portfolio assessment second trimester (see Figure 2). These scoring guides tended to focus on the presence of the required portfolio pieces, the overall organization of the portfolio, and the quality of the reflection sheets. In no way did the guidelines reflect a student's ability in mathematics.

Although students seemed a bit insecure about grading their portfolios, they all believed it was not only a good idea, but a "fair" assessment. There seemed to be some security in having their peers also grade the portfolios in case they made a mistake in their self-assessments. The teacher's score, students' self-assessments, and peer assessments were all within one point of each other.

When the students were asked if it was fair that 50% of the trimester grade was based on their portfolio, half of the students claimed it was because it gave them an opportunity to have more voice in their grades. The students who did not think it was fair stated reasons based on the novelty of the situation or lack of time to finish the portfolio due to other projects. On the other hand, when students were asked how they felt about having 50% control over their grade, all but two said they liked it. Some students also viewed the portfolios as a way to balance the various skill levels within the classroom, thus giving all students a stronger chance of getting a good grade. The two students who claimed it was too much control were concerned about students' abusing this power.

Figure 1

Portfolio Contents, First and Second Trimesters

First trimester's portfolio contents chosen by teacher:
- Math in another subject area
- Individual student math journals
- One best piece
- One piece from the beginning, one from the middle, and one from the end of the trimester
- Biography of a famous mathematician
- Math autobiography

Second trimester's portfolio contents chosen by students:
- Problem solving ability
- Use of mathematics in another subject area
- Improvement in mathematics during the trimester
- Use of mathematics in a career chosen by the student
- Understanding mathematics content areas covered during the trimester (solving algebra equations, functions, number theory
- Use of writing to express understanding of mathematics problems and procedures
- One most valuable piece

Figure 2

Portfolio Scoring Guide

6
Extra time and effort put into portfolio
Extra pieces included to demonstrate abilities in mathematics
Turned in on time
All requirements for a 5 present

5
All required pieces are in portfolio
Every piece has a well-thought-out reflection sheet
Contents well organized
Turned in on time

4
One reflection sheet not as well thought out or detailed
One reflection sheet may be missing
One piece may not reflect what it is intended to reflect
Turned in on time

3
Reflection sheets lack thoughtfulness as a whole
Reflection sheets missing from two or more pieces
Pieces are not solid reflections of desired outcomes or may be missing more than two pieces
Portfolio not well organized
Turned in one day late

2
Three or more pieces missing
Pieces do not reflect desired outcomes as a whole
Reflection sheets missing from more than half of pieces
Not organized at all
Student obviously did not spend much time on portfolio
Two or more days late

1
Portfolio contents do not reflect any thought or prepartion
Pieces do not demonstrate any of desired outcomes but instead appear to have been just thrown into folder
No reflection sheets on papers
More than two days late

All students gave themselves passing grades for the second trimester, basing grades on their efforts rather than skill level. The chance to redo work in the portfolio seemed to have a profound affect on the students overall perception of their grades since they were allowed an opportunity to demonstrate increased understanding of concepts and skills—and replace poor grades with better ones.

Was there evidence of growth in self-assessment through the reflection sheets and students' self-perception of their abilities to reflect on their work?

There was a great deal of evidence of growth, as demonstrated through the artifacts of their reflection sheets and their perceptions of skill improvement when asked during the interviews. An example of this improvement can be seen in Roger's first and second trimester's reflection sheets (see Figure 3). But, this improvement may have been the result of the teacher's coaching and teaching. It seems that this skill does not come naturally for students in the initial stages of their growth as self-assessors. The emphasis placed on the reflection sheets in the portfolio scoring guide may have also forced some of this improvement.

Reflections on Using Portfolios in Mathematics Classes

It is evident by this study that students were empowered to take control over their learning and assessment through portfolios in mathematics. They did this through revisiting the items in their working portfolios, taking ownership in the portfolios' contents, reflecting on their portfolio pieces, and assessing their own and each other's portfolios. The majority of the students claimed that this control over 50% of their grade was fair, and they knew that their efforts were directly tied to their grades. Stiggins (1994) claims that student achievement and academic self-concept are determined mainly on the basis of students' perceptions of their own success in the classroom and that students rely almost completely on the assessments conducted by their teachers to judge their current success. Although students count on their teachers to know what they are doing, harm can come to students through teachers' mismeasurement—in both academic achievement and self-concept. The "fairness" that students talked about in terms of ownership in grades made sense in that students' assessments of themselves are often different from and more "true" than what might arise from the teacher's attempt to gauge the qualities in question (Rowntree, 1987).

"If students are to function as independent learners, they must reflect on their progress, understand what they know and can do, be confident in their learning, and ascertain what they have yet to learn" (NCTM, 1995, p. 14). The portfolios seemed to provide an opportunity and forum in which students could do all of these things. But the contents of the portfolios alone did not tell the whole story. What was interesting was that when students were asked what the portfolio said about them, their assessments included traits that were both visible and invisible in the portfolio. In many cases, it was the actual reflection sheets

Figure 3

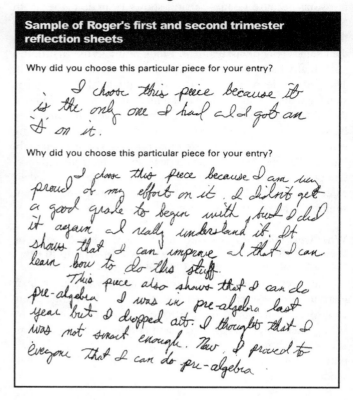

Sample of Roger's first and second trimester reflection sheets

attached to the portfolio pieces that gave students an opportunity to address some of these important elements—elements which defined their "sense" of their own mathematical power. With the inclusion of the reflection sheets, the portfolio included artifacts of learning which could not be captured in any other way. This has important implications for the use of portfolios as a form of self-assessment. As teachers guide students in their growth of self-critical skills, they need to encourage students to talk about some of these more implicit characteristics.

The teacher expected students to choose almost the same portfolio contents second trimester that she had chosen first trimester. This did not occur. It seemed important to students to include pieces that indicated skills in the content they had covered—they wanted to be able to "prove" that they could do these things. The students seemed proud of demonstrating their learning in mathematics. Another indication of this pride was through the inclusion of pieces that showed improvement in mathematics. Many of the students considered their most valuable piece to be a test that they were able to redo based on their acquired understandings. This had a profound effect on many of the students. In fact, Roger started taking so much pride in his work that he now considers himself good at mathematics. Stiggins (1994) claims that through portfolios students develop feelings of pride in their work that are just not possible with more traditional forms of assessment.

The working portfolios gave students an opportunity to revisit their work and not view their assessment as a one-time event—a concern expressed by many students early in the school year. It seemed a powerful factor for students to be able to see their own improvement in mathematics. Some students also saw the portfolios as a way of creating equity in a heterogeneous classroom since students could redo work and demonstrate increased understanding in mathematics. The students who claimed this to be unfair tended to be the high-ability students who viewed this as equating grades to effort rather than ability. But, the majority of the students seemed quite tolerant of students' differences and sympathetic to students who needed to redo things.

NCTM (1995) claims that students become mathematically powerful independent learners when they critique the work of their peers and productively use the critiques of others. For the majority of the students, the peer-review process with their portfolios was viewed as being quite valuable, especially since they were able to choose peers that they trusted. This seemed to offer a balance to their individual assessments of their portfolios and give the teacher another perspective in case she "missed" something. Students said they worked harder knowing that peers would also look at their portfolios. They were bothered when their friends did not take the time with the portfolios that individuals believed was warranted and viewed their work as "trivialized" by their peers. Students found out that their closest friends did not always give the portfolios the consideration they deserved.

Many of the students viewed the initiation of portfolios in the classroom as a way of demonstrating the fact that the teacher cared for her students. She was both touched and surprised by this revelation. This reinforces how teachers usually do assessment "to" rather than "with" their students. The teacher found that, by giving students opportunities to write about their learning—especially through their journals—a whole new world opened up to her about them. They talked about many things besides school work—she assumed this is why they did not want to include journals in their second trimester's portfolios. She respected that decision, even though she knew the journals gave her great insights into how her students constructed their knowledge of mathematics.

So, were the portfolios instrumental in removing many of the obstacles her students claimed were preventing them from being successful in mathematics? This was the first time the teacher had not given an "F" as a trimester grade. But, success needs to be defined as much more than the grade they received. Students' self-efficacy improved as evidenced by revisiting the mathematics in their portfolios, caring about their understanding in mathematics, believing they had control over their

grades, seeing mathematics in the world around them, and smiling a lot more in mathematics class.

Did their attitudes towards the value and importance of mathematics change? Perhaps the answer to this question can be best exemplified in Jenny's last journal entry:

> Mathematics is the most important class in school because it is in every job there is, even if it is selling drugs on a street corner, you still have to know a lot of math. I feel that right now is the most important time to learn different types of mathematics because next year we will need to be figuring out our future careers and the mathematics we need to know for it. I feel that a few years ago I would have laughed at what I just wrote and say like always, "I hate math."

Karen M. Higgins teaches in the College of Home Economics and Education at Oregon State University, Corvallis. Mary Ann Heglie-King teaches mathematics at Shasta Middle School, Eugene, Oregon.

References

Arter, J., & Spandel, V. (1992). Using portfolios of student work in instruction and assessment. *Educational measurement: Issues and practices*. Portland, OR: Northwest Evaluation Association.

Calfee, R., & Perfumo, P. (1993). Student portfolios: Opportunities for a revolution in assessment. *Journal of Reading, 36*(3), 532–537.

Chittenden, E. (1991). Authentic assessment, evaluation, and documentation of student performance. In V. Perrone (Ed.). *Expanding student assessment* (pp. 21–33). Alexandria, VA: Association for Supervision and Curriculum Development.

National Council of Teachers of Mathematics. (1995). *Assessment standards for school mathematics*. Reston, VA: Author.

Paulson, L., Paulson, P., & Meyers, C. (1991). What makes a portfolio a portfolio? *Educational Leadership, 48*(5), 60–63.

Perrone, V. (Ed.). (1991). *Expanding student assessment*. Alexandria, VA: Association for Supervision and Curriculum Development.

Rogers, V., & Stevenson, C. (1988). How do we know what kids are learning in school? *Educational Leadership, 45*(5), 68–75.

Rowntree, D. (1987). Assessing students: How shall we know them? New York: Nichols.

Stiggins, R. (1994). *Student-centered classroom assessment*. New York: Merrill.

Viechnicki, K., Barbour, N., Shaklee, B., Rohrer, J., & Ambrose, R. (1993). The impact of portfolio assessment on teacher, classroom activities. *Journal of Teacher Education. 44*(5), 371–377.

Wolf, D. (1989). Portfolio assessment: Sampling student work. *Educational Leadership, 46*(7), 35–39.

From *Middle School Journal* Vol. 29, No. 1, September 1997, pages 22–29. Copyright © 1997 by National Middle School Association. Reprinted with permission from National Middle School Association.

DISMANTLING THE FACTORY MODEL OF ASSESSMENT

Frank W. Serafini
University of Nevada–Las Vegas, NV, USA

The Factory Models of the 1900's had a significant and lasting impact on the educational curriculum and testing frameworks developed in America's public schools. The child was viewed as a product, the school was designed as an educational factory, and standardized testing became the quality control mechanism for measuring educational progress. The effects of these structures can still be seen in today's public school organizations. Breaking free of the limiting effects of standardized testing requires changes in teacher education, school organization, curriculum frameworks, and especially, the methods of assessment currently used in public schools. Viewing assessment as 'reflective inquiry' rather than the measurement of accumulated facts, requires time, a new perspective, and dialogue among educators.

"School cannot be a place of pleasure, with all the freedom that would imply. School is a factory, and we need to know which workers are up to snuff....The teachers in charge are the floor bosses, so don't expect them to praise the virtues of free intellectual development when everything, absolutely everything in the school setting—the classes, grades, exams, scales, levels, orientations, streams—enforces the competitive nature of the institution, itself a model of the workaday world." (Pennac, 1994, p. 92)

Standardized testing and the "Factory Model of Education" have had an enormous impact on educational structures and practices since the early 1900s (Callahan, 1962). As referred to in the above quotation by Daniel Pennac, school has been traditionally designed as a factory, with the child seen as a product and all of the other educational components supporting that premise.

It is no coincidence that large-scale efforts to develop standardized tests began at approximately the same time as these "Factory Models" were being introduced into education. Both the Factory Model of Education and the Standardized Testing Programs of the early 1900s were intended to bring "hard science" into their respective endeavors to reduce uncertainty, standardize products, and create more efficient schools (Bracey, 1995).

These educational developments, the factory model of education and standardized testing, are aligned with modernist, philosophical assumptions that are based on "the point of view that all nature (including human nature) is governed by invariable laws and that these laws can be discovered and unerringly applied by means of science" (Hanson, 1993, p. 13). In this sense, assessment, namely standardized testing, is a form of measurement based on modernist philosophy (Elkind, 1997).

Educational theorists intended to bring their version of "science" into their respective models to reduce uncertainty in order to ensure a standardized product and create more efficient educational institutions. This "scientific" initiative is expressed by Murphy (1997): "Th[e] abundance of testing in contemporary American society is just one more manifestation of the desire to control, to be 'scientific' and to leave nothing to chance". Murphy adds that, "[s]tandardized testing is, perhaps, a prototypical exemplar of this broader desire to control chance. The ultimate reward for using standardized tests, then, was that education could be made more efficient and effective".

The adoption of these "scientific principles" into educational arenas forced educational administrators to view themselves as business managers concerned with efficiency and production rather than as scholars or educators (Callahan, 1962). Efficiency (namely, time well spent) and accountability (namely, money well spent) took precedence over the concern for providing a quality education for individual children. Control and cost effectiveness were prioritized over educational excellence.

This "scientific" movement was predicated on three main concepts; (1) The School as Factory, (2) The Child as Product, and (3) Standardized Testing as Quality Control. The child was thought of as a piece of raw material to be shaped by the educational "factory" into a quality "product." Teaching became viewed as a form of training, and schools were expected to operate more like assembly lines, working on children as they passed through various stages of the curriculum. Once these factories were "up and running" and the standards for the "child as product" were determined, standardized testing became the means for measuring the quality of this product.

In what follows, I first address the concept of "Standardized Testing as Quality Control." Next, I briefly discuss the types of assessment used in today's schools and the need for a new perspective concerning assessment. Then, I outline a different perspective for assessment, one based on reflective inquiry rather than measurement. Following that discussion, I describe several factors that have helped support teachers (including myself) in making this "paradigm shift" from assessment as measurement to assessment as reflective inquiry. Using examples from my experience as a staff development facilitator working with teachers in their classrooms, I will explain the characteristics that have helped support this change in perspective. In closing, I will briefly describe some of the challenges we face as educators in supporting teachers changing their perspectives towards assessment.

STANDARDIZED TESTING AS QUALITY CONTROL

The effects of the standardized testing movement of the early 1900s had a profound impact on the way schools viewed assessment. This impact can still be felt today as we spend millions of dollars each year on standardized testing programs nationwide in order to judge the efficiency and effectiveness of schools (Hanson, 1993).

This standardized testing, along with grade level structures, has been a predominant factor in supporting the "school as factory" model of education. Originally, these standardized testing programs were designed to measure the specifications set out by administrations for the development of their educational "products" and to provide public accountability for external audiences, such as business leaders and legislative bodies (Bracey, 1995). Once the standards for the quality of each "child as product" were devised and the "assembly line" of education was up and running, the next logical step was to devise a method to judge the quality of each product. In this sense, standardized tests became the quality control mechanism used to regulate public schools and ensure a quality product.

These standardized tests were designed according to a "consumption view of knowledge" (Crebbin, 1992). According to this view, knowledge was seen as a product, a set of discreet facts and skills to be "consumed." Standardized tests were then developed to measure the amount of consumption that took place. From this perspective, knowledge is seen as a value-free body of concepts and objectives that are independent of time, place, and individuals. This view of "assessment as measurement" is closely aligned with a modernist philosophy and supports the factory model of education.

In today's educational environment, it is fairly certain that large-scale standardized testing programs are not fading away; rather, they are increasing in number and frequency (Berliner & Biddle, 1995). The desire to control education through "scientific" principles and to be able to "objectively" measure student learning still influences educational decisions today. Large-scale assessments, particularly norm-referenced, standardized tests, still dominate assessment frameworks in educational institutions in the United States and Canada (Murphy, 1997).

THE NEED FOR A NEW PERSPECTIVE

The types of assessments needed by classroom teachers to guide instruction and support a quality education for every child are different from the traditional, "assessment as measurement" devices of the standardized testing industry (Bertrand, 1991). As our view of learning has changed from the consumption of discreet skills and isolated bits of knowledge to the construction of more complex, contextually grounded processes, assessment practices need to change to acknowledge this new perspective on learning (Johnston, 1992). As Cambourne (1997) suggests, "the prevailing paradigm of evaluation has not kept pace with the emerging paradigm of learning and language". Unfortunately, this change may not occur until teachers and other educators begin to question the foundations upon which the assessment-as-measurement paradigm is built.

By shifting the focus of assessment programs from large-scale accountability to the individual needs of the child, teachers are better able to use these "classroom-based" assessment procedures to gather information, influence learning, and guide their decisions concerning classroom instruction. Where standardized tests are concerned with "commonalities," universals, and regularities in data, classroom-based assessment is more concerned with individual student abilities and needs (Bridges, 1995). Classroom-based assessment helps support teachers to direct curriculum and instruction based on students as individuals rather than as pieces coming along an assembly line in need of identical services.

Teachers that use classroom-based assessment procedures to make decisions about instruction are "reflective inquirers," not simply the dispensers of someone else's mandated curriculum. These reflective inquirers use classroom observations and their knowledge of learning theories to make decisions regarding curriculum and classroom procedures. Because of this change in their view about learning and teaching, they begin to change their view about assessment. When knowledge is no longer seen as a value-neutral, objective commodity to be delivered to students, assessment is no longer viewed as the "instrument" to measure how much has been delivered.

If we change our perspective towards assessment from a concern about accountability, objective measurement, and cost effectiveness to a concern about the quality of educational opportunities afforded individual children, our assessment programs and procedures will need to change as well. The large-scale standardized testing programs no longer offer internal audiences (such as teachers, students, and parents) the type of information needed to make day to day curriculum and instructional decisions concerning individual students. Not only will this require a change in perspective, "paradigm shift" if you will, but also an accompanying change in assessment procedures, instruments, purposes, and audiences (Serafini, 1997).

ASSESSMENT AS REFLECTIVE INQUIRY: ANOTHER PERSPECTIVE

The assessment as reflective inquiry perspective has different purposes and audiences, as compared to a traditional, assessment-as-measurement perspective (Farr, 1992). The three primary goals of the assessment-as-reflective-inquiry perspective are (1) helping students learn, (2) helping teachers teach more effectively, and (3) helping teachers articulate their knowledge of children and children's learning processes to external audiences, starting with parents and moving beyond the classroom walls to school districts and state educational organizations.

The assessment-as-reflective-inquiry perspective attempts to achieve these goals by heightening the teacher's awareness, understandings, and perceptions of individual student abilities, student's conceptual frameworks, the learning environment created in the classroom, the role of the teacher, the quality of the educational experiences provided, and the attitudes and behaviors of individual students (Serafini, 1995). This is a different stance towards assessment when compared to the factory model of assessment, where the main purpose was accountability, comparison, and economic efficiency.

In the assessment-as-reflective-inquiry paradigm, assessment is a social activity involving human beings, interpretive processes, and the social construction of knowledge (Johnston, 1997). It is not based on "modernist" assumptions; rather, it is based on an "interpretivist" perspective (Erickson, 1986). Teachers and students, not standardized tests, become the primary instruments used to assess children's literate abilities. Teachers, and in many instances students, collect evidence of student's learning and use this information to guide curricular decisions. In this way, the curriculum is responsive to the assessment process, and the assessments we choose are responsive to the experiences we provide children.

Assessment may be responsive, but it is not separated from the classroom learning experiences. Rather, assessment is ongoing, embedded in the authentic learning context of the classroom environment (Bergeron, 1996). From this perspective, assessment is a "bottom-up" process, beginning with teachers and students in the context of the classroom, and "working up" to provide information to external stakeholders, such as school districts and departments of education. Assessment is grounded in actual classroom learning events, not reduced from all of its complexity and ambiguities (Cambourne & Turbill, 1990).

This list represents some of the basic characteristics concerning the assessment-as-reflective-inquiry paradigm. Assessment as Reflective Inquiry:

1. is done in an authentic context.
2. provides information to help teachers make curricular decisions.
3. is non-competitive.
4. begins with learner's strengths, not their deficits.
5. helps the learner to engage in self-evaluation and reflection.
6. includes teacher intuition and tacit knowledge.
7. is grounded in observation, inquiry, and reflection.
8. uses the teacher and student as assessment instrument.
9. uses a variety of sources and methods to collect information.
10. is on-going, continuous, and extends over a long period of time.
11. views learning as a social process.
12. cannot be standardized.
13. provides a knowledge base for teachers to articulate their understandings to parents and other audiences.
14. should not privilege one gender, race, social class, ethnicity, or group over another.

Many of these characteristics align with qualitative research methodologies and with a constructivist perspective towards knowledge (Erickson, 1986). It is my belief that assessment as reflective inquiry honors the individual student as learner rather than conceiving of the student as a product or raw material on the "assembly line" of the educational factory.

TIME, DISTANCE, AND DIALOGUE

For any type of educational reform to be successful, teachers need time to work through the proposed changes, a critical perspective from which to examine their beliefs and practices, and the opportunity to collaborate and dialogue with other interested educators (Fullan, 1994). The support for educational change can come from internal sources, such as school level administrators, staff development opportunities, colleagues, parents, or students, as well as from external sources, such as local universities, state departments of education, and legislative bodies. I would like to discuss three general characteristics that support changes in classroom practice, and then discuss three specific characteristics that support a change in assessment paradigms. I feel that both these general (as well as these specific) characteristics are important in helping classroom teachers change their beliefs about assessment practices.

Changing classroom practices or a teacher's perspectives demands adequate time to work through these new ideas plus the opportunity to collaborate with other educators. Teachers need time to understand how these new assessment practices, or teaching practices for that matter, will impact their classrooms and improve their student's educational experiences. Time to work through changes is the first characteristic that supports changes in classroom practice and assessment procedures.

In the schools where I have worked, administrators and teachers themselves have tried different ways to create additional time for the professional development necessary to support these changes in classroom practices. Many school districts have designated up to seven work days as professional development days during the school year, often allowing school sites to design how these days will be utilized. Another district that I have worked with lengthened the work day on Monday, Tuesday, Thursday, and Friday by twenty minutes so that they could use every Wednesday afternoon as professional development time. Students were released early on Wednesdays, and teachers met to work on various projects and support groups. This schedule offered more ongoing opportunities for teacher collaboration and in-depth development than was previously available to teachers during the work day. It also demonstrated the district's commitment to quality, long-term staff development.

The school I am working in now offers each teacher a substitute teacher to work in their classroom for two days a year so that the full-time teacher may visit other classrooms, attend professional conferences, or explore other professional development opportunities. Other districts I have worked with have created a summer "academy" where teachers are provided a stipend to attend. Well-known speakers and educators from across the country are invited to speak at this summer academy. This summer academy provides teachers with the opportunity to learn from other educators before returning to their classrooms. These are a few of the possible ways that schools and school districts have been creative in finding time for teachers to work through the changes being implemented in their classrooms.

The second general characteristic I have called "distance," or more specifically, the ability to achieve a more "critical" perspective towards one's beliefs and classroom teaching practices. In my opinion, this is a crucial aspect to changing one's practice, but it is also one that is hard to define and harder yet to achieve. The questions seem to be, "How do we as teachers 'step outside ourselves' to view ourselves as actors in the classroom drama? How do we achieve a better perspective to understand the impact we have on the learning experiences and learning environment we provide our students?"

In my present position as a staff development facilitator, my job entails working in elementary classrooms to support teachers in becoming more effective literacy educators. I provide responses to teacher's lessons, demonstrate different approaches to literacy instruction, share articles and other professional resources for teachers to read, and provide general support for teachers in their journey to becoming more reflective educators. I believe that my role as staff development facilitator provides a form of support for teachers to achieve a critical perspective towards their classroom practice. By creating an atmosphere of trust and collegiality, I hope to encourage teachers to try new ideas and challenge their present understandings. I provide another perspective for them to view their teaching practice, offering my observations, responses, and advice when needed. It is my goal to help teachers implement classroom-based assessment procedures, to come to know their students more extensively, and to provide more effective literacy experiences in their classrooms.

There are other ways that teachers can achieve this critical perspective towards their practice. Reflective notebooks or journals (Cochran-Smith & Lytle 1992, p. 26), teacher research projects (Shagoury-Hubbard & Miller-Powers, 1993), classroom peer visitations and alternative forms of teacher evaluation (Searfoss & Enz, 1996) may all provide new means to support a critical perspective towards one's practice. These other "reflective instruments" help teachers step back and see their practice from new perspectives.

I have been keeping a reflective notebook since I began my teacher preparation program many years ago. I have filled about twenty-five hardcover notebooks with my thoughts, concerns, notes from articles I have read, and ideas from the classes I have taken. These notebooks allow me to go back and find patterns in my thinking, to revisit earlier experiences, and to come to a better understanding of the way that I view myself as teacher and educator. For me, it has been an invaluable tool for providing a critical perspective towards my practice and beliefs.

The third general characteristic I would like to present is "dialogue." Dialogue is the opportunity to collaborate with colleagues in an open, trusting environment about concerns and ideas that are important to the teachers themselves. It is an engaged discussion where participants invest themselves in the dialogue, sharing their ideas and learning from the insights and experiences provided by other collaborative participants. Without this opportunity, many teachers feel isolated and left to fend for themselves.

Dialogue requires participants to be actively involved in discussions as well as open to accepting others views and perspectives. It requires active listening and the co-production of meaning. Peterson (1992) states, "Dialogue encompasses two qualities that are central to learning: *critique* and *inquiry*. It is dependent upon people who can rise to the challenge of paying attention and thinking critically" (p. 104).

Different ways that have supported dialogue in the schools where I have worked are team teaching structures, teacher dialogue groups, restructured staff meetings, professional development days, e-mail discussion groups, and school-based professional development classes.

Probably the most powerful professional development experience of my teaching career was the three years I spent in a team-teaching setting. I taught an intermediate, multiage class with another teacher, working with approximately fifty children, ages nine through twelve, in fourth, fifth, and sixth grades, respectively. Being able to spend every day working closely with a respected, intelligent, dedicated colleague that pushed my thinking and constantly caused me to reflect upon my practice helped me to develop into a better teacher. We were able to bounce ideas off of one another, critique each other's practice, and reflect together about the day's experiences. It was not easy finding someone that I could work with this well and I do not recommend trying to mandate this in schools, but for me it was an incredible professional experience.

On a different level, teacher dialogue groups that meet together after school once a week to discuss ideas can be very supportive. Teachers at my schools have been meeting regularly for several years, on a voluntary basis, to discuss educational issues, classroom approaches to literacy instruction, teacher research, and new assessment procedures. Teachers have told me how important the opportunity to talk to other interested colleagues about their practice has been, and I continue to this day to participate in these support groups at the school where I work. These dialogue groups help break down teachers' feelings of isolation and helps them understand the experiences of other teachers.

E-mail "chat groups" have been able to provide discussion with colleagues from different countries and school locations. I have been writing back and forth with several colleagues from Australia and parts of the United States about reflective practice and various assessment processes for several years now. This is not a substitute for face-to-face interaction; however, it is a viable alternative for those that do not have anyone to engage in dialogue.

I have been fortunate to work with several administrators that value dialogue as part of their staff professional development process. These administrators have redesigned staff meetings and in-service days to accommodate and promote teacher dialogue opportunities. For the business news and day-to-day announcements, these administrators have begun to use e-mail and handwritten notes to facilitate information distribution.

Doing so has opened up more time during staff meetings for teacher interactions and discussions.

Many of the agendas of these meetings are designed by the teachers themselves about the issues they need to discuss. It is through this ongoing, open dialogue that teachers have been able to openly express their concerns, discuss their own practice and instructional approaches, get ideas about classroom activities, and come to a better understanding of their own practice and beliefs.

The three characteristics mentioned above are general in scope and are essentially foundational for any educational reform process. I would now like to discuss three characteristics that are specifically designed to address the changes in assessment perspectives mentioned earlier. These three characteristics are 1) teacher as knowledgeable, reflective participant, 2) meaningful student involvement, and 3) the negotiation of criteria for assessment and evaluation. These three characteristics have arisen out of my work with teachers, my readings from professional literature, and my own classroom practice.

TEACHER AS KNOWLEDGEABLE, REFLECTIVE PARTICIPANT

The teacher as a knowledgeable, reflective participant is a different stance to teaching as compared to the traditional "teacher as program deliverer" models of education that have dominated schools for decades (Goodlad, 1983). Reflective participants, like Schon's "reflective practitioners" (1983), are not simply "test givers" or "deliverers" of a prepackaged curriculum. Rather, these teachers are astute observers of children, active participants in the assessment process, and judges of student progress and growth. Reflective practitioners do not simply follow commercially produced teacher manuals; instead, along with their students, they are "co-creators" of the classroom curriculum (Short & Burke, 1994).

Foremost these teachers are knowledgeable practitioners. Their practice is grounded in their close observations of students and the current learning theories and practices published in educational books and professional journals. Many of these authors are reflective practitioners who are widely read, are active in professional teacher organizations, and frequently speak at regional and national education conferences. They are deeply committed to their profession and usually have advanced degrees in their area of expertise.

However, knowledge of these reflective practitioners is not simply learned by reading educational journals; it is also grounded in their close observations of children, reflections on their actions and observations, and dialogue with other knowledgeable educators. Often these teachers belong to an informal "community of scholars" that share their expertise and observations through teacher–educator dialogue groups.

Reflective practitioners are able to articulate their underlying beliefs and theories that inform their practice. These teachers don't just engage in activities because they are "cute" or because they are what everyone else is doing; rather, they engage in particular activities because they believe that these activities are important vehicles to enhance students' literate abilities.

Second, reflective practitioners often assume the stance of "teacher-as-researcher," reflecting on their classroom practice through teacher research projects (Cochran-Smith & Lytle, 1990). They are collaborators and inquirers. They use research methodologies to inform their own practice and to help them understand the needs and abilities of individual children in their classrooms.

Their reflective stance is not simply a "navel-gazing" activity but is an active, participatory stance, using the knowledge they create to guide their practice and inform their instructional decisions. These teacher researchers are not merely "consumers" of university-based research but are producers of research, often publishing their findings in teacher research journals.

Reflective participants practice what I have termed "knowledgeable uncertainty." These teachers are very knowledgeable about learning theories, children's language development, and classroom practice, but they approach all knowledge from a position of uncertainty. They are inquirers themselves, unable to blindly accept the mandates of externally prescribed programs. They do not allow themselves to be reduced to the role of "program operator."

Third, these reflective participants are "active" participants in the assessment process. Many of the teachers I work closely with have created their own teacher portfolios so that they can understand this process from the inside. I have my own portfolio that I use to demonstrate to student teachers what one may look like and the power of developing one of their own.

Reflective participants are promoters of "reflective learning communities," inviting students to reflect alongside the teacher about their classroom learning experiences. They create a democratic atmosphere, one of trust and collaboration, where students feel safe to express themselves and inquire about the world. In these communities, teachers share the "control" of the classroom, and all participants become more empowered because of this sharing.

In these reflective learning communities, teachers are seen as learners and students are invited to become teachers. Knowledge is co-constructed, and students are deeply involved in the decision-making process, often discussing classroom procedures, curriculum design, and behavioral expectations. Reflective participants do not represent the sole voice of authority; rather, they invite the student's voice to be heard and involved in the life of the classroom.

In many of the schools where I have worked, to assume the stance of reflective practitioner is to "teach against the grain" (Cochran-Smith, 1991, p. 280). It is a politically charged stance and one that has caused many teachers, myself included, to be ostracized from various teaching communities. However, in my case and for many of my colleagues, it is the only stance worth teaching from. We find it empowering, liberating, and professionally redeeming. In my opinion, I am obligated to help students receive the most effective educational experiences possible and not obligated to simply perform mandated activities for external agencies.

MEANINGFUL STUDENT INVOLVEMENT

Along with promoting a reflective stance to teaching, involving students in the assessment process is an important aspect of the assessment-as-reflective-inquiry paradigm. Involving students in the assessment process sounds so logical that it is often taken for granted. However, traditionally designed assessment programs have operated with little, if any, student involvement other than as "test-takers." Rather than being "objects of measurement," students need to be actively involved in the assessment and evaluation of their academic progress.

Portfolio assessment processes (Tierney, Carter, & Desai, 1991), student-led conferences (Anthony, Johnson, Mickelson, & Preece, 1991), and retrospective miscue analysis (Marek, 1991) have each involved the student in the assessment process in a meaningful way. It has been shown that when students are involved in the assessment process, they become more involved in their own learning (Kohn, 1993).

In my intermediate, multiage classroom, students were involved in assessing their academic progress on a daily basis. At the end of each day, students spent time discussing and writing about their experiences at school in their "learning logs." Students filled out a form that we developed together, listing our areas of study (such as science topics, reading genres, writing topics, and behavioral aspects) that would go home each Friday for parents to review with their child. This form evolved over the course of the year from a "What I Did Today" list to a "What I Learned Today" reflection. What began as a list of the day's events expanded into a reflective journal that students used to assess their growth. Parents found this log extremely helpful in understanding their child's experiences at school and the expectations set forth in our classroom. They often expressed to me that this was a tremendous help in finding out what was going on in our classroom each week. Many parents used the learning log to talk with their child about their child's experiences at school.

Students were also deeply involved in their own assessment as part of our portfolio assessment process. At the beginning of the year, students were given a file folder and were invited to begin collecting some artifacts of their learning. Students could be found throughout the week putting things into and maintaining their portfolio collections. We set aside a special time every Friday to talk about these collections and learn different ways to use these collections to promote student reflection.

These portfolio collections were used by the students to prepare for student-led conferences during the spring semester of each school year. They collected and organized their portfolio and presented it to their parents at conference time. These collections were designed to help students reflect upon their growth and to help them write a self-evaluation in the form of a narrative report card. Knowing the purpose and the audience for these collections was crucial in helping to establish the importance of their collection.

By establishing portfolios, allowing for discussion concerning these collections, and involving students in daily reflec-

tions about their progress, I was able to involve my students in the assessment of their academic progress.

NEGOTIATION OF CRITERIA

In the assessment-as-measurement paradigm, the criteria for assessing students' work and educational progress are preset by test developers, state standards documents, and curriculum designs. In contrast, the assessment-as-reflective-inquiry paradigm allows for the criteria to be negotiated between the teacher, the mandated curriculum documents, state standards documents, and the students themselves. Boomer (1991) described a similar process for negotiating the curriculum. From this perspective, teachers are actively involved with their students in negotiating and creating the criteria for assessing student work and academic progress. These criteria are flexible and can change throughout the course of the years to reflect student growth and experience.

A good example of negotiated criteria are rubrics developed within individual classrooms (Rickards and Cheek, Jr., 1999). These rubrics are a list of statements concerning the qualities a particular product should exhibit. They are created by the students and teachers themselves before they begin the project and are expanded as the actual work is being done.

The *process* of creating these rubrics, the negotiation itself, is more important in helping students understand what is involved in producing a quality poem, for example, than the actual rubric itself that is created. State testing agencies that have produced performance-based assessments, and have created numerous rubrics for teachers to use to judge the quality of student work. The problem with these, I believe, is that neither the teachers nor the students were involved in the discussions or negotiations, from which these rubrics were developed.

In my elementary classroom as well as my college literacy education courses, I regularly present an outline of my expectations for my students to read over and consider as we develop the criteria for a project or piece of writing. This initial outline is my "platform statement" concerning my beliefs, values, and expectations about a particular project we are undertaking (Kottkamp, 1990). Together we consider the expectations I put forth in my platform statement and my students ideas about the topic. Then we look at the district curriculum guidelines and state standards documents to develop a working criteria to assess our progress and our work. By beginning with our expectations and criteria and then looking at the externally mandated criteria, we can develop criteria that are grounded in our understandings and experiences. These "classroom negotiated criteria" are usually more extensive than those prescribed from external agencies. In this way, we are meeting the externally mandated requirements—but on our own terms.

During the semester or school year, these criteria change and enlarge to reflect our current understandings. My students and I use the rubrics we develop to assess individual pieces of writing and determine the quality of the piece. We use this information to set goals for our next piece of writing.

For example, in my intermediate, multiage class, we developed the following rubric for pieces of narrative writing, entitled "Criteria for Quality Writing." It reads as follows:

1. poetic language/appropriate word choice
2. not "generic" /unique ideas
3. correct spelling, punctuation, and capitalization
4. makes sense/understandable to the reader
5. has emotional impact
6. interesting/the reader wants to finish it
7. proper sentence structure
8. proper form or format
9. neatly written or published

These criteria were used by my students to assess their own writing and by myself to give responses to their efforts. This rubric initially began as items numbered one through four in the above list. As the year progressed and our understandings enlarged, so did our rubric. By the end of the year, it incorporated all of the items listed above. An important consideration when using classroom rubrics is that these rubrics are designed to support student learning and growth, not to create blueprints for standardization of student work. Therefore, they must remain flexible, open to revision as new insights arise and new experiences change our understandings.

The main difference between this negotiated, reflective assessment and the assessment as measurement paradigm is that there is not an external agent solely responsible for telling the class what constitutes a quality effort. It is a negotiation between the district-created curriculum documents, state standards documents, and other externally prepared criteria, and the ideas of students and teachers working in classrooms, where the actual learning is taking place.

CHALLENGES FOR THE FUTURE

One of the tensions we face concerning assessment is how to provide public accountability and the information required by state departments of education while at the same time diminishing the dominance of standardized testing programs and all of the problems associated with them (Garcia & Pearson, 1994). Can classroom-based assessment provide the information required by these public institutions while still maintaining its primary objective of helping students learn and teachers teach? It seems that until these tensions can be resolved to the satisfaction of these different audiences, standardized tests will continue to dominate assessment programs in schools.

Tierney stated that all too often, classroom-based assessment frameworks were co-opted in favor of the comparative purposes of large-scale testing programs (Tierney & Clark, 1998). The comparative designs of the large-scale assessment programs took precedence over the individual needs of students addressed by classroom-based assessments. In fact, Tierney (1998) held little hope in finding a common ground, a functional blend of these two assessment frameworks, mainly because they have such diverse purposes and audiences.

In the state of Arizona, where I teach, we are in the middle of yet another transformation of large-scale testing. This new test, entitled "Arizona's Instrument to Measure Standards" (AIMS), has been designed to measure students progress in acquiring the knowledge, skills, and processes described in the Arizona state standards documents. This test has now been linked to student high school graduation, requiring a passing score on reading, mathematics, and writing portions of the test by those intending to graduate in 2002. One of the primary intentions of this test is to measure whether students have learned the required curriculum delineated in the standards. There is no further negotiation. The instrument to measure students' progress is in effect designed to provide accountability for the general public. It has been proposed that schools that "produce" students that can't "measure up" will be taken over by the state department. How far is this from the original Factory Model of Assessment described in the opening section? For me, not far enough. The standards, and the instruments designed to measure these standards, may have changed, but the intentions remain the same: to measure how much knowledge children have consumed.

Another challenge facing us would be the changes needed in teacher education programs to support this new perspective on learning and assessment. Some programs would have to be redesigned to promote reflective practitioners instead of creating "program delivery specialists." In fact, in universities across North America, teacher education programs are beginning to make this change in perspective in light of new understandings of learning processes and research on effective teaching and reflective participants (Zeichner, 1987).

Traditionally, universities have relied on "methods" classes to educate teachers in the best way to "deliver curriculum." This philosophy aligns with the modernist, factory model of education discussed earlier in this article. In order to support the shift from assessment-as-measurement to assessment-as-reflective-inquiry, teacher education programs would need to provide time for reflection, establish more school-based teacher education programs, create partnerships with reflective teachers, and provide the time, distance, and dialogue opportunities to support these changes in perspectives. Many of the teacher education programs are currently making these changes in their programs and are promoting reflective practice in their coursework and apprenticeships.

An important question will be whether the school structures that have long supported these standardized tests, a modernist philosophical perspective with teachers working in isolation, will be able to adapt to the demands this new assessment paradigm would place on the teachers, schools, and educational communities. Teachers working with students in traditional grade levels for a single year may become problematic when we place the needs of the individual children ahead of economic efficiency. The school structures and the design of the school day may need to be changed to allow children and teachers to work together for more than a single year and across age levels.

I am fully aware that these suggestions challenge the dominant political views of education that currently influence schools. I am also aware that this is a political as well as an educational battle. Smith (1992) once wrote, "People who don't trust children to learn, will always rely on a program to do their job". I believe that this pertains to the current state of assessment programs as well. Assessment has been traditionally designed to provide accountability rather than support the educational needs of individual students. These new methods of assessment, with their focus on the individual student, are necessary if we are ever going to break the stranglehold that standardized testing has on public schools in America. As Smyth (1992) writes, "It is becoming increasingly clear that they [teachers] are being acted upon by educational systems and governments in ways that bear an uncanny resemblance to the oppressive treatment meted out to minority groups. Indeed, only when teachers take an active, reflective stance, are they able to challenge the dominant factory metaphor of the way schools are conceived, organized, and enacted".

I believe that we as teachers need to "step up" and challenge the current assessment paradigm. We need to question the traditional school structures and assessment practices that limit the possibilities of children, especially children from non-mainstream cultures. The more we can articulate our understandings of student learning to wider external audiences, the less these audiences will have to rely on standardized tests to understand the quality of educational experiences provided in public schools. Assessment programs that view children as "products on an assembly line" need to be redesigned to honor the individual student, provide as many opportunities as possible for each child, respect students of diverse backgrounds, and help teachers to become more effective facilitators of children's literacy development.

Address correspondence to Frank Serafini, 9599 W. Charleston Blvd, #1074; Las Vegas, NV 89117. E-mail: serafini@unlv.edu

REFERENCES

Anthony, R., Johnson, T., Mickelson, N., & Preece, A. (1991). *Evaluating literacy: A perspective for change*. Portsmouth, NH: Heinemann.

Bergeron, B. (1996). Seeking authenticity: What is "real" about thematic literacy instruction? *The Reading Teacher, 49*(7), 544–551.

Berliner, D. C., & Biddle, B. J. (1995). The manufactured crisis: Myths, fraud, and the attack on public schools. Reading, MA: Addison-Wesley.

Bertrand, J. (1991). Student assessment and evaluation. In B. Harp (Ed.), *Assessment and evaluation in whole language programs* (pp. 17–33), Norwood, MA: Christopher Gordon.

Boomer, G. (Ed.). (1991). *Negotiating the curriculum: A teacher-student partnership*. Sydney: Ashton-Scholastic.

Bracey, G. (1995). *Final exam: A study of the perpetual scrutiny of American education*. Washington: Technos Press.

Bridges, L. (1995). *Assessment: Continuous learning*. York, ME: Stenhouse.

Callahan, R. (1962). *Education and the cult of efficiency*. Chicago, IL: University of Chicago Press.

Cambourne, B., & Turbill, J. (1990). Assessment in whole language classrooms. *Theory Into Practice, 90*(3), 337–349.

Cambourne, B., & Turbil, J. (Eds.). (1997). *Responsive evaluation*. Portsmouth, NH: Heinemann.

Cochran-Smith, M. (1991). Teaching against the grain. *Harvard Educational Review, 61*(3), 279–309.

Cochran-Smith, M., & Lytle, S. (1990). Research on teaching and teacher research: The issues that divide. *Educational Researcher, 19*(2), 2–11.

Cochran-Smith, M., & Lytle, S. (Eds.). (1992). Inside/Outside: Teacher research and knowledge. New York: Teachers College Press.

Crebbin, W. (1992). Evaluation: A political issue. In C. Bouffler (Ed.), *Literacy evaluation: Issues and practicalities* (pp. 7–11). Portsmouth, NH: Heinemann.

Elkind, D. (1997). The death of child nature: Education in the postmodern world. *Educational Leadership, 78*, 241–245.

Erickson, F. (1986). Qualitative methods in research on teaching. In M. Wittrock (Ed.), *Handbook of research on teaching* (pp. 119–161). New York: MacMillan.

Farr, R. (1992). Putting it all together: Solving the reading assessment puzzle. *The Reading Teacher, 46*(1), 26–37.

Fosnot, C. T. (1996). Constructivism: A psychological theory of learning. In C. T. Fosnot (Ed.), *Constructivism: Theory, perspectives and practice* (pp. 8–33). New York: Teachers College Press.

Fullan, M. (1994). Why teachers must become change agents. *Educational Leadership, 50*, 12–17.

Garcia, G. E., & Pearson, P.D. (1994). Assessment and diversity. In L. Darling-Hammond (Ed.), *Review of research in education, 20* (pp. 337–391). Washington, DC: American Educational Research Association.

Goodlad, J. (1983). *A place called school: Prospects for the future*. New York: McGraw-Hill.

Hanson, F. A. (1993). Testing, testing: Social consequences of an examined life. Berkeley, CA: University of California Press.

Johnston, P. H. (1992). Nontechnical assessment. *The Reading Teacher, 46*(1), 60–62.

Johnston, P. H. (1997). *Knowing literacy: Constructive literacy assessment*. York, ME: Stenhouse.

Kohn, A. (1993). Choices for students: Why and how to let students decide. *Phi Delta Kappan, 75*, 8–20.

Kottkamp, R. B. (1990). Means for facilitating reflection. *Education and Urban Society, 22*(2), 182–203.

Marek, A. M. (1991). Retrospective miscue analysis: An instructional strategy for revaluing the reading process. In Goodman, K. S., Bird, L. B., & Goodman, Y. M. (Eds.), *The whole language*. Santa Rosa, CA: American School Publishers.

Murphy, S. (1997). Literacy assessment and the politics of identity. *Reading and Writing Quarterly, 13*, 261–278.

Pennac, D. (1994). *Better than life*. Toronto: Coach House Press.

Peterson, R. (1992). *Life in a crowded place*. Portsmouth, NH: Heinemann.

Rickards, D., & Cheek Jr., E. (1999). *Designing rubrics for K–6 classroom assessment*. Norwood, MA: Christopher-Gordon.

Schon, D. A. (1983). *The reflective practitioner: How professionals think in action*. New York: Basic Books.

Searfoss, L., & Enz, B. (1996). Can teacher evaluation reflect holistic instruction? *Educational Leadership, 56*(2), 38–41.

Serafini, F. (1995). Reflective assessment. *Talking Points: Conversations in the Whole Language Community, 6*(4), 10–12.

Serafini, F. (1997). Stances to assessment. *Talking Points: Conversations in the Whole Language Community, 8*(3), 2–4.

Shagoury-Hubbard, R., & Miller-Powers, B. (1993). *The art of classroom inquiry*. Portsmouth, NH: Heinemann.

Short, K., & Burke, C. (1994). *Creating curriculum*. Portsmouth, NH: Heinemann.

Smith, F. (1992). Learning to read: The never-ending debate. *Phi Delta Kappa, 73*, 432–441.

Smyth, J. (1992). Teacher's work and the politics of reflection. *American Educational Research Journal, 29*(2), 267–300.

Tierney, R. J. (1998). Literacy assessment reform: Shifting beliefs, principled possibilities and emerging practices. *The Reading Teacher, 51*(5), 1374–1390.

Tierney, R. J., Carter, M. A., and Desai, L. E. (1991). *Portfolio assessment in the reading–writing classroom*. Norwood, MA: Christopher Gordon.

Tierney, R. J., & Clark, C. (1998). Portfolios: Assumptions, tensions, and possibilities. *Reading Research Quarterly, 33*(4), 474–486.

Zeichner, K. (1987). Preparing reflective teachers: An overview of instructional strategies which have been employed in preservice education. *International Journal of Education Research, 11*, 565–575.

UNIT 7

Critical Literacy Perspectives

Unit Selections

Key Points to Consider

- How do textbooks transmit culture?

- How can content area teachers meet the needs of diverse students in their classroom?

- What reading strategies have been found to be effective in assisting secondary students to read their content area textbooks?

- How can classroom teachers adapt their content area textbooks to meet the needs of students?

 **Links: www.dushkin.com/online/**
These sites are annotated in the World Wide Web pages.

Critical Issue: Addressing Literacy Needs in Culturally and Linguistically Diverse Classrooms
http://www.ncrel.org/sdrs/areas/issues/content/cntareas/reading/li400.htm

While we have a right to be free, public education was not included in the Bill of Rights. However, few would argue against its necessity in a nation committed to democracy. Many of us reference John Dewey as the father of education for a democratic citizenry, much like we laud Thomas Jefferson as one of the founding fathers of the United States as a democratic nation. Jefferson has been quoted as having said, "If a nation expects to be ignorant and free, in a state of civilization, it expects what never was and never will be." And similarly he has been quoted, "Educate and inform the whole mass of the people... They are the only sure reliance for the preservation of our liberty." I would like to believe that the 2001, No Child Left Behind, legislation is in the spirit of this ideal. State mandates that require secondary schools to eliminate remedial and vocational preparation classes and encourage all students to work towards a Core 40 curriculum may be an effort to insure that all students receive the education necessary for college entrance. This theory can only become a realized practice if teachers are committed to meeting the needs of the diverse learners in their classrooms.

Pre-service and in-service teachers must be prepared to address the needs of ALL the learners assigned to their classrooms. State and national standards require that schools accommodate ALL students. Principle #3 from the Interstate New Teacher Assessment and Support Consortium (INTASC) states that "The teacher understands how students differ in their approaches to learning and creates instructional opportunities that are adapted to diverse learners." Among the teacher-performances identified by INTASC are these two:

> The teacher makes appropriate provisions (in terms of time and circumstances for work, tasks assigned, communication, and response modes) for individual students who have particular learning differences or needs.

> The teacher can identify when and how to access appropriate services or resources to meet exceptional learning needs. (1992)

While ALL secondary students need instruction on how to utilize their content area textbooks, this unit focuses on strategies that have been found to be particularly successful with secondary students who read below the level of the Core 40 curriculum. The articles in this unit present strategies for aiding secondary students who have difficulty reading textbooks. Strategies include previewing, vocabulary preparation, predicting, and concept mapping. Reading activities should include reciprocal teaching, mapping, and cooperative learning strategies. Follow-up or post-reading strategies connect back to pre-reading activities and expanding understanding through analysis questions.

On another level, this unit challenges readers to critique the cultural politics of education by raising critical questions about cultural transmission and domination through textbook bias. Diversity has always been a key component of the democratic ideal. Critical literacy defined by multiple perspectives requires that students read their textbooks with an openness to hear diverse views and with a critical lens through which they can question bias views that sometimes dominate texts.

In "Tales from Two Textbooks: A Comparison of the Civil Rights Movement in Two Secondary History Textbooks" (1994), Terrie L. Epstein shows the problems of textbook presentation of the civil rights movement in two secondary History books. The article gives concrete examples of how differences in information presentation result in creating biased accounts of history. In "The Story of Ourselves: Fostering Multiple Historical Perspectives" (1996), Michael O. Tunnell and Richard Ammon argue in favor of teachers exposing students to multiple points of view through trade books. Likewise, the authors suggest teachers guide students in a critique of the texts to surface the ways that texts omit some voices and include others.

In "Using Textbooks with Students Who Cannot Read Them" (1995), Jean Ciborowski summarizes existing literature on textbook instruction, providing many practical strategies to develop skills for utilizing textbooks. In "Guidelines for Adapting Content Area Textbooks: Keeping Teachers and Students Content" (1991), Jeanne Shay Schumm and Kelly Strickler present several ways of substituting. In "Assisting Students with Difficult Textbooks: Teacher Perceptions and Practices" (1994), Jeanne Shay Schumm, Sharon Vaughn, and Linda Saumell examined successful teachers of diverse learners for perceptions and practices with regard to adapting textbooks for their students to promote understanding. The article provides teachers' ratings of desirability, feasibility, and use of textbook adaptations by elementary, middle, and high school groupings.

I conclude this section and the manual with "Dialogue in Teaching as Critical Instruction" (2003), an article I began while still teaching middle school students in East Texas. I further developed the article while completing my doctoral studies, presented it in draft form at The New England League of Middle Schools Annual Meeting and The Texas Middle School Association Conference in 2000, and submitted it for publication in 2002. I present dialogue in teaching as critical instruction for engaging students in reading, writing, speaking, and listening—four key components of literacy.

Tales from Two Textbooks

A Comparison of the Civil Rights Movement in Two Secondary History Textbooks

TERRIE L. EPSTEIN

Recent controversies in California and New York over the adoption and use of history textbooks and other social studies curricular materials in schools have brought to the fore what historians and others have noted for years—history, as a written account of the past, is a humanly constructed interpretation of the causes, course, and consequence of past events (Holt 1990; Megill 1989; Cronon 1992). As such, the historical narrative—that is the written text—that forms the foundation of history textbooks, will differ as history textbook authors' interpretations of past events vary. Differences in interpretations between or among historical narratives are significant, for they have implications for citizenship education. A historical narrative, for example, that presents the causes, course, and consequences of historical change primarily from the perspectives of elites, contains few lessons about the roles marginalized groups have played in transforming and attempting to transform their lives and their society, especially in the face of unjust laws, customs, and institutions. Conversely, historical narratives that present non-elites or subordinated people as capable of creating, participating, and experiencing the effects of historical change provide not only a richer and more complex portrayal of how historical change occurs, but a more positive, powerful, and relevant image to young people from marginalized groups of the risks, opportunities, and alternatives people like themselves have pursued in the past.

In this article, I illustrate how the historical interpretations in selected sections of the text in two secondary level history

textbooks differ significantly. The selections on the civil rights movement from the first textbook present elites and one or two selected African-American leaders as the driving force for change, whereas the other textbook presents marginalized people as intelligent actors working in concert to pursue a range of alternative strategies and actions in attempting to transform their lives. The first interpretation, by presenting marginalized people in a passive light, contains few portrayals of empowerment for young people from marginalized groups to draw upon. The interpretation in the second textbook promotes a more active and empowered portrayal of marginalized people as those capable of confronting and living with the consequences of change. I conclude by proposing that historical interpretations that present empowered rather than passive portrayals of marginalized people should be considered as a basis for textbook selection, especially, but not exclusively, for young people from marginalized groups.

Methodology

Below is a comparison of two secondary-level United States history textbooks' narratives on the civil rights movement. They were chosen because they present two very different perspectives on the roles of elites and marginalized groups. The first narrative described in each section is taken from Daniel J. Boorstin and Mather Kelley's (1992) *A History of the United States*. One of the five top-selling textbooks in the country, the Boorstin and Kelley textbook

was chosen as an example of a textbook whose authors give greater weight to political and military history and present events from the perspectives of elites (Davis et al. 1986; Gagnon 1988; Sewall 1987). The second set of examples is taken from Winthrop D. Jordan, Mirium Greenbelt, and John S. Bowes' (1991) *The Americans: A History*. Winthrop Jordan, a specialist in African-American history, has presented the civil rights movement from the perspectives of African Americans as instrumental in causing, setting the course, and being affected by the consequences of historical change.

The handling of the civil rights movement in each text is analyzed in the following way. Three separate sections of the text are compared by contrasting the authors' perspectives on the causes, course, and consequences of change. Specifically, I focus on who the author credits with causing particular acts, actions, or events within the civil rights movement, the relationship between the actions and ideologies of elites and mass movements in causing change, and the perspective from which the author describes the consequences of change.

Two Textbook Accounts of the Civil Rights Movement

Brown v. the Board of Education

In a five-page section entitled "The Fight for Equality," the Boorstin and Kelley textbook begins by noting that African Americans in the 1940s and 1950s "struggled to be equal." "Soldiers who had fought for democracy, and workers who had helped bring victory, refused to be second class citizens. They objected to segregation and every other kind of inequality." In the following section, "The Supreme Court Fights for Equality," African-Americans' sense of objection and struggle is lost. After a short review of the 1896 *Plessy v. Ferguson* case that established court-sanctioned segregation, the authors write,

Who had the power to complain if the schools were not really equal? Most blacks were kept from voting in the South, so they had no way of forcing government officials to listen. The Supreme Court had okayed the two-nation South.

In the South, blacks continued to have the worst of everything. In any case, people who are forced to use separate washrooms and water fountains and schools not used by other Americans are not being allowed to be equal…

Finally in a series of decisions the United States Supreme Court began to outlaw southern practices and laws that had taken from blacks their full rights as Americans. In three separate decisions—in 1944, 1947 and 1953—the court declared that the laws that kept blacks from voting in the Democratic primaries violated the Fourteenth Amendment…. And in 1950, after hearing a case argued by the persuasive Thurgood Marshall for the NAACP, the Court declared that the black law school in Texas could not possibly be made equal to the prestigious University of Texas Law School.

In 1953, President Eisenhower appointed former Governor Earl Warren of California as the Supreme Court's new Chief Justice…. He was to be deeply influenced by two of the Court's most forceful justices, Hugo Black and William O. Douglas. During the Warren years the Supreme Court would make many far-reaching decisions on segregation, the rights of criminals and legislative apportionment within the states.

Perhaps no decision of the Warren Court was more significant than *Brown v. Board of Education of Topeka, Kansas.* This case too had been argued by Thurgood Marshall, who would become the first black to sit on the Supreme Court when he was appointed by President Johnson. A unanimous Court ordered that, under the Constitution, public schools could not be separated by race. Americans had the right to go to school with all other Americans of their age and

grade. This was a part of their education. No American should be deprived of that right. The opposite of separation was "integration"—bringing together into one. And the Supreme Court now seemed to say that all public schools in the United States had to be "integrated." (p. 738)

Although the Boorstin textbook begins by crediting African Americans with "objecting to segregation and every other kind of inequality," it then renders them powerless three paragraphs later by noting that because African Americans were denied the right to vote, they had no other recourse, no way of "forcing government officials to listen." The text then notes how African Americans in the South had the worst of everything, yet did little to change their conditions. The driving force for change is the Supreme Court, remedying African Americans' problems by granting them the rights they needed but apparently did little to procure. The Supreme Court "insisted," through a series of Court actions, that separate was not equal. With the help of the persuasive powers of one great African American, Thurgood Marshall, the Court systematically chiseled away at segregation.

The discussion of the *Brown* case and its consequences similarly are written about from the perspectives of Supreme Court and congressional actions. The text concentrates on the composition of the Court and the decision making of the justices over the years. The text also credits the contribution of one prominent African-American attorney and notes he, too, becomes a member of the Court in later years. Who brought the case, the conditions that led the plaintiffs to sue the courts, and its influence on African Americans and others is left undiscussed.

In the comparable section entitled "Minorities Make Some Progress," the Jordan et al. text, like the Boorstin and Kelley text, lays the groundwork for discussing the *Brown* case by noting that African Americans made progress in "the continuing struggle to end racial discrimination throughout the United States." Unlike the Boorstin text, however, the Jordan text notes progress resulted both from court action and from "the political technique of civil disobedience." The Jordan text describes the individuals and issues involved in the cases leading up to the *Brown,* the case itself, and its consequences from the perspective of individual and collective actions of African Americans. In a section entitled, "Americans Try to End Discrimi-

nation," the Jordan et al. text includes the following:

Beginning with the mid-1930s, the NAACP had concentrated its limited resources on winning equal educational opportunities for black Americans. By the mid-1950s, the effort resulted in a precedent-shattering decision by the Supreme Court.

Early Cases. The first significant challenge to the "separate but equal" doctrine established by *Plessy v. Ferguson* occurred in 1938. Lloyd Gaines, an African American, wanted to study law at the University of Missouri. Since the state did not have a law school for black students, it offered to pay Gaines' tuition at a Canadian school. Gaines sued. The Supreme Court held that since Gaines expected to practice law in Missouri, he was entitled to receive his legal training there….

Over the next fifteen years, the Supreme Court heard several similar cases…. A typical case was *Sweatt v. Painter* (1950). Texas had organized a separate law school for a single black applicant, Herman N. Sweatt. Sweatt refused to attend on the ground that the school was inferior. The Court agreed, and Sweatt was finally enrolled at the University of Texas Law School….

The Brown Case. All this legal action was a rehearsal for the 1954 decision in the case of *Brown et al. v. Board of Education of Topeka* (Kansas)….

Oliver Brown, a black resident of Topeka, brought legal action against the school board on behalf of his eight-year-old daughter Linda. She had been denied admission to the all-white elementary school a few blocks from her house. Instead, she had to cross a railroad yard and then take a bus for twenty-one blocks to an all-black school. The attorney for the NAACP, which represented Brown, was Thurgood Marshall, who later became the first black Supreme Court justice.

Reaction to the Decision. *Brown v. Board of Education* affected 12 million children. It has been called the most important event in black history since the Thirteenth Amendment. African Americans throughout the nation greeted it with joy and hope. (pp. 801–02)

The Jordan textbook presents a very different conception of historical change reflected in the *Brown* case. Rather than locating the causes of change in law solely in the courts, the authors give considerable credit to the organization and efforts of many African Americans. The text notes the NAACP had worked since the 1930s to obtain equal educational opportunities for African Americans, an effort that paid off with the *Brown* decision. In explaining the court cases leading up to *Brown,* the text describes them from the perspectives of the individuals who had the courage to bring the case to court and the circumstances that led them to take action. In contrast to the Boorstin description of *Sweatt v. Painter,* where it only mentions Thurgood Marshall argued the case, the Winthrop text raises how Sweatt's refusal to attend an inferior school paid off.

Similarly, Jordan begins the discussion of the *Brown* case from the perspective of Oliver Brown. Whereas the Boorstin text explains the background to the court case by describing the membership and future influence of the Court, the Jordan textbook details the social conditions Oliver Brown's daughter and other African-American children endured, which motivated Oliver Brown to sue the court in the first place. Jordan also notes Oliver Brown, the NAACP, and Thurgood Marshall each played a part in the development and success of the case. Although the text credits the boycott for unleashing other forms and acts of nonviolent civil disobedience, it makes no connection between the mass actions thousands of African Americans participated in and the passage of the early Civil Rights Acts, the consequences of which are described in terms of congressional and national politics. And unlike the Boorstin textbook, the Jordan text explicitly explains the significance of the ruling to African Americans, placing it within the broader context of African-American history. In short, the two textbooks present very different portrayals of the roles marginalized people have played in the making and significance of historical change.

As the following section illustrates, the Boorstin and Kelley textbook sets the context for the Montgomery Bus Boycott of 1955 in terms of the inspired leadership of one great man, Martin Luther King.

Martin Luther King and Mrs. Rosa Parks. In the 1950s the nation was ready for the work of Martin Luther King, Jr. He began in a small way and in one place. Within a few years his message had carried out to the world....

On December 1 1955, Rosa Parks, a tired black seamstress returning from work, boarded a crowded bus in Montgomery, Alabama. She took a seat in the front row of the section of the bus reserved for black passengers. When she was told to give up her seat to a white man and move farther back in the bus, she refused. The police arrested her for violating the law.

Martin Luther King, who was then a Baptist minister in Montgomery, agreed with Mrs. Parks that it was time for action. It was time to stop any Americans from being degraded.

The nonviolent way. Although King was indignant and saddened, he was not angry. He was a thoughtful man, and a Christian, and he decided to try another way.... It was the way of massive and nonviolent opposition to unjust laws.... So he preached to the blacks of Montgomery. He told them to stop using the buses until the buses gave them their place as Americans. Of course many blacks were angry. But Martin Luther King begged and pleaded with them to keep their heads, and to keep love in their hearts, even while they joined the bus boycott. (pp. 740-41)

Although later on in the section, the authors credit "the blacks and all the decent people of Montgomery" for the success of the Montgomery boycott, the entire boycott is set within the context of the work of Martin Luther King. Rather than viewing King's message or methods as a reflection of a movement, Boorstin sets the context of the civil rights movement within the context of one man's mystique and message. Rosa Parks' courageous act is written about, not as a significant act in and of itself, but as a springboard for King's decision that it "was time for action." It also appears King single-handedly came up with the idea of a boycott, and his preaching of nonviolence alone motivated thousands of African Americans to boycott Montgomery's buses. Given this account, one wonders if there would have been a boycott if Martin Luther King had not directed it.

In the Jordan et al. textbook selection cited here, a very different interpretation of the Montgomery bus boycott and King's role within it is described.

Integrated Public Facilities. Even before Little Rock had shown that the struggle for school integration would be long and difficult, African Americans in the South had begun using direct action rather than court cases to bring about change. The shift in tactics was triggered by a black woman in Montgomery, Alabama. **Rosa Parks.** On December 1, 1955, a seamstress Rosa Parks was returning home on a city bus. Tired after a long day's work, she sat down in the front section, which was reserved for whites. A white passenger entered and the bus driver ordered the seamstress to give up her seat, as the laws said she must. As Rosa Parks told it afterwards, "For a long time I resented being treated a certain way because of my race. We had always been taught that America was the land of the free and the home of the brave and that we were all equals." So, Rosa Parks said "No." At the next bus stop, she was arrested and, later, fined ten dollars.

Within forty-eight hours, the black community of Montgomery had organized a one-day boycott of the city's bus line. It was a complete success, and it set black leaders to thinking. There were 25,000 black people in the city, and they made up about 75 percent of the bus company's customers. Suppose they refused to ride the buses until certain conditions were met, such as allowing black people to sit wherever they wanted, hiring black drivers for buses in black areas, and instructing white bus drivers to be polite to black passengers. If the bus company lost three-fourths of its customers, surely it would eventually be forced either to agree to the conditions or to go out of business.

Martin Luther King, Jr. At the head of the association formed to carry out the boycott was a twenty-six year old minister named Martin Luther King, Jr.... King persuaded his fellow blacks to keep their protests entirely nonviolent....

The struggle in Montgomery was not easy. Negotiations between black leaders and the bus company broke down early. The boycott continued for more than a year....

Hope for the Sixties. The Montgomery bus boycott was a bright spot in the civil rights movement. It produced an organization, a leader, and a technique. Additional groups, mostly church centered, sprang up and were brought together by King in the Southern Christian Leadership Conference. This organization was to play a major role during the 1960s. (pp. 803-04)

Unlike the Boorstin and Kelley textbook, which organizes the Montgomery bus boycott around Martin Luther King's philosophical beliefs and political acumen, the Winthrop textbook credits African Americans in the South generally and the African-American community in Montgomery in particular for the organization and success of the boycott and for the effects of mass action on future developments. The authors also credit Rosa Parks' courageous actions for being the catalyst that mobilized a community, and they quote her directly. They also credit the logic and deliberations of several black leaders, including King, in figuring out a direction for change. The authors also look at the effect of the boycott in terms of it having produced an organization and a technique that were instrumental in accomplishing change in other times and places.

Early Civil Rights Acts

In describing the Civil Rights Acts of 1957 and 1960, the Boorstin and Kelley textbook presents the consequences of the acts not in terms of the thousands of African Americans they intended to benefit but from the perspectives of congressional actions and national party politics.

Civil Rights Laws. Now the federal government moved, too. In August 1957 the Eisenhower administration finally won the first Civil Rights Act since the days of Reconstruction. It was not an earthshaking law. The main thing that it did was to give the Justice Department the right to bring suits on behalf of blacks who were denied the right to vote. The real significance of the measure was that it passed and that it was a truly bipartisan measure. Republicans and Democrats working together overcame the resistance and filibusters of the southern members to pass this bill....

This was followed in 1960 by another Civil Rights Act, again passed with bipartisan support. It gave even more aid to blacks who wanted to vote. When the Republicans and the Democrats met in their conventions to draw up platforms and select candidates for the Presidency in 1960, both parties supported desegregation. (p. 741)

Conversely, the Jordan et al. text describes the 1957 Civil Rights Act based on its potential effects on the millions of African Americans it sought to serve.

Also significant for the future was the Civil Rights Act of 1957. It was the first such act since Reconstruction, and it was passed only after a legislative struggle that included a Senate debate lasting three days. The act set up a Civil Rights Commission and gave the Justice Department the power to file suits on behalf of black citizens who were denied the right to vote.

Black voter registration in the South was 1.2 million in 1956, but it was estimated that throughout the region, at least 5 million African Americans were eligible to vote. (p. 804)

Race Riots and Black Power

In explaining the race riots that erupted in the North in the mid-1960s, the Boorstin textbook begins by explaining that civil rights laws did little for African Americans in the North, who faced housing and employment discrimination. Although the text mentions the rioting in Watts, followed by more than 100 other riots in the following three years, the reader learns nothing about the causes of rioting from the perspectives of the people involved. Rather, the text describes the causes and consequences of violence from the perspective of President Johnson.

LBJ was stunned by Watts. He had just signed his great Voting Rights Act into law—and now this. "How is this possible," he asked, "after all we've accomplished?" Johnson was understandably bitter. For the riots hurt his Great Society programs. They seemed so aimless and only served to destroy, when what was needed was to build.... The President tried to understand. "God knows how little we've really moved on this issue," he said, "despite all the fanfare. As I see it I've moved the Negro from D + to C −. He's still nowhere. He knows it. And that's why he's out in the streets. (p. 806)

Similarly, the diversity of opinion in the African-American community on how historical change should occur is downplayed and discredited. Whereas the text's approval of the political philosophy and strategy of Martin Luther King is obvious, it barely describes and then discredits alternative perspectives within the African-American community. Malcolm X is described as a handsome ex-convict who called all whites "devils." And although the text relates something about Malcolm X's changing views on white Americans, it tells little else about the appeal of his views to the thousands of African Americans and how his views were a response to the racism that spawned riots throughout the North.

Malcolm X. He thought whites and blacks should be separate and that blacks should have a nation of their own. Malcolm's eloquent voice carried a message of hate. "When I speak," he said, "I speak

as a victim of America's so-called democracy."

.... He did not follow Martin Luther King's Christian gospel of nonviolence. But after a pilgrimage to Mecca, where all true Muslims were supposed to go once in their lives, he began to change his view that all whites were born evil. For true Muslims believed that all races were equal. Malcolm X's career ended in a blaze of gunfire from several of his many black opponents in February 1965. His powerful *Autobiography,* which came out after his death in 1965, fanned both black anger and black pride. (pp. 806-07)

Similarly, the text describes Stokely Carmichael as a young black radical who "preached black power" and negatively compares him to Martin Luther King. "Martin Luther King had preached love and human brotherhood. Now the angry champions of Black Power mainly wanted to be able to 'get even.' They wanted their chance to lord it over others." Again, the text tells nothing about the views of Stokely Carmichael nor the meaning of the black power movement nor the movement's effect, if any, on the changes African Americans sought. The text describes the consequences of rioting and the black power movement in a negative light, solely as ones of loss and ineffectiveness.

By the fall of 1966 the civil rights movement was divided and in disarray. White backlash grew stronger. For the first time in recent years, a civil rights measure failed to pass Congress. The summer of 1967 saw the worst rioting in United States history. Blacks went on the rampage, destroying their own neighborhoods. (p. 807)

In concluding this section on the civil rights movement, Boorstin and Kelley turn to LBJ's actions or abilities, or lack thereof, in effecting change. "Again during 1967, LBJ asked for new civil rights laws, but Congress was no longer sympathetic. About all that LBJ could do that year was to appoint Thurgood Marshall to the Supreme Court...."

Like the Boorstin and Kelley textbook, the Jordan et al. textbook locates the cause of the riots and the black power movement in terms of racial discrimination in the North. The text then, however, views the riots from the perspectives of people in the African-American community who were affected. Rather than quoting President Johnson's interpretation of why African Americans in northern cities rioted, the text quotes Bayard Rustin, a "moderate black leader," who quotes in turn a young black man on the cause of the riot: "We won," the young African American told Rustin. "We won because we made the whole world pay attention to us. The police chief never came here before; the mayor always stayed uptown. We made them come" (p. 843).

Perhaps the most obvious difference between the two textbooks in interpreting the civil rights movement is in their explanations and significance of the black power movement. The Jordan et al. textbook describes Malcolm X not as a "handsome ex-convict" but as the founder of the organization for Afro-American Unity. The text describes the difference between King's philosophy and Malcolm X's not by simply discrediting Malcolm X's views but by quoting him directly, "The day of nonviolent resistance is over. If they have the Ku Klux Klan nonviolent, I'll be nonviolent.... But as long as you've got somebody else not being nonviolent, I don't want anybody coming to me talking any nonviolent talk" (p. 843). The quote reveals a logic and what many in the African-American community believed a legitimacy to Malcolm X's views on the needed course of change in the civil rights movement.

Unlike the Boorstin and Kelley book, which describes the black power movement simply as a message of hate and desire to get even, the Jordan et al. textbook describes the black power movement as a series of strategies to empower the African-American community, including "(1) the development of black-owned businesses in black communities, (2) local control of schools in black communities, (3) the use of black police officers in black communities, (4) bloc voting to elect black representatives who would give priority to the needs of black communities, and (5) the development of a sense of pride in being black" (pp. 843-4).

Finally, unlike the Boorstin and Kelley textbook that only attributes negative consequences to the black power movement and concludes the segment on civil rights by noting President Johnson's limited options in furthering the course of change, the Jordan et al. textbook finds a balance in judging the consequences of the black power movement and describes both positive and negative results. Whereas the Boorstin text credits President Johnson with appointing Thurgood Marshall to the

Supreme Court, the Jordan text includes Marshall's appointment as one of six consequences of the black power movement. In addition, he credits the movement with electing more African Americans to public office, increasing employment opportunities and business ownership, and pushing Congress to pass the 1968 Civil Rights Act. The Jordan textbook also describes the movement's negative aspects by noting how the effects of statements and actions of more militant African Americans helped to cause the loss of white support for civil rights (p. 844). Overall, the authors present Malcolm X and the black power movement as legitimate and logical voices and visions in causing and influencing the course of historical change.

Implications

Of late, educators have been concerned with providing school policies and practices to empower students who have not been well served by the public schools. In the area of curriculum, James Banks (1991) has called for a "transformative and empowering curriculum." Such a curriculum, he writes, "cannot be constructed merely by adding content about ethnic groups and women to the existing Euro-centric curriculum or by integrating or infusing ethnic content or content about women into the mainstream curriculum". Rather, he and others argue, a curriculum must be constructed that, among other things, presents content that will enable students to develop their own "sense of empowerment and efficacy over their lives and their destinies".

In the case of history textbooks, the differences that exist in historical interpretations can serve to further or diminish these ends. As part of a large literature assessing history textbooks, a number of articles have critiqued history textbooks in terms of their inclusion or lack thereof of marginalized groups, such as African Americans (Garcia and Tanner 1985), women (Tetreault 1984, Tetreault 1986), Native Americans, and others who traditionally have been excluded. None of these studies, however, has looked at the differences among textbooks and specifically, how differences in interpretations tell very different tales about a marginalized group's historical experience. Such differences are

significant, for they can serve as a curricular foundation for providing images of empowerment for young people of color and others whose histories in many textbooks and other curricular materials have barely moved beyond lionizing the heroic.

In selecting history textbooks, parents, teachers, and school and state committees interested in providing more positive and powerful images of marginalized groups need to consider not just the amount of information included on people of color, women, and working people but the perspective from which the information is presented. Historical interpretations in history textbooks that present people of color, women, working people, and other marginalized groups as active participants not only provide images of empowerment for young people who can identify most directly with those groups, but provide the foundation for a curricular framework to enable all students to respect the roles marginalized people have played in causing, pursuing the course, and living with the consequences of historical change.

TERRIE L. EPSTEIN teaches in the School of Education at the University of Michigan at Ann Arbor.

REFERENCES

Banks, J. 1991. A curriculum for empowerment, action and change. In *Empowerment through Multicultural Education,* edited by C. Sleeter, (pp. 125–42). Albany: SUNY Press.

Boorstin, D. J., and M. Kelley. 1992. *A history of the United States.* Needham, Mass.: Prentice-Hall.

Cronon, W. 1992. A place for stories: Nature, history, and narrative. *The Journal of American History* 78: 1347–1376.

Davis, O. L., G. Ponder, L. M. Burlaw, M. G. Garza-Lubek, and A. Moss. 1986. *Looking at history: Review of major U.S. history textbooks.* Washington, DC: People for the American Way.

Gagnon, P. 1988. Why study history? *The Atlantic Monthly* 262: 43–66.

Holt, T. 1990. *Thinking historically: Narrative, imagination and understanding.* New York: College Board.

Garcia, J., and D. E. Tanner. 1985. The portrayal of black Americans in U.S. history textbooks. *The Social Studies* 76: 200–203.

Jordan, W., M. Greenblatt, and J. S. Bowes, 1991. *The Americans: A History.* Evanston, Ill.: McDougal, Littel

Megill, A. 1989. Recounting the past: Description, explanation and narrative in historiography. *American Historical Review* 75: 627–53.

Sewall, G. T. 1987. *American history textbooks: An assessment of quality.* New York: Educational Excellence Network.

From *The Social Studies,* May/June 1994. © 1994 by Heldref Publications, 1319, Eighteenth St., NW, Washington, DC 20036-1802. Reprinted with permission of the Helen Dwight Reid Educational Foundation.

THE STORY OF OURSELVES

Fostering Multiple Historical Perspectives

MICHAEL O. TUNNELL AND RICHARD AMMON

In Chicago, Native Americans marched in protest, proclaiming Columbus Day a day of infamy. Not long after, Italian Americans paraded in the streets to honor their hero, the Admiral of the Ocean Sea. The controversy surrounding the quincentennial commemoration of Columbus's voyage provided a clear reminder that people will always view historical events from different perspectives. Although it may be unsettling at times, the debate about the merits of Columbus and his "discovery" suggests to us important questions about how we should view history and how we should study it in our classrooms.

We have often presented a narrow view of history to our school children, giving them the impression that there is little, if any, variation in the interpretation of our past. We should remember, however, that the recounting of history is subjective, and, according to Hayden White (1980, 23), "unless at least two versions of the same set of events can be imagined, there is no reason for the historian to take upon himself the authority of giving the true account of what really happened."

Making Judgments About History

Recognition of multiple historical perspectives is fundamental to good history teaching. But Bardige (1988) points out that simply presenting children with multiple perspectives may give them the impression that all perspectives are of equal worth. Therefore, teachers must help students learn how to evaluate the merit of particular interpretations of historical events. Making judgments based on a well-rounded gathering of information is a vital critical thinking procedure, and "part of that exploration [of the past] includes an opportunity to study and evalu-

ate human behavior in a developmentally appropriate context" (Levstik 1989, 136). Levstik also believes that trade book literature provides a better context for the young history student than do textbooks by "inviting the reader to enter into a historical discussion that involves making judgments about issues of morality. ... What was it like to be a person here? What was the nature of good and evil in that time and place, and with whom shall my sympathies lie?".

Comparing Textbooks and Trade Books

One of the problems with most elementary and secondary school history textbooks is that history is presented from a single perspective with few conflicting ideas. "When a textbook is used as the only source of information, students tend to accept the author's statements without question" (Holmes and Ammon 1985, 366). Holmes and Ammon suggest that incorporating trade books (fiction and nonfiction) into content area studies aids in developing critical reading skills such as determining the reliability and authenticity of printed sources. Teachers should guide students toward trade books and other materials that present conflicting points of view, a practice that not only encourages students to make historical judgments but also increases students' interest in the subjects.

William Bigelow (1989, 635) goes a step further, pointing out in uncompromising terms the weakness of history textbooks: "Students don't know ... that year after year their textbooks, by omission or otherwise, have been lying to them on a grand scale." Milton Meltzer (1992, 1) softens this indictment by calling such lying "selective forgetfulness." Patrick Shan-

non (1989, 101) calls it covert censorship, which he defines in part as "the unconscious presentation of just one side of an issue which distorts reality by making it seem that the one position is all there is worth considering about the issue." For example, one recently published sixth grade level social studies textbook does not mention Malcolm X or the viewpoint of his followers in its eight pages on equal rights. The Holocaust is given a single paragraph, hardly room for any perspective at all. Moreover, this popular text does not even include the words *art, music,* or *poetry* in its index. This omission seems to suggest that political and military affairs are the only important matters in history.

Whether intentional or unintentional, the omission of multiple perspectives has debilitating effects on students. Bigelow (1989) uses the treatment of Columbus as an example, pointing out that even the word *discovery*, as used in textbooks, is a loaded term that subtly suggests a particular perspective. It echoes the perspective of "the invaders, masking the theft" and makes it more difficult for students to empathize with the native populations.

In fact, textbooks avoid the Native American perspective of Columbus. Most fifth grade American history textbooks limit the coverage of Columbus to a page or two of print, and in that brief space offer only a Eurocentric point of view. Any reference to his conquest or cruel treatment of the native peoples is missing. For instance, some fifth grade texts hardly mention the Taino or Arawak people whom Columbus encountered, except to describe them as peaceful. Many of the texts do not mention that Columbus, during his first voyage, captured several of the Indians and later forced them to parade in front of Ferdinand and Isabella, his royal sponsors. Note, however, the following textbook excerpt in which this incident is included.

> The two peoples exchanged gifts. ... But these friendly Native Americans offered no silks or spices or gold, for they had none of these to give. Columbus was disappointed that he had found no gold and had not yet found China or Japan. But he was sure he had reached Asia. To prove it, he brought six Indians with him when he returned to Spain. (Bass 1995, 123–124)

Although the text does say that Indians returned to Spain with Columbus, the language conveys a completely positive connotation. The Indians were friendly, so the reader can easily assume that when Columbus brought them along they came voluntarily. Words like *forced* or *captured* would give another, more accurate impression.

Multiple Perspectives in Trade Books

Many picture books, biographies, novels, and informational books have been published about Columbus's voyages of exploration. Some of these trade books deal with Columbus in more varied and accurate terms than do textbooks. Compare the following trade book excerpt with the textbook excerpt quoted earlier.

> ... Lief [ship's boy] heard a heartrending shout. He looked and saw one of the natives standing in a canoe, his hand raised toward them. Lief would never forget the look of grief on his face. He was the father of some of the children in the group. He begged to be allowed to join his family in captivity. Columbus had the man pulled on board and added to the captives, pleased to have a "volunteer" living specimen. (Foreman 1992, 30–31)

Information in trade books often does not agree from title to title. Therefore, when used together, these books give students the best opportunity to compare, contrast, and evaluate the so-called facts of history. Some titles paint Columbus in purely heroic colors. Others present a balanced view of his positive and negative attributes, while still other titles come close to vilifying the explorer and his conquest.

The American Revolution is another topic often taught from a single perspective that can be approached from multiple perspectives through trade books. Before 1960, authors of children's books about the Revolution used the Whig interpretation exclusively, described by Christopher Col-

lier (1976, 132) as "moralistic and pedantic, depicting simple, freedom-loving farmers marching in a crusade." The classic novel *Johnny Tremain* (Forbes 1943) exemplifies this viewpoint.

After 1960, children's novels began to provide a broader choice of perspectives about the American Revolution. The consensus interpretation, a more refined version of the Whig interpretation in which good and evil are no longer assigned to sides in the war, was common in the 1970s (Taxel 1983). But some unusual books [*My Brother Sam if Dead* (Collier and Collier 1974); *Who Comes to King's Mountain* (Beatty and Beatty 1975); *When the World's on Fire* (Edwards 1972)] featured young protagonists who are indecisive about or uncommitted to the Patriot cause or even go so far as to reject it. Edwards's *When the World's on Fire* (1972) takes several unusual yet valid approaches to presenting the Revolution. First, the story is told by a black protagonist, thus confronting the paradox of a war fought for individual liberties in which many leaders held slaves. Also, Edwards does not concentrate on the Whig-Tory division among the colonists, but rather exposes the divisions among the patriots–artisans versus aristocrats.

In the 1980s, a number of books about the American Revolution were published that contained more realistic characters and that examined a wider range of human motives for and emotions about the conflict. In Avi's *The Fighting Ground* (1984), the young protagonist, Jonathan, changes from being a zealous Patriot to wondering which side, if any, he is on. It is interesting that the battle in Avi's story is against Hessian mercenaries, who suddenly seem to Jonathan no worse than the American corporal who has directed the execution of a Tory family. *Sarah Bishop* by Scott O'Dell (1980) shows a girl from a Tory family who is brutalized by the war and eventually flees to a place safe from the Patriots and the British alike. James Lincoln and Christopher Collier (1981) wrote *Jump Ship to Freedom*, the first in a trilogy [*War Comes to Willy Freeman* (1983), *Who Is Carrie?* (1984)] that has young black protagonists. Set against the background of the Constitutional Convention, this novel focuses on the futile hopes of American blacks, including war veterans, that the new government might actually provide liberty and justice for all.

Reading about the Constitutional Convention from the black American perspective will help students better understand

the human motives leading to the U.S. Civil War. The seeds of civil conflict were sown in 1787 with The Great Compromise, which granted the newly formed states representation based on population. Levy's *If You Were There When They Signed the Constitution* (1987, 50–51) clearly alerts young readers to the ticking time bomb: "The problem was how to count the slaves. The southern states wanted to count their slaves as people. The northern states didn't want to count the slaves. Gouverneur Morris [of Pennsylvania] asked, 'Are they men? Then make them citizens and let them vote.'" The question of slavery was not to be answered for another seventy-seven years.

Trade books also offer young readers a variety of perspectives about the War Between the States. In *Voices from the Civil War*, Milton Meltzer (1989) presents multiple points of view by drawing on documents and letters written by eyewitnesses to the actual events. In *Walk Together Children* (Bryan 1974) and *I'm Going to Sing* (Bryan 1982), students experience the agony of slavery through spirituals, especially the sorrow songs such as "Deep River," "Motherless Child," and "Nobody Knows the Trouble I See."

Just as students often believe that all Colonials were Patriots, they often think that all Yankees were Abolitionists. Clinton Cox (1991, 5) in *Undying Glory* wrote, "Pro-slavery sentiment was so widespread in the North at the beginning of the war that many Union generals allowed slave owners to come into their camps and seize escaped slaves." Using the Draft Riots in New York City as an example, Meltzer (1989, 83) dispels the myth of a unified North: "Whites were being drafted to fight to free the hated 'niggers,' who would then come North to take their jobs at even lower pay."

Ina Chang (1991) in *A Separate Battle* examines female perspectives of the Civil War by looking at such notable women as Sojourner Truth, Harriet Tubman, Clara Barton, Louisa May Alcott, and Dorothea Dix–as well as dozens of women who disguised themselves as men to fight in the army. Also, more than 250,000 children and young adults fought in the Civil War and recorded their perspectives in letters and diaries. In *The Boy's War*, Jim Murphy (1990) shares accounts that paint a disturbing picture of the senseless waste and brutality that transformed children into hardened veterans.

In his historical novel *Bull Run*, Paul Fleischman (1993) develops sixteen characters with diverse backgrounds and viewpoints on the events surrounding the war's first major land battle. Another historical novel, *Across Five Aprils* by Irene Hunt (1964), tells the story of the Civil War through the experiences of nine-year-old Jethro Creighton. He watches his family and southern Illinois farming community split asunder by divided loyalties.

By examining the black American perspective of the American Revolution and the Civil War, students may be better equipped to connect the past with the present as they learn about the civil rights movement in the twentieth century. In *Reconstruction: America After the Civil War*, Zak Mettger (1994) spells out the conditions that brought us to the civil rights movement in the 1950s and 1960s, and even to some current states' rights initiatives of the 1990s. She writes, "Slavery was a thing of the past. ... [But] with bureau agents and federal troops no longer on the scene to protect freed slaves, white planters felt free to write restrictive labor contracts, use physical punishment, and create slave-like working conditions".

"Jim Crow" laws kept blacks and whites separated for nearly another hundred years. In a biography titled *Duke Ellington*, James Lincoln Collier (1991, 92) emphasizes these restrictions: "[Ellington] could not, even though he had been invited to the White House, get into the best white hotels and restaurants even in the North. ..." Patricia and Frederick McKissack, Jr. (1994) tell a similar story of black professional athletes who were deprived of equal living and working conditions in *Black Diamond: The Story of Negro Baseball Leagues*.

Young readers may appreciate another perspective of the African American plight found in the paintings of Jacob Lawrence (1993) as reproduced in *The Great Migration*. This collection depicts the exodus of African Americans from the poverty of the South to jobs in the North. Music and poetry also can illuminate a historical perspective with unusual power, like the stirring poems of Langston Hughes that capture the African American experience. Students may feel the spirit of the civil rights movement when singing freedom songs or other popular folk songs of that era, such as "If I Had a Hammer," found in *Gonna Sing My Head Off!* (Krull 1992).

Few perspectives of the same issue seemed as different as those of Martin Luther King, Jr., and Malcolm X. In his biography, *Martin Luther King, Jr.*, David Adler (1989) credits King's strategy of nonviolent protest to his study of Mohan-

das Gandhi. Walter Dean Myers's (1993) biography of Malcolm X fleshes out this black leader, telling of the circumstances that led to his espousing a call to arms. In *Witnesses to Freedom*, Belinda Rochelle (1993) profiles nine ordinary people who helped desegregate schools, boycotted buses in Montgomery, joined sit-ins in North Carolina, or marched on Washington.

Ideas for Helping Students Compare and Evaluate Historical Accounts

William Bigelow (1989) suggests a strategy for questioning historical accounts about Columbus that can be readily applied to other historical topics. The following questions create an atmosphere of critical inquiry that necessitates the inclusion of multiple historical perspectives.

1. How factually accurate was the account?
2. What was omitted ... that in your judgments would be important for a full understanding of Columbus? [Or Frederick Douglass?]
3. What motives does the book give to Columbus? [Or American Revolution Patriots?] Compare those with his real motives. [Or with motives discussed in other books.]
4. Who does the book get you to root for, and how do the authors accomplish that?
5. What function do pictures in the books play? What do they communicate about Columbus [or Martin Luther King?] and his "enterprise"?
6. In your opinion, why does the book portray the Columbus/Indian encounter the way it does? [Or the encounters between trade unions and factory owners?]
7. Can you think of any groups in our society that might have an interest in people having an inaccurate view of history? (Bigelow 1989, 639)

With Bigelow's questions in mind, teachers and students are able to use a variety of trade books and other materials to examine history in broader contexts. Here are a few examples of this sort of teaching drawn from actual classroom experiences.

- A fifth grade class placed Columbus on trial, complete with prosecution and defense teams. Evidence was gathered from sources reflecting differing perspectives about Columbus.
- High school students took the roles of Loyalists and Rebels in an emotion-

laden debate before a judge concerning this question: "Resolved: The British government possesses the legitimate authority to tax the American colonies." Teachers observed a change in attitude among class members.

> At the beginning of the research days, the loyalist position was ridiculed, and students failed to see how any rational person could have resisted the rebels' call to arms. By studying documents favorable to the Tory position, however, students came to see that both sides had merit and that the issues were anything but simple (Wineburg and Wilson 1991, 410).

- American history classes created a multiethnic data chart for the American Revolution listing Black Americans, Native Americans, Anglo Revolutionaries, Anglo Loyalists, and Europeans (e.g., French, Germans). Then students asked and answered questions about each group, such as "What social effects did the Revolution have on them?" and "What overall changes did the Revolution cause in their group status?" (Gay and Banks 1975).

- A class searched for newspaper articles about current issues that relate to the historical topics they were studying, such as the Civil War issue of states' rights that is being debated once again in Congress.

Conclusion

Philosopher Ernst Nagel (1961) said that understanding history is a matter of understanding human motives. Because motive is inextricably intertwined with individual perspective about life's events, we must consider these multiple viewpoints if we hope to make sense of our heritage.

Russell Freedman (1993) called history "the story of ourselves." Others have noted that presenting history in terms of a strong, well-defined story seems to provide a natural framework for dealing with these human aims and values (Levstik 1993). Therefore, history-related trade books (both fiction and nonfiction) are one of the finest sources for providing young students with a broader, more complex, and more fascinating approach to telling "the story of ourselves."

References

Adler, D. *A Picture Book of Martin Luther King, Jr.* Illustrated by R. Casilla. New York: Holiday House, 1989.

Avi. *The Fighting Ground.* New York: Lippincott, 1984.

Bardige, B. "Things So Finely Human: Moral Sensibilities at Risk in Adolescence." In *Mapping the Moral Domain: A Contribution of Women s Thinking to Psychological Theory and Education*, edited by C. Gilligan, J. V. Ward, J. M. Taylor, 37–110. Cambridge, Mass.: Harvard University Press, 1988.

Bass, H. J. *Our Country.* Morristown. N.J.: Silver Burdett Ginn, 1995.

Beatty, J., and P. Beatty. *Who Comes to Kings Mountain?* New York: Morrow, 1975.

Bigelow, W. "Discovering Columbus: Rereading the Past" *Language Arts* 66 (1989): 635–43.

Bryan, A. *Walk Together Children.* New York: Atheneum, 1974.

———*I'm Going to Sing.* New York: Atheneum, 1982.

Chang, I. *A Separate Battle: Women and the Civil War.* New York: Lodestar, 1991.

Collier, C. "Johnny and Sam: Old and New Approaches to the American Revolution." *The Horn Book* 52 (1976): 132–38.

Collier, J. L. *Duke Ellington.* New York: Macmillan, 1991.

Collier, J. L., and C. Collier. *My Brother Sam Is Dead.* New York: Four Winds Press, 1974.

———*Jump Ship to Freedom.* New York: Delacorte, 1981.

———*War Comes to Willy Freeman.* New York: Delacorte, 1983.

———*Who Is Carrie?* New York: Delacorte, 1984.

Cox, C. *Undying Glory.* New York: Scholastic, 1991.

Edwards, S. *When the World's on Fire.* New York: Coward, McCann and Geoghegan, 1972.

Fleischman, P. *Bull Run.* New York: HarperCollins, 1993.

Forbes, E. *Johnny Tremain.* Boston: Houghton Mifflin, 1943.

Foreman, M. *The Boy Who Sailed with Columbus.* New York: Arcade (Little, Brown), 1992.

Freedman. R. "Bring 'Em Back Alive." In *The Story of Ourselves: Teaching History Through Children's Literature*, edited by M. O. Tunnell and R. Ammon, 41–47. Portsmouth, N.H.: Heinemann, 1993.

Gay, G., and J. A. Banks. "Teaching the American Revolution: A Multiethnic Approach." *Social Education* 39 (1975): 461–65.

Holmes, B., and R. Ammon. "Teaching Content with Trade Books." *Childhood Education* 61 (1985): 366–70.

Hunt, I. *Across Five Aprils.* New York: Follett, 1964.

Krull, K. *Gonna Sing My Head Off!* New York: Knopf, 1992.

Lawrence, J. *The Great Migration.* New York: HarperCollins, 1993.

Levstik, L. "A Gift of Time: Children's Historical Fiction" In *Children's Literature in the Classroom: Weaving Charlotte's Web*, edited by J. Hickman and B. Cullinan, 135–145. Needham Heights, Mass.: Christopher-Gordon, 1989.

———" 'I Wanted to Be There': The Impact of Narrative on Children's Historical Thinking." In *The Story of Ourselves: Teaching History Through Children's Literature*, edited by M. O. Tunnell and R. Ammon, 65–77. Portsmouth. N.H.: Heinemann, 1993.

Levy, E. *If You Were There When They Signed the Constitution.* Illustrated by R. Rosenblum. New York: Scholastic, 1987.

McKissack, P., and F. McKissack, Jr. *Black Diamond: The Story of the Negro Baseball Leagues.* New York: Scholastic, 1994.

Meltzer, M. *Voices from the Civil War.* New York: Crowell. 1989.

———"Selective Forgetfulness: Christopher Columbus Reconsidered." *The New Advocate* 5 (1992): 1–9.

Mettger, Z. *Reconstruction: America After the Civil War.* New York: Lodestar, 1994.

Murphy, J. *The Boys' War.* New York: Clarion, 1990.

Myers, W. D. *Malcolm X: By Any Means Necessary.* Scholastic, 1993.

Nagel, E. *The Structure of Science: Problems in the Logic of Scientific Explanation.* New York: Harcourt, Brace and World. 1961.

O'Dell, S. *Sarah Bishop.* Boston: Houghton Mifflin, 1980.

Rochelle, B. *Witnesses to Freedom: Young People Who Fought for Civil Rights.* New York: Lodestar, 1993.

Shannon, P. "Overt and Covert Censorship of Children's Books." *The New Advocate* 2 (1989): 97–104.

Taxel, J. "The American Revolution in Children's Fiction." *Research In Teaching English* 17 (1983): 61–68.

White, H. "The Value of Narrativity in the Representation of Reality." *Critical Inquiry* 7 (1980): 5–27.

Wineburg, S. S., and S. M. Wilson. "Models of Wisdom in the Teaching of History." *The History Teacher* 24 (1991): 395–412.

Michael O. Tunnell is Associate Professor of Education at Brigham Young University where he teaches children's literature. Besides numerous professional articles, he has written or edited several books, including The Story of Ourselves: Teaching History Through Children's Literature (Heinemann), Children's Literature, Briefly (Merrill/Prentice Hall), *and several titles for young readers. Richard Ammon is Associate Professor of Education and teaches children's literature and language arts at The Pennsylvania State University/Harrisburg. He has published professional articles in numerous journals, edited* The Story of Ourselves: Teaching History Through Children's Literature *(Heinemann), and written several nonfiction books for young readers.*

Using Textbooks with Students Who Cannot Read Them[1]

ABSTRACT

Too many students have difficulty comprehending information presented in the textbooks intended for their use. One reason for this is that textbooks are often organized so that the task of reading and thinking about them is made unduly difficult. Further, teacher editions offer little in the way of helping teachers improve the textbook's usability for students who struggle with reading. This article summarizes the existing literature on effective textbook instruction. The author then proposes how special educators and content instructors can combine their talents to compensate for poorly written books and maximize good books when teaching all their students, but particularly those students who do not learn in the expected ways.

JEAN CIBOROWSKI

STUDENTS WHO ARE BEHIND THEIR PEERS IN textbook reading do not need "watered down" textbooks, nor do they need "different" or "slower" instruction. Rather, they need instructors to help them discover how to gain or regain the confidence in their abilities and the control of their learning lost through years of an accumulation of academic frustrations and failures.

One way this can be achieved is through specific instructional techniques that are woven into three distinct but recursive phases of teaching and learning. These phases do not segment teaching and learning content into easier parts and pieces, but rather, they are techniques that help students connect and expand concepts in their reading, writing, and thinking behaviors.

For the student with low reading skills, the most critical phase is Phase 1 (before reading), because it is rooted strongly in the belief that all students have a reservoir of knowledge and experiences that can be utilized as a way to prep them for textbook learning. Once students feel that their prior knowledge is seriously recognized and valued, they can begin to see the connections between their unique experiences and what they are about to learn. Feeling empowered, students whose reading skills are low can slowly regain the confidence to learn and invent strategies for organizing and integrating the textbook content into what they already know.

Phase 2 (during reading) and Phase 3 (after reading) are opportunities for instructors to challenge their students who are poor readers as seriously as they challenge more adept readers. Once teachers learn to teach strategies for comprehending, studying, and consolidating the dramas, events, and phenomena found in the history, social studies, and science textbooks, they

may find that even those students once thought to be disinterested can discover new reasons for reading, grow in the capacity to think critically, and develop more positive attitudes toward school and learning.

BACKGROUND

The Struggle to Learn How to Read

More than likely, students who experience problems reading their textbooks encountered difficulty when learning to read in the early grades. Growing evidence supports the notion that for the young child, the most critical factor in forming the necessary building blocks of reading is phonological awareness (Chall, 1983; Haskell, Foorman, & Swank, 1992; Stanovich, 1986a; Vellutino, 1991). Typically, this awareness develops during the first grade, allowing the child to discover how letter-sound relationships are used to decode the printed word. Once the beginning reader can decode words both quickly and accurately, a level of automaticity is achieved that in turn facilitates reading fluency. Feeling gratified, the child is more likely to engage in reading practice so that speed and accuracy continue to increase. Like a train leaving the station, slowly mounting speed and power, the beginning reader accumulates enough successes to travel down the track toward increasingly satisfying reading experiences.

Unfortunately, for reasons that are not entirely clear, some children do not develop the necessary phonological awareness. As a result, they are unable to experience the intrinsic gratification that spurs reading speed and accuracy (Stanovich, 1986a,

1986b). Instead, for these children, early reading experiences are stressful and defeating. The children stay stuck on a stalled or painfully slow-moving train, acutely aware of their classmates moving past them with apparent ease.

For the child stuck in the early stages of reading, other areas of academic development will also suffer. Not only are spelling and writing skills intimately related to reading skills, but also, the struggling reader will be denied the opportunity to expand his or her knowledge base and vocabulary through reading experiences (Snider & Tarver, 1987). Presumably, what begins as a highly specific reading disability later compromises the development of other literacy skills. Ultimately, early reading difficulties spiral out of control, negatively affecting a child's ability to manage more conceptually dense materials such as the expository text found in textbooks. Because these children have not learned to read efficiently, reading to learn from their textbooks is overwhelmingly difficult. As they move up in the grades, many never catch up to their peers. As the gap between what they can read and what they should read continues to widen, learning and reading problems become more generalized, compromising word attack skills, comprehension and thinking strategies, attention, and sadly, self-esteem. The train never acquires quite enough steam, and invariably, slows down and may even slide backward.

Because poor readers spend less time reading and are exposed to less text than facile readers, they are unable to benefit from reading practice. To make matters worse, sometimes poor readers receive a qualitatively different kind of instruction than good readers. More time is spent on isolated skill work, workbooks, phonic sheets, or other decontextualized tasks than on reading connected text. Exposed to less appealing and "stilted" text, the poor reader's problem is exacerbated while the good reader's reading gets better.

By the time students with reading problems are old enough for textbook learning, they may be unable to concentrate well when reading and appear easily distracted or anxious, particularly when called upon to read orally in front of their classmates. They may make careless errors or fail to reflect carefully before answering a question, instead "jumping in" with an impulsive guess. They are anxious and uncertain about their reading ability, and their uncertainty or anxiety generalizes to other learning tasks. Such students may seem passive, beaten down by the feelings of defeat that come from the cumulative effects of years of frustrations and failures in reading. Not surprisingly, they are often ill-equipped with strategies for organizing their materials and studying for tests. They seem to lack awareness of their learning style (i.e., their error patterns, their limitations, their strengths) and the demands of the task at hand. As a result, these students tend to plod through the textbook reading assignment, rarely rereading or self-questioning when they are confused or in doubt of a word or meaning.

The Mismatch Between the Student and the Textbook

Although textbooks remain relatively unchallenged in their role as a primary instructional tool, they have in recent years been the focus of repeated controversy (Britton, Woodward, & Bin-

kley, 1993; Herlihy, 1992). Among other things, textbooks have been criticized for decreasing difficulty (Chall & Conard, 1991), stilted writing (Britton, 1988; Tyson-Bernstein, 1988), covering too much information in too little depth and avoiding controversy (Chall, Conard, & Harris, 1977; Gagnon, 1987; Larkins & Hawkins, 1987; Tyson-Bernstein & Woodward, 1989), and poor instructional design (Armbruster & Gudbrandsen, 1986). A study that involved training teachers to analyze textbooks (Education Development Center & RMC Research, 1989), revealed, among other things, that teacher editions lacked important information about prior knowledge, student misconceptions, text structures, comprehension-monitoring techniques, study strategies, chapter mapping, and critical thinking. As a result, critics argue that today's textbooks do an inadequate job of helping teachers learn ways to motivate students to read more about a topic and do little to influence the development of comprehension and higher-order thinking skills.

THE TEXTBOOK TEACHING–LEARNING MODEL

While the debate rages on about the nature of textbook content, quality of instructional design and writing style, and indeed what role textbooks should play in the larger curriculum, classroom teachers are faced with a more immediate dilemma: how to ignite their students' interests in the content and inspire them to read and study when so many lack the necessary skills to do so.

Special and General Educators Pooling Their Talents

Many students with low reading skills are participating in special education, Chapter 1, or other kinds of remedial or tutorial programs. Therefore it is recommended that teachers learn to collaborate with one another in working toward acquiring new knowledge and beliefs about (a) teaching and the way children and youth learn and (b) novel and effective teaching techniques to better meet the needs of a more diverse student population.

Indeed, the content instructor must acquire an appreciation for the developmental and connected nature of reading, thinking, and learning content; and the remedial or special needs instructor must acquire an appreciation for the depth and breadth of the content to be covered during the school year (Education Developmental Center & RMC Research, 1989).

Collaborating teachers must be good planners and must be able to set aside brief but regularly scheduled planning time. Administrative support for planning is therefore essential. When teachers from the different disciplines are encouraged to begin talking and problem solving together, a sense of camaraderie can develop. Together, amelioration of student failure can be addressed more quickly, and recognition for student achievement can be shared more equally. Collaborative textbook teaching thus must involve the student's special or remedial educator and content teachers meeting and planning on a regular basis. It must include (a) regular assessments of the needs of the students having difficulty; (b) emphasis on the integration of content and learning and reading strategies; and (c) encouragement of teachers to solicit constructive feedback from one another about how they are teaching.

If teachers pool their resources and talents to collaborate in making the teaching decisions on a regular basis, substantial benefits can be reaped for students with a wide range of abilities. The decisions of collaborating teachers should address the following issues of content:

1. What chapters will be covered?

2. In what order?

3. When will they be covered?

4. In what depth?

Collaborating teachers should also address the following issues regarding the specific strategies:

1. What strategies will be taught to learn this content?

2. How will they be taught?

3. In what setting? (i.e., resource room, learning center, content classroom, after school tutorial)

4. How will strategies be reinforced over time?

5. Who will teach the strategies or support the strategies that prove to be useful over time?

In the event that students who are low readers do not participate in academic support programs, the content teacher must learn to implement the three-phase textbook teaching and learning model alone.

THREE PHASES OF THE TEXTBOOK TEACHING–LEARNING MODEL

The three phases of teaching and learning are generative and interconnected. Phase 1 (before reading) readies students for Phase 2 (during reading), which in turn prepares students for Phase 3 (after reading). Ideally, learning a lesson or a chapter is viewed as a thoughtful, well-planned construction of knowledge that continually undergoes the processes of rebuilding, readjusting, and extension of that knowledge. And, what holds this construction of knowledge together are the meaningful and logical connections between what has already been learned and experienced and what is about to be learned in the textbook.

There is more to instructing students who are low readers in the content area than preparing them to read their textbooks. Indeed, specific guided reading and after reading activities are also vital parts of the methodology.

The three-phase model is also based on an understanding of the characteristics of students who are low readers and how they compare to good readers when engaged in textbook learning. A closer look at how the two groups compare in before, during, and after reading behaviors strongly suggests that students who are low readers are not prepared to begin reading from their textbooks, and further, tend not to possess the necessary reading strategies for efficient comprehension. Figure 1 compares the characteristics of students who are good readers and students who are poor readers in each of the three stages of the textbook teaching-learning model.

Good Readers	Poor Readers
Before Reading	
• Think about what they already know about a subject	• Begin to read without thinking about the topic
• Know the purpose for which they read	• Do not know why they are reading
• Are motivated or interested to begin reading	• Lack interest and motivation to begin reading
• Have a general sense of how the BIG ideas will fit together	• Have little sense of how the BIG ideas will fit together
During Reading	
• Pay simultaneous attention to words and meaning	• Over-attend to individual words; miss salience
• Read fluently	• Read slower and at the same rate of speed
	• Have difficulty concentrating, particularly during silent reading
• Concentrate well while reading	• Unwilling to "risk"; easily defeated by words and text
• Willing to "risk" encountering difficult words and able to grapple with text ambiguities	• Unable to construct efficient strategies to monitor comprehension
• Construct efficient strategies to monitor comprehension	• Seldom use a "fix-it" strategy; plod on ahead, eager to finish
• Stop to use a "fix-it" strategy when confused	• Reading progress is painfully slow
• Reading skills improve	
After Reading	
• Understand how the pieces of information fit together	• Do not understand how the pieces of information fit together
• Able to identify what's salient	• May focus on the extraneous, peripheral
• Interested in reading more	• See reading as distasteful

FIGURE 1. Characteristics of good and poor readers using textbooks.

Phase 1 (Before Reading): Activating Prior Knowledge

The rationale for Phase 1 is that general class discussions are not enough; instead, teachers must spark the interest of students who are low readers by activating their prior knowledge (Palincsar & Brown, 1986, 1988) and focusing them on the purpose for reading (Flood & Lapp, 1988; Idol, 1987). Teacher-led explanations about the upcoming chapter are insufficient to reach the reluctant learner who has a history of feeling incompetent in reading and disconnected from traditional class discussions. Students experiencing reading problems have experienced a loss of control over their ability to learn from textbooks; therefore, Phase 1 is the most critical phase for low readers. Given the opportunity the day before to preview what they will be reading, they will be better prepared for the introduction of the lesson when it is presented in the content classroom. Giving low readers a head start can be accomplished by asking open-ended questions formulated to accomplish three important objectives: (a) to get students to think about what they already know about a topic, (b) to direct their focus and attention on a purpose for which they will be reading, and (c) to spark their interest and curiosity in the upcoming topic.

What students comprehend, remember, and infer from text has to do primarily with the "old" knowledge they are able to access. That, in turn, allows them to make sense of the new knowledge in the text. Their old knowledge can be general or highly specific about the upcoming topic. For example, a student may have general knowledge about navigation because of personal experiences with boats. When accessed, this old knowledge can make reading and thinking about Columbus's ocean voyages and his decisions about the routes he navigated far more meaningful.

Instruction, therefore, must help readers build upon and activate their prior knowledge and make meaningful connections between what is familiar, what is known, what is experienced, and what is about to be learned. Then attention is better focused on a reason to read, and reading becomes more gratifying because its purpose becomes more apparent.

One obvious way to begin the process of recognizing and valuing students' prior knowledge is to conduct informal and frequent inventories about students' interests, strengths, and meaningful experiences. When teachers deliberately capitalize on the unique interests and attributes of their students, reluctant readers can be wooed into participation in discussions, learning becomes more relevant, and discovering, constructing, and reconstructing ideas is more likely to occur. No matter what their reading capacity, all students have some knowledge that is pertinent, and strengths and interests that can be tapped. When teachers arm themselves with this powerful information to use when formulating prereading questions and discussions, they are recognizing the uniqueness of the individual student, and in doing so, helping him or her feel good about learning once again.

During Phase 1, teachers can also determine how much a student knows and does not know about a topic. These discussions can offer both teachers and students the opportunity to identify strongly held myths and misconceptions that can be used to build more meaningful bridges between old and new ways of thinking. When teachers view misconceptions or gaps in knowledge as fruitful learning opportunities, students who are reluctant learners begin to see that mistakes are not only OK but, in fact, useful and instructional.

Activating students' prior knowledge and focusing their attention on the purpose for reading will give low readers a head start by allowing them to (a) think about what they already know about a subject, (b) acquire a general understanding of how the big ideas will fit together, and (c) increase their confidence and motivation to read more.

SETTINGS AND TECHNIQUES FOR PHASE 1. Figure 2 presents the recommended settings in which instruction in each of the three phases of the textbook teaching-learning model might occur. As shown in Figure 2, the settings for Phase 1 might be a small group in the general classroom, a resource room, a learning center, an after-school study tutorial, or any other setting prior to the introduction of the lesson in the content classroom.

Following are examples of Phase 1 techniques.

1. *Select core vocabulary.* The teacher introduces carefully selected words and terms that appear in the text. Textbook chapters contain a vast amount of information. The teacher selects core vocabulary by determining those words the student is likely to encounter again, or only those words germane to the main ideas of the lesson. The teacher presents words and terms on the board or on a simple form such as the one in Figure 3. The teacher urges students to write an answer, even if only a guess. The teacher then collects papers and returns them to the students during Phase 3 or at the end of the lesson so they can fill in the last column and have the opportunity to review their initial responses. Initial mistakes or omissions should be viewed as instructional and used to help students become more aware of their own thinking and learning patterns.

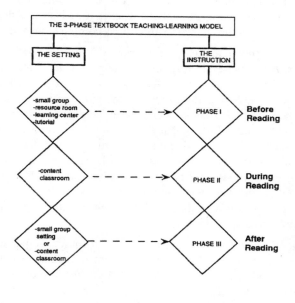

FIGURE 2. The three-phase textbook teaching–learning model.

Grade 5
CHAPTER 6
The First Colony, Jamestown

New chapter words/terms	What I think I already know	(to be completed in Phase III) What I *now* know
What is a *colony*?	ANTS hare coloNYS	
Where was *Jamestown*?	?	
What is a *stockholder*?	?	
What is a *profit*?	MONEY MONEY	
What is an *indentured servant*?	?	
What is *prosperity*?	good times	
What is a *plague*?	don't kNow	

FIGURE 3. Before reading—vocabulary task.

2. *Writing predictions.* When students learn how to make reasonable predications about what they will be reading, they are anticipating what they think the author is going to say and begin thinking about the purpose for which they read. There are no right and wrong predictions. Therefore, students who have less confidence in their learning abilities can feel they can respond without risking yet another incorrect answer.

Triangle frames, as shown in Figure 4, can be used to record the reader's prediction. Teachers can distribute triangle frames and emphasize that the base or bottom of the triangle is the largest area, where students will be expected to do the most writing. The teacher encourages students to write freely, creatively, and phonetically (if they are unsure of how to spell a word). This is an excellent activity for pairs or small groups of students. The teacher collects the frames to redistribute during Phase 3, when the chapter instruction is coming to an end.

3. *Use analogies and visual images in prereading discussions.* Analogies and visual images help students make meaningful links between what is familiar to them, what they know, and what they are about to read. Analogies and visual images can be fun to think about because they help students construct mental pictures of ideas. They can also help students organize new information, rendering it less arbitrary and thus facilitating retention and recall. Analogies should be easy to learn and remember. Once students begin to exhibit analogous thinking, it should be enthusiastically reinforced because it is a clear sign that in spite of low reading skills, students are developing their capacity to think abstractly.

4. *Distribute concept maps.* Semantic maps are simple, easy-to-read maps of words and terms presented to students before, during, and after they read the textbook. When maps are presented before reading, their purpose is to serve as an advance organizer for giving students a *preview* of the important concepts and ideas in the textbook chapter and how they are related to

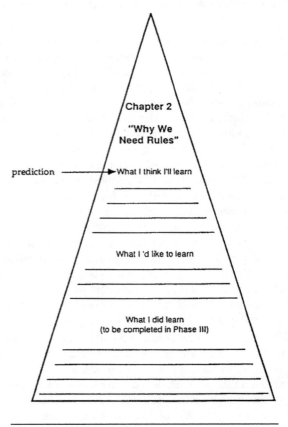

FIGURE 4. Before reading—predictions task.

one another. Maps can differ depending on whether they reflect a lesson that has flowed from the previously learned lesson or whether they present entirely new information. Basic guidelines to follow when designing maps include the following:

1. If students already possess some conceptual knowledge about the upcoming lesson, less detailed, more general, maps can be constructed.
2. A map is effective when it conveys the relationships among ideas in a meaningful and explicit way rather than in arbitrary or implicit ways.
3. A map is *not* effective when it is too specific, too literal, or when it presents summaries or mere outlines.

Maps can also be powerful tools for collaborating teachers. Forced to clarify lesson goals in order to design the maps, instruction becomes more focused and illustrates yet another way of thinking about information. Maps and organizers are also excellent ways to communicate to parents, offering them a *preview* of what their children will be expected to learn.

Distributed before the chapter is discussed, maps serve to prep students, giving them confidence to participate more fully in the upcoming textbook lesson. Maps can by partially complete, allowing the students to view the large structure of the new information but not all the important details. Later, as students read, they can add to the map's design with new information. An example of a semantic map is presented in Figure 5.

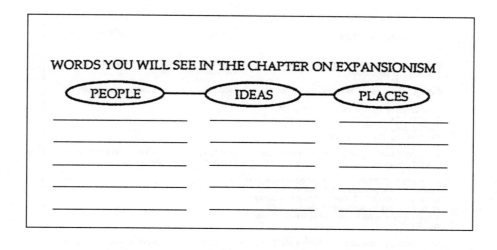

FIGURE 5. Before reading—semantic map.

Once the instructor selects and completes the most appropriate Phase 1 techniques, the student is ready to complete Phase 1 and make the transition to Phase 2 learning. In Phase 1, the student gathers the big ideas into a neat and manageable package that will equip him or her with the confidence, prior knowledge, and interest in the lesson about to be presented in the content classroom. Armed with a preview of the new lesson, the student feels more in control and is more self-assured, more confident, and considerably more ready to read and understand the textbook.

Phase 2 (During Reading): Helping Students Become More Active Comprehenders and Thinkers

The rationale for Phase 2 is that children and youth who have low reading skills often do not respond well to teacher-dominated, lengthy lectures and do not interact well with their textbooks during traditional oral or silent reading. When lectures are lengthy, the student who is a low reader feels little control over his or her own learning and becomes passive, losing track of what has been said as attention fades.

When engaged in textbook reading, students who are low readers tend to expend more time and energy struggling with individual words than on constructing meaning from the text. Unlike good readers, who are automatic in their ability to recognize familiar words and skilled in decoding less familiar words, students who are low readers often exhibit a labored and choppy reading style that strains their attention and interest. This is particularly true during the sustained silent reading that typifies homework assignments. Further, as low readers overattend to individual words, they are less able to utilize the context to predict meaning. The result is a failure to activate or invent self-help strategies as they encounter ambiguous points in the text. These strategies ordinarily include rereading the passage more slowly, rehearsing a salient point, self-talking, or jotting down notes.

Finally, matters are made worse for the student who is a low reader because too many popular textbooks are organized so that main ideas are embedded, structures are implicit, and too many concepts are treated superficially. As these readers proceed to stumble on words, lose their place and concentration, they often lose the battle of understanding the meaning. They simply give up or refuse to read the textbook altogether. At this point, the obvious question becomes: How do we teach low readers the strategies they need to succeed when the strategies can be mastered only while they are engaged in reading, a task in which they are so inept?

Whereas the success of Phase 1 lies in the teacher's belief in the power of prior knowledge, the success of Phase 2 depends upon the teacher's shift to more student-centered strategy learning. The teaching methodology referred to as strategy instruction requires that the content teacher relinquish the role of lecturer and instead learn to teach specific instructional techniques that will draw the low reader into a more strategic and participatory role in the learning or reading activity.

Strategy instruction takes time to teach. It requires careful reflection on the teacher's part about how to teach and why, when, and in what problems or circumstances to use a strategy. It also involves frequent modeling and reteaching of specific strategies when necessary (Ellis, 1993; Gaskins & Elliot, 1991; Swanson, 1989).

The success of strategy instruction depends heavily on three criteria: (a) the commitment the teacher makes to acquire a repertoire of instructional strategies that have shown promise with students who are low readers, (b) how well teachers can model their own strategic thinking, and (c) how well students are convinced that strategies are useful in improving their grades. Experts in the field of strategy instruction (e. g., Ellis, Deshler, Lenz, Schumaker, & Clark, 1991; Pressley, 1990; Swanson, 1989; Wong, 1985) have made a number of useful observations about teachers and strategy teaching. Figure 6 displays characteristics of skilled and less skilled strategy teachers.

Not all strategies are appropriate for all students who struggle with reading, nor can they be universally applied across all reading tasks. Further, not all strategies have been scientifically validated. However, teachers can discover the reading and

<table>
<tr><th>Good Strategy Teachers</th><th>Not So Good Strategy Teachers</th></tr>
</table>

Good Strategy Teachers

- Make sure that strategy instruction is well planned and continuous

- Overtly "model" covert self-regulation thoughts;

  for example; ["In class today...we're going to do 3 things. The first thing we're going to do is...The second thing we're going to do is...and the third thing we're going to do is..."]

- Identify and teach strategy prerequisites before teaching strategy;

  for example; ["Before we open our books to learn how to preview text structures, let's make sure we all remember the 3 most common structures found in history books. If you think you might forget these structures later, what should you do now?"]

- Focus strategy instruction on what we are doing and why

  for example; ["Remember, we're looking for text structures so we can improve our chances of remembering the important ideas here and therefore do better on the chapter test next week. Look back on the 6 pages you read yesterday. What did you decide were the common structures?"]

- Work hard to get students to self-regulate, set their own goals and self-reinforce

- Know that strategy learning takes time and effort

  for example; ["It may be several weeks before you'll be able to recognize the structures in your textbook. Give yourself time. It takes practice."]

Not So Good Strategy Teachers

- Provide fragmented, "hit or miss" strategy instruction

- Tend to be unaware of own mental processes

- Tend to ignore prerequisites or teach them and the strategy at the same time

- Focus strategy instruction on memorization of strategy steps

- Set goals for students/exaggerate praise/use extrinsic reinforcers

- Expect students to benefit immediately

FIGURE 6. Behaviors of good and not-so-good strategy teachers.

thinking strategies that work best over time in order to help students in their ability and desire to (a) better attend to words and meaning simultaneously, (b) cope more effectively with text ambiguities, (c) develop self-help comprehension and study strategies. and (d) be motivated to read more.

Following are examples of Phase 2 techniques.

1. Reciprocal teaching techniques. As presented by Palincsar and Brown (1986. 1988). reciprocal teaching techniques are particularly effective in helping students who are low readers acquire a sense of control over their learning because students assume more dominant roles in the learning process. This is achieved by teaching students how to lead discussions about the text. In reciprocal teaching, teachers and students are partners in jointly constructing the meaning of the text through four processes that require initial teacher modeling, followed by less teacher and more student involvement. As more opportunities for student participation occur, the diversity among students' cultural and linguistic backgrounds, prior knowledge, experiences, and unique strengths and interests can be more effectively utilized. Executed carefully, the steps in reciprocal teaching can build upon Phase 1 learning. With careful plan-

ning, the method takes approximately 10 days for the teacher and students to master.

2. Insert. As presented by Vaughn and Estes (1986), Insert is an active reading technique. It is a particularly useful way for students who are low readers to become more aware of a breakdown in comprehension so that they can remember to clarify the ambiguity at a later point in time. This is a particularly useful strategy when students own their own books and are free to mark in them. But if marking or photocopying the reading assignment is not possible. students can use adhesive notes or strips of paper in the margin of the text. Assign students pages to read for homework or class work by first reviewing the following marking scheme for Insert.

    X   I thought differently

    +   New information

    !   WOW

    ??   I don't understand

    *   Very important

Ask students to copy the symbols on a sturdy blank bookmarker to use while they are engaged in the reading activity. Students can also be encouraged to invent their own codes or symbols. In doing so, they will think about the way they think and move more steadily toward independent learning.

3. *Mapping strategies.* Prepare reading maps or teach students how to construct their own. Reading maps can be extensions of concept maps (introduced in Phase 1) or newly constructed maps for reading. Maps can be particularly effective during Phase 2 because they can help readers focus on what is salient in the text, as well as help them monitor their comprehension. Because reading maps can combine visual or graphic symbols with words and phrases, they tend to be a more appealing task than traditional note taking or outlining.

As in reciprocal teaching, teachers should regularly model how to construct reading maps by using an overhead projector or the board. Teachers must also speak clearly about the reasons behind each part of the map construction. Teachers should construct reading maps that will teach readers to think about text structures. Readers should be encouraged to construct additions, pictures. or any other "cue" that will help them organize and remember the text. Gradually, students should be able to independently construct their own maps.

To begin, teachers should distribute reading maps such as those displayed in Figure 7 immediately prior to the reading assignment, having students fill in the missing information as they read or distributing chapter maps as an alternative to note taking or outlining.

4. *Transactional strategy instruction.* Transactional strategy instruction emphasizes the coordinated use of a variety of strategies through direct explanations and modeling (see Pressley et al., 1992, for a complete review of transactional instruction). This method requires teachers to pay as much attention to helping students understand the thinking behind their responses as to the teaching of the strategies per se. The goals of transactional strategy instruction include not only improving academic performance through strategy use but also strengthening students' commitment to learning. More specifically, transactional strategy instruction involves (a) teachers and students jointly constructing and reconstructing meaning from the text, (b) offering students a small number of strategies during any given lesson and demonstrating how to use and coordinate them with previously learned strategies, (c) frequent discussions about the natural use of strategies and how they are related to the textbook content, and (d) building motivation and a commitment to reading. For example, Mrs. Romaine begins her fifth-grade social studies class by discussing what reading strategies her students like best and why (e. g., thinking aloud, rereading, imaging the text, discovering an analogy, jotting down short summaries, mapping the text, using Insert, predicting, paraphrasing, etc.). She reviews (a) the nature of the strategies, (b) why they are valuable, and (c) her student's ideas about when to use them. Together. Mrs. Romaine and her students make the relationship between the strategy and the content explicit as she models her own strategic thinking and reading behavior by reading a short text aloud to the class.

At the same time, Mrs. Romaine is sensitive to each individual student's responses to the task, particularly how efficient and flexible her students become in strategy use. She emphasizes the connections between old knowledge and new knowledge and works hard over time to get her students to make these connections without her.

Phase 3 (After Reading): Consolidating and Extending Textbook Knowledge

The rationale behind Phase 3 is that paper-and-pencil tests are not sufficient to help students retain new knowledge. Instead,

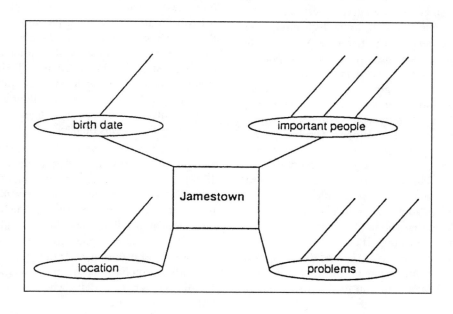

FIGURE 7.   During reading—chapter mapping ideas.

teachers should help students keep track of their progress and extend what they learn in their textbooks to their personal world. Although part of the success in Phases 1 and 2 lies in the teacher's belief in the power of students' prior knowledge and a commitment to student-centered learning, the success of Phase 3 has much to do with the teacher's ability to guide students in learning to connect and consolidate new knowledge based on previous learning and experiences both in and out of the classroom. Phase 3 strategies will help students to (a) understand how the pieces of the information fit together, (b) learn how to identify what is salient and what is extraneous, and (c) become more interested in reading.

Following are examples of Phase 3 techniques.

1. *Complete vocabulary/prediction forms from Phase 1.* To implement this technique, the teacher redistributes the vocabulary forms from Phase 1 (see Figure 3) and has students complete the third column. Most importantly, the teacher has students study their own shifts in thinking by comparing their responses in column 2 to those in column 3.

2. *Have students analyze end-of-the-chapter questions.* Students enjoy this activity because it does not require them to answer questions. Rather, it helps them learn about ways to use questions to think about the content. Teach students how to discriminate among three types of end-of-the-chapter questions: (a) questions looking for literal or factual answers, (b) questions asking students to make inferences or analyses, and (c) questions asking students for their opinions. When students learn how to discriminate among types of questions, they can learn how to formulate their own questions when reading and learn that when answers to questions are required in an assignment, they can save time by not looking for the answer to an opinion question.

3. *Have students extend their concept maps.* Once again, mapping is an effective way to consolidate learning once the text has been read and can be an alternative to test taking. For those students who have found reading to be distasteful, mapping exercises can serve as an incentive to reread. Moreover, by Phase 3, mapping should be a familiar task, because practice and repetition produce feelings of success and confidence. Students who are low readers can begin to discover ways to become better at mapping, improving and creating new maps as they proceed through the textbook chapters. Students can add on from previous maps or make new ones. Gradually, they should experiment with more symbols, pictures, colors, words, or phrases. Students might also work collaboratively or independently in study groups. The idea is for students to use words and visual cues to make connections among ideas in the textbook. In this way, they begin to process information at a deeper and more meaningful level that should subsequently facilitate retention and recall. Even more importantly, though, students should spend time discussing the reasons behind their map construction decisions. This technique can enhance not only classroom interactions but also motivation to read, thus enhancing reading competence.

A Shift in the Way to Teach Low Readers in the Content Classroom

	Old Way	New Way
Before Reading	Teacher provides a brief discussion of the new chapter	Teachers regard this as a critical phase of instruction; (e.g., pre-reading activities may take place in the resource room prior to the introduction of the chapter in the content classroom).
During Reading	Assigns pages to read and end of the lesson questions to write for homework, and asks students to be prepared to discuss text lectures, discusses and asks questions.	Assigns part of reading and writing in class so that guided reading and other strategies can be practiced; connections to material are frequently made explicit.
After Reading	Written tests	Students collaborate and study with one another to prepare for tests. Novel Projects such as chapter maps that demonstrate comprehension are encouraged; the transition to the next chapter begins.

FIGURE 8. Old and new ways to think about teaching content.

4. *Have students go back and look for text structures.* Initially, text structures can be made explicit to the reader by distributing frames identifying the structure(s). Then, over time, the teacher can provide frames containing less information, forcing readers to identify the structures (e.g., cause/effect, problem/solution, compare/contrast, listings, etc.) on their own. When students are able to independently identify text structures, they will improve not only their ability to remember important information, but also their ability to organize and express their thoughts on paper.

As noted in recent works in the textbook teaching-learning area (e.g., Ciborowski, 1992; Fiore & Nero, 1993; Guerin, 1992), to teach the diverse population of students currently enrolled in America's schools, teachers must abandon the traditional role of dispenser of knowledge and adopt a new instructional paradigm in which learning from textbooks is viewed as a recursive, interactive process involving a variety of activities before, during, and after reading. Figure 8 summarizes the shift in emphasis between the old way and a new way of teaching content to students who have traditionally experienced difficulty in reading.

DISCUSSION AND RECOMMENDATIONS FOR TEACHERS

Good teachers can maximize the use of even a mediocre textbook, particularly if they love to teach, are excited about their subject area, are willing to collaborate with the student's remedial teachers or tutors, and enjoy making learning fun. In a climate of increasing student diversity, teachers who possess the ability to foster trust between themselves and their students may be the teachers who are ultimately the most successful. Trust between the teacher and the student who has experienced considerable academic failure and frustration can foster in the student self-determination, a willingness to take risks, and ultimately the confidence to want to learn more (Ensminger & Dangel, 1992). An effective teacher of content is a lover of content, a strategic thinker, and a collaborator.

More specifically, the content teacher who uses the textbook well (a) spends time thinking about ways to capitalize on her or his students' strengths and helps students make connections between their experiences and learning textbook content; (b) believes that how one learns is as important as what one learns; (c) has high expectations for all students, especially students who are low readers; (d) challenges students of all ability levels; (e) teaches reading, thinking, and content concurrently; (f) is a strategy teacher who models his or her own strategy by thinking out loud or in other observable ways; and (g) works closely with the remedial teacher to set up paired reading structures, peer tutoring, after-school study sessions, or other cooperative learning structures in or out of the content classroom.

Students who use textbooks well (a) learn how to think about their prior knowledge when reading new ideas in their textbooks; (b) learn how to better monitor their comprehension (and confusion); (c) gradually acquire a repertoire of reading, thinking, and study strategies, and master the ones that work best; (d) become confident enough to create and test their own strategies; and (e) are able to make connections with what they learn from their books to their personal world and community.

This article has presented a textbook teaching-learning model describing strategies that special educators and content instructors can utilize when their classrooms contain students with a wide range of reading abilities. However, before teaching and learning can begin, teachers must determine the best match between the level of instruction and the reader, given that for some students the textbook may be too easy, for others too difficult, and for still others, just about right.

JEAN CIBOROWSKI is the director of Educational Services in the School Function Programs at Children's Hospital in Boston. She earned her PhD in 1986 from the joint doctoral program at San Diego State University and the Claremont Graduate School. She has recently completed a book about how to use and select textbooks for students with reading difficulties. She is also involved in work with children and youth without homes. Address: Jean Ciborowski, Division of General Pediatrics, Children's Hospital, Boston, MA 02115.

NOTES

1. From Textbooks and the Students Who Can't Read Them: A Guide to Teaching Content, by Jean Ciborowski, 1994, Cambridge, MA: Brookline Books. Copyright 1994 by Brookline Books. Adapted with permission.

REFERENCES

Armbruster, B. B., & Gudbrandsen, B. (1986). Reading comprehension in social studies programs. *Reading Research Quarterly, 21,* 36–48.

Britton, B. (1988). *The impact of good and bad writers on learners.* Paper presented at the annual meeting of the American Educational Research Association, New Orleans.

Britton, B., Woodward, A., & Binkley, M. (1993). (Eds.). *Learning from textbooks: Theory and practice.* Hillsdale, NJ: Erlbaum.

Chall, J. S. (1983). *Learning to read: The great debate.* New York: McGraw-Hill.

Chall, J. S., & Conard, S. S. (1991). *Should textbooks challenge students?* New York: Teachers College Press.

Chall, J. S., Conard, S., & Harris, S. (1977). *An analysis of textbooks in relation to declining SAT scores.* Princeton, NJ: College Entrance Examination Board and Educational Testing Service.

Ciborowski, J. (1992), *Textbooks and the students who can't read them: A guide for the teaching of content.* Cambridge, MA: Brookline.

Education Development Center & RMC Research. (1989). *Improving textbook usability: Final report.* (ERIC Document Reproduction Service No. ED 310 585)

Ellis, E. S. (1993). Integrative strategy instruction: A potential model for teaching content area subjects to adolescents with learning disabilities. *Journal of Learning Disabilities, 26,* 358–383, 398.

Ellis, E. S., Deshler, D. D., Lenz, E. K., Schumaker, J. B., & Clark, F. L. (1991). An instructional model for teaching learning strategies. *Focus on Exceptional Children, 23*(6), 1–24.

Ensminger, E. E., & Dangel, H. L. (1992). The foxfire pedagogy: A confluence of best practices for special education. *Focus on Exceptional Children, 24*(7), 1–15.

Fiore, T. A, & Nero, R. (1993). *Integrating diverse learners into mainstream education: The role of instructional materials, adoption and selection.* Research Triangle Park, NC: Research Triangle Institute.

Flood, J. Y., & Lapp, D. (1988). Conceptual mapping strategies for understanding information texts. The *Reading Teacher, 4,* 780–783.

Gagnon, P. (1987). Democracy's untold story. *American Educator, 11*(2), 19–25.

Gaskins, I., & Elliot, T. (1991). *Implementing cognitive strategy training across the school.* Cambridge, MA: Brookline.

Guerin, G. R. (1992). *Improving instruction for students at risk using history-social science textbooks.* Sacramento: Resources in Special Education.

Haskell, D. W., Foorman, B. R., & Swank, P. R. (1992). Effects of three orthographic/phonological units on first grade reading. *Remedial and Special Education, 13*(2), 40–49.

Herlihy, J. G. (1992). *The textbook controversy: Issues, aspects and perspectives.* Norwood, NJ: Ablex.

Idol, L. (1987). A critical thinking map to improve content area comprehension of poor readers. *Remedial and Special Education, 8*(4), 28–40.

Larkins, G. A., & Hawkins, M. L. (1987, April). *Trivial and noninformative content of social studies textbooks in the primary grades.* Paper presented at the annual meeting of the American Educational Research Association.

Palincsar, A. S., & Brown, A. L. (1986). Interactive teaching to promote independent learning from text. *The Reading Teacher, 39,* 771–777.

Palincsar, A. S., & Brown, A. L. (1988). Teaching and practicing thinking skills to promote comprehension in the context of group problem solving. *Remedial and Special Education, 9*(1), 53–59.

Pressley, M. (1990). *Cognitive strategy instruction that really improves children's academic performance*. Cambridge, MA: Brookline.

Pressley, M., EI-Dinary, P. B., Gaskins, I., Schuder, T., Bergman, J. L., Almasi, J., & Brown, R. (1992). Beyond direct explanation: Transactional instruction of reading comprehension strategies. *Elementary School Journal, 92,* 511–554.

Snider, V. E., & Tarver, S. G. (1987). The effect of early reading failure on acquisition of prior knowledge among students with learning disabilities. *Journal of Learning Disabilities, 20,* 351–356.

Stanovich, K. (1986a). Matthew effects in reading: Some consequences of individual differences in the acquisition of literacy. *Reading Research Quarterly, 21,* 360–407.

Stanovich, K (1986b). Cognitive processes and the reading problems of learning disabled children: Evaluating the assumptions of specificity. In J. K Torgesen & B. Y. L. Wong (Eds.), *Psychological and educational perspectives on learning disabilities* (pp. 85–116). Orlando, FL: Academic Press.

Swanson, H. L. (1989). Strategy instruction: Overview of principles and procedures for effective use. *Learning Disability Quarterly, 12*(1), 3–16.

Tyson-Bernstein, H. (1988). *A conspiracy of good intentions: America's textbook fiasco*. Washington, DC: Council for Basic Education.

Tyson-Bernstein, H., & Woodward, A. (1989). Why students aren't learning very much from their textbooks. *Educational Leadership, 47*(3), 14–17.

Vellutino, F. (1991). Introduction to three studies on reading acquisition: Convergent findings on theoretical foundations of code-oriented versus whole-language approaches to reading instruction. *Journal of Educational Psychology, 83*, 437–483.

Vaughn, J. L., & Estes, T. H. (1986). *Reading and reasoning beyond the primary grades*. Boston: Allyn & Bacon.

Wong, B. Y. L. (1985). Issues in cognitive behavioral intervention in academic skill areas. *Journal of Abnormal Child Psychology, 2,* 123–131.

Guidelines for Adapting Content Area Textbooks:

Keeping Teachers and Students Content

Textbook adaptations are often necessary in working with mainstreamed special education students

By Jeanne Shay Schumm
and Kelly Strickler

Reading specialists and content area reading teachers have recognized the inappropriateness of traditional textbooks for students in terms of level of difficulty (Johnson & Vardain, 1973) and level of interest (Baldwin, 1985; Graves et al., 1988). This phenomenon is hardly new. Indeed, Huey (1908, p. 382) questioned traditional textbook dependency and recommended the following: "Far more extensive reading should be done in the upper grades and in the high school, as compared with the usual intensive analytical study of a few texts and authors." Some have even advocated "bookless" instruction for students with persistent reading problems (Silberberg & Silberberg, 1969).

Nonetheless, recognizing that students, particularly those who are college bound, must ultimately be able to extract salient information from textbooks and retain that information for subsequent tests, secondary teachers have persisted in using the textbook/lecture instructional routine as the primary mode of operation (Applebee, Langer, & Mullis, 1987; Weiss, 1978). This practice has become even more challenging to execute with the addition of mainstreamed special education students in the general classroom.

The success of mainstreaming is dependent, in part, on teachers' ability and willingness to make adaptations to accommodate individual differences. (Stainback, Stainback, Courtnage, & Jaben, 1985). While general classroom teachers see the use of alternative methods and materials as desirable, implementation is not always feasible (Schumm & Vaughn, 1991). Moreover, because general classroom teachers often have not been trained to make such adaptations (Schumm & Vaughn, 1990), problems arise in coping with student diversity. A recent critic of mainstreaming offered the following observation of differentiated instruction: "The Robins can read the whole book; the Blue Jays need read only half; the Pigeons can copy the table of contents five times. The Robins can dissect a frog; the Blue Jays can watch a movie about a frog; the Pigeons can play leapfrog" [Ohanian, 1990, p. 221).

Our view of teacher avoidance or misuse of textbook adaptations and alternative instructional practices to adjust to student diversity is not as caustic. It is our contention that general education teachers are anxious to accommodate individual needs

(Schumm & Vaughn, 1990) but are often unaware of how to do so. Consequently, the purpose of this article is to provide a description of practitioner and researcher-identified textbook adaptations that can be used in working with children with special needs. The adaptations are intended for use in content area classrooms as well as exceptional student resource rooms where students are working in textbooks intended for general education students.

Where elaboration of individual adaptations is warranted but not feasible within the scope of the present article, citations are provided. It is our intent that special educators and reading resource specialists use this compilation of textbook adaptations for inservicing content area teachers.

The textbook adaptations were gleaned from two sources. The first was a review of literature. Our literature search included research and practical articles focusing on textbook adaptations for mainstreamed special education students, as well as content area reading textbooks and reading methods compendiums.

The second source of textbook adaptations was transcripts of a series of focus group interviews. It was our impression that an adaptation list should be buttressed with adaptations teachers actually use. Therefore, a series of focus group interviews was conducted to further extend a list of adaptations found in the review of literature and to build a reality base for our instrument. A focus group interview is a structure originally used in marketing research for probing perceptions of individuals (Bellenger, Bernhardt, & Golstucker, 1976; Patton, 1980). Unlike individual interviews, the group setting of the focus group interview enables participants to exchange ideas and elaborate on them through discussion. Although guided by a core of questions and facilitated by a discussion leader, participants are not confined to a highly structured question-answer sequence. Rather, the interview is flexible and fluid, encouraging exploration and elaboration of ideas.

In order to determine what adaptations teachers actually use, we interviewed both teachers and students. Three focus group interviews were with teachers. One group consisted of general education middle and high school content area teachers, and a second group was made up of reading resource specialists. The third group consisted of special education teachers (LD and varying exceptionalities) who teach in both resource and self-contained classes. The other three focus group interviews were with high school students. The three groups interviewed were mainstreamed special education students, low achieving students, and high achieving students. Each interview session included a minimum of four and a maximum of six participants.

" 'The Robins can read the whole book; the Blue Jays need read only half; the Pigeons can copy the table of contents five times. The Robins can dissect a frog; the Blue Jays can watch a movie about a frog; the Pigeons can play leapfrog' (Ohanian, 1990, p. 221)."

The interviews were audio-recorded and later transcribed. Data were reduced using the Glaser and Strauss (1967) constant comparison procedure as described in Lincoln and Guba (1985). Finally, the list of adaptations derived from the focus group interviews was merged with information from the review of literature.

The type of adaptations that teachers select will be dependent, in part, on the match between the textbook and the reader. Therefore, the first section of this article provides suggestions for how classroom teachers can detect the compatibility of the textbook with the students' reading and interest levels. Next, adaptations are presented in four categories based on student needs: Substitute the textbook (students with severe word recognition problems); simplify the textbook (students with moderate word recognition and vocabulary problems); highlight key concepts in the textbook (students with reading comprehension problems); and structure opportunities for retention of textbook material (students with problems remembering text material for subsequent tests).

Determining the Goodness of Fit

Quite often, classroom teachers do not have the opportunity to select the content area textbook. If a choice can be made, that choice is often limited to a brief list of district- or state-adopted textbooks. Consequently, teachers are often "stuck" with "one size fits all" textbooks that are too difficult for many students in the classroom. Before teachers can make necessary adaptations, it is important that they obtain evidence about the student, the textbook, and the student/textbook interaction. This is by no means an exact science, but general knowledge of the "goodness of fit" is imperative to accommodate diverse student needs.

Student Reading Level

* *Investigate student records to identify students with potential problems with textbook reading.* Check cumulative folders or IEPs or interview special education teachers to determine students' scores on standardized reading tests or more informal reading inventories.

Textbook Level

* *Determine the readability level of the textbook.* One way to estimate the level of difficulty of a textbook is to ascertain its readability level. Readability levels are often reported as grade levels determined by formulas based on semantic and syntactic elements. The problems of readability formulas are well documented (Klare, 1984); nonetheless, they do provide an estimate of text difficulty and are helpful when used in conjunction with other measures (Fry, 1989).

If publishers do not provide the readability level of the textbook, teachers can *estimate* the grade level of the textbook by using one or more readability formulas (e.g., Fry, 1977; Raygor, 1977). Computer software is now available to avoid cumbersome hand calculations.

* *Determine the degree of "considerateness" of the textbook.* Research indicates that text features (e.g., preposed questions, headings and subheadings, new vocabulary in boldface type, etc.) that make the text "friendly" or "considerate" to the reader are critical for students with reading problems (Osborn, Jones, & Stein, 1985). Several teacher checklists for evaluating the considerateness of textbooks have been devised (Armbruster & Anderson, 1981; Irwin & Davis, 1980; Readence, Bean, & Baldwin, 1985; Singer, 1986; Steinley, 1987). These checklists typically include items related to text organization, conceptual density, instructional aids, explicitness, and ability to motivate or engage students. Recently, a system for student evaluation of text considerateness has been suggested (Schumm & Mangrum, in press).

Student/Text Interaction

* *Administer a close test based on the textbook.* The cloze procedure can be used to determine how well a textbook "matches" the reading achievement levels of students. A cloze test consists of a passage extracted verbatim from a target textbook from which words have been systematically deleted. Students' ability to interact and construct meaning from the textbooks is gauged by how well they can supply the missing words. Readence, Bean, and Baldwin (1985) have provided a comprehensive description of how to construct and administer a cloze test.

* *Administer a content reading inventory.* A content reading inventory is a teacher-constructed assessment that provides teachers with specific information about how students can learn from a particular textbook. The items of the inventory include questions about reading and study aids, vocabulary knowledge, and reading comprehension questions. Students use their assigned textbook to answer the questions during a group administration of the instrument. Several authors (e.g., McWilliams & Rakes, 1979; Readence et al., 1985) provide directions for writing a content reading inventory.

> *"Our view of teacher avoidance or misuse of text-book adaptations and alternative instructional practices to adjust to student diversity is not as caustic. It is our contention that general education teachers are anxious to accommodate individual needs (Schumm & Vaughn, 1990) but are often unaware of how to do so."*

- *Preview the textbook with students to determine their knowledge of textbook organization and learning tools.* Conduct a textbook scavenger hunt to ascertain students' awareness of such text features as the table of contents, index, glossary, and so forth (Irwin & Baker, 1989; Schumm & Mangrum, in press).

Substitute the Textbook

After evaluating the textbook and making an initial estimate of student reading ability, the teacher may determine that the "goodness of fit" is very poor. In such cases, even with many adaptations and prompts, the students would be unable to learn from the textbook independently. For students who have severe word recognition problems, it may be necessary to substitute textbook reading assignments with more appropriate learning tools. In many cases, students can comprehend content if it is presented in a form other than print. It is our belief that if such substitutions are implemented, they should be as unobtrusive as possible so that the student is not stigmatized in any way. Middle school and high school students are very sensitive to changes in the textbook that result in their having a different textbook than other students in the class (Vaughn, Schumm, Johnson, & Daugherty, 1991).

- *Audio-tape textbook content.* Adult or student volunteers can audio-tape textbook chapters. Students with reading problems can listen to the tapes at home or in their special education resource room (Bender, 1985; Wood & Wooley, 1986).
- *Read textbook aloud to students.* Once again, adult or student volunteers can read aloud to students during study hall time or in the special education resource room (Dupuis & Askov, 1982; Rhodes & Dudley-Marling, 1988).
- *Pair students to master textbook content.* Good and poor readers can be paired to learn a section of a chapter and then present it to the class as a whole (Masters & Mori, 1989; Schula & Turnbull, 1984).

- *Use direct experiences, films/ video-tapes/recording, and computer programs to substitute textbook reading.* Many students who cannot learn through print can learn through direct experiences or through auditory or visual means (Forgan & Mangrum, 1985; Lapp, Flood, & Farnan,1989).
- *Work with students individually or in small groups to master textbook material.* Organize after-school or study hall tutoring sessions to work one-to-one or in small groups with students having similar needs. Quite often, school volunteers or student service groups can be enlisted to help in tutoring sessions (Masters & Mori, 1989; Schula & Turnbull, 1984).

Simplify the Textbook

Many students have mastered basic word recognition skills, but their reading level is far below that of the textbook used in class. In these cases, the textbook may need to be simplified.

- *Construct abridged versions of textbook content or use publisher's abridged versions.* This is a labor-intensive task, but perhaps can be managed if members of a department (or school district using the same textbook) divide the rewriting task into manageable units. Beech (1983) has offered a comprehensive guide for rewriting text for mainstreamed students.
- *Provide students with chapter outlines or summaries.* Students appreciate Cliff Notes for a reason: Key concepts are highlighted; extraneous fluff is omitted. Key concepts and vocabulary can be outlined or summarized in a simplified form on handouts (Schula & Turnbull, 1984; Wood & Wooley, 1986).
- *Use a multilevel, multimaterial approach.* Allow students to read from various sources representing a variety of readability levels to achieve a common goal (Bos & Vaughn, 1988; Forgan & Mangrum, 1985; Radencich & Schumm, 1985).

Highlight Key Concepts

At the middle and high school level, many students have satisfactory word recognition skills but have difficulty comprehending textbook material. For these students, adaptations need to focus on im-

proving and enhancing comprehension of information.

- *Preview reading assignments with students to orient them to the topic and provide guidelines for budgeting reading/study time.* Show students how to examine headings, subheadings, graphics, introductions, and summaries so that they can use this information to orient themselves to main ideas and key concepts (Rhodes & Dudley-Marling, 1988; Thomas & Robinson, 1982). Also demonstrate to students how to chunk the chapter into manageable study units (Schumm & Mangrum, in press).
- *Provide students with purposes for reading.* Introduce assignments with a reading goal so students know what they need to focus on during a reading assignment (Blanton, Wood, & Moorman, 1990; Moore, Readence, & Rickelman, 1989).
- *Provide an overview of an assignment before reading.* Diagram and discuss major concepts or events before initiating the reading assignment (Heimlich & Pittelman, 1986; Moore et al., 1989).

> *"Teachers are often 'stuck' with 'one size fits all' textbooks that are too difficult for many students in the classroom."*

- *Structure opportunities for students to activate prior knowledge before starting a reading assignment.* Brainstorm about the topic, develop mental imagery, construct semantic maps, and share common experiences/reflections about the topic before reading (Heimlich & Pittelman, 1986; Irwin & Baker, 1989; Moore, Readence, & Rickelman, 1989).
- *Introduce key vocabulary before reading an assignment.* Discuss specialized terms and preview new words in context. Be sure students understand not only the definition of the word but also how the term is used in the particular context (Bos & Vaughn, 1988; Nagy, 1988; Schula & Turnbull, 1984).
- *Develop a study guide to direct learning from the textbook.* Create participatory organizers to be filled in during reading to involve student engagement. The guided questions are outlines that encourage student involvement and guide the student to key ideas and concepts. Paragraph-by-paragraph study guidelines are also

helpful (Irvin, 1990; Roe, Stoodt, & Burns, 1987).

- *Summarize/reduce textbook information to guide classroom discussions and independent reading*. Put most salient concepts on overhead or on chalkboard to reinforce ideas presented in the textbook (Irwin & Baker, 1989; Wood & Wooley, 1986).
- *Color-code textbooks*. Use different color markers to highlight key vocabulary words, definitions, and important facts. Many students have a difficult time deciding what is the most salient information in a textbook. By highlighting key information, students learn to focus on what is most important. Ultimately, students can be provided guided lessons on highlighting relevant information (Wood & Wooley, 1986).
- *Reduce length of assignments*. Divide chapters in manageable units. Encourage students to master one unit at a time (Polloway, Patton, Payne, & Payne, 1989; Wood & Wooley, 1986).
- *Slow down the pace of reading assignments*. Cover less material. Allow time for students to reread assignments (Polloway et al., 1989; Wood & Wooley, 1986).
- *Provide assistance for answering text-based questions*. Reword text questions in easier terms. Provide page number where answer can be found (Readence et al., 1985; Wood & Wooley, 1986).
- *Demonstrate/model effective reading strategies and comprehension techniques*. Use teacher think-aloud procedures to demonstrate how to use fix-up strategies when you don't understand what you read, to identify main ideas, and to select important details (Irwin, 1986; Tierney, Readence, & Dishner, 1990).
- *Place students in cooperative learning groups to master textbook content*. Organize students into groups of three or four to read and discuss textbook material (Irvin, 1990; Rhodes & Dudley-Marling, 1988; Vacca & Vacca, 1989). Reward students for working together so that everyone masters the material.
- *Teach comprehension-monitoring techniques to improve ongoing understanding of text material*. Encourage students to ask questions when they do not understand. Teach students to take notes on information they do not understand during independent reading and to ask the teacher about the material either during or after class (Irwin & Baker, 1989; Irvin, 1990).
- *Teach students to use graphic aids to understand information presented in textbooks*. Provide direct instruction in using illustrations, pictures, tables, charts, and graphs to understand text content (Lapp et al., 1989; Masters & Mori, 1989).

Idea Retention

Finally, some students can read the words and can comprehend material during ongoing reading. Nonetheless, some students do not perform well on tests due to difficulty with long-term memory. For these students, the most important textbook adaptations are those that focus on retention of ideas.

- *Structure postreading activities to increase retention of content*. Have students answer text-based questions and write summaries to promote memory of text material (Tierney et al., 1990; Vacca & Vacca, 1989).
- *Teach reading strategies to improve retention of textbook material*. Reading strategies such as the classic SQ3R (Robinson, 1941) include a memory component.
- *Teach students to record key concepts and terms for study purposes*. Techniques such as semantic mapping, underlining/annotating text, outlining, and taking notes from textbooks help students to write information that can be rehearsed at a later time (Heimlich & Pittelman, 1986; Irvin, 1990; Irwin & Baker, 1989).
- *Teach memory strategies to improve retention of text material*. Demonstrate mnemonic tricks and rehearsal tactics to students (Crawley & Mountain, 1988; Mastropieri & Scruggs, 1989; Roe et al., 1987).

A Final Note

A potpourri of research-based, classroom-tested techniques are available to make textbook adaptations for students with special needs. At first glance, the task of making adaptations to adjust to the needs of individual students may seem time-consuming. However, the adaptations described here can be integrated into the instructional routine, thus enhancing learning for all students. Moreover, many of the adaptations are designed to foster development of skills and strategies that promote student independence in learning. Such outcomes warrant the investment of time.

Jeanne Shay Schumm is an assistant professor and project codirector of the Teacher Planning Project at the University of Miami. **Kelly Strickler** is a research associate with the Teacher Planning Project at the University of Miami. Address: Jeanne Shay Schumm, Teacher Planning Project, University of Miami, School of Education, PO Box 248065, Coral Gables, FL 33124.

Authors' Notes

1. We gratefully acknowledge support for this study from the United States Department of Education, Grant Award No. H02E90014, Research on General Education Teacher Planning and Adaptation for Students with Handicaps, to the School of Education, University of Miami. Any opinions, findings, or conclusions expressed in this paper are those of the authors and do not necessarily reflect the views of the United States Department of Education.

2. We are also grateful for the assistance of Sharon Vaughn, Twila Grandchamp, Yaro Sojka, Eleanor Levine, Keith Scott, the Florida Diagnostic and Learning Resources System, and the principals and teachers in Dade County Public Schools.

References

Applebee, A.N., Langer, J.A., & Mullis, I.V.S. (1987). *Literature and U.S. history: The instructional experience and factual knowledge of high school juniors*. Princeton, NJ: Educational Testing Service.

Armbruster, B.B., & Anderson, T.H. (1981). *Content area textbooks* (Reading Education Report No. 23). Champaign, IL: Center for the Study of Reading.

Baldwin, R.S. (1985). Children's literature and the reading program. In L.W. Searfoss & J.E. Readence (Eds.), *Helping children learn to read* (pp. 393–408). Englewood Cliffs, NJ: Prentice-Hall.

Beech, M.C. (1983). Simplifying text for mainstreamed students. *Journal of Learning Disabilities, 16,* 400–402.

Bellenger, D.N., Bernhardt, K.L., & Golstucker, J.L. (1976). *Qualitative research in marketing*. Chicago: American Marketing Association.

Bender, W.N. (1985). Strategies for helping the mainstreamed student in secondary social studies classes. *Social Studies, 76,* 269–271.

Blanton, W.E., Wood, K.D., & Moorman, G.B. (1990). The role of purpose in reading instruction. *The Reading Teacher, 43*, 486–493.

Bos, C.S., & Vaughn, S. (1988). *Strategies for teaching students with learning and behavior problems.* Boston: Allyn & Bacon.

Crawley, S.J., & Mountain, L.H. (1988). *Strategies for guiding content reading.* Boston: Allyn & Bacon.

Dupuis, M.M., & Askov, E.N. (1982). *Content area reading: An individualized approach.* Englewood Cliffs, NJ: Prentice-Hall.

Forgan, H.W., & Mangrum, C.T. (1985). *Teaching content area reading skills: A modular preservice and inservice program* (3rd ed.). Columbus: Merrill.

Fry, E. (1977). Fry's readability graph: Clarifications, validity, and extension to level 17. *Journal of Reading, 21*, 242–252.

Fry, E.B. (1989). Reading formulas—Maligned but valid. *Journal of Reading, 32*, 292–297.

Glaser, B.G., & Strauss, A.L. (1967). *The discovery of grounded theory.* Chicago: Aldine.

Graves, M.F., Slater, W.H., Roen, D., Redd-Boyd, T., Duin, A.H., Furniss, D.W., & Hazeltine, P. (1988). Some characteristics of memorable expository writing: Effects of revisions by writers from different backgrounds. *Research in the Teaching of English, 22*, 242–265.

Heimlich, J.E., & Pittelman, S.D. (1986). *Semantic mapping: Classroom applications.* Newark, DE: International Reading Association.

Huey, E.B. (1908). *The psychology and pedagogy of reading.* New York: Macmillan.

Irvin, J.L. (1990). *Reading and the middle school student.* Boston: Allyn & Bacon.

Irwin, J.W. (1986). *Teaching reading comprehension processes.* Englewood Cliffs, NJ: Prentice-Hall.

Irwin, J.W., & Baker, I. (1989). *Promoting active reading comprehension strategies: A resource book for teachers.* Englewood Cliffs, NJ: Prentice-Hall.

Irwin, J.W., & Davis, C.J. (1980). Assessing readability: The checklist approach. *Journal of Reading, 24*, 124–130.

Johnson, R.E., & Vardain, E.B. (1973). Reading, readability and social studies. *The Reading Teacher, 26*, 483–488.

Klare, G.R. (1984). Readability. In P.D. Pearson (Ed.), *Handbook of reading research* (pp. 681–744). New York: Longman.

Lapp, D., Flood, J., & Farnan, N. (1989). *Content area reading and learning: Instructional strategies.* Englewood Cliffs, NJ: Prentice-Hall.

Lincoln, Y.S., & Guba, E.G. (1985). *Naturalistic inquiry.* Beverly Hills, CA: Sage.

Masters, L.F., & Mori, A.A. (1989). *Teaching secondary students with mild learning and behavior problems: Methods, materials, strategies.* Rockville, MD: Aspen.

Mastropieri, M.A., & Scruggs, T.E. (1989). Constructing more meaningful relationships: Mnemonic instruction for special populations. *Educational Psychology Review, 1*, 83–111.

McWilliams, L., & Rakes, T.A. (1979). *Content inventories: English, social studies, science.* Dubuque, IA: Kendall/Hunt.

Moore, D.W., Readence, J.E., & Rickelman, R.J. (1989). *Prereading activities for content area reading and learning* (2nd ed.). Newark, DE: International Reading Association.

Nagy, W.E. (1988). *Teaching vocabulary to improve reading comprehension.* Newark, DE: International Reading Association.

Ohanian, S. (1990). P.L. 94-142: Mainstream or quicksand? *Phi Delta Kappan, 72*, 217–222.

Osborn, J.H., Jones, B.F., & Stein, M. (1985). The case for improving textbooks. *Educational Leadership, 42*, 9–16.

Patton, M.Q. (1980). *Qualitative evaluation methods.* Beverly Hills, CA: Sage.

Polloway, E.A., Patton, J.A., Payne, J.S., & Payne, R.A. (1989). *Strategies for teaching learners with special needs* (4th ed.). Columbus: Merrill.

Rodencich, M.C., & Schumm, J.S. (1985). Script 'n scribe: Parallel study/writing strategies for college students. *Reading World, 24*, 88–96.

Raygor, A. (1977). The Raygor readability estimate: A quick and easy way to determine difficulty. In P.O. Pearson (Ed.), *Reading: Theory, research, and practice. Twenty-sixth yearbook of the National Reading Conference* (pp. 259–263). Clemson, SC: National Reading Conference.

Readence, J.E., Bean, T.W., & Baldwin, R.S. (1985). *Content area reading: An integrated approach* (2nd ed.). Dubuque, IA: Kendall-Hunt.

Rhodes, L.K., & Dudley-Marling, C. (1988). *Readers and writers with a difference: A holistic approach to teaching learning disabled and remedial students.* Englewood Cliffs, NJ: Prentice-Hall.

Robinson, F.P. (1941). *Effective study.* New York: Harper & Row.

Roe, B.D., Stoodt, B.D., & Burns, P.C. (1987). *Secondary school reading instruction: The content areas* (3rd ed.). Boston: Houghton Mifflin.

Schula, J.B., & Turnbull, A.P. (1984). *Mainstreaming handicapped students: A guide for classroom teachers.* Boston: Allyn & Bacon.

Schumm, J.S., & Mangrum, C.T. (in press). FLIP: A framework for fostering textbook thinking. *Journal of Reading.*

Schumm, J.S., & Vaughn, S. (1990, December). Planning for mainstreamed special education students: Perceptions of regular classroom teachers. Paper presented at the meeting of the National Reading Conference, Miami Beach.

Schumm, J.S., & Vaughn, S. (1991). Making adaptations for mainstreamed students: General classroom teachers' perspectives. *Remedial and Special Education, 12*(4), 18–27.

Silberberg, N.E., & Silberberg, M.C. (1969). The bookless curriculum: An educational alternative. *Journal of Learning Disabilities, 20*, 302–307.

Singer, H. (1986). Friendly texts: Description and criteria. In E.K. Dishner, T.W. Bean, J.E. Readence, & D.W. Moore (Eds.), *Reading in the content areas: Improving classroom instruction* (pp. 112–118). Dubuque, IA: Kendall/Hunt.

Stainback, W., Stainback S., Courtnage, L., & Jaben, T. (1985). Facilitating mainstreaming by modifying the mainstream. *Exceptional Children, 52*, 144–152.

Steinley, G.L. (1987). A framework for evaluating textbooks. *Clearing House, 61*, 114–118.

Thomas, E.L., & Robinson, H.A. (1982). *Improving reading in every class: A sourcebook for teachers* (3rd ed.). Boston: Allyn & Bacon.

Tierney, R.J., Readence, J.E., & Dishner, E.K. (1990). *Reading strategies and practices: A compendium* (3rd ed.). Boston: Allyn & Bacon.

Vacca, R.T., & Vacca, J.L. (1989). *Content area reading.* Glenview, IL: Scott-Foresman.

Vaughn, S., Schumm, J.S., Johnson, F., & Daugherty, T. (1991). *What do students think when teachers make adaptations?* Manuscript submitted for publication.

Weiss, I.R. (1978). *Report of the 1977 national survey of science, mathematics, and social studies education.* Washington, DC: U.S. Government Printing Office.

Wood, J.W., & Wooley, J.A. (1986). Adapting textbooks. *The Clearing House, 59*, 332–335.

From *Intervention in School and Clinic* Vol. 27, No. 2, November 1991, pages 78–84. Copyright © 1991 by PRO-ED, Inc. Reprinted with permission.

Assisting Students with Difficult Textbooks: Teacher Perceptions and Practices

Jeanne Shay Schumm
Sharon Vaughn
University of Miami
School-Based Research Project

Linda Saumell
University of Miami

ABSTRACT

The primary purpose of this investigation was to examine teachers' perceptions and practices pertaining to textbook adaptations and instructional strategies to facilitate understanding of textual material. Subjects included 20 elementary, 20 middle, and 20 high school teachers. Each teacher completed the Textbook Adaptation Evaluation Instrument, a Likert-type scale that consists of 31 textbook adaptations. Teachers rated each adaptation in respect to desirability, feasibility, and use. Analyses provided a comparison of teachers' overall rankings of desirability, feasibility, and use for each of the three grade groups (elementary, middle, and high). Findings are discussed in respect to types of adaptations preferred, grade grouping differences, and implications for future research.

Since the early 1900's the type of discourse contained in textbooks has been criticized because it is often difficult to derive information from the text and impedes readers' ability to organize and recall information (Bartlett, 1932; Huey, 1908). Many content area textbooks (particularly in social studies and science) have readability levels superseding their target grade level (Hill & Erwin, 1984) and are inconsistent in their inclusion of considerate text features (Anderson & Armbruster, 1984).

The dilemma of difficult text has been exacerbated with the broadening range of linguistic, cultural, and academic diversity of students in the United States. The increasing numbers of students whose first language is other than English, the passage of the Education for All Handicapped Children Act (PL 94-142) that requires all students with disabilities to be educated in the least restrictive environment, and the current trend away from ability grouping (Au, 1991; Barr, 1989) have all contributed to a burgeoning heterogeneity in the classroom.

In response to this diversity and heightened awareness of the deepening chasm between the learner's reading level and text demands, more and more teachers find themselves in the position of having to find instructional methods to cope with this apparent student/text mismatch. Eliminating textbooks does not seem to be a realistic solution since as much as 90% of teacher decision-making is governed by textbooks (Muther, 1985). Indeed, many administrators expect teachers to rely on textbooks for instructional planning (Shannon, 1987). It is unlikely, then, that content area teachers will abandon textbooks completely

and that some adaptations will be necessary to help students read and learn from text. However, because teachers' guidebooks provide little information to help teachers deal with the full range of student diversity (Schumm & Vaughn, 1992), teachers are often left to their own devises to cope with the one-size-fits-all textbooks issued to them.

Recognizing that students need to become proficient in learning from textbooks, particularly in preparation for the text-driven instruction they will encounter in post-secondary settings (Orlando, Caverly, Swetnam, & Flippo, 1989), a number of content area reading professionals advocate making instructional and textbook adaptations to foster learning (Herber, 1978; Robinson, 1975; Pressley, Johnson, Symons, McGoldrick, & Kurita, 1989; Schumm & Strickler, 1991). For purposes of this investigation, textbook adaptation was broadly defined as any instructional accommodation used to facilitate reading of textbook material (for a review see Schumm & Strickler, 1991). In this context textbook adaptations include: determination of the student/textbook match (e.g., determining readability level), actual changes to the textbook (e.g., abridging textbook content), classroom instructional practices (e.g., pre-teaching vocabulary), and instruction in reading/study strategies that promote independence in textbook reading (e.g., SQ3R).

Numerous research efforts have focused on demonstrating the effectiveness of strategies and adaptations for learning from textbooks (Alvermann, 1981; Moore & Readence, 1984). Indeed, empirical evidence supports the use of a variety of reading strategies and textbook adaptations, although the effectiveness of particular strategies does appear to vary in accordance with the students' grade level, ability level, and content area (Alvermann & Swafford, 1989). Recent inquiry in content area reading has focused on evaluating whether teachers affirm such adaptations and actually incorporate them into their regular instructional repertoire (Alvermann & Moore, 1991). This research suggests that a discrepancy exists between what reading specialists recommend and what occurs in the classroom (Hinchman, 1987; Ratekin, Simpson, Alvermann, & Dishner, 1985; Rich & Pressley, 1990). Wood and Muth (1991) dubbed this discrepancy a gulf between "prevailing and preferred practice."

The alternative to textbook adaptations, traditional textbook assignments that involve student independent reading of text and answering of text-based questions, has long permeated content area instruction. In our study of students' perceptions of teachers' instructional practices (Schumm, Vaughn, & Saumell, 1992), one student described this routine, "Some teachers give you the page number in the textbook, sit down and read a book, leaving you on your own, understand or tough luck if you don't." Another student stated, "I find it most annoying when teachers make us read, and then immediately ask questions without teaching it." Our survey of over 1,800 middle and high school students (Schumm & Vaughn, 1992) as well as individual interviews with over 90 secondary students (Vaughn, Schumm, Saumell, & Klingner, in review) provide evidence that students do not feel they are learning very much from typical textbook assignments and that they need adaptations to promote learning from text.

A number of explanations have been proposed for the disparity between prevailing and preferred practice. Certainly a subgroup of teachers is skeptical about the instructional value of textbook adaptations (Ratekin, et al., 1985). As Edelsky (1989) commented, "doing tricks with print" is a feeble substitute for engaging encounters with genuine text. On the other hand, teachers may view content reading practices as valuable but not part of their responsibility (Gee & Forrester, 1988) or unacceptable in terms of the time required to teach the strategy. Teachers may perceive strategy use as facilitating one goal at the expense of another more important goal (Rich & Pressley, 1990). Professional and environmental constraints may impede teachers' ability to incorporate these practices into their own instructional routines (Davey, 1988; O'Brien, 1988). Also, while many teachers may express a desire to make adaptations, they may see such practices as not feasible given the reality of the classroom condition (Schumm & Vaughn, 1991) and do not feel they are particularly skilled in making such adaptations (Schumm & Vaughn, 1992).

The extent to which teachers value and use reading strategies and adaptations remains unclear. Little research seems to have been conducted in this area, and that which exists has yielded broad variation in the estimates of the number of teachers who actually incorporate instructional adaptations into their classroom routines (see Alvermann & Moore, 1991 for a review). The present investigation was designed to examine teachers' perceptions and practices pertaining to textbook adaptations and instructional strategies to facilitate student understanding of

textual material. We decided to investigate teachers' perceptions of textbook adaptations in terms of **desirability** (value of an adaptation), **feasibility** (potential for implementation within the constraints of the classroom), and **use**. We also decided to examine teachers' perceptions of textbook adaptations across elementary, middle, and high school grade groupings. Recent evidence indicates that teachers' willingness to make instructional adaptations varies across grade groupings (Schumm & Vaughn, 1992), and to our knowledge no studies have been conducted that compare teachers' perceptions and practices regarding textbook adaptations across grade groupings. A secondary purpose of this investigation was to develop an instrument that teacher educators or reading resource specialists might use to structure discussions about textbook adaptations.

METHOD

Subjects

Subjects were 20 elementary (grades 2-5), 20 middle school (grades 6-9), and 20 high school (grades 10-12) teachers from a metropolitan school district in Southeastern United States. Demographic information for the initial cohort of 60 teachers is presented in Table 1. Overall, the gender, highest degree held, ethnicity, and years of teaching experience mirrored the school district as a whole.

Understanding the variability typical of classroom teacher practice in using textbook adaptations (Alvermann & Moore, 1991), we decided to examine a well defined subset of teachers who instruct a diverse student population in their classrooms and who currently teach students representing a wide range of cultural, linguistic, and academic diversity. We felt that identifying a well defined subset of teachers who instruct diverse learners was important because these teachers would have good reason to make adaptations. Thus, all subjects were principal, special education teacher, and self-identified as being effective in meeting the needs of diverse learners, e.g., mainstreamed special education students. We recognize the limitations of using nomination procedures, but also recognize that researchers have few options when attempting to identify "effective" teachers (Leinhardt, 1990).

All regular classroom elementary teachers were eligible for consideration in our initial teacher pool (music, reading resource, and other specialists were not included). In the secondary areas we limited our pool of teachers to social studies and science teachers because other than elective classes, these were the content areas in which special education students were most likely to be mainstreamed, thus increasing the range of student diversity.

The school district's urban setting ensured that each teacher had at least one student whose native language was other than English. Also, to assure a range of academic diversity, teachers were selected who had in their class at least one mainstreamed special education student, one low achieving student, and one average/high achieving student.

Table 1

Background Information Percentages for Sample as Compared with School District Personnel as a Whole

Background Category	District	Total Sample	Elementary Sample	Middle Sample	High Sample
Gender					
Male	26	37	0	28	80
Female	74	63	100	72	20
Highest degree					
Bachelor	51	45	20	55	40
Master	41	40	65	30	25
Specialist	6	13	15	10	15
Doctor	2	2	0	0	0
Ethnicity					
Black/Afro American	27	21	30	22	11
Caucasian/Non-Hispanic	52	50	35	56	58
Caucasian/Hispanic	21	23	35	17	21
Other	4	6	0	5	10
Years teaching					
1 to 5	24	26	10	47	21
6 to 10	16	13	15	10	16
11 to 15	17	11	5	5	21
16 to 20	18	18	20	11	21
20+	25	32	50	27	21

Table 2
Operational Definitions for Superordinate Categories Used to Classify Inventory Items

Category	Operational Definition
Student/Text Interaction	Adaptations that are concerned with the student's overall ability to comprehend the required textbook for a course. (Ex: determine student reading levels and textbook difficulty; preview textbook with students; or do not use textbook.)
Provide Direct Assistance	Adaptations in which direct human assistance is provided by the student's teacher or peers. (Ex.: reading aloud; individual or small group instruction; cooperative learning group; or lectures.)
Simplify Textbook/ Assignments	Adaptations in which the actual textbook is changed. (Ex.: color code or highlight text; construct abridged versions of the text.)
Supplement the Textbook	Adaptations in which other materials augment or replace textbook assignments. (Ex: computer programs, films, videotapes, recordings, field trips, or experiments; and use of multi-level, multi-material approaches.)
Structure Lessons to Promote Comprehension of Textual Material	Adaptations involving teacher methods that enhance student learning of text material. (Ex.: provide summaries, outlines, questions to guide reading, views of assignments; introduce key vocabulary; set purpose for reading; slow pace of assignments; guide class discussions; provide assistance for answering text questions; activate prior knowledge; create interest for reading; or structure post-reading activities to increase retention of material.)
Teach Reading/Study Strategies	Adaptations in which the teacher provides direct instruction that teaches students strategies that can be used independently by students to enhance their comprehension and retention of textbook material. (Ex.: develop study guidelines or outlines; model effective comprehension strategies; teach students to use graphic aids, record key concepts or use SQ3R; or teach memory strategies.)

Measure: Textbook Adaptation Evaluation Instrument

An extensive literature review yielded no one scale that encompassed the full range of textbook adaptations teachers might use to accommodate individual needs. The one instrument that was most closely aligned was the *Instructional Practices Checklist for Reading in the Content Areas* (Shannon, 1984). However, many of the items were unrelated to our concerns (e.g., recreational reading, teacher responsibility for content area reading instruction), and no reliability or validity information was provided.

The Textbook Adaptations Evaluation Instrument (TAEI) was developed to examine teachers' evaluations of the desirability, feasibility, and use of textbook adaptations (See Appendix). It consists of two parts: evaluation of adaptations and teacher ratings of knowledge and willingness to make adaptations. Part I, Adaptations Evaluation, consists of a list of 31 possible textbook adaptations. The instrument directs teachers to rate (on a Likert-type scale; 1 = low, 7 = high) each adaptation in terms of desirability, feasibility, and use. The list of adaptations was derived from two sources: an extensive review of literature and transcripts of a series of six focus group interviews. Our literature search included research and practical articles which focused on textbook adaptations, as well as content area reading textbooks and reading methods compendiums.

A series of six focus group interviews (Stewart & Shamdasani, 1990) was conducted so that the list of adaptations constructed for the TAEI would be buttressed with adaptations teachers actually use and would be written in language familiar to classroom teachers. Separate focus group interviews were conducted with groups of reading resource specialists, ESL teachers, and special education teachers. In addition three focus group interviews were conducted with elementary teachers and content area teachers assembled by grade grouping: middle school and high school. Each interview session included four to five teachers. Procedures for focus group interviews described by Vaughn, Schumm, and Sinegub (in review) were followed. Each interview was audio taped and then audio scanned by two researchers to identify adaptations and to attend to the language teachers used to refer to adaptations.

After both the literature review and focus group interviews were completed, we compiled a master list of textbook adaptations. To organize the individual items into meaningful categories for discussion purposes, two independent coders read the inventory items and generated possible categories using an "open coding" category generating process (Strauss & Corbin, 1990) that yielded a total of 14 initial categories. After combining related categories, the initial list of categories was then reduced to six. Each category was operationally defined (see Table 2). Then, using the revised six category scheme, two raters independently sorted the items with an interrater agreement rating of .82. The resulting superordinate categories were: student/text interaction (3 items), direct assistance (5 items), simplify textbook (8 items), supplement textbook (3 items), structure lessons to promote comprehension (6 items), and teach reading/ study strategies (5 items). One item which could not be labelled as a textbook adaptation was included as a gauge of teacher reliance on text based instruction. That item was Item 31 (avoid use of textbooks). The superordinate categories were not placed on the scale and individual items were randomly ordered on the protocols. Part II of the TAEI scale consists of 3 items assessing teacher ratings (on a four point scale) of their knowledge of and willingness to make textbook adaptations.

A pilot study with 82 teachers was conducted to field test items and to ascertain scale reliability. Item intercorrelations were calculated and three items were eliminated, reducing the original 34 item scale to 31 items. Pilot data yielded Cronbach's alpha coefficients of .91 for the desirability subscale, .82 for the feasibility subscale, and .81 for the use subscale.

Procedures

Following the pilot testing and refinement of the TAEI, the instrument was hand delivered to all participating teachers and then collected one week later. All 60 instruments were completed and returned.

RESULTS

Scale Reliability

The revised 31 item version of the TAEI yielded the following Cronbach's alpha coefficients: .93 for the desirability subscale, .92 for the feasibility subscale, and .87 for the use subscale.

Table 3

Means, Standard Deviations, and Medians for Teacher Ratings of Desirability, Feasibility, and Use of Textbook Adaptations

	Desirability Mean SD	Mdn	Feasibility Mean SD	Mdn	Use Mean SD	Mdn
Student/Text Interaction						
1. Determine student reading levels	6.05[a,b] 1.38	7	4.93[c] 1.79	5	4.22 2.12	4
2. Preview textbook with students	6.07[a,b] 1.36	7	6.12[c] 1.26	7	5.77 1.75	7
3. Determine level of difficulty of textbook	6.03[a,b] 1.41	7	4.64[c] 2.02	5	3.86 2.10	4
Provide Direct Assistance						
4. Read textbook aloud to students	4.48[a,b] 2.22	5	4.83[c] 2.08	5	3.93 2.36	3.5
5. Explain textbook information thoroughly in lectures	6.51[a,b] .92	7	6.20[c] 1.05	7	5.90 1.26	6
6. Pair students	5.52[a,b] 1.83	6	4.72[c] 2.03	5	3.68 2.23	4
7. Work with students individually	5.58[a,b] 1.72	6	3.88[c] 1.80	4	3.32 1.90	3
8. Organize cooperative learning groups	5.77[a,b] 1.59	6	5.07[c] 1.89	5	4.35 2.03	5
Simplify Textbook/Assignments						
9. Audiotape textbook content	4.61[a,b] 2.12	5	3.29[c] 1.89	3	2.45 1.94	1
10. Write abridged versions	5.19[a,b] 2.17	6	3.90[c] 2.20	4	3.02 1.93	3
11. Summarize/reduce textbook information to guide classroom discussions	6.35[a,b] .95	7	5.75[c] 1.23	6	5.50 1.51	6

continued

Table 3 (cont.)	Mean SD	Mdn	Mean SD	Mdn	Mean SD	Mdn
12. Write study guides	6.00[a,b] 1.25	6	5.21[c] 1.48	5	4.78 1.76	5
13. Color code textbooks	5.03[a,b] 2.08	5.5	3.87[c] 2.08	4	2.93 2.15	2
14. Reduce length of assignments	5.93[a,b] 1.56	7	5.66[c] 1.48	6	5.31 1.67	5
15. Use multi-level reading materials	5.85[a,b] 1.68	7	4.51[c] 2.15	5	4.15 2.12	4
16. Provide assistance in answering text-based questions	5.97[a,b] 1.37	6	5.43[c] 1.31	6	4.95 1.61	5
Supplement the Textbook						
17. Use film/videotape/recordings	6.25[a,b] 1.27	7	6.00[c] 1.24	6	5.28 1.70	6
18. Use computer programs	5.81[a,b] 1.80	7	3.84[c] 2.13	4	2.52 1.77	2
19. Provide direct experiences (field trips, etc.)	6.35[a,b] .99	7	4.95 1.78	5	4.78 1.82	5
Structure Lessons to Promote Comprehension						
20. Preview reading assignments	5.97[a,b] 1.46	7	5.43[c] 1.62	6	4.97 1.82	5
21. Provide purposes for reading	6.55[a,b] .79	7	6.18[c] 1.05	7	5.95 1.24	6
22. Create interest in reading assignments	6.47[a,b] .83	7	5.47[c] 1.54	6	4.95 1.88	5
23. Introduce key vocabulary	6.47[b] .98	7	6.44[c] .99	7	6.14 1.27	7
24. Provide questions to guide reading	6.49[b] .94	7	6.38[c] 1.01	7	6.12 1.32	7
25. Structure post-reading activities	6.14[a,b] 1.09	7	5.41[c] 1.43	6	5.07 1.59	5
Teach Reading Strategies						
26. Teach comprehension monitoring techniques	6.56[a,b] .84	7	5.81[c] 1.43	6	5.47 1.59	6
27. Model effective reading strategies	5.83[a,b] 1.45	6	5.00[c] 1.59	5	4.49 1.78	5
28. Teach students to record key concepts	6.15[a,b] 1.39	7	5.16[c] 1.86	6	4.30 2.05	4.5
29. Teach students to use graphic aids	6.48[a,b] 1.07	7	6.27[c] 1.09	7	5.75 1.48	6
30. Teach memory strategies	5.93[a,b] 1.47	7	5.10[c] 1.62	5	4.57 1.69	5
31. Avoid use of text	3.15 2.11	3	3.17 2.02	3	3.37 2.12	3

Note: a = Wilcoxon Matched-Pairs Signed Ranks Test comparisons between ratings of desirability and feasibility significant at .05 level; b = Wilcoxon Matched-Pairs Signed Ranks Test comparisons between ratings of desirability and use significant at .05 level; c = Wilcoxon Matched-Pairs Signed Ranks Test comparisons between ratings of feasibility and use significant at .05 level.

Overall Ratings of Adaptations

The means, standard deviations, and medians by item from the TAEI for all participating teachers are presented in Table 3. Items are categorized by superordinate category and not the order on which they appeared on the scale. Mean desirability ratings were the highest ranging from 4.44 to 6.59, feasibility ratings were somewhat lower ranging from 3.15 to 6.43, and use ratings were the lowest ranging from 2.16 to 6.12.

The Kendall Coefficient of Concordance was used to measure the association among teachers' rankings of desirability, feasibility, and use for each item. In every case except one, Item 31 (avoid the use of textbooks), the difference between the rankings proved to be statistically significant. If there were statistically significant differences among the three sets of rankings, the Wilcoxon Matched-Pairs Signed Rank statistic was employed to conduct post hoc analysis of the data. This analysis revealed that in the majority of cases, mean desirability ratings were significantly higher than both feasibility and use ratings. Similarly, feasibility ratings in each case were higher than use ratings. On Items 23 (introduce key vocabulary) and 24 (provide questions to guide reading), no differences between desirability and feasibility were noted, although in both cases desirability/use and feasibility/ use differences were observed.

Ratings of Adaptations by Grade Grouping

The Kruskal-Wallis test was used to assess significant differences among elementary, middle and high school teachers on their ratings of each item. Grade grouping differences proved to be statistically significant on three desirability, five feasibility, and seven use items. Table 4 reports the means and standard deviations for each item by grade grouping.

When there were significant differences among the grade groupings, the Mann-Whitney-Wilcoxon statistic was employed for the purposes of post hoc analysis. This analysis indicated that elementary teachers differed from their secondary counterparts with elementary teachers' item ratings being substantially higher. Elementary teachers' desirability ratings of Item 4 (read textbook aloud to students) was significantly higher than those of high school teachers. The two other items in the desirability subscale that reached traditional significance levels were both related to student grouping: Item 6 (pair students) and Item 8 (cooperative learning groups).

Elementary teachers' ratings were significantly higher than their secondary counterparts on four of the feasibility items: Item 1 (determine student reading levels); Item 6 (pair students); Item 8 (cooperative learning groups); and Item 15 (multi-level reading materials). Elementary and middle school teachers' ratings were significantly lower than those of high school teachers on Item 11 (summarize/reduce textbook information to guide class discussions).

In terms of use of adaptations, elementary teachers' ratings were significantly higher than both middle and high school teachers on five items: Item 1 (determine student reading levels); Item 6 (pair students); Item 8 (cooperative learning groups); Item 15 (multi-level materials); and Item 18 (computer programs). Both elementary and middle school teachers reported use of Item 4 (read textbook aloud to students), more frequently than high school teachers. Yet high school teachers reported more frequent use of Item 11 (summarize/reduce textbook information to guide classroom discussions) than both elementary and middle school teachers.

Teachers' Knowledge of How to Make Textbook Adaptations and Willingness to Do So

Part II of the TAEI asked respondents to react to three general statements pertaining to textbook adaptations on a four point rating scale. In response to the first statement, "Overall, my knowledge and skills for making textbook adaptations are....", teachers reported that their knowledge and skills in making adaptations were high. Eighty-five percent of the elementary teachers, 80% of the middle school teachers, and 74% of the high school teachers rated their skills as good or excellent. There was more diversity among grade groupings in their responses to the second statement: "Overall, my willingness to use my planning time to create textbook adaptations to meet individual student differences can be described as ..." Seventy percent of the elementary teachers, 90% of the middle school teachers, and only 53% of the high school teachers rated their willingness as extremely high or high. The third statement was as follows: "If textbook publishers, district or school curriculum specialists, etc. were to provide specific textbook adaptations for me to use in my classroom, my overall willingness to use such textbook adaptations to meet individual student differences can be described as ..." Ninety-five percent of the elementary and middle school teachers rated their willingness as extremely high or high, while only 68% of the high school teachers had such positive ratings.

Table 4

Teacher Ratings of Desirability, Feasibility, and Use of Textbook Adaptations by Grade Grouping

	Desirability			Feasibility			Use		
	Elem. School	Mid. School	High School	Elem. School	Mid. School	High School	Elem. School	Mid. School	High School
	Mean SD	Mean SD	Mean SD	Mean SD	Mean SD	Mean SD	Mean SD	Mean SD	Mean SD
Student/Text Interaction									
1. Determine student	6.60	6.05	5.50	5.85a,b	4.70	4.25	5.55a,b	3.70	3.40
reading levels	.75	1.15	1.85	1.60	1.46	1.97	1.82	1.98	1.98
2. Preview textbook	6.35	6.20	5.65	6.25	6.25	5.85	6.25	3.85	5.20
with students	1.09	1.15	1.73	1.21	.97	1.57	1.37	1.42	2.24
3. Determine level of	5.95	6.11	6.05	4.20	5.26	4.50	3.70	4.47	3.45
difficulty of textbook	1.54	.99	1.67	1.80	2.00	2.21	1.81	2.20	2.24
Provide Direct Assistance									
4. Read textbook aloud	5.45b	4.55	3.45	5.32	4.80	4.40	5.05b	3.65	3.10
to students	2.04	2.14	2.11	1.95	2.31	1.96	2.19	2.37	2.17
5. Explain textbook	6.53	6.40	6.60	5.79	6.20	6.60	5.47	5.90	6.30
information	.96	.88	.94	1.18	1.06	.75	1.43	1.12	1.13
thoroughly									
in lectures									
6. Pair students	6.50a,b	5.15	4.90	5.95a,b	4.35	3.85	5.50a,b	2.65	2.90
	.95	1.73	2.22	1.40	1.90	2.16	1.61	1.87	2.02
7. Work with students	5.47	4.05	5.40	3.37	4.05	4.20	3.25	3.05	3.65
individually	1.90	1.67	2.01	1.67	1.67	2.02	1.94	1.82	1.98
8. Organize cooperative	6.65a,b	5.50	5.15	6.15a,b	4.35	4.70	5.65a,b	3.60	3.80
learning groups	.67	1.67	1.81	1.53	1.81	1.90	1.66	1.86	1.96
Simplify Textbook/Assignments									
9. Audiotape textbook	4.90	4.72	4.21	3.37	3.33	3.16	2.79	1.74	2.21
content	1.94	1.84	2.55	1.74	1.65	2.29	2.12	1.41	2.15
10. Write abridged	5.95	5.35	4.30	4.32	3.95	3.45	3.00	3.10	2.95
versions	1.68	1.98	2.52	1.97	2.14	2.46	1.80	2.02	2.06
11. Summarize/	6.20	6.35	6.50	5.15b	5.80	6.30	4.95b	5.47	6.05
reduce text-	.95	1.04	.89	1.27	1.15	1.03	1.39	1.65	1.36
book information to									
guide classroom									
discussions									
12. Write study guides	6.05	6.20	5.75	5.05	5.30	5.26	4.53	4.55	5.26
	.91	.83	1.77	1.39	1.74	1.88	1.74	1.70	1.82
13. Color code textbooks	5.20	4.85	5.05	3.60	4.15	3.85	2.95	2.60	3.25
	1.99	1.98	2.35	1.70	2.03	2.39	1.79	2.30	2.36
14. Reduce length of	6.40	6.35	5.05	5.74	6.21	5.05	5.53	5.84	4.60
assignments	1.14	.88	2.06	1.28	1.08	1.79	1.30	1.39	2.01
15. Use multi-level	6.30	6.05	5.20	5.60a,b	4.21	3.70	5.40a,b	3.65	3.40
reading materials	1.13	.23	2.29	1.50	1.93	2.49	1.82	1.79	2.23
16. Provide assistance in	5.95	6.30	5.65	5.00	5.50	5.80	4.65	4.95	5.25
answering text-based	1.32	.87	1.76	1.45	1.00	1.36	1.73	1.36	1.74
questions									

Table 4 (cont)

Teacher Ratings of Desirability, Feasibility, and Use of Textbook Adaptations by Grade Grouping

	Desirability			Feasibility			Use		
	Elem. School	Mid. School	High School	Elem. School	Mid. School	High School	Elem. School	Mid. School	High School
	Mean SD	Mean SD	Mean SD	Mean SD	Mean SD	Mean SD	Mean SD	Mean SD	Mean SD
Supplement the Textbook									
17. Use film/videotape/ recordings	6.35 .88	6.50 .83	5.90 1.83	5.90 .97	6.25 .97	5.85 1.66	5.20 1.51	5.80 1.28	4.85 2.13
18. Use computer programs	6.40 1.39	6.06 1.21	4.95 2.32	4.60 1.57	3.67 2.20	3.17 2.43	3.55[a,b] 1.85	2.00 1.28	1.89 1.64
19. Provide direct experiences (field trips, etc.)	6.35 .81	6.65 .75	6.05 1.28	5.10 1.62	4.85 1.81	4.90 1.97	5.00 1.52	4.53 1.90	4.80 2.07
Structure Lessons to Promote Comprehension									
20. Preview reading assignments	5.85 1.66	6.10 1.25	6.10 1.51	5.45 1.91	5.30 1.42	5.55 1.57	5.00 2.00	5.00 1.81	4.90 1.74
21. Provide purposes for reading	6.65 .67	6.40 .75	6.60 .94	6.45 .83	5.95 1.05	6.15 1.23	6.40 .94	5.55 1.47	5.90 1.17
22. Create interest in reading assignments	6.45 .76	6.30 1.03	6.65 .67	5.50 1.36	5.30 1.69	5.60 1.60	4.95 1.96	4.70 1.84	5.21 1.90
23. Introduce key vocabulary	6.80 .52	6.30 1.08	6.30 1.17	6.80 .52	6.21 1.08	6.30 1.74	6.45 1.05	5.74 1.52	6.20 1.15
24. Provide questions to guide reading	6.47 1.07	6.40 .99	6.60 .75	6.25 1.21	6.30 1.03	6.60 .75	5.95 1.57	6.05 1.36	6.35 .98
25. Structure post-reading activities	6.30 1.08	5.95 1.78	6.15 1.04	5.25 1.52	5.39 1.20	5.60 1.57	5.15 1.60	4.94 .55	5.10 1.68
Teach Reading Strategies									
26. Teach comprehension monitoring techniques	6.55 .76	6.63 .76	6.50 1.00	5.65 1.35	5.79 1.55	6.00 1.45	5.37 1.42	5.58 1.64	5.45 1.76
27. Model effective reading strategies	6.25 1.12	6.00 1.33	5.25 1.71	5.30 1.30	5.37 1.50	4.35 1.79	5.00 1.52	4.63 1.80	3.85 1.87
28. Teach students to record key concepts	6.20 1.47	5.90 1.62	6.37 1.01	5.05 1.73	4.80 2.09	5.67 1.72	4.35 1.81	3.75 2.15	4.83 2.10
29. Teach students to use graphic aids	6.55 1.91	6.30 1.13	6.60 .88	6.30 1.22	6.00 1.26	6.50 .69	5.90 1.55	5.40 1.60	5.95 1.28
30. Teach memory strategies	6.00 1.33	6.10 1.65	5.70 1.46	5.05 1.51	4.90 1.68	5.35 1.69	4.80 1.51	4.25 1.77	4.65 1.81
31. Avoid use of textbook	3.56 2.09	3.06 2.16	2.83 2.12	2.75 1.57	3.28 1.99	3.42 2.39	3.69 2.24	3.18 1.88	3.26 2.31

Note: a = Mann-Whitney U comparisons between means of elementary and middle school teachers significant at .05 level; b = Mann-Whitney U comparisons between means of elementary and high school teachers significant at .05 level; c = Mann-Whitney U comparisons between means of middle and high school teachers significant at .05 level.

DISCUSSION

The primary purpose of this investigation was to examine elementary, middle, and high school teachers' evaluations of the desirability, feasibility, and use of textbook adaptations in their classrooms. This research was conducted with classroom teachers who had been identified as being effective in their instruction with diverse student learners and who were currently teaching diverse learners during the time of the investigation.

Our findings indicate that these teachers value textbook adaptations, and despite the constraints of the classroom condition, that they implement a variety of adaptations, at least to a moderate degree. The moderate to high ratings of the desirability of all items except one (Item 31, avoid use of textbooks) provide evidence that classroom teachers find most textbook adaptations to be at least somewhat desirable. The highest rated items on the desirability subscale fell in two of the categories used to classify inventory items: structure lessons to promote learning of text material and teaching reading/study strategies.

The lowest items on the desirability subscale were primarily those from the categories: simplify the textbook and provide direct assistance. It appears that the more desirable adaptations were linked to encouraging student engagement with text and promotion of comprehension or study skills. Adaptations more closely aligned with meeting the needs of students with decoding problems (e.g., read the textbook aloud, audiotape textbook, abridging the textbook) were viewed less favorably. Teacher open-ended comments indicated that even though teachers identified such adaptations as desirable, they were not always considered feasible.

Feasibility ratings were significantly lower and represented a broader range of ratings. Of the five items rated highest on the feasibility subscale, three were related to structure lessons to promote comprehension, one related to provide direct assistance (explain information thoroughly in lectures), and one was to teach reading/study strategies. Least feasible adaptations related to simplify the text, avoid the text, and provide direct assistance (work with students individually). Apparently teachers question the feasibility of providing students with adaptations that assist in decoding and that are individualized in nature. Many of the lowest rated feasibility items (e.g., construct abridged versions, audiotape textbook content, color code textbooks) entail a great deal of preparation time on the part of teachers. On the other hand, the most highly rated feasibility items are likely to be applied during teaching (introduce vocabulary, provide purposes for reading, create interest) and require little, if any, preparation. Not surprisingly, these findings suggest that if teachers make adaptations, they are likely to be ones that do not necessitate a great deal of advance preparation and can be implemented "on the spot" during instruction.

Use ratings were generally lower than both desirability and feasibility. Results indicated that while teachers use a variety of adaptations (19 of the 31 items had a median rating of 5 or higher), a number of adaptations are rarely, if ever implemented [e.g., Item 9 (audiotape textbook content) and Item 18 (computer programs)].

Few grade grouping (elementary, middle school, high school) differences emerged on *any* of the three subscales in Part I of the inventory. The most notable differences were: determining student reading levels (more likely to occur in elementary classes that are self-contained and where the classroom teacher has fewer student reading levels to know), use of multilevel reading materials (more likely to occur when students' reading levels are known), and use of a variety of student groupings (more likely to occur in elementary classrooms where teachers are not constrained by 50 minute class periods).

The lack of statistically significant differences among grade groupings on the majority of inventory items is not unexpected. We recognize that our findings are based on the self-reports of teachers identified as being effective in working with diverse student needs. Additional research using the TAEI with other teacher groups needs to be conducted. Similarly, research using classroom observations is also warranted. We have conducted some initial analyses of teachers' use of textbook adaptations using interviews and classroom observations from an extant data base (Schumm, Vaughn, Haager, McDowell, Rothlein, &

Saumell, in press). Our initial findings suggest that classroom teachers make adaptations for the class as a whole, rarely for individual students with learning disabilities or for students who speak English as a second language. It has been suggested if inclusion is to be successful, that success is largely dependent on teachers' willingness to make accommodations for individual student needs (Stainback, Stainback, Courtnage, & Jaben, 1985). Yet it is unclear whether those adaptations need to be individualized in nature or whether alterations to general classroom instruction (e.g., strategy instruction and interactive teaching) can facilitate learning of students with special needs. Indeed, some recent evidence suggests that low achieving students are resistant to adaptations that may single them out or draw attention to their disabilities (Vaughn, Schumm, & Kouzekanani, 1993; Vaughn, Schumm, Niarhos, & Daugherty, 1993). We also observed that teachers did not have a systematic, regular plan for adaptation use. We are conducting additional research to confirm or disconfirm these findings.

As has been reported elsewhere (Graham & Harris, 1993), strategy instructional procedures have been effective largely in the hands of the researcher and have yet to "go to school" and be used regularly by classroom teachers. This gap between documented effective instructional practice by university based researchers and actual practice, even by teachers who are considered effective by their colleagues, needs to be considered in the educational community (Wood & Muth, 1991). We advocate the development of effective strategies that can be incorporated into teaching routines with little materials preparation on the part of teachers, and that can be taught to the class as a whole with practice and rehearsal in small groups.

We also propose that when developing such strategies, it is imperative to keep a "reality principle" in mind. In considering the research literature on training for teachers working with "at-risk" children, Gersten and Woodward (1990) proposed a "reality principle" that attributes success in staff development to the inclusion of "concrete, usable ('classroom friendly') remedies to instructional problems". If we are to close the gap between "prevailing and preferred practice" (Wood & Muth, 1990), then two realities must be recognized.

First, teachers are unlikely to utilize adaptations that require a great deal of advance preparation. It would seem advantageous for publishers and district and state curriculum supervisors to provide teachers with materials that they can use to accommodate individual student differences. Also, when adaptations are proposed to teachers through the professional literature or professional development programs, attention should be paid to how suggested adaptations can be implemented in classrooms including students with a wide range of needs.

A second reality is that accommodations that teachers are most willing to make are more related to reading comprehension and study skills. Adaptations that have been posed in the literature for helping students who literally cannot read the text are deemed undesirable and are simply not used. This finding is particularly alarming given the trend in some school systems to eliminate mandatory reading instruction beyond the elementary grades and to delegate reading instruction to content area teachers. Research in this area needs to be continued.

For years the reading community has been coaxing teachers to determine the readability of textbooks, rewrite materials, develop study guides, etc. However desirable such activities may be, teachers are unlikely to do them. If we want teachers—even highly dedicated and skilled teachers—to make adaptations, the adaptations need to be palatable, realistic, and manageable.

The secondary purpose of this investigation was to develop and evaluate an instrument that could be used to explore teachers' perceptions about textbook adaptations. The findings concerning the reliability of the measure are encouraging. It appears that the TAEI is a reliable measure that has discriminative properties. We have found the TAEI to be useful in undergraduate content area courses and professional development workshops to trigger discussion about textbook adaptations.

REFERENCES

Alvermann, D. E. (1981). The compensatory effect of graphic organizers on descriptive text. *Journal of Educational Research, 75*, 44-48.

Alvermann, D. E., & Moore, D. W. (1991). Secondary school reading. In R. Barr, M. L. Kamil, P. Mosenthal, & P. D. Pearson (Eds.), *Handbook of reading research* (Vol. 2, pp. 951-983). New York: Longman.

Alvermann, D. E., & Swafford, J. (1989). Do content area strategies have a research base? *Journal of Reading, 32*, 388-394.

Armbruster, B. B. & Anderson, T. H. (1984). Content area textbooks. In R. C. Anderson, J. Osborn, & R. J. Tierney (Eds.), *Proceedings of the conference on learning to read in American schools: Basal readers and content text*, 193-226. Champaign, IL: University of Illinois.

Au, K. (Ed.). (1991). Organizing for instruction [Special issue]. *The Reading Teacher, 44* (8).

Barr, R. (1989). The social organization of literacy instruction. In S. McCormick & J. Zutell (Eds.), *Cognitive and social perspectives for literacy research and instruction*. Thirty-eighth Yearbook of the National Reading Conference (pp. 19-33). Chicago: National Reading Conference.

Bartlett, F. D. (1932). *Remembering*. Cambridge, MA: Cambridge University Press.

Davey, B. (1988). How do classroom teachers use their textbooks? *Journal of Reading, 31*, 340-345.

Edelsky, C. (1989). *Challenge to educators: The development of educated persons*. Paper presented at the Appalachian State University's Distinguished Scholars Colloquim.

Gee, T. C., & Forrester, N. (1988), Moving reading instruction beyond the reading classroom. *Journal of Reading, 31*, 505-511.

Gersten, R., & Woodward, J. (1992). The quest to translate research into classroom practice: Strategies for assisting classroom teachers' work with "at risk" students and students with disabilities. In D. Carnine & E. Kameenui (Eds), *Higher cognitive functioning for all students* (pp. 201-218). Austin, TX: Pro-Ed.

Graham, S., & Harris, K. R. (1993). Cognitive strategy instruction: Methodological issues and guidelines in conducting research. In S. Vaughn, & c. Bos (Eds.), *Learning disabilities research: Theory, methodology, assessment and ethics*. New York: Springer-Verlag.

Herber, H. L. (1978). *Teaching reading in the content areas*. Englewood Cliffs, NJ: Prentice Hall.

Hinchman, K. (1987). The textbook and three content-area teachers. *Reading Research and Instruction, 26*, 247-263.

Hill, W., & Erwin, R. (1984). The readability of content textbooks used in middle and junior high schools. *Reading Psychology, 5*, 105-117.

Huey, E. B. (1908). *The psychology and pedagogy of reading*. New York: Macmillan.

Leinhardt, G. (1990). Capturing craft in teaching. *Educational Research, 19,* 21-23.

Moore, D. W., & Readence, J. E. (1984). A quantitative and qualitative review of graphic organizer research. *Journal of Educational Research, 78,* 11-17.

Muther, C. (1985). What every textbook evaluator should know. *Educational Leadership, 42,* 4-8.

O'Brien, D. G. (1988). Secondary preservice teachers' resistance to content reading instruction: A proposal for a broader rationale. In J. E. Readence & R. S. Baldwin (Eds.), *Dialogues in literacy research* (pp. 237-244). Chicago, IL: National Reading Conference.

Orlando, V. P., Caverly, D. C., Swetham, L. A., & Flippo, R. F. (1989). Text demands in college classes: An investigation. *Forum for Reading, 21,* 43-48.

Pressley, M., Johnson, C. J., Symons, S., McGoldrick, J. A., & Kurita, J. (1989). Strategies that improve memory and comprehension of what is read. *Elementary School Journal, 90,* 3-32.

Ratekin, N., Simpson, M. L., Alvermann, D. E., & Dishner, E. K. (1985). Why teachers resist content reading instruction. *Journal of Reading, 28,* 432-437.

Rich, S. & Pressley, M. (1990). Teacher acceptance of reading comprehension strategy instruction. *The Elementary School Journal, 91,* 43-64.

Robinson, H. A. (1975). *Teaching reading and study strategies: The content areas.* Boston, MA: Allyn and Bacon.

Schumm, J. S., & Strickler, K. (1991). Guidelines for adapting content area textbooks: Keeping teachers and students content. *Intervention, 27,* 79-84.

Schumm, J. S., & Vaughn, S. (1992). Planning for mainstreamed special education students: Perceptions of general education classroom teachers. *Exceptionality, 3,* 81-98.

Schumm, J. S., & Vaughn, S. (1991). Making adaptations for mainstreamed students: General classroom teachers' perceptions. *Remedial and Special Education, 12,* 18-27.

Schumm, J. S., Vaughn, S. & Saumell, L (1992). What teachers do when the textbook is tough: Students speak out. *Journal of Reading Behavior, 24,* 481-503.

Shannon, A. J. (1984). Monitoring reading instruction in the content areas. *Journal of Reading, 28,* 128-134.

Shannon, P. (1987). Commercial reading materials: A technological ideology, and the de-skilling of teachers. *Elementary School Journal, 87,* 311-313.

Stainback, Stainback, Courtnage, & Jaban T. (1985). Facilitating mainstreaming by modifying the mainstream. *Exceptional Children, 52,* 144-152.

Stewart, D. W., & Shamdasani, P. N. (1990). *Focus groups: Theory and practice.* Newbury Park, CA: Sage.

Strauss, A., & Corbin, J. (1990). *Basics of qualitative research.* Newbury Park, CA: Sage.

Vaughn, S., Schumm, J. S., Klingner, J., & Saumell, L (in review). *Students' views of instructional practices: Implications for inclusion.*

Vaughn, S., Schumm, J. S., & Kouzekanani, K. (1993). What do students with learning disabilities think when their general education teachers make adaptations? *Journal of Learning Disabilities, 26,* 545-555.

Vaughn, S., Schumm, J. S., Niarhos, F., & Daugherty, T. (1993). What do students think when teachers make adaptations? *Teaching and Teacher Education, 9,* 107-118.

Vaughn, S., Schumm, J. S., & Sinagub, J. (in review). *The Focus group interview: Use and application in education research.*

Wood, K. D., & Muth, K. D. (1991). The case for improved instruction in the middle grades. *Journal of Reading, 35,* 84-91.

From *Reading Research and Instruction* Vol. 34, No. 1, 1994, pages 39–56, published by the College Reading Association. Copyright © 1994 by Jeanne S. Schumm. Reprinted with permission of the author.

Dialogue in Teaching as Critical Instruction

by: Glenda Moss

While state tests are driving many middle school teachers to use traditional classroom practices centered around impersonal drill and practice, interpersonal communication patterns and dialogue in teaching offer potential for students to develop critical thinking skills. My students grew from critically dialoguing with me about the cultural differences evidenced in test answer choices on the state test that held me accountable. While this dialogue helped my minority students to successfully choose correct answers on the test, my hope was that their consciousness of the influence of culture on education would empower them to become critical thinkers and critical citizens capable of contributing towards building a more democratic society. By doing so, dialogue in teaching as critical instruction would produce in practice what Dewey (1916) wrote about in theory—democracy and education as integrally related. The following, drawn from my reflexive memory, is an example of typical dialogical conversations I experienced while teaching classes of predominantly African-American students in East Texas.

DIALOGUE EXAMPLE I

Teacher: 15 of you missed question 10 on our practice test yesterday. That question is testing to see if you understand double negatives. Let's see if we can figure out why we are missing that one. Look at your answer and think about why you picked the answer you picked.

Raylon: I picked the one that sounded right.

Yolanda: So did I.

Marcus: I did too.

Shakeisha: Me too.

John: I put the one that sounded right, and I got it right.

Teacher: Why do you think putting what sounds right worked for John, but not for others?

Marcus: Maybe John talks right and we don't.

Teacher: What does it mean to talk right?

Yolanda: You know.

Teacher: White?

Yolanda: Yeah.

Marcus: Who says what is correct grammar? What's wrong with the way we talk?

Teacher: That's a good question. Who decides?

Jason: The TAAS test.

Teacher: Who makes the TAAS test?

Jason: Who does make it?

The example dialogue evidences how allowing students to dialogue about the state test, which holds teachers accountable for learning, results in a critical dialogue about power issues that are implicit in the test. These types of dialogues frequently resulted in extended conversations about what is fair and not fair in state testing that seemed to favor middle class students who tended to speak the same English usage as what appeared on the test. Many of the students in my classes were not middle class, and most were African-American. Most spoke a dialect of English that would result in incorrect responses on the TAAS test if the student chose the answer based on "what sounded right."

Allowing the above example of critical dialogue often opened a door for me to enter into a relationship with my students based on understanding. We would talk about when and how people learn language that results in the differences that were evident in the classroom and on resultant performance on state tests. Most found it easy to understand that they learned what is considered non-standard usage when they were infants and toddlers. They could also understand the difference between what was considered the standard North American English lan guage that I was hired to teach them and the dialectical English that they spoke in most settings—home, neighborhood, church.

I found that building relationship with my students and working within the interpersonal group process were key elements to creating a learning environment. Drawing on middle school research that promotes cooperative learning, interdisciplinary teaming, and interdisciplinary projects-based instruction, I physically restructured my classroom and instructional patterns to give my students more control over their learning. I replaced the rows of desks with tables and chairs. I supplemented the one adopted text with a small classroom library of resources. The better job I did at creating a learning environment where my students could access information from a variety of resources as well as draw on their own experiences, the higher level of student engagement I observed and the less discipline problems I encountered. This was not an easy transition.

It took several months of allowing my students to work on their writing in a cooperative group setting before they began to accept responsibility for their own work and contribute to the success of their peers. I replaced my desks with tables, allowing four or five students to sit at the same table. I became comfortable with students talking about their writing while writing. Talk considered "off task" eventually evolved into talk that appeared essential to learning. I came to appreciate this "social talk" between students as it contributed to building the learning relationship necessary for the students to become participants in a learning group. What follows are brief examples of talk that went on during work time.

DIALOGUE EXAMPLE II

Mike: How do you spell environment?

Tisha: e-n-v-i-r-o-n-m-e-n-t

Crystol: Are you going to Drew's party Friday?

Ebony: Yeah

Chrystol: What time is it?

Ebony: 7

Jarrod: Listen to this. [Jarrod reads his paper to Andre.]

Andre: You gotta give more reasons. It's not convincing.

Jermaine: Would you read this and see how it sounds?

Jeremy: [After reading.] It sounds good, but you got fragments and misspelled words.

Tina: I hate doing the work.

Nia: It's easy.

LaKeisha: Yeah, for you maybe.

Nia: Just write what you thinking like Miss Moss says then fix it up after.

Tina: Would you read what I got so far?

Nia: Yeah.

REFLECTIVE WRITING PRODUCT

- If I planted my dreams, I would want a dream tree to grow. I would have one of my dreams on each leaf. Every time I pick one that dream comes true. I would have lots of fun and hope. (seventh-grade student, 1993)
- If the little voice inside me became bigger it would help me in life. I would listen to it and what it said. I would be involved more in life. (seventh-grade student, 1993)

While cooperative learning groups and reflective journal writing are frequently used teaching strategies in middle school education, the more we understand the interactive dynamics embedded in those strategies, the better we can focus on the learning process rather than disconnected instructional strategies. Central to reflective journal writing and cooperative learning is dialogical interaction. Lemke's (1989) written statement, "spoken language is the medium through which we reason to ourselves and talk our way through problems to answers" (p. 136), captures the role that the dialogical process plays in learning.

What follows in this essay are the basic principles of dialogue in teaching (Burbules, 1993) and examples from educational literature of how dialogue is used in middle school classrooms to enhance critical thinking. The first section is a review of Burbules's book, *Dialogue in Teaching*. The second section is a discussion of dialogue as conversations that transform the student-teacher relationship and the learning environment, resulting in critical instruction. The third section presents a review of educational literature that shows how middle school classroom teachers are using the principle of dialogue in teaching. The essay concludes with a suggestion for beginning the process of dialogue in teaching for critical instruction.

DIALOGUE IN TEACHING

In *Dialogue in Teaching*, Burbules (1993) presents dialogue as a form of communication and sets it up as a viable pedagogical alternative to lecturing and explaining. In contrast to the teacher-centered and teacher-as-authority point of view, dialogue "tends toward a de-centered and non-authoritarian view of learning," (p. 9). Dialogue embodies "reciprocal teaching." It is central to the human practices fostered by education—language, reason, morality, and social organization. It is open-ended, evolving with each new thought or reflection shared. It is a building process described as scaffolding by some thinkers. It is dynamic.

Several characteristics of dynamic dialogue have emerged in Burbules's (1993) writing. There is a "climate of open participation of two or more participants putting forth alternating statements" as time allows. This exchange includes "questions, responses, redirecting, and building statements." It is not sequential in terms of concrete to abstract, but "a sequence that is continuous and developmental" with a guiding "spirit of discovery." The climate is one of "exploratory and interrogative" with "commitment to the process of communication" as contrasted to the competitiveness of debate for the purpose of substantiating a preconceived point of view. There is an "attitude of reciprocity," including "interest, respect, and concern" that continue even when there is "tension and disagreement" (p. 7-8). It is in the tension and even confusion that reconstructive processes are at work and growth and development are taking place. Central to the process is relationship. Learning takes place as learners in a learning community relate with each about an object or concept of study. It is in critical dialogue that one's thoughts and concepts are challenged with the opportunity to think reflectively out of a newly introduced perspective.

Burbules (1993) describes dialogue in instruction as a game. He describes the game as one of making connections, paths of learning, strands of thought, inclusive and supportive. He outlines clear rules for successful play. All must participate; statements must be connected cognitively to the topic or affectively out of one's feelings; one player at a time speaks. There is no ending, only pauses based on time limitations. It is more like a time out to rest or do something else. The three guiding principles are "participation," "commitment," and "reciprocity." Why rules? Burbules (1993) poses that they broaden the scope of communication and have a critical function that keeps play moving; learning them is learning how to dialogue; and they are a basis for diagnosis when there is a breakdown.

DIALOGUE AS CRITICAL INSTRUCTION

Bacon and Thayer-Bacon (1993) refer to classroom dialogue as "real talk" and believe that dialogue that represents real conversation among learners about a topic leads to critical thinking. Bacon and Thayer-Bacon (1993) contrast "real talk," or conversational talk in the classroom from didactic, teacher-led question and answer discussion. Dialogue, or "real talk," according to the authors, "is a conversation based on cooperation and reciprocity as opposed to domination" (p. 182). It "encourages people to suspend their disbelief in other people's positions in order to try to understand them" (p. 182).

This view of dialogue can be traced to the work of physicist David Bohm (1985, 1992). A common theme in Bohm's (1992) definition of dialogue among a group of participants is the suspension of judgment of others' views in order for all participants to become "one mind" in the sense that all participants "have the *same content* — all the opinions, all the assumptions" (p. 204). Humans bring to any and every conversation preconceptions and assumptions that are based on their prior experience and sense of knowledge. Preconceptions and assumptions that are held as absolutes and essential are sources of conflict between people because emotions are connected to the sense of knowledge (Bohm, 1992).

Often it is because of preconceptions, assumptions, and the inability to suspend judgement based on one's belief system that conflict and discipline problems occur in the classroom. Disrespect is a good example. It is not uncommon for a teacher to interpret a student's response, verbal or body language, as disrespect. Teachers, who hold the belief that their perspective is to be held as truth and authority in the classroom, will spend much of their time experiencing perceived disrespect. Every time a student disagrees with a teacher and fails to accept a teacher's perspective, the potential for perceived disrespect is there.

This reminds me of the time I was teaching the novel, *The Contender*, by Robert Lipsyte. As a white teacher in a predominantly African-American classroom, nothing in my background prepared me for the storm which erupted as we read and processed the fictional novel about Alfred Brooks, a seventeen-year-old African-American high school drop-out, who struggles with the pressure of gangs in Harlem. Brooks discovers a gym and becomes a boxer but in the end decides to become a "contender" in life instead of the ring. He goes back to school to become a teacher.

I began to read out loud from chapter 1 in *The Contender*. The chapter was filled with stereotypical images of populations of people as well as sociological power issues: Jews, Blacks, life in Harlem, and gangs. It was on page three that a critical dialogue erupted in my classroom. In the opening scene, Alfred, the main character in the novel, enters the Harlem "clubroom" to pick up his friend James to go to the movies. Alfred has money because he works a job sweeping and delivering goods

for a Jewish family that owns a store. On the receiving end of racial terms, such as "nigger" and "Uncle Torn," from "club members," Alfred has to deal with peer pressure that contests his participation in work of a low social status. The reader immediately is challenged with critical thinking. The disturbance in my classroom erupted when I read the word "nigger" out loud to my students from the text. The dialogue that followed went something like this:

DIALOGUE EXAMPLE III

Teacher: Alfred took a step backward, nearly knocking over an old wooden chair. "Let's go, James."

Major swaggered across the room, the metal tips on his pointed shoes clicking on the concrete floor. "How much them Jews give you for slavin', Uncle Alfred ?"

"Jews squeeze the eagle till it screams," said Hollis. "The eagle screams, "Faster, Alfred, sweep that floor, you skinny nigger.'"

Class: Gasp!

Marquisha: Miss Moss, you can't say that word!

Teacher: I'm just reading it in a novel.

Marquisha: That's wrong!

Jason: You're white. It ain't right for you to say that word.

Carlisa: I'm gonna tell my mama on you.

Teacher: What's wrong with me reading it in a novel?

Marquisha: It's not right for a white person to say that word in front of blacks. You shoulda let one of us read that part of the book.

Teacher: But, it's just a book. I'm not calling anyone that word.

Marquisha: Yeah, but it's not right for you to do that. You're gonna get in trouble.

My African-American students challenged my tacit assumption that they would experience the novel from the same perspective as me. Implicit in that assumption was my hope that my poor, African-American students would be inspired to resist gang activity, graduate from high school, and perhaps go on to become classroom teachers. I was operating under the presupposition that all students have the same opportunities to achieve such goals. I had not begun to recognize that I represented the very system that reproduces the status quo-white dominant norms that prevent minority students from achieving such goals.

Viewed now through the lens of multiculturalism, I am beginning to understand critical instruction, and dialogue is part of that. Crossing cultural boundaries unaware, I did not consider the level of offense to my black students to hear me read the word "nigger" out loud in class even if it was in the context of oral reading from a novel. Teaching the novel was an opportunity to engage my students in a critical look at their own identity in relationship to history, cultural norms, and their future that lay before them to be shaped by their educational decisions.

What resulted were critical conversations with and among my black students, black parents, black teachers in the school, and my black principal. Retrospectively, the conflicts were the result of lack of understanding and respect for the cultural diversity of my students. The dynamics, though, did result in my eighth-grade students voicing their discontent with the visibility of my whiteness overshadowing the study of the novel. In retrospect, the conflict was an opportunity to move towards constructivist education in practice by "seeking to understand students' points of view," (Brooks & Brooks, 1993, p. 60). More importantly, it was an opportunity for critical constructivism as my students challenged my cultural presuppositions. Only now is it clear that my whiteness was invisible to me and the other adults who had grown accustomed to the socially dominant norms that have shaped the construction of knowledge and education in the past.

In retrospect, through my present understanding of critical instruction, it is clear that text, context, and pedagogy converged to bring out the issue of racism in my classroom. The novel was a written text through which I intended to engage my students. Engaging the novel in the context of a white teacher reading the word "nigger" in a predominantly African-American class created a living or experiential classroom that made it possible for the students and I to engage in critical thinking that challenged us to consider both my students' African-American identity and my identity as an outsider.

My students raised their voices at me, and the looks in their eyes and faces expressed their anger towards me. I could have written several of them up for disrespect. I didn't do that. I was in shock and afraid of what was going to happen, but I didn't think I had done anything wrong. I felt afraid and distant from my students during the interaction, but I did not judge their behavior as disrespect. It was clear that they were the ones who felt like I had disrespected them. It was cultural disrespect. As teachers, we should consider the subjective nature of defining disrespect.

Daily, I listened to the stories of classroom confrontations resulting in students being sent to the office for disrespect—a serious offense in the school where I taught. I was reluctant to ever judge a student's behavior as disrespect in the sense of breaking a school rule. When I encountered disagreement and confrontational behavior from students, I saw it first as communication and tried to understand what was being communicated. I had decided early on as a middle school classroom teacher that I would not take my students' behavior and verbal responses toward me too personally. I knew that I would not last long if I did. Rather, I interpreted a student talking back as their attempt to communicate what they felt and thought in a given situation. While I sometimes resorted to my position of authority to end interactions because of time limits, I viewed those endings as pauses in the developmental process. Given the number of students I had to daily interact with and the time constraints within which I worked, I had to trust that over time relationship would emerge and allow us to move beyond the division of roles and authority that accompany the education system as it presently exists.

Knowledge based on positivist thinking has been produced and reproduced by a closed system of education and traditional teaching styles that position teacher as authority and student as empty vessel to be filled. Learning and knowledge have been viewed as external to the self and commodities to be attained as capital. The system of education, embedded in the social system, reflects and reproduces society's way of knowing and viewing the world. The recent trends emphasizing content, standardized testing, rules, and policies have continued to foster a closed system, rather than critical thinking and inquiry for the purpose of developmental growth and maturity. If education for the purpose of developing a critical citizenry as foundational to a democratic society (Dewey, 1916) is still held as a goal, the perspective that the testing movement fosters workers for market at the expense of empowering students as critically thinking citizens, illuminates the need for systemic change in 21st century education and society.

Herein lies an educational paradox, for education is funded by society for its perpetuation. At the core of education is the production of social values, including freedom, equity, and the pursuit of happiness, but the history of our society cannot escape the presence of paradoxes: slavery in a free nation, separate but equal schooling, preach individualism but manage from a collective point of view, honor personal freedom but assimilate through cultural dominance, and espouse education for upward mobility yet use tracking to reproduce a closed class system.

Classroom teachers must recognize the role they play in reproducing the current educational system and the potential they have to participate in changing the system, beginning with their own classroom. Stone (1999), interviewing Goodlad, asked, "What do you see as the role of teachers today?" Goodlad responded:

> No different than it has always been—to provide for every child the richest kind of environment where the youngster can develop as a responsible human being. All the teacher can do is to create an environment. (p. 265)

Teachers can use the dialogical process to allow all the students in their classrooms to participate in designing the learning process. This requires that teachers give up traditional control of their students' learning, and shift to a critical and reciprocal process of mutual learning. It requires that teachers recognize that each scheduled class of students has the potential to develop a group culture that influences the learning process (Smagorisnky & Fly, 1993). Teachers must negotiate their place within this group process to both model and mediate interpersonal interactions as a "function of the overall classroom discourse" (p. 170) that leads to student independence, characteristic of critical thinking.

DIALOGUE IN MIDDLE SCHOOL INSTRUCTIONAL PRACTICE

Examples from research show the ways that teachers are transforming their pedagogy from one of teacher as dispenser of knowledge to one of mutual construction of knowledge. Dialogue has been central to whole language approaches that integrate instruction, silent reading, and written responses to literature and science in dialogue journals, providing a medium for interpersonal communication between students and teachers or students and students (Atwell, 1987; Oberlin & Shugarman, 1989; Alvermann, 1989; McWhirter, 1990). Urzua (1992) reported "how teachers are learning how to turn talk into dialogue" through the study of literature. These strategies require a shift from teacher as the knowing authority, to teacher as learner with the students. The teacher becomes "one among" the student participants, works within the group process that develops group integrity, models through participation, and shares from experience (Urzua, 1992).

Using literature circles is another strategy for creating an opportunity for dialogue in teaching in the middle school. The dialogical community process results in the development of responsibility among the members through "choice, ownership, and empowerment" (p. 40). These are classroom conversations that promote critical thinking and self-discipline.

Dialogue in teaching is not limited to reading and literature instruction. Gaskins, Satlow, Hyson, Ostertag, and Six (1994) found that talk is important in constructing meaning in science instruction. The authors stated, "It is through talk that students negotiate the meaning of text" (p. 558). Gaskins, and others (1994) are critical of the traditional results of science instruction that results in "inert knowledge" that is owned by the student but not usable by the student. The authors attribute the accumulation of inert knowledge "with a discourse model in which the teacher *initiates* talk by asking a question, a student responds, and the teacher evaluates the adequacy of the response" (558).

BEGINNING THE DIALOGICAL PROCESS IN THE MIDDLE SCHOOL CLASSROOM

Where should a teacher begin dialogical classroom conversations for critical instruction? Smith and Smith (1994) present a simulated discussion strategy that gives students the opportunity to learn the art of discussion in the classroom. The process reinforces participatory democracy by requiring all students to participate and practice various roles. It teaches the negotiation process, which is becoming central to problem solving in all types of relationships. Finally, the process allows students to develop social-personal relationship skills as well as critically self-reflect on their experiences (Smith & Smith, 1994).

From my 13 years' experience as a middle school teacher and academic study of scholarship, I would say that the way to begin is by the teacher opening the idea of dialogue in teaching up to students. A teacher desiring to shift from teacher-directed instruction to a conversational style of teaching should read current literature on dialogue in teaching and conduct an open class dialogue about dialogue. Give students a chance to think about dialogue and share their ideas about how it could be used for critical thinking and learning. Listen to what the students have to say. Build from there.

DIALOGUE EXAMPLE IV

Paul: How, as future teachers, as teachers, could we assimilate new information into existing schema: What do you think are some ways you could draw on student's prior knowledge and make it applicable to what they are learning in the classroom?

Sarah: Well, I have some students that are from lower socio-economic status and this is how I used World War II and required prior knowledge. I asked them what they thought a ghetto was and they could relate. They told me what their ghetto was and what it was like to live in their ghetto. And I said, "Well, did you know that Jewish people also lived in a ghetto?" And then they were able to connect their past knowledge to our lesson.

Glenda: In my eighth grade class, I was going to teach the novel, *The Contender* The word "nigger" is used in the text. Just before we read that section, we talk about what that word means. Some of my white students learned from the African-American students what that word means and why it is not appropriate for white people to use it, but it is okay for African-American students to use it.

It had been four years since reading the word "nigger" caused conflict in my classroom. I had talked about that incident with many educators in the context of presenting dialogue in teaching as critical instruction. It was not until the dialogue opportunity presented by one of my students that I realized how to translate "schema theory" into practice as a critical strategy for introducing the novel *The Contender*. I was able to connect my prior teaching experience to Sarah's example of introducing her students to the plight of the Jews during World War II. Thus, I learned from my student, and all in the class learned from the dialogical practice as critical instruction.

My students also learned from the critical reading and critical dialogues in my preservice teacher preparation classes. One student called me early this semester after contacting her cooperation teacher for student teaching. She was excited because she was going to get to teach *The Contender*. She asked me if I would be willing to come and lead an introductory critical dialogue in a predominantly African-American class. With her cooperating teacher's support, I introduced the students to the concept of critical dialogue by leading a dialogue to explore what the term meant. With a common understanding that critical dialogue is the open exchange of ideas, thoughts, and feelings about issues such as race, gender, and social class in a setting where the participants do not judge others' opinion, the student teacher and I engaged the students in a critical dialogue about the word "nigger." We reconstructed the dialogue from memory as best we could.

DIALOGUE EXAMPLE V

Visiting Professor: The way this is going to be a critical dialogue is that we're going to talk about a word that has been connected with race issues, and it's what some people would call a kind of a hard word. It's a difficult word for me to even verbalize in this setting today because right now, as I get ready to say this word, I'm conscious I'm white and you all have a darker skinned color, and the word that we're going to have a dialogue about today is the word "nigger."

Student: ooooo

Students: snickering laughter

Visiting Professor: I need you to write on a piece of paper what that word means to you.

Student: nigga?

Student Teacher: No, the word nigger.

Female Student 2: we use an "a" at the end of that word

Student Teacher: "n-i-g-g-e-r"

Female Student 2: We sayan "a" at the end of that word.

Student Teacher: Or you can write it how you say it.

Visiting Professor: I'm going to begin by saying I don't understand that word.

Female Student 1: Pass.

Female Student 1: I don't want to talk.

Female Student 2: That word means all the black Africans who were brought here as slaves. "Nigger" was used by a white slave-owner.

Female Student 3: I feel that word is like she [referring to the professor] said, it's not understandable, but it also is a word that the slave owners used to call the slaves. It brought a tear to my eye in "Roots." That's a painful movie for somebody to watch. Some of us just don't know how really good we got it because it used to be bad.

Male Student 1: I think it's a word for Negroes.

Male Student 2: I have to pass.

Male Student 3: It's a word slave owners called slaves back then. Now it's a word black people call each other.

Female Student 3: Can I say something else?

Visiting Professor: After everybody's had a turn.

Male Student 4: I don't know. It was just used back when there were slaves.

Male Student 5: Nigger is a name white folks use to identify or disrespect us because of our color, because we are not as pure as the water as they are.

Female Student 4: I don't know what it means.

Student Teacher: I don't have a personal knowledge of the word. I know what the connotation of it is. I know what it means and I think that each of you has stated it extremely well. It's a painful work I think, and I've grown up in a time when I've heard it used negatively.

Female Student 3: I feel that the word "nigga" and "nigger" are two totally different words. "Nigga" is something you call your people and "nigger' is what other people call you.

Visiting Professor: The reason that we are using this critical dialogue as an introduction to *The Contender* is because that word appears on the third page of the story. I used to teach eighth graders. When I read the word out loud, my students got upset. My students said that because I was white that it was wrong for me to read that word out loud in front of them. We ended up having this very critical dialogue. Maybe that will help you to understand the term critical dialogue on a deeper level. It wasn't a planned dialogue, like we have a planned dialogue today. My students engaged me in a conversation I wasn't prepared to have. It all turned out good because we started talking about the differences in culture, but I've never taught that book since then. The next year, I started my doctoral program and became a teacher of teachers. In my class this last semester, we were talking about these issues and critical dialogue and what is appropriate. More and more, white teachers find themselves in classrooms where all their students are African Americans, and issues like certain words and the ways to do things are

coming up in far more critical conversations. So, today, this next critical conversation is going to be an opportunity for you to give input into how should teachers handle, and specifically, in teaching *The Contender*, when we know that word is on the third page of that book, what is your opinion about how a teacher should handle that.

Female Student 1: I'm listening.

Female Student 3: That's like us coming across a harsh cuss word. Would you be mad if we came across a harsh cuss word in a book and read it out loud in class? I wouldn't be mad because you can't help it that the word is in there. Would you get mad if we came across a harsh cuss word and we read it?

Male Student 1: The way I see it, I don't care as long as you're not calling me the word. I don't care about you saying the word in the book because you didn't write the book, so I don't care. I guess it depends on how you read it. As long as you don't have bad feelings toward us.

Visiting Professor: I want to understand a little more about what you were saying. I hear you saying that it doesn't matter what a person's background is; if it's in a book, it doesn't matter who reads it. But if a white person reads it, they shouldn't have bad feelings towards you. What determines how it comes across to you? How would you know how to take it? You said as long as the person reading it didn't have the same meaning behind that word and didn't mean it personally toward their students. How would you know?

Male Student 1: It depends on their heart.

Visiting Professor: Do you have some teachers that you know that if they read that in the book it wouldn't feel good to you?

Male Student 1: Nope.

Visiting Professor: Have you ever had a teacher like that?

Female Student 3: Last year, my eighth-grade teacher, if we had a word like that in our book, I would very personally feel a little hurt because she was rude. She was rude to all people. We don't have any teachers that feel like that because we have a lot of mix here, like we have lots of blacks, lots of whites, and lots of Hispanics here. We have mixed teachers too.

Student Teacher: I wanted to have this kind of a conversation because I thought it was good to have this experience because people need to communicate on a level that you can understand someone without getting upset or angry when you put out your thoughts. That, to me, is critical dialogue when we try to understand them. I wondered about trying to haves a dialogue about this word that we're going to encounter in the book because I didn't want to make it a real big issue or focus, but it came to light just a couple of days ago in one of my other classes when we were listening to a tape and I had read the story in our book. The story was different than the tape. On the tape, there was a negative word, but it had been left out of the book. The students reacted when they heard the word on a tape, and that wasn't even me reading it to them. It was on a tape, and some of the students said, "What did that person say?" It made me stop and think that maybe we need to discuss before we get into *The Contender* about how you feel about it and if it's okay for us to talk about it openly or to read that in the text. That's why I felt like it was important to go ahead with this discussion, this critical dialogue today.

At this point, the student teacher transitioned the class by focusing on a short, associated press article, "N-word connotation depends on race, age group of those using it," by Paul Shepard. The student teacher read the article to the students as a textual base to take the dialogue about the word "nigger" to a deeper level. The dialogue began as one student asked a question in response to the last paragraph of the article.

Student Teacher: "Documentary use" is OK, he said. "Can a white schoolteacher, in that context, use the word? In some disciplines, I see nothing wrong in using it."

Student: disciplines

Student: What's that mean? By some disciplines.

Student Teacher: Some classrooms, or in a discussion.

Female Student 2: Why do you use "N-word"? Why can't you just say "nigger"?

Student Teacher: The question has been raised whether it is appropriate. If you noticed, in one place I read it and one place I didn't. It depends on how a person is using that word. But, how do you feel about a white teacher reading that word in a book?

At this point, one of the quieter students walked to the center of our dialogue circle, picked up the talking stick (a wooden walking stick), stood very straight as though he had thought his thoughts through to understanding and position, and stated with authority.

Male Student 5: I think it shouldn't be used at all because while we came here to read a book with it in it, none of our history classes talk about that word. Ya'll might say it's just in a book, but ya'll don't even teach the word or what it means in our history class.

Student Teacher: You don't know what it means?

Male Student 5: I know what it means, but our history teachers don't teach it in school, so why use it at all?

Rest of students: Amen. [applause]. Praise God!

After class, I asked the teacher if Raymond (Male Student 5) is usually that articulate with his thoughts. She said he is usually very quiet and seldom speaks. She was surprised at how he had evidenced empowerment when given the opportunity to express his thoughts on a critical issue in a dialogical setting.

FINAL REFLECTIONS

After her student teaching experience was completed, my pre-service teacher reflected on her initial experience with using critical dialogue in the classroom. While she had been very apprehensive about trying to initiate a dialogue on a racial issue in a classroom with students of color, it turned out to be a positive experience for both the students and my pre-service student teacher. From her perspective, the students were immediately intrigued when they came into the classroom to see the desks in a circle instead of the usual rows. All the students participated by actively listening, and most expressed their thoughts and opinions. The next time the class met, the first question several asked was "Are we going to do that dialogue thing again?" While my pre-service student teacher did not attempt another critical dialogue as a student teacher, she considers it a highlight of her student teaching experience and something she plans to use regularly when she has her own classroom.

REFERENCES

Alvermann, D. E. (1989). Teacher-student mediation of content area texts. *Theory Into Practice*, 28 (2), 142-47.

Atwell, N. M. *In the Middle: Writing, Reading, and Learning with Adolescents.* Upper Montclair, NJ: Boynton/Cook.

Bacon, C. S., & Thayer-Bacon, B. J. (1993). "Real talk": Enhancing critical thinking skills through conversation in the classroom. *Clearing House*, 66 (3), 181-84.

Bohm, D. (1985). *Unfolding Meaning.* New York: Routledge.

Bohm, D. (1992). *Thought as a System.* New York: Routledge.

Brooks, J. G. & Brooks, M. G. (1993). *The case for constructivist classrooms.* Alexandria, Virginia: Association for Supervision and Curriculum Development.

Burbules, N. (1993). *Dialogue in teaching: Theory and practice.* New York: Teachers College Press.

Dewey, J. (1916). *Democracy and Education. An introduction to the philosophy of education* (1966 edition). New Yark: Free Press.

Gaskins, I. W., Satlow, E., Hyson, D., Ostertag, J., & Six, L. (1994). Classroom talk about text: Learning in science class. *Journal of Reading*, 37 (7), 558-565.

Lemke, J. L. (1989). Making text talk. *Theory Into Practice*, 28 (2), 136-141.

McWhirter, A. M. (1990). Whole language in the middle school. *The Reading Teacher*, 43 (8), 562-565.

Oberlin, K. J., & Shugarman, S. L. (1989). Implementing the reading workshop with middle school LD readers. *Journal of Reading*, 32 (8), 682-87).

Scott, J. E. (1994). Literature circles in the middle school classroom: Developing reading, responding, and responsibility. *Middle School Journal*, 26 (2), 37-41.

Smagorinsky, P., & Fly, P. K. (1993). The social environment of the classroom: A Vygotskian perspective on small group process. *Communication Education*, 42 (2),159-71.

Smith, L. J., & Smith, D. L. (1994). The discussion process: A simulation. *Journal of Reading*, 37 (7), 582-585.

Stone, S. J. (1999). A conversation with John Goodlad. *Childhood*, 75 (5), 264-268.

Urzua, C. (1992). Faith in learners through literature studies. *Language Arts*, 69 (7), 492-501.

Index

Index

Test Your Knowledge Form

We encourage you to photocopy and use this page as a tool to assess how the articles in *Annual Editions* expand on the information in your textbook. By reflecting on the articles you will gain enhanced text information. You can also access this useful form on a product's book support Web site at *http://www.dushkin.com/online/*.

NAME:

DATE:

TITLE AND NUMBER OF ARTICLE:

BRIEFLY STATE THE MAIN IDEA OF THIS ARTICLE:

LIST THREE IMPORTANT FACTS THAT THE AUTHOR USES TO SUPPORT THE MAIN IDEA:

WHAT INFORMATION OR IDEAS DISCUSSED IN THIS ARTICLE ARE ALSO DISCUSSED IN YOUR TEXTBOOK OR OTHER READINGS THAT YOU HAVE DONE? LIST THE TEXTBOOK CHAPTERS AND PAGE NUMBERS:

LIST ANY EXAMPLES OF BIAS OR FAULTY REASONING THAT YOU FOUND IN THE ARTICLE:

LIST ANY NEW TERMS/CONCEPTS THAT WERE DISCUSSED IN THE ARTICLE, AND WRITE A SHORT DEFINITION:

We Want Your Advice

ANNUAL EDITIONS revisions depend on two major opinion sources: one is our Advisory Board, listed in the front of this volume, which works with us in scanning the thousands of articles published in the public press each year; the other is you—the person actually using the book. Please help us and the users of the next edition by completing the prepaid article rating form on this page and returning it to us. Thank you for your help!

ANNUAL EDITIONS: Critical Reading in the Content Areas 04/05

ARTICLE RATING FORM

Here is an opportunity for you to have direct input into the next revision of this volume.
We would like you to rate each of the articles listed below, using the following scale:

1. **Excellent: should definitely be retained**
2. **Above average: should probably be retained**
3. **Below average: should probably be deleted**
4. **Poor: should definitely be deleted**

Your ratings will play a vital part in the next revision.
Please mail this prepaid form to us as soon as possible.
Thanks for your help!

RATING	ARTICLE
	1. Exploring the Links Between Critical Literacy and Developmental Reading
	2. Saving Black Mountain: The Promise of Critical Literacy in a Multicultural Democracy
	3. What Do We Mean By Literacy Now?
	4. Creating a Middle School Culture of Literacy
	5. Building Sound Literacy Learning Programs for Young Adolescents
	6. Improving Young Adolescent Literacy Through Collaborative Learning
	7. A Culture of Literacy in Science
	8. Affective Dimensions of Content Area Reading
	9. Activating Student Interest in Content Area Reading
	10. Enhancing Young Adolescents' Motivation for Literacy Learning
	11. Reading and Understanding Textbooks
	12. Assessing Students' Skills in Using Textbooks: The Textbook Awareness and Performance Profile (TAPP)
	13. Fostering Students' Understanding of Challenging Texts
	14. Searching for Information in Textbooks
	15. Teachers' Views of Textbooks and Text Reading Instruction: Experience Matters
	16. Teacher-Directed and Student-Mediated Textbook Comprehension Strategies
	17. The Directed Questioning Activity for Subject Matter Text
	18. Scaffolding Adolescents' Comprehension of Short Stories
	19. Developing Critical Understanding of the Specialized Language of School Science and History Texts: A Functional Grammatical Perspective
	20. Learning from Social Studies Textbooks: Why Some Students Succeed and Others Fail
	21. Reading Across the Great Divide: English and Math Teachers Apprentice One Another as Readers and Disciplinary Insiders

RATING	ARTICLE
	22. The Effect of Learning Mathematical Reading Strategies on Secondary Students' Homework Grades
	23. Comprehending Multiple Texts: A Theme Approach Incorporating the Best of Children's Literature
	24. Celebrating Literature in a Comprehensive Middle School Program
	25. Literature for Children and Young Adults in a History Classroom
	26. Using Alternative Assessment to Provide Options for Student Success
	27. Giving Voice to Middle School Students Through Portfolio Assessment: A Journey of Mathematical Power
	28. Dismantling the Factory Model of Assessment
	29. Tales from Two Textbooks: A Comparison of the Civil Rights Movement in Two Secondary History Textbooks
	30. The Story of Ourselves: Fostering Multiple Historical Perspectives
	31. Using Textbooks with Students Who Cannot Read Them
	32. Guidelines for Adapting Content Area Textbooks: Keeping Teachers and Students Content
	33. Assisting Students with Difficult Textbooks: Teacher Perception and Practices
	34. Dialogue in Teaching is Critical Instruction

ABOUT YOU

Name   Date

Are you a teacher? ❑   A student? ❑
Your school's name

Department

Address   City   State   Zip

School telephone #

YOUR COMMENTS ARE IMPORTANT TO US!

Please fill in the following information:
For which course did you use this book?

Did you use a text with this ANNUAL EDITION? ❑ yes ❑ no
What was the title of the text?

What are your general reactions to the *Annual Editions* concept?

Have you read any pertinent articles recently that you think should be included in the next edition? Explain.

Are there any articles that you feel should be replaced in the next edition? Why?

Are there any World Wide Web sites that you feel should be included in the next edition? Please annotate.

May we contact you for editorial input? ❑ yes ❑ no
May we quote your comments? ❑ yes ❑ no